1 MONTH OF FREE READING

at

www.ForgottenBooks.com

By purchasing this book you are eligible for one month membership to ForgottenBooks.com, giving you unlimited access to our entire collection of over 1,000,000 titles via our web site and mobile apps.

To claim your free month visit: www.forgottenbooks.com/free632726

* Offer is valid for 45 days from date of purchase. Terms and conditions apply.

ISBN 978-0-656-10466-6
PIBN 10632726

This book is a reproduction of an important historical work. Forgotten Books uses state-of-the-art technology to digitally reconstruct the work, preserving the original format whilst repairing imperfections present in the aged copy. In rare cases, an imperfection in the original, such as a blemish or missing page, may be replicated in our edition. We do, however, repair the vast majority of imperfections successfully; any imperfections that remain are intentionally left to preserve the state of such historical works.

Forgotten Books is a registered trademark of FB &c Ltd.
Copyright © 2018 FB &c Ltd.
FB &c Ltd, Dalton House, 60 Windsor Avenue, London, SW19 2RR.
Company number 08720141. Registered in England and Wales.

For support please visit www.forgottenbooks.com

historical & archaeological
to Montgomeryshire and its borders

v. 14

DA
740
M7C6
v.14

SOUTHEY AND HEBER IN POWYSLAND.

By REV. D. R. THOMAS, M.A., Vicar of Meifod.

THE footsteps of "Men of Note" possess an attraction which does not attach to those of ordinary people, and we like to trace their movements, and to observe the impressions which our every-day world makes upon them. Hence the charm of a well-written biography. When, moreover, the biographer tells his own story, and we are brought face to face with the thoughts and expressions of the man himself, and that, too, in language of singular grace and power, the pleasure is vastly enhanced. And when it further happens that the scenes described, and the characters alluded to, are otherwise familiar to us, we have all the elements of an attractive subject, backed by the conditions of a highly instructive treatment. Such appears to me to be eminently the case with the subject I have chosen for this paper, the "Visit of Southey and Heber to Powysland"—a visit, in the case of Heber, not unconnected, it may be, with his nomination to the See of Calcutta; and in the case of Southey, a link in an intimate and life-long friendship. They were the fellow-guests of the Right Hon. C. W. Williams-Wynn, for so long a period the representative of this county in the House of Commons, and, at that time, a member of the Cabinet. This intimacy was begun, like so many of the truest and most enduring friendships, in their days of boyhood, when they were schoolfellows together at Westminster; was cemented by the strongest proofs of esteem and affection through many years of good and evil fortune;

and was only closed by death. Indeed, I believe I am not wrong in saying that it was owing to this friendship, and to the material help which Mr. Williams-Wynn extended for so many years to the poet in his early career, that we owe it that Southey was enabled to pursue that literary course, to which he was so devoted, and which has conferred so much pleasure and benefit upon us, his countrymen. And I know no greater encomium that has ever been passed upon that able statesman; certainly none that will excite so vivid a sense of his personal worth, as that in which Southey describes him as

"My earliest friend, whom I
Have ever, through all changes, found the same
From boyhood to grey hairs,
In goodness and in warmth of heart."

The interesting old hall at Llangedwyn, with its beautiful surroundings, in the valley of the Tanat, was Mr. Wynn's country residence; and here it was that Robert Southey and Reginald Heber, while they formed a mutual friendship, enjoyed his genial hospitality, and made their first acquaintance with Powys-land. And we can well imagine how these two high-souled and congenial spirits must have enjoyed the society, the intercourse, and the pleasant excursions in which they shared. In an "Ode on Bishop Heber's portrait", Southey thus alludes to the occasion:—

"Ten years have held their course
Since last I looked upon
That living countenance,
When on Llangedwyn's terraces we paced
Together to and fro;
Partaking there its hospitality,
We with its honoured master spent
Well pleased the social hours."

Here, before passing on to the descriptions which the poet gives of the scenes they visited together, it may not be amiss to put on record two little episodes, of a literary character, for which I am indebted to the "honoured master's" son, each of which has an interest of its own. It was during this visit, that Heber, after hearing the old Welsh air of "Ar hyd y nos" played upon the harp, and while the tune was still ringing in his ears, composed to its music his well-known Evening Hymn.

> "God, that madest earth and heaven,
> Darkness and light;
> Who the day for toil has given,
> For rest the night,
> May Thine angel guards defend us,
> Slumber sweet Thy mercy send us,
> Holy dreams and hopes attend us,
> This livelong night.
>
> "Guard us waking, guard us sleeping,
> And when we die,
> May we in Thy mighty keeping,
> All peaceful lie;
> When the last dread call shall wake us,
> Do not Thou, our God, forsake us,
> But to reign in glory take us
> With Thee on high."

And it was when accompanying Mr. Wynn to Meifod, when the latter was about to purchase the Humphreys property in that parish, that Southey extended his expedition to the ruins of Mathraval, and there, after careful investigation into the stories and legends of the place, collected the materials for one of the chief scenes, if not for the whole scheme of his poem, entitled "Madoc in Wales":—

> "He came
> Where Warnway rolls its waters underneath
> Ancient Mathraval's venerable walls,
> Cyveilioc's princely and paternal seat."

Few are the vestiges that remain of this once famous palace of the Princes of Powys—nothing to betoken its royal splendour. The lofty mound, first raised to guard the river ford, and afterwards converted into a keep, when the castle was erected on its bank; the broken ground which shows roughly where the foundations of the buildings ran; an angle of the walling, upon which it is probable that a wooden superstructure was raised, and the deep foss which enclosed the whole space: these are all that remain, perhaps all that ever survived the disastrous fire on the 2nd of August 1212, when King John set it ablaze, in order to check the victorious rising of Llewelyn ap Iorwerth, and the chieftains of Powys. Decay and silence have been its after portion, a strange contrast to that life and splendour of its earlier days, which the poet has re-awakened in those vivid lines,—

"From Cyveilioc's hall
The voice of harp and song commingled came,
It was that day the feast of victory there;
Around the Chieftain's board the warriors sate;
The sword and shield and helmet on the wall
And round the pillars were in peace hung up;
And as the flashes of the central fire
At fits arose, a dance of wavy light
Played o'er the reddening steel. The Chiefs who late
So well had wielded in the work of war
Those weapons, sate around the board to quaff
The beverage of the brave and hear their fame.—
Mathraval's Lord, the Poet and the Prince,
Cyveilioc stood before them—in his pride;
His hands were on the harp, his eyes were clos'd,
His head, as if in reverence to receive
The inspiration, bent; anon, he raised
His glowing countenance and brighter eye
And swept with passionate hand the ringing harp,
'Fill high the Hirlas Horn.'"

To return from this digression to the two friends, Southey and Heber. One of their excursions was to Sycharth, in the adjoining parish of Llansilin:—

"Together there we traced
The grass-grown site, where armed feet once trod
The threshold of Glendower's embattled hall."

Burnt down in revenge for that chieftain's rising in arms, there are no vestiges left of the ancient palace and its surrounding buildings. The site, however, is unmistakably marked out by the enclosing foss, and the outer ward, and the inner keep, on which once stood the fair house of wood, "Ty pren glân, yn nhop bryn glas". Happily, too, we have a minute description of it, as it stood, from the pen of Iolo Goch, Glyndwr's domestic bard and Laureate. It is the more interesting as picturing a typical moated mansion of the end of the fourteenth century, with its picturesque outlines, and its domestic arrangements. The palace, he tells us, was surrounded by a well-filled moat, and was entered through a spacious gate, standing on a bridge. It had a tower of Irish type, that reminded him of the Cloisters at Westminster, with their vaults and arches, and gilded chancel. The basement (apparently of stone) comprised eighteen compartments, and above were four stories, raised on four firm and richly-carved pillars, each story being subdivided into eight sleeping chambers. The whole was covered with a shingle roof, and there were chimney stocks to carry off the smoke. In the rooms were wardrobes, stored with apparel, not unlike the shops in London. It had a church, too, quadrangular in form, with chapels richly glazed. Around the palace he enumerates an orchard and a vineyard, a park with deer, a rabbit warren, meadows, and cornfields, a mill, a pigeon-house, and a fish-pond, stocked with pike and gwyniaid; and here, in the poet's trysting place,

"Yn Sycharth, buarth y beirdd,"

was abundance of Shropshire ale and malt liquor.

There are so many local traits in this roughly rendered description, that we have less difficulty in accepting the account of those parts which have disappeared. The nearest house to it is still called *Parc Sycharth*, probably the old deer park,

"Gerllaw'r llys
Pawr ceirw mewn parc arall."

And not far off is Pentref y Cwn, which tells of the pack of staghounds. The present Pandy (fulling mill) was, in earlier times, a corn mill, the "Melin deg ar ddifreg ddwr", and one[1] who has studied the question well has identified the site of the fishponds.

"Pysgodlyn—a fo raid i fwrw rhwydau."

Hither, too, some fifty years later, hied another genius, that gossipy, amusing and rather credulous traveller, George Borrow, who, if not a poet, had a good deal of the poetic spirit about him, as is testified by his translation of Iolo Goch's poem; a translation which he made, as he tells us, in the days of his boyhood, and which he chanted anew on the opposite hill, after visiting the scene described. It is so spirited, that it will not be amiss to reproduce it, as it may be more interesting to many of our readers than the original itself.

"Twice have I pledged my word to thee
To come thy noble face to see;
His promises let every man
Perform as far as e'er he can!
Full easy is the thing that's sweet,
And sweet this journey is and meet;
I've vow'd to Owain's Court to go,
And I'm resolv'd to keep my vow;
So thither straight I'll take my way
With blithsome heart, and there I'll stay,
Respect and honour, whilst I breathe,
To find his honor'd roof beneath.
My chief of long lined ancestry
Can harbour sons of poesy.
I've heard, for so the muse has told,
He's kind and gentle to the old;
Yes, to his castle I will hie;
There's none to match it 'neath the sky:
It is a baron's stately court,
Where bards for sumptuous fare resort;
There dwells the lord of Powis land,
Who granteth every just demand.
Its likeness now I'll limn you out:
'Tis water girdled wide about;
It shows a wide and stately door
Reached by a bridge the water o'er;

---

[1] Rev. Walter Davies, who wrote a History of Llansilin Parish in *Cambro-Briton*, 1820.—See *Gwaith Gwallter Mechain*, iii, 66.

SOUTHEY AND HEBER IN POWYS-LAND.

'Tis formed of buildings coupled fair,
Coupled is every couple there;
Within a quadrant structure tall
Muster the merry pleasures all.
Conjointly are the angles bound—
No flaw in all the place is found.
Structures in contact meet the eye
Upon the hillock's top on high;
Into each other fastened they
The form of a hard knot display.
There dwells the chief we all extol
In timber house on lightsome knoll;
Upon four wooden columns proud
Mounteth his mansion to the cloud;
Each column's thick and firmly bas'd,
And upon each a loft is plac'd;
In these four lofts, which coupled stand,
Repose at night the minstrel band;
Four lofts they were in pristine state,
But now partitioned form they eight.
Piled is the roof, on each house-top
Rise smoke-ejecting chimneys up.
All of one form there are nine halls
Each with nine wardrobes in its walls
With linen white as well supplied
As fairest shops of fam'd Cheapside.
Behold the church with cross uprais'd
And with its windows neatly glazed;
All houses are in this comprest—
An orchard's near it of the best,
Also a park where void of fear
Feed antler'd herds of fallow deer.
A warren wide my chief can boast,
Of goodly steeds a countless host.
Meads where for hay the clover grows,
Corn-fields which hedges trim inclose,
A mill a rushing brook upon,
And pigeon tower fram'd of stone;
A fish-pond deep and dark to see
To cast nets in when need there be,
When never yet was known to lack
A plenteous store of perch and jack.
Of various plumage birds abound;
Herons and peacocks haunt around.
What luxury doth his hall adorn,
Showing of cost a sovereign scorn;

His ale from Shrewsbury town he brings;
His usquebaugh is drink for kings;
Bragget he keeps, bread white of look,
And, bless the mark! a bustling cook.
His mansion is the minstrels' home,
You'll find them there whene'er you come.
Of all her sex his wife's the best;
The household through her care is blest;
She's scion of a knightly tree,
She's dignified, she's kind and free.
His bairns approach me, pair by pair,
O what a nest of chieftains fair!
Here difficult it is to catch
A sight of either bolt or latch;
The porter's place here none to fill;
Here largess shall be lavish'd still,
And ne'er shall thirst or hunger rude
In Sycharth venture to intrude.
A noble leader Cambria's Knight,
To take possession, his by right,
And midst that azure water plac'd,
The castle, by each pleasure grac'd.

Another excursion, in which Southey and Heber joined, was to the secluded, but wildly beautiful valley of Pennant:—

" Melangel's lonely church—
Amid a grove of evergreens it stood,
A garden and a grove, where every grave
Was deck'd with flowers, or with unfading plants
O'ergrown, sad rue and funeral rosemary."

There they

" Saw the dark yews, majestic in decay
Which in their flourishing strength
Cyveilioc might have seen—
Letter by letter traced the lines
On Yorwerth's fabled tomb:
And curiously observe what vestiges
Mouldering and mutilate
Of Monacella's legend there are left."

From the epithet "fabled", we may gather that Southey was misled by the legendary tradition (as given in *Pennant's Tours*), that it was the tomb of

Iorwerth Drwyndwn, the eldest son of Owen Gwynedd, with whom he very effectively connects it in his *Madoc*.

> "His glancing eye fell on a monument
> Around whose base the rosemary droop'd down
> As yet not rooted well. Sculptured above
> A warrior lay; the shield was on his arm,
> Madoc approach'd and saw the blazonry....
> A sudden chill ran through him—as he read—
> 'Here Yorworth lies'.. it was his brother's grave."

The legend on the effigy, "Hic jacet Edwart", and the tradition that the neighbouring *Bwlch Croes Yorwerth* took its name from a memorial cross, erected in the pass where Iorwerth Drwyndwn fell, harmonise well with the idea; but "the blazonry" of the shield claims it for another Iorwerth. The rampant "wolf" proclaims that it belonged to Edward ap Madoc ap Rhirid Flaidd, the potent Lord of Penllyn. And it is probable that the female effigy, which has so often done duty as "the rude image of St. Monacel, is that of Gladus, the daughter and heiress of Gwrdendu, Lord of Bryn, with whom Bryn and Pennant passed, as a marriage portion, to Rhirid Flaidd.

They marked well the legend carved by skilful hand upon the holy screen which

> "Told how here a poor and hunted hare
> Ran to the Virgin's feet and look'd to her
> For life."

But no notice is recorded of the giant Rib, "Asgwrn or Asen y Gawres", still preserved within the church, or of the small square room at its east end, called "Cell y Bedd", said to mark the burial place of the founder. Here I hold that the shrine stood which preserved her relics; and I would suggest that the early Roman capitals, built into the south wall of the church, were part of this shrine. The room itself may have supplied a lodging for those who sought "sanctuary" within these precincts. For, by the laws of Howell Dda, which treat of "Church Protection", it is enacted that "whoever shall take protection, is to walk about within the churchyard and the burial-ground, without relics upon him". And "the measure of the burial-ground is a legal 'erw' in length, with its end toward the churchyard; and that circling the churchyard is to be its compass".[1]

The importance of this privilege, and the extent of the cultus, may be gathered from the fact, that at the period of the Reformation, the "oblaciones ad reliquias" amounted, in the money of those days, to the respectable sum of £2 16s. 8d. per annum.

With this use and purpose of Cell y Bedd, I would compare that of Eglwys Gwyddvarch, which once stood in the west end of Meifod churchyard. For to Meifod, I believe, and not to Chirk, *i.e.*, to Mechain, and not to Y Waun, we must assign the grant referred to in the *Worthenbury MSS.*, Hist. MS. Commission, quoted in the *Arch. Cambr.*, 1880, p. 150, "1467, April 4 or 14. Grant by several Cardinals, of remission of one hundred days, to those who should go to the chapel of St. Gwyddvarch, confessor and abbot, or to the cemetery at Chirk, of St. Tysilio, confessor, and hear mass of Richard ap J (ohn ap David), priest of the said diocese, or give to him support, or say *Pater Noster* and *Ave Maria* for the souls of his parents on certain days". There is, however, this difference between the two, that whereas "Cell y Bedd" still remains to the church, Eglwys Gwyddfarch has been alienated and secularised.

There is one legend mentioned by Southey, which I have met with no reference to elsewhere; although similar ones do occur in connexion with other places. The old house alluded to is evidently, from his account of it, "Llechweddgarth", an ancient mansion of the Thomas's, from whom it passed by marriage to the late Mr. Griffiths of Caer-Hun:—

We " together visited the ancient house
   Which from the hill-top takes
Its Cymric name euphonious : there to view,
   Though drawn by some rude limner inexpert,

---

[1] Quoted in "Pennant Melangell", *Mont. Coll.*, 1879, p. 76.

> The faded portrait of that lady fair,
> Beside whose corpse her husband watched,
> And with perverted faith,
> Preposterously placed,
> Thought, obstinate in hopeless hope, to see
> The beautiful dead, by miracle, revive."

The legend is not mentioned in Mr. Hancock's parochial account in the *Montgomeryshire Collections*, 1878-9; and though I have made inquiries, I can hear of no such tradition now surviving in the parish. It does not, indeed, follow that the lady was an actual resident here; and a similar story exists relating to a former lady at Newtown Hall. Perhaps the inquiry may lead to further information relative to the Pennant legend and clear up the mystery.

NOTE ON
PRICE OF PERTHEIRIN.

In the *Montgomeryshire Collections*, Vol. xi, p. 266, the opinion is given that Mary Sheinton, heiress of Pertheirin, and wife of Lewis Price, was a daughter of Richard Sheinton. I am inclined to think, for the following reasons, that she was the daughter and heiress of Hugh Sheinton, *son* of Richard Sheinton.

PEDIGREE OF SHEINTON, FROM LEWYS DWNN, Vol. I, p. 305.

Hugh Shenton, Gent. ⟂ Margt., dau. Wm. Wright, Esq.

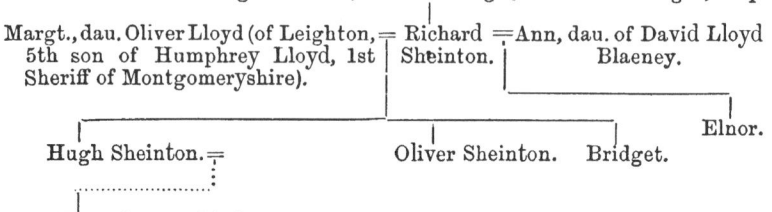

Margt., dau. Oliver Lloyd (of Leighton, = Richard = Ann, dau. of David Lloyd
5th son of Humphrey Lloyd, 1st │ Sheinton. │ Blaeney.
Sheriff of Montgomeryshire).

Hugh Sheinton. =   Oliver Sheinton.   Bridget.   Elnor.

? Mary, dau. and heir.

Oliver Sheinton was churchwarden, with Richard Middleton, of Chirbury Parish, in 1615. His elder brother, Hugh Sheinton, would therefore have a marriageable daughter on 8th October 1647. By the pedigree Richard Sheinton had no daughter Mary. Lewis Price, husband of Mary Sheinton, the heiress of Pertheirin, was living, by the date of his will, in 1700. Mary, the heiress, his relict, it seems, did not die till 1712. I think it exceedingly improbable that she was the daughter of the Richard who is described as "Ricus Sheynton de Llanwonvge gen." on a county grand jury as far back as 3 James I, 1605-6. By the Lloyd of Leighton pedigree (*Vis. of Salop, Harl. MSS.*, 1396 and 1982) it appears that Margaret Lloyd had been previously married to Francis Hordley.

It is erroneously stated (p. 265) that "Ricus Sheinton de Llanwnog, gen.", living in 1618, was a *son* of the last named Hugh Sheinton on the Dwnn pedigree. He was the latter's father. W. V. Ll.

PEDIGREE OF SIR WILLIAM HUMFREYS, BART.

WE are indebted to the Rev. D. R. Thomas, the Vicar of Meifod, for the loan of the following correspondence and pedigrees. They are of a rare character, comprising three original letters of the celebrated Herald, Peter le Neve Norroy, skeleton pedigrees of the Humfreys family, with autograph notes by Humphrey Humphreys,[1] Bishop of Hereford, and certain alterations therein, in which he points out various sources of genealogical information.

Sir William Humfreys, whose pedigree and armorial bearings gave rise to the correspondence, was the son of Nathaniel Humphreys, who (one of the letters states) "was a tinman in London, and dyed very rich", and who was the grandson of Humfrey Griffith, "a substantial freeholder, in the lordship of Deyddur (about 50 or 60^{li} per ann.)", which, at the then value of money, would represent a much larger rental than at

[1] Humphrey Humphreys was born at Penrbyn Deudraeth, in the county of Merioneth, and was educated in part, at least, at Oswestry School. He was accounted to be a great antiquary, and the documents we now print show the high estimation in which he was held in the College of Arms. The inscription upon his gravestone gives a biographical synopsis of his career:—

"H. S. E.
Humphredus Humphreys, S. T. P.
Primo decanus A.D. 1680 ⎫ Bangorien-
Mox Episcopus A.D. 1689 ⎭ sis factus.
Inde Herefordiam translatus A.D. 1701.
Tandem vitæ satur & cœlo maturus,
Obiit 20 Novemb. 1712 Ætatis suæ 64.
Ejus ad exemplum si vixeris, amice lector,
Mori non timebis."

its present value). Sir William became an Alderman of the city of London, and in 1704 served the office of Sheriff, when he was knighted by Queen Anne. It was on this occasion, Peter le Neve, Norroy King of Arms, applied to Bishop Humphreys for information respecting the pedigree of the sheriff. The Bishop had presented to the Herald's College MSS. of pedigrees of Wales, and evidently was considered an authority on the subject. The sketch of pedigree sent by Norroy in the first instance to the Bishop, was a very imperfect and unauthentic production. The Bishop, whilst residing at Whitborne, the ancient seat of the Bishops of Hereford, had communication with Thomas Humphreys, possibly a relative, who gave him much interesting information, in a characteristic and racy letter, reporting the result of his enquiries. Thomas Humphreys remarks that "he did not find any great curiosity, that way, in this part of the country". He, however, enclosed to the Bishop a pedigree of the Penrhyn's "of Penrhose", but ending with "Owen ap Griffith". At this point of the enquiry, none of them seemed to have hit upon the link by which Sir William is afterwards stated to be connected with this branch of the Brochwel tribe, and in right of which descent he was afterwards held to be entitled to the "Nag's Head" shield.

The pedigree sent by Thomas Humphreys is stated by him to have been derived from Mr. Edwards, who was interested in Mr. Price, the son of the celebrated antiquary, Thomas Price, of Llanfyllin, then recently dead. The correspondence here ceases; but, doubtless, the sketch of pedigree was forwarded by the Bishop to Norroy. To Norroy's first letter there is an interesting postscript, in which he shows he had a keen eye for business, and gives information as to the charges made by heralds at their visitations, for entering arms and pedigrees of persons of different grades of rank.

In 1707, the correspondence was renewed by Norroy, stating, as a reason, that Sir William Humfreys "would have the arms fixed for him", and the Bishop was asked to point out any faults in the pedigree then enclosed, and " to certify so much thereof which is correct; and that it is the common report that Sir William Humfreys is descended in this manner".

Here the Bishop is appealed to as an authority. There are two pedigrees with the letters, which we print for the purpose of showing the Bishop's notes, and how his mind was gradually brought to the conclusions ultimately arrived at; the two pedigrees are nearly identical, and both show the missing link which Thomas Humphreys' pedigree lacked. Griffith ap Rinalt is stated to have had two sons. (1) Owen, father of John Derwas, of Penrhose;[1] and (2) David Vychan, the grandfather of Humphrey Griffith, the father of Nathaniel Humfreys, the wealthy tinman, and grandfather of Sir William Humfreys, the Sheriff of London. This, the Bishop states, was taken out of the card of "Mr. Derwas of Penrhose".

There is a slight scent of "cooking" in this part of the pedigree, and it would be interesting to know whether the Derwas ancient and authentic pedigree does really show the second son David Vychan, and his above-mentioned descendants. The Bishop's notes give interesting information as to the authenticity of the main descent of the Brochwel pedigree, now universally received, and which stands chiefly on the authority of Robert Vaughan of Hengwrt, whom the Bishop repeatedly calls "the greatest antiquary we have had of late". It is to be observed, however, that the five later descents do not rest on that authority, but on the "card" of the Derwas's. The term "card" seems to be used in these documents in the sense of "pedigree".

[1] He was not the ancestor of the Penrhyns. The Penrhyns were descended from Griffith Vaughan of Deuddwr, a different branch of Brochwels. The pedigree given, p. 16 *seq.*, is the line of Penrhyn. Griffith Vaughan of Deuddwr, and Sir G. Vaughan, were different persons.

THE HUMFREYS PEDIGREE.

We shall now be indebted to Burke's *Extinct Baronetage*, and Hasted's *History of Kent* (of which county Sir William became an important landowner) for material to complete this sketch.

In the first year of George II, Sir William Humfreys was Lord Mayor of London, and had the honour of entertaining the King and Queen; and he was, in consequence, created a baronet on the 30th November 1714. In 1715, Sir William purchased the castle of Hever, and several manors in Kent. By his first wife, Margaret, daughter of William Wintour, Esq., of Dymoke, and granddaughter of Sir William Maxey, Bart., he had an only surviving child, Orlando, his heir. He died in October 1735, and was succeeded by his son, Sir Orlando Humfreys, who married Ellen, daughter and co-heir of Robert Lancashire, and had issue, three sons and two daughters; two of the sons died young. "Robert, the second, had the castle and manors, and died before his father, possessed of them, as appears by his epitaph in 1736." Ultimately, in 1745, the two daughters and their husbands conveyed Hever Castle and the manors to Sir Timothy Waldo,[1] Knight. Sir Orlando died 14th June 1737, when the baronetcy became extinct. Thus, in twenty-two years, this title, conferred upon a Montgomeryshire man, came to an end. As to the arms borne by the Humfreys, there seems to be some discrepancy. In *Burke's Extinct Baronetage*, the arms are given as "*sable*, three nags' heads erased

[1] Of Sir Timothy Waldo, of Hever Castle, an anecdote is told, shewing that the old and expensive custom of vails-giving received its death-blow from him at Newcastle House. "Sir Timothy Waldo, on his way from the Duke's dinner-table to his carriage, put a crown into the hands of the cook, who returned it, saying, 'Sir, I do not take silver.' 'Don't you, indeed?' said Sir Timothy, putting it into his pocket; 'then I do not give gold.'" Sir Timothy was the grand-nephew of Sir Edward Waldo, knight, who was knighted in his own house, in Cheapside, opposite Bow Church, by Charles II, in 1677. This house was taken down in 1861, and at the sale of the materials some finely carved oak panelling was purchased and removed to Gungrog, near Welshpool, in the dining-room of which house it is now fixed.

arg."; the shield, attributed to Brochwel Yscithrog, pure and simple.

In Hasted's *History of the County of Kent*,[1] it is stated "he was descended from Nathaniel Humfreys, citizen of London, the second son of William ap Humfreys, *of the County of Montgomery.* He bore for his arms—1 and 4, *sable*, two nags' heads erased *arg.*; 2 and 3, *or* and *gu.*, two lions rampant, endorsed and counterchanged". The statement that the grandfather was of the county of Montgomery, without specifying any precise locality, and the omission of one nag's head in the arms, which omission may have been a difference imposed, seemed at first sight to be not without significance, and may have implied that the Brochwellian descent was not deemed to be conclusively proved.

By the kindness of Sir Albert W. Woods, Garter, however, we are enabled to give the correct blazon of the arms of Sir William Humfreys, which sets the matter at rest :—

"By Patent dated 22nd April 1717, the arms and crest following were granted to Sr. William Humfreys of Bloomsbury square, in the County of Middlesex, Knt. and Bart. Alderman and sometime Lord Mayor of the City of London, who had by letters represented unto his Lo'p—That he being now the only son of Nathaniel Humfreys, Citizen of London, who was second son of William ap Humfrey of Penrhyn Vayor in Deyddur, and of Llandrinio, in the County of Montgomery in North Wales, which William ap Humfrey was descended from Sr. Griffith Vychan of Penrhyn Vayor in Deyddur aforesaid, who bore for his coat armour two coats quarterly.

"*Arms.*—Two coats quarterly, viz., *sable* three naggs' heads erased argent, as descended from Kynan Gwarwin, son of Brochwel King of Powis. Secondly, per pale, *or* and *gules*, two lions rampant, endors'd counterchanged as descended from Brochwell son of Aedden.

"*Crest.*—On a wreath argent and *sable* a lion sejant *or*, reposing his dexter foot upon a nagg's head coupe *ermines.*"

---

[1] Vol. i, p. 395.

CORRESPONDENCE.

Herald's College, London, 14th *November* 1704.

My Lord.—'Tis to your Lordship as to a great Oracle, both in divinity and other sciences, that persons continually make their application; amongst the rest therefore of your Lordship's suitors be pleased to give leave to Sir William Humphreys, now Sheriff of London, by your most humble servant Norroy, to desire the favour of letting him know the pedigree of that gentleman; the information which I have is that one Esqr. of Penthrin, in Deuthur, had 7 dau'rs, one of which married to William Humphrey, a male ancestor of Sir William's, as I am told his grandfather; another married to Matthews of . . . Montgom. an ancestor of Mr. Matthews, late one of the judges of Wales; the coat Sir William thinks belongs to him is that of *sable* 3 Horse heads coupt *arg.* which is said to belong to Brochwell Ysgythrog, King of Powis, Earle of Chester, of whom are said to descend the Lloyds of Powis land and others—qre what others? he quarters a coat very like that of Ithel Anwyl of Northop, found also in the office of Arms, being p. pale *or* and *gules* 2 lyons rampt. indorsed counterchanged which with ¶ in the midle was born by Ithel. I have lookt over the MSS. of pedigr. of Wales you was pleased to p'sent to the office, but in that find no descent as hereafter sent to your Lordship; be pleased, my Lord, to favour me with your answer to the heralds office to
My Lord, your Lordships most dutyfull
and obedient servant,
Peter Le Neve Norroy.

As your Lordship is a lover of Heraldry I will beseech your Lordship to ask as many Gent. of North Wales as you shalbe accidentally in company with if they shall be well pleased if Norroy, King of Arms, should come down to visit their several countys and will enter their arms and pedigrees with him, the charge whereof will be but small, scil.: 1*l*. 7*s*. 6*d*. for a gent., 1*l*. 17*s*. 6*d*. an Esqr., 2*l*. 07*s*. 6*d*. for a knight or baronet, and for the greater nobility and corporations what they are pleased to present.

Griffith, Lord of Guilsfield, Bromouth and deythur......[torn]
No address.
[The Bishop of Hereford]

THE HUMFREYS PEDIGREE.

Fragment of Pedigree enclosed in Norroy's Letter.
[Torn.]

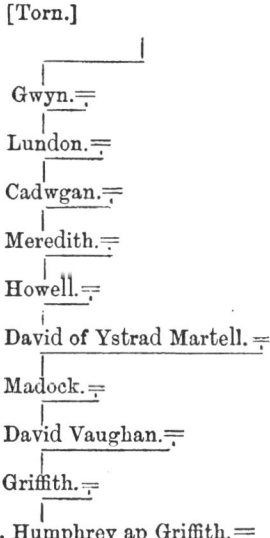

Gwyn.=

Lundon.=

Cadwgan.=

Meredith.=

Howell.=

David of Ystrad Martell.=

Madock.=

David Vaughan.=

Griffith.=

of Llandrinion, Com. Montgomery, Humphrey ap Griffith.=
[torn.]
... of the other house...William Humfreys, Esq., of Penthryn ⊤ ...d. and coheir
... son or grandson   Vayor, in Deuthur, in Com. Mont-   of Penthryn,
of this man.   gomery.   of

Nathaniel Humfreys, of City of London ⊤ dr. of Winton of Abington, Berks.

Thomas Humfreys ⊤ ... dr. of   Sr William Humfreys, ⊤ Margt, d. of Wm.
citizen of London. ... house   of London, Kt., Sheriff   Wintour, of Dy-
                    of London. of London.   mock, in Gloucester,
                                                          dead, 1704.

Orlando Humfreys, Esq.; unmarried; only child.

Addressed on back (being apparently the cover for the letter).
To the Right Reverend
    HUMFREY, LORD BISHOP OF HEREFORD, Hereford Palace.
Postmark, "Go." } "1s. 8d."
         "No. 14."

Decr. 30, 1704.

MY GOOD LORD,—Yor Lo'ps of ye 4th from Whitborn I had not until the 13th, and pursuant to y'r Lo'ps com'ands have ever since made all ye enquiries I co'd into ye affair menconed in it. Mr. Tho. Price[1] has been dead since last spring, w'ch I thought I might have acquainted y'r Lo'p of

---
[1] This would be the celebrated antiquary of Llanfyllin.

whn I was at Whitburn. His son was abroad for some time and Mr. Edwds. who had an interest in him, co'd not have ye perusal of y'r papers till within these 2 days, tho' it seems they contained nothing of moment in relation to any of the families in Deyddwr. Mr. Edwds. being acquainted with M. Evans' executors gave himself the trouble of perusing all his papers and has made the enclosed transcript w'ch I have sent y'r Lo'p for y'r satisfaction, tho' I believe it may be upon mistake, the other being likeliest to be Sir Wms. paternal line, and if taken out of a card[1] of the Derwas's of Penrhos, and if y't happens to be the paternal line y'n y'r Lo'p has ye Penrhyn at large in Mr. Edwds. paper. There are those alive and well remember Nathaniel, Sir William's father, who was a Tinman in London and dyed very rich, ye father Humphrey Griffith was a substantial freeholder in the L'dship of Deyddur (ab. 50 or 60 li. per ann.) as I am informed, but sold it and it is now in ye possession of one Davies and Rogers, both men of some note in the neighbourhood. Mr. Clopton of Llandrinio inherits ye Penrhyn's Estate by his Lady, I have made w't enquiry I co'd there but co'd meet with nothing satifactory as yet, some friends have promised me w't further information can be got in this matter tho' I do not find any g't curiosity y't way in this part of the country. W'ever I can add to the enclosed y'r Lo'p shall have as soon as possible, and if either of these accounts happen to be approved by y'r Lo'p it may be had in form.

Mr. Davies of Colfryn, who is employed under my L'd Bradford to receive the rents of Lo'p of Deyddwr, has promised me a sight of all ye old Rent Rolls, and if anything can be made out of y'm y't may furthur illustrate this matter y'r Lo'p shall have the trouble of it if worth while, if it be of any service or any satisfaction to y'r Lordship. In case these enquiries prove ineffectual I will readily send on to Mr. Lewis Jones for y'r Lo'p's Book, and send to Pontsbury, whence I p'sume it may easily be conveyed to your Lo'p. Wishing y'r Lo'p and Madme Hums. long life and health and many happy new years, I humbly beg y'r Lo'p's blessing and am, my Lord,

Your Lo'p's most obliged, faithfull, humble servant,

THO. HUMPHREYS.

W'tever com'ands yo'r Lo'p may have further in this matter I shall sooner have by London y'n any other way.

---

[1] This word is used frequently in this correspondence for "pedigree".

THE HUMFREYS PEDIGREE.

Brochwel Yscithroc, a Prince of Powys and Earl (or as some books stile him), Consul of Chester A.D. 603. He was general of ye Britains ag'st Ethelfred, K. of Northumberland. The arms of Brochwel Yscithroc: *S.*, 3 naggs' heads erased *ar.*, or, as some say, a chevron between 3 naggs' heads erased *arg.*; but I think there should be no chevron.	*a* Brochwel ap Aeddan. His arms, party per pale *or.* and *g.*, 2 lyons rampt. endorsed counterchanged.
|	|
Conan Garwyn, son of Brochwel Yscithroc	Selyf or Seleu ap Brochwel.
|	Beli ap Selyf.
Selyf ap Conan.	Griffith ap Beli.
Mael Mynan ap Selyf.	Gwyn ap Griffith.
Beli ap Mael Mynan.	Cadwgan Wenwys ap Gwyn.
Gwyliawe ap Beli.	Madoc ap Cadwgan.
Elise ap Gwyliawe.	Evan ap Madoc.
Cyngen ap Elise.	Griffith ap Evan,
Aeddan (or Aethan) ap Cyngen.	Sr Griffith Vau'n.
	Rinallt ap Sr Griffith.
	Griffith ap Rinallt.
	Owen.
	[This paper is addressed] For the Rt. Rev. The LORD BISHOP OF HEREFORD, at Whitbourn, near Worcester
a	No. 21.

31 *May* 1707.

MY LORD,—On behalf of Sir William Humfreys, I humbly begg of your Lordship to know whether, amongst your papers, you have not found the enclosed descent to be true? if so, be pleased, my Lord, to subscribe it, or to attest so much thereof as, to the best of your Lordship's knowledge may be true, especially that Griffith Vychan wore two coats quarterly; first, *sable*, two naggs' heads erased *arg.*, as descended from Brochwel, *Brenin* Powis; second, p. pale *or* and *gules*, two lions rampant, endorsed counterchanged, as descended from Brochwel ab Aeddan, if the whole in the pedigree should be unknown to your Lordship, which I can hardly think, be pleased to inform me of the faults thereof, if any, and to certifye so much thereof which is correct, and that it is the com'on report that Sir William Humphreys *(sic)* is descended in this manner.

I am, my Lord, y'r Lordship's most dutyfull servant,

P. LE NEVE NORROY.

Lre. for the Lord Bishop of Hereford.

THE HUMFREYS PEDIGREE.

My Lord,—About four months since I sent to your Lordship a packet, wherein was a pedigree of Sir William Humfreys, of which I begged your Lordship's thoughts, and, if you approved of it, your attestation; but not having heard from your Lordship since, I would beg now to know whether you received it, and your approbation, or dislike thereof, for that Sir William Humphreys *(sic)* would have the arms fixed him.

I am, my Lord, y'r Lordship's most humble servant,
Colledge of Arms,   Peter Le Neve Norroy.
London, 13 *November* 1707.

Drawing of Arms.
Sa, 3 coursers' heads erased *arg*.

Brochwel Skithrog, King of Powis and Earl of Chester, bears *sable*, 3 coursers' heads erased *argent*.
|
Conan Garwyn.   [1][=Leucy, d. of Clothien, of Cardigan.]
|
Selyff or Salmon Sarff Cadu.   [=? Hum, d. of Yner ap ......, Earle of Hereford.]
|
Mynan.
|
Maye Mynan.   [=Evah, d. of Meiric ap Kadvan, Lord of Raddevar,]
|
Belin [Beli].   [=Leucy, d. of Tewdur Mawr, Prince of South Wales.]
|
Glisseu [Elisseu].   [=Ann, d. of Kynrick ap Rhiwallon, a nobleman of Bromfield.]
|
Gwylawn [Gwylawe].   [=Alis, d. of Ivor ap Cadwgan ap Elyssau, Prince of Ferlix.]
|
Kyngen [or Congen].   [=Ysabel, d. of L. Selin Vraise K^t. of the Red.]
|
Aethan.   [=Ales, d. of Rodrick ap Tewdur Mawr.]
|
Brochwel [ap Aeddan].   [=Eva, d. of Meuric (?) Hen ap......[2]]
|
Salmon [Selyf or Seleu.]
|
Belin [Beli].
|
Griffith.   [=Jonet, d. of Sr William Camber, of Bretton, Kt.]
|

[Drawing of Arms—*or* and *gu*, 2 lyons endorsed counterchanged.]
Erased.—[I cannot recollect anything as to this coat; perhaps it might have been Ye Atachement of Cadwgan Wenwys below, or of Brochwel ap Aedan before. But I know it not at present.]

[1] The parts in square brackets were added in the Bishop's autograph.
[2] 'Card of my mother's family whose ancestor married ye dau. of Gwyn, as you may see in Vincent's *Carnarvonshire*, in ye College of Arms.

THE HUMFREYS PEDIGREE.

[But I think that this was not the bearing of Gwyn ap Griffith. His coat in all the books I have seen is the same as Brochwel Yscythrog, s. and ar., 3 naggs' heads erased s., as before.]

Gwyn ap Griffith bears party per pale *or* and *gules*, between two lyons counterchanged.

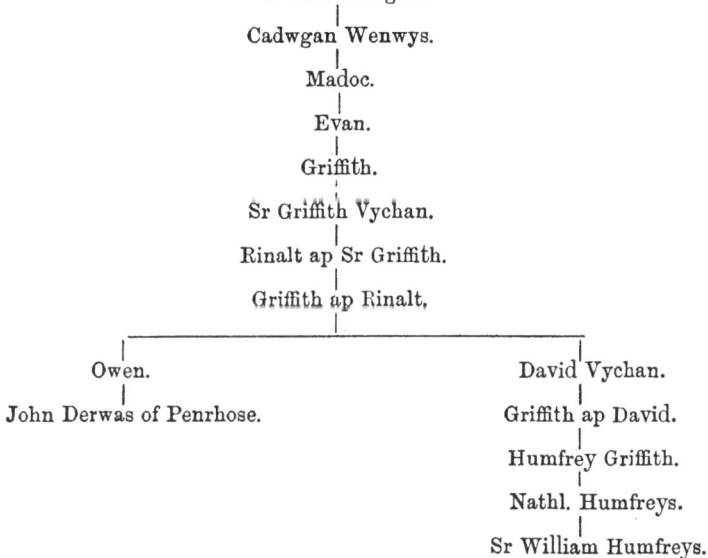

Cadwgan Wenwys.

Madoc.

Evan.

Griffith.

Sr Griffith Vychan.

Rinalt ap Sr Griffith.

Griffith ap Rinalt.

Owen.
John Derwas of Penrhose.

David Vychan.
Griffith ap David.
Humfrey Griffith.
Nathl. Humfreys.
Sr William Humfreys.

Nov. 22, 1707.—This was taken out of ye card of Mr. Derwas, of Penrhose. And I find by this, and several accounts I have out of Montgomeryshire and elsewhere, that Humfrey Griffith, ye grandfather of Sir William Humfreys, was a considerable freeholder in Deythur and Llandrinio, and descended fraternally from Brochwel Ysgithroc, whose coat, as above, I conceive he has a right to.

H. HEREFORD.

[On second page]. N.B.—Since I writ, as is on ye other side, concerning the two lyons endorsed, I am fully satisfied they were the Arms of Brochwel ap (Aeddan or) Aethen, for so I find in Mr. Robert Vaughan's (the best genealogist we have had in Wales), in his additions to Dr. Powel's *History*, printed at Oxon, but not finished by reason the author died when they were in the press; but twenty sheets were printed, and page 26, he says thus: "Brochwel ap Aeddan's coate, p' p' pale *or* and *g.*, two lyons rampant, endorsed counterchanged"; upon this I conceive Sir William hath a just right to ye three nagg's heads and two lyons (as drawn on the other side) quarterly.

Nov. 24, 1707.   H. HEREFORD.

THE HUMFREYS PEDIGREE.

In another account of ye descendants of Griffith Va'n of Deudwr, I find it thus:—

Griffith Va'n, of Penthryn Vawr, in Llandrinio. ⊤ Margt., d. of Oliver ap Evan Gethin ap Madoc Kyffin, Esq.

N.B. This Madoc Kyffin was ye paternal ancestor of ye Earl of Carbery, and the last Earl bore his arms (viz.), party per fene s. and a. a lyon ramp. counterchanged, as descended from Enion Evell.

Llewelyn ap Griffith, of Penrhyn, af's'd. ⊤ Angharad, dau. of Howel ap Madoc ap Iorwerth Goch, of Mochnant, Esq.

Griffith ap Llewelyn, of Penrhyn. ⊤ Beatrix, dau. and heir of William Kynaston, brother of S'r Roger Kynaston.

Humphrey Griffith, of Penrhyn. ⊤ Agnes, dau. of Meredyth ap William Griffith, of Swinere.

[1]Willm. Humfreys. ⊤ Dau. of William Penrhyn. Llewelyn ap Humfrey. ⊤ Catherine, dau. of David ap Howel, of Mochnant.

William ap Llewelyn, ancestor of the Penrhyns.

Nathaniel Humfrey, citizen of London, etc.

[1] I do not think this can be true, for it makes this Willm. marry his brother's son's daughter; but I take ye pedigree on the other side to be the true [one]. H. H.

Endorsements [in Bishop's autograph]. This out of ye Card of Derwas.

[In another handwriting.] S'r William Humphrey's pedigree found out amongst the papers of Lord Bishop Humphreys, late Bishop of Hereford.

WILLIAM GRIFFITH.

DRAWING [Sa., 3 naggs' heads ar.]   DRAWING.—[Or and gu., two lyons rampt., endorsed counterchanged.]

Brochwel Skithrog, King of Powis and Earl of Chester, bears sable, 3 coursers' heads erased a, g.
|
Conan Gwarwin.
|
Selyf or Salmon Sarff Cadu.
|
Mynan.
|
Mayl Mynan.
|
Bely.
|
Elissey.
| a

Gwyn ap Griffith bears party p' pale or and gu., 2 lyons ramp., endorsed counterchanged.[1]
|
Cadwgan Wenwys.
|
Madoc.
|
Evan.
|
Griffith.
| c

| b

[1] [This was ye bearing of Brochwel ap Aeddan, above-named, ancestor to this Gwyn. See Mr. Robt. Vaughan, our best genealogist, p. 26 of his additions to Dr. Powel, printed at Oxon in part, but never finished, because he dyed while it was in the press.] H. H.

THE HUMFREYS PEDIGREE.

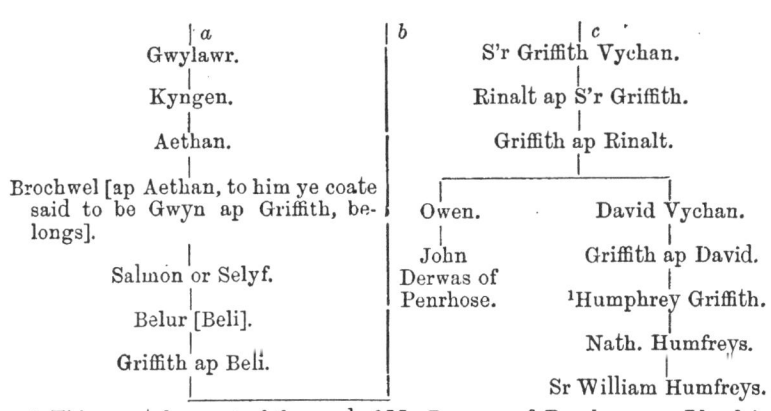

```
    | a                                  | b              | c
 Gwylawr.                                         S'r Griffith Vychan.
    |                                                    |
 Kyngen.                                          Rinalt ap S'r Griffith.
    |                                                    |
 Aethan.                                          Griffith ap Rinalt.
    |                                                    |
 Brochwel [ap Aethan, to him ye coate       ┌─────────────┴─────────────┐
   said to be Gwyn ap Griffith, be-       Owen.                David Vychan.
   longs].                                  |                       |
    |                                    John                 Griffith ap David.
 Salmon or Selyf.                      Derwas of                    |
    |                                   Penrhose.           ¹Humphrey Griffith.
 Belur [Beli].                                                      |
    |                                                         Nath. Humfreys.
 Griffith ap Beli.                                                  |
    |                                                        Sr William Humfreys.
```

¹ This was taken out of the card of Mr. Derwas, of Penrhose, nr. Llandrinio; and I find by this and several accounts I had from that country, that Humfrey Griffiths, S'r William's ancestor, was descended from Brochwel Scythroc and Brochwel ap Aeddan, and therefore conceive S'r William Humphreys has a just right to ye two coates above. H. HEREFORD.

Whereas, on ye other side, I referr to Mr. Robert Vaughan's account for ye descents, from Brochwel Yscithroc to Gwyn ap Griffith inclusive. You are to understand that ye said Robert Vaughan was Robert Vaughan of Hen Gwrt in Com' Merioneth, Esq., one of the greatest antiquaries wee had of late, and who was oft consulted by the learned primate Usher (as may be seen in Bishop Usher's letters, at the end of his life, by Dr. Parr). He left behind him a very large methodical collection of ye pedigrees of North Wales, containing twenty-four quires of paper, if I remember right, which, after his son's death, came into ye hands of Sir William Williams, the lawyer, and I presume it may still be in the hands of his son, Sir William Williams of Llanforda, com' Salop.

Mr. Vaughan published a litle-book (at Oxon, 1662) call'd *British Antiquitys*, revived and begun to print there. Dr. Powel's *Chronicle or History of Wales*, with large additions of his own, of which twenty sheets were printed off. But then, he dying at that time, ye work went no further, and w‍ᵗ. was wrought was sold off by the printer. I, being yn in Oxon, I got one copy; and out of the 26th page of that, had the confirmation of the descent above mentioned. H. H.

NOTES BY REV. W. V. LLOYD, R.N.

THE letters respecting Sir William Humfreys' arms are very interesting. Statements made therein are, in some cases, without authority and inaccurate. The only reliable pedigree given is that of "Derwas of Penrhos", down to their ancestor Owen, said to be a son of Griffith ap Reginald (of Garth) ap Sir Griffith Vaughan. It is unnecessary to ascend higher for our purpose. This Owen is given as the common ancestor of the Derwas and Humfreys families. The Derwas pedigree is to be found in *Brit. Mus. Add. MSS.*, 9864-5, under "Derwas of Llandrinio". I cannot find any other traces of this Owen ap Griffith ap Reginald. No authority of repute notices him. Lewys Dwnn names but two sons of Griffith ap Reginald of Garth. These were John Wynn (ap Griffith ap R.), of Garth, and David Lloyd (ap Griffith ap R), lord of half Broniarth and Gaervawr. Mr. Joseph Morris, in transcriptions of the Herald's visitations of 1584 and 1623, follows Lewys Dwnn. The *Cedwyn MS.* (about A.D. 1636) states that Griffith ap Reginald had but these two sons. It, however, adds, "and some illegitimate children". It also gives the issue of Anne, "natural daughter" of Griffith ap Reginald. (*Mont. Coll.*, vol. x, pp. 37-8-9.) Owen may have been one of these children, and as such is styled "Owen of Llandrinio", and his wife Anne, daughter of Hugh Say of Pool, by Ellen, daughter of Gwil. ap Griff. Derwas of Cemmes. (*Mont. Coll.*, vol. ix, p. 6.) But what about David Vychan, brother of Owen, and supposed ancestor of the Humfreys, Baronets? "Vychan" implies that his father must have been some David, not Griffith ap Reginald. The Derwas family I can trace in jury lists, from the 20th Eliz. down, but nothing of the baronet line. Humfrey Griffith, the freeholder in Deythur, if the pedigree is authentic, would be a contemporary of "Owen Derwas de Penrhyn Vechan, gen.", on a jury list in 1623 (see "Mis. His." in *Mont. Coll.* for that year), but I can find no trace of him.

Although the "David Vychan" generation puzzles me, and may be an error, I still think it probable that Sir William Humfreys was descended from a son, probably illegitimate, of Griffith ap Reginald of Garth. The Wynne of Garth pedigree (*Mont. Coll.*, vol. xii,

p. 258), says that Griffith ap Reginald had issue, as before stated, " David Lloyd ap Gr. of Broniarth, and John Wynne ap Gr. of Garth, etc." Whatever this " etc." may mean, it leaves room for further issue. The question is, does the pedigree or " card" of Derwas of Llandrinio, or Penrhos, show this " David Vychan"? To me, he is rather an ugly missing link. He bears out the suspicion of "cooking". The Mr. Derwas referred to in the correspondence was probably the Rev. Richard Dorwas, then (1707) vicar of Meivod. Another question arises : was the Bishop's information derived from the living Mr. Derwas, or from the "card" of the family? All the Bishop says is, that "this", the descent of Sir William Humfreys, "was taken out of ye card of Mr. Derwas of Penrhose". It will, doubtless, occur to you that the Mr. Derwas, the contemporary, and of the corresponding generation to Sir William, would be his fourth cousin, and therefore a reliable local authority.

The Bishop seems to have been exercised about the arms assumed by Aeddan ap Kyngen, party per pale, *or* and *gu.*, two lions, addorsed counterchanged. John Salisbury of Erbistocke, in the Wynne of Garth pedigree, says "some suppose them to be given him (Aeddan ap Kyngen) for a reward of his good service in the warrs with the Princes of Powis and of South Wales, whose arms they have united in one escutcheon ; but others rather think this bearing an assumption of his own, as being a pretender to both those principalities, in the male line, the elder houses of both being terminated in daughters". (*Mont. Coll.*, vol. xii, p. 256.) I quite agree with Mr. Salisbury ; and if I could get the world to believe the same, I should immediately put in my claim to the principality of Powys, as the senior male representative of Brochwel ap Aeddan ap Kyngen. (See *Mont. Coll.*, vol. vi, p. 78.)

Although the Bishop may have been considered an " oracle" in divinity, Peter le Neve, Norroy, ought to have known better than to accept him as such in heraldry. The autograph additions, the matrimonial alliances of the early generations of the "Derwas card", are altogether too good. Take, for example, the spouse of Gwylawg, viz., "Alis d. of Ivor ap Cadwgan ap Elystan, Prince of Ferlix". Cadelh, great-grandson of Gwylawg (the latter being one of the Princes of Powys, recorded on the pillar of "Eliseg, filius Guoillanc"), is known to have died about A.D. 800. Cadwgan ap Elystan is said, by Lewys Dwnn, on the Pryce of Newtown pedigree, to have had, as his second wife "Jane (fourth in descent from Gwylawg), daughter of Brochwel ap Aeddan of Powys". In the same pedigree it states that "William the Conqueror fell upon this Cadwgan, and took all the English country from him". So that the Bishop marries Alis, the granddaughter of a man living in 1085, to a prince of Powys, living in the eighth century. . The Bishop, I believe, has the credit of being the first generous individual who has found wives for our early Brochwellian Princes of Powys. At all events, his additions are so far curious to me, that I have never seen them before.

I find that Sir Orlando Humfreys left a daughter, Mary, who married John, a younger son of Robert Honywood of Evington, Hants, or Charing, Kent, by Mary, heiress of Sir Richard Sandford, Bart. (See Betham's *Baronetage*, under Honywood, baronets of Evington, Hants. Ed., 1802, vol. ii, p. 133, note.) I add, in pedigree form, the genealogy of "Derwas of Llandrinio"[1] (*Add. MSS.*, 9864-5, Brit. Museum), with David Vichan, the alleged ancestor of Sir William Humfreys, introduced. W. V. LL.

LLANDRINIO PARISH.[1]
Add. MSS. 9865, *Brit. Mus.*

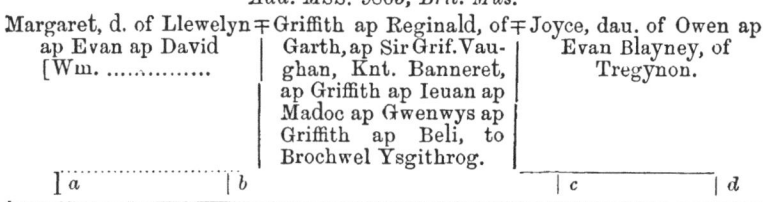

Margaret, d. of Llewelyn ⫛ Griffith ap Reginald, of ⫛ Joyce, dau. of Owen ap
ap Evan ap David | Garth, ap Sir Grif. Vau- | Evan Blayney, of
[Wm. .... | ghan, Knt. Banneret, | Tregynon.
 | ap Griffith ap Ieuan ap |
 | Madoc ap Gwenwys ap |
 | Griffith ap Beli, to |
 | Brochwel Ysgithrog. |

| a | b | c | d

[1] We are indebted to Mr. T. W. Hancock for making a copy of this pedigree.

THE HUMFREYS PEDIGREE.

a	b	c	d
[¹David Vy-⊤ chan.	Owen.⊤Anne, dau. of Hugh Say, of Pool, by Ellen, dau. of Gwilim ap Griffith Derwas, of Kemes.	David Lloyd, of Broniarth and Gaervawr.	John Wynne, of Garth.

Griffith ap David ⊤

Humfrey Griffith. ⊤

Nathaniel Humfreys. ⊤

Sir William Humfreys, ⊤ Bart,

Sir Orlando Humfreys,⊤ 2nd Bart., died 14, June 1737.

Mary, wife of John Honeywood.]

Ellen, dau. of⊤ John ⊤Anne, dau. of Richard Sandford, of the Isle. 1st wife.
Edwin Lloyd. | Derwas.
2nd wife.

Owen Derwas.⊤Joyce, dau. of David Lloyd Geoffrey.

David Derwas,⊤ Blanch, dau. of Edw. Thomas, of Hendre Hen,
of Penrhyn Vechan.

John Derwas.⊤Catherine, dau. of John Kynaston, of Llwyn y Mapsis.

David Derwas. = Dorothy, dau. of John Edwards, of Ness Lestrange, Esq.
of Llwyn y Mapsis, 1700.

Richard Derwas ⊤Margaret, dau. of Jeffrey Penrhyn, Esq.

Hugh Derwas,⊤Mary, dau. of Jeffrey ap Llewelyn ap Griffith ap Adda.
of Penrhyn.

John Derwas. ⊤ Gwen, dau. of Thos. ap Reginald of Llandrinio.

Richard ⊤ Margaret, dau. of Thos. ap William of Waynowddyn.
Derwas.

John Derwas, of= Elizabeth, dau. of William Tanat, of Trewylan Issa.
of Penrhyn, in 1700.

William Derwas.⊤ Maly, dau. of Humffr. Lloyd, of Coedd Deuddwr.

Griffith Derwas, ⊤Catherine, dau. of David Tanat, of Tredderwen, Gent.
of New Chapel.

Hugh Derwas, ⊤ Margt., dau. of Oliver Lloyd, of Goitre.
of Penrhos.

Richard Derwas,⊤ ....
Vicar of Meivod, | Y Rondal. Vicar of
1700 | Meifod.

Elizabath, 1700.

Mary, 1700.

John Derwas, (? a brother of=.....................
Rev. Rich. Derwas.)

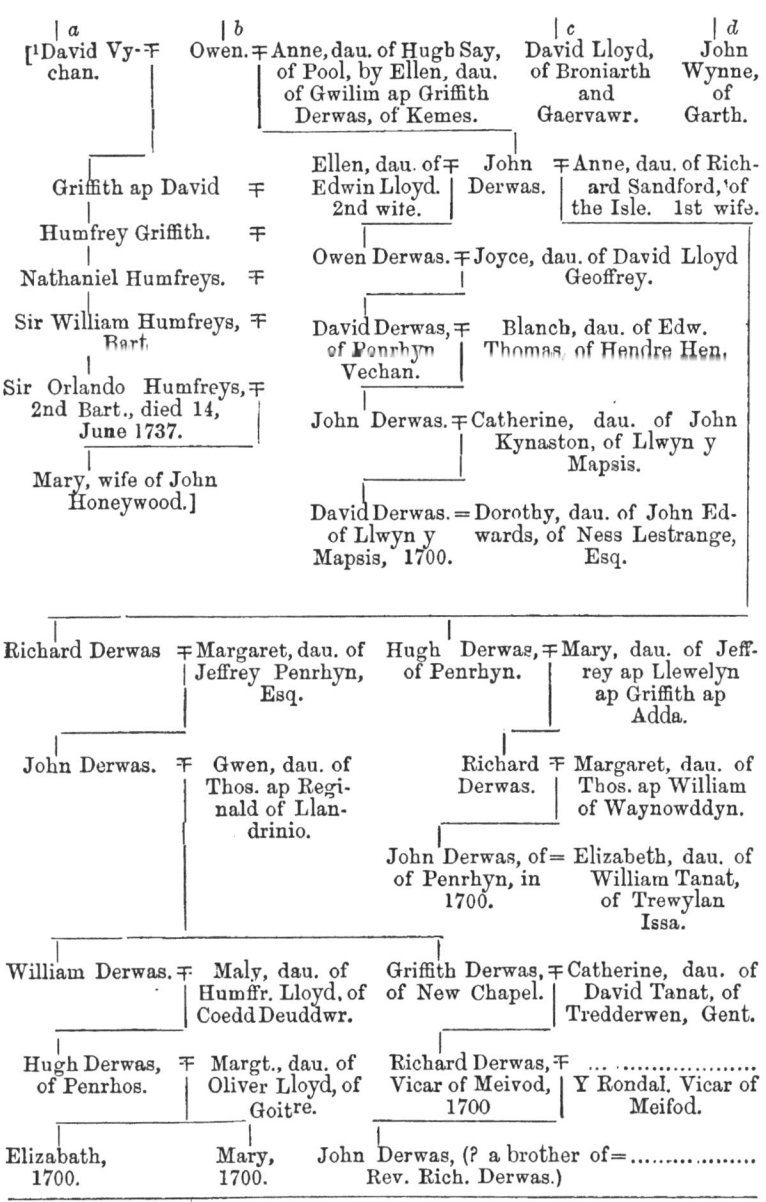

¹ "David Vychan" and his descendants have been here introduced to show their supposed connection with Owen and his descendants, as given in the "Derwas" pedigree.

PEDIGREE OF MR. AND MRS. SEYMOUR DAVIES OF HIGHMEAD, CARDIGANSHIRE, AND DOLGADFAN, LLANBRYNMAIR, MONTGOMERYSHIRE.

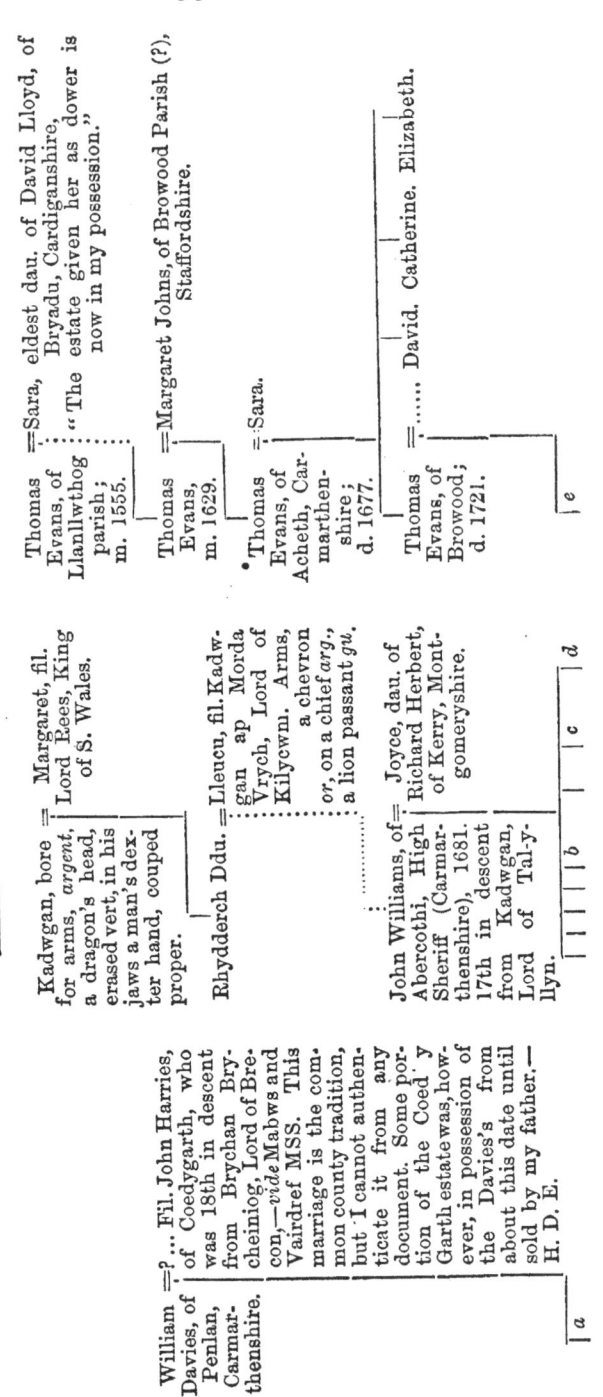

William =?... Fil. John Harries, Davies, of Penlan, Carmarthenshire. of Coedygarth, who was 18th in descent from Brychan Brycheiniog, Lord of Brecon,—*vide* Mabws and Vairdref MSS. This marriage is the common county tradition, but I cannot authenticate it from any document. Some portion of the Coed' y Garth estate was, however, in possession of the Davies's from about this date until sold by my father.—H. D. E.

Kadwgan, bore for arms, *argent*, a dragon's head, erased *vert*, in his jaws a man's dexter hand, couped proper. = Margaret, fil. Lord Rees, King of S. Wales.

Rhydderch Ddu. = Lleucu, fil. Kadwgan ap Morda Vrych, Lord of Kilycwm. Arms, a chevron *or*, on a chief *arg.*, a lion passant *gu.*

John Williams, of Abercothi, High Sheriff (Carmarthenshire), 1681. 17th in descent from Kadwgan, Lord of Tal-y-llyn. = Joyce, dau. of Richard Herbert, of Kerry, Montgomeryshire.

Thomas Evans, of Llanllwthog parish; m. 1555. = Sara, eldest dau. of David Lloyd, of Bryadu, Cardiganshire, "The estate given her as dower is now in my possession."

Thomas Evans, m. 1629. = Margaret Johns, of Browood Parish (?), Staffordshire.

Thomas Evans, of Acheth, Carmarthenshire; d. 1677. = Sara.

Thomas Evans, of Browood; d. 1721. = ... David. Catherine. Elizabeth.

| a | b | c | d | e |

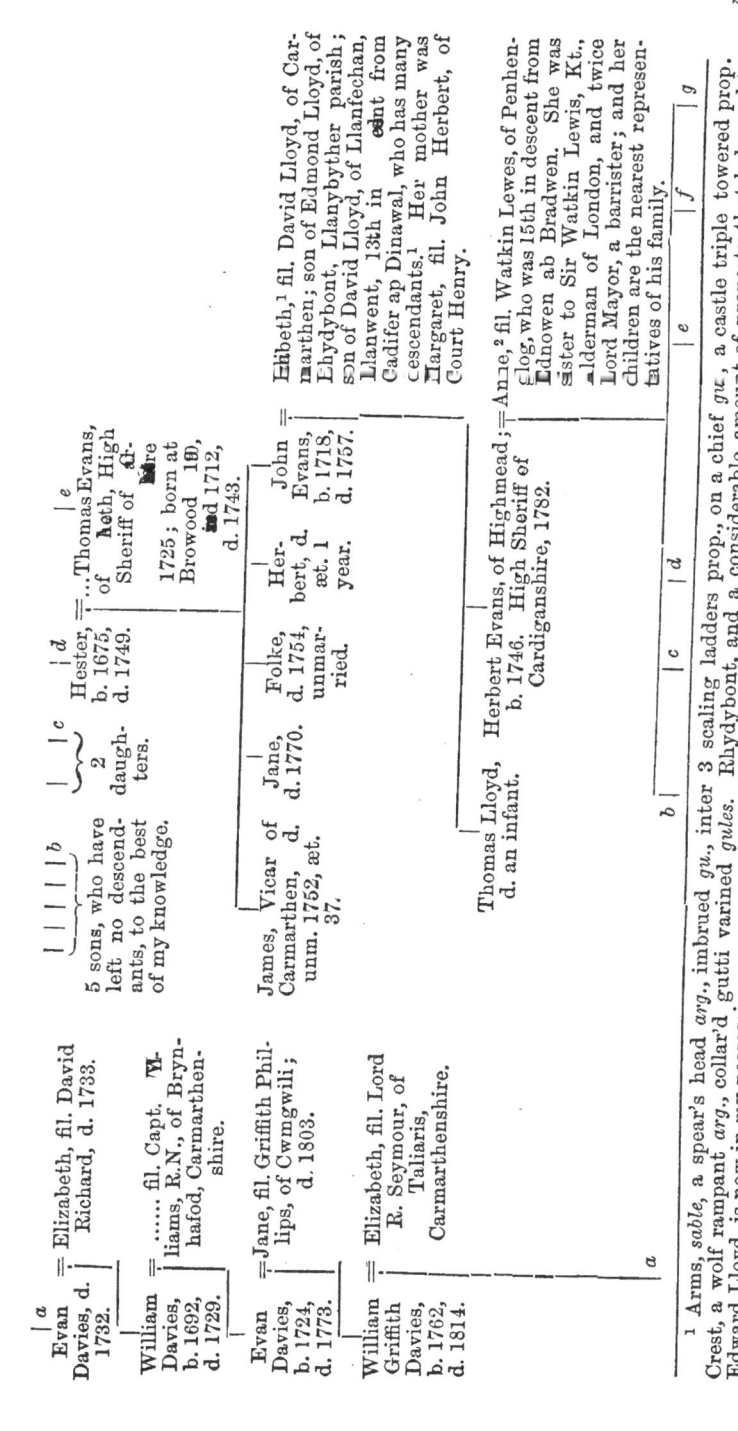

PEDIGREE OF MR. AND MRS. SEYMOUR DAVIES. 31

[Pedigree chart:]

a — Evan Davies, d. 1732. = Elizabeth, fil. David Richard, d. 1733.

b — William Davies, b. 1692, d. 1729. = ... fil. Capt. Williams, R.N., of Brynhafod, Carmarthenshire.

5 sons, who have left no descendants, to the best of my knowledge.

c — 2 daughters.

d — Hester, b. 1675, d. 1749. = ...Thomas Evans, of Aeth, High Sheriff of ...... 1725; born at Browood 10, and 1712, d. 1743.

e — Elizabeth,[1] fil. David Lloyd, of Carmarthen; son of Edmond Lloyd, of Rhydybont, Llanybyther parish; son of David Lloyd, of Llanfechan, Llanwent, 13th in descent from Cadifer ap Dinawal, who has many descendants.[1] Her mother was Margaret, fil. John Herbert, of Court Henry.

Evan Davies, b. 1724, d. 1773. = Jane, fil. Griffith Phillips, of Cwmgwili; d. 1803.

James, Vicar of Carmarthen, d. unm. 1752, æt. 37.

Folke, d. 1754, unmarried.

Jane, d. 1770.

Herbert, d. æt. 1 year.

John Evans, b. 1718, d. 1757.

William Griffith Davies, b. 1762, d. 1814. = Elizabeth, fil. Lord R. Seymour, of Taliaris, Carmarthenshire.

Herbert Evans, of Highmead, b. 1746. High Sheriff of Cardiganshire, 1782. = Anne,[2] fil. Watkin Lewes, of Penhenclog, who was 15th in descent from Ednowen ab Bradwen. She was sister to Sir Watkin Lewis, Kt., Alderman of London, and twice Lord Mayor, a barrister; and her children are the nearest representatives of his family.

Thomas Lloyd, d. an infant.

a **b** **c** **d** **e** **f** **g**

[1] Arms, *sable*, a spear's head *arg.*, imbrued *gu.*, inter 3 scaling ladders prop., on a chief *gu.*, a wolf rampant *arg.*, collar'd gutti varined *gules*. Rhydybont, and a considerable amount of property that belonged to Edward Lloyd, is now in my possession.

[2] Arms of Sir Watkin Lewes. Quarterly; 1st and 4th, *Or*, three serpents conjoined in triangle vert, 2nd and 3rd *arg.*, a lion rampant *sable*. Crest, an eagle displayed *sable*, the feet resting on the wreath, in the beak and enwrapped around the body a serpent proper.

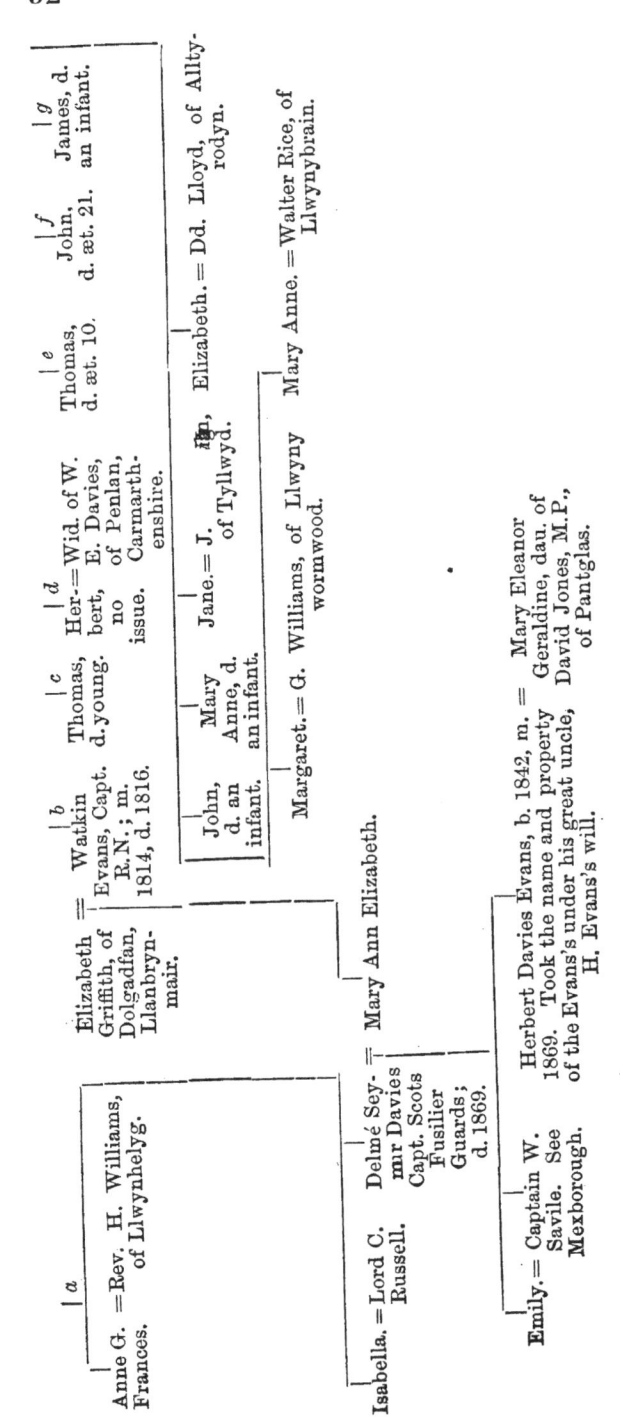

PEDIGREE OF MR. AND MRS. SEYMOUR DAVIES.

a. Anne G. Frances = Rev. H. Williams, of Llwynhelyg.

b. Elizabeth Griffith, of Dolgadfan, Llanbrynmair, = Watkin Evans, Capt. R.N.; m. 1814, d. 1816.

c. Thomas, d. young.

d. Herbert, Wid. of W. E. Davies, of Penlan, Carmarthenshire. no issue.

e. Thomas, d. æt. 10.

f. John, d. æt. 21.

g. James, d. an infant.

John, d. an infant.

Mary Anne, d. an infant.

Jane. = J. ⟨⟩, of Tyllwyd.

Elizabeth. = Dd. Lloyd, of Alltyrodyn.

Margaret. = G. Williams, of Llwyny wormwood.

Mary Anne. = Walter Rice, of Llwynybrain.

Mary Ann Elizabeth.

Isabella. = Lord C. Russell.

Delmé Seymr Davies Capt. Scots Fusilier Guards; d. 1869. = Mary Ann Elizabeth.

Emily. = Captain W. Savile. See Mexborough.

Herbert Davies Evans, b. 1842, m. 1869. Took the name and property of the Evans's under his great uncle, H. Evans's will. = Mary Eleanor Geraldine, dau. of David Jones, M.P., of Pantglas.

SCULPTURED TOMBSTONE IN MEIFOD CHURCH.

SCULPTURED TOMBSTONE IN MEIFOD CHURCH.

IN the July number (1880) of the *Archæologia Cambrensis* (p. 184), the Rev. D. R. Thomas, present vicar of Meifod, has given a paper on this subject, and has kindly permitted us to reprint it in the *Montgomeryshire Collections*, of which permission we gladly avail ourselves, being anxious to collect therein all information obtainable on Montgomeryshire subjects. Mr. Thomas seems somewhat fanciful in his interpretation of the alleged symbols, which it is very difficult to discover, even in Mr. Worthington Smith's beautiful woodcut of the sculptured stone. However, if these sculptures are really "the well reasoned designs of some thoughtful mind", it seems well they should have so able and strongly imaginative an interpreter as the present Vicar of Meifod.

"The history of Meifod has been twice published, first in the *Cambrian Quarterly Magazine*, 1829, by the Rev. Walter Davies, M.A., who had been Curate of the parish from 1796 to 1805; which account has been reprinted in the third volume of his Works, edited by the Rev. D. Silvan Evans, B.D. (*Gwaith Gwallter Mechain*, Cyfrol, iii, p. 99); and more recently in the *Montgomeryshire Collections*, 1875, 1876, and 1877, by the Rev. Canon Wynne Edwards, vicar of the parish from 1860 to 1877. In both of these histories there is a brief account of this stone; but neither of them is quite satisfactory, as the former describes but does not illustrate it, and the latter illustrates it without describing the details. A much better account, accompanied with a far more faithful illustration, is given in Professor Westwood's *Lapidarium Walliæ*, p. 154, and Plate lxxii, fig. 1. The stone, however, is so interesting, and its ornamentation so curious, that it deserves a place in the pages of our Journal, where Mr. Worthington G. Smith's admirable drawing will greatly enhance its value.

"Mr. Walter Davies states that 'near the font is an antique tombstone without inscription save rude sculpture, in bas-relief, of a St. Catherine's wheel in chief, a sword, and the edges garnished with figures in humble representation of what are called 'true love's knots'. What is here taken to be a sword is the stem of the cross, and the 'true love's knots' are the Celtic interlacings and other designs with which it is embellished. Its position has been changed to the west end of the south aisle, where it now stands upright against the west wall. 'It was removed,' Mr. Wynne Edwards informs us, 'to this place about forty years ago, from a recumbent position in which it was previously placed near the chancel-rails.' It stands 4 feet 10 inches high from the floor of the church; and its width is at the top 22 inches, and at the bottom 16 inches. From the way in which the lower portion has been worn away it is evident that it must have been continually trodden upon by the feet of the ministrant in the celebration of the Holy Communion; and having been on the north side, its position would correspond with that generally assigned to the founder's tomb. With this corresponds the tradition that assigns it to one of the Princes of Powys; and if I be right in the surmise that 'St. Mary's Church in Meifod', which was consecrated A.D. 1154, was a Lady chapel built on to the east end of the earlier St. Tysilio's, then this might be the memorial of 'Madoc ap Meredydd, Prince of Powys, who was buried with honour in Meifod, where was the watch-tower in St. Tysilio's Church.' 'Ym meiuot yn y lle yd oed y wylwa yn eglwys Tyssiliaw sant y cladwyt yn enrydedus.' (*Brut y Tywysogion*, ed. 1870, p. 627 b.)

"But Professor Westwood, whose authority must be allowed to be of the highest weight in all matters of Celtic palæography, claims for it a much earlier date: 'There is no inscription on the stone; but I apprehend, from its general appearance, that it is considerably older than the twelfth century'; [during which century (the Professor adds) it is recorded 'that here, besides the earlier princes of the family of Mervyn and Convyn were interred at a later period Madoc ap Meredydd, Prince of Powys, in 1159, and his eldest son Gruffydd Maelor in 1190']. (*Lapidarium Walliæ*, p. 184.) Leaving, therefore, as needs we must, its date and appropriation still unsettled, let us examine a little more closely its ornamental details. 'The ornamentation,' Mr. Westwood tells us, 'is very peculiar, since in addition to the large cross in the middle of the stone, decorated with interlaced ornaments, there is a wheel-cross in the upper part, within which is very rudely carved the figure of our Lord crucified, with raised pellets in the spaces within the limbs of the cross. In addition to the various interlacements there are, on the right side of the stone, several small, ill-shaped quadrupeds, one with a wide, gaping mouth.' It is not, however, on the right side alone that these animal forms are found; but all around the edge, where it remains undestroyed by wear and tear. Thus, while on the right hand-side a grotesque, cat-like, creature appears to be gnawing away at a worm, and above it a hare seems to be running for its life, at the top a coiled snake is seen rolling out its forked tongue; and on the left the outline of a dragon, or some similar malignant beast.

"Looking, as I have often done, at these details, the question has again and again occurred, Have they any meaning? Are they merely the skilful devices of some ingenious craftsman? Or are they the well-reasoned designs of some thoughtful mind that would thus engrave its lessons in stone? And I have come to the conclusion that they are the latter; that they are symbolical in their meaning, and eminently Christian in their character.

"In the first place I would interpret the interlacements, which occupy positions in all parts of the stone, as indicating the interweaving of circumstances in the life of man; or, indeed, in time itself; whilst those which have no beginning or ending will represent eternity. Between them they may teach the immortality of the soul. Next, I would compare the grotesque and malignant forms along the outer edge to the similar forms which may be seen on gurgoyles, and generally on the exterior of churches. These I would read as signifying the evil spirits by whom the fall of man was wrought, and by whose influence the moral evil of the world is perpetuated; the spirits of revenge, of fear, of cunning, and of malice. In high relief, above all these, and filling the central portion, stands the cross surrounded with the *triquetra*, the emblem of the Holy Trinity, and various forms of the cross and crown. Above the arms of the cross, again, are labels on either side, figured with the ribbon-pattern, which may have been intended to represent the superscription over the cross, just as in some large churches is done by a double transept. And last, but chiefest of all, and heading the sculpture, on a cross contained within a crown, is 'Jesus Christ and He crucified.'

"Meifod. *May* 1880. "D. R. T."

STONE, WITH MASON'S MARKS (?), MEIFOD.

WE re-produce from *Lapidarium Walliæ* (p. 154), the plate representing a sculptured stone, now built in the south-east wall of the church of Meifod, about 15 feet from the ground. Professor Westwood says that "it is 2 feet 4 inches long, and 4 inches wide, and is covered with a variety of small crosses, some enclosed within oblong oval spaces and other marks, apparently cut with a knife or chisel, the object of which it is not possible to discover, unless they can be considered as masons' marks".

The repetition of the same figures seems to negative the idea of their being masons' marks. By being engraved in so splendid a work as the *Lapidarium Walliæ*, it is questionable whether it has not had attributed to it undue importance.

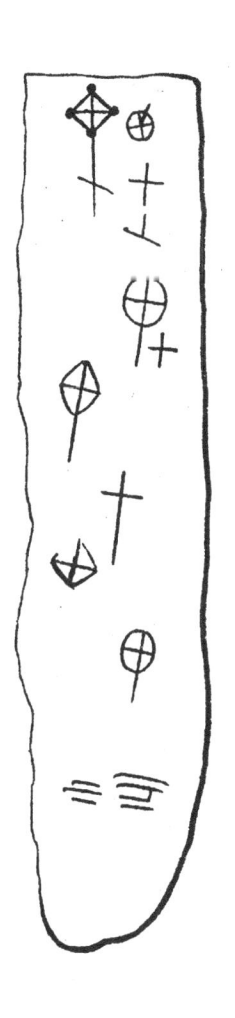

THE STONE WITH MASON'S MARKS.?
Meifod.

A LIST OF MEMBERS OF PARLIAMENT FOR MONTGOMERYSHIRE.

In the second volume of *Montgomeryshire Collections*, Mr. E. R. Morris compiled a List of Members for the County and Boroughs, giving as his authorities Browne Willis's *Notitia Parliamentaria*, Beatson's *Chronological Register*, Cobbet's *Parliamentary History*, and Oldfield's *Representative History*. During the past year a " Blue Book" has been issued, entitled, "Return of *Members of Parliament;* ordered by the House of Commons to be printed, March 1878". This List, we are informed, "has been compiled from Writs and Returns preserved in the Public Record Office, checked with the Books of Parliamentary Returns preserved at the Crown Office." Being thus official, I have thought it would be interesting to copy the list, with all its variety of spellings of names, and point out where it differs from that compiled by Mr. E. R. Morris.

ASKEW ROBERTS.

Croeswylan, Oswestry.

COUNTY.	BOROUGHS.
1541-2. Jacobus Leche, armiger.	Willielmus Herbert.
1545. (No Returns found.[1])	
1547. (Return omitted in list.)	
1552-3. Edwardus Herbert, armiger.	Ricardus Herbert, generosus.
1553. Edwardus Herbert, armiger.	Johannes ap Edmunde, generosus.
1554. Edwardus Herbert, armiger.	Ricardus Floyd, generosus.
1554. Edwardus Herbert, armiger.	(No Return found.)
1555. (Return omitted in list.)	
1557-8. Edwardus Herbert, armiger.	Willielmus Herbert, senior, armiger.

[1] No Returns found for England or Wales in 1545.

LIST OF MEMBERS OF PARLIAMENT

COUNTY.	BOROUGHS.
1558-9. Edward Herbert, Esq.	John Man, Esq.
1562-3. Edward Herbert, Esq.	John Price, gent.
1572. John Price, Esq., of New Town.	Roland Pughe, Esq.
1584. Richard Harbert, Esq., of Montgomery.	Richard Harbert, gent., of Gray's Inn.
1586. Oliver Lloid, Esq.	Matthew Harbert, gent.
1588-9. Edward Herberte, Esq.	(Return torn.)
1592-3. Reginald Williams, Esq.	Richard Morgan, gent.
1597. William Herbert, Esq.	Thomas Jucks, Esq.
1601. (Return torn.)	John Harries, Esq.
1603-4. (No Returns found.)	
1614. (No Returns found.[1])	
1620-1. Sir William Herbert, Knight of the Bath.	Edward Herbert, Esq.
1623-4. Sir William Herbert, Knt.	George Herbert, gent.
1625. Sir William Herberte, Knt.	George Herberte, Esq.
1625-6. Sir William Herbert, Knt.	Sir Henry Herbert, Knt.
1627-8. Sir William Herbert, Knt.	*Richard Lloyd, gent.
1640. Richard Herbert, Esq.	Sir Edward Lloyd, Knt.
1640. Sir John Price, Bart.[2]	Richard Herbert, Esq.
[Edward Vaughan, Esq.]	[George Devereux, Esq.]
1653. (No Return.[3])	
1654. Sir ...... Bart.	Charles ......
1656. (No Returns found.)	
1658-9. (No Returns found.)	
1660. John Purcell, Esq.	Thomas Myddleton, Esq.[4]
1661. (No Return found.)	John Purcell, Esq.
[Andrew Newport, Esq.[5]]	
1678-9. Edward Vaughan, Esq.	Matthew Price, Esq.[6]
1679. Edward Vaughan, Esq.	Matthew Pryce, Esq.
1680-1. Edward Vaughan, Esq.	Matthew Price, Esq.
1685. Edward Vaughan, Esq.	William Williams, Esq.
1688-9. Edward Vaughan, Esq., of Llandiarth.	Charles Herbert, Esq., of Aston.

[1] There were no Returns found for Wales of this year.

[2] The Long Parliament. ": Sir John Price, Knt." (sic) and Richard Herbert " disabled to sit".

[3] There are no Returns for England or Wales given in this year.

[4] Another Indenture of the same date (still amongst the Returns) returning Herbert Evans, Esq., was disallowed, and the above declared duly elected by order of the House, 27th June 1660. (*Commons' Journals.*)

[5] Elected 25th October 1661, *vice* Edward Vaughan, deceased.

[6] Double Return of the same date. That by which Edward Lloyd, Esq., was returned was declared void by order of the House, dated 1st April 1679. (*Commons' Journals.*)

FOR MONTGOMERYSHIRE.

	COUNTY.	BOROUGHS.
1689-90.	Edward Vaughan, Esq.	Charles Herbert, Esq.
		[Price Deverux, Esq.[1]]
1695.	Edward Vaughan, Esq.	Price Devereux, Esq.
1698.	Edward Vaughan, Esq.	Price Devereux, Esq.
1700-1.	Edward Vaughan, Esq.	John Vaughan, Esq.
1701.	Edward Vaughan, Esq.	John Vaughan, Esq.
1702.	Edward Vaughan, Esq.	John Vaughan, Esq.[2]
1705.	Edward Vaughan, Esq., of Lloydiarth.	Charles Mason, Esq.
1708.	Edward Vaughan, Esq.	John Pugh, Esq.
1710	Edward Vaughan, Esq.	John Pugh, Esq.
1713.	Edward Vaughan, Esq.	John Pugh, Esq.[3]
1714-15.	Edward Vaughan, Esq.	John Pugh, Esq.
	[Price Devereux, Esq.[4]]	
1722.	Pryce Devereux, Esq.	John Pughe, Esq.
1727.	Price Devereux, Esq.	William Corbet, Esq.[5]
1734.	Price Devereux, Esq.	William Corbet, Esq.
	[Robert Williams, Esq.[6]]	
1741.	Sir Watkin Williams Wynn, Bart., of Llwydiarth.	James Cholmondeley, Esq.
	[Robert Williams, Esq.[7]]	
1747.	Edward Kynaston, Esq.	Henry Herbert, Esq.
		[Francis Herbert, Esq.[8]]
1754.	Edward Kynaston, Esq.	William Bodvill, Esq.
		[Richard Clive, Esq.[9]]
1761.	Edward Kynaston, Esq.	Richard Clive, Esq.
1768.	Edward Kynaston, Esq.	Richard Clive, Esq.
	[Watkin Williams, Esq.[10]]	[Frederick Cornewall, Esq.[11]]

[1] Of Vaynor, elected 18th November 1691, *vice* Charles Herbert, Esq., deceased.

[2] "Montgomery, Llanidloes, Pool and Llanfylling Borough" (heretofore it has been "Montgomery Borough" only).

[3] Again described as "Montgomery Borough" only.

[4] Elected 9th January 1718-19, *vice* Edward Vaughan, Esq., deceased.

[5] Double Return. The Indenture by which Robert Williams, Esq., was returned was taken off the file by order of the House, dated 16th April 1728.

[6] Elected 12th December 1740, *vice* Price Devereux, Esq., called to the Upper House as Lord Viscount Hereford.

[7] Elected 2nd April 1742, *vice* Sir Watkin Williams Wynn, who elected to serve for the county of Denbigh.

[8] Elected 16th April 1748, *vice* Henry Herbert, deceased.

[9] Elected 21st November 1759, *vice* William Bodvill, deceased.

[10] Elected 9th June 1772, *vice* Edward Kynaston, deceased.

[11] Elected 15th June 1771, *vice* Richard Clive, deceased.

40 LIST OF MEMBERS OF PARLIAMENT

	COUNTY.	BOROUGHS.
1774.	William Owen, Esq.	Whitshed Keene, Esq.[1]
1780.	William Owen, Esq.	Whitshed Keene, Esq.[2]
1784.	William Owen, Esq.	Whitshed Keene, Esq.
1790.	William Owen, Esq., of Bryngwyn. [Francis Lloyd, Esq.[3]]	Whitshed Keene, Esq.
1796.	Francis Lloyd, Esq. [Charles W. Williams Wynn, Esq.[4]]	Whitshed Keene, Esq.
1802.	Charles W. W. Wynn, of Llwydiarth.	Whitshed Keene, Esq.
1806.	Charles W. W. Wynn, Esq., of Pentrefgoe.	Whitshed Keene, Esq.
1807.	Charles W. W. Wynn, Esq., of Penhygoe.	Whitshed Keene, Esq.
1812.	Charles W. W. Wynn, Esq.	Whitshed Keene, Esq.
1818.	Charles W. W. Wynn, Esq.	Henry Clive, Esq.
1820.	Charles W. W. Wynn, Esq.[5]	Henry Clive, Esq.
1826.	Charles W. W. Wynn, Esq.	Henry Clive, Esq.
1830.	Charles W. W. Wynn, Esq.[6]	Henry Clive, Esq.
1831.	Charles W. W. Wynn, Esq.	Henry Clive, Esq.
1833.	Charles W. W. Wynn, Esq.	David Pugh, Esq. [John Edwards, Esq.[7]]
1835.	Charles W. W. Wynn, Esq.	John Edwards, Esq.
1837.	Charles W. W. Wynn, Esq.	John Edwards, Esq.
1841.	Charles W. W. Wynn, Esq., of Pentrego.	Hugh Cholmondeley, Esq.
1847.	Charles W. W. Wynn, Esq. [Herbert W. W. Wynn, Esq.[9]]	David Pugh, Esq.[8]

[1] Re-elected 4th July 1777, after accepting the Stewardship of the Chiltern Hundreds. Re-elected 1st January 1779, after appointment as Surveyor-General of Wales.

[2] Re-elected 16th April 1783, after appointment as one of the Lords Commissioners of the Admiralty.

[3] Of Domgay, elected 4th April 1795, vice William Owen, deceased.

[4] Of Glascoed Hall, elected 14th March 1799, vice Francis Lloyd, deceased.

[5] Re-elected 18th February 1822, after appointment as First Commissioner for the Affairs of India.

[6] Re-elected 15th December 1830, after appointment as Secretary at War.

[7] Elected 8th April 1833, vice David Pugh, whose election was declared void.

[8] Double Return. The Indenture returning Hugh Cholmondeley, Esq., was taken off the file by order of the House, dated 14th February 1848.

[9] Of 18, St. James's Square. Elected 11th October 1850, vice Charles W. W. Wynn, Esq., deceased.

	COUNTY.	BOROUGHS.
1852.	Herbert W. W. Wynn, Esq.	David Pugh, Esq.
1857.	Herbert W. W. Wynn, Esq.	David Pugh, Esq.
1859.	Herbert W. W. Wynn, Esq.	David Pugh, Esq.
	[Charles W. Williams Wynn, Esq.[1]	[John Samuel Willes Johnson.[2]]
		[Charles Richard Douglas Hanbury Tracy, Esq.[3]]
1865.	Charles W. W. Wynn, Esq.	C. R. D. Hanbury Tracy, Esq.
1868.	Charles W. W. Wynn, Esq.	C. R. D. Hanbury Tracy, Esq.
1874.	Charles W. W. Wynn, Esq., of Coedymaen	C. D. R. Hanbury Tracy, Esq., of 63, Eccleston Square.
		[Frederick Stephen Archibald Hanbury Tracy, Esq.[4]]

The *Blue Book* ends with the election of 1874. In April 1880, at the General Election, Stuart Rendel, Esq., was returned for the County, and the Hon. Frederick Hanbury Tracy was re-elected for the Boroughs. I will now, in as short a space as possible, point out where the official list varies with the one compiled for the second volume of *Montgomeryshire Collections*:—

1541-2. *For* Edward Leeche (in *Mont. Coll.*) *read* Jacobus Leche (in *Blue Book*).

1554. *For* Lewis Owen *read* Edwardus Herbert.

1558-9. *For* John Price *read* John Man.

1571. *Mont. Coll.* gives Arthur Price as member for the Boroughs. The *Blue Book* omits the year and the name.

1625-6. *For* Lewis Powell *read* Sir Henry Herbert, Knt. After the entry of Powell's name follows: " In whose place Thomas Myddleton, Knt." This name does not occur in the *Blue Book* until 1660. In the same year *Mont. Coll.* adds another name for the Boroughs, viz., Hugh Owen. This does not occur at all in the official list.

1627-8. *For* Richard Lloyd, Knt., *read* Richard Lloyd, gent.

1640. *For* Henry Lloyd, Knt., *read* Edward Lloyd, Knt.

1661. *For* Purcell, as member for County, *read* Borough.

1661. *For* Purcell (County) *read* Andrew Newport.

---

[1] Elected 14th July 1862, *vice* Herbert Watkin Williams Wynn, deceased.

[2] Captain, R.N., elected 4th May 1861, *vice* David Pugh, deceased.

[3] Elected 20th August 1863, *vice* Captain Johnson, deceased.

[4] Of Toddington, elected 17th May 1877, *vice* C. D. R. Hanbury Tracy, called to the Upper House as Lord Sudeley.

1680-1. *For* Edward Lloyd *read* Matthew Price. Edward Lloyd's name does not again occur.

1688-9. *For* Lord Herbert *read* Charles Herbert Esq., of Aston.

1747. *For* William Herbert *read* Francis Herbert.

1820. Mr. E. R. Morris says, in a note, that Whitshed Keene continued to represent the Boroughs till 1820, when Henry Clive was elected. The *Blue Book* gives the first return of Mr. Clive in 1818. Mr. Morris also states that all the Boroughs save Montgomery were disfranchised in 1728. In the official list, these names are left out in 1702, and never again restored.

As it will make this paper more complete, I have copied, below, from *Mont. Coll.*, vol. ii, the names of members for the years missing in the *Blue Book*.

	COUNTY.	BOROUGH.
1545.	William Herbert.	
1547.	William Herbert.	
1554.		• Richard Lloyd.
1555.	Edward Herbert.	
1588-9.		Rowland Pugh.
1601.	Edward Herbert.	
1602-4.	Sir W. Herbert, Knt.	Edw. Whittingham.
1614.	Sir W. Herbert, Knt.	Edw. Herbert.
1654.	Sir John Price, Bart.	Charles Lloyd.
1656.	Hugh Price.	Charles Lloyd.
1658-9.	Edward Vaughan.	Charles Lloyd.
1661.	John Pursell.	

THE FAMILY OF JONES OF CHILTON AND CARREGHOVA.

By H. F. J. VAUGHAN, B.A., S.C.L.Oxon.

On page 389 of the *Montgomeryshire Collections*, vol. xiii, under the head of "Parochial History of Llanymynech", occurs a pedigree of the Family of Jones of Chilton, which was divided into two chief branches, one seated at Chilton, the other at Shrewsbury, the latter being now represented by Sir Henry Tyrwhitt, Bart., of Stanley Hall, near Bridgnorth; and it was to this branch that the Carreghova property, which is situated in the parish of Llanymynech, belonged.

The date at which the pedigree before us was compiled was about 1733; and, consequently, it participates in the interest which attaches to genealogical rolls of that period, when the heralds had ceased to make their visitations, and many families ceased to record their members and descent. That the science of heraldry and genealogy then languished may, we think, be sufficiently seen from the specimens which are extant of the family pedigrees of that date, which are, for the most part, not only defective, but full of inaccuracies as to the names and the blazons of arms. Had the visitations of the several counties, and the importance which formerly attached to a long line of ancestors been kept up, undoubtedly many families would have had the opportunity of recording their descent, which was lost when the burthen of going up to the College of Arms in London was cast upon them. But if English families suffered by this means, *à fortiori*, Welsh ones were far worse off, since, the heralds, being Englishmen, were often utterly devoid of all knowledge of the Welsh language and history. We are not surprised, then, that families sometimes had an account of their forefathers drawn up by men in their own neighbourhood who were eminent for their knowledge upon the subject; and Morris Evans (a Welshman, as the name shows) was thus peculiarly fitted to draw out the pedigree of a family which represents not only one of the noble tribes of Wales, but also a branch of the first royal tribe. A somewhat greater accuracy in the names, however, might have been expected. In the heading of the pedigree occur the names of Griffith Hiravrho, no doubt meaning Gruffydd Hiraethog, a Denbighshire author of the sixteenth century, who wrote from 1520 to 1550, and is buried at Llangollen; William Lleyn (Llyn) and Simwnt Vychan (Simon Vaughan) were his pupils. Rhys Cain (Rees Kine) was a Merioneth man, and born at Trawsvynydd. He flourished in the latter part of the sixteenth century. Robert Vaughan is, of course, the celebrated antiquary of Hengwrt, whose MSS., together with those of John Jones of Gelli Lyvdy, and others, form the well-known collection now at Peniarth.

The writer proposes taking each descent of the pedigree, and giving from other pedigrees of the family, MSS. in public collections, as the College of Arms, the British Museum, the Bodleian Library, etc., together with private records, papers, deeds, wills, and parish registers, corrections where necessary, and further information. For the sake of reference, a number will be placed before each descent. It must not, however, be supposed that a full account could be given in the limited space of an article.

1. EDNOWAIN BENDEW, or, as in the pedigree before us, Eden Owen, a name apparently taken from Henwain, prince of Cornwall, his ancestor, is called in the pedigree of Colonel Jones, the regicide, "chiefest of the fifteen peers of North Wales". In *Harl. MS.* 2,299, which formerly belonged to Hugh Thomas, and is in the autograph of Vaughan of Hengwrt, is the following: "Ednywen Bendew y Pennafor 15 Llwych Gwy-

nedd . . . Arglwydd Tegaingl, Ano 1079", and another MS. of the British Museum confirms his being Prince of Tegaingl in 1070. He was the son of Cynan Veiniad, Lord of Trefgarnedd, or, as others give it, Lord of Tegaingl, or Ingle, by Efa, sister of Iestyn ap Gwrgan, Prince of Glamorgan, and grandson of Gwaithvoed, Prince of Cardigan, by Morfydd, daughter and heir of Ynyr Ddu, King of Gwent. Here we are brought face to face with the question, were there one or two Gwaithvoeds, one of Cardigan and one of Powys? It would be beside our purpose to enter into the matter, since it is sufficient to know that our Gwaithvoed was Prince of Cardigan and Cibwyr, the former probably in right of his wife, Morfydd, daughter and heir of Odwyn ab Teithvalch, of Keredigion, a descendant of Cunedda Wledig. He was son of Eunydd ab Cadifor ab Peredur Peiswyrdd ab Einion ab Eunydd ab Brychvael ab Ussa ab Idris Gawr ab Gwyddno Garanhir, Prince of Cantref Gwaelod when the sea inundated it and formed the present Cardigan Bay, ab Gorvyniawn ab Dyvnwel Hên, King of Gwent, ab Ednyvet ab Macsen Wledig (Maximus), whose wife was Elen, sole daughter and heiress of Eudav (Octavius), Prince of Ewas and Wrekenfield. The origin of the royal and noble tribes of Gwynedd was the effect of a diligent inquiry into family pedigrees, instituted by the princes Gruffudd ab Cynan of Gwynydd, Rhys ab Tewdwr of Dyvet, and Bleddyn ab Cynvyn of Powys in the twelfth century. It should be well borne in mind that the old British did not recognise any rights in primogeniture, and therefore all sons of a father in Welsh pedigrees are equal. The law favoured the youngest, if any, since it gave him the family place, but distributed the lands equally amongst the other sons. The arms attributed to Ednowain are, *argent* a chevron between three boars' heads, *sable*, couped, langed and snouted *gules*, tusked *or*. Of course the arms of the ancient British kings and princes were ascribed to them at a later date; but they often have a foundation in some tradition, and are useful as marks by which to distinguish families. The arms of Ednowain are taken from the fact of his having, single-handed, killed a monstrous and very fierce wild boar; and the crests borne by his descendants have the same origin, that of Jones of Chilton being a boar's head, as in the arms, pierced with a dagger ppr., and that of Evans of Northop the boar's head on a ducal coronet ppr., which doubtlessly has reference to the rank of Ednowain as prince of his country. Some of the old heralds add to these arms quarterings derived from the ancestors of Prince Ednowain, as *azure*, three open crowns in pale *or*, and *azure*, three ducal coronets, two and one, *or*, for the Belyns; *or*, an eagle with two heads displayed for Macsen Wledig; *argent*, a lion passant guardant, *gules*, between three fleurs-de-lis *sable* for Gwyddhno Garanhir; *or*, a lion rampant regardant *sable* for Gwaithvoed, quartering *sable* a lion rampant, *argent*, and *sable*, three roses *argent* for his mother; and, again, for Morfydd, wife of Gwaithvoed, party per pale *azure* and *sable*, three fleurs-de-lis *or;* *vert*, a lion rampant *argent*, head, feet, and tail *gules* for Cynan Veiniad, father of Ednowain. He married Gwerfyl, the daughter of Llyddocca ab Tudor Trevor, who is called Earl of Hereford, party per bend sinister, *ermine* and *ermines*, a lion rampant *or;* her mother being Angharad, daughter of Iago, Prince of North Wales 1021 to 1031, son of Idwal ab Meurig ab Idwal Voel ab Anarawd, son of Rhrodri Mawr, King of all Wales, slain 877. In reverting to the pedigree before us, we may pass over Tegengel as sufficiently near to the Welsh Tegaingl, but the truer name of Englefield should be substituted for that of Enghtffild; Seissyltt is the true form of Sisell; and, on the wife's side, Llyddocca should stand for Llyddoen; while, in the account of the blazon, *ermines* should stand for *erminois*, the latter term being used in heraldry to signify a fur the field of which is gold and the spots sable.

Ednowain is said to have had eleven sons and two daughters.

2. MADOC AB EDNOWAIN—*i.e.*, Madoc, son of Ednowain—of Tegaingl, or, as the pedigree says, Madock, Baron Englefield, married Arddun, or, as it is spelt in Lewis Dwnn, Jarddyn, daughter of Bradwain (or Bradwen), Lord of Dolgelley (as now spelt), in Merioneth, North Wales. Bradwain was the chief of another of the noble tribes of North Wales, and had his residence (called, from him, Llys Bradwain) upon the high ground above Arthog, not far from Dolgelley, and then on the borders of a lake. The writer, who visited the spot, may state that of this palace scarcely anything now remains, and its foundations can only be discerned by the regular position of certain large stones. It is close upon a brook, which fed the lake, and which subsequently discharges itself, by a precipitous descent, into the estuary of the Mawddac. Bradwain was the son of Idnerth ab Davydd Esgid Aur ab Owain Aurdorchog ab Llewelyn Aurdorchog (so called from wearing the torque bracelets and anklets of gold as ensigns of sovereign power instead of a crown) ab Coel ab Gwerydd ab Cynddelw Gam ab Elgyd ab Gwerysnadd ab Dwyi Lythyr ab Tegawg ab Dyfnrath ab Madoc Madogion ab Sandde Bryd Angel, who is said to have been so beautiful that he escaped from the battle of Camlan, since every one thought he must be an angel, and so let him pass. He was the son of Llywarch Hên, formerly a chief of the Strathclyde Britons, but who retired to the neighbourhood of Bala Lake, and died *circa* 656. Bradwain had a son, Ednowain, who has been confused with Ednovain Bendew. The arms of the wife of Madoc ab Ednowain are rightly—*gules*, three snakes, enowed or knotted *argent*.

3. IORWERTH (*Anglicè*, Edward), Baron Englefield, or, as others say, of Tegaingl, had one, if not two, brothers; but since it would swell this article to too great a bulk if all the other branches were noticed, the writer will content himself with those mentioned in the pedigree.

He married Arddyn, daughter of Llewelyn ab Owain ab Edwyn, King of Tegaingl and one of the noble tribes. In the time of Gruffudd ab Cynan, the last who bore the title of King of Wales, the above-named Owain joined Hugh, Earl of Chester, against his sovereign, who was also his son-in-law, and thus earned the unenviable epithet of Vradwr, or traitor. He subsequently died, in the earlier part of the twelfth century, from a disease of the lungs. Owain's wife was Morfydd, daughter of Grono ab Ednowain Bendew. His father, Edwyn, King of Tegaingl (*Harl. MS.* 2,299, etc.) married Gwerydd, the daughter of Cynfyn ab Gwerystan ab Gwaithvoed, Prince of Powys in right of his wife, Angharad, relict of Llewelyn ab Seissyllt, Prince of North Wales, and daughter and heir of Meredydd ab Owain ab Howel Dda. Meredydd derived his right to the principality of Powys through his mother, Angharad, daughter and heir of Llewelyn ab Meuric ab Mervyn ab Rhrodri Mawr. Edwyn was slain by Rhudosa ab Rhys ab Owain near Rhuabon, and buried at Northop, co. Flint. The father of Edwyn was Grono, who married Edelfleda, the widow of Edmund Ironsides of England, and daughter of Edwyn, Earl of Mercia, whence probably the name. The *Saxon Chronicle* says—"1039. The Welsh kill Edwin, brother of Leofric the Earl, and Thurkill, and Elfget, and very many good men with them." Edwyn was son of Owain ab Howel Dda by Angharad, Queen of Powys in her own right. His father, Howel Dda—*i.e.*, the Good— was Prince of South Wales, and married Elen, whose ancestry is traced through Constans to Constantine, the Roman Emperor (*vide Annales Cambriæ*, Preface). Howel Dda was the great law-giver of Wales, and son of Cadel ab Rhrodri Mawr, Prince of South Wales. It may be remarked that some write the name of Iorwerth's wife Ardduard; and, apparently, he had also another wife, Nest, daughter of Rhyn ab Meirchion. The arms are rightly given in the pedigree.

4. RIRID AB IORWERTH married, as in the pedigree,

Agnes, daughter of Sir Robert Pulford, a family much connected with Cheshire. In several MSS. she is called Tibot, and her mother was Elizabeth, daughter of Lord Corbet by Blanche, daughter to Sir Hugh Bukley by a daughter of Kynric Sais ab Ithel Vychan (Vaughan, *Anglicè*) of Mostyn (*Harl. MS.*, 1972). The arms are correct in this generation also. They are sometimes called—*sable*, a cross patonce *argent*.

5. IORWERTH AB RIRID married Nest (*Anglicè*, Agnes), daughter and heir of Iorwerth ab Grono ab Einion ab Seissyllt of Merioneth. On consulting the great pedigree of Colonel Jones the Regicide (*Harl. MS.*, 1977, etc., Vincent's *Wales*, in the College of Arms, and other authorities), we find that this lady's grandfather, Grono, married Middyfis, or Maude, daughter of Owain Cyfeilioc, Lord of Powys (*or*, a lion rampant, *gules*), whose wife was Gwenllian, daughter of Prince Owain Gwynedd of North Wales. Einion ab Seissyllt married Nest, daughter of Cynvelin ab Bosfyn ab Rhiwallon ab Madoc ab Cadwgan ab Bleddyn of Nannau, *or*, a lion rampant, *azure*. Seissyllt, who married Nesta, daughter of Grono ab Einion of Tegaingl, was descended from Gwyddno Garanhir, *argent*, a lion passant guardant, *sable*, between three fleurs-de-lis *gules*.

6. ROBERT AB IORWERTH is called in the *Welsh MSS.* Rhotpert, and in Vincent's *Wales*, in the College of Arms, his wife is called Alicia, daughter of Ithel Vychan. The name, however, is ordinarily called Adles in Welsh pedigrees. She was the daughter of Ithel Vaughan, or Vychan, of Mostyn (*azure*, a lion passant *argent*), son of Ithel Lloyd ab Ithel gam ab Meredydd ab Uchtred ab Edwyn of Tegaingl. The wife of Ithel Vychan, and mother of Adles, was Ales, daughter of Richard (by Alice, daughter of Gwyn ab Einion ab Colwyn ab Tangno), son of Cadwaladr (by Alice, daughter of Richard, or Gilbert, Earl of Clare), son of Gruffudd ab Cynan, King of Wales, by Angharad, daughter of Owain ab Edwyn of Tegaingl. It will be

remembered that Gilbert de Clare married Joan of Acre, daughter of Edward I of England; and his father, Richard, who died in 1261, married Margaret, daughter of Hubert de Burgh; and his grandfather, Gilbert de Clare, married Isabella, one of the co-heirs of William Marshall, Earl of Pembroke, by Isabella, his wife, the heiress of Richard Strongbow and Eva, daughter and heir of Durmot, King of Dublin and Leinster, of the line of the old kings of Ireland. From what has been said, it is evident that the arms impaled by Robert ab Iorwerth ought to be *azure*, a lion passant *argent*—*i.e.*, those of Ithel Vaughan of Mostyn, rather than those of his ancestor Edwin of Tegaingl, as given in the pedigree. Robert was living in 1339, and Ithel, his eldest son, was archdeacon of Tegaingl, and no doubt a celibate, who died without issue.

7. KYNRICK AB ROBERT succeeded his father. In the *Welsh Pedigrees* he is called Cynric ab Rhotpert, and some difficulty has been met with respecting his two wives (both of whom were named Angharad) and their respective issue. His first wife was Angharad (written, by mistake, in the pedigree, Auckred), daughter of Madoc Lloyd of Bryncunallt, son of Iorwerth Voel ab Iorwerth Vychan ab Iorwerth Hên, descended from Tudor Trevor, party per bend sinister, *ermine* and *ermines*, a lion rampant *or*. His second wife was Angharad, daughter of Gruffudd Vychan ab Gruffudd ab Davydd Goch, Lord of Denbigh, and by this wife he was father of Ithel Vychan—*Anglicè*, Vaughan (*Harl. MSS.*, 1977, 1972, Vincent's *Wales*, College of Arms, etc.) Upon reference to the pedigree of the first Royal Tribe, it will be seen that Gruffudd Vychan married twice. By Gwervyl, daughter of Uchtred goch ab Meredydd ab Llewelyn, he had issue Howel Coetmore, etc. His other wife was Gladys, daughter of Gruffudd ab Sir Howel y Pedolau (so called because he was strong enough to bend horse-shoes), son of Gruffudd (by Gwenllian, daughter of Iorwerth ab Madoc ab Ririd Vlaidd), son of Iorwerth ab Meredydd

ab Mathusalem ab Hwfa ab Cynddelw. It may be observed that the wife of Hwfa ab Cynddelw, Lord of Llys Llwon, in Anglesey, was Ceinfrid, daughter of Ednowain Bendew. It appertained to the office of this Hwfa to place the royal crown on the head of the Prince of Wales after he had been anointed at his coronation by the Bishop of Bangor. By Gladys, Gruffudd Vychan had issue Moruff and Angharad, wife of Cynric ab Robert, so that she would appear to have been his heir by this wife. Gruffudd Vychan was son of Gruffudd of Nant Conway by Margaret, daughter of Tudor ab Iorwerth ab Gwrgeneu ab Ryfauth ab Rhun ab Nevydd Hardd (*i.e.*, the handsome), *gules*, a lion rampant between three roses *argent*, though others say *argent*, three spear-heads imbrued, *gules*. Arms not being hereditary at this time, the two coats probably simply belong to two different generations. Gruffudd was son of Davydd Goch, Lord of Denbigh (*sable*, a lion rampant *argent*, in a bordure engrailed *or*), by Angharad, daughter of Sir Heilin ab Tudor ab Ednyvet Vychan, living 1241, *gules*, a chevron *ermine* between three Englishmen's heads, couped at the neck proper, arms given to commemorate his prowess against the English; they were also the ensigns of his descendants, the Tudors, kings of England. Davydd Goch (*i.e.*, the red) was the son of Sir Davydd Lloyd, Baron of Denbigh, by Tangwystl, daughter of Owain le Flemming of Dehebarth, *gules*, fretty *or*, a fess *azure*, but others call her daughter and heir of Owain Blaine. Sir Davydd Lloyd was son of Gruffudd, Prince of North Wales, who died in 1250, having broken his neck by a fall from the battlements of the White Tower, in the Tower of London, wherein he was imprisoned, while endeavouring to escape; quarterly *gules* and *or*, four lions rampant counterchanged. His wife was Senana, daughter of Caradoc ab Thomas ab Rhodri ab Owain Gwynedd. Prince Gruffudd was son of Prince Llewelyn the Great (quarterly *gules* and *or*, four lions passant counterchanged), who died in 1244, and was buried in

Conway Abbey. His wife was Tanglwystl, daughter of Llowarch Goch ab Llowarch Holbwrch, Lord of Rhos. Prince Llewelyn was son of Prince Iorwerth Dryndwn (*sable*, a lion rampant in a bordure engrailed *or*) by Margaret, daughter of Madoc ab Meredydd, Prince of Powys; and, finally, Prince Iorwerth Dryndwn (*i.e.*, of the broken nose) was son and heir of Prince Owain Gwynedd, of North Wales (*vert*, three eagles displayed in fess *or*), by Gladys, daughter of Llowarch ab Trahaiarn ab Caradoc ab Gwyn ab Colwyn, *sable*, three fleurs-de-lis *argent*. Such is the descent of the mother of Ithel Vaughan of Northop, or Holt, as it is put in the pedigree; but since many genealogists make him the son of Angharad, daughter of Madoc Lloyd, of Bryncunallt, in the lordship of Bromfield, it may be well to show why this is erroneous. Madoc Lloyd, of Bryncunallt, married twice, his first wife being Margaret, daughter of Llewelyn ab Ieuaf ab Adda ab Awr ab Ieuaf ab Cuhelyn of Trevor, by whom he was ancestor of the Trevors of Bryncunallt and others. His second wife was Dyddgu, daughter and heir of Llewelyn ab Grono Vychan ab Grono (*obt.* 1269) ab Ednyvet Vychan, and by her he was father of Angharad, wife of Cynric ab Robert (*Harl. MS.*, 2299, *Add. MS*, Brit. Museum, *Pennant's MS.*, 9865). But this Dyddgu was also wife of Robert ab Meredydd ab Howel, of whom more will be said hereafter, and by him was mother of a sole daughter and heiress, Angharad, who was the wife, as we shall presently see, of Ithel Vaughan, son of Cynric ab Robert. If, therefore, Angharad, daughter of Madoc Lloyd, was mother of Ithel Vaughan, then her daughter, by Robert ab Howel, would be the wife of her grandson, by Madoc Lloyd. In other words, Ithel Vaughan would have married his aunt, which, if not impossible, is, to say the least, highly improbable. Such being the case, instead of Auckred, daughter of Madoc Lloyd, with the arms as described in the pedigree, it should be Angharad, daughter and heir of Gruffudd Vychan ab

Gruffudd ab Davydd Goch, and the arms *sable*, a lion rampant *argent*, in a bordure engrailed *or*, with its quarterings as above.

8. ITHEL VYCHAN AB CYNRIC. Vychan being the same name as Vaughan, and signifying the less or younger, in the present instance it was no doubt used to distinguish him from his uncle Ithel, Archdeacon of Tegaingl. The marriage of Ithel Vaughan with the heiress of one branch of the first royal tribe of North Wales is the great match of the family, since it constituted his descendants representatives of the royal family of Wales. *The History of the House of Gwydir*, several of the Harleian MSS., the Additional MSS. in the British Museum, and Vincent's *Wales*, in the College of Arms, all call her Angharad; and as Sir John Wynn, the historian, probably knew as much of his own family as anybody, the account given by him is worthy of reception. Angharad, then, was the sole daughter and heir of Robert or Robin, by Dyddgu, daughter and heir of Llewelyn ab Grono Vychan ab Grono ab Ednyvet Vychan. The family mansions of this Robin or Robert were at Cefn y fan and Cesylgyfarch. He was the son of Meredydd, who dwelt in Evionydd, and held the lordship of Gest, 6 Richard II, by his wife Morfydd, daughter of Ievan ab Davydd ab Trahaiarn Goch ab Madoc ab Rhys Gloff, *i.e.*, the lame; *sable*, a lion rampant, within a bordure engrailed *or*, the arms of his ancestors, the princes of South Wales. Meredydd was the son of Howel of Rhiwlwyd, who married Eva (by some called Myfanwy), daughter and coheir of Ievan, living in the month of May, 2 Henry IV, son of Howel ab Meredydd of Cefyn y fan in Evionydd, descended from Colwyn ab Tangno; *sable*, a chevron between three fleurs-de-lis *argent*. Howel was son of Davydd, lord of Rhiwlwyd, by his wife Efa, daughter and heir of Gruffudd Vychan ab Gruffudd ab Moreiddig of Penyfed in Evionydd. She brought the land in Penyfed called Gwely Griffri. There were two persons named Moreiddig, one of South and the other of North Wales. The above Eva seems to have been the

descendant of the latter, who was Lord of Burton and Llai, and married Tanglwystl, daughter of Cadwgan ab Cadwalader, lord of Cardigan, who resided at Aberystwith Castle. Cadwalader was second son of Gruffudd ab Cynan, King of Wales; *gules*, three lions passant in pale *argent*. The father of Moreiddig was Sandde Hardd (the handsome), who, for his services in the wars against the English, received from the Prince of Powys the lordship of Burton and Llai, in the parish of Gresford. He bore *vert*, semée of broomslips, a lion rampant *or*. The mother of Moreiddig was Angharad, only daughter and heir of Gruffudd ab Cadwgan of Nannau; *or*, a lion rampant *azure*. Her mother being Angharad, only daughter and heir of Davydd ab Owain Gwynedd, Prince of North Wales, and Emma, his wife, daughter of Geoffrey Plantagenet, Count of Anjou, and sister of Henry II of England. Quarterly, 1 and 4, *or*, a lion rampant *azure*, 2 and 3 *vert*, three eagles displayed in fess *or*. The arms of Moreiddig are *azure*, three boys' heads couped at the shoulders, proper, crined *or*, each wreathed round the neck with a snake *vert*. He having been said to have been born with a snake round his neck. Moreiddig Warwyn of South Wales was son of Drym Bennog, lord of Cantref Selyff, son of Maenarch ab Dyffryn, Prince of Brecknock (*Harl. MS.*, 2289). Davydd, the father of Howel, was the only son of Gruffudd ab Caradoc, who, with his brother Eignion ab Caradoc, took part with their nephew, Prince Llewelyn, at the battle of Buellt. Sir John Wynn says that there was a tradition among the men of Evionydd to the effect that when Prince Dafydd ab Llewelyn, who was made prince by the aid of his uncle, the English king, came to Pwlheli in Llûn, to treat of peace with these two brothers, Eignion and Gruffudd ab Caradoc, they met him accompanied by so large a force that the prince told them they were too strong for subjects, but they replied that he rather was too weak to be prince, and so they separated. However, they lost their possessions in continuous wars, and joined Prince Llewelyn ab Gruffudd, who gave them other great possessions near Denbigh, and subsequently restored their former lands. After the death of the last Prince Llewelyn, these brothers were forced out of their lands by Henry Lacy, Earl of Lincoln, who wished to accumulate a large territory round Denbigh Castle; and, by Justice William Sutton, on behalf of the queen of Edward I, by whom they were compelled to exchange their patrimony for other lands. The wife of Gruffudd ab Caradoc ab Thomas was Lleuki, daughter of Llowarch Vychan ab Llowarch Goch ab Llowarch Holbwrch ; *vert*, a stag *argent*, antlered *or*. Caradoc ab Thomas ab Prince Rhrodri of Anglesey, married Efa, daughter of Gwyn ab Gruffudd of Cegidfa, *sable*, three nags' heads erased *argent*, who was a descendant of Brochwel Yscithrog, Prince of Powys in 607. During the reign of Prince Llewelyn ab Iorwerth, the descendants of Prince Rhrodri of Anglesey were kept under lest they should aspire to the princely dignity which their ancestors had held. Thomas ab Prince Rhrodri, married Marged, daughter of Einion ab Seissyltt, lord of Merioneth, and descended, as previously stated, from Gwyddno Garanhir ; *argent*, a lion passant *sable*, between three fleurs-de-lis *gules*. Prince Rhrodri of Anglesey, son of Owain Gwynedd, Prince of Wales, by his second wife, Christian, daughter of Grono ab Owain ab Edwyn of Tegaingl or Englefield, was buried in the Collegiate Church of Caergybi, *i.e.*, Holyhead, where his tomb was found in 1713, when the choir of that church was repaired, and upon it a brass shell wrought with network. He was imprisoned (1175) when young, by his brother, Prince Davydd at Buellt, but, escaping into Anglesey, he remained there, and took under his protection Llewelyn ab Iorwerth (*Anglicé*, Edward), the son of his eldest brother, Iorwerth Dryndwn, who afterwards became Prince of Wales. Prince Rhrodri married his first cousin once removed, Agnes, daughter of the Lord Rhys of South Wales (by Gwenllian, daughter of Madoc ab Meredydd, Prince of Powys), son of Prince Gruffudd of South Wales (by

Gwenllian, daughter of Gruffudd ab Cynan, King of North Wales), and his posterity enjoyed large tracts of country in Denbighland, called Rhuvoniog, near Denbigh Castle, as well as lands in Evionydd, etc. It seemed necessary to enter more fully into the genealogy of Angharad, the heiress of the great Holt property, which subsequently became the seat of the family, because of its intrinsic interest, and also because the pedigree, by dismissing her so curtly as "Tanghwyst, daughter and heir of Robert Davis of Holt, gent.", gives no idea of the position and importance of her family. Holt is a town in Bromfield, co. Denbigh, situated upon the river Dee, and having the remains of a castle, which was garrisoned by the friends of the Parliament in 1643, but taken and destroyed by the Royalists next year. It was a curious pentagonal structure, with towers at the corners, surrounded by a deep moat, which was fed by the Dee, and in the midst of which was a tower, to which there was a drawbridge from the castle, and from which there was a drawbridge to the main land. A few scarce prints remain of it, one of which is in possession of the writer. The Holt estate, which was brought into the family by the wife of Ithel Vaughan, consisted probably of lands which had been given in exchange for those which had been taken away by the wife of Edward I of England. The arms are correct as given in the pedigree, but are generally given with many quarterings, *e.g.*, 1, *vert*, three eagles displayed in fess *or*; 2, *gules*, three lions passant in pale *argent*; 3, *sable*, three nags' heads erased *argent*; 4, *azure*, a cross patée fitchée *or*, for Cadwaladr last called King of the Britons, *obt.* 689; 5, *sable*, a lion rampant *argent*, for Angharad, Queen of Rhroderic the Great; 6, *azure*, three boys' heads couped at the shoulders proper, crined *or*, each wreathed round the neck with a snake *vert*, for Moreiddig; 7, *sable*, a chevron between three fleurs-de-lis *argent*, for Colwyn ab Tangno; 8, *gules*, a chevron ermine between three Englishmen's heads couped, proper, for Ednyvet Vychan; 9, *gules*, a Saracen's head erased, proper, wreathed *argent* and *sable*, for Marchudd.

9. KYNRICK AB ITHEL VAUGHAN of Holt, or, as the Welsh pedigrees, Cynric ab Ithel Vychan, succeeded to and settled upon his mother's estate at Holt, co. Denbigh. The pedigree seems quite correct as to his wife, and her arms, though they are often blazoned, *vert*, a stag trippant *argent*, attired *or*, being those of her ancestor, Llowarch Holbwrch. She was the daughter of Gruffudd Lloyd (by Bedylan, daughter of Tudor ab Ithel ab Cynric ab Iorwerth ab Madoc), son of Davydd ab Meredydd of Demeirchion ab Rhys ab Gruffudd ab Llewelyn ab Meilr (by Maud, daughter of Heilyn ab Howel), son of Pill ab Cynan ab Llowarch Vychan (by Angharad, daughter of Cloddien ab Meredydd ab Trahaiarn of Emlyn), son of Llowarch Goch (by Tangwystl, daughter of Llowarch ab Bran), son of Llowarch Holbwrch of Rhos in Denbighland, lord treasurer of Gruffudd ab Llewelyn, Prince of Wales, son of Pill ab Cynvyn ab Gwrydyr Goch ab Heli ab Glanawg ab Gwgan ab Caradoc Vreichvras, *i.e.*, of the brawny arm, who was one of the knights of Arthur's round table, and Earl of Hereford. He bore, *sable*, a chevron between three spears' heads *argent*, imbrued *gules*, and married Tegairvron, daughter and heir of King Pelinor; *argent*, a griffin's head erased *vert*, holding in its mouth a dexter hand *gules*. He was also grandfather of Bleddyn ab Maenarch of Brecknock.

10. JOHN AB KYNRICK of Holt, is called in *Harl. MS.*, 1971, John ab Cynric ab Ithel Vychan of "Plase in llanassa", and he is there said to have married Ionnett, daughter of John Conway, "the ould ayer of Conway", 38 Hy. VI, and 14 Ed. IV. There were two families of Conway, but the older pedigrees are in favour of John ab Cynric, having married a daughter of the House of Conway of Bodrhyddan, not Conwey of Bryn Euryn. It is true that sometimes the name is written Jonet or Sionet, sometimes Margaret. There is also a difference as to the generation, some making her the

daughter of the above-mentioned John Conway, others his granddaughter, and daughter of his son, also named John. Lewis Dwnn makes the wife of John ab Cynric of Holt, Sionet, daughter of John Conway of Bodrhyddan, by Janet, daughter of Thomas Salsberie hên, and her sister, Margaret, "yn gynta gwr Gruffudd Lloid ab Ievan, ag wedy, gwr Elis ab Harry ab Kynfrig", the last husband's arms being those of Ednowain Bendew. A reference to the full pedigree of the Chilton family shows that this Elis was the son of Harry (by Alis, daughter of Simon Thelwall), who was brother of John ab Cynric of Holt. It would appear, therefore, that some confusion has arisen between the names of these two sisters (or aunt and niece), who both married into the same race. The father of John Conway, who married Janet, daughter of Thomas Salsbury Hên, *i.e.*, the elder, was John Conway, who married Jonet, daughter of Edmund Stanley, *argent*, on a bend *azure*, three stags' heads caboshed *or*, by Angharad, sole daughter and heir of Howel ab Tudor ab Ithel Vychan of Mostyn ab Ithel Llwyd ab Ithel Gam ab Meredydd ab Uchtred ab Edwin of Tegaingl. This Edmund was second son of Sir William Stanley of Holt Castle, co. Denbigh, which explains the fact of the Chilton family having been called the descendants of ancestors who lived at Holt Castle. Sir William Stanley of Holt Castle, K.G., was younger brother of Thomas, first Earl of Derby, and son of Sir Thomas Stanley, King of Man, by Joan, daughter and coheir of Sir Robert Goushill. The wife of Sir Robert Goushill was Elizabeth, daughter and coheir of Richard Fitzalan, fourteenth Earl of Arundel and Surrey, K.G., by his first wife, Elizabeth, daughter of William de Bohun, Earl of Northampton. Richard was beheaded in 1397, and was the son and heir of Richard Fitalan, thirteenth Earl of Arundel, by his second wife, Eleanor Plantagenet, daughter of Henry, Earl of Lancaster, and widow of John, Lord Beaumont. But, to return to the Conways, the last, John, was son of Jenkyn, by Marsli, daughter of Meredydd ab Howel ab Dafydd ab Gruffudd, and so aunt of the wife of Ithel Vaughan. Jenkyn was son of John, by Anne (the *Golden Grove Book* says Elen), daughter and heir of Sir Henry Torbois, son of Richard Conway, by Anne, daughter of Sir Richard Ratclyffe, Kt., son of Sir Hugh Conway, by Ancreda, sole heir of Sir Harry Crevecœur, lord of Prestatyn (the *Golden Grove Book* says Elizabeth, daughter of Hugh Courtenay, Earl of Devon), son of Sir John Conway, by Avicia, daughter of Sir James Butler of Wormwood. But here the *Golden Grove Book* is probably more correct in making Sir Hugh, son of Sir Henry de Conway, by Ancred, daughter and heir of Sir Hugh Crevecœur, lord of Prestatyn, which Sir Henry was son of Sir John Cogniers of Richmond, co. York, brother to Lord Conyers, who came to Conway in the time of Edward I. Sir John was son of Sir Ralph, by Joyce, daughter of Sir Peter Croft, son of Sir Richard, by Sybil, daughter of Sir Roger Mortimer of Wigmore, son of Sir Richard, by Felis, daughter of Sir Robert Corbet of Caus Castle, son of Sir William, High Constable of England, by Isabel, daughter of Baldwyn, Earl of Blois. Considerable interest attaches to this match with the Conways, since, as the late Mr. Morris of Shrewsbury stated, the Chilton property came into the family from them by this means. Another consideration is that probably by this means they became more drawn into the Wars of the Roses, which were so disastrous to the older nobility of England, being connected with the Stanleys, and the House of Tudor, from which Henry VII sprang. John ab John, or Jones, as the English called it, the eldest son of John ab Cynric and Janet Conway, was the first to settle at Chilton in Shropshire, but, as will be hereafter seen, was succeeded by his brother's son, having fallen in the Wars of the Roses, it is believed; from which time the family gave up the sword and took to the study of law. In the pedigree, then, the wife of John should be Jonèt, daughter of John Conway of Bodrhyddan, and the arms, *sable*, on a bend cotized *argent*, a rose between two annulets *gules*, for Conway;

quartering, *azure,* a cross of the field double voided *or,* for Crevecœur.

11. RICHARD JONES, or in Welsh, Ab John, of Holt, the brother of John Jones of Chilton, and son of John ab Cynric of Holt. He married Margaret, daughter of Llewelyn Vychan of Mold, co. Denbigh, and there is some difficulty in *exactly* giving her descent, because some pedigrees make Llewelyn Vychan, or Vaughan, the son of Ieuan ab Cynric, others make him the son of Ieuan ab Davydd ab Cynric. It may, therefore, be well to give both descents. Llewelyn Vaughan married Sionet, or Jonet, daughter of Evan (by Catherine, daughter of Gruffudd ab Rhys ab Davydd ab Howel) ab Davydd (by Angharad, daughter and heir of Cynric Vychan ab Cynric ab Ieuan, or Madoc, of Wepre) ab Ithel Vaughan of Northop, the descendant of Ednowain Bendew, as given above. Ieuan, the father of Llewelyn Vaughan, if the son of Cynric, married Nest, daughter of Ednyvet ab Grono, by Gwladys, daughter of Bleddyn ab Ithel Anwyl. This Ithel Anwyl was a son of the above Ithel Vaughan, though others call him son of Bleddyn ab Ithel Lloyd, and lived at Northop, in Flintshire, in the time of Edward I. He lies buried in the parish church there, 1284. If, however, Llewelyn Vaughan, who is also called of Llewenni, was the son of Ieuan ab Davydd (and this seems to have the better MSS. authority), then Ieuan married Gwenllian, daughter of Rhys ab Grono, the son of Owain (by Efa, daughter and co-heir of Madoc Goch, a natural son of Gwenwynwyn, and Lord of Mawddwy and Caer Einion) ab Bleddyn (by Annes, daughter of Llewelyn ab Iorwerth, but the *Cae Cyriog MSS.* say ab Idnerth Lord of Buellt ab Meredydd Hen ab Howel ab Seissyllt ab Cadwgan ab Elystan Glodrydd, Prince of Fferlis). Bleddyn was son of Tudor, Lord of Whittington and Maelor, by Jane (or Janet), daughter of Rhys Vychan ab Rhys ab Meredydd Goch, or, as others say, Rhys Vychan ab Gruffudd ab Rhys ab Tudor Mawr. Tudor was the eldest son of Rhys Sais (descended from Tudor Trefor),

by Efa, daughter of Gruffudd Hir ab Gruffudd ab the Lord Rhys of South Wales. Rhys Sais died in 1070. Davydd ab Cynric, the father of Ieuan, married Angharad, daughter of Bleddyn Vychan ab Bleddyn ab Grono Goch of Heurthig, a descendant of Llowarch Holbwrch. Davydd was son of Cynric ab Ieuan Vychan of Rhuddlan, by Tangwystl, daughter of Robert ab Iorwerth, descended as above from Ednowain Bendew. Ieuan Vychan of Rhyddlan was the son of Griffith (ab Madoc of Rhuddlan ab Ririd ab Llewelyn ab Owain ab Edwyn of Tegaingl) by Gwladys, daughter of Bleddyn ab Owain Brogyntyn, who was a natural son of Madoc ab Meredydd, Prince of Powys. It will be noticed that this marriage of Richard Jones with Margaret, daughter of Llewellyn Vaughan, was one of the last Welsh alliances of the family, and it brings in two, if not three, strains of their own blood, though otherwise this race is singularly free from intermarriages with its relatives. The pedigree is correct in this descent, both as to names and arms.

12. WILLIAM JONES, born at Holt, Co. Denbigh, but succeeded his uncle John in the property at Chilton, near Shrewsbury, which came from the Conways. This seems to have been the time when the family became scattered, and their estate at Holt broken up and lost in the changes and chances of the Civil Wars of the Roses, wars which naturally affected a family related to the Stanleys and Tudors, and which changed the face of England, destroying and ruining most of the ancient nobility, while they raised others to eminence and affluence. Henceforth, the family estate was so curtailed that it could only support one branch, and that quietly, while the offshoots, with one brilliant exception, *i.e.*, the Shrewsbury branch, sank out of the number of those who held landed estates, and for the most part seem to have taken up the profession of the law. The Chilton estate, which lies about three miles from Shrewsbury, consists of some eight hundred acres, and though it may formerly have been larger, certainly

was not one of the great estates of Shropshire. William Jones married Alice, daughter of Richard Brereton of Brereton, in Cheshire, or, as he is called by others, Ralph, who was a younger son of William Brereton of Brereton, and Alice, daughter of John Corbet of Leighton, and sister and sole heir of Richard Corbet of Leighton. William was son of Sir William Brereton, by Amylla, daughter of Hugh Venables, married in 1386, and Sir William was son and heir of another Sir William Brereton by his first wife, Ellen, daughter and heiress of Sir Philip Egerton of Egerton, co. Cheshire. Upon reference to a pedigree of the Egerton family, kindly lent to the writer by Sir Philip de-Malpas Grey Egerton, Bart., and of the date 1651, we find that Sir William de Brereton (mentioned above) married Audella, daughter of Sir Hugh Venables, Baron of Kinderton, *azure*, two bars *argent*, and his father, Sir William de Brereton, *argent*, two bars *sable*, married Ellen, daughter and co-heir of Phillip de Malpas, *alias* Egerton, surnamed Le Large, and with her he obtained a part of the Barony of Malpas. Ellen was named apparently after her mother, Ellen, daughter of John de St. Pierre, son of Urien de St. Pierre, by Idonea, daughter and co-heir of David le Clarke, by Constance, daughter of Owain Cyfeilioc, Prince of Powys. Beatrix, the other co-heir, married William Patrick, and had an only daughter and heir, Isabel, who married Richard de Sutton; *or*, a lion rampant *vert*, from whom descended the Barons Dudley and Ward, and also the present Earl of Dudley. Sir William Brereton was son of William, by Margery, daughter of Richard de Bosley, son of Sir William, 1321, by Rohesia, daughter of Ralph de Vernon, son of Sir William, by a daughter of Richard de Sandbach, son of Sir Ralph de Brereton, by Ada, daughter and co-heir of David, Earl of Huntingdon, by Maud, eldest daughter and co-heir of Hugh Cyfeilioc, Earl of Chester; *azure*, six garbs, 3, 2, and 1 *or*. David, Earl of Huntingdon, *or*, three piles *gules*, was the son of Prince Henry of

Scotland (by Adama, daughter of William, Earl of Warren and Surrey), whose father, David, King of Scotland, married Maud, daughter of Woldeofus, Earl of Northumberland; and his father, Malcolm Canmore, who died in 1093, married Margaret, sister of Edgar the Atheling, and so heir of the Saxon line of English kings. The Lady Adama, mentioned above as wife of Prince Henry of Scotland, was the daughter of William, Earl of Warren (grandson of William the Conqueror), by his wife, Isabel or Elizabeth, daughter of Hugh the Great, Count of Vermandois, in right of his wife, Adelheid, daughter of Herbert, Count of Vermandois; and Hugh was the son of Henry, of the Capetian line of the kings of France, by Agnes, daughter of George, King of Russia, whose father, Wlademir, King of Russia, married Anne, daughter of Romanus, and sister of Basilius II and Constantine VIII, Emperors of the East. In the pedigree, William Jones, though born at Holt, was of Chilton, co. Salop, the name of his wife's father was Brereton, not Broueton, and the arms of that family are *argent*, two bars *sable*.

13. RICHARD JONES of Chilton, in the year 1488, 4 Henry VII. It may be noticed here how carefully the date is marked, and what took place at this time —namely, a change of the family arms. This seems to show that the compiler of the pedigree was in possession of the family tradition that Henry VII, in his passage through Shrewsbury, visited Chilton, or, at least, was visited by the owner of Chilton at that time, who proffered what assistance he could give; and that Henry Tudor, who claimed the throne not only through his relation to the House of Lancaster, but also as the descendant of the old blood royal of the Britons, and who was very jealous of those who bore the old Royal arms, changed the insignia which had been borne so long by the family, wherein the arms of the old kings of Wales appeared, and caused them to assume their present coat, *argent*, a lion rampant *vert*,.

armed and langed *gules* (sometimes borne wounded in the breast, proper). There are reasons for believing that Chilton was formerly a much larger mansion than now, since the writer, when there, was informed by R. L. Burton, Esq., the present owner of the estate, that during some alterations of the drive and flower-beds in front of the house, the workmen came upon what appeared to be the remains of a courtyard. There is also some reason in favour of the pedigree before us being correct as to this Richard Jones being the one who succeeded to Chilton, since there is a record that *John* Jones of Chilton paid twenty-six shillings and eightpence to the benevolence, as it was called, of the 7th Henry VII; and we know that John Jones was the man who was succeeded at Chilton by the son, or perhaps grandson, of his brother Richard. Richard Jones of Chilton married Elizabeth, daughter of Lee of Gloucester, as the pedigree says, and so the heralds leave it in their visitations. The object of stating that she belonged to the Gloucestershire Lees is to distinguish her from the family of Lee of Langley, a very ancient Shropshire race. The pedigree of the great Cheshire family of Lee, or Leigh, or Legh, is in itself a genealogical study, so many and various are its branches; and it would appear, from the arms in the pedigree, that the author of it considered her as belonging to the same branch as that of Sir Thomas Leigh, Lord Mayor of London in 1555, who married Alice, daughter of John Barker of Wolverton by Elizabeth, daughter of Thomas Hill, but they were not connected with Gloucestershire until a later date. This Elizabeth was the daughter of Richard Lee and Elizabeth, his wife, daughter and co-heir of William Saunders of Oxfordshire by Joane, daughter of John Spenser of Wormleighton, in that county. This branch of the Lee family was connected with Gloucestershire through the marriage of Margaret Lee with Thomas Lane, who bought the lands of Mattesdon and the lands of Llanthony Abbey from the city of Gloucester, to which they had been granted by Henry VIII. The Lee family seem to have been great purchasers of Church lands. John Lee of Lee, county Chester, married a daughter of Dutton, and had issue John, who married a daughter of Sir Thomas Foulshurst, by whom he had a son, Thomas, who, by a daughter of Sir John Aston of Aston, co. Stafford, was father of John Lee of Lee, who married Margaret, daughter of — Hocknell, and their fifth son was Benedict Lee of Quarndon, county Bucks, who, by his wife, Elizabeth, daughter of — Wood of Warwickshire, was father of Richard Lee, whose daughter, Elizabeth, married Richard Jones. *Harl. MS.*, 1535, says that this Richard Lee changed his arms from *argent*, a chevron engrailed between three leopards' heads *sable*, to *argent*, a fess between three crescents *gules*; so that the arms stand, quarterly —(1) the new coat; (2) the old coat, as above; (3) *argent*, a fess between three unicorns' heads, erased *sable*; (4) *or*, a lion rampant *azure* in a bordure of the second charged with estoiles of the first. John Lee, the elder brother of the above Benedict, seems to have settled at Aston, near Stone, co. Stafford, and married Grace, daughter of — Bagott, by whom he was father of Sir William Lee of Aston, who changed his arms to *sable*, a scythe in pale *argent*, and, having married Maud, daughter and heir of Sir John Cheyney (*argent*, a fess, and in chief three martlets *gules*), had issue Sir James Lee of Aston, father of a daughter and heir, Elleyn Lee of Aston, who married Sir Humphrey Stanley of Pipe, co. Stafford. Sir John Spenser of Wormleighton, previously mentioned, died in 1521, having married the sister of Sir Richard Empsonne, Knt., of Southam, co. Warwick. In the pedigree it would be well to change the arms for those given above. The arms of Jones (*i.e.*, *argent*, a lion rampant *vert*) are by some said to be those of Gwaithvoed. Before passing on to the next generation, it may be well to remark that the *Heraldic Visitations* of Shropshire say that Thomas Jones of Uckington (wrongly spelt Vekington in the pedigree) was the younger brother of this Richard Jones of Chilton, though there seems reason to believe that a pedigree of the family is correct which makes him a younger son of this Richard.

14. WILLIAM JONES of Chilton was dead in 1600. He married Joan, daughter of Richard Blakeway of Cronkhill, an estate adjoining that of Chilton. She was born in 1534, and her father was still living in 1592. Her mother was Elizabeth, daughter of William Oteley, who was Sheriff of Shropshire in 1500. Richard Blakeway was the son of Edmund Blakeway of Bridgnorth by Anne, daughter of William Farmer, a family much connected with Berrington, the next parish to that of Atcham, wherein Chilton is situated. The Blakeways bore *argent*, on a bend engrailed *sable*, three bezants. In Blakeway's *Sheriffs of Shropshire*, speaking of William Oteley, he says, "William Ottely of Pitchford was son and heir of Thomas Ottely of the same place, third son of Philip Oteley, Lord of Oteley", a manor in the lordship of Ellesmere. The arms borne by the family are *argent*, on a bend *azure*, three garbs (*i.e.*, oat-sheafs) *or*. Thomas Oteley, being a younger son, engaged in the wool trade, and acquired so much wealth thereby that in 1473 he was enabled to purchase the Pitchford estate, near Shrewsbury. *Harl. MS.*, 1396, gives the following pedigree, which is not without interest, as showing how this marriage connected the Chilton family with many of the principal ones in Shropshire. George Oteley married Anne, daughter of Robert Corbet of Lee (called Roger in other pedigrees). Their son, Philip, married Anne, daughter of John Lacon, fourth son of Sir Richard Lacon of Willey by Alice, daughter of Thomas Hoorde of Bridgnorth, son of William Lacon of Willey by Magdalen, daughter of Richard Wisham of Holt, co. Worcester, son of Sir Richard Lacon by Elizabeth, daughter and heir of Sir Hamon Peshale of co. Stafford by Alice, sole heir of Robert Harley of Willey by Joan, daughter

of Sir Robert Corbet of Morton Corbet. Philip Oteley and Anne Lacon had issue Thomas of Pitchford, who married Anne, daughter of Robert Scriven of Frodesley, near Shrewsbury, by Alice, daughter of Thomas Corbet of Lee, her mother being Jane, daughter of Sir John Burley of Bromcroft Castle, in Corvedale, co. Salop. But the wealth of the Oteley family was greatly increased by the marriage of William, son of the above Thomas, with Margery, daughter and heir of John Bruyn of Bridgnorth, whose mother was Joan, daughter of John Leighton by Angharad, one of the daughters and co-heirs of Sir John Burgh of Mowddwy. This Sir John, who married Jane Clopton, daughter and heir of Sir William, was son of Hugh Burgh (*obt.* 18th August 1439) by Elizabeth, daughter and heir of John ab William ab Griffith de la Pole, her mother being Elizabeth, daughter and heir of Sir Fulke Corbet. The wife of William ab Griffith de la Pole was Margaret, daughter and co-heir of Thomas ab Llewelyn, and sister of Eleanor, mother of Owain Glyndour. This Margaret married as a second husband Sir Tudor ab Grono of Penmynydd, in Anglesey, by whom she was mother of Sir Owain Tudor, grandfather of Henry VII. From which it is evident that Angharad de Burgh, wife of John Leighton, was second cousin of the half blood to King Henry VII. The pedigree is correct as to William, but the name of his father-in-law was Richard Blakeway, which should be put as a correction, and the arms of the family are as above stated, *argent*, on a bend engrailed *sable*, three bezants. Moreover, Thomas Jones of Uckington, the ancestor of the Shrewsbury branch, was a younger brother of this William Jones of Chilton (the heralds call him his uncle), and ought so to be placed; indeed, it is manifestly improbable that there should be two sons of the same name living at the same time and the same generation, as in the pedigree. The issue of William Jones of Chilton and Joan his wife was a son, Thomas, and a daughter, Elizabeth, born in 1549.

15. THOMAS JONES of Chilton, born in 1550, married at Hodnet, 14th June, Margaret, daughter and co-heir of John Gratwood of Wollerton, co. Salop. He was of Stoke in his own right, and Wollerton came through his wife, Joan, or Johanna, sister of Sir Rowland Hill, and one of his co-heirs. Thomas Jones was in possession of the Chilton estate at the time of the Heralds' Visitation of 1623, and his son and grandson were living, so that he was then an old man. His wife's name is entered on the Herald's books as Mary, very possibly the error of a copyist, since Mary is entered in another MS. of the British Museum as wife of Sir Richard Leveson. Most of the Gratwood estates passed away with the eldest daughter, Alice, who married Reginald Corbet of Stoke. John Gratwood was the son of William Gratwood, by Mary, daughter of Thomas Newport of High Ercal. It is curious that in two generations of the Newport family daughters married persons of the name of William Gratwood; firstly, the one mentioned, and secondly, the daughter of Sir Richard Newport, who married William Gratwood, the brother of these co-heirs, who died without issue. The Gratwoods did not enter their pedigree at the Heralds' Visitation, though they were evidently people of position, William having been Sheriff of Shropshire in 1572 and 1581, nor are there any impressions of his arms as Sheriff. Blakeway, therefore, in his *Sheriffs of Shropshire*, leaves the shield void. There are, however, in the writer's possession impressions of some family seals of this date, one of which is Jones impaling *gules*, a bend *argent* (Gratwood), then Jones quartering this coat, and a third with these two quartered impaling Burton of Longner, which will be explained hereafter. This proves that the arms used by the family were *gules*, a bend *argent*. There is, in *Harl MS.*, 1241, a short pedigree, which seems defective, giving three generations of Gratwoods—*i.e.*, Nicholas, son of Robert, son of Thomas. The Thomas Newport mentioned above married Anne, daughter of Sir Robert

Corbet, of Morton Corbet Castle, by Elizabeth, daughter of Sir Henry Vernon, of Tong Castle, co. Salop, and Haddon Hall, co. Derby, Governor of Prince Arthur, the eldest son of Henry VII. Sir Henry's wife was Lady Anne Talbot, daughter of John, second Earl of Shrewsbury, by Elizabeth, 1473, daughter of James, the White Earl of Ormond, 1452, and his wife, Lady Jane, daughter of Gerald, fifth Earl of Kildare. Sir Henry died 13th of April 1515, having rebuilt his residence, Tong Castle, co. Salop, and is buried in the parish church there. Thomas Newport was son and heir of John Newport of High Ercal, who died 13th October 1512, by Alice, daughter of Sir Thomas Swinnerton, who was son and heir of William Newport, of High Ercal, by Elizabeth, the eldest daughter and co-heir of Sir John Burgh, Knt., previously mentioned. Joan or Johanna Hill, the wife of John Gratwood, was the sister and co-heir of Sir Rowland Hill, the first Protestant Lord Mayor of London, and daughter of Thomas Hill of Malpas and Hodnet, by Margaret, daughter of Thomas Wilbraham of Woodhay, co. Chester, son of Humphrey Hill, or Hull, by Anne, or Agnes, daughter and co-heir of John Bird of Charlton, by the niece and heiress of David David de Malpas. A reference to the Egerton pedigree shows that Roger, natural son of Sir William de Malpas, had issue David, father of David of Bickerton and Hampton (*gules*, a chevron between three pheons, points downwards, *argent*), who married Katherine, daughter of Hugh de Bickerton, *argent* on a chevron *sable*, three pheons of the field. They had issue John, whose son, David, died without issue, thus leaving his aunts his co-heirs. Humphrey Hill, or Hull, as the name was formerly spelt, was the son of Griffith Hull of Buntingsdale and Wlonkeslow by Margaret, or Mary, sister of Griffith Warren of Ightfield, son of William Hull, the son of Hugh Hull of Hull by Eleanor, daughter and heir of Hugh de Wlonkeslow. The arms of Hill, or Hull, are— *ermine* on a fess *sable*, a castle, triple-towered, *argent*;

THE FAMILY OF JONES OF CHILTON.

and those of Wlonkeslow, *sable*, a lion rampant *or*, crowned *gules* between three crosses formée fitchée *gules*. Thomas Jones, by his wife, Margaret, or Mary, daughter and co-heir of John Gratwood of Wollerton, had issue two sons, William, the successor of his father, and Edward. In the pedigree, for Gracewood read Gratwood, and for the arms of Gratwood, *gules*, a bend *argent*. As an heiress, Margaret Gratwood's coat would be quartered by her descendants with its quarterings as follows : 1. *Gules,* a bend *argent,* for Gratwood; 2. *ermine* on a fess *sable*, a castle, triple-towered, for Hull; 3. *sable*, a lion rampant *or*, crowned *gules*, between three crosses formée fitchée *gules*, for Wlonkeslow; 4. *argent*, a cross fiory, between four martlets *gules*, and a canton *azure*, for Byrd ; 5. *azure*, a bend *argent*, cotized *ermine* between six martlets *or*, the ancient arms of Byrd; 6. *gules*, a chevron between three pheons, points downward, *argent*, for David of Malpas.

(To be continued.)

PAROCHIAL HISTORY OF LLANYMYNECH.

BY JOHN FEWTRELL.

(*Concluded from* Vol. xiii, p. 416.)

CHAPTER IX.—NONCONFORMITY.

NONCONFORMITY had not commenced in this parish earlier than the year 1823. Rev. Walter Davies (Gwallter Mechain), writing in 1795, says, "There are no professed Dissenters in this parish—they are all either of the established religion, or of no religion at all". Probably the earliest attempt to spread views differing from the Established Church, took place under the Commonwealth, when the "Committee of Sequestration" deprived the Rev. G. Griffiths of his living, but allowed him residence, and one fifth of the tithe proceeds to support his family. The rector did not forsake his faithful band of followers, but continued to administer to them, both here and at Llandrinio. It is not known who was recognised as the legal minister for the time being. At the Restoration, the living was immediately given to Dr. J. Edwards, whose name is unhappily remembered, on account of his persecution of the Quakers, while Chancellor of the Diocese. A long interval then ensues, till the introduction of Independent views in 1796.

INDEPENDENTS.

Llanymynech is situated between two early settlements of the Independents, Oswestry and Penrhos. From these centres, itinerant preachers went out to establish churches in the surrounding parishes. Hence the history of Independency here is closely connected with that of Oswestry. At the Commonwealth, the Rev. Rowland Nevett, M.A., was appointed minister of the parish church of Oswestry, by the "Assembly of Divines." He retained the living at the Restoration, but was deprived, in 1662, by the Act of Uniformity. He then retired to Sweeny Hall, the residence of a Puritan lady, Madame Baker, where he continued to minister to those of his former congregation who chose to follow him. When greater toleration appeared, this small party of Puritans removed to a more commodious meeting-house in the town, and were known simply as "Protestant Dissenters". In course of time the old chapel was erected, and the "Protestant Dissenters" became the nucleus of the Independents of Oswestry, styling themselves by the latter name.

It was during the pastorate of the Rev. John Whitridge in 1796, that an attempt was made to establish an Independent church in this parish. He was one of the first to establish in Oswestry, a day-school for the education of the children of the poor. He established a day-school at Pant, in this parish, about the same time. At first his preaching was in the open air, sometimes at Pant, and other times nearer the village, the county stone being a favourite site. In the year 1820 Mr. Whitridge induced six of his congregation to become members of the Oswestry church, and to form a branch in Llanymynech. In the following year, 1821, funds were raised to erect a chapel. A difficulty arose as to the purchase of a site. It was desirable to build in the village, and a piece of land purchased by the Primitive Methodists was offered to them. As this was adjoining the parish church, disputes arose, and they relinquished the offer. A site was afterwards obtained from the late Mr. Thomas of Morton, at the boundary line between the parishes of Llanymynech and Morton. The chapel is a small rectangular brick building, and has a central aisle, with pews accommodating 200 persons. The cost of the building amounted to the modest sum of eighty pounds. The trust deed is dated 9th

July 1823. The chapel was opened for divine service in January 1822.

Until 1823 the officiating minister was supplied by the Oswestry church; but in that year the Pant members formed themselves into a separate church. The following is an extract from a pastoral charge, found among the muniments of the Old chapel, and has reference to this change.

"As we cannot know anything of the members at Pant and Blodwel, and as they have a place of worship of their own; and as they do not in their present connection benefit us nor we them, we recommend them to separate from us, and to form a church of themselves. They can, until they have an ordained minister of their own, have either our ministers or others to administer to them."

In the following year, 1824, the Rev. John Griffiths was appointed to the congregation at Pant, taking along with it the ministry of the church at Dovaston. He remained pastor of Dovaston and Pant for many years, the only change in his pastoral oversight being that, after a time, Domgay took the place of Dovaston, he residing at Llanyblodwel. The pastorate of Domgay and Pant, he retained, until the infirmities of old age necessitated retirement from the public ministry in 1858.

From the death of Mr. Griffiths until 1878, the services were conducted by ministers from neighbouring churches. At that date Rev. D. H. Shankland was appointed to the charge of the Pant, and Domgay churches. At the latter place a beautiful residence has recently been erected.

Primitive Methodists.

About the year 1822, the Nantwich circuit of the Connexion appointed Mr. William Doughty to open a mission in North-west Shropshire. Whitchurch was the scene of his first efforts, and from that place he proceeded to Wem, Ellesmere, and Oswestry. A chapel was built in Oswestry, where Mr. Doughty afterwards resided, and the mission was extended to the adjacent villages and hamlets. He visited and preached at Sweeney, Morton, Porthywaen, Pant, Llanymynech, and Llandrinio. He and a colleague, Mr. Fitzgerald, carried on their labours at Pant and Llanymynech, holding their meetings in the open air. Mr. S. Ward, a member of the body, then purchased a piece of land near Pant, and presented to them a site, whereon the chapel was built, at a cost of £350. It is a neat structure of bricks, with large plain Gothic windows. Formerly the chapel was included in the Oswestry circuit; it is now the centre of a circuit, and has several neighbouring stations associated with it. The present minister, Rev. J. Clare, is the first whom the Conference has appointed here. A residence is provided for the minister in the village.

Calvinistic Methodists.

About the year 1849, a project was entertained by the Calvinistic Methodists, to erect a chapel in this parish, but it was frustrated for many years, by some dispute about the title to the land which had been purchased for the purpose. In 1864 the difficulties were overcome, and the plans for a chapel were prepared by Mr. W. H. Spaul of Oswestry, and the first stone was laid, on the 11th of June in that year, by Edmund Cleaton, Esq., J.P., of Llanidloes. In the following October it was opened for religious worship. It is constructed of lime-stone, in the Gothic style, with facings of red sandstone. The front, facing the south, is lighted by large Gothic windows, and the south-east corner has a spire. This is said to have been the first chapel of the Calvinistic Methodists which had a spire. When the chapel was opened, the Rev. J. Ffoulkes was appointed the first minister. He was succeeded by the present minister, the Rev. R. Jones. A residence is provided in the village.

Chapter X.—Education.

The education of the poorer classes in this parish, in bygone years, seems to have been neglected, and much ignorance and superstition prevailed. A resident here during the latter part of the last century says of them—"There is scarcely an inhabitant here who is not able, with the greatest ease and indifference, to speak both English and Welsh. The Welsh language being still spoken on the confines of Offa's Dyke, is a proof of its permanency. Strength, courage, and activity have always been the characteristics of the men of this parish, but, unfortunately, too often applied to sinister purposes. It is a melancholy fact that more coroner's inquests have been held here within thirty years, than have been, perhaps, in any other parish in Wales. The source of these misfortunes must be the prevailing vice of drunkenness. The disposition of the people in general, is open-hearted and communicative. Nature has not been niggard in the endowment of their minds." The parish registers show that, out of 204 marriages solemnised here since 1837, there were 116 cases in which one or both parties were unable to sign their names. In 58, of these neither of the married persons signed; of the remainder, there are 29 instances in which the bridegroom alone could write, and an equal number in which only the bride could write. The witnesses appear to have been better educated. There are but 66 cases when one or both were unable to sign. In nine of these neither party signed, in 14 cases the male witness alone signed, and in 13 the female witness alone could write. Some of these persons were strangers to the parish, but the above analysis proves a deficiency in the education of many who, after marriage, settled here.

Private Schools.—Two schools appear to have been in existence during the last century; one conducted by the curate in charge of the rectory, and held at the rectory house; the other, a parish school, held in the tower of the old church. In country districts the curates often became the schoolmasters, especially when the stipend was small. The first record of a school in the parish is found in a memorandum book kept by the Rev. J. Whitridge, pastor of the Old Chapel, Oswestry. Amongst other accounts are the following :—

1796.—Remaining towards the school, Llanymynech, 13s., balance of an account received, to be paid to him (Enoch Thomas, Schoolmaster), of Mr. Lewis, Superintendent of the School, and Mr. Lewis of Wrexham, £12 0s. 0d., paid £11 7s. 0d.; balance, as above, 13s.

1797.—Enoch Thomas. Paid to him for teaching the Charity School at Pant-trwstan, near Llanymynech, at various times, and inserted in Day Book, £10 7s. 9d.

N.B.—The school commenced November 8th, 1796, ended September 18th, 1797.

From the latter date the school appears to have been conducted at Llanyblodwel, as shown by the next entry :—

"Paid for teaching the school at Blodwel, from September 18th, 1797, to May 28th, 1798, £7 12s. 3d."

This school, which was held at Pant, was one of the circulating schools established in the Oswestry district by the Independents, just before the close of the last century. The idea originated with the Rev. Griffith Jones, rector of Llanddowror. This clergyman undertook long tours, for the purpose of preaching in districts remote from places of worship. Wherever it was practicable he established schools, and teachers were employed to conduct them for a few months, and then pass on to other places, returning again to the school they originally commenced to teach. Through the benevolence of a Madame Bevan, he was enabled to found a school for the training of these itinerant teachers. At his death, in 1761, it was found that he had established no less than 215 of these circulating schools, attended by 8,637 scholars; and in twenty-four years he had been the means of teaching more than 150,000 Welsh people to read the Bible in their mother tongue. The system was the same as that adopted in later years by Mr. Whitridge, when Enoch Thomas became the itinerant schoolmaster. Unfortunately, the book referred to, does not state in what year the Llanymynech school was finally closed. In 1800 a subscription was commenced, to enable Enoch Thomas "to maintain his family one quarter of a year, during which time he hopes to establish a school adequate to their maintenance". The same year Mr. Powell was appointed schoolmaster of the "Salopian Circulating Charity Schools".

The old rectory school was probably held at the same time as this "circulating" school. It was attended principally by the sons of farmers and tradesmen of the village and district, and a fair education seems to have been given. At the commencement of this century Mr. Hughes was the master. Since his time it has been discontinued.

A similar private school was afterwards opened at the old house, known as Siamber Wên, between the church and the rectory. This place was very commodious for the purpose, containing some very large rooms. It was held in a room on the second story, and approached by a flight of steps from the inside. The other portion of the house was then kept as an inn. When the present National School was built, the master of the church school, Mr. Robert John Baugh, resigned, and commenced the Siamber Wên School, but it was closed at his death.

Several other schools of this class have been carried on at various times. One was held in a house in the row belonging to the Earl of Bedford. The principal was an auctioneer, named Cooke. Later, a gentleman, who had formerly been a Baptist minister, opened a school in another part of the village, and for a short time it was known as the "Llanymynech Academy". At present there are two schools for young ladies; one at Verniew Bank, the other at Ashfield House.

Free School.—The parish, or free school, was held for a number of years in a room on the ground floor, beneath the belfry of the old church. The room was small, and did not contain many scholars. It was chiefly supported by subscriptions from the landed proprietors and farmers. The education was free until a certain age, when the weekly payment amounted to a penny. Many of the children were sons of farmers, and were known as "pay scholars", on account of paying a higher rate of fees, usually five shillings per quarter. The free scholars were popularly known as "paupers", a name which was often the cause of schoolboys' riots. The subscribers were appointed visitors, a duty taken in rotation, notice being sent each week to those expected to attend.

National School.—About the year 1825 the present schoolroom was built, subscriptions being raised by the Rev. W. E. Evans, curate of the parish, and son of Dr. Evans of Llwynygroes. It is erected on the east side of the churchyard, and is built of lime-stone. It was enlarged and improved in 1870, and again in 1878.

Sunday School.—In addition to the religious education given in the day school, there is a Church Sunday School, held on each Sunday morning and afternoon. The number of children and adults attending, amount to about 120, with a staff of nine teachers.

APPENDIX.

Blasting Experiments.—Various attempts have been made by the proprietors of the limestone quarries, to introduce some method of obtaining the stone in sufficient quantities, to enable them to compete successfully with other quarry proprietors, principally those of Staffordshire. The primary idea seems to have been, to offer the fluxing stone to the iron-masters, at a lower price than formerly. This they were unable to do as long as the old, slow method of drilling holes, and blasting on a small scale was continued. The experiments were carried out in a similar manner to those in use at Holyhead, viz., by forming shafts and chambers to contain a large quantity of powder, and firing by a "time-fuse", or electricity. The stone at Holyhead was used for the harbour works, and the quarrying took place under the direction of Capt. G. R. Hutchinson, an officer of the Engineers. Reports of the scheme were published by the Government, and the success appears to have influenced the proprietors of these rocks. The great difficulty they had to fight against, was popular prejudice among the quarrymen. They looked upon the affair as a means of abolishing much manual labour, which it would certainly have done, unless there was a corresponding increase of trade.

The first experiment took place 17th September 1867. Preparations were made by sinking a shaft, at a distance of 12 yards from the edge of the perpendicular face of the rock, and to a depth of 60 feet. From the bottom of this, a chamber was cut, inclining at an obtuse angle to the shaft, and towards the face of the rock. It measured 7 feet long, 5 feet wide, and 4 feet in height, and was intended as a receptacle for the blasting material. The powder used weighed 1½ tons, and to it were attached three fuses, inclosed in gutta-percha, and computed to burn from fifteen to twenty minutes. Great precautions were taken to avoid any accident, either in the quarries, or the immediate neighbourhood. Men were stationed at various points along the hill with signals, and traffic was stopped along the roads adjoining. The firing signal was given, and in sixteen minutes the explosion occurred, and an immense mass of rock was brought down, considered to amount to eight or nine thousand tons, and about half that quantity loosened.

At the next experiment it was intended to make use of electricity, and operations were at once commenced for the purpose. The plan adopted was somewhat more elaborate than in the preceding trial. A level was driven into the rock a few yards above the base, and to a distance of 12 yards. At the end of the level, a cross level was driven, cutting the main one at right angles, both to the right and left of it. At equal distances small shafts were sunk in the cross level, until the base of the rock was reached. From the bottom of these shafts chambers were cut to contain the blasting powder. The total number of cubic yards to be operated upon, was assumed to be about 25,000, and, as the specific gravity of limestone is about two tons to the cubic yard, the quantity to be removed would be about 50,000 tons, or nearly four tons to each pound of powder. The three chambers were charged respectively with 6,000 lbs., 4,000 lbs., and 3,000 lbs, making a total of 13,000 lbs., or 6½ tons of Messrs. Curtis and Harvey's L.C.B. blasting powder. Two of Grove's powerful electrical batteries were used, one consisting of eighteen cells, and the other of ten.

cells. The largest battery was connected with insulated wire to the two largest charges, and the other battery to the small charge; this arrangement enabled the three charges to be exploded simultaneously. The batteries were placed in a small structure, or hut, and amply protected from danger, the operator being Mr. Edward Gledhill of Penpompren Mines, Aberystwith, an eminent electrician. All was in readiness by 11th March 1868, and a large concourse of people had assembled to witness the explosion. An eye-witness thus describes the result:—" The arrangements being pronounced complete, a few minutes after the hour appointed for the explosion, three o'clock, signals were given to ascertain that the precautions previously arranged to ensure safety were also complete. These being satisfactory, Mr. Savin gave the final signal for the explosion, which, it is almost needless to say, was instantaneous. The effect was terrific. The huge rock was burst from base to summit with tremendous force, and poured down, with a fearful roar, on to the floor of the quarry, the dull thunder of the explosion causing a tremor to pass through the rock." Some of the *débris* fell at an immense distance, a portion of the tramway bridge was destroyed on the Oswestry road, beneath the rocks, and a large quantity of fragments of powder was carried upwards of a mile distant. The report of the explosion was distinctly heard at Welshpool, a distance of ten miles. No other experiment of the kind has since taken place, with the exception of one by the British Dynamite Company, and it is apparent the results were not satisfactory.

Nelson's Monument.—In the early part of this century, a movement was commenced, to celebrate the victories of Lord Nelson, by raising a monument to his memory on Llanymynech Hill, similar to that of Lord Rodney on Breidden Hill. Meetings were held here, and the scheme was decided,[1] but finally it was abandoned, though the reason is not known.

---

[1] See "Bye-Gones", 1880.

OLD PARR OF WINNINGTON.

By ASKEW ROBERTS.

It might reasonably be supposed that a name so well known all over the kingdom as that of "The Olde, Old, very Olde Man, or Thomas Par", would be a household word in the district where he was born; but I question if many of those who live round Rodney's Pillar know how near to the Breidden Hills he was reared, and lived so long a period as to have become fabulous. The juniors of the present generation vaguely associate his name with a quack medicine, and many of the elders, who would hesitate to swallow his pills, take in the old-age theory without investigation.

One day during the summer of 1876, accompanied by a friend, I paid my third visit to the cottage at Glyn, in which Parr lived for so many years, and for the first time was able to get inside, the woman who has occupied it for more than thirty years having been from home on my two former visits. The cottage is in much the same state as it was when Parr left it two centuries ago, to journey to London, and the present resident has, on the walls of the kitchen, two likenesses of Parr himself, and one of his so-called son, who was also reputed to have been a centenarian. Of course the custodian of the place believes in the Old Parr fiction, and in support of it triumphantly told us she had seen it all in a book! We asked her what the book said? and she replied that when they came for Old Parr "to take him to the Parliament" they went into the house, and said to "an owd mon by the chimbley cornel, ' owd mon we'en cum for yo', but un said, 'Tinna me it's me fayther', and ther the fayther wun in the oak tree afore the door, and they ta'ed 'un out'n the tree". "But", I ventured to suggest in answer to this circumstantial narrative, "Parr had no children who lived beyond infancy", when I was met with the prompt reply, "Oh! it wun the base child he had by the ooman he dun penance for in Abberbury Church". To the narrator this was conclusive, nevertheless it might be objected that Parr was said to be 105 when he did penance, and 152 when he was taken to London, so the age of the junior by the fire-side, if he existed, could only have been 47 years, at the time of the visit, certainly not an age at which he would have been mistaken for a patriarch. For all this we have a well-engraved picture purporting to be a likeness of the elderly son of Old Parr, which my readers can see for themselves if they are fortunate enough to visit the cottage on a day when its occupant is not out "nurse-tending".[1]

My purpose in this paper is to give a short history of Thomas Parr, and to see how far it is reasonable to suppose that he lived in this world more than a century and a half, and then died prematurely! For his history we usually turn to the metrical account by Taylor the Water Poet; interesting enough, but scarcely trustworthy. The best account of him that has yet appeared was written a few years ago by Sir Baldwyn Leighton, Bart., for the *Alberbury Almanack,* and from this I take the following extract :—"It appears from contemporary records that John Parr, the father of Thomas, was a petty farmer at Winnington, holding his cottage and a few acres of land on lease from a Mr. Lewis Porter. Thomas lived with his father till he was 17, and then went to service; there is a tradition that he was in service at Rowton Castle, and the picture (a half length of the School of Vandyke) which hangs in that dining-room is one of the best extant of him.[2] At the age of 35 he returned home on his

[1] Parr's cottage is only half a mile from the Middletown station, on the Shrewsbury and Welshpool railway; so is very accessible.
[2] There is an excellent copy of this picture at Sweeney Hall, Oswestry, the seat of Stanley Leighton, Esq., M.P.

father's death, who left him four years of the lease of the place. In 1522, at the age of 39, he renewed his father's lease from Mr. Lewis Porter, for twenty-one years; and at the age of 60 (in 1543) he renewed again for twenty-one years from Mr. John Porter, the son of Mr. Lewis Porter; and at the mature age of 80 he married Jane Taylor, by whom he had a son and daughter, both of whom died young. In 1585, at the age of 102, he renewed his lease again from Mr. Hugh Porter, the son of Mr. John Porter; and three years afterwards, at the discreet age of 105, he did penance in Alberbury Church for disorderly conduct with Katharine Milton. When, towards the end of his life, King Charles I. asked him, after having lived so long what he had done more than other men? he is said to have related to him this occurrence:—

'How for having satisfaction 'twas thought meet
He should be purged by standing in a sheet;
Which aged (he) one hundred and five yeare,
In Alberbury's Parish Church did weare,
Should all that so offend such Penance doe,
Oh what a price would linen rise unto.'

"In 1595, when Thomas Parr was 112 years old, his wife Jane, to whom he had been married thirty-two years, died, and ten years afterwards this mature juvenile, at the age of 122, married another Jane, perhaps in memory of his first. She was the daughter of John Lloyd (or Flood) of Gilsells (possibly Guilsfield) in Montgomeryshire, and the widow of a Mr. Anthony Adda. He lived with her thirty years, but had no children. After having again renewed his lease (this time for life, of which he saw fifty years) from Mr. John Porter, the son of Hugh, and grandson of John, who had granted him his second lease, his fame reached the Court, and in 1635 Charles I. sent for him."

Sir Baldwyn goes on to say that most of his facts are taken from Taylor's narrative, "who evidently obtained them direct from Thomas Parr and his relations, so they have nearly the value of an autobiography". In his preface, Taylor says that the Earl of Arundel, being on a visit to Shropshire on some business connected with lands he held in the county, heard of this "remarkable piece of antiquity", and went to see Parr; and, being pleased with his visit, "in his inated noble and Christian piety, he took him into his charitable tuition and protection". This included the dragging of the poor old fellow off to London to see— or rather to be seen by—the king.[1] To make the journey easy and pleasant for the old rustic, his daughter-in-law, Lucy, attended him; "and to cheer up the old man, and make him merry, there was an antique-faced-fellow, called Jack, or John the fool, with a high and mighty no beard, that had also a horse for his carriage". One of the earl's own servants attended the party, and defrayed expenses. The fame of the old man went before him, and at some of the halting places "the rabble were so unruly" that Parr was nearly stifled by the crush, "so greedy are the vulgar to hearken to or gaze after novelties".[2]

[1] "One *Thomas Parr* is dead at a wonderful greate age, being, it is said, 150 yeares old. The Earle of *Arundell* had him brought to *Whitehall*, and the change did shortly affect his Health; no marvel, poore old Man, he would have beene better pleased, methinks, to have beene lett alone."—*Diary of Lady Willoughby*, November 24th, 1635.

[2] Taylor thus describes the journey to London:—"Winnington is a hamlet in the parish of Alberbury, near a place called the Welsh Poole, eight miles from Shrewsbury, from whence he was carried to Wim, a town of the Earl's aforesaid; and the next day to Shefnall, a manor house of his Lordship's, where they likewise staid one night; from Shefnall they came to Wolverhampton, and the next day to Brimicham, from thence to Coventry: and although Master Kelley had much to do to keep the people off that pressed upon him in all places where he came, yet at Coventry he was most oppressed; for they came in such multitudes to see the old man, that those that defended him were almost quite tired and spent, and the aged man in danger to have been stifled; and in a word, the rabble was so unruly, that Bryan was in doubt he should bring his charge no further; so greedy are the vulgar to hearken to or gaze after novelties. The trouble being over, the next day they past to Daventry, to Stony Stratford, to Redburn, and so to London, where he is well entertained and accommodated in all things, having all the aforesaid attendants at the sole charge and cost of his Lordship."

The " poet" does not seem to have been aware of the satire conveyed in his reflections on "the vulgar"; and he goes on to state that his hero had outlived most part of the people living near him round the Breidden, three times over; and that his children, of which he only had two, died in infancy.

When in London, Old Parr was turned into a show in the Strand, where "the vulgar" went to see him, and where authors wrote him up and artists depicted him. When he died—which event took place during the same year—Dr. Hervey made a *post-mortem* examination of his body, the result of which showed that Parr might have lived "a great while longer" had he not undergone such a change in life as the journey to London necessitated.

From all this, Sir Baldwyn Leighton comes to the conclusion that "Thomas Parr did attain to something like twice the alloted span of man's ordinary life—to twice the three-score years and ten of the Psalmist David". Sir Baldwyn thinks "Taylor's and Hervey's accounts so minute and graphic", that he cannot but conclude "that, either from some accidental strength of constitution, or owing to the moderate and healthy life he led", Parr did attain the fabulous age recorded. In common with a host of sceptics, may I venture totally to differ with him in this opinion. To me, Taylor's evidence seems utterly worthless. He found a show, and he became the showman. He greedily swallowed all the stories told him, to enhance the value of the article exhibited, and was not particular to investigate the truth of what he wrote. He tells us that Parr never had any children to grow to man's estate, yet quotes a daughter-in-law, Lucy. He speaks of the "cyder" manufactured where Parr lived, and the "nightingales" that sang round his home. In short, he takes "poetic licence" with such a vengeance that his plain prose becomes quite apochryphal. Dr. Hervey too, could be no authority. He is asked to make a *post-mortem* examination on the body of a man he is told died at the age of 152 years. He finds the body wonderfully healthy, and his examination goes far to prove that Parr was nothing like so old as his friends asserted he was. Still, the old age theory was accepted, and, in course of time, a will[1] makes its appearance, which, by the way, utterly ignores the statement of Parr's leaving no descendants, and of one of Taylor's reasons for the extreme age of his hero—that he took no physic. The will is doubtless as authentic as the narrative Taylor has put into verse, and the pills it indicates as genuine as the likeness on the outside of the boxes in which they are contained.[2]

[1] The audacity of this document is only surpassed by its extraordinary results. It was revealed to the world some time about the year 1843, as follows:—

"A most singular document has recently been brought to light, written by the celebrated OLD PARR, who attained the almost incredible age of 152 years. It is written on parchment, and, although upwards of 200 years old, it is in an excellent state of preservation. The following is an extract:

"'These do certifie yt ye undermentioned is ye method of preserving health, which by ye grace of Almighty God has caused me to attain to my miraculous old age. Albeit, in my youth I was afflicted with ye bloody flux and King's evil, but which left me by using some dayes ye herbs as herein written.'"

"(Here follows the receipt).

"Moreover, I bequeath to my second Great Grandson ye method I employ for preparing ye medicament.

"Given this day, and in the 147th year of my age.

"THOMAS PARR.

"Winnington, Salop, Januarie 17th, 1630."

Messrs. Ingram and Cooke, two unknown young men, were the fortunate "discoverers". They set up the *Illustrated London News*, and with it, and "Parr's Life Pills", made a princely fortune.

[2] This likeness represents Parr dressed in a flowing wig, and eyes wide open; although Taylor describes him as having long been blind. He says, in the introduction to his metrical account of Parr, and in allusion to this:—"One remarkable passage of the old man's policy must not be omitted or forgotten, which is thus; his three leases of sixty-three years being expired, he took his last lease of his landlord, one Master John Porter, for his life; with which lease, he hath lived more than fifty years, as is further hereafter declared; but this old man would, for his wife's sake, renew his lease for years, which his landlord would not consent unto; wherefore Old Parr, having long been blind,

The old Parr fable has had a long run, and no one seems to have attempted to investigate it until 1869, when Mr. W. J. Thoms took up the subject in *Notes and Queries*. Failing to get any satisfactory replies, he wrote to the Shrewsbury newspapers, to the vicar of Alberbury, and to other parties who were likely to render assistance. All his labour was in vain. One reply, indeed, he did get to his newspaper query, by a correspondent who said—"Alberbury Church adjoins Loton Hall, the residence of Sir Baldwin, and *I have no doubt* the particulars of Parr's penance may be found in the church records, *to which I would refer all sceptics*". Unfortunately for the writer, these church records had already been overhauled, and no mention of Parr found in them. Where, then, are "the records and true certificate" Taylor speaks of as shown to the Earl of Arundel? All the records we have are the veriest hearsay evidence; and there is little doubt "the vulgar" of two centuries ago were easily led to believe in monstrosities, and were not confined to the rabble.

There are several portraits of Old Parr extant. In addition to the one already noticed, "of the school of Vandyke", there is the well-known picture by Dobson, in which he is represented as a very old man, and blind. A copy of this was exhibited at the Wrexham Fine Art Exhibition of 1876, also one representing a much younger-looking man, the property of the Earl of

sitting in his chair by the fire, his wife looked out of the window, and perceived Master Edward Porter, the son of his landlord, to come towards their house, which she told her husband, saying, 'Husband, our young landlord is coming hither.' 'Is it so?' said Old Parr; 'I pr'ythee, wife, lay a pin on the ground near my foot, or at my right toe,' which she did, and when young Master Porter, yet forty years old, was come into the house, after salutations between them, the old man said, 'Wife, is not that a pin which lies at my foot?' 'Truly, husband,' quoth she, 'it is a pin indeed'; so she took up the pin, and Master Porter was half in a maze that the old man had recovered his sight again; but it was quickly found to be a witty conceit, thereby to have them to suppose him to be more lively than he was, because he hoped to have his lease renewed for his wife's sake, as aforesaid."*

Powis. Colonel Heyward of Crosswood, writing to *Bye-gones* of April 14th, 1880, says he saw the portrait by Rubens, "lot 94 of the Novar collection", knocked down for 180 guineas, at Christie's, in 1878. Sir Baldwyn Leighton mentions seven portraits in his memoir of Parr, but some of these he has reason to think are duplicates. A good engraving of Parr's cottage appeared in the *Gentleman's Magazine* some years ago, and it has recently been copied into Chambers's *Book of Days*.

Old Parr was buried in Westminster Abbey, and, says Mr. Thoms, in his *Longevity of Man*, "the inscription which marked his resting-place has lately been carefully re-engraved, by order of the present Dean [Stanley], and is as follows:—'Tho: Parr of ye County of Sallop, Borne in A$^{o.}$ 1483. He lived in ye reignes of Ten Princes viz: K. Edw. 4. K. Ed. 5. K. Rich. 3. K. Hen. 7. K. Hen. 8. K. Edw. 6. Q. Ma. Q. Eliz. K. Ja. & K. Charles Aged 152 yeares & was Buried Here Novemb. 15, 1635'."

ROADS, BRIDGES, CANALS, AND RAILWAYS IN MONTGOMERYSHIRE.

By A. HOWELL, Rhiewport.

(*Continued from* Vol. ix, p. 192.)

III.

We have noticed the changes brought about by the extension of the canal systems of England into Montgomeryshire, and now propose giving some account of the leading incidents in the history of that extension.

This closely followed upon the improvement of our main lines of road on their conversion into turnpike roads, and which took place chiefly under the first "Montgomeryshire Roads Act", which was passed in the year 1769. In 1793 the Ellesmere Canal Act, 33 George III, was passed, and in its title it is stated to be—

"An Act for making and maintaining a navigable canal from the river Severn, at Shrewsbury, to the river Mersey, at, or near, Netherpool, in the county of Chester; and also for making and maintaining certain collateral cuts from the said intended canal."

The Act in its preamble recited that—

"Whereas, the making and maintaining a canal, for the navigation of boats, barges, and other vessels, from the river *Severn*, at *Shrewsbury*, through, by, or near to, the towns of Ellesmere and Wrexham, the city of Chester, and through the several counties of Salop, Denbigh, Flint, and Chester, and the county of the city of Chester, and also certain collateral cuts to be connected with the said canal, as hereinafter described, will open a communication for the cheap and easy conveyance of goods, wares, provisions and merchandise, and all heavy commodities, between the rivers Severn, Dee, and Mersey, and the ports of Liverpool, Chester, and Bristol, and the several intermediate towns and places, will greatly promote and facilitate the intercourse of trade and commerce between the several places aforesaid, will encourage and increase manufactures, and will materially assist the agriculture of the country throughout the line and neighbourhood of the said canal and collateral cuts, by a supply of lime and other manure at a moderate expense; and the said canal and collateral cuts will tend very much to reduce the price of coals in the neighbourhood thereof, and will be in other respects a great public utility." The Act then incorporated some 1,500 or more persons named in it, and their successors, with others to be named by them, into a Company for making such canal and cuts, by the name and style of "The Company of Proprietors of the Ellesmere Canal", and empowered such Company to make such canal and cuts, to be called "The Ellesmere Canal", from and out of the river Severn, within the liberties of the town of Shrewsbury, above a bridge called Bagley Bridge, and also at a place adjoining a close of land called Warehouse Field, through the several parishes, townships, and places named, lying in its way in the counties of Salop, Denbigh, Flint, and Chester, to unite with the river Mersey at or near Netherpool, and also to make a collateral cut to branch out of such canal in Horderley, in the county of Salop, passing through the several parishes, townships, or places of Hordley, Whittington, Frankton, Felton, Rednal, Sutton, Wooton, Oswestry, Aston, Twyford, Maesbury, Moreton, Criccieth, and Llwyntydman to Llanymynech; and other branches, which are described in like manner, to Brumbo Holt and Prees, in Denbighshire and Flintshire. Surveys and plans, signed by the Speaker of the House of Commons, were to be deposited with the clerks of the peace of the respective counties.

The Company were authorised to raise and contribute among themselves a competent sum for making the canals, tents, and works, not exceeding £400,000, and further sums if needful, not exceeding £50,000, by shares or by mortgage, and an additional sum of £50,000 by mortgage. The first general assembly was to be held at the sign of the *Royal Oak*, in Ellesmere, on the 3rd of July 1793. The act appointed the persons resident within the counties, through which the canal or branches passed, possessing certain qualifications, to be commissioners to settle the amounts payable to landowners for or in respect of their lands, subject to appeal to a jury, and for determining differences between the company and any other persons. Powers were given to elect officers and a committee for the management of their affairs. The company were authorised to take tolls for coal, lime, limestone, and rock salt at 1½d. per mile; for freestone, timber, slate, ironstone, lead ore, iron, and lead, 2d.; and for all other goods and things, 3d. per ton per mile, with powers to lower those rates, and with the consent of the commissioners to fix the rates for the conveyance of small parcels. There were exemptions for manure (except lime) for the improvement of the lands through which the canal or cuts should pass, and for road materials, powers to landowners to carry manure toll free, reservation to them of the fisheries, and a right to use pleasure boats, and other exemptions and privileges. The navigation was to be free to all parties on payment of the rates and subject to regulations and restrictions. And after authorising a further collateral cut from the Llanymynech Branch at Maesbury Marsh to Morda Bridge, near Oswestry, and after stating that it was conceived to be practicable to make a navigable canal from the summit of the Ellesmere Canal, thereby authorised at or near Morton Hall Farm, in the township of Prees Henlle, by or near, as conveniently might be, to the town of Oswestry, to the limestone quarries at Porthywaen, there to communicate with a navigable canal which had been proposed to be made from the said quarries to Welshpool, and to substitute such canal from Prees Hentle to Porthywaen, or some other cut or canal between Prees Henlle and Porthywaen, or Llanymynech, more advantageous to the public, in lieu of the branch hereby authorised from the Ellesmere Canal to Llanymynech, and application might at a future session of Parliament be made for that purpose; and it had been proposed that, previous to the making of such authorised branch, an investigation should take place as to whether such a substituted canal, more advantageous to the public, might be made in lieu of the branch thereby authorised from the Ellesmere Canal to Llanymynech, and application might, in a subsequent session of Parliament, be made for that purpose ; and it had been proposed that, previous to the making of such authorised branch, an investigation should take place as to whether such a substituted canal, more advantageous to the public, could be made, then the construction of the authorised Llanymynech branch was thereby suspended for two years, in order to give time for such investigation and application to Parliament, and engineers were appointed to report thereon.

Another Act of the 36th year of George III (1796) was passed to explain and amend the Act of 1793 :—

"And for varying and altering certain parts of the Whitchurch line of the said canal and collateral cuts, and for extending the same from Franckton Common to Sherryman's Bridge, in the parish of Whitchurch, and for making and maintaining several other branches and collateral cuts to communicate therewith."

In the preamble of that Act, after references to the Act of 1793, it is stated that commissioners were appointed for carrying its powers vested in them into execution, and that the company had begun to make the canal and cuts, and had raised and contributed amongst themselves a considerable sum of money, part whereof had been laid out and expended in the undertaking, and the company were desirous to complete and finish the said canal, but it was found that the powers given by the said Act required to be altered and amended ; and that it appeared, upon a re-survey of the country through which the company were by the said Act empowered to make and complete those parts of the canal and collateral cuts which yet remained unfinished, that it would be convenient to vary and alter some parts of the line of the canal and collateral cuts, and. to make, extend, and maintain several other collateral cuts and branches to communicate therewith, as thereinafter mentioned. The Act then made provisions accordingly, and it restrained the company from taking water from the Ellesmere Lakes or meres, or any other lakes or meres belonging to Francis Duke of Bridgwater, in the county of Salop.

By another Act of the same session, power was given to alter the previously authorised line between Ruabon and Chester, and the construction of several branches. In that Act also, after stating that upon a survey it was found practicable to make a branch from the Ellesmere Canal at Morton Hall, within the township of Prees Henlle, to communicate with the Montgomeryshire Canal at Porthywaen, and whereby the making of the proposed branch from Maesbury Marsh to Morda Bridge would be saved, then authority was given to construct such branch to Porthywaen, in a line described, or other line as near as conveniently as might be to the town of Oswestry and make a feeder out of the river Tannat at Abercynlleth on the landowners' consent being obtained, or failing which, on obtaining Parliamentary powers to go through the lands, and in default of the Ellesmere Company doing this, power was given to the Montgomeryshire Canal Company to do it. By an Act of the 41st of George III (1801), power was given in furtherance of the power of the Act of 1790, to extend the Whitchurch branch from the New Mills, in the parish of Whitchurch, to the Chester Canal, in the township of Stoke, in the parish of Acton, in the county of Chester; and by a subsequent Act, after stating that the making of the portion of the line between Pontcysyllte and the upper end of Cegedog Valley, near Brymbo, would be considerable an exemption of coal, coke, culm, lime, and limestone was repealed, and powers were given to raise additional capital, amounting to £67,000. The company were exempted from repairs of roads over the approaches to the canal bridges after such roads should be made and put into good and durable repair; and after stating that steam engines had become of great use for various purposes, and such engines consumed considerable quantities of coal, and could be used only where sufficient cold water could be obtained to condense the steam, then power was given to supply them therewith by pipes from the canal.

It does not appear there was anything further done in regard to the proposed branches to Morda Bridge and Porthywaen, or the proposed canal from Porthywaen Quarries to Welshpool and the Montgomeryshire line, as afterwards made, as a continuation of the Ellesmere Company's Llanymynech branch, seems to have been substituted. The Ellesmere Company accordingly constructed their main line from Shrewsbury to the right of Ellesmere by Chirk, Pontcysyllte, Ruabon, to the right of Wrexham, and by Gresford and Chester to Ellesmere Port on the Mersey, also the branch from near Frankton to Llanymynech, and another from the same point in the opposite direction by Ellesmere, Whitchurch, and Wrenbury, to join the Chester Canal, near Nantwich, with other smaller branches.

Those lines of canal were as necessary to Montgomeryshire as to the districts through which they passed, and the Act for and the construction of the Montgomeryshire Canal followed on the heels of those lines. The Montgomeryshire Canal Act was passed in the 34th year of George III (28th March 1794), being the next year after the year in which the first Ellesmere Act was passed. By the Montgomeryshire Act the following persons, viz. :—

George Baker, George Baxter, clerk, Jane Baxter, William Baxter, Samuel Yate Benyon, Arthur Blayney, Evan Bowen, William Brown, clerk, Thos. Brown, Pryce Buckley, Aaron Bywater, John Palmer Chichester, The Right Hon. Edward Lord Clive, Thomas Colley, Robert Corbett, Phillip Wyatt Crowther, Ann Davies, Pryce Davies, Thos. Dadford, Richard Edmunds, John Edwards, Susannah Edwards, Edmund Edye, Thos. Evans, Henry Foulkes, Ambrose Gethyn, Geo. Gould, Robert Griffiths, Athelstan Hamer, John Herbert, Geo. Hodson, John Home, Samuel Home, Charles Gardner Humphreys, David Jones, Evan Jones, Humphrey Jones, John Lloyd Jones, Matthew Jones, Oliver Jones, Robert Jones, Thomas Jones, clerk, Thos. Jones, surgeon, Thos. Jones of Lymore, Thos. Jones of Garth, Richard King, clerk, Whitshed Keene, Sir Edward

Lloyd, Bart., Edward Pryce Lloyd, Joseph Lyon, Maurice Lloyd, Devereux Mytton, Arthur Davies Owen, Pryce Owen, Margaret Parry, Martha Parry, The Right Hon. Geo. Edward Henry Arthur Earl of Powis, Clopton Phrys, Henry Proctor, John Probert, John Pryce, clerk, Catherine Pugh, John Pugh, William Pugh, Evan Stephens, Maurice Stephens, Thomas Sturkey, Henry Lord Viscount Tracy, Richard Tudor, James Turner, William Turner, John Williames the elder, John Williames the younger, John Williams, Martha Williams, John Winder, and Sir Watkin Williams Wynn, Bart., and their successors, executors, administrators, and assigns,

Together with such other person or persons, bodies politic, or corporate, or collegiate, as they or the major part of them at their first general meeting should appoint, were incorporated into a company under the name of "the Company of Proprietors of the Montgomeryshire Canal", with power to make and maintain a canal to be called "the Montgomeryshire Canal", from or near Porthywaen Lime Rocks, in the parish of Llanyblodwell, to the town of Pool, and from thence, by Berriew and Garthmill, to or near the river Severn, opposite to the east side of the town of Newtown; and also a branch out of such canal at or near Porthywaen, to, or near to, Llanymynech Lime Rocks; another branch in the township of Burgedin, in the parish of Guilsfield, to Sarney Crowner Bridge, in that parish, and to supply those canals with water from the river Tannatt, at Abercynlleth, and from the rivers Verniew, Rhiew, and Severn, and from all brooks and watercourses within 2,000 yards thereof, and to divert the Tannatt between Abercynlleth Hall and Carreghovah Hall, and to erect one or more fire engine or fire engines, or other machine, to supply the canals with water, and also feeders, aqueducts, and channels for supplying the canals, fire engine, and reservoirs with water. But not to take water from the Lledan, Country House Brook, and Llivior Brook, except the water of the Lledan Brook at Welshpool, for twenty-four hours in every week, from twelve o'clock on Saturday night to twelve o'clock on Sunday night.[1] And in case the company should take any water to the injury of Aberbechan, Berriew, Brithdir, Luggy, Dommin's Green, Guilsfield, Ceunant, Mardu, and Carreghovah Mills respectively, and if any injury to any of those Mills should be caused, then the company were, if required by the owners, to purchase the mills. The owners of estates in the counties of Salop, Denbigh, or Montgomery, to the annual value of £40, and the heirs apparent of the owners of such estates, value £200, or possessing personal property value £800, were appointed commissioners to settle all questions between the company and the owners of property, but none to act in cases wherein they were interested; appeals to juries were given. The company were authorised to raise the capital among themselves to defray the cost, not exceeding £72,000, in shares of £100 each; and, if that amount should be insufficient, a further amount not exceeding £20,000, and with the option to raise the last-mentioned sums by shares or mortgage. The first general meeting was to be held at the *Royal Oak*, Pool, the 7th July 1794, the second meeting on the 28th of that month, and subsequent meetings on the first Monday in July annually. Power was given to appoint at such meetings thirteen proprietors, possessing £500 of the share capital respectively, to be a committee to manage the company's affairs and to appoint other offices. The company were authorised to levy tonnage not exceeding, for limestone, 1d. per ton per mile; for coal and lime, 2d.; for other stone, pig-iron, brick, timber, tiles, slates, gravel, sand, lead ore, and all other raw materials, 3d.; for bark, cordwood, coke, charcoal, lead, wrought iron, plank and deal, 3½d.; and with the higher rates of 2¼d., 3d., 5d., 5½d., and 6d. in respect of such things respectively

[1] This was enacted to protect the supply of water to the Old Domen Mill, and was observed by an arrangement at the aqueduct there, until a few years ago, when the Mill was removed, and the road to the Smithfield then constructed was made over its site.

between Llivior Brook and Newtown. But dung, soil, marl ashes, or other manure, (except lime and limestone,) used for improvement of the lands through which the canals passed, and also stone, gravel, sand, or other materials for the roads in the parishes passed through, were exempted from the tonnage, provided the water should, at the time of the passing of the boats containing such things, be flowing over the waste weirs. The right of fishing was given to the lords of the manors and the landowners, as were also powers to use pleasure boats. The minerals, and also powers to construct railways and roads communicating with the canal wharves, were given to them. And, after stating that the Ellesmere Company intended to apply for an Act for the making of a canal from Preeshenlle to communicate with the Montgomeryshire Canal at Porthywaen, the Act provides and regulates between the two companies the supply of water by a feeder from the Tannatt at Abercynlleth.

It does not appear that there was any subsequent Act obtained in respect of the Montgomeryshire Canal until the Western Branch Act in 1815, and the Ellesmere Company, not having constructed their branch to Porthywaen, the portion of the Montgomeryshire main line to that place appears to have been abandoned, and the Llanymynech Branch substituted, that is, the Montgomeryshire Canal was made as a continuation of the Ellesmere and Llanymynech Branch, as the main line, and which thence as far as Garthmill, and the Guilsfield branch were completed within the first decade of the present century. Until very lately there were persons alive who well remembered the completion and opening of it to Welshpool, about the middle of that decade.

We cannot do anything better than, or as well as, give here, in his own words, the following, from the Rev. Walter Davies's very interesting book, published in 1813, entitled, *General View of the Agricultural and Domestic Economy of North Wales.*

"The Ellesmere Canal, which connects the rivers Severn, Dee, and Mersey, commencing from the latter at a place now called Ellesmere Port, crossing the Hundred of Wirrall to Chester, and from the Dee proceeding in a direction nearly south, enters the county of Denbigh near Pulford, it then crosses the Alan, and proceeds to Gwersyllt; from thence a branch turns off westerly to Brynbo Iron and Coal Works, to Ffrwd Colliery, in the county of Denbigh, and to Talwern Colliery and Nant y Ffridd Lime Rocks, in the county of Flint, where it terminates in a reservoir of eighty-two acres; the water whereof, when necessary, is to supply the summit-level of the canal. The main trunk proceeds from Gwersyllt to Bersham Iron Works; and, by a connection of iron railroads pervading the Ruabon collieries, it appears a second second time upon the Dee at Pont Cyfsylltau, where it crosses both river and dale upon an aqueduct of the following extraordinary dimensions:—

	Ft.	In.
Length of the cast-iron trough, which supports the water	1007	0
Height from the bed of the Dee to the top of the side plates	126	8
Breadth of the water-way, within the iron-work	11	10
Number of freestone pillars, including abutments, 20.		
Distance between the pillars at the top, being of a pyramidal shape	45	0
Depth of the iron sides of the canal	5	3
Length of the earthen embankment, formed for the carriage of the canal to the level on the south bank of the Dee	1503	0
Height of the embankment at the south abutment	75	0

"The iron-work was cast in a foundry erected for the purpose on the spot, and the stones for the pillars were raised in a neighbouring quarry at Plas Kynaston.

"This magnificent aqueduct was opened with great ceremony on the 26th day of November 1805, in the presence of about 8,000 spectators.

"The three great Italian aqueducts have celebrated the names of as many Roman Pontiffs, and that near Maintenon has displayed the magnificence of the Grand Monarch;[1] but neither of them had the principle of commerce for its foundation; in which light this aqueduct over the Dee is the first in Europe. Its expense was estimated at £40,000.

"On the north side of the Dee a branch extends to Llangollen and to the vicinity of the Oernant slate quarries. From

---

[1] Louis XIV, who built it to convey the river Bure to Versailles.

the end of the embankment at the aqueduct, the main canal proceeds to the west of the Park du Collieries, the east of Bronygarth lime rocks, and between Chirk Castle and village to the bank of the river Ceiriog; which, together with the dale, it crosses upon a freestone aqueduct 700 feet in length, consisting of ten arches, and 70 feet above the surface of the plain. At this place it quits the North Wales district for a space, and enters Shropshire. Having proceeded towards Shrewsbury as far as Frankton, a branch, near that place, takes a south-western direction to Llanymynech lime works, where it re-enters the county of Denbigh,[1] and where the property of the Ellesmere Canal Company terminates, and that of the Montgomeryshire commences. From the lime rocks at this place, about two-and-a-half miles of railway have been formed for the easier conveyance of limestone into the boats. From thence the Montgomeryshire branch proceeds, and crosses the river Vyrnwy upon an aqueduct of five arches, 40 feet in each span, and 25 feet above the ordinary surface of the water; exclusive of a number of arches adjoining the aqueduct to discharge the surplus water of floods. From thence the canal proceeds along the Severn Vale to Welshpool and towards New Town as far as Garthmill, which is the limit of its present extent. This branch may most peculiarly be styled the Agricultural Canal; the chief articles of its import into the county being limestone and coal; and of its export, timber, grain, and the produce of the dairy. The whole expense of the Montgomeryshire canal amounts to upwards of £70,000, including the sum of £2,000 expended in bringing a branch, the extent of three miles, towards the village of Guilsfield."[2]

---

[1] This refers to Careghova township at Llanymynech, which then was a detached portion of the county of Denbigh; but was, subsequently, some thirty years ago, more or less, by Act of Parliament, made part of Montgomeryshire.

[2] The author adds:—"Notwithstanding the Montgomeryshire Canal being formed chiefly for the encouragement of agriculture, yet farmers are loth to grant that they derive any advantage from it. Those through whose farms it was cut, complain of loss of land without any reduction in rent; and that their meadow-lands lying below it become rushy, owing to the oozing of the water. A farmer already keeping a team, would rather take it the distance of from ten to eighteen miles to the lime-rocks or coal-pits, where he has the article at prime cost and superior weights or measures. But these land-carriage advantages are counterbalanced by others arising from the local conveniences of the canal. A team cannot return from the Ruabon coal-pits to the upper parts of the Vale of the Severn in less

The period of and following upon the construction of the canal to Garthmyl, which portion afterwards took the name of the Eastern Branch, was, as is well known, a period which may, perhaps, without exaggeration, be called one of unparalleled pressure upon the nation's resources, arising mainly from the gigantic and ruinous war by sea and land with our neighbours, and subsequently our very good friends and allies, the French, in which England took such prominent part. The scarcity of money, and great increase in the cost of labour and materials, continued to increase at an advancing rate as the work proceeded and afterwards. The efforts and means of the Company were exhausted by the construction of that portion of their undertaking, though at the commencement it was thought sufficient for the cost to Newtown. The work, therefore, there stood for a good many years, and was not taken up again until after the close of that war. It became

than four days, exclusive of two days' rest; whereas, within a moderate distance of the canal, only one day is lost for the necessary work of the farm. Lime also cannot be procured in sufficient quantity by land-carriage at a great distance. A farmer who could lately procure but fourteen loads in a season from the rocks, at the distance of twenty miles, and for which he paid about £10, is now enabled to carry thirty loads from the canal wharf, the distance of five miles, though at the expense of £54. This farmer could not carry his fourteen loads with one team, in less than seven weeks, but he can carry the thirty loads in five weeks. By this means he gains twelve days to work his summer-fallow or turnip-ground, and sixteen loads more of lime; besides a saving in gate-tolls, ale- and victual-money, wear-and-tear of horses, gearing, waggon and wheels, towards counterbalancing the £44 extra lime bill; and if the soil he cultivates be improveable by the additional quantity of lime, he need not be long before he is fully reimbursed. Nothing, therefore, but either penuriousness or want of foresight will cause the farmer to prefer the distant carriage; especially if the profits of the Canal Vendors would permit them to give equal measures of lime, and equal weights of coal, with those of the rocks and pits. One other advantage arising from the convenience of the canal is, that the farmer within a moderate distance is enabled to lime his Lent crops before sowing; by which means the lime becomes incorporated with the soil, and one load may have greater effect than two, spread as usually, upon the growing grain."

necessary, before it could be proceeded with, to obtain a new Act of Parliament constituting a new Company, and with new capital. During that gloomy period, hopes were kept up, first by our naval successes, afterwards by the success of our arms in the Peninsula, and revived by the subsequent successes of England and her allies, which in 1814 culminated in the reduction and occupation of Paris and the abdication of the Emperor. The Bill for the new Act was introduced into Parliament in the Session of 1815. The period of its passing through Parliament was an eventful one. The enthusiastic feelings and rising expectations of the country were doomed to temporary disappointment by Napoleon's escape from Elba and landing on the coast of France on the 1st of March, and the renewal of the war which followed. Then came the crowning Battle of Waterloo, which was fought just four days before the Act obtained the Royal assent.

That Act (55 Geo. III, c. 83) was passed on the 22nd of June 1815, and was known as "The Western Branch Act". It was entitled

"An Act to authorise the raising of a further sum of money to complete the Montgomeryshire Canal, and to extend the power of deviating from and making certain alterations in part of the original plan; and for explaining and rendering more effectual an Act of the thirty-fourth year of his present Majesty for making the said canal."

In its preamble, it stated in general terms the object of the prior Act, to which we have above referred:—

"And that the Company of Proprietors had proceeded in the execution of the prior Act, and had raised and contributed among themselves £71,100, part of the £72,000 authorised by that Act, in 711 shares of £100 each, and had expended that amount in carrying out the undertaking. Also that the Company had nearly completed the main line of the canal from Garthmill eastward, and also the collateral cut in the parish of Guilsfield. That the continuing of the canal from Garthmill westward, to or near to Newtown, and the varying of part thereof from the course authorised by the original Act, and carrying the same by Bryn-y-derwen Bridge to Aberbechan, and thence to or near to the Severn, at or near Newtown, would be more beneficial to the Company and useful to the public, and would preserve a better level and save a considerable expense; and for the purpose of so completing the canal, it was expedient to raise a further sum of money as thereinafter mentioned. And it would tend to the better carrying of the purposes of the original Act into effect if the powers and provisions thereof were in various other respects explained, altered, and amended."

Then it was enacted that John Davies, clerk; John Edwards; John Hunter; Evan Jones, clerk; Sir Edward Pryce Lloyd, baronet; Sir Arthur Davies Owen, knight; David Pugh; Evan Stephens; and Charles Hanbury-Tracy (being proprietors of the Montgomeryshire Canal Company), together with such other persons as should be nominated, were thereby incorporated into a Company for the making and completing of such continuation, in accordance with the powers of the original Act, and with similar powers except as thereby altered. The number of shares possessed by proprietors at their general meetings, to enable them to choose a committee, and for other purposes, to be 150, instead of 500, as in the original Act. The commissioners were to be paid 10s. 6d. a day for their attendance at meetings. The Company were prohibited from constructing wharves, except with the consent of the landowners to whom the sites belonged, and the same in regard to lime-kilns. And after stating that the original Company had constructed a feeder for the supply of water from the Severn to the terminus at Garthmill, such feeder was transferred to the new Company. The new Company were authorised to raise and contribute, in addition to the £71,100 already contributed, and to the £9,000 residue of the original £72,000 and £20,000 authorised by the original Act, the sum of £40,000, in shares of £100 each, and all the said sums were to make one joint capital stock of the Company of proprietors of the Montgomeryshire Canal. After the completion of any portion of the Western

Branch, and until such branch should, under this Act, be vested in the Company of proprietors of the Montgomeryshire Canal, the profits from the completed portions or entire branch were to go to the Western Branch proprietors to the extent of five per cent. per annum on their shares, and the rest applied to the completion of the canal. The portion of the canal east of Garthmill was to be called " the Eastern Branch", and the portion on the west side of Garthmill to be called " the Western Branch", but after the Western Branch should be completed and certified, as thereinafter mentioned, the whole was to be under the control of the proprietors of the Montgomeryshire Canal. When the whole of the Western Branch should be completed, and certified to be navigable by the justices of the Court of Great Session of the county of Montgomery, then from the first Monday in July next following, all the powers given to the proprietors of the Western Branch, and the powers given to the committee for the time being of the Eastern Branch, were to cease, and the Western Branch powers were to vest in the Company of proprietors of the Montgomeryshire Canal; the proprietors of the Western Branch thereupon becoming proprietors of the Montgomeryshire Canal, and at a general assembly of the united proprietors, a new committee was to be appointed, and both branches were thenceforth to be one concern.

In the preamble to this Act the portion of the main line authorised by the original Act to be made to Porthywaen is referred to as a collateral cut from Porthywaen to Llanymynech, and it was enacted that, until the union of the eastern and western branches as one concern, the construction of that collateral cut was not to be commenced, and was not at any time to be constructed unless by an order of the majority of all the proprietors of the entire concern at a general assembly. As already mentioned, it was never constructed. Until such consolidation of the two branches, the surplus profits of the eastern branch, after payment of five per cent. per annum on the eastern branch capital, were to go in aid of the completion of the western branch, and, after such completion, in augmentation of the dividends of the western branch proprietors, until they should receive five per cent. per annum on their shares ; and when the proprietors of both branches received five per cent., then all the capital of both branches was to be united as one capital, and on an equality in all respects.

The rates of tolls authorised by the original Act were repealed, and, in lieu thereof, on the eastern branch, the tolls were to be for limestone, $1d.$ per ton per mile ; for coal, culm, and lime, $2d.$; for stone, pig-iron, brick, timber, tiles, slates, gravel, sand, lead ore, iron ore, and all other raw materials, $3d.$; for bark, cordwood, coke, charcoal, lead, wrought iron, baulk and deals, $3\frac{1}{2}d.$; and for all other goods and things, $4d.$ per ton per mile. And, on the western branch, for limestone, $2\frac{1}{4}d.$; for coal, culm, and lime, $3d.$; for stone, pig-iron, brick, timber, tile, slates, gravel, sand, lead ore, iron ore, and other minerals, $5d.$; for bark, cordwood, coke, charcoal, lead, wrought iron, baulk and deals, $5\frac{1}{2}d.$; and, for all other things, $6d.$ per ton per mile. If the canal should not be completed in five years, the powers were, at the expiration of that period, to be void.

As is well known, an exceedingly bad harvest followed the close of the war in 1816, such as was never seen again—at least, until 1879. That, and a great stagnation of trade and commerce, the pressure which continued after the close of the war from the heavy taxes imposed to meet the enormous public burdens caused by the long-continued and heavy war, the depreciation of the currency by the suspension of cash payments, and a large issue of notes during the war, the change now from war prices and return to a metallic currency caused, it may be said, even a greater pressure than was felt during the war. Foreigners at this time began to compare Great Britain to a stately but strained vessel which, after having weathered the fury of the storm, was sinking amidst the heaving waves before their agitation subsided, little knowing the vitality inherent in British energies, or anticipating the force of the elasticity with which the people of this country bore the pressure, and, by degrees, repaired their disasters and continued to maintain the high position which they held during the heavy trials of the preceding twenty years.

The pressure, however, retained its force during all the period of the construction of the western branch, yet by reason, it may be said, of the indomitable energy and devotion to that work of the late Mr. William Pugh of Brynllywarch, and a few devoted friends of his, the means were found, and the work was done within the five years, being the period of the powers of the Act, or thereabouts; not, it is true, without very serious sacrifices to Mr. Pugh and his family, and which were never retrieved, and heavy losses, to a smaller extent, to others. That work, invaluable as it was to the inhabitants and proprietors of Newtown and its surrounding country, was not the only great benefit which they derived from Mr. Pugh's devotion to their interests. To him was almost wholly owing the construction of the superior roads from Newtown to Llandrindod, and from Abermule into Radnorshire, and other public works, for which Newtown and its district have ever since owed to him and his family a heavy debt of gratitude. The eastern branch was a fairly paying undertaking to the proprietors, but the western branch was far from being so for many years, and never became remunerative during the time it remained in the hands of the original proprietors; the two branches were, therefore, never consolidated as proposed by the Act. There was subsequently an Act for, among other things, further defining and regulating the relative positions of the two branches towards each other. The affairs of the two branches were conducted by the local proprietors and their committees until the sale of both to "The Shropshire Union Railways and Canal Company" on the incorporation of that Company in 1846, and when, also, the Ellesmere and other canals passed into the hands of that Company. The original intention was to convert the canals into railways, but that it was afterwards found would not answer. The opening of the canal to Welshpool made, as previously stated, a great and very beneficial change, affecting nearly the entire county, and this was greatly increased afterwards, as to a large portion of it, by the extension to Newtown. The navigation of the Severn to Pool Quay soon came to an end after the opening of the eastern branch. The estuary of the Dovey and its Derwenlas Port near Machynlleth continued even after the opening of the western branch as the place of embarkation of the exports and disembarkation of the imports of the Dovey Valley and its adjoining districts; but the rest of the county above Newtown changed its intercourse with that port, partially, at first, to Berriew and Garthmyl, and afterwards more completely to Newtown. A considerable portion of the exports and imports of the lighter commodities continued to be conveyed by stage waggons along the improved turnpike roads between Shrewsbury and the Montgomeryshire towns of Welshpool, Newtown, Llanidloes, and Machynlleth, until the construction of the railway, which wholly superseded them and to a great extent the canal also, as it did also the Dovey, and its once famous Derwenlas Port, which was physically destroyed in the construction of the railway, and the traffic whereof the railway appropriated to itself.

(To be continued.)

107

THE DESCENT OF DAME MARGARET BROUGHTON,

WIFE OF SIR GRIFFITH VAUGHAN,

KNIGHT BANNERET OF AGINCOURT.

THE following pedigree is taken *verbatim* from Mr. Joseph Morris' *MS. Visitations of Salop.* His voluminous MSS. have this introductory preface:—

"From the *Herald's Visitations of Shropshire*, made by Robert Treswell, Somerset Herald, and Augustine Vincent, Rouge croix Pursuivant, Marshalls and Deputies to Wm. Camden, Clarencieux King-at-Arms, 1623.

"Together with the former visitations made by Richard Lee, Richmond Herald, Marshall to Robert Cook, Clarencieux King-of-Arms, taken in the years 1564 and 1584, with notes and additions from the visitations of Lewys Dwnn, Deputy-Herald for the Principality of Wales and the Marches thereof, in the reign of Queen Elizabeth and King James the First, and from other sources.

"To which are added continuations and further pedigrees from public and accredited private authorities to the present time.

"Collected and arranged
"By JOSEPH MORRIS, Shrewsbury."

⚭ Madoc or Roveries (*alias* Roveras or de Overs), near Bishop's Castle, Salop, son of Einion, son of Godrys Vawr, son of Sir Wm Godrider, Knt., son of William Glandford, Lord D'Eolbœuf in Normandy, whose mother was sister to William the Conqueror.

Madoc de la Home. *Temp.* K. Ed. I. ⚭

Walter. ⚭   Sir Robert ap Madoc, Knt., ⚭ Joyce, dr. to Peter Corbet,
             Lord of Home.   of Leigh.

Walter de Broughton, 18 Edw. II, 1325. Arms, *sab.*, ⚭ Avicia, f. h. Thos. three owls (2 and 1) *argt.*; some places a chevron   de Winsbury. between.

BROUGHTON PEDIGREE.

```
                    | a
Walter de Broughton, 18 Edw. II. ⚭
    |
John Broughton, of Broughton and Home. ⚭
    |
Jenkin Broughton, of Broughton and Home, ⚭ Elen Verch Griffith ap Gwen-
                     co. Salop.                    |   wynwyn ap Owen Cyveilioc.
    |
Griffith Broughton, alias ⚭ Gwenhwyver, dr. and h. of Dav. Vychan ap Ieuan
   Griffith ap Jenkin, of  |  ap David Goch ap Ieuan ap Tudyr Vychan ap
   Broughton, Esq.         |  Tudyr Goch ap Tudyr Lloyd ap David ap Gwyn
                           |  ap Ednowen ap Bradwen.  Her mother was
                           |  Gwervyl, dr. of Evan Lloyd ap Ieuan Vogan to
                           |  Llowdden.
    |
Margaret Broughton, dr. and co-heir. ⚭ Sir Gruffydd Vychan, Knt. Banneret.
                                       |
                                       v
```

Lewys Dwnn, deputy to Robert Cook, Clarencieux, thus follows the latter "Sir Robert ap Madoc, ap Sir Einion Goodrich, Knt., ap Goodrich Vawr, ap Sir William Goodrich, ap William Lord Elbeth". He is thus described as the ancestor of the Edwards of Pentre, or Castle Trynn;[1] and of Griffith Fordyn,[2] steward of Over and Nether Gorddwr manors to his father-in-law Ralph, Earl of Stafford. The Cedwyn MS., which has been found tolerably accurate in its genealogical details, styles Madoc (the father of Sir Robert fitz Madoc) the "Good Knight", and makes him the son[3] of William Glandford, the sister's son of William the Conqueror. This statement is not inconsistent with what is recorded. The three generations introduced by the Shropshire and Welsh heralds between a nephew of the Conqueror and Madoc, whom we can show to have been living in 1174, cannot stand the test of chronology. Some modern annotator of the Cedwyn MS., questioning, however, the possibility of Madoc's descent from a sister of William the Conqueror, has qualified his opinion by pronouncing it "apocryphal".[4] This is rather hard upon the fairly respectable authority who compiled the MS., *circa*

[1] *Visitations of Wales*, vol. i, p. 323.
[2] *Ib.*, vol. i, p. 285, and note.
[3] *Mont. Coll.*, vol. x, p. 14.   [4] *Ib.*, p. 41.

1630. There is certainly the possibility of a sister of William the Conqueror having given birth to a son. Of course we can only reason on such matters, and this we can do in connection with the dates of known events. There is historical evidence to prove that Madoc "Godrider", or the "Good Knight", was living in 1174, that he was the father of Sir Robert fitz Madoc, and that he became a Monk, perhaps a Knight of the Holy Sepulchre, before the year 1200. Since the name of the lady is not given, and as many of the natural issue of Robert Duke of Normandy doubtless find no place in the records of history, it seems a hopeless effort to pursue this portion of the inquiry further. That the ancestor of Dame Margaret was a nephew of William the Conqueror must remain a tradition, but need not, in the absence of records, be considered "apocryphal". The further tradition, that this ancestor built Goodrich's Tower in Bishop's Castle, must not be considered void of every element of truth, nor must it in the absence of records be allowed to discredit the general accuracy of the family descent. Thanks to the laborious and conscientious researches of the Rev. R. W. Eyton, and their results in his invaluable *Antiquities of Shropshire*, we are enabled, on the undoubted authority of our public records, to show not only the existence of the individuals mentioned in the pedigree of Dame Margaret Broughton, but also to illustrate, by many interesting incidents, the personal history of these individuals for such periods as there are records extant. It is needless to remark how few of our received English pedigrees can bear the test of critical historical investigation from so early a period as the middle of the twelfth century. This Welsh family is, however, in all essential particulars, able to stand such a test; and this may also be affirmed of many of those families whose descent is recorded in the visitations of Lewys Dwnn; that where the testimony of contemporary records has been available, there their general accuracy has been vindicated. It is not reasonable, because the sources of family local or national history have been often contaminated by the unwisely prolific imagination, or the carelessness of transcribers, that all Welsh family history is to be pronounced apocryphal when the charters and deeds of their Norman invaders are not always forthcoming in evidence.

Leaving the sister's son of William the Conqueror as a tradition, to share the tender mercies of that opinion which is popularly entertained of the general accuracy of Welsh pedigrees, we will, as briefly as the subject will permit, proceed to enumerate certain evidences of the family descent.

The ascertained era of Madoc de Overs will chronologically suit his assumed position as a grandson, if not a son, of the Conqueror's nephew. If we are to favour the tradition it may be taken as very probable that the Sir William Glandford, Sir William Goodrider, knt., and Godrys Vawr, refer to that and the same individual who has been assumed to be the Conqueror's nephew.

There is a Linley deed, quoted by Mr. Eyton, to the effect that, in the year 1174, about the time when Robert Foliot succeeded to the Bishopric of Hereford, he found in his chatellany of Lidbury a certain Madocus, Radulphus, and Agneta, his wife, in possession of the manor of Linley.[1] This Madocus was also a tenant *in capite* of Overs and Home (near Bishop's Castle), of Mucklewick (in the parish of Hissington), of Middleton and Brompton, a feudatory of the Barony of Caus for Weston Madoc, and of the Bishop of Hereford's feudal Barony of Lydbury North for Broughton. In the face of the tradition it is significant that Overs and Mucklewick were royal demesne. As Madoc de Overs was of mature age in 1174, and had retired, as we shall see, from secular life to assume the cowl by the year 1200, his grandfather, whoever he may have been, would be a contemporary of the Conqueror's nephew. Assuming that the latter was living at the time of his first cousin's

[1] *Antiquities of Shropshire*, vol. xi, p. 208.

(Henry I) death, in 1135, we can admit but one intervening generation between the Conqueror's nephew and Madoc de Overs.

Speaking of Middleton, in the parish of Chirbury, Mr. Eyton says[1] its tenants were first those of De Boulers, Lord of Montgomery, "and afterwards *tenants-in-capite* of the Crown. Madoc, the earliest of these tenants whom I can name, became a monk early in the year 1200. His son, Robert Fitz Madoc, instantly proffered a fine of fifteen merks to King John, that he might have seizin of such lands as his father had held by right hereditary on the day when he put on the habit of religion, which thing he had done recently, saving to the seigneural lords of such lands all services and reliefs, and saving the claims of all persons. The king ordered the sheriff to take security for the above fine. Later in the year it was renewed—or, rather, increased—by a palfrey. No instalment of Robert Fitz Madoc's debt had yet been received at Michaelmas 1202. At the Salop Assizes of October 1203, Robert Fitz Madoc sat as a juror, and, apparently, a knight, in some principal causes. In 1209 he occurs as one of the manucaptors, or sureties, concerned in the forest trespass of Robert Corbet of Caus.

On February 6th, 1224, King Henry III orders his treasurer to make Robert Fitz Madoc a present of 20s. towards his expenses. Another writ, of July 16th, 1224, orders Godescall de Maghelines (then Bailiff of Montgomery) to restore the house and lands of which he had disseized the said Robert, and to protect him. A third writ, of October 4, 1224, is addressed to Baldwin de Hodnet, then Seneschal and Custos of Montgomery. He is to give Robert Fitz Madoc such seizin of Middleton and Bromton as he had when he set out to see Llewellyn on the King's affairs. Moreover, the challenge or appeal made by one Thomas Fitz Ivette against Robert Fitz Madoc, for murdering his (Thomas's) daughter, is to be adjourned till the King

[1] *Antiquities of Shropshire*, vol. xi, p. 85.

should visit those parts. On November 28th, 1224, Robert Fitz Madoc being dead, the King, at the instance of Lewellyn, orders Godescal de Maghelins to deliver to the widow of the said Robert such portions of his lands and chattels as was customary in those parts, she having been nurse to the King's niece, Lewellyn's daughter. On February 13th, 1225, the same functionary is ordered to take lawful men of the honour of Montgomery, and go to the late Robert Fitz Madoc's estate of Weston, and, after assigning his widow her dower therein, to deliver the residue up to Thomas Corbet, of whose fee Weston was. Another precept of February 25th extends the above order to any other lands of the deceased, besides Weston, the King repeating the grounds of his personal interest in the widow—viz., that she had nursed his niece. A writ of March 21st, 1225, aims to secure to Thomas Corbet his seignural rights in Weston."[1]

Now there is enough in the above to warrant the belief that some such relationship as the heralds describe existed between King John and Sir Robert Fitz Madoc; for we find him a *tenant-in-capite* of a portion of the royal demesne; that during his lifetime he was the object of some consideration to both John and Henry III; that he was employed by the latter king on delicate and important state affairs, as a mediator between the King and his brother-in-law, Prince Lewellyn; and that after his death we find King Henry III taking a personal interest in the welfare of his widow, inasmuch as she had nursed his niece. This lady is said, in the pedigrees, to have been a Corbet of Caus, or Legh, and, by the light of the above connection, might be a sister of Thomas, and daughter of Robert Corbet of Caus, but certainly not a daughter of the first *Peter* Corbet of Caus, who, chronologically, would be her nephew.

On April 3rd, 1225, we have yet another writ, implying that Howen ap Robert ap Madoc was of full age.[2] Sir Robert Fitz Madoc left another son, Meurich

[1] Eyton's *Antiq.*, vol. xi, p. 85.   [2] *Ib.*, vol. xi, pp. 85, 86.

de Hope, who in 1240 held the eighth of a knight's fee in Rhiston and Brompton, which William de Boulers afterwards succeeded to in 1346.[1] Some doubt having existed as to Owen's legitimacy, we find another son of Sir Robert—viz., Howell, or Hoel, de Brompton—who died seized of all Brompton and all Weston about the year 1242.[2] From this Howell the Edwards' of Pentre, or Castle Trynn, claim descent. We are, however, immediately concerned in a second

MADOC DE OVERS and HOME, a brother of Sir Robert Fitz Madoc. We have seen that their father, Madoc, became a monk, and therefore took no part in secular affairs after the year 1200. Overs is situate a mile S.W. of Ratlinghope, to which it parochially belongs. Of the status of this Overs, and its feudal tenants, Mr. Eyton affords the presumption that, like Stitt and Ratlinghope, it formed part of the demesne of King Henry II. As there is no positive record of its seigneural lords, it was afterwards probably annexed to one of the Abbot of Haughmond's estates, such as Stitt, Linley, or the Boveria on the Long Mynd.[3] This family of De Overs had an estate at Mucklewick, near Hyssington. They also held under what was called the *Fee of la More;* and a certain Robert de Overs, probably identical with Sir Robert Fitz Madoc, held as early as the reign of King John (1199 to 1216) a virgate and a mill in the fee of More, of the gift of Roger de la More,[4] the ancestor of the Mores of Linley. Between the years 1200 and 1216, we have Grenta de Middleton releasing, for a consideration, to Haughmond Abbey, his right in three half-virgates in Linley. The first witness is " Robert Fitz Madoc", and the third witness " Madoc de Overes".[5] Another Linley deed, of the year 1220, has among its witnesses Madoc de Ham (Home), Philip de Ploudene (Plowden). This Madoc de Overs, Lord of Overs and Mucklewick, granted Little Radley Wood, together with his body, to Haughmond Abbey, where his father, Madoc the monk, had

[1] Eyton's *Antiq.*, vol. xi, p. 72. [2] *Ib.*, p. 150.
[3] *Ib.*, p. 297. [4] *Ib.*, p. 293. [5] *Ib.*, p. 210.

probably assumed the cowl. He was succeeded by his son, Robert de Overs, in 1221; but Mr. Eyton thinks it probable that he was deceased before 1216. He left, besides Robert, several other sons, of whom one was—

WALTER FITZMADOC, in whom we are principally interested. He was a mesne lord in Bishop's Castle in 1255, and, like his progenitors, a military vassal of the Bishop of Hereford for Broughton in the bishop's manor of Lydbury North.[1] To give you an idea of the enormous extent of this manor, Mr. Eyton states "that if restored to its Domesday integrity, and leased out at a modern rental, it would furnish forth the average endowment of four English bishoprics. Its importance is implied in its very name, for it was called Lydbury North to distinguish it from a manor of the same bishop's which lay many miles south of Hereford, and which is now spelt *Ledbury*. The possession of Lydbury North may almost be said to have made a Lord Marcher of every Bishop of Hereford till Wales was conquered. The foundation of Bishop's Castle was a feudal obligation, no less than a secular precaution, and to protect or control the tenantry of more than 18,000 acres."

The mention of Broughton (now Upper and Lower Broughton, near Bishop's Castle) and the circumstance that the De Overs family were military retainers of the Bishops of Hereford, recall the tradition to which we have before alluded. "The Good Knight", and "Knight of Rhodes,"[2] although an anachronism, are cognomens given to Madoc de Overs, the monk of the year 1200. We might assume, in connection with his era and what follows, that he was a Crusader or Knight of the Holy Sepulchre. His neighbour and contemporary, Roger de Plowden, is said to have been at the Fall of Acre in 1191, as a vassal of the Bishop of Hereford. It can readily be imagined, then, that Madoc de Overs, returning from the toils and turmoil of Palestine, after

[1] Eyton's *Antiq.*, vol. xi, p. 204.
[2] See Cedwyn MS., *Mont. Coll.*, vol. x, p. 19.

a victorious career with Richard Cœur de Lion, should, with the advance of age, retire to the quiet seclusion of Haughmond Abbey, an institution which we have seen enriched by the pious offerings of his family. It requires no flight of poetic imagination in this case to surmount anything improbable. The accidents of the position were such as to call forth the chivalry and pious instincts of the neighbourhood. Plowden, Oakley, Walcot, and Broughton were all members of Lydbury North or Bishop's Castle. They gave family names to the mesne lords who owed feudal service to the mitred semi-military barons who sat enthroned in Hereford Cathedral, and who, when holy war was proclaimed against the enemies of the Cross, or when serious Welsh combinations of Llewellyns and Gwenwynwyns made life on the borders bristle with excitement, had to rally their retainers within the precincts of their feudal fortress of Lydbury North. It is well known that William de Vere, Bishop of Hereford, preached up and urged on the crusade with ardent zeal. The recorded benefactions of the local families to abbeys and churches would alone indicate the spirit likely to be shown in the cause of oppressed Christianity, and the family traditions of the Plowdens, Oakleys, and Walcots, as well as the arms[1] borne by their lineal descendants, indicate the crusader spirit and origin of the family honours. "It is worth observing", says Mr. Eyton, " that the ancient coat of the Walcots was charged with a cross and *fleur-de-lys*. The coat undoubtedly belongs to the same origin, whatever that origin may be, as the coats of Plowden and Oakley; but whereas the Walcots bore a cross in addition to the *fleur-de-lys*, and the Oakleys three crescents, it becomes exceedingly probable that all

[1] It may here be convenient to state that the coat borne by the Plowdens was "*Az.*, a fesse dancettée, the two upper points terminating in fleurs-de-lis *or*"; by the Oakleys, "*Ar.*, on a fesse between three crescents *gu.*, as many fleurs-de-lis *or*"; and by the Walcotts, "*Ar.*, on a cross flory *sa.*, three fleurs-de-lis *or*".

these coats originated at the time of the Crusade, and in some such way as tradition relates when referring to the Plowden arms in particular."

After this digression we return to the few but reliable historical details which refer to the grandson of Madoc the Monk and assumed Crusader, viz. :—

WALTER FITZ MADOC OF BROUGHTON, whom we have also shown as a mesne lord of Bishop's Castle in 1255. "In August 1252 an inquest was ordered as to the immunities theretofore enjoyed by the men of Ludlow, in the markets of Montgomery. Six of the jurors belonged to the district of Lydbury, viz., Roger de Walcote, Roger de Plaueden, *Walter de Borchton*, William de Munedey, Roger Fitz Celestria, and William de Pleweden.[1] As Walter's elder brother, Robert de Overs, succeeded his father in 1221,[2] and died in 1255, we may assume that the following relates to Walter, son of Walter Fitz Madoc.

WALTER DE BROUGHTON (II). He, as "Walter de Broughton", April 3, 1282, witnesses an obligation of John de Linley.[3] His marriage with the *Avicia* of the pedigree is thus confirmed under "Upper and Lower Broughton". "In Easter term, 1305, a conventional fine was levied, whereby David de Burgheton, Deforciant, is allowed to have a right of 5 messuages, 60 acres of arable land, 12 acres of meadow, 60 acres of bosc, and 12s. annual rent in *Burghdon.* The said David forthwith settled the premises on Walter de Burgheton, his wife *Hawise* (Avicia), and his heirs by Hawise—to hold of the lords of the fee, with remainder to the right heirs of Hawise".[4] This Hawise, or Avicia, the pedigree tells us, was a daughter and heiress of Thomas de Winsbury, in the parish of Chirbury. It was doubtless her son, who, as

WALTER DE BURGHTON (III) is entered as Lord of the vill of Burghton in the *Nomina Villarum* of 1316.[5] We find a *Walter de Boritton*, who sat as seventh

[1] Eyton's *Antiq.*, vol. xi, p. 220.   [2] *Ib.*, p. 211.
[3] *Ib.*, p. 212.   [4] *Ib.*, p. 224.   [5] *Ib.*, p. 224.

juror for Purslow Hundred at the assizes of 1292, and who is called Walter de Brohton in a Minton jury list of 1295. These may refer to the husband of Hawise. On December 13, 1310, he, as *Walter de Borton*, witnesses a grant of Griffin de la Pole, Lord of Longnorle to William de Acton Burnell, clerk.[1]

"In 1316, the sheriff of Shropshire having to serve the king's writ on Griffin de la Pole, being unable to find him, notified its contents on the lands of the said Griffin and his tenements at Deuder in Powys, by Edmund de Langdon and *Walter de Burghton*, in the presence of Peter Corbet and Thomas de Wynnesbury."[2]

According to the Shropshire Heralds' *Visitation*, Walter de Broughton III was succeeded by his son—

JOHN BROUGHTON, of Broughton and Home. Mr. Eyton's account of Upper and Lower Broughton closes with the year 1316. Earlier members of the family, however, occur in connection with Ham, or Home, as early as 1220, when the king's writ, surrendered to the Seneschal of Haghmon Abbey, is witnessed by Roger de More, *Madoc de Ham*, Philip de Ploudene, and Walter de Newton. This Madoc is probably identical with the Madoc de Overs, who granted Little Radley Wood and his body to Haghmon Abbey in 1216.[3] At an inquisition, held 28th July 1260, on the death of Roger de la More, king's constable in the Welsh wars, Robert de Overes, William and John de la Hom appear as witnesses.[4] He was succeeded by his son—

JENKIN BROUGHTON, of Broughton and Home. The Shropshire Heralds inform us that he married Elen daughter of Griffith ap Gwenwynwyn ap Owen Cyfeiliog, Prince of Powys, by his wife Hawise, daughter of the John le Strange (III) of Nesse and Stanwardine. This must be an error in transcription, for Ellen, daughter of Griffith (de la Pole, fifth son) ap Griffith ap Gwenwynwyn. "Walter de Burghton" seems to have

---

[1] Eyton's *Antiq.*, vol. vi, p. 62 *et seq*.
[2] *Mont. Coll.*, vol. i, p. 72.
[3] Eyton's *Antiq.*, xi, p. 210.   [4] *Ib.*, p. 288.

been the *locum tenens* of Griffith de la Pole on his lands of Deuddwr in 1316. Griffith was living in 1330, and is known to have had female issue, two of his daughters being incidentally mentioned as having married Sir Roger Chamber and Hugh Montgomery; so it is not improbable that Ellen, daughter of Griffith de la Pole, married a grandson of the above "Walter de Burghton", or Broughton, viz., the above Jenkin Broughton. He was succeeded by his son—

GRIFFITH BROUGHTON, or Griffith ap Jenkin, of Broughton and Home, who married Gwenhwyver, daughter and heiress of David Vychan, as given in the pedigree, descended from Ednowen ap Bradwen, whose arms were *gules*, three snakes entwined in a triangular knot, *argent*. The remains of "Llys Bradwen", or the palace of Bradwen, are near the River Krogennan, under Cadir Idris, and measure nearly thirty yards square. This Griffith is also styled "Griffith ap Jenkin[1] of Mochdre", which appears to have been the inheritance of one of his daughters and co-heiresses. His uncle, Philip ap Jenkin, was living in 1461, when, with Thomas Corbet of Lee, he enfeoffed John Middleton on a feofment of land by John de Boulers, or Bowdler, of Marrington, Chirbury.[2]

By his wife Gwenhwyver he left three daughters and co-heiresses, whose seniority is not known, of which TANGLWYST married Morris ap Madoc ap Einion, of Mochdre, descended from Elystan Glodrydd. David Lloyd ap Einion, ancestor of the Prices of Newtown, and Madoc ap Einion, were brothers.[3] Their great granddaughter, Elizabeth,[4] daughter of John Lloyd of Gwernygo, Kerry, (ap Jeuan ap Morris ap Madoc) married John ap Cadwalader, also descended from Elystan Glodrydd, whose

[1] Lewys Dwnn, *Vis.*, vol. i, p. 276.   [2] *Ib.*, p. 277.
[3] *Mont. Coll.*, vol. x, p. 10.
[4] Her brother Morris ap John Lloyd of Gwernygo, married Lucy, daughter of David Lloyd Vaughan of Marrington. Hugh ap John Lloyd, another brother, left a daughter and heiress, Jane, who married William Herbert of Kerry, third son of Sir Richard Herbert of Montgomery.—*Mont. Coll.*, vol. x, p. 43.

son Robert took the surname of Broughton of Lower Broughton or Owlbury, doubtless so styled in reference to the arms (the owls) of the old Broughton family.

Als, or Alice, another daughter and co-heiress, married David ap Howell of Arwystley. Their daughter and heiress Margaret married Ririd Myddleton, ancestor of the Myddletons of Chirk Castle, Gwenynog, and Garthgynan, in the county of Denbigh, and brother of Philip Middleton of Middleton, Chirbury.[1]

DAME MARGARET, wife of Sir Griffith Vaughan, Knight Banneret of Agincourt, was another daughter and co-heiress of Griffith ap Jenkin. They had issue three sons and three daughters. David Lloyd of Mathavarn, in his elegy to the memory of Sir Griffith Vaughan, thus alludes to them in addressing the spirit of his departed friend :—

"Lie not in thy grave and stones
In St. Mary's chancel, my comely friend;
See the course of fraud and fear,
To the Lord of Llai, the brave Lloyd,
Six stags are yonder hiding
That were hunted in the Black Ridge."[2]

The inheritances of Sir Griffith and Dame Margaret were thus apportioned to their sons :—Llai or Leighton went to David Lloyd ; Maesmawr and Trawscoed to Cadwallader Lloyd ; Reginald, the youngest, took the paternal seat, Garth, in Guilsfield, and a portion of his mother's inheritance of Broughton and Owlbury, near Bishop's Castle. Gwenhwyver, the eldest daughter, married Griffith ap Aron ap Ednyved of Peniarth, Merionethshire, who was living 2nd November, 9th Henry VI (1430).[3] Their son Rhys was on a Merionethshire grand jury, 23 Henry VI.[4] Anne, their second daughter, married Ieuan Vaughan ap Ieuan ap Griffith of Llanuchllyn, in Merionethshire. Their son David was the ancestor of the Vaughans of Glanllyn, and

[1] *Lewys Dwnn*, vol. ii, p. 335.
[2] See *Mont. Coll.*, vol. vi, p. 93.
[3] Lewys Dwnn's *Vis.*, vol. ii, p. 238, and note.
[4] *Mont. Coll.*, vol. vi, p. 98.

subsequently of Llwydiarth. Margaret, their youngest daughter, married, first, Morris Ludlow, son of Sir Richard Ludlow of Stokesay. "Mauricius Ludlowe armiger" occurs on an inquest held at Shrewsbury, 11th Edward IV, 1471, on the death of Sir John Burgh, Lord of Mawddwy. She married secondly Sir Walter Inglis Knight.[1]

The three owls, the arms of Dame Margaret's family, without the chevron elsewhere introduced, are still to be seen as a quartering on a shield, with two griffins as supporters, at Marrington Hall, the seat of her grandson, David Lloyd Vaughan; and the same on a shield of six quarterings, with the griffins as supporters, in old stained glass, at Garth, the seat of her son Reginald.[2] The owls also appear as prominent ornaments in the carved oak of Guilsfield Church to this day.

UPPER BROUGHTON became the property of, and gave a surname to, John Wynn ap Reginald ap Sir Griffith Vaughan, alias JOHN BROUGHTON of Broughton. He first occurs as "John Brockdyn", one of nineteen witnesses in a suit between Griffith ap Howell ap David Bowdler, of Churchstoke, and Margaret Middleton, wife of David Lloyd Vaughan and heiress of Marrington,[3] in 5th Henry VII, 1489. He last occurs as John Broughton, King's Bailiff of Montgomery, 29 Henry VIII, and as John Broughton, Gent., on a county grand jury, 35 Henry VIII. He left an only son, Edward, and several daughters, by his wife Ellen, daughter of David Lloyd ap Evan ap Griffith Vaughan. Of these

Lucy married Randolph Hanmer of Penley, Sheriff of Montgomeryshire, in 1561.

Margaret married Walter Hockleton of Hockleton, Chirbury, son of the "John Hockleton", another of the nineteen witnesses with "John Brockdyn" in 1489.

Petronella married John Harris of Stockton, perhaps

[1] *Mont. Coll.*, vol. vi, p. 99.   [2] *Ib.*, vol. vi, p. 140.
[3] *Ib.*, pp. 67, 68.

another of the nineteen witnesses, called "John Penry (ap Henry) of Stockton".

Jane married Robert Broughton ap John ap Cadwalader, descended from Elystan Glodrydd.

EDWARD BROUGHTON, by his wife, Joan Pilsworth, left four sons and four daughters. Jane, one of the latter, married the imaginative old chronicler, Oliver Matthews of Bishop's Castle. Their sons and grandsons are given in a tabulated form in Lewys Dwnn's visitation of Montgomery.[1] It is not known who succeeded to the estate, or for how long the Upper Broughton property was in the possession of this line.

LOWER BROUGHTON seems to have been called Owlbury, and became the property of a family descended from Elystan Glodrydd, viz., of Robert ap John ap Cadwalader,[2] who doubtless assumed the name of Broughton on his marriage with Jane, daughter of John (Wyn ap Reginald ap Sir Griffith Vaughan of) Broughton.[3] He was succeeded by his son

RICHARD BROUGHTON of Owlbury. He first occurs to our notice in the enrolment of a grant, 2 March, 12 Eliz., wherein it is stated that Richard Broughton for twenty-one years is to enjoy, under the Crown, numerous lands and tenements in the lordship of Kerry and Kedewen, mines and slate in Corndon Forest, as well as lands and tithes of the dissolved monastery of Chirbury, at Lydham, Hissington, Hurdley, Castlewright, and elsewhere. Certain of the lands enumerated were those of Enor ap Ieun ap DD and Ieu'n ap Enor, attainted; and Fern Vill and Brinllowarch, Brenor Vill, Arthnill, Keven y Beren, etc., in the lordship of Kerry, the property of John ap Meredith, attainted; Pengelley, in Kerry lordship, part of the possessions of the said John ap Meredith, who was doubtless of Glanmeheli, in the parish of Kerry. How the latter incurred the disgrace of attainder is not known, his father, Meredith ap Rhys, having filled the position of steward

[1] See *Lewys Dwnn*, vol. i, p. 329.
[2] *Ibid.*   [3] *Ibid.*

of the lordships of Kerry and Kedewen, and Constable of Montgomery Castle, under King Henry VII.[1]

Richard Broughton, or "Brogden", is given by Lewis Dwnn as "one of the Council of the Marches" at Ludlow, and therefore in a favourable position to have acquired Crown grants. He also includes (in the year 1586) his name amongst "the aristocracy, by whom I was permitted to see old records and books from religious houses, that had been written, and their materials collected, by abbots and priors."[2] John Rhydderch, the transcriber of a portion of Dwnn's *Visitation*, tells us that he wrote concerning all England and parts beyond seas; and that he had a commission to search the ancient records of the White Tower of London, where the Welsh records are said to have been kept. "Richard Broughton, Esq., of Broughton and Owlbury, near Bishop's Castle", was admitted of the Inner Temple in 1568; and, since he was born in 1524, must have adopted the profession of the law late in life. He was an original fellow of the Society of Antiquaries, and esteemed by Sir John Wynn of Gwydir "the chief antiquary of England". He married Anne, daughter of Richard Bagot, Esq., of Blithfield, and, from some letters to this gentleman, he appears to have been a retainer of Devereux, Earl of Essex. The interest of the latter, he being a member of the Council of the Marches, and having certain influential family connections, procured for him the office of "deputy judge of Chester". In this capacity we find "wine geven to Mr. Justice Broughton, 6s. 4d." by the corporation of Shrewsbury, in the year 1596. On the death of Edmond Walter, the Chief Justice, in 1594, he had aspired to succeed him as Chief Justice of South Wales. "My Lord Essex," he writes, "told me her Majestie said I should have any favor, for my lord's father's sake." But, in spite of his reliance on royal promises,

---

[1] *Mont. Coll.*, vol. iii, p. 148; and *Lewys Dwnn*, vol. i, p. 315.
[2] *Lewys Dwnn*, vol. i, p. 7.

his ambition had to satisfy itself with the position of deputy judge of Chester.[1]

The *Cedwyn MS.* has the following reference to Owlbury as the resort of antiquarian gleaners. Giving the particulars of the issue of Catherine, daughter of David Lloyd ap Sir Griffith Vaughan, it says, "These notes were had at Owlberry, drawn in a table by Richard Lloyd of Marrington, Esq."[2] The latter, as well as Richard Broughton, is commended by Lewys Dwnn for his assistance to the Herald on his visitation tours.

Hugh Broughton, styled, for his eminence as a Hebrew scholar, Rabbi Broughton, was a younger brother of Richard Broughton. Their sister married Thomas Lingen of Whitton, whose daughter and heiress, Elizabeth,[3] gave her hand and Whitton to Alexander Topp, ancestor of the Topps of Whitton. Richard Broughton had a son Robert, who must have died without issue, as his daughter and heiress married, and conveyed the Owlbury estate to Edmund Waring, son of Thomas Waring of Lea, Staffordshire, and of Llandinam, in Montgomeryshire. Walter Waring, fourth in descent from this marriage, was M.P. for Coventry, and sold Owlbury to Lord Powis.[4] Walter Waring of Owlbury was sheriff for Montgomeryshire in 1724. It is probably to his widow that the following memorial was erected in Aberhavesp Church: "In memory of Mrs. Abigail Waring, who, after a life spent in great piety and virtue, and every amiable quality that could adorn her sex, died 12th day of November 1753, in the 88th year of her age." This lady was the daughter of Matthew Morgan, Esq., of Aberhavesp; and on a monument in the same church to her sister, "Mrs. Anne Morgan", is described as "her only surviving sister and executrix, Mrs. Abigail Waring, the wife of Walter Waring of Owlbury, in Com. Salop, Esq."[5]

[1] Owen and Blakeway's *Hist. of Shrewsbury*, vol. i, p. 399.
[2] *Mont. Coll.*, vol. x, p. 35.
[3] Blakeway's *Sheriffs*, p. 142.   [4] *Ib.*, p. 132.*
[5] From inscriptions kindly communicated by the Rev. F. W. Parker, formerly Rector of Aberhavesp, but now Rector of Montgomery.

BROUGHTON PEDIGREE.

The following genealogical table has been formulised from information afforded of the family in Mr. Eyton's *Antiquities of Shropshire*, and gives the correction for several inaccurate dates in the *Herald's Vis.* pedigree.

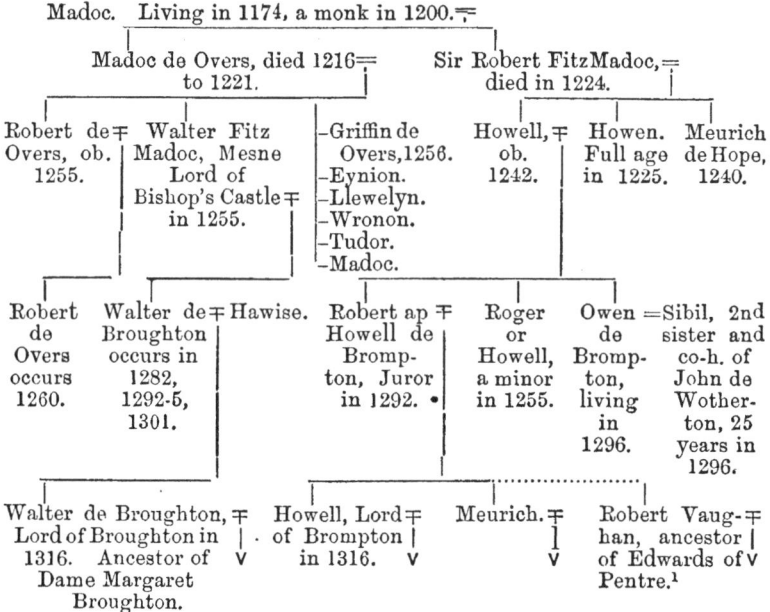

```
Madoc. Living in 1174, a monk in 1200.⚌
    |
    ├─────────────────────────────────┬──────────────────────────┐
Madoc de Overs, died 1216⚌         Sir Robert FitzMadoc,⚌
    to 1221.                            died in 1224.
    |                                       |
┌───┴───┬──────────┬──────────┐    ┌────────┼────────┬────────┐
Robert de⚌ Walter Fitz  -Griffin de   Howell,⚌  Howen.    Meurich
Overs, ob. Madoc, Mesne  Overs,1256.   ob.     Full age  de Hope,
1255.      Lord of      -Eynion.      1242.   in 1225.   1240.
           Bishop's Castle⚌ -Llewelyn.
           in 1255.       -Wronon.
                          -Tudor.
                          -Madoc.
    |
┌───┴────┬──────────────┬──────────┬──────────┬──────────┐
Robert   Walter de⚌Hawise. Robert ap⚌  Roger    Owen =Sibil, 2nd
de       Broughton       Howell de    or       de    sister and
Overs    occurs in       Bromp-       Howell,  Bromp- co-h. of
occurs   1282,           ton, Juror   a minor  ton,   John de
1260.    1292-5,         in 1292.     in 1255. living Wother-
         1301.                                 in     ton, 25
                                               1296.  years in
                                                      1296.
    |
┌───┴──────────┬──────────────┬──────────┬──────────┐
Walter de Broughton,⚌ Howell, Lord⚌ Meurich.⚌  Robert Vaug-⚌
Lord of Broughton in  . of Brompton            han, ancestor
1316. Ancestor of  v  in 1316.   v       v     of Edwards of v
Dame Margaret                                  Pentre.¹
Broughton.
```

Griffin de Forden, steward of the manors of Over and Nether Gordwr to his father-in-law, Ralph, Earl of Stafford, is said to have been fourth in descent from Meurich ap Robert ap Howell.[2] On July 8th, 1389, Griffin, son of Griffin de Forton, was presented to the rectory of Lydham by his first cousin John de Cherlton, Lord of Powys; and, on 22nd December, 1391, exchanged preferments with Sir Roger Bromelowe, late rector of Machynllaith."[3]

Eliza Constantia, daughter of the Rev. Samuel D'Elbeuf Edwards of Pentre Hall,[1] Montgomeryshire, married, 3rd March 1795, Richard Pryce of Gunley, Sheriff of Montgomeryshire in 1817, and was the mother of the late Rev. R. H. Mostyn Pryce of Gunley.

W. V. LL.

---

[1] See their pedigree in *Mont. Coll.*, vol. xii, p. 425.
[2] Lewys Dwnn's *Visitations*, vol. i, p. 285, note 3.
[3] Eyton's *Antiquities of Shropshire*, vol. vi, p. 283.

PETITION OF RICHARD GREY, LORD POWYS, TO KING HENRY VI.

WE are indebted to the research of Mr. Morris C. Jones, for the discovery of the following document. After an interval of four hundred and ten years, it unexpectedly comes to light, and affords a further ray of confirmation and testimony to the truthfulness of our local bards. It made its appearance in the *Trevelyan Papers*,[1] printed by the Camden Society in 1857, and records the fact of the arrest of Sir Griffith Vaughan, for rebellion in the very year, 1447, that Welsh poets and chroniclers say that he was beheaded in the court yard of Powys Castle. It is a petition to King Henry VI by Richard Grey, Lord Powys, for five hundred marks which had been due to Henry Grey, Earl of Tankerville, his father, as the captor of Sir Griffith Vaughan. Neither the king's proclamation, the act of council referred to, nor the petition, appear in the published "Acts of the Privy Council", but the document itself must have come into possession of John Trevelyan, in his capacity of "keeper of the Council Chamber, at Westminster, and Usher of the receipt of the Exchequer", to which offices he was appointed in the year 1447, but held them only a short time.[2]

Before we refer to its contents, it may be remarked that there is no part of our history since the conquest of England so obscure, so uncertain, so little authentic or consistent as that of the Wars of the Roses; historians differ about many material circumstances, and are without records to settle or enlighten their doubts. It seems incredible that there should not be scattered about,

[1] *Trevelyan Papers*, p. 36, recently presented to the Powys-land Museum and Library by Mr. T. B. Barrett.   [2] *Ibid.*, p. 32.

perhaps mouldering, in many libraries, the works in MS. of many Welsh poets of the fifteenth and sixteenth century, capable of furnishing this dark period with many historical illustrations nowhere else to be found. These, if we ever hope to complete the history of the period, must be published in a collected form, and then submitted to our most competent Welsh scholars for translation. Many of these poet-historians enable us to throw much light upon the contents of the following document:—

A.D. 1446.—*Petition of Richard Lord Powes to Henry VI.*

Sheweth unto your highnesse your humble sujet and true liegeman, Richard Gray Lord Powes, son and heir of Henry Grey sumtyme Lord Powes, That where as ye sov'ain Lord, by your letters of prive seal, beryng date at Westm̄ the XX day of July the XXV yere of your most gracious regne, com̄aunded the Tresorer and Chambelleyns of your Eschequer to pay and content the seid Henry Grey, that tyme Lord Powes, the some of V^c mark, to be had of your yeft, by wey of reward for takyng of Griffith Vaghan, of Wales, open Rebell unto your Lord, which some of V^c marcs was p'mytted by open proclamacion in your behalf made to that persone that might take your seid Rebell: as in the seid proclamacion it is att large conteyned. Wherfor, your most gracious sovran Lord, in asmoche as the said some of V^c marcs was not payed to the seid Henry in hys lyf, according to your com̄aundment, ne your seid letters of prive seale put in execucion, that it plese your highnesse to graunt newe letters of prive seale to be made in due forme, direct to the Tresorer and Chamberleyns of your seid Eschequer, chargying and com̄aundyng them straitely to pay and content your seid suppliant the seid some of V^c marcs, due unto his fadre for the cause above rehersed, to be had of your yeft. And your seid suppliant shal ever pray to God for your.

It may be remarked that 1446 is not the date of Richard Grey's petition, but is a part of the 25th regnal year of Henry VI (Sep. 1, 1446 to Aug. 31, 1447), in the "spring" of which, according to Lewys Glynn Cothi, Sir Griffith Vaughan was ensnared and beheaded. Henry Grey, second Earl of Tankerville, and Lord of Powys, did not die until the year 1450, and therefore Richard Grey, Lord Powys, could not have presented a petition as " son and heir of Henry Grey, sum tyme Lord Powes," until after that year. The capture having taken place in the spring of the year, 1447, we find the sovereign's "letters of prive seal" dated July 20, 1447, with an order to the Treasury for the reward of 500 marks.

The document seems to strengthen the arguments already adduced,[1] to show that the Barony of Cherleton, or Cherleton de Powys, falling into abeyance between Sir Edward de Cherleton's two daughters, was revived and transmitted through the family of Grey. Sir John Grey having predeceased his father-in-law, would not be styled Lord Powys, but his son Henry, on the death of his mother, Joan de Cherleton, in 1425, although then a minor, was knighted under the title of *Dominus de Powys*. In ordinances of the king, and in various public records, this title was given him up to his death; still there is no evidence that he ever had a writ of summons to, or sat in Parliament with that title. In the absence of this testimony, the barony, if not taken out of abeyance in his time, was certainly so in that of his son Richard, who sat in the seat of his ancestors, the Cherleton's, in the thirty-third Parliament of Henry VI. But as no subject would dare to assume for himself or his father in a petition to the sovereign himself, a dignity to which they were not entitled, this interesting document is inferentially a proof that the barony of Powys was out of abeyance before the year 1446-7. Joyce de Cherleton, Lady Tiptoft and Powys, and co-heiress with Joan, Countess of Tankerville, left a son John who, as " John Typtoft, Lord of Powys," confirmed charters, granted by his ancestors the Cherleton's, to the burgesses of Llanidloes in 26 Henry VI (1447-8), and was beheaded for his adherence to the house of York about the year 1470.

[1] "Feudal Barons of Powys", *Mont. Coll.*, vol. i, p. 362 *et seq.*

The person styled by Richard Grey Lord Powys, "Griffith Vaughan of Wales, open Rebell unto your Lord", was no less a person than Sir Griffith Vaughan, Knight Banneret of Agincourt, of Garth, Lord of Guilsfield, Burgedyn, Trelydan, Gaervawr, and Lord of the Manor of Broniarth. It was the custom of the age to be liberal in discourtesy to political or religious opponents. The illustrious Lollard and reformer, the great and good Sir John Oldcastle, Knight and Baron of Cobham, in a charter of privileges granted by Edward de Charlton, Lord Powys, to Sir Griffith Vaughan and his brother Ieuan, for the capture of Lord Cobham, is described as "John Oldcastell, a heretic, perverter of the Catholic Faith, and a traitor to our most illustrious Sovereign, King Henry the Fifth, now King."[1]

The document itself confirms what we are told by contemporary Welsh writers,[2] that Sir Griffith Vaughan, being suspected of holding correspondence with some adherents of the House of York, incurred the ill-will of the Government. This suspicion having been insinuated to the Queen, Margaret of Anjou, and her Council, a Treasury warrant is said to have been sent to Henry Grey, Lord Powys and Earl of Tankerville, for the apprehension of Sir Griffith; and accordingly, under some pretence or other, the knight was summoned to appear at the Castle of Pool. He at first demurred, but on receiving what David Lloyd of Mathavarn, his relative and eulogist, describes as a "safe conduct", he resolved to confront his accusers; but as soon as he arrived at the courtyard of the castle he was apprehended, and, in the presence of Henry Grey, beheaded on the spot, "without judge or jury".

The warrant for his arrest is not forthcoming in the minutes of the Council. The only reference of the year 1447,(19th March) to any apprehension of political disturbance in Wales is the following:—"Item, that letters be written to the constables and others

[1] *Mont. Coll.*, vol. i, p. 321.
[2] See "The Feudal Barons of Powys", *Mont. Coll.*, vol. i, p. 335.

having places in Wales that they see to the safeguard of the said places, as they will answer to the king." It appears that Henry Grey had certain authority of the king, Henry VI, for this summary proceeding, as is stated in the petition, by the reward of v^c marks " p'mytted (? promised) by open proclamation in your behalf made to what persone that might take your said rebell". Letters of Privy Seal, bearing date at Westminster the 20th of July, the 25th Henry VI, 1447, gave an order on the Treasury for the five hundred marks to Henry Grey for the capture; but it is still a question whether Henry Grey, under the ægis of this royal proclamation, of which he may have been the instigator, did not, for the sake of a very ample reward, or from an instinct of jealousy, commit an unjustifiable murder. Before the discovery of the above document, the very year, 1447, was the one given by the Welsh bards as that of Sir Griffith's decapitation in the courtyard of Powys Castle. If their writings have been found authoritative as to facts, their testimony must be accepted as to motives. Although Lewys Glyn Cothi certainly, in the following, ascribes the act to the king—

> " 'Twas a marvel that, in the presence of all men,
> King Harry, with his councillors,
> Should honour the head that protected us,
> And having honoured it, cut it off!"

still, he traces the motive of the act as one of summary vengeance to a secret foe.

> " For his enemy's sake, hath a man been doomed,
> Of his doom were his arms the seal,
> Where he was guileless,
> They were full of guile."

David Lloyd of Mathavarn, addressing the dead, names the man.

> " May God avenge thy fair brow;
> No man even with a vengeful hand
> Could kill thee but the demon of jealousy.

My loved one, I did not advise
Reliance on a Saxon's word.
Was not the *safe conduct* detestable
When his head was killed (severed) from anger?
That safe conduct which a double-tongued Earl broke,
Harry Grey—may he be long crucified!"[1]

Causes of jealousy there probably were. The Greys, although of ancient standing in the north,[2] were new to the dignity and people of Powys. Griffith Vaughan represented the line of the ancient princes of the land through his ancestor, Brochwel ap Aeddan ap Cyngen, second son of Eliseg, Prince of Old Powys,[3] and had claims upon the inheritance of Griffith de la Pole, fifth son of Griffith ap Gwenwynwyn, Prince of Powys. This Griffith de la Pole had a life-long struggle to retain his inheritance of Powys, which he had seen, through his niece Hawise, transmitted to a Norman adventurer. Gathering together all the resources he could command, by the sale of Longnor to his cousin, Fulke le Strange, and other outlying estates, and by the enlistment of connections and compatriots, he, in 1312, laid claim and siege to the Castle of Powys, and nothing but the energy of the powerful Roger de Mortimore of Wigmore, instructed by Edward II to support Hawise and her husband, Sir John de Charlton, prevented Griffith from capturing the princely seat of his ancestors. The living representatives of the parties to this disputed interest in 1447 were Henry Grey, the descendant of Sir John Charlton, and Sir Griffith Vaughan, the representative, through his wife, of Ellen, the daughter of Griffith de la Pole.

Moreover, the illustrious descent, local connection, valour, and general popularity of Sir Griffith commanded an influence in Powys-land, which, on the eve of the impending struggle for supremacy between the

[1] *Mont. Coll.*, vol. vi, pp. 92-96.
[2] Of Berwick, Heaton, and Chillingham.
[3] *Mont. Coll.*, vol. vi, p. 78.

rival houses of York and Lancaster, was of considerable importance in the scale. Mourning his loss, Lewys Glynn Cothi says—

"Not a day passes, but I ail,
Bowed down with grief for Sir Gruffydd Vychan.
For the man that here was so honoured,
In memory of the valorous Knight."

Speaking of Powys—

"Gono is her name, her Beloved,
Her head, her owner, her guide.
. . . .
From hence to York it has been a dreary autumn
And sad spring for the Gwenwys."[1]

David Lloyd of Mathavarn, alluding to his decapitation, says—

"The head of *Gruffud* with the fine lurid spear of lightning.
Vaughan, the active lion, him they killed.
The worthy knight, with the arm of an impetuous thruster.
A head of priceless value,
A lovely head, like that of John,[2]
A fair head when presented—
The Chief Judge of broad Powysland,
A happy head—a head that was deceived!"

The rebellious act which brought such a man to the block is not specified in the petition of Richard Grey. We are left partly to the statement of the bard, "from hence to York it has been a dreary autumn", and partly to the consideration of the current events of the period, to conclude that he had been in correspondence with certain local emissaries of the Duke of York. We know that public discontent began to prevail about this period. The loss of France, with the exception of

---

[1] Alluding to Sir Griffith's family and descent (ap Griffith ap Ieuan ap Madoc ap Gwenwys ap Griffith ap Beli ap Brochwel, etc.)
[2] The Baptist?

Calais, the king's weakness of intellect, the prejudicial influences of his foreign wife, whom he had recently (1445) married, the mal-administration of a clique of Court favourites and adventurers, to whom the king had committed the government of the realm, all combined to favour the pretensions of the Duke of York, whose administration of affairs, both in France and Ireland, had gained him a reputation for wisdom, moderation, and valour. Through his mother, Anne, and her father, Roger Mortimer, who in 1385 had been nominated heir-apparent by Parliament, he had certain rights of succession to the throne; but what is more relevant to our subject, he succeeded to her estates, and could command the support of the chief families of Shropshire, Herefordshire, and the Marches of Wales, who then held dependencies of the heir of Mortimer. Issuing from their princely possessions, the castles and lordships of Wigmore, Montgomery, Kerry, and Kedewen, armies of military tenants and retainers, had ever been willing to support any cause a Mortimer might elect to promote. Generally speaking, the Welsh of the Marches were faithfully attached to the house of Mortimer, and it is in accordance with the popular feeling of his countrymen and the best interests of his country that we should expect to find Sir Griffith a Yorkist. In those times, any one burdened with troublesome convictions, or serving interests opposed to those of the party in power, was either deemed, or could be easily proclaimed, a rebel. Nothing was then known of the amenities of political life. There was no interchange of courtesies between majorities and minorities. An expression of what we euphemistically style "advanced opinions" would be considered rank treason, and, though called the age of chivalry, the only strength of an argument then lay in the amount of brute force with which you were prepared to maintain it.

Since, in the opinion of Richard Grey, Sir Griffith was an "open rebell", what are we to say of the loyalty and consistency of Lord Powys himself. Richard Grey, presumably like his father Henry Grey, was a Lancastrian. As a Lancastrian we find him sueing for the 500 marks—the price of blood—which the needy Henry VI had promised, but had hitherto failed to pay. The proper date of his petition must be subsequent to 1450, the year of his father's death. In 1459 what does history record? Why that this same loyal "humble sujet and true liegeman" was an "open rebell" in arms against his king on the field of Ludford, and after the defeat and flight of the Duke of York to Ireland, is found, in the company of prominent Yorkist partisans, sueing for mercy; and the king, more generous than his subject, mindful perhaps of the more faithful services of his father, Henry Earl of Tankerville, refused his consent to Richard Grey's attainder. On the fall of his sovereign he was considered too new a convert to Yorkist principles to be trusted, and was, on the accession to power of the Duke of York, deprived of his governorship of Montgomery Castle.

The conflict of interests, the internecine feuds and vicissitudes of families, arising from the Wars of the Roses, is amply exemplified in the family connection of Richard Grey and of Sir Griffith Vaughan. Humphrey Duke of Gloucester, grandfather of Richard Grey, and a companion in arms of Sir Griffith, was murdered in the same year, 1447, as the latter. Richard Grey's father-in-law, James Lord Audley, was slain by the hand of Sir Roger Kynaston, the brother-in-law of Richard Grey. Lucy, the neice of Sir Roger Kynaston, married David Lloyd of Leighton, the eldest son of Sir Griffith Vaughan, beheaded by Richard Grey's father, and this picture of family horrors must need be complicated and overshadowed by a hypocritical petition for 500 marks on the plea of loyalty and good faith.

The doctrine of a retributive justice would also seem to trace its evidences and find its exposition in the events of which we are treating. 500 marks, it will be remembered, was the original amount offered for the apprehension of Lord Cobham, the Lollard, in 1414, the year after his escape from the Tower. This failing to secure him, Archbishop Chicheley, and the Church generally, being anxious for his capture, induced King Henry V, in 1416, to increase the reward to 1,000 marks and an annuity of £20. These sums offered considerable inducements to an energetic search, and an estimation of the social influence and position of the assumed culprits. Taking the decrease in the purchasing value of money in our day to be sixteen times what it was in 1414 or 1447; 500, if they were silver, marks would represent £2,000 of our currency; if gold marks £10,000.

The discovery of this document affords an important link in a chain of interesting local personal history of which we have already the following occasional records from 1406 to 1447 :—

In 1406 "Sir Griffith Vaughan ap Gwenwys, Knt.", appears on the roll of burgesses of Welshpool, found by Lewys Dwnn on the Inspeximus Charters of Edward de Charleton Dominus Powys, 29 June, 7 Henry IV. Looking at the wording of certain clauses of that charter we can almost acquit Sir Griffith of being "out" with Owen Glendower; for Sir Edward Charleton avers that the burgesses "in the time of the rebellion of Owen ap Griffith (Glendower) were always faithful to our sovereign lord the king and to us". A particular clause states—" That no Welshman ought to be taken into the said liberty from this time except those who are faithful to our lord the king and us, and *were always with us in the time of the rebellion aforesaid."* He perhaps committed no overt act of rebellion, but it is certain that his heart must have been in the cause espoused by his father, Griffith ap Ieuan of Caus, and by his uncles, " David Lloit ap Ieuan ap Madoc de Southstrad-Margell" and "Mer'd ap Ieuan ap Madoc ap Gwenwys; the former pardoned in 1408, the latter attainted in 1405 for participation in the rebellion of *Owen de Glendoudoy*".[1]

In 1415 the battle of Agincourt was fought. "Griffin Fordet" appears on a roll (in French) which purports to be that of the retinue of the Duke of Gloucester. Sir John Grey, afterwards created Earl of Tankerville, father of Henry Grey, had a retinue of thirty lances with him at the battle. Sir John Grey and Sir Hugh Stafford, both known to have been at Agincourt, are neither of them on the roll. Of the "six knights, one hundred and ninety-three esquires, and six hundred horse archers" of the Duke of Gloucester's retinue, only one hundred and forty names are recorded; so we have no means of ascertaining, as the roll is manifestly incomplete, on whose particular retinue Sir Griffith Vaughan served. Sir John Grey and Sir Hugh Stafford were probably part of the Duke of Gloucester's retinue. The former was Lord of Powys, the latter of the Barony of Caus, and Sir Griffith Vaughan was a military retainer of both baronies.

In 1417 he and his brother Ieuan captured Lord Cobham, the Lollard, on their estate at Broniarth. In 1419 they received certain privileges by charter of Sir Edward de Charleton, Lord Powys, for the said capture.

In 1420, in the month of March, Sir Griffith, his brother Ieuan, and two of their armed retainers, parties to the capture, wrote a letter to Sir Edward Charleton, Knight, Lord of Powys, stating that they had "ben fully satisfied" as to the "guerdonn and rewarde" offered by the king's proclamation, and that the matter had been "compownyd with us and fynaly accorded".[2] A testing clause is appended to this letter of agreement, stating that they had set their seals thereto "in the hie and noble presence of our said sovereigne lord (Henry V), and also of the hie and mighty prince the Duc of Gloucestre, brother unto oure soveraigne lord

[1] *Mont. Coll.*, vol. vi, p. 86; vol. iv, pp. 336-7.
[2] The letter is printed in *Mont. Coll.*, vol. i, p. 295.

byforesaid, and also of Umfray, Erle of Stafford, John Lord Fornyvall," and others, " at Shrosbery the iiij day of March, the yere of oure said soveraigne lord the viijth." A Latin endorsement states that the parties to the letter of agreement appeared at Wattlesborough Castle, *vicesimo die Aprilis anno presenti*, and acknowledged and bound themselves by its contents in the presence of John de Talbot Lord Furnyvall,[1] and the Abbot of St. Peter's, Salop.

The date of the month (iiij) of March, in the 8th year of Henry Vth, is manifestly an error of the transcriber of the original letter.

The critical observation of Mr. Morris C. Jones detected this discrepancy, and in his " Feudal Barons of Powys" led him to conclude that King Henry Vth could not have been present at Shrewsbury when the letter was said to have been sealed in his presence. He argues, with apparent force, that " the King tested a charter on the 2nd March of that year (8th Henry V) at Windsor, and on the 5th of the same month we find him testing several documents at the Castrum Rothomagi (Rouen). The Royal movements", he says, "must have been rapid for the King to have been at Windsor on the 2nd, at Shrewsbury on the 4th, and at the Castrum Rothomagi on the 5th of the same month. It was not possible. It is safer to conclude", continues Mr. Morris Jones, " that the letter was not sealed in the *actual* presence of the Sovereign".[2]

The 8th regnal year of King Henry V commenced on the 21st March 1420, and ended 20th March 1421, so that Mr. Morris Jones' dates refer to acts of the Sovereign at Windsor and Rouen in 1421, and are, therefore, no proof that he was not at Shrewsbury in March 1420. The wording of the endorsement, "cognoverunt scriptam prædictam", shows that the date of the letter must be antecedent to the act of recognisance recorded thereon ; and as the date of the endorsement

---

[1] First Earl of Shrewsbury.   [2] *Mont. Coll.*, vol. i, p. 296.

is 20th April 1420, the date of the letter must, to have been in the 8th Henry V, have been on or subsequent to the 21st day in the previous month of March 1420. The discrepancy is better overcome by assuming that the transcriber wrote iiij for xxij, than, in the face of the explicit declaration in the letter, to conclude that it was not possible that it could have been sealed in the *actual* presence of the king.

After the 20th April 1420, no incident of Sir Griffith's eventful life occurs to us until that of its disastrous close in 1447. He, like Sir John Grey, was a soldier by profession. They had been companions in arms at Agincourt, and doubtless throughout the French wars; and he is not likely to have led an inactive and uneventful life at home, when ample facilities presented themselves for military adventure abroad. Sir John Grey, having died during the life-time of his father-in-law, Sir Edward de Cherleton, never attained the dignity of Lord Powys; but doubtless commanded all the feudal interests and military services of the Barony. Of the latter was the Commot of South Strata Marcella, held in fee by Sir Griffith Vaughan and his family, who, both by tenure and inclination would be found in the following of Sir John Grey. In 1417 the latter was retained by indenture to serve king Henry V in the wars of France with forty men at arms, and for his valiant services he had a grant of the Castle and Lordship of Tilye, in Normandy; and in the following year that of the Earldom of Tankerville, the Governorship of Harfleur, and of the Castle of Gournay, in Normandy. On the 3rd April 1421, one year after the above incident of the letter, the Earl of Tankerville fell on the field of Beaugé. With him were slain the Duke of Clarence, brother of Henry V, the Earl of Kent, and others. The Earl's body is said to have been recovered from the field, brought home, and buried in the chancel of Welshpool Church. Who could have been a more likely and suitable custodian of the honoured and venerated remains, than his companion of the battle field, the chief feudal retainer of the Lordship of Powys?

The bard, in his elegy recording the incidents of the Earl's burial, might seem to echo Sir Griffith's plaintive sympathy, when he says:—

> " Alas the time when on his grave I stood,
> And on my honoured chief I placed my foot."

The poet's doleful strain is appropriately prophetic of his end.

> " Woe to the cheerless country! to watch over the oak
> Whose top the wind has broken off."

And the very wail of Joan Charlton, the youthful[1] widow of the Earl—

" The Countess of the land of Gwent, with the varied coloured mansions,
So feeble was she that once she swooned,
Uttered a scream with voice so loud,
That it echoed through the chancel of Trallwng"[2],

might describe, as the mutilated remains of Sir Griffith also lay "in S. Mary's Chancel",[3] the horror and prostration of his bereaved ones.

W. V. Ll.

[1] She was twenty at the time the Earl was killed.
[2] *Mont. Coll.*, vol. i, p. 332.   [3] *Ibid.*, vol. vi, p. 95.

ARCHAIC WORDS, PHRASES, ETC., OF MONTGOMERYSHIRE.

By the REV. ELIAS OWEN, M.A.

(Continued from Vol. XII, p. 324.)

FROM the names of places in the border land between England and Wales it will be seen that Welsh was spoken in places where at present it is not heard; and from places' names, however strangely disfigured by the tongue of the foreigner, we learn how tenacious of life is the name of a place. What is going on, and has gone on in Wales, has likewise occurred in other parts of England, and many an English town, river, and brook, mountain and dale, owes its name to the Celt, who, in ages long gone by, inhabited the whole country and freely roamed over the downs in the south of England and along the valleys of Derbyshire, and other parts of the kingdom, and gave names to the places therein that have come down to our days. These names, though, can in the lapse of time be hardly recognised in their modern garb even by a Welsh-speaking Welshman. It requires an ingenious aptitude for such a work ere the present name of an English place can be referred to its undoubtedly Celtic original appellation. The writer does not lay claim to such a gift, but in his various journeys, the somewhat disguised names of places, evidently at one time Welsh, strike his ear, and he has thought that it would be well to record a few, if only a few, of these names, merely to indicate what may be done by local word-worms who have the curiosity and time for collecting a list of place names undoubtedly derived from the Welsh in former years. Such an undertaking would be interesting and useful, and there is ample scope for it in many parts of England, and particularly in the English counties adjoining Wales, as well as in the English-speaking parts of Wales.

The other day I was in the parish of Buttington, near Welshpool, and I had several instances of the corruption of the names of places from an intelligent lad who accompanied me in my walk. Pointing to a conical summit of a branch of the Breidden Hill, I asked him what it was called. He said, "That point there is called Pennyrozin."

Pennyrozin. This word I took down just as the boy pronounced it. The first part was clear—the *pen*—but what could the *rozin* mean? This was the crux, but upon looking round the difficulty vanished. Stretching before me right up to the *Long Mynd Mountains* was a valley, which, before its cultivation, was a regular *rhos*, or moist meadow land. On the other side, again, was the Severn; and ere the land at the foot of the mountain was drained, that, too, must have been a *rhos;* hence, the plural of rhos, *rhosydd*. The *Penny* is made to do duty for *Pen y* (the top of), and the name undoubtedly at one time was *Pen-y-rhosydd*, which in the course of years has been corrupted into Pennyrozin.

A summit not far from Penyrhosydd was called by the boy *Molly golfa*. Here, again, a similar change to that which Penyrhosydd underwent was evident. The *Molly* of to-day was the *Moel y* of former days. *Moel* means a conical hill void of wood. The latter part of the name, viz., *golfa*, is not clear. There are those who derive it from *collfa*, a place of execution; others, again, think it comes from *gwylfa*, a watching-place. The *g* is certainly often dropped when an initial in Welsh words in Montgomeryshire, but other changes would be required to convert *wylfa* to *collfa*, and such changes as do not occur. Perhaps the root of the word is to be looked for in *coll*, hazel wood; thus, *Moel-y-gollfa* would mean the hazel wood hill.

Near Newtown, on the road to Kerry, is a place called locally *Vastry*. The present form of the word is rather obscured, but with a little thought the darkness is dispelled, and it is soon seen that Vastry comes from *Maes*, an open space, plain, or field, and *tref*, a homestead.

Rossett, a parish adjoining Cheshire, is evidently a corruption of *rhosydd*, marshy land.

Gresford derives its name from Croes, a cross, and fford, a road. A few hundred yards from the village is still to be seen the pedestal or base of a wayside cross.

Cytte, a place in Whittington parish, comes from *coed*, wood, and *ty*, a house.

Such changes as those now referred to are common; but there is another peculiarity observable in various parts of Wales, but more particularly so on the border land, that is the translating of the names of places from Welsh into English, both names being current at the same time. Thus in the valley of Trefeglwys there is a house known as *Tycoch*, and it is always so called by the Welsh-speaking population of those parts, while the English-speaking people call it *Redhouse*. Thus, too, we have *Whitehouse* for *Tygwyn*. In the neighbourhood of Denbigh stands the mother church of that parish. It is also one of those places that have the peculiarity alluded to. It is known to the Welshman as *Eglwyswen*, and to the Englishman, Whitechurch.

Whitechurch, the terminus of the Cambrian railway line, was once Eglwyswen.

Bettisfield, a station between Oswestry and Whitechurch, and which is also an ecclesiastical district, seems to be an attempt at a translation of the word *Caerbettws*. The *cae*, field, is translated, and the *bettws* is judiciously left alone, and this gives us the mongrel word Bettisfield.

I have no doubt that the key to the meaning of many names of places will be got by bearing in mind that partial or literal translations of Welsh names often took place.

There is another peculiarity in reference to the names of places which shall be referred to, viz., the addition of a word in English, to make the meaning of the term intelligible to English-speaking people. Thus, not far from Llanymynech is a bridge now commonly called "*Pont Meredith Bridge*". *Pont* is the Welsh for bridge. This the English population either is ignorant of, or it has Anglicised the term, to make it a descriptive term to them. In the same manner *yr ogof*, the cave on the Llanymynech Hill, has been converted into "the ogo hole". In the uplands of Radnorshire, between Buillt and Knighton, is a lake, locally called Lynbucklyn Pool, llyn meaning pool, or lake. This combination of synonymous words is not uncommon.

Passing on from the names of places to words used in ordinary conversation, it is in this case also observable that there is an interchange of words between the Welsh and English. Some of these I have already mentioned in the course of these papers, such as *pendre*, for the sickness to which sheep are subject, and which affects their heads, and causes them to turn round and round; *glasder* for *glasdwr*, etc. Words like these are common. In this manner do concurrent languages affect each other.

In this paper I will put down, without alphabetical order, Welsh words, or words used by Welsh-speaking people in Montgomeryshire, that are either not used, or are not commonly used, in other parts of the principality.

Shettin, a hedge. In other parts of Wales a hedge is a *gwrych*. In Carnarvonshire, where stones are plentiful and trees scarce, the hedge becomes *clawdd*, a mound; but the divisions between field and field there are stone-built walls. *Shettin* has an English sound about it, and probably it is derived from *shut in*, to enclose.

Wttra, a lane; sometimes the *w* aspirated as *hwttra*. In Carnarvonshire a wttra is a lōn; in Denbighshire, a rhewl.

Cog, a lump. A short, lusty fellow is called a cog—
"Mae o yn glamp o gog lusti". The *cog* may be applied to thick-set, short men, but it is usually applied to children, as "Pan oeddwn i yn gog bach"—"When I was a little cog". "Cymmerwch *gog* o gaws"—"Take a cog, or lump, of cheese".

Anferth, which Dr. Owen Pugh gives as "without beauty, monstrous", is a word of wide application in Montgomeryshire. It answers somewhat to the word *ofnadwy*, terrible, frightful. It is one of those words intended to intensify an expression. "Yn sal anferth"—"very ill indeed", or "extremely ill". "Y mae yn rhewi yn anferth"—"It freezes very hard, or tremendously".

Manwes. An open sow that has not had pigs.

Mwlwg mawn, the peat-ash, or remains of peat after they are burnt. In some parts this is called *mwnws mawn*.

Caenen, a heavy fall of snow. This word is commonly used in Carno parish. In Cardiganshire the word used for the same thing is *Haen*.

Talch, coarse meal.

Stican, a spoon. In Carnarvonshire, and other parts of Wales, the usual word for a spoon is *llwy*. There is, however, a piece of wood used to stir the porridge called a *stican* in Carnarvonshire.

Grwn, a seed bed, called in parts of Wales *Gwely*. Thus, in Llanfair Caereinion they would say, "Dyma grwn o foron anferth o fawr"—"This is a very large bed of carrots". In Anglesey the same information would be conveyed thus—"Dima wely o *garaitch* mawr ofnadwy."

Moron, carrots. In some places called moron cochion, or red carrots, to distinguish them from parsnips, called moron gwynion, or white carrots. The usual name for this vegetable is a corruption of carrots, as given above.

Ffebrys, gooseberries. In Carnarvonshire the word used is a corruption of the English word, as coesberrins. Similar corruptions are used in other parts. In Llanfyllin, I have heard gooseberries called Eirin-Mair, Mary's plums.

Gomedd, to refuse. The common word is gwrthod, or nacâu, but gomedd is the word used in Llanfair, Montgomeryshire, and the parts there about. Thus, there a person would say, "Yr oedd o yn *gomedd* dod getha i", which in Flintshire would take the form—"Yr oedd o yn naca dod gyda mi"—"He refused to come with me."

Dannod, to upbraid, is a word that, while it is good Welsh, is, nevertheless, a local word. The usual word in other parts of North Wales is *edliw*, to upbraid, or reproach.

Ffwrn, an oven. The use of this word strikes a person from Carnarvonshire as singular, where an oven is a pobty, or baking-house.

Ffwrna, to bake, or, in Flintshire, "I rhoi yn y pobty"—is to put into the bakehouse.

Cligeth, a funeral. This is a word common to South Wales, as well as Montgomeryshire. It is an abbreviation of Claddedigaeth. In Anglesey and Carnarvonshire, a funeral is a cynhebrwng. In Montgomeryshire hebrwng is the word used when a person goes "to send a person on his way".

Gythge, necks. Gythge seems to be a corruption of the word gyddfau, plural of gwddf, neck.

Gwddwg, neck. A word heard in Llanfair, Montgomeryshire. "Y mae llawer a dolur gythge y mis yma"—"Many suffer from sore throats this month."

Enfedd, ripe. The usual word is addfed.

Modyd, for teimlo, to feel.

Moyn, to go for a thing, or to fetch a thing. The usual words in other parts of Wales are "Yn hol". The common use of the word moyn in Montgomeryshire would strike a Carnarvonshire person as very strange.

Da, cattle. This is a good Welsh word, but as applied to cattle it is not often heard out of the county; at least, I have not heard it. The usual word for cattle is *gwartheg*, or *anifeiliaid*. In Denbighshire, cattle becomes *cattal*. Thus, in a booklet, by Robert Davies, Nantglyn, published in 1803, p. 27, is the line—

"Ac ar ei *gattal* gyrn."

Nant, a brook. In most counties in North Wales a nant is a dingle, or narrow valley, and not a brook. Thus sings the bard of Nantglyn of his native valley, Nantglyn—

"Nantglyn drwy'r flwyddyn yn flith—nant gyrchog,
　　Nant gorchwyl y fendith,
　　Nant winwydd, nant o wenith,
　　Nant is law, hwyl glaw, haul, gwlith."

Clwyd, a hen-roost.

Clwyd, a sort of a gate, which is not secured to its posts by hinges, but by a straw, or other kind of, rope. The word is in Dr. Owen Pugh's *Dictionary*, and is defined by him as a hurdle and wattled gate. It is a local term, and it is interesting to find it current in Montgomeryshire. It is common in Trefeglwys parish.

Plancio, to protest, or affirm a thing, as "Yr oedd yn *plancio* na wyddai ddim am y peth."—He protested that he knew nothing of the matter. This word is heard in Llangadfan parish.

Burr, a whetstone. It is called *calenhogi* in Flintshire. In some parts it is called *maen hogi*, and in other parts of Wales it goes by other names. *Burr* is heard in Llangyniew parish, Montgomeryshire.

Penty, a cottage standing alone, a detached house without land belonging thereto, a farm-servant's house built by itself, a hovel. The word is in Dr. Owen Pugh's *Dictionary*, but there it is defined as "a building added to the main house; penthouse, a shed; also, the head house". It is used in quite a different sense to this in Montgomeryshire, for instead of being "the head house", it is a mean building, standing by itself, without any pretension to distinction of any kind.

Blaid, cowhouse. The general term for cowhouse in

Welsh is *Beudy*. " Dew'ch a getho i i'r *blaid*"—"Come with me to the cowhouse"—is heard in Llangyniew for "Deuwch gyda mi i'r beudy" in more northern parts of Wales. In Flintshire a cowhouse is called a cor.

Wap, soon, immediately. The sense in which the word is used may be seen from the following example: "Ni a fyddwm wedi darfod *wap*"—" We shall finish in the twinkling of an eye". *Wap* is a slang term. In some parts of Wales the equivalent is *wap* is *toc*, which means instantaneous; thus, "Fyddwn wedi darfod toc."

Dyl means the same as *toc*, or *wap*.

Allusion has already been made in a former paper to the dropping of *ch*, when an initial letter, in the neighbourhood of Llanidloes. It appears, though, that this peculiarity extends to other parts of the county. Thus I am informed by my friend, the Rev. G. Edwards, M.A., that it is common in Llangadfan, of which parish the reverend gentleman is rector. My friend Mr. Griffiths, schoolmaster, Llangyniew, tells me that such also is the case in that parish. In Llanwnog and Llanidloes I have myself noticed repeatedly this provincialism. There is, however, a difference, which I think I have observed, in the pronunciation of such words as begin with *ch* in the eastern and western parts of the county; thus, in the western parts, where Welsh only is the language of the people, the *w* is preceded by the aspirate—thus, *chwech* becomes *hwech*; whilst in the eastern parts of the county there is a tendency to drop the aspirate altogether, and the *chwech* becomes *wech*; this, however, will require further corroboration. The peculiarity of dropping the *ch* leads to the abbreviation of words; thus, *chwyad* becomes *hwyd*, and *chwyaden* *hwyden*. In such words as these, where the initial is aspirated, it is difficult to state with certainty whether the *h* precedes or follows after the *w*. In the English word, *when*, and such like, the aspirate appears after the *w*, but it is a question whether in sound it does not precede it.

(To be continued.)

MONTGOMERYSHIRE WORTHIES.

By RICHARD WILLIAMS.

(*Continued from Vol. viii, p. 382.*)

Lewis ab Maredydd ab Ieuan Vychan of Llanwrin, a generous, wealthy, and influential person, a warrior, and an esquire of the body-guard to Henry VI, to whom Lewys Glyn Cothi has addressed a spirited Ode. (*Works*, p. 452.) He was a nephew of Sir Richard Gethin, a brave and warlike knight, who fell at one of the sieges of Rouen, in Normandy.

Lewis ab John ab Jenkin, Vicar of Darowen, was one of the bards who attended the great Eisteddfod at Caerwys in 1567.—(*Arch. Camb.*, 1st series, iv, p. 146.)

Lewis Powys, was another bard who attended the same Eisteddfod.—(*Ibid.*)

Lloyd, Humphrey, of Leighton, was the *first* Sheriff of Montgomeryshire. He served that office for the year ending Michaelmas 1541. He was a grandson of Sir Griffith Vaughan of Guilsfield, Knight Banneret (who was knighted, as is alleged, on the field at Agincourt, and who in 1447 was decapitated by Henry Grey, Lord of Powys) and a descendant of Brochwel Ysgythrog. Prior to the dissolution of the Abbey of Strata Marcella, he held (in 1523) the appointment of steward or judge of the Abbey Court, and subsequently that of receiver of the Abbey lands. He was also Ringild, or Crown receiver of rents of assize, of the Crown demesnes of Tregynon, Llanllwchaiarn, Kerry, Egville and Teirtref; and in 1553 was high constable or steward of the barony of Caus. His name appears on the roll of magistrates as late as the 2nd Eliz. (1560). He was the ancestor of the Lloyds of Leighton, Talgarth, Forden, and other Montgomeryshire families. —(*Mont. Coll.*, ii, pp. 139, 211.)

LLOYD, LUDOVICK or LODWICK, fifth son of Oliver Lloyd of Marrington, was sergeant-at-arms to Queen Elizabeth, and a distinguished herald. Anthony Wood mentions Lodowyke Lloyd as one of the contributors to Richard Edwards' *Paradise of Dainty Devises* (London, 1578, qu.). In 1590 was also published "*The Consent of Time*, disciphering the errours of the Grecians in their Olympiads, the uncertain computations of the Romanes in their Penteterydes and buildinge of Rome, of the Persians in their accompt of Cyrus, and of the vanities of the Gentiles in fables of antiquities disagreeing with the Hebrews, and with the sacred histories in consent of time. Wherein is alsoe set down the beginninge, continuance, succession, and overthrowe of kinges, kingdoms, states, and governments, by Lodowick Lloid, Esquire." An illustrated coloured Geography was also published by the same author. The three above named were probably one and the same person.—(Wood's *Athenae Oxon.*, i, 152; *Mont. Coll.*, vi, 112; *Byegones*, Oct. 8, Nov. 15, Dec. 17, 1873.) 29 Eliz., May 31.—By letters patent of this date "of her Maiesties speciall grace certain knowledge and meere motion did graunt and to fearme sett (for 40 years) unto Ludovick Lloyd, esquier, then one of her Maiesties seriant-at-Armes, amongst other things : All that then Chapell of FFording al's FForden" . . . . . "all manner of Tythes of corne and hey, and all other tyethes in great Heme, little Heme, Kelekewith, FFording, Nantcreba, Penylan, Brinkendrithe, Akley, Lettinwynwarethe, sometymes belonging unto the late Priory of Chirbury."—(*Mont. Coll.*, iii, 325.)

LLOYD, REV. MAURICE, of Aberhavesp, is mentioned by Calamy among the clergy who in 1662 were ejected for nonconformity, but his name is not given in the list of Rectors in Thomas's *History of St. Asaph*. He appears to have afterwards conformed.—(Calamy's *Noncon. Memorial* (1803) iii, 494.)

MADOG DANWR ("Ignifer") a descendant of Tudor Trefor, was a faithful and brave soldier, who served under Gwenwynwyn, Lord of Powys, who as a reward for his services, bestowed upon him the lordship of Llangurig with an addition to his arms. He bore, according to Mr. Joseph Morris, *argent* a lion rampant *sable*, within a bordure *gules*, in which six lions passant *argent*, one of them in chief, another in base. The new arms which he had the privilege of bearing in augmentation of his paternal coat were a border *gules* charged with eight mullets *argent*. He married a daughter of Idnerth ab Meredydd Hen, lord of Buallt, by whom he had three sons, Meredydd, Idnerth, and Gruffydd. He resided at Clochfaen, Llangurig, and was the progenitor of the Lloyds of Clochfaen, one of the oldest and at one time most powerful of Montgomeryshire families.—(*Mont. Coll.*, ii, 269; Jos. Morris's *MSS.*)

MARCHELL (Lat. *Marcella*), the daughter of Arwystli Gloff, by Tywanwedd or Dwywannedd, daughter of Amlawdd Wledig, was a British saint (not canonised by the church of Rome) who flourished between 566 and 600. She is the reputed original foundress of Ystrad Marchell, where the famous Cistercian abbey bearing that name was afterwards established; also of Capel Marchell near Llanrwst.—(*Cam. Briton*, iii, 336; *Mont. Coll.*, iv, 9.)

MATTHEWS, OLIVER, was a member of an old and respectable family settled for many generations at Park in the parish of Llanwnog, where he appears to have been born about the year 1520. He removed to Shrewsbury, where he became a prosperous mercer, being a resident in that town in the year 1576. After retiring from business he settled, according to the *Heraldic Visitations* of Shropshire, at Bishop's Castle. He married Jane, daughter of Edward Broughton, of Broughton, who was buried at Bishop's Castle 9th

January 1611. On the 18th March 1615 (being then 95 years old), he wrote a letter "to his 2 lovinge frends of the Cittie of Bristowe", namely, "Mr. Phillip Jenkins, my naturall Countreyman, and Mr. Thomas Taylor, my loving and faithfull frind", in which, after having at some length shewed them his " knowledge and judgement as towchinge the Antiquitie and Foundation of your famous Cittie of Brennus Towne, which was built about 369 yeres before Christ's Incarnation by Brennus, that noble Brittaine", he concludes thus, " I, being aged 95 years, and by reason thereof decayed in memorie, praie you to have me excused yf I have not performed to the full your expectacion herein. And nowe, not ever thinckinge to see you in this transitory World, I take my last and *ultimum vale* of you bothe, bequeathinge unto you, and to that famous Cittie of Brennus, and to Mr. Maior, with the Magistrates and Commynaltie thereof, my best love, wishinge yt with all my harte all prosperity and happiness. Dated at Snead neere Bu[shops] Castle the xviii[th]daie of March, *anno Domini* 1615. Your old Frind and Brittaine, OLIVER MATTHEWS." The following May (1616) he wrote, "An Abbreviation of divers most true and aunciect Brutaine Cronicles, briefelie expressing the foundation of the most famous decayed Cittie Caer Souse or Dinas Southwen, most auncient in Britaine, (Troy Newyth onlie excepted) and of some other famous Citties in Greate Brutaine"; to which is added "The Cause of the Brittaines Captivitie". These first appeared in print in Hearne's *History and Antiquities of Glastonbury.* Lastly, he wrote an account of " The Scituacion, Foundation, and auncient Names of the famous Towne of Sallop, not inferiour to manie Citties in this Realme, for Antiquitie, godlie Goverment, good Orders, and Wealth. The Lord so continue yt, to his good pleasure and theire good. Amen. By Oliver Matthews, gen., Julie 1616." The exact date of his death I have not been able to ascertain. A reprint of all these quaint and curious compositions was issued in 1877 by Messrs. Bickley and Son, Shrewshury.

MEISIR, one of the daughters of Cyndrwyn, Prince of Powys, and who resided at Llystinwennan, in Caereinion, about the close of the fifth century. She was a sister of Cynddylan, in whose elegy Llywarch Hen thus refers to her—

> "Eryr Eli gorthrymed heno,
> Dyffrynt Meisir mygedawg
> Dir Brochwael; hir rygodded."

(The eagle of Eli let him oppress this night
The valley of Meisir, the celebrated
Land of Brochwael; long has it been afflicted.)

"The valley of Meisir", her patrimony, is said to be identical with Maesbury, near Oswestry. There is also an old mansion in Berriew parish called *Bryncaemeisir.*—(*Four Anc. Books of Wales*, i, 453, and ii, 283; Llyw. Hen's *Works*, p. 81.)

MELANGELL (*St. Monacella*), a virgin saint, daughter of Tudwal ab Ceredig, by Ethni the Irishwoman. See her legend in *Mont. Coll.*, xii, 53; see also *Cam. Briton*, iii, 337; *Arch. Cam.*, 1st series, iii, 139; L. G. Cothi's *Works*, 362.

MEREDYDD AB BLEDDYN, Prince of Powys, succeeded his father, Bleddyn ab Cynfyn, as such in 1072. In the year 1101 Robert de Belesme, Arnulph Earl of Pembroke, and Iorwerth, Cadwgan, and Meredydd (Bleddyn ab Cynfyn's three sons) rebelled against the King of England, Henry I. The following year, however, Iorwerth made his peace privately with the king, and betrayed his brother Meredydd, who was taken and cast into the king's prison, where he remained four years. He then broke out of prison, " and came home, and gat his owne inheritance againe, and enioied it quietlie". He also obtained possession of the territories of his brothers, Iorwerth and Cadwgan, both of whom were slain in 1109—the one at Caereinion, the other at Welshpool. In 1118 the king invaded Wales, when Meredydd defended the passes into Powys with great ability and success, and the king himself narrowly escaped with his life. Peace was afterwards made up between them. He was a prince of undoubted abilities, but his ambition to reunite under his own rule the various divisions of Powys led him to commit or sanction many acts of cruelty even towards his nearest relatives. He was twice married—first, to Hunydd, the daughter of Eunydd ab Gwernwy, by whom he had several children; secondly, to Eva, daughter of Bledrws ab Ednowain, and granddaughter of Ednowain Bendew, by whom he had a son named Iorwerth Goch, who was father to Sir Gruffydd Vychan, Lord of Criggion and Burgedin. With regard to the time of his death, various dates are mentioned. *Brut y Tywysogion* gives 1124 as the date, adding that he died "in his old age, a thing not often witnessed in the family of Bleddyn ab Cynfyn". *Brut y Saeson*, and another copy of *Brut y Tywysogion*, gives the date as 1129, and the latter speaks of the death of Meredydd, "the fairness and safety of all Powys, and its defence, after taking upon his body salutary penance, and in his spirit pure repentance, and the Communion of the body of Christ, and oil and fasting". Powel, however, gives the date as 1133, speaking of Meredydd as "the greatest lord and cheefest man of Powys; as he that had gotten his brethren and nephewes lands by hooke and by crooke into his owne hands". Upon his death, Powys was again divided between his eldest son, Madog (whose share was thenceforth called Powys Fadog), and his grandson Owain Cyfeiliog, whose moiety descended to his son Gwenwynwyn, and was from him called Powys Wenwynwyn. His arms were *or*, a lion's gamb in bend *gules*, armed *sable* and erased. (Williams' *Em. Welshmen*; Powel's *Hist. of Cambria*, 162-188; *Myv. Arch.*, 622, 676, 707; Jos. Morris's *MSS.*)

MEREDYDD AB ROTPERT, a descendant of Tegonwy ab Teon, styled Lord of Cedewain, was a chieftain of power and note during the struggles of the last Llewelyn for the liberty of his country. In 1211 his name appears among the list of Welsh chieftains who, joining the army of King John, marched to Chester, and caused Llewelyn to retreat towards Snowdon for a time. During the minority of Henry III, the Castle of Kinnerley, in the county of Salop, was ransacked and demolished by Llewelyn's forces. Llewelyn afterwards engaged upon his corporal oath to make satisfaction for the damage then done, as appears by the Patent of 7th Henry III, m. 2, dorso, his surety for the performance of the treaty being Meredydd ab Rotpert. "Omnibus, etc., *Meriduc filius Roberti* salutem. Sciatis nos manucepisse et jurasse ad preces Leuelini P. Norwalliae, quod nisi satisfecerit Dni Henrico R. Angliae, ego eis inde satisfaciam." In his latter years he became a monk, and died at the Abbey of Strata Florida, in 1244 : "Maredut filius Roberti obiit sumpto religionis habitu apud Stratam Floridam.—(J. Morris's *MSS.; Lit. Kymry,* 255; *Annales Cambriae,* 85.)

MORGAN, REV. EDWARD, of Dyffryn, Merionethshire, an eminent minister with the Welsh Calvinistic Methodists, was born at a small hamlet called Pentre, near Llanidloes, on the 20th September 1817. He was one of a family of eleven children, his father being a small farmer and flannel manufacturer, who in 1829 removed to Llanidloes, where, in addition to his manufacturing business, he opened a retail shop. His mother died in May 1831. About this time he joined the Cymreigyddion at Llanidloes, which no doubt gave an impulse to his literary tastes and aspirations. He had but little schooling, but an ardent desire for knowledge was kindled within him, to gratify which he made the best use of every means and opportunity. He served an apprenticeship to the drapery business with Mr. E. Cleaton, during which his habit was to sit up until two o'clock in the morning, or later, to study such books as came within his reach. When about eighteen years of age, he made his first appearance as a public speaker on behalf of total abstinence, and his talents were speedily recognised. In 1839 he entered college at Bala, in order to qualify himself for the ministry with the Calvinistic Methodists, but only remained there a few months, leaving Bala to undertake the management of a day-school at Dyffryn. Here, in 1841, he began to preach, and early in 1842 he returned again to Bala, which the following year he left again to resume his scholastic duties at Dyffryn. About the beginning of 1846 he studied theology for a few months at New College, Edinburgh, then conducted by Dr. Chalmers, and other eminent professors. He was fully ordained as a minister at Bala in 1847, and soon afterwards undertook the pastoral care of a church at Dolgelley. On the 19th July 1849, he married Janet, daughter of the Rev. Richard Humphreys of Dyffryn, where soon afterwards he took up his residence. From July 1854 to December 1856 he edited, with considerable ability and taste, a small monthly magazine called *Y Methodist*. Mr. Morgan's talents as a preacher, and his tact, energy, and administrative ability, soon won for him great influence and a leading position in the denomination to which he belonged. In 1870, his brethren, by electing him Moderator of their General Assembly, conferred upon him the highest honour within their power. Although endowed with a weakly frame and a very fragile constitution, and for the last sixteen years of his life a great sufferer from bronchial affections, Mr. Morgan, in addition to his pastoral labours, undertook, and brought to a successful issue, undertakings before which many stronger men might well have quailed. About the end of 1856 he undertook the collection of an Endowment Fund of £20,000 for the Denominational College for North Wales, at Bala. In this he succeeded so well, that at the end of five years the fund amounted to £26,000, in addition to which he subsequently collected about £7,000 more towards the Building Fund of the new college, which was completed and opened in 1867. In acknowledgment of these services, Mr. Morgan was presented with a well deserved testimonial of 220 guineas in money, and a handsome tea and coffee service of the value of 50 guineas. Mr. Morgan also took a very active part in his own county in the political struggles of his day, which ended in the return of a Liberal member for Merionethshire, a result which probably he, by his eloquence and personal influence, did as much, at least, as any single individual to accomplish. His active and laborious life was brought to a close in his fifty-fourth year, on the 9th May 1871, and on the 16th of the same month he was buried in the burial-ground attached to Horeb Chapel, Dyffryn, his funeral being, it is said, the largest ever seen in Merionethshire. His wife and eight children survived him. Since his death a selection of his sermons has been published. They are characterised by purity of diction and chasteness of expression, as well as by glowing eloquence and great fervour of feeling, and many of them display considerable depth and originality of thought.—(*Y Gwyddoniadur, etc.*)

MORGAN, ROBERT, D.D., an eminent Bishop of Bangor, was born in 1608 at Fronfraith, in the parish of Llandyssil. He was the third son of Richard Morgan of that place (who represented Montgomery in Parliament in 1592-93), by his wife Margaret, daughter of Thomas Lloyd of Gwernybuarth, in the same parish. He received his school education under Mr. Lloyd, the father of Archdeacon Simon Lloyd, who lived near, and was afterwards admitted to Jesus College, Cambridge, where in due course he graduated M.A. On the elevation of Dr. Dolben to the see of Bangor he became his chaplain, and was by him promoted, first to the vicarage of Llanwnog, in his native county, in 1632, and then to the rectory of Llangynhafal, Denbighshire. Upon the death of Bishop Dolben, he returned to Cambridge, and settled at St. John's College, where he took the degree of B.D. Upon the promotion of Dr. William Roberts, in 1637, to the bishopric of Bangor, he returned to Wales as his chaplain, and received from him the vicarage of Llanfair Dyffryn Clwyd. He resigned Llangynhafal, and in 1642 was instituted to Trefdraeth, Anglesey. The same year he resigned Llanfair, and was instituted to Llanddyfnan, Anglesey, a living which was then worth only £38 per annum, the tithes having been leased for ninety-nine years to the Bulkeleys of Baron Hill, prior to the Statute of Limitation. Mr. Morgan, at a cost of about £300, bought out the remainder of the term, about fifteen years, and this enabled him to keep this preferment when he was deprived of his other livings during the Commonwealth, and he subsequently left it to the church free of charge. He suffered much during the Civil War and the Commonwealth, and chiefly resided at Henblas, in Anglesey. On the Restoration of Charles II, he was restored to his preferments, was made Archdeacon of Merioneth, and obtained the degree of D.D. In July of the same year (1660), he was made comportioner of Llandinam, Montgomeryshire. Upon the death of Dr. Robert Price, he was elected Bishop of Bangor, and consecrated July 1st, 1666. On the death of Archdeacon Mostyn of Bangor, in 1672, he took that archdeaconry *in commendam*, and secured it in the same manner for his successor, who so enjoyed it, and had it annexed to the bishopric by Act of Parliament. He performed the sacred duties of his office with exemplary diligence and conscientiousness. He died September 1st, 1673, and was buried in the cathedral, on the south side of the altar, in the grave of Bishop Robinson. He married Anne, daughter and heir of the Rev. William Lloyd, rector of Llanelian, Anglesey (uncle of Dr. William Lloyd, Bishop of St. Asaph), by whom he had four sons and four daughters. His wife survived him. He did much to repair and improve the interior of the cathedral, and, with some assistance from the neighbouring gentry, furnished it with an excellent organ. He left behind him several compositions, which he had once intended for publication, but because, as he said, they were ill-transcribed, he forbade them to be published. It is said of him that "he was a man of great prudence in business, good learning, and eloquence in preaching, both in the English and his native tongue, and he perfectly spent and wore himself away by his constant preaching". There is a portrait of Bishop Morgan at Cefn, near St. Asaph.—(Williams' *Em. Welshmen;* Humphreys' *Additions to Wood's Athenæ Oxon.; Mont. Coll.,* vi, 345.)

OLIVERS, THOMAS, was born at the village of Tregynon in the year 1725. His baptismal entry in the parish register is dated September 8th, 1725, and he is described as the son of Thomas Oliver and Penelope, his wife. His parents were respectable, and owned a small estate. His father died in December 1728, and was buried at Tregynon on the 31st of that month, and his mother died in the March following. He was then taken charge of by his father's uncle, a man of some property, who at his death left him a small fortune, and also placed him under the care of his granddaughter Elizabeth Tudor, who, being unmarried, committed him to the care of her father Thomas Tudor, a large farmer in the parish of Forden. Here he was boarded, and sent to a local school until he was eighteen years of age, when he was bound apprentice. He appears to have been at this time of a particularly gay and lively disposition, fond of dancing and company, for in his autobiography he states "that out of sixteen nights and days, he was fifteen of them without ever being in bed". Some years afterwards he went to Shrewsbury, where he lived for some time, and thence to Wrexham, and other places. At Bristol he went to hear the celebrated Whitfield preach, whose sermon he ever afterwards considered the means of his conversion. Thenceforth his whole demeanour and conduct were entirely changed. Leaving Bristol, he went to Bradford in Wiltshire, where he joined the Wesleyan Methodist Society, and was afterwards admitted a lay preacher. When he had been a local preacher for about twelve months, he had the small-pox in its most virulent form. On his recovery, he paid a short visit to his native county "to receive his fortune, which had remained so long in Mrs. Tudor's hands". With the money he bought a horse, "and rode far and near, paying all he owed in his own country"; which seems rather to have astonished the people, and particularly Lord Hereford, who, in fact, sent him to the stocks because he had turned Methodist. Having paid every farthing he owed in his own country, he went to Shrewsbury and did the same. From Shrewsbury he went to Whitchurch on purpose to pay sixpence, and thence to Wrexham, and satisfied every one there. He also visited Chester, Liverpool, Manchester, Birmingham, and Bristol, preaching wherever he went, and finally returned to Bradford. Having paid about seventy debts (which he could not accomplish till he had sold his horse, bridle, and saddle), he, with the small remains of his money, and with a little credit, set up in business. Before, however, he was half settled, he, at Mr. Wesley's request, gave it up, sold all his effects, and went to Cornwall, setting out on foot from Bradford, October 24th, 1753, preaching on his way; and for the next twenty-four years he devoted himself entirely to itinerant preaching in various parts of England, Scotland, and Ireland. His preaching appears to have been of an earnest, convincing character, and to have been attended with much success. About 1758 he was married at Whitehaven, "after consultation with Mr. Wesley", to a Miss Green. In 1764, he paid another visit to his native county, and preached at Montgomery, Newtown, Llanidloes, Tregynon, and other places. About 1777 he undertook "the care of Mr. Wesley's printing", superintending, among other things, the publication of the *Arminian Magazine*. This office he held for twelve years, but the work was not altogether satisfactorily done, as the following entry in Mr. Wesley's journal, under the date of August 9th, 1789, shews:—"I settled all my temporal business, and, in particular, chose a new person to prepare the *Arminian Magazine*; being obliged, however unwillingly, to drop Mr. O—— for only these two reasons : 1. The errata are unsufferable. I have borne them for these twelve years, but can bear them no longer. 2. Several pieces are inserted without my knowledge, both in prose and verse. I must try whether these things cannot be amended for the short residue of my life." This affair, however, does not seem to have in the least disturbed the friendly relations which previously existed between Mr. Olivers and the great leader of English Methodism. Mr. Olivers continued to reside in London, where he exercised his ministry, as the infirmities of age permitted, until his death, which took place somewhat suddenly in March 1799. His remains were deposited in Mr. Wesley's tomb, behind the City Road Chapel. Mr. Olivers was certainly a man of considerable natural abilities, and, besides being an argumentative and sometimes a powerful preacher, he took a prominent part in the theological controversies of those days. He was the author of several excellent hymns printed in most hymn-books, the best known being that commencing

"The God of Abraham praise."

He was also the composer of "Helmsley" and other sacred tunes, which were at one time very popular. The following is a list of Mr. Olivers' publications :— 1. *A Hymn on the Last Judgment*, set to music by the author. 2. *A Hymn of praise to Christ*, to which is added a Hymn on Matt. v, 29, 30. 3. *A Hymn to the God of Abraham*, adapted to a celebrated air sung by Leoni in the Jews' Synagogue. 4. *A Letter to Mr. Thomas Hanby*, occasioned by the sudden death of several near relations. 5. *Twelve reasons why the people called Methodists ought not to buy or sell uncustomed goods.* 6. An *Answer* to a pamphlet, entitled "A few thoughts and matters of fact concerning Methodism, offered to the consideration of the people who attend, encourage, and support Methodist teachers, in a letter to the author. 7. *A full Reply* to a pamphlet, entitled, " An Answer to a late pamphlet of Mr. Wesley against Mr. Erskine. 8. *A Letter to the Rev. Mr. Toplady*, occasioned by his late letter to the Rev. Mr. Wesley. 9. *A Scourge to Calumny*, in two parts, inscribed to Richard Hill, Esq. Part the first, Demonstrating the absurdity of that gentleman's "Farrago". Part the second, containing a full answer to all that is material in his "Farrago Double-distilled". London 1774. 10. *A full Defence of the Rev. John Wesley*, in answer to the several personal reflections cast on that gentleman by the Rev. Caleb Evans. 11. *A Rod for a Reviler;* or an Answer to Mr. Rowland Hill's Letter to the Rev. Mr. John Wesley. 12. *An Account of the Life of Mr. Thomas Olivers*, written by himself. 13. *A full refutation of the doctrine of Unconditional Perseverance*, 12mo. 14. *A Defence of Methodism*, 12mo. 15. *A descriptive and plaintive Elegy on the death of the late Rev. John Wesley*, 8vo. 16. *An Answer to Mr. Mark Davis's Thoughts on Dancing;* to which are added, Serious considerations to dissuade Christian parents from teaching their children to dance, 12mo.—(*Jackson's Lives of Early Methodist Preachers.*)

WELSH POOL:

MATERIALS FOR THE HISTORY OF THE PARISH AND BOROUGH.

(*Continued from* Vol. xiii, p. 286.)

IN a deed dated 7 James I (1608), being a mortgage from "Rees Davies ap Howell Bedow of Brithdir, in the county of Montgomery, gent., Alexander ap Rees, son and heir apparent of the said Rees, and Gwen his wieffe, of the one part; and Richard ap Lewis of Disserth, in the said county, yeoman, of the other part", the mortgage money is made payable "on the feast of the Annuntiation of the blessed Virgin Mary, *at or upon the Stone Crosse within the church yeard of the parish church of Poole,* in the said county, between the houres of seaven and eleaven of the clock in the afternoon."

This is the only mention we have met with of this cross, of which no remains exist to mark its site. It is clearly distinct from and not to be mistaken for the Market Cross which, according to Bleaze's plan of "the Welshpool", stood in the middle of the "High Street", a little to the south of the modern Cross Pump.

There is a house in Broad Street, Welshpool, on the east side, with an engraved stone upon its front lettered thus :—

"N.
W.S.
1721."

Although by no means the oldest house, it bears the earliest inscribed date; but we have not been able to identify the owner whose initials it gives.

In 1722 William Earl of Powis (and second Marquis

and Duke) obtained restitution of his estates, including Powis Castle and the Manor of Welsh Town.

There are two silver maces belonging to the Corporation of Pool. They are inscribed "The gifte of Edward Vaughan". There was an Edward Vaughan who was a member for the county of Montgomery in 1660, and was of the House of Glanllyn, but by marrying the heiress of the Purcells, became possessed of Llwydiarth *jure uxoris*. There was also another Edward Vaughan—probably of the same family—who was one of the bailiffs of the borough in 1754. The tops of the maces are ornamented with the royal arms, which appear to be those of Queen Elizabeth. It is not possible to determine whether Edward Vaughan, the county member, or Edward Vaughan, the bailiff, was the donor of the maces; but whichever it may have been, how came it to pass that the royal arms of Elizabeth should adorn municipal insignia, presented either in the 17th or 18th century? The only solution of the knotty question that occurs to us is, that the maces given by the donor, Edward Vaughan, were ornamented with the heads of earlier maces, which had been in use in the time of Queen Elizabeth, and had borne her arms. James I's charter says that there were to be two maces; one to bear the royal arms, and the other the arms of the Lordship of Powis. There is no mace bearing the latter arms.

In November 1727 there was a fire at Powis Castle, when the buildings which then stood upon the site of the present ball-room were burnt down. There is an old plan extant of the part of the castle which was then burnt, shewing the "store-room, still-house, brew-house, bake-house, laundry, slaughter-house, candle-house, and common-room", where the ashes lay, extending a length of 169 feet. The fact of this fire having taken place is also mentioned by Lord Littleton,[1] in a letter written in 1756, describing his tour through Wales, and his visit to Powis Castle.

[1] *Works of George Lord Littleton* (1774), p. 739.

In 1728 there was a great dispute in the parish, and litigation in the Ecclesiastical Court between the parishioners, respecting the erection of a gallery at the east end of the church. A "quorum interest" was obtained out of the Consistory Court of St. Asaph by Mr. William Powell and Griffith Griffithes Tanner, "for erecting a gallery over the loft which lay over the passage out of the body of the church into the chancel", extending in length about 28 feet, and in breadth 9 feet. William Powell and Griffith Griffithes wished to erect it at their own cost, they having liberty to dispose of the seats in the new gallery to any persons willing to buy them. Mr. Thomas Parry, an attorney, who lived "near the bridge in Pool", opposed the application most strenuously, and it is from the correspondence between him and his proctors, the particulars of this famous contest are gathered. His grounds for the opposition appear to have been, that the proposed gallery would darken the two seats of him (Thomas Parry) who always had had the benefit of the chancel-light to read and pray by. Many reasons were alleged for the opposition; that the vestry at which the alterations was agreed upon was not duly constituted; that a gallery would be better placed at the western or steeple end of the church; that it would necessitate a staircase in the chancel, which would be objectionable, one never having been there before; that the gallery was intended to subserve the private interest of the promoters, and not the public interest— it being insinuated that the promoters would "if the prices be like extraordinary, if persons yt want doe not like, then the project will have its intended effect, and the projectors will have the gallery entirely to themselves". The next reason we quote, because it gives some interesting particulars of the ancient rood loft, which then existed across the entrance of the chancel.

"This loft is also to be 28 feet or thereabouts in length, which cannot possibly be, unless it be built over the Lord

Duke of Powis's seat, which will assuredly darken two of his seats, the Bayliff's of the corporation seats, and some other seats below them, and the reading desk in great measure. But to bring this over my Lord's seat, ye one end of the present loft must be struck out and taken away, which end, as a peece of antiquity, is very curiously wainscoted, cut, and neatly carved, in which end is six pedestalls on which in former days were the effigies of the Apostles, or some other of the Saints, supposely finely cut to stand with proper distances between each other, which it's a pity it should be throun down."

This gives a glimpse of a finely carved rood-screen, ornamented with sculptured figures of Saints and Apostles, no account of which has come to light from any other source; the opposition[1] failed. In ten years afterwards, the strife was renewed with unabated vigour, but with the same result. The gallery was erected, and remained until within sixty years ago, and within the memory of several persons now living.

We mention this contest here, rather than in the ecclesiastical chapter, as it was a lay dispute although about an ecclesiastical subject.

We now come to the Minute Books of the ancient corporation of the borough of Pool, of which we have been permitted to have inspection. They were called "Tensors' books", but why they were so named it is not easy to determine. We refer to a foot-note as to the meaning of the word "Tensor".[3] The earliest

[1] Some further particulars of this dispute are given in Thomas's *Diocese of St. Asaph*, p. 791.

[2] We derived much information from a printed statement prepared by Mr. A. Howell, Mayor of Welshpool in 1855, entitled "A Statement of the Result of an Examination and Enquiry by the Mayor and Council respecting the Books, Documents, Property, Rules, Regulations, and other Matters relating to the Borough and District of Welshpool"; also to another printed document containing "Memoranda extracted from the various Minute Books now in the possession of the Corporation, by D. P. Owen, Mayor of Welshpool", which was laid in the foundation stone of the Town Hall, on September 15th, 1873.

[3] "Tensers" or "tensors" were such as traded in a town without being burgesses, for which liberty they paid such fines as by the Court leet were set upon them (Philips, p. 168, cited in Owen and

WELSH POOL. 165

Minute Book now in the possession of the corporation commences in 1728. There was an earlier one, but that has been missing since 1729.

The new Tensors' Book, or Minute Book, begins with the following entry :—

Burgus de Pola.—At a Common Hall, held by the Bailiffs, Aldermen, and Burgesses of the Burrough aforesaid, at the Guildhall, in the Towne of Poole, within the said Burrough, on the 16th day of July, in the first year of the reign of our Sovereign Lord, George the Second, by the Grace of God of Great Britain, France, and Ireland, King, Deffender of the Faith, etc., Anno Dom. 1728, upon due summons and warning given by the Sergeants-at-Mace of the Burrough of Welshpool.

Blakeway's *History of Shrewsbury*, vol. i, p. 217, note 1). Those learned authors in the "Corrections and Additions", vol. ii, p. 525, add the following remarks: "Tenser is certainly a corruption of *tenancier*, *i.e.*, tenant"; and they quote an award by "John Talbot Knyght, sone & eyr to John Erle of Shrewsbury", which is contained in the books of the Corporation of Shrewsbury, and which recites "that diversez cont'versies & variancez wer had & meoved in the ton of Schrovysbury be twyn burges of the seid ton on that oon p'tie & the tenans[rs] of the same ton as that other p'tie . . . in especiall amongz other thinges, as for the makyng of burges by the said tenans[rs] tenderly desired". It appears, therefore (Owen and Blakeway proceed to remark), "that the tensers were the same with the king's tenants who aspired to a share in the government of the town, but of whom the burgesses were excessively jealous".

This seems a satisfactory explanation of the meaning and origin of the word tenser or tensor. But the reason why the minute books of the bailiffs and burgesses of Welshpool were called tensors' books is not evident. One would have expected that they would rather have been called Burgesses' Books. The "Old Ile" and the "New Ile" were a list of the burgesses as they were admitted, and would, we conceive, be the "Burgenses Boke" referred to in the ancient record quoted in *Mont. Coll.*, vol. xiii, p. 203.

We annex an extract from Gough's *History of Middle*, which shews the distinction between "Tensorship" and "Burgesship".

"This Richard Mucklestone was a person of a bould and dareing spirit; hee could not brooke an injury offered him. Hee commenced a suit against the towne of Shrewsbury for exacting an imposition upon him which they called *tensorship*, and did endeavor to make voyd theire Charter, butt they gave him his *burgesship* to be quiet; hee was accounted a just man in all his dealings.—(*The Antiquities and Memoirs of the Parish of Myddle, co. Salop*, by Rd. Gough, 1700, p. 128.)

At which generall meeting of the Bailiffs, majority of the Aldermen, and Burgesses, all the Bye-laws, orders, rules, and Decrees contained and written in the old Booke of Bye-laws, commonly called the Tensors' Books, were carefully inspected and examined, upon which inspection and examination we whose names are hereunto subscribed, finding the same to be of singular use for the well government of the said Corporation, doe hereby allowe and approve of the same; and doe ratify and confirm all and every of the said bye-laws, orders, rules, and decrees therein contained and written; and haveing a tender regard to the welfare and future prosperity of the said Burrough or Corporation, doe, as much as in us lyes, will, command, and unanimously direct and require all Aldermen and Burgesses that now are, as also all such that shall for the future be and become members of the said Burrough or Corporation, strictly to obey, observe, preserve, and keepe the same under the paines and penalties therein denounced against all that shall hereafter in any wise violate or transgress against them, or any of them, in any respect or respects whatsoever.

Wm. Nichols, } *Bailiffs.*
Hen. Parry,

Thomas Parry, *Cler. Cur.*
David Thomas,
Richard Edmunds,
R. Tudor,
W. Powell,
Henry Parry,
Griffith Griffith,
Jno. Gwynn,
} *Aldermen.*

Burgesses.—Jno. Peers,
John Evans,
Humphrey Tudor,
John Owen,
Humphrey Parry,
Edwd. Parry,
Peers Roberts,
Humphrey Tudor,
Edwd. Lloyd,
Edwd. Jones,

It will be noticed that a distinction is drawn between the borough and town, the town being described as being in the borough.

The next entry we give as a specimen of the receipts for the corporation documents given by the new bailiffs to their predecessors on their entering on their office. These are interesting, inasmuch as they afford information of what documents and articles were in existence at the time, and also show at what period some of them were lost.

Received this 22nd day of Oct. 1728, from William Nicholls and Henry Parry, gent., late Bailiffs, by us, Thomas Parry and

Richard Powell, Esqs., ye present Bailiffs of the Burrough of Poole, the severall pieces of writings hereunder written, together with the four silver maces, one brass Winchester measure or bushell, one brass quart and pint, two fire hooks, five Holbards also.

One Charter from Jn°. Charleton, then Lord of Powis.

One other Charter from Edward de Charlton, then also Lord of Powis.

One charter granted by King James the First contains three skins of vellum or parchment.

The Bye-laws and decrees of the Marches of Wales containing 3 skins of parchment.

The Tensors' Books.

The old Ile contains 14 skins or peeces of parchment.

The new Ile contains 24 skins or peeces of parchment.

Testes.   (Signed)   Thos. Parry,
S. Tudor,   Richard Powell.
Rich. Parry.

Dav. Coupland,
Jacob Humphreyes, jun.,
John Owen,
Richard Humphreys, jun,

This receipt is repeated in the same terms every year (with few exceptions) until 1743, when the receipt only included three silver maces, instead of four (the word "four" being struck out, and the word "three" interlined). No intimation is given as to what became of the fourth mace. Perhaps one or two of them were much worn, and two amalgamated, or made into one mace; but this is conjecture only.

The next entry relates to the repairing of the Cross, which, according to Bleaze's plan of 1629 (*Mont. Coll.*, vol. xiii, p. 242), was standing in the middle of the High Street, and to the south of the Market Hall.

At a Common Hall, upon due summons and warning, held this 10th day of March, in the year of our Lord 1729, it was then agreed that the sum of £20 be forthwith assessed, collected, and leavyed from the severall and respective inhabitants and occupiers of houses and lands within the Towne of Poole, for and towards the erection and rebuilding of the Cross within the said Towne, and repairing the High Street of the Town aforesaid, and in case of refusall, to distrain for the same; and if any overplus be, to render the overplus to the owner or owners thereof. As witness our hands, the day and yeare above written.

      Thomas Parry,   Mich. Parry,   } *Bailiffs.*
      Wm. Parry,   Richard Edmunds, }
      W. Powell,
      Henry Parry,
      Griffith Griffiths,
      Hen. Parry, jun.

This sum of £20, it will be observed, is to be levied upon houses and land situate in the town, and if not all expended, the surplus is to be returned to the "owner or owners" thereof, by which it is presumed the persons upon whom the rate was levied. The distinction between the town and borough is again made, but the boundaries are not distinguished. Possibly, the town may mean the parish, or three divisions of the parish. The modern corporation may take this as a precedent. The Cross would be the Market Cross, and in the immediate vicinity of the Market-house. This is the last that is heard of it. We have not been able to learn when it was removed. The plan on page 243 of *Mont. Coll.*, vol. xiii, may possibly be of the foundations of it, as they are near the site where, according to Bleaze's plan of 1629, the Cross stood.

In 1730 and 1731 similar receipts are given for documents, etc., as that already set out.

Sir William Herbert, having succeeded, in 1594, to the Powys estates, which his father, Sir Edward Herbert, had purchased in 1585 from Edward Grey, the illegitimate son of Edward Grey, last Lord of Powys of that line, was made Knight of the Bath on the coronation of James I, and four years after the accession of Charles I, viz., in 1629, he was created "Baron Powys of Powys".[1] The elevation of the possessor of the Powys estates to the peerage or barony of

[1] This nobleman's title was "Powys", not Powis, as the subsequent creations were; but his successors spelt the name "Powis".

Powys is one of several illustrations (to which we shall hereafter allude) of the Powys estates being treated as a barony by tenure. The title and estates remained with direct descendants to the fourth generation, and the former became extinct in 1748, when William, the fifth Lord Powis (and third Earl, Marquess, and Duke of Powis) died without issue.

We next give two extracts from the Tensors' Book which relate to the erection of a pump "at the upper end of the town". No trace of its site now remains

Burgess de Pola.—At a Common Hall, upon due summons and warning, held this 30th day of Nov. 1731, it was then, at the Guildhall of the said Town and Burrough of Poole aforesaid, agreed that, whereas Henry Parry, sen., late one of the Bailiffs of the said Burrough, having paid the sum of £6 11s. 8d., being the balance of his account as Bailiff for the last year, into the hands of Rd. Tudor, the capital Bailiff for this present year, it is unanimously agreed that a pump be made and set up in sume convenient part of the upper end of the said Town such as shall hereafter be appointed by ye present Bailiffs and some two substantial persons inhabiting in the upper part of the said [Town], and that the said pump be erected and set up with all convenient speed.

Pool Borough. *7th December* 1733.

At an adjournment of a Common Hall lately held, and upon due summons and warning given by the Serjeants-at-Mace then given, it was then further agreed by the persons hereunder named that the above-mentioned £6 11s. 8d., now in the hands of the said Richard Tudor, be fourthwith paid by ye said Richard Tudor into the hands of Richard Pryce, Esq., Capital Bailiff of the said Borough, to be laid out and disposed of by the said Richard Pryce and Richard Edmunds, jun., in order to sink further in the place now begun, and to fix a pump there, and not elsewhere, being the place now agreed upon by the persons present, and whose names are hereunto subscribed. It is further agreed that a further sum of £4 5s. 11d., received from Mr. Richard Parry, be likewise laid out and disbursed by the said Bailiffs towards carrying on and perfecting the said work. And if soe happen that the above several sums, both amounting to the sum of £10 17s. 7d., be not sufficient to compleat the said work, that then in such a case that they may, out of the further perquisites owing from the said Town, lay out and disburse soe much thereof as may be sufficient to finish soe good an intended work.

Thos. Parry,	R. Tudor,	Pearce Morgan,
Rd. Edmunds,	Humph. Tudor,	R. Pryce,
Richd. Lloyd,	Griffith Griffith,	R. Edmunds,
W. Nichols,	Hen. Parry, jun.,	Edward Parry.

In 1734 the Corporation learnt that the county authorities were about to erect a house of correction in Montgomery, in lieu of the one which had time out of mind existed in the borough of Welshpool, and been maintained at the expense of the county. A public meeting, or common hall (as it was called), was convened, and a subscription raised, and the following minute appears in the Tensors' or Minute Book of the Corporation.

At a Common Hall held at the Guildhall of the said Borough, by adjournment, 17th September, 8th George II, 1734,
At which said Common Hall and General Meeting of the said Bailiffs and majority of the Aldermen and Burgesses then present it was then and there unanimously agreed that whereas the house of correction for the County of Montgomery which now is and stands in the Towne of Poole, within the said County, has been time out of mind, and far beyond the memory of any person and persons now living, errected, built, and continued there, at the expense, costs, and charges of the said County in generall, and has at several times, at the said County's charge, been amended and repaired. But now soe it is, that at a General Quarter Sessions, held at the Towne of Poole by the Justices of the Peace of the said County, an order was by them made for erecting a house of correction, omitting the place where; that omission gives some gentlemen an opportunity of believing that a new house of correction may, at the charge of the said County, be erected and built at Montgomery expressly contrary to the statute made in the 7th year of King James the First of gratious memory. We whose names are hereunto subscribed, the Bailiffs, Aldermen, and Burgesses present, being made sensible of the desire of removing the said house of correction, and erecting a new one in the said Towne of Montgomery, doe hereby unanimously for ourselves, and for absent Brethren, Aldermen, and Burgesses, agree that a *certiorari* be immediately sued out returnable at our next Great Sessions, to be held for the said County of Montgomery before

Her Majesty's Justices there, at the expense of the said Bailiffs, Aldermen, and Burgesses, and that the sum of £30 be forthwith, by a subscription of the said Bailiffs, Aldermen, and Burgesses, raised for removing of the said order, and for reinstating, rebuilding, and continuing the said house of correction in Pool aforesaid, as antiently it has been, and for utterly avoyding the puting the said County to such an unnecessary expense of erecting a new one, as intended in Montgomery. And wee further doe agree that the present Bailiffs do procure and make ready such a subscription paper forthwith, to be handed about to all Aldermen and Burgesses for the purpose aforesaid. As witness our hands the day and year aforesaid,

Richard Parry,	John Hughes,	Ed.Edmunds,sen.,
Edward Parry,	Adam Coupland,	Randle Parry,
Richard Evans,	Richd. Humphrey,	R. Tudor,
Humph. Tudor,	Humphy. Rogers,	Henry Parry,
R. Morgan,	William Howell,	Henry Parry, jun.,
John Owen,	Edward Griffiths,	Edward Parry,
Jno. Brisco,	R. Pryce,	Morris Jones,
Rees Jones,	R. Edmunds, jun.,	Richard Jones,
Edward Parry,	Thos. Parry,	John Cappock.
Humphrey Parry,		

The excitement must have been great to induce so many and influential burgesses to attend the meeting and to append their signatures, but we have not been able to ascertain whether the opposition proceeded any further. Where the building called the house of correction was, it is not easy at this time to ascertain. There is an old man of eighty[1] years old now living (1879), who says that his father told him that the old house of correction was on the site where the present house called "Park Lane" now stands. We are not able to say whether this house of correction is identical with the gaol, the site for which John de Charleton granted to the burgesses of La Pole by the document dated 24th April, 1 Henry IV (1400), which we have already printed.[2] If it be, the county authorities must have

---

[1] *Ex inf.*, Mr. S. Powell.
[2] See *Mont. Coll.*, vol. vii, p. 338.

built the house of correction upon a site belonging to the burgesses.

The next extract seems of considerable interest.

1735.—At a Common Hall, held on 1st day of April 1735, William Rogers of Poole, Malster, having on the 31st December last pulled up and carryed away two posts, one at the upper end of the Town Hall of the said Town of Pool, and the other at the lower end of the same hall (which had been there fixed to prevent carts and carriages from running under ye said hall), to the public damage of the corporation, the Bailiffs were authorized to commence an action against him for the trespass.

This shews the Town Hall to have been erected on pillars, so that carts and carriages could run underneath it. The Town Hall is called, in the previous minutes quoted, the Guildhall. It formerly stood on the eastern side of the High Street (now called Broad Street), the upper end or side being parallel with the south side of Upper Church Street (now called Hall Street). There is a plan of the site in a book in the possession of the corporation, entered by the late Mr. Mickleburgh in 1819, with the dimensions added by him in 1852. We reproduce this plan for comparison with Bleaze's plan of 1629.

The next extract discloses a commendable economy on the part of the corporation in utilising the old church clock, by setting it up in the Town Hall.

Borough of Poole.—At a Common Hall held at the Guildhall of the said Burrough the 2nd day of September, in 9th year of George II, 1735.

At which time and Common Hall and General Meeting of the Bailiffs, Aldermen, and Burgesses then present it was then and there by the persons then present agreed that the Old Clock, now in the Steeple belonging to the parish church of Pool, when taken down, to be disposed of by the Churchwardens, the Ordinary, and Parishioners, at a Vestry to be hereafter called, that it be bought by the Bailiffs, and afterwards be set up, by their consent and directions, in the Town Hall of the said Town, and that the price thereof be paid out of the perquisites of and arising from the said Town, as witness our hands the day and year above mentioned.

"A MAP OF THE TOWN HALL IN POOL.

WITH THE SCITE OF THE OLD TOWN HALL.

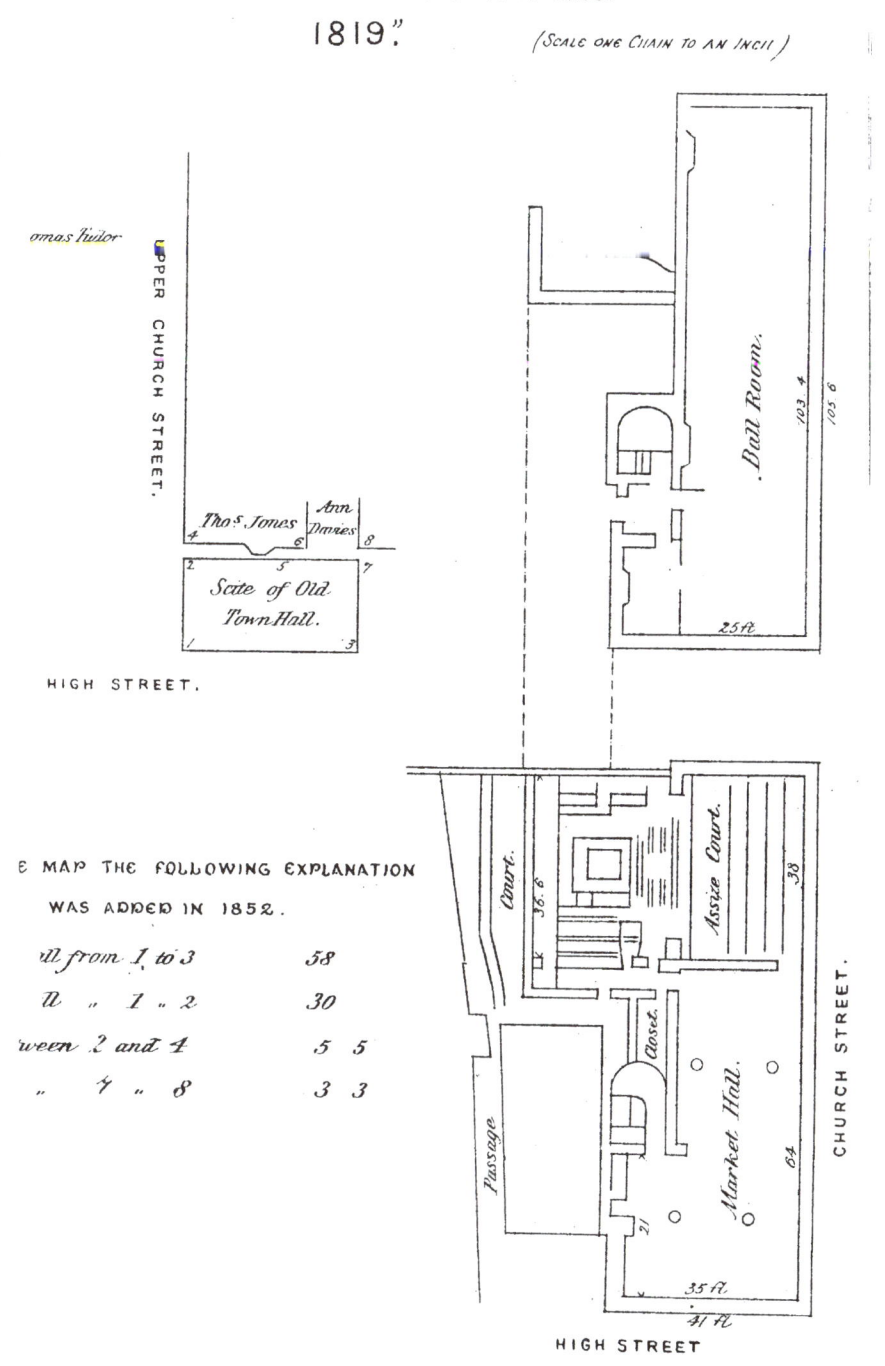

1819."

(Scale one chain to an inch)

omas Tudor

UPPER CHURCH STREET.

Thos. Jones | Ann Davies

Scite of Old Town Hall.

HIGH STREET.

Ball Room.

103.4
105.6
25 ft.

E MAP THE FOLLOWING EXPLANATION
WAS ADDED IN 1852.

ill from 1 to 3	58
1 " 2	30
'ween 2 and 4	5 5
" 4 " 8	3 3

Court.
36.6
Assize Court.
38
Closet.
Passage
Market Hall.
64
21
35 ft.
41 ft.

CHURCH STREET.

HIGH STREET

WELSH POOL.   173

Henry Parry, } *Bailiffs.*
Hen. Parry,
Rd. Edmunds, sen.,
Edward Parry,
Rd. Pryce,
Rd. Edmunds, jun.,
Humphrey Parry,
John Edmunds,
Richard Lloyd,

Rd. Jenkins,
John Rees,
David Endon,
Edward Griffiths,
Joseph Newell,
John Owen,
Humph. Francis,
William Rogers,
Pearce Morgan,
Thomas Davies.

In 1736, measures were taken for the safe custody of the corporation documents, which, however, did not prevent the loss of some of them at a future period.

At an adjournment of a Common Hall, held this 11th day of January 1736,

It was agreed by the Bailiffs and Aldermen then present, also the Burgesses then likewise present, that a good firme and strong coffer, or chest, be made of strong planks, with three iron hoops about it; and that there also be bought three locks, the keys whereof to keep, one of the keys to be kept in the hands of the Head Bailiff for the time being, the other key to be kept by ye Second Bailiff for the time being, and the third key to be likewise kept by the Town Clerk for the time being, soe that neither of the persons for the time being may hereafter ye one without the other have any access to it, whereby any further alteration be hereafter made in the Ile of Burgesses; and that a partition be made in some convenient place in the Jury Chamber, with a door and lock thereupon, for the greater security and safety of the charters and Iles of Burgesses; which coffer and partition is to be made, or ordered to be made, by the present Bailiffs within the space of two months next ensuing the date hereof, and the Charters and Iles to be put therein, and each key to be delivered up as aforesaid, to all which we whose names are hereunto subscribed are unanimously agreed, as witness our hands,

Aldermen.
Thos. Parry,
Henry Parry,
Hen. Parry, jun.,
Edwd. Parry,
R. Pryce,
Richd. Edmunds, jun.

Burgesses.
Humphrey Parry,
Jno. Peers,
Richard Humphreys,
John Roberts,
William Howell,
Hugh Meredith,
William Rogers,
Richd. Evans,

John Jones,
Will. Rogers,
David Humphreys,
John Owen,
Henry Parry, jun.,
Henry Owen,
Richard Edmunds,
Michl. Parry.

In 1738, in a *Trip to North Wales*[1] (London : J. Tarbuck), supposed to be written by a lawyer on circuit last century, the writer thus describes his hotel at Welshpool:—"The first town we stopp'd in was Welshpool in Montgomeryshire, where we were so commodiously lodged that it may be presumed *Marius*, when in the *Fens of Misturnum*, lay in a palace compared with this ill-favoured resemblance of an inn." If this account be true, it affords a striking contrast to the good hotel accommodation which Welshpool at present affords.

In 1739, the corporation were placed in a dilemma by the refusal and disability of the second bailiff to act as such in the election of the new bailiffs. The emergency was met by the chief bailiff being empowered to act in his stead, and, in the ballot, to take out the second ball, usually taken out by the second bailiff, as well as the first ball of wax, which it was his duty as capital bailiff to take out. It shows that great importance was attached to the regularity of the proceedings on the election of bailiffs, and that the corporation assumed that it possessed inherent powers sufficiently elastic and extensive to meet any ordinary emergency that may arise.

Burrough of Poole.—At the General Meeting of the Capital Bailiff, Aldermen, and Burgesses of the Town and Burrough of Pool aforesaid, in the County of Montgomery, at the Guildhall, in the said Town, on Saturday, the 29th day of September, in 13th George II, 1739,

We, the Capital Bailiff, and the majority of the Aldermen and Burgesses of the Burrough aforesaid, at the Common Hall there, held the said 29th day of September 1739, being Michaelmas Day, unanimously assembled together, do, upon the refusall and disability of John Peers, who was sworn to serve the office of second or other Bailiff for the said Burrough for one year, ending this present Michaelmas Day, and until another should be duly elected in his stead, to act or join in the electing or making of two new Bailiffs for the ensuing year, by one assent and consent agree and do hereby order that the names of all the Aldermen of the

---

[1] *Bygones*, 1871-3, p. 184.

said Towne or Burrough, or the names of as many of them as are here now present, being the time accustomed for election of officers of the said Town, shall be written in several billetts of paper or parchment by the Town Clerk for the time being, the Recorder for the time being not being present, which Town Clerk shall receive a corporall oath of the said Capitall Bailiff for the true usage thereof. And all the names so written by the said Town Clerk shall be severally rolled up together in baggs of wax of like quantity, and put into a close bagg with the names therein, which bagg shall be shaken by the Town Clerk, and delivered to the said Capitall Bailiff, who, turning up his sleeve, shall take out one ball, and the Alderman whose name doth therein appear shall name eight discreet, honest, and substantial Burgesses, commorants within the said Town, and likewise the said Capitall Bailiff, having his sleeve turned up, shall take out one other ball, and the Alderman whose name doth therein appear shall name seven honest, discreet, and substantial Burgesses, likewise inhabiting within the said Town; so that these fifteen Burgesses shall receive a corporall oath from the said Capital Bailiff that they, or nine of them at the least, shall nominate and appoint two of the most honestest, discreetest, and substantialest Aldermen, or Burgesses of the same Town and Borough to be Bailiffs for the year ensuing, which two Bailiffs shall be duely sworn by the said Capitall Bailiff, pursuant to such election, to serve in the office of Bailiffs for the said Burrough for one year ensueing as duly and effectually as when there were two Bailiffs duly qualified and did each of them take up a separate ball or lott, in order to the electing and swearing of Bailiffs of the said Corporation. And that the election of Serjeants and Catchpoles for the said Burrough be as hath been heretofore used and accustomed.

W. Powell,	Richard Powell,	Rd. Cappock,
Henry Parry,	Thomas Parry, Town	Pearce Morgan,
Hen. Parry, jun.	Clerk,	John Evans,
Ed. Parry,	Rd. Edmunds, sen.,	Richd. R. Price,
Rd. Edmunds, jun.,	Heny. Parry,	his mark,
	Thos. Cappock,	John Jervis,
	John Edmunds,	Robt. Powell,
	Humphrey Parry,	John Humphreys,
	Cesar Griste,	Richard Lloyd.

Again, in 1742, the recorder failed to make his appearance at the time of election, and to perform the duty that had been imposed upon him of making up the balls of wax. The corporation, by the following order, wisely directed the town clerk to perform this duty for the recorder.

At a Common Hall and General Meeting held this 6th day of April 1742, by Michael Parry, Esq., the surviving Bailiff, the Aldermen, and Burgesses of the said Town and Burrough, upon due notice and summons by the Serjeants-at-Mace of the said Burrough.

By virtue of an order made the 19th day of May, in 37th year of Elizabeth, &c., for the election of a Bayliffe of the sayd Town or Borough, in the room of one Humphrey Owen, gent., then deceased, wherein it was then ordered that the balls of wax therein mentioned should be made up by the then Recorder of the said Town and Burrough, as by the said order is directed. And whereas the Right Hon. Pryce, Lord Viscount Hereford, now Recorder of the said Town and Burrough, is now absent, and not ready to attend for the purpose aforesaid, It is thereupon ordered that Thomas Parry, gent., Town Clerk of the said Town and Burrough, shall, at the next Common Hall and Generall Meeting to be held for the said Town and Burrough, on the 20th day of this instant April, make up the said balls of wax as the said order doth direct for the purpose therein mentioned, in order to proceed to the election of a Bayliff in the room of Griffith Griffiths, late one of the Bayliffs of the said Town and Burrough, now deceased. The which being done shall be as effectual to all intents and purposes as if the said Recorder was personally present. In witness whereof we have hereunto set our hands this 6th day of April 1742.

Aldermen.	*Burgesses.*	
Thomas Parry, Town Clerk,	Humphrey Parry,	Gilbert Jones,
Rd. Edmunds, sen.,	Charles Lloyd,	Will. Rogers,
Henry Parry,	Wm. Nicholls,	John Edwards.
Hen. Parry, jun.,	John Edmunds,	Michl. Parry.
Richard Powell,	John Owens,	
Edward Parry,	Olliver Evans,	
Rd. Edmunds, jun.,	William Lloyd,	
Richard Lloyd.	Samuel Bowdler,	
	Edwd. Tudor,	

On a house situate in Church Street (formerly called Bull Street), and opposite the Bull Inn, there is an inscription " Briscoe, W. S., 1742", which we think it well to record, although we are not able to identify the owner of the initials.

In 1744, the sheriff of the county must have shown an intention of encroaching upon the privileges of the borough, and action was taken by the corporate authorities to prevent such a trespass. The corporation claimed exclusive jurisdiction within the borough, and resented the intromission of the county magistrates. The Municipal Corporation Commissioner thought the charter of James I. did not contain any non-intromittent clause in and by which the magistrates of the county were expressly mentioned and excluded. But there is no doubt there is a clause prohibiting the sheriffs of the county from intruding or entering into the borough without the license of the bailiffs, and this clause has been referred to as granting a jurisdiction to the borough justices, exclusive of the county magistrates. The Commissioner thought it was plain that there was no reason whatever in this borough to allow the county magistrates to intromit themselves. He suggested that the charters prior to that of James I. may possibly have had the effect of granting an exclusive jurisdiction. But these earlier charters were granted to the borough before Montgomeryshire was constituted shire-ground, and had received a commission of the peace from the British Crown appointing a county magistracy; and, consequently, in this abnormal state of things, it is not easy to predicate what was the effect of these ancient charters.

At a Common Hall and General Meeting held the 10th day of July 1744, by the Bayliffs, Recorder, Aldermen and Burgesses of the said Burrough, upon due notice and summons given by the Serjeants-at-Mace of the said Burrough, or one of them.

We, the Bayliffs, Recorder, and the majority of the Aldermen and Burgesses of the Burrough aforesaid, there and then present, do unanimously assent and consent, agree, and do hereby order, that in case the present or any future Sheriff for the County of Montgomery do at any time or times hereafter execute any precept or process whatsoever within the

Burrough, contrary to the charter granted to the said Burrough, without the leave and consent of the Bayliffs of the said Burrough for the time being, or on their defect or refusal, that such Sheriff shall be sued and prosecuted for his so doing, at the expense of the Corporation, provided that every such Sheriff shall, soon after he shall be sworn into his office, have a copy of the clause contained in the charter, whereby the Sheriff is prohibited from executing any authority within the said Burrough, delivered to him by the Town Clerk of the said Burrough for the time being. And that no person or persons whatsoever shall at any time hereafter (not being an hereditary Burgess of the said Burrough) be admitted or sworn as Burgess of the said Burrough unless such person or persons to be admitted or sworn shall first respectively pay into the hands of the Bayliffs for the time being, or one of them, the sum of Five pounds of lawful money of Great Britain to the use of the said Corporation. And that all other person and persons not paying the said sum of £5, as aforesaid, who shall be elected or sworn, such election shall be void.

Jno. Peers, } *Bailiffs.*
Richard Lloyd,
Hereford, *Recorder.*

Richard Mytton,
W. Powell,
Richard Edmunds, sen.,
John Davies,
Henry Parry,
Edward Parry,
Rd. Edmunds, jun.,
Hen. Parry, jun.,
Richard Powell,
Michl. Parry,
William Nicholls,
} *Aldermen.*

Gab. Wynne,
George Devereux,
Edwd. Devereux,
Richd. Mytton, jun.,
Richd. Cappock,
× Thomas Jenking's Marke.
William Nicholls,
Charles Rocke,
George Jones,
David Parry,
Wm. Owen,
Thomas Cappock,
John Owen,
Brockwell Griffiths,
} *Burgesses.*

In 1745, the feeling that members of the Corporation should be residents, seems to have increased in strength, and an order was made that a non-resident alderman, "drawn out of the bag", should have no benefit of the lot unless he would reside within the borough and take the office of bailiff the next year; and if he refused, that another alderman should be elected who should be entitled to the benefit of the toll, or, if a resident burgess were elected, the toll should go to the use of the Corporation. The reason for making a distinction in this respect between an alderman and a burgess is not apparent. It will be observed, the office of alderman is treated as one of emolument,—"the benefit of the toll".

Burrough of Poole, County of Montgomery, to wit.—At a Common Hall and General Meeting held the 17th day of September 1745, by the Bailiffs, Aldermen, and Burgesses of the said Burrough, upon due notice and summons given by the Serjeants-at-Mace of the said Burrough, or one of them.

We, the Bailiffs, and the majority of the Aldermen and Burgesses of the Borough aforesaid, then and there present, do unanimously assent, consent, and agree, and do hereby order that every Alderman of the said Burrough residing out of the same who shall appear at the time of election of the Bailiffs of the said Burrough for the future, and shall happen to be drawn out of the bagg, such Aldermen shall have no benefit of the said lot unless he will reside within the said Burrough for the ensuing year, and take upon him the office of Bailiff of the said Burrough; and in case he shall refuse to do that, one of the Aldermen residing within the said Burrough shall be elected and sworn Bailiff in the room and stead of such Alderman so refusing to reside within the said Burrough as aforesaid, and shall be entitled to receive the benefitt and advantage of the Toll of the said Corporation for that year. And in case any one or more of the Burgesses resident within the said Burrough shall be elected Bailiff or Bailiffs, instead of such person or persons who shall refuse to reside as aforesaid, that then the profitts of the Toll shall be paid and applyed for the use of the said Corporation for that year.

Richard Edmunds,
R. Tudor,
Hen. Parry,
Hen. Parry, jun.,
Edward Parry,
Michl. Parry,
Richard Lloyd,
Jno. Peers,
} *Aldermen.*

Jno. Briscoe,
Roger Bowdler,
Gilbert Jones,
} *Burgesses.*

In 1748, upon the death of William, fifth Lord Powis (also third Earl, Marquess, and Duke), he left all the Powis estates, including Powis Castle and Pool Town Manor, unto Henry Arthur Herbert, who, as nearest kinsman to the last Lord Herbert of Chirbury, of the Ribbesford branch, had in 1743 been created Lord Herbert of Chirbury; and in the same year he was created Baron Powis, Viscount Ludlow, and Earl of Powis, which is a second illustration of the title accompanying the Powis estates, as if the latter were considered a barony by tenure.

In three years afterwards, viz., in 1751, Lord Herbert, then Earl of Powis, married Barbara, sole daughter and heir of Edward, only brother of William, fifth Lord of Powis. But his honours only continued for one generation, viz., until the death of his son, George Henry Arthur, Earl of Powis, s.p. in 1801, as we shall subsequently see.

In 1750 the following minute occurs:—

At a Common Hall held in the Guildhall of the said Burrough, upon due summons and warning given before Richard Tudor and William Coupland, Esqs., Bailiffs of the said Burrough, and the Aldermen and Burgesses of the said Burrough, whose names are hereunto subscribed, the 22nd day of May, in the year of Lord 1750,

Whereas the Recordership of the said Burrough became vacant on the death of late Right Honourable Price, Lord Viscount Hereford, deceased, late Recorder of the said Burrough, and no person has been duly and legally elected in his stead. Now, therefore, we whose names are hereunto subscribed, being the Bailiffs and the majority present of the Aldermen and Burgesses of the said Burrough, met and assembled at the said Common Hall, do hereby nominate, elect, and appoint Edward Kynaston of Hardwicke, in the County of Salop, Esq. (Member of Parliament of the said County of Montgomery), to be Recorder of the said Burrough.

Bailiffs.
R. Tudor,
Wm. Coupland,

Aldermen.
W. Powell,
Richard Powell,
Edwd. Parry,
Richard Edmunds,
Michl. Parry,
Richd. Mytton,
Thos. Lloyd,
Price Jones,
Richard Lloyd,

Burgesses.
Henry Wynne,
John Colley,
Henry Parry, jun.,
Humphrey Thomas,
David Parry,
Jno. Pugh,
William Owen,
John Morgan,
Wm. Lloyd,
Thos. Ffelton,
Dd. Jones,
  The Mark of
Samuel "B." Bowdler.

In 1748, there is a similar minute appointing Mr. Kynaston, but it is not signed by the bailiffs and majority of aldermen and burgesses. The name of Mr. Kynaston is written on an erasure. This appointment must have failed in some particular, for the above minute states "no person had been duly and legally elected in his stead".

It seems fitting to record the following instance of longevity in this borough:—"On January 26, 1752, Jonathan Evans, near Welshpool, died aged 117. He left a son aged 91 and a daughter aged 87." (*Gentleman's Magazine,* 1752.)

In 1755, the first step was taken for the enclosure of Pool Common. The following minute appears:—

Borough of Poole.—At a Common Hall held in the Guildhall of the said Borough, upon due summons and warning given by the Serjeants-of-Mace of the said Borough before Henry Parry and John Pugh, Esqs., Bailiffs of the said Borough, and the Aldermen and Burgesses of the said Borough whose names are hereunto subscribed, the 7th day of January 1755.

We, the Bailiffs, and the majority of the Aldermen and Burgesses of the said Borough, then and there present, do unanimously assent, consent, and agree, and do hereby order that the part of the Common called Gwern y Goe, which belongs to the resiant Burgesses within the Towne of Poole, in the said Borough, be with all convenient speed inclosed and sett to the best advantage by the present Bailiffs, and that the rents and profits thereof (after the expense of inclosing the same shall be discharged) shall from time to time, as the same shall become due and payable, be paid into the hands of the Bailiffs of the said Borough for the time being, to be by them applied and disposed of for the public use and benefit of the Corporation.

Henry Parry, jun., } *Bailiffs.*
Jon. Pugh,
Richd. Edmunds, } *Aldermen.*
Jno. Peers,

Thomas Ffelton,
John Morgan,
Humph. "H." Thomas,
Rich. "H." Humphrey, his Mark,
Elijah Jones.

In 1755, a curious robbery was perpetrated at Powis Castle and Buttington Hall. Four persons were tried for stealing lead from Powis Castle and Buttington Hall. Neither of these residences could have been constantly occupied, and probably Buttington Hall (which, in Grose's *Antiquities,* and there alone, so far as we can discover, is called " Buttington Castle", see Vol. vii, p. 62*), was then falling into disrepair. The tradition in the neighbourhood is that it at one time contained no less than thirty rooms of considerable size. At present it is divided into two houses, not in actual contact with each other ; and in part of the stables, of late years taken down and rebuilt, there was a Gothic arch, evidently part of an Early English ecclesiastical building. The roof, being of lead, would evidence it being a mansion of importance.

An account of the robbery, and of the trial of the thieves and receivers, is contained in the following letter from Mr. George Morris of Pentrenant to the Earl of Powis.—

"Pentrenant, *March 26th,* 1755.

" My Lord,—As your Lordship was pleased to order me to be employed in the prosecuting the severall persons concerned in stealing and receiving the lead from Powis Castle and Buttington Hall, I thought it a duty incumbent on me to give your Lordship a detail of the whole transactions that happened at the Sessions in relation to that affaire, which ended this morning. It appeared on the face of the examination that no less than eight persons have been concerned in the felony, four whereof were stealers, and most of them fled, and four receivers, amongst the latter of which one of the present Bayliffs of Pool happens to be one. This being the case, I was obliged to advise with Counsel, and to get severall indictments drawn according to the nature of the offences, which were all found by the Grand Jury (Mr. George Devereux being foreman) except one against one Ratcliffe, a clockmaker of Poole, and how that escaped I am at a loss to know. One of the felons who was imprisoned for stealing the lead from Buttington Hall took his tryall with one of the receivers, and were both acquitted for want of proving the property of the lead in your Lordship, as laid in the indictment. The Counsell on behalf of the prisoners insisting that Buttington Hall, from whence the lead was taken, was only a Trust Estate, and consequently the property of the lead was not vested in your Lordship. Your

Agent, Mr. Clough of the Royal Oak, was called upon to prove that fact. The rest of the persons indicted for receiving stolen goods have entered into recognisances of £200 a piece, with sufficient sureties, to appear and take their tryalls at next Sessions, the Chief Justice having consented to baile them on these terms. I assure your Lordship that no pains or care were wanting to convict the offenders, having taken the ablest Counsell's advice on the circuit. I am apprehensive more villainy of this kind will be yet discovered. . . I am, etc.,

"To the Right Hon. The Earl of Powis, GEORGE MORRIS.
11, Dover Street, London."

The following minute occurs respecting the enclosure of Pool Common, for which the Earl of Powis and the Corporation petitioned the House of Commons :—[1]

---

[1] The following is a copy of the Petition :—

"*To the Honourable the Commons of Great Britain in Parliament assembled.*

"The Petition of the Right Honourable Henry Arthur, Earl of Powis, and the Bailiffs, Aldermen, and Burgesses of the Town of Pool, in the County of Montgomery.

"Sheweth,—That there are within the Manors of Llanverchidol and Street Marcel, alias Street Marshall, in the parishes of Pool and Guilsfield, in the County of Montgomery, severall parcells of Moor, Common, or waste ground, called Pool Common, containing in the whole 156 acres, or thereabouts.

"That your Petitioner, Henry Arthur, Earl of Powis, is Lord of the Manor of Llanverchidol and Street Marcel, alias Street Marshall, in the said parishes and county, and as such is seized of or entitled to the soil of the said Common, Moor, or waste ground, as being parcell of, or belonging to, the said Manors.

"That your Petitioners, the Bailiffs, Aldermen, and Burgesses of the Borough of Pool, in the said County of Montgomery, are entitled to common of pasture therein daily for their cattle of all kinds.

"That the said Moor, Common, and waste grounds, so long as they lye open and uninclosed, produce little profit to your Petitioners, who are the sole proprietors and owners thereof, and, in their present situation, incapable of improvement.

"That your Petitioners are desirous that the said Moor, Commons, and waste grounds may be divided and inclosed, and that a specifick part thereof may be assigned and allotted to and between your Petitioners in proportion to their rights and interests in the said premises.

"That, although the making such inclosure, division, and allottment, will tend greatly to the advantage of your Petitioners, and be

In a Common Hall, held in the Guildhall of the said Borough, upon due summons and warning, given by the Sergeants-at-Mace of the said Borough, before Richard Edmunds and Humphrey Lloyd, Esq., Bailiffs of the said Borough, and the Aldermen and Burgesses of the said Borough whose names are hereunto subscribed, 29 June 1760.

We, the Bailiffs, Aldermen, and Burgesses of the said Borough, then and there present, and being all the persons as members of the said Borough then assembled, do unanimously assent, consent, and agree, and do hereby order that that part of the Common called Gwern y goe, which belongs to the Burgesses of the said Borough, be, with all convenient speed, enclosed, sett, let out, and farmed to the best advantage by the present Bailiffs of the said Borough, and their successors for the time being; and that the rents and profits thereof (after the expense of enclosing the same, and all other expenses incident thereon shall be discharged), shall from time to time, as the same shall become due and payable, be paid into the hands of the Bailiffs of the said Borough for the time being, to be by them applyed and disposed of for the public use and benefit of the said Corporation and Borough, and to be by them accounted for from time to time at the time of paying their general accounts, when they are discharged of their respective offices. And it is hereby further ordered and agreed that such inclosures be made by and with the consent and approbation of the Right Hon. the Earl of Powis, as Lord of the Mannor, to whom the soil thereof belongs, he having a seventh part allotted him thereout for such his consent and confirmation of this order and agreement. In testimony whereof we have hereunto subscribed our names.

Richard Edmunds } *Bailiffs.*
W. Lloyd

The mark of
" H "
John Hughes.

---

a great improvement of the respective interests and properties in the said Moor, Common, and waste lands, and be of public utility, yet, as the same cannot be effectually made and established to answer the intentions of the parties interested in the same without the aid of an Act and authority of Parliament,

" Your Petitioners, therefore, humbly pray that leave may be given for bringing in a Bill for dividing, inclosing, assigning, and allotting the said Moor, Common, and waste grounds, or such other relief in the premisses as to this Honourable House shall seem meet.

" And your Petitioners shall ever pray, etc."

Jno. Rees, *Town Clerk.*

R. Tudor
Wm. Coupland
Henry Parry, jun.
Jno. Pugh
Thos. Briscoe
} *Aldermen.*

The mark of
Samuel " B." Bowdler.
John Edwards, jun.

Witnesses to signing the marks of John Hughes and Samuel Bowdler
Daniel Turner
Francis Adams.

The site of the Market Hall[1] is shown in Bleaze's plan of 1629 to have been in the centre of the street then called "High Street", a little to the north of the site of the present Cross Pump. It seems that over it there was a large room, which was used for the Great Sessions and other Courts, and for the Flannel Market.

This ancient building was in a frail condition for some years, but, in the year 1758, matters came to a crisis. The *Gentleman's Magazine* of that year, under the date of August 11, 1758, p. 391, records that :—

"At Poole, in the County of Montgomery, whilst the Court of Great Session was sitting in the hall there, *over the market place*, an alarm was given that the floor gave way, which occasioned so great crowding at the door and stairs that six of the common people were trampled to death, and many others bruised."[2]

A curious incident which occurred on this occasion has been handed down. An old lady[3] used to relate

[1] Mr. A. Howell and Mr. D. P. Owen, in their printed statements, seem to have taken the "Market House" and the "Town Hall" as being one and the same building; but Bleaze's plan of 1629, and also the minute subsequently quoted, clearly show that they were distinct buildings.

[2] In the Register of burials of Pool the following entries occur :—
1758. Aug. 12. Mary Lewis of . . . .
" " 12. Edward Williams.
" " 12. Jane Jones.
" " 13. Shuzan Robetts.
No further entries occur in August. Probably these were four of the people killed on this occasion.

[3] The grandmother of Mr. Richard Williams of Celynog, Newtown, a member of the Powys-land Club.

that a ladder was placed against the wall for the Judge to get down out of the ruinous building. A man stepped upon the ladder, and, when remonstrated with for his rudeness, replied that his life was as valuable to him as the Judge's, and persisted in descending first. The name of this unmannerly person has not been preserved.

This accident ultimately led to the old building being pulled down. At a Common Hall, held on September 29th, 1761, it was reported that the Market Hall was in so bad a state that it was ordered to be pulled down, and the market removed to the lower end of the Guildhall.

The Guildhall, which occupied part of the site of the present Town Hall, was afterwards used for holding the Great Sessions, and other Courts (temporary structures for which purpose being put up every time these Courts were held), the Common Hall, and the Flannel, Grain, and other Markets.

Borough of Pool, in the County of Montgomery, to wit.—
At a Common Hall held at the Guildhall of the said Borough, the 29th day of September 1761, before Price Jones and John Pugh, Esqs., Bailiffs of the said Borough.

Ordered that the Corn Market for the future be kept under the Guildhall of the Town of Pool in the said Borough, and that the Flannel Market be kept in the upper part of the said Guildhall, and that the remaining part of the Market House which is now standing be removed to the lower end of the said Guildhall, to be made use of for selling, and exposing for sale, all other things (except corn, cattle, and grain) brought to the said Town of Pool for that purpose; and it is hereby further ordered that the timber, tiles, and other materials of the late Market House be sold and disposed of, and the money arising from such sale be laid out and employed for the public use of the Corporation and Borough of Pool aforesaid; and it is hereby further ordered that Mr. Wm. Pritchard of Shrewsbury shall be employed to view and survey the state and condition of the said Guildhall, and that the expense of his survey, and the methods by him directed for securing the safety of the said Guildhall and edifice, or the repair thereof, be paid out of the money contributed or subscribed towards the repair of the said Guildhall.

It is convenient here to mention that in the Manorial Roll for the manor of Pool Town for 1766 the inhabitants were presented,—

"For not repairing that part of the street adjoining on the side to the Market House, and opposite to the dwelling houses of Humphrey Meredith, Lewis Lewis, and John Lloyd, containing fifteen yards in length and three in width."

This presentment shows that, even in 1766, the Market House was not wholly removed, and also, what is important to note, that its dimensions from north to south were 45 feet, and that it was so wide that it occupied all the present street except 9 feet, the width of the roadway, which the inhabitants had omitted to repair. How the traffic of the Town could have been conducted through so narrow a gut in its principal thoroughfare it is difficult to conceive. But the fact of there having been intermediate buildings, which have been removed, explains how Welshpool came to have so fine and wide a street as Broad Street, the equal to which few country towns can boast of.

On the house now occupied by Mr. John Sayce there is an inscription, $\frac{M M}{1808}$, the initials of Margaret Meredith, which identifies the house with that of Humphrey Meredith, her predecessor, mentioned in the presentment.

Mr. William Parry, formerly of the Farm, died a few years ago, at Welshpool, at a great age (about 96, it is believed). His memory went back to a distant period.

He used to relate that an old building stood in the middle of Broad Street, opposite the site of the *Plough Inn*,[1] which was like an umbrella, being supported by one large piece of timber in the centre, and that the prop of timber was sawn through one night by some mischievous persons, whereby the structure fell. This,

[1] It has ceased to be an inn, but it is the house now occupied by Mr. John Sayce, and formerly by his maternal grandfather, Mr. Roderick.

probably, was the last remnant of the old Market Hall.[1]

Shortly before 1762, a substantial freeholder, a resident of one of the out townships, situate in the borough, died, and we are enabled to give an inventory of his effects and the amounts at which they were valued, which is interesting as showing the then value of the different kinds of stock and the nature and value of the furniture then used.

AN INVENTORY of all and singular the goods and chattells, rights, creditts, and personal estate of J. D., late of D., in the county of Montgomery, Esq., deceased, taken and appraised by us whose names are subscribed, this 24th day of Novr., in the year of our Lord, 1762.

	£	s.	d
Cattle—			
Two oxen	9	0	0
Twelve bullocks	30	10	0
One hundred and twenty-two sheep	20	6	8
Two oxen sold at Welshpool fayre	11	14	6
One black mare	3	10	0
One black filley	2	15	0
One chesnut colt	2	15	0
One bay colt	2	15	0
One black horse	3	10	0
One sow and ten pigs	2	10	0
Implements of husbandry	6	6	6
Wheat in the barn and in a stack	14	0	0
Barley unthreshed	7	10	0
Oats unthreshed	6	0	0
In the room over the large parlour—			
Two feather beds, bedsteads, bed cloathes and hangings	6	6	0
One oak beaureau	2	5	0
Two looking-glasses	0	7	0
One chair	0	1	6
On the staircase—			
One clock and case	3	3	0
Two chairs and a small square table	0	6	6
Room over the kitchen—			
One feather bed, cloaths, bedstead, and hangings	3	3	0
One chest of drawers, square table, and three chairs	1	10	0
One close stool	0	4	0

---

[1] Mr. William Parry used to say that he remembered the time when there were no glass shop windows in Welshpool. The front of the shops were "bulkheads", opening with folding shutters, one falling down and the other lifting up.

	£	s.	d.
In the closet—			
One hanging press and a piece of ticking	1	5	0
In the yellow room—			
One feather bed, bed cloaths, bedstead, and hangings	4	10	0
Three chairs, one square table, and glass	1	0	0
Room over the pantry—			
One feather bed, bed cloaths, and hangings	1	10	0
Three chests and three chairs	0	14	0
Twenty-three pair of sheets and table linen	3	15	0
In the garret—			
Two feather beds, bedsteads, and bed cloaths	2	5	0
One table and two chairs	0	2	0
In the large parlour—			
Twelve chairs	2	8	0
Two tables and a corner cupboard	0	14	0
In the kitchen—			
One dresser, shelves, and other kitchen furniture	4	0	0
Brass furniture, copper, and tin	3	15	0
Pewter	5	0	0
Iron jack and other iron furniture	1	10	0
Two tables, six chairs, one salt-box, and skreen	1	2	0
In the little parlour—			
Four chairs, two tables, and a corner cupboard	0	14	0
In the room over the skullery—			
One feather bed, bed cloaths, and bedstead	0	15	0
In the pantry—			
One dresser and square table, and four chairs	0	9	6
One square table and drawers	0	2	6
In the dairy and brewhouse—			
One copper and brewing vessels, etc.	3	0	0
In the cellar—			
Barrels, pails, and butter tubs	1	2	0
Plate—			
One silver tankard	4	10	0
One half-pint	1	10	0
Eight silver spoons, two salts	3	0	0
Six teaspoons and tongs	0	15	0
One silver watch	2	0	0
One cream jug	0	10	0
Six gold rings and two ditto, enameled	3	12	0

Edward Parry.
Richard Dixon.

In four years afterwards there was some litigation respecting his children, and a commission was held for taking evidence therein.

The following is a copy of the bill of expenses of the witnesses at a Welshpool inn :—

A bill of expenses at the Castle Inn for the commission in the Chancery cause of D.'s infants against S. :—

		£	s.	d.
1766.	Breakfast for four gentlemen	0	2	0
April 16.	Dinner for seven	0	7	0
	Ditto for seven witnesses	0	3	6
	Sixteen quarts of ale	0	5	4
	Red wine	0	2	0
	White ditto	0	2	6
	Supper for five	0	2	6
	White wine wey	0	1	0
11.	Breakfast for five gentlemen	0	2	6
	Dinner for four	0	4	0
	Dinner for five witnesses	0	2	6
	Hay	0	0	3
	Supper for five	0	2	6
	Fifteen quarts of ale	0	5	0
	Four pints of negus	0	4	8
	Ale for gentlemen	0	0	6
	Wey	0	1	0
12.	Breakfast for five gentlemen	0	2	6
	Dinner for three ditto	0	3	0
	Dinner for three witnesses	0	1	6
	Supper for five	0	2	6
	Eighteen quarts of ale	0	6	0
	Seven tankards of negus	0	8	2
	Three quarts of ale upstairs	0	1	0
	Wey	0	1	0
13.	Breakfast for four	0	2	0
	Pen, ink, and paper	0	2	0
	Ale	0	1	0
	Wine	0	1	0
	Horses, hay, and corn	0	13	6
	For the commission room	0	7	6
	For servants	0	4	0
		£5	5	5

Received the 3rd of June 1766 of Mr. S. the full contents of ye within bill for ye use of my brother, Mr. William Jones, by me, Mary Jones.

£5 : 5 : 5.

In the Manorial Courts (which, it may be incidentally mentioned, were generally held at the *Royal Oak*, which shows the antiquity of the name of that hotel),[1] by presentments, the sanitary and public regulations of the town were enforced. In 1763, by the Manorial Roll of Pool Town Manor, there were the following presentments.

"The Inhabitants of this Town for not repairing the causeway and highway leading from the dwelling house of Ann Rowlands down to the River Severn.

"The Inhabitants of this Manor for not repairing one half the bridge across the River Lledan, leading from the *Bull* to the Church of Pool, which ought to be repaired by such inhabitants.

"The same for not repairing half the bridge from John Humphrey's shop

"The same for not repairing that part of the highway leading from the *Lower Sun* to the Cross, and from Llangollen Bridge to the *Bull*."

Also, in 1764,—

"The Serjeants of Mace present John Ward and Edward Jones for throwing muck and rubbish in Sealing Lane, leading to the dwelling house of Peter Turner, to the nuisance of His Majesty's subjects passing that way.

"They also present that three great stones now fixed in the ground opposite the house, the property of Mrs. Anne Lloyd, are a great nuisance, and ought to be removed by her."

These presentments are given as examples of frequent occurrence.

In the Manorial Roll for Teirtreff Manor, for 1763-4, the inhabitants of Welsh Town were presented and amerced in £5, "for not keeping in repair half a bridge

[1] Jane Gilmour, who is ninety-three years old, being born on St. David's day, 1788, states that her mother, who died thirty years ago in her ninety-eighth year, used to say that she remembered a large oak tree standing in the middle of the street near where the Cross Pump stands, from which tree the *Royal Oak* Inn was named. The *Royal Oak*, she says, was formerly kept by Mr. Keate, afterwards by Mr. Colley, and afterwards by Mr. and Mrs. Whitehall, both of whom had been in the service of the Earl of Powis—the former as master of the horse, and the latter as lady's maid. When their eldest daughter was born, the Duchess of Northumberland and Lady Harriet Wynn (both of them daughters of the earl) stood as her sponsors, and, in commemoration of the occasion, the Duke of Northumberland sent an emblazonment of his coat of arms, which is now in the *Royal Oak* Inn.

over the Lledan, leading from the Town Hall by John Humphrey's garden wall to Close Bach".

In a book entitled "*A Survey of the Roads of England and Wales*—showing all the cities, towns, villages, etc.; with distances; engraved by Emanuel Bowen; with an accurate historical and topographical description of the cities, towns, and places of note; with maps of the counties; by John Owen (1764)"—there is a map of Buttington Bridge, which shows two streams into which the River Severn was divided at this point, there being another bridge shown near the church. Possibly the little brook now there may have been at one time a larger stream, and been a branch of the Severn.

In 1765 (September 29), John Pugh and Richard Edmunds were drawn up to serve as bailiffs, and, inasmuch as a sufficient number of burgesses did not appear to elect them according to the constitution of the borough, the court was adjourned to December 7. There is no record of its having subsequently taken place. The next entry is in 1765, when the formal receipt is given for the charter, bye-laws, etc.; but the maces, etc., are not mentioned.

The entries in the Tensors' Book from 1761 are not so regular as in previous years, but an account current is begun, showing the receipts and payments of each bailiff in each successive year.

The first account is that of Henry Parry, Esq., Capital Bailiff for the year beginning at Michaelmas 1761, and ending at Michaelmas 1762.

In the receipts the following items occur:—

"March 1762. Received for slates of the Market House of Mr. Yearsley - - £1 10 6
18 October. For bricks in arches - - - 1 1 0
From Mr. Copeland for the old timber of the Market House - 1 11 6
To Richard Davies for taking down the walls - - - - 0 1 6"

From these items we may infer that the Market House was then being gradually removed.

There are other items of payment showing that temporary arrangements were made for the accommodation required for the holding of the Great Sessions, such as,—

"To Dixon for putting up and taking down the Court - - - - - - - £0 15 0
To Dixon for erecting and taking down the Court against the Session - - - - 0 15 0
To boards for the use of the Hall - - - 2 10 0"

The following item appears in this account:—
"For wine for the Judge, and money given the Servants - - - - - - - £3 8 0"

This is continued throughout the accounts, and was a burden upon the slender corporate funds. We will notice it occasionally, and it will be seen that in more recent days it greatly increased.

The accounts were examined by the incoming bailiff, and sworn to by the outgoing bailiff, and were sometimes signed by several burgesses. The receipts and payments were small in this year, the former being £9 3s. 8½d., and the latter £12 6s. 10d., leaving an adverse balance of £3 13s. 1½d. The receipts afterwards much increased.

In 1765, similar items occur for putting up the court, and for wine for judge. The corporation servants' clothing also.

"Sept. 15. Paid Edw. Rowland for making the Bellman's cloathes - - - £0 8 0
" 18. Paid Mr. Fleming for Bellman's cloathes - - - - - 2 5 0"

This branch of expenditure afterwards considerably increased.

In 1764,—

"April 24. Paid Mr. Draycot for a piece of Timber for the use of the Market House Pump - - - - - - £0 4 6
Paid Mr. Price for Posts for guarding the Market House Pump - - 0 2 6"

These items probably relate to the pump authorised

to be erected in 1731. The rents (£45 4s.) of the common lately enclosed, came into this account, and the Town Hall produced £5, and "4d. received for an old crank from the Market House", swell the receipts to £50 4s. 4d. But an item of disbursement appears of £31 7s., payment to Lord Powis of three years' interest on £224 2s. 7d., the expenses of the enclosure.

In 1768,—

" Paid for two dozen of wine for the Judge - £2 8 0
    Paid to the Judge's Servants - - - 1 0 0
    Paid for treating the Burgesses at Michaelmas 2 0 0"

What wine it was is not stated, but the price is not extravagant, £1 4s. per dozen.

In 1761, John Pugh was appointed treasurer.

In 1769, John Wesley visited Welshpool, and met with a sorry reception. The bailiffs were applied to for permission for him to preach in the Town Hall. One of them was willing to grant him leave, but the other refused. He therefore quitted the town without his voice being heard therein, and went on to Newtown, where he met with a welcome.[1]

The following is an extract from John Wesley's diary, under date September 1765 :—

"Monday, 23. The next day I spent at Shrewsbury. Wednesday, 25. I took horse a little after four, and, about two, preached in the Market House in Llanidloes, two or three and forty miles from Shrewsbury."

He would then pass through Welshpool, and possibly it was the occasion above referred to.

On January 30, 1773, a society " of young men, inhabitants of Welshpool and places adjacent", was established and called the "Young Society". The articles of the society had the following exordium :—

" Whereas it hath been and is a laudable custom in this kingdome of Great Britain for artists and others charitably disposed to meet together and form themselves into societies to promote friendship and Christian charity, and, upon all just occasions, to assist and support each other."

---

[1] *Ex inf.*, Robert Jones, " Prothonotary's Clerk".

The rules were of a rather singular character, but it would occupy too much space to print them. It was the first friendly society formed in Welshpool.

In 1773, by a minute of the Corporation, it was " ordered that a new pump be made at the end of the Guildhall, and the clock be put in order, and the court painted, and the cock upon the top of the Town Hall be put in order, and all other necessary repairs". This pump (or rather the well) was discovered within recent years, when alterations were made at the Town Hall.

In 1774, the receipts had increased to £60, and the balance of £14 was ordered to be laid out in buying cushions for the court, and altering the staircase and enlarging the market place, "where corn was sold", and the crier of the court was ordered a new suit of livery, which cost no less than £8 2s. 8d. The Corporation seemed to indulge in gorgeous livery.

The following is a list of county voters who voted in the great contest for the county of Montgomery, between W. Mostyn Owen, Esq., and Watkin Williams, Esq., in October 1774, and whose residence is given as being in Welshpool, or within the borough :—

List of those who voted for MOSTYN OWEN.

Name	Qualification.	Name.	Qualification.
William Turner	Kerry.	John Cross	Pool.
John Edmunds	Forden parish.	David Lloyd	Pool.
William Griffith	Pool.	Richard Edmunds	Pool.
John Heyward (Guilsfield)	Buttington.	Evan Evans	Pool.
Edward Jones	Castle.	William Foulkes, Esq. (Trelydan)	Trelydan.
Evan Morris	Castle.	Thomas Griffith	Pool.
David Pugh (of London)	Llanerchydol.	Rev. Daniel Griffith (Trowscoed)	Guilsfield.
Humphrey Parry	Dyserth.	Robert Griffith	Pool.
Arthur Pearce	Pool.	Richard Hinley	Pool.
Richard Parry	Pool.	Edward Heyward (Trowscoed)	Guilsfield.
John Smith, Dyserth	Pool.	John Jones	Pool.
Thomas Addenbrook	Pool.	Joseph Morgan	Pool.
Griffith Adams (Llanerbrochwell)	Guilsfield.	John Morris	Pool.
Edward Astley (Tyrymynech)	Guilsfield.	Jeremiah Meredith	Pool.
William Coupland	Pool.	William Nichols (Cai Athrow)	Guilsfield.
Richard Cappock	Pool.	William Richards	Pool.

List of those who voted for MOSTYN OWEN—*continued.*

Name.	Qualification.	Name.	Qualification.
Charles Rocke	Pool.	John Williams	Llanfihangel.
John Tudor	Pool.	Joseph Pughe	Pentirch, Llanfair.
John Thomas (Varchwell)	Pool.	David Powell (Trehelig)	Castle Caereinion.
Richard Tudor, Esq. (Garth)	Guilsfield.	Richard Brown	Manafon.
Thomas Waring	Pool.	Samuel Fox	Berriew.
William Watson	Pool.	Thomas Powell	Berriew.
Samuel Pierce	Meifod.	Evan Vaughan	Newtown.

List of those who voted for WATKIN WILLIAMS.

Name.	Qualification.	Name.	Qualification.
John Evans	Pool.	Robert Lloyd, Esq. (Oswestry)	Gungrogfechan
Thomas Francis	Buttington.	Robert Morris	Pool.
Vaughan Jones	Pool.	Maurice Stephens	Llandinam.
John Meredith	Forden.	Ambrose Gethyn (of Berriew)	Berriew.
Jeremiah Nichols	Buttington.	Arthur Davies Owen (Shrewsbury)	Berriew.
Henry Wynne, Esq.	Castle.		
John Dicken	Pool.		

In 1775, by a minute of the Corporation, it is ordered, " that the bailiff repair the roof of the Town Hall, which was then in ruinous condition, and all other repair that was necessary, at the expense of the Corporation". The sergeants-at-mace were ordered to have " an upper garment and hats".

In 1776, Llanerchydol Hall was built. "It is a stone mansion, in a castellated style (as it was then called), and is by no means a bad example of the school of eighteenth century gothic."[1] We have not been able to ascertain who was the architect.

In the Manorial Roll for 1776, for the manor of Pool Town (which included the principal portion, but not the whole of the town), there is given a list of the inhabitants in the town of Pool, with their occupations added for the first time. This ancient directory we think it well to print.

John Williams, attorney.
Edward Davies, carpenter.
Richard Davies, tailor.
Charles Davies, labourer.

Humphrey Tudor, barber.
Joseph Morgan, shoemaker.
Richard Syer, labourer.
Richard Clayton, labourer.

[1] *History of the Gothic Revival*, by Charles L. Eastlake, p. 57.

WELSH POOL.

David Matthews, labourer.
William Oliver, labourer.
Samuel Evans, gardner.
John James, labourer.
Mary Lloyd, widdow.
Edward Owen, carpenter.
Arthur Jones, labourer.
Isaac King, Supervisor of Excise.
Elizabeth Pryce, widow.
Richard Davies, labourer.
Thomas Howells, labourer.
William Cook, tayler.
Edward Mores, innkeeper.
Evan Evans, innkeeper.
Hugh Hughes, saddler.
Arthur James, blacksmith.
Thomas Waring, carpenter.
Humphrey Parry, currier.
Ann Roberts, widow.
Edward Lewis, grocer.
David Hughes, Officer of Excise.
Thomas Nickolas, sawyer.
Thomas James, labourer.
Joyce Stephens, widdow.
John Corbett, weelwright.
Thomas Griffiths, maltster.
Thomas Davies, shoemaker.
James Powell, labourer.
Vaughan Pryce, maltster.
Humphrey Pugh, weaver.
John Richards, mason.
Francis Powell, cowper.
Elizabeth Luke.
William Jones, maltster.
Anne Watson, widdow.
Evan Davies, maltster.
Edward Davies, shoemaker.
Sarah Meredith, widdow.
Richard Jones, butcher.
Richard Griffiths, innkeeper.
Jeremiah Nickolas, shoemaker.
William Lewis, sadler.
David Jones, tayler.
Francis Morris, labourer.
David Davies, innkeeper.
Edward Davies, maltster.
George Lloyd, ironmonger.
Vaughan Jones, surgen.
Susannah Birkett, widdow.
Roger Bowdler, attorney.
Lloyd Turner, tanner.
John Meredith, attorney.
John Pugh, ironmonger.
John Bromley, jun., mercer.
Humphrey Holloway, butcher.
Evan Williams, ironmonger.
Elinor Morris, spinster.
John Bromley, senior.
Martha Owen, spinster.
James Matthews.

John Foulkes, mercer.
Charles Jones, Esq.
John Williams attorney.
John Morris, innkeeper.
Richard Evans, butcher.
William Foulkes, saddler.
David Salmon, stationer.
Sarah Yearsley, widdow.
John Dickin, attorney.
Evan Jones, taw dresser.
William Coupland, apothecary.
Evan Evans, tayler.
Catherine Daxon, widdow.
Francis Evans, labourer.
John Pugh, currier.
Moses Roberts, cowper.
Margaret Edward, widdow.
Mary Momford, widow.
John Momford
John Evans, shoemaker.
Jane Morris, widdow.
Edward Thomas, sawyer.
Elizabeth Jones, widdow.
Robert Sambrook, labourer.
Griffith Griffiths, malster.
Margaret Edmonds, widdow.
John Edwards, weaver.
Thomas Francis, labourer.
John Hughes, shoemaker.
John Evans, labourer.
Thomas Dax, carpenter.
Alice Thomas, widdow.
Robert Burrows, shoemaker.
Samuel Edwards, gardener.
Elena Hinley, spinster.
John Francis, cooper.
David Davies, labourer.
John Edmunds.
Anne Elliss, widdow.
James Davies, labourer.
Evan Dixon, joyner.
Francis Powell, maltster.
Richard Gardner, blacksmith.
Elizabeth Tipton, widdow.
Richard Morris, shoemaker.
Robert Sambrook, blacksmith.
John Oliver, labourer.
Thomas Artcher, serg.-major.
Lewis Jones, innkeeper.
Pierce Reynolds, postmaster.
Evan Griffiths, turner.
John Williams, labourer.
Sarah Bowdler, widdow.
David Evans, labourer.
John Williams, shoemaker.
Edward Turner, carpenter.
Anne Richards, spinster.
Owen Owens, labourer.
Griffith Morris, tanner.
Thomas Davies, labourer.

WELSH POOL.

Edward Jones, labourer.
John Evans, labourer.
Henry Oliver, labourer.
Joseph Pugh, mason.
Morgan Jones, labourer.
Abigail Prowdley, widdow.
Jane Edwards, spinster.
Elizabeth Jones, widow.
David Humphreys, labourer.
Jane Herbert, widdow.
Owen Owen, glover.
Anne Jones, widdow.
John Thomas, glover.
Anne Evans, spinster.
Edward Jones, labourer.
John Jones, postman.
Edward Howell, shoemaker.
Sarah Jones, widdow.
Jane Powell, widdow.
Thomas Stockton, labourer.
John Wooding, labourer.
William Williams, breechesmaker.
John William, labourer.
Thomas Dax, jun , carpenter.
Thomas Humphreys, carpenter.
Owen Morris, innkeeper.
Matthew Morris, sawyer.
John Edwards, labourer.
David Randle, shoemaker.
John Rogers, miller.
Jonathan Griffiths.
John Jones, weaver.
Richard Thomas, labourer.
Richard Evans, tanner.
Hugh Thomas, labourer.
Thomas Davies, hatter.
Robert Elliss.
Rodrick Hughes, tanner.
John Williams, mason.
James Stockbridge, gardner.
John Roberts, glover.
Edward Moses, weaver.
John Humphreys, weaver.
John Griffiths, shoemaker.
James Pugh, postman.
Henry Humphreys.
Henry Wynne, Esq.
Reece Williams.
John Pugh.
Charles Rocke, attorney,
Susannah Pryce, spinster.
Richard Morris, glover.
Clement Williams, shoemaker.
John Jenkins, shoemaker.
Mary Humphreys, widdow.
John Morris, maltster.
William Elliss, labourer.
Elizabeth Hughes, widdow.
David Davies, labourer.
Robert Morris, soapboyler.

Evan Griffiths, innkeeper.
Richard Morris, innkeeper.
Edward Rowland, tayler.
Joseph Meredith, weelwright.
William Richards, shoemaker.
Samuel Hudson, tanner.
William Griffiths, innkeeper.
John Matthews, currier.
John Evans, innkeeper.
John Crace, butler.
Anthony Morris, barber.
Thomas Griffiths, gunsmith.
Joseph Morris, innkeeper.
Jane Perry, widdow.
William Pryce, hatter.
Arthur Ryder, shoemaker.
Evan Davies, gardner.
Thomas Ashford, glazier.
William Rider, butcher.
Dorothy Wilhams, widdow.
Margaret Vaughan, spinster.
Ann Perry, widdow.
Samuel Bowdler.
Thomas Williams.
James Davies, shopkeeper.
Thomas Clark, staymaker.
Mary Barnett, spinster.
Edward Lewis, hatter.
Thomas Peplow, weaver.
William Turner.
Elizabeth Williams, widdow.
Sarah Davies, widdow.
Edward Morgan, hatter.
James Meredith, basketmaker.
Evan Evans, labourer.
Robert Owens, shoemaker.
William Richards, cowper.
Mary Evans, widdow.
John Draycott, grocer.
Robert Jolley.
Charles White.
Thomas Wilkes.
Anne Hughes, widdow.
Elizabeth Watson, widdow.
Richard Lloyd, weaver.
Martha Lewis, widdow.
George Baker, grocer.
Henry Owens, butcher.
Sarah Tudor, widdow.
William Bowen, glover.
Thomas Morris, barber.
Thomas Howells, barber.
Thomas Powell, currier.
Elinora Williams, widdow.
John Weaver, skinner.
Humphrey Meredith, saddler.
Richard Brown, grocer.
Elizabeth Walter, widdow.
Richard Cappock, barber.
Richard Hurley, tailor.

WELSH POOL. 199

Oliver Jones, grocer.
John Johnson, shopkeeper.
John Jones, saddler.
Samuel Sayce, mason.
Lewis Lewis.
John Howells, innkeeper.
Thomas Davies, wheelwright.
Robert Jones, innkeeper.
Owen Ratcliff, clockmaker.
Anne Owen, widow.
William Thomas, innkeeper.
Richard Rowland, tailor.
George Richards, mason.
Mary Llewellin, widdow.
Mary Main, widdow.

Lowry Williams.
Thomas Pryce, maltster.
John Thomas Owens, saddler.
William Davies, tayler.
Elizabeth Plimmer, widdow.
Elizabeth Reeves, widdow.
John Evans, labourer.
Sarah Griffiths, widdow.
Thomas Pryce, Officer of Excise.
William Roberts, joyner.
Richard Pugh, currier.
John Rogers, blacksmith.
Robert Morris.
Richard Maddox.
Watkin Thomas, malster.

The number in each profession or trade was as follows :—

38 of each of the following, widows.
25 ,, ,, labourers.
14 ,, ,, innkeepers.
13 ,, ,, shoemakers
9 ,, ,, tailors and breeches makers.
8 ,, ,, maltsters.
7 ,, ,, spinsters.
6 ,, ,, attornies, carpenters and joiners, sadlers, weavers.
5 ,, ,, grocers, butchers, glovers.
4 ,, ,, barbers, tanners, hatters.
3 ,, ,, supervisors of excise, ironmongers, gardeners, sawyers, coopers, curriers.
2 ,, ,, esquires, surgeons and apothecaries, mercers, masons, postmen, wheelwrights, shopkeeepers, curriers, blacksmiths.
   ,, carrier, blacksmith, wheelwright, stationer, taw (tow ?) dresser, glazier, baker, miller, soapboiler, gunsmith, staymaker, basketmaker, skinner, clockmaker.

Matthew Williams, a tragedian, was born in Welshpool; little is known about him. In Anthony Pasquin's *Children of Thespis*, published in 1789, there is a notice of him, from which it may be inferred he must have been an actor of some note to have met with Pasquin's notice, and from which we glean the following :—

"To Decency dear, and to Merit long known,
See Williams' advance to Calliope's throne;
Though the tones of his voice are restrain'd within bounds,
They form a sweet concord of heavenly sounds;
If to greatness unequal, each essay prevails,
For his diffidence aids where ability fails,
As encircled he stood in the Temple of Fame,
'Twas himself that alone had a doubt of his fame."

"His *début* was at Birmingham, in the New Theatre, where he enacted *Hamlet* on the memorable 27th of July, 1778. After a probation at Bath, he joined the dramatic regiments at Old Drury in 1779. His weekly salary was £5."

Matthew Williams's fame probably would have been transient, and his name passed away, but for his unfortunate end. He was killed in a duel by Quin. Dr. Doran, in *Their Majesties' Servants*, thus describes the occurrence:—

"It was Quin's hard fate to kill two actors—Bowen and Williams, who was Decius to Quin's Cato. Williams, in delivering the last line, 'Cæsar sends health to Cato', pronounced the last name so like Keeto, that Quin could not help exclaiming, 'Would he had sent a better messenger'. This irritated the little Welsh actor, the more that he had to repeat the name in nearly every sentence of his scene with Cato, and Quin did not fail to look so hard at him when he pronounced it, that Williams' irritation was at the highest, and, in the green-room, the irascible Welshman attacked Quin on the ground that he had rendered him ridiculous in the eyes of the audience. Quin treated the matter as a joke, but the Welsh actor would not be soothed. After the play, he lay in wait for the offender in the piazza, where much malapert blood was often spilt. There Quin could not refuse to defend himself, and, after a few passes, Williams lay lifeless on the flagstones, and Quin was arrested by the watch. Of course, as he had only defended himself, he was acquitted."[1]

In the book of the churchwardens of Pool, under date of October 17th, 1777, the following minute occurs:—

"It was agreed that the churchyard wall and buttresses and the steps are to be repaired as soon as opportunity may be,

---

[1] *Bygones*, 1871-3, pp. 5-10.

Montgomeria XIV. P.101   THE PACKHORSE INN WELSHPOOL

and that the expenses and charge of the same be paid out of Poor Lewn of the middle division of the parish."

A memorandum is subjoined in another handwriting.

"The above belongs to the town part to repair, as appears by the Terriers."

According to the Church Terrier of 1730 the repair of the churchyard fences was as follows :—

"The stile gate at the east end is repaired by the Vicar; the wall from thence, down the south side to the Greedle, is repaired by the town part of the parish; the Greedle gates by his Grace the Duke of Powis; and the rest of the fences by the other townships."

In a letter in the *Archæologia Cambrensis* for 1858 (p. 111), the experience of a person who remembered the last twenty years of the eighteenth century, is related. When a boy, the only public mode of travelling in Wales, or medium for transmission of goods and parcels, was the pack-horse; for when he went to Shrewsbury to school he was given in charge to the carrier, and mounted on one of the train of horses. The train varied in number and length according to the exigencies of the carrier for the time. As it took four or five days, there were stages or places of rest on the way. Amongst them the sign of the *Packhorse*, in Welshpool, was then a well known and established hostelry, which must in those days have borne some resemblance to an eastern caravanserai; the name as that of an inn still remains, but its ancient occupation is gone. We give an autotype of a sketch made by a lady, Mrs. Howell, of Rhiewport, as it at present appears.

Jane Gilmour, an old inhabitant before referred to, says that before the canal was completed the traffic through Welshpool by waggons was very great. As many as twenty carts and waggons might be seen in the town at one time, each having large teams of horses, as the roads were very bad. From Llanfair to Welshpool the traffic was carried on by pack-horses, which started from the *Upper Pack-horse*, a very ancient inn.

In 1779, the corporation accounts show that a payment was made

"To Mr. Campbell on account of building the
Bailiffs' seat and canopy in the Church - £10 10 0"

The usual receipt was given for the charters by the bailiffs.

"Paid Mr. John Morris, Crown, for wine for the
Judges - - - - - - - £1 14 0
Paid Mr. Bayley, Castle Inn, for wine for Judges 1 12 0"

In 1781 there is the item—

"Paid Mrs. Morris, Crown, for dozen wine for
Judges - - - - - - - £3 6 0"

The quality of the wine given was better.

In 1783, the common called Gwern y goe was ordered to be let for any time not exceeding three years.

In 1785, three lamps were ordered to be set up, one at the end of the Town Hall, and another at that part of the Town Hall that faces Upper Church Street, to be lighted during the dark nights in the winter season at the expense of the corporation. This is the first notice of the public lighting of the borough.

The recorder, the Earl of Powis, not being able to attend personally, the bailiff was ordered to act in his place at the election, and make up the balls of wax, etc.

In 1788, in consequence of the illness of Price Jones, one of the bailiffs, a special arrangement was made for carrying out the election of bailiffs.

In Davies's *Agricultural Survey of North Wales*, p. 481, the following particulars are given of the poor-rate from 1733 to 1788, with other curious information.

Pool, Middle Division.

						Amount of Rates		
1733	at	0	6	per	pound	23	11	8
1736	,,	0	6	,,	,,	27	1	6
1749	,,	1	0	,,	,,	53	5	4
1755	,,	1	6	,,	,,	65	0	0
1763	,,	2	6	,,	,,	105	12	8

```
1774 at  3  6  per pound  155  6  6
1783  ,,  4  6   ,,   ,,    227 15  6
         By an old rate.
1788  ,,  4  0   ,,   ,,    253  8  0
```
By a new rate at three-fourths of the present value.

1794. The poor received into the house.
```
1800 at 12  0  per pound  866  8  0
```
Being thirty-six times the amount of the rates in the year 1733. The present population of this division is 1,311, about one-third part more than it was sixty years back.

	Years fatal.	No buried.	Years favourable.	No buried.
Welshpool	1747	70	1748	32
,,	1796	54	1797	37[1]

In the first enclosure of Powis Castle Park there are three fine elm trees growing on the south side of the carriage drive, standing close together in the form of a triangle, and they are called the Three Sisters. They are each fully fourteen feet in circumference at the ground, and tower to a great height. Old Mr. Edmund Edye told our informant[2] that he was present when these trees were planted, and assisted in planting them. He came to Montgomeryshire (his son, Mr. Thomas Edye, still flourishing at the age of ninety, says) in 1779, when he was twenty-two years of age.[3]

According to a memorandum in Powis Castle Office, these trees were planted in 1789; the one nearest the castle being planted by Mr. Probert, the middle one by Mr. Edmund Edye, and the third by Mr. Robert Wilding. These trees, planted ninety-two years ago, are of

---

[1] On page 466, the author gives the following information as to the local measures of the county and town :

"In Montgomeryshire, a cylindrical vessel containing twenty quarts is called a hoop, two of such hoops make a strike or measure, and two strikes or measures make a bushel of eighty quarts, equal to a Denbighshire hobed.

"A bushel of oats at Welshpool is seven hoops, or half strikes heaped; a bushel of malt is nine-tenths of the corn measure."

[2] *Ex inf.*, Mr. J. Pryce Davies of Fronfelin.

[3] He was born 2nd January 1757, and died 23rd January 1849, aged ninety-two years and three weeks. An engraved portrait of him is in the Powys-land Museum.

large size, and particularly fine specimens of elms. It is said that the same persons also, about the same time, planted the elm trees now standing on the "Domen", near the bowling green, and near to which the old Domen mill formerly stood.[1]

In the borough accounts, there are frequent payments for repairs and alterations of the old Town Hall to 1795.

In 1790, at a Common Hall it was ordered that the court for holding the Great Sessions in the Guildhall "be altered, enlarged, and improved in a commodious and elegant manner"; and again, in 1791, in a Common Hall held on the 27th of September, the flagging and railing were declared to be ruinous, and were ordered to be repaired in a "substantial and handsome manner". These orders do not seem to have been carried out except by temporary repairs, until, in the year 1795, another catastrophe occurred, although fortunately of not so serious a character as the accident in the Market Hall in 1758. The Great Sessions were held therein on Saturday, the 8th of August 1795, before the Hon. Edward Bearcroft and Francis Burton. During the trial of a man named Edward Barrett for burglary, the *Cambrian Register*[2] records that "some of the timbers which support the Town Hall gave way, and the floor sank several inches. The court was cleared of those who were not concerned in the trial without accident, and was finished". The prisoner was found guilty of grand larceny only, the evidence not being sufficient to convict him of the burglary (conviction of which might have cost him his life), and he was sentenced to be transported for seven years. Then the remarkable fact is recorded that "the remaining business of the Sessions were done *in the church*".[3]

[1] For some particulars respecting a large oak tree, see *Mont. Coll.*, vol. xiii.   [2] Vol. i, p. 457.

[3] Mrs. Edward Jones, an old inhabitant of Welshpool, who died in 1879, aged 92, used to say that she remembered the Assizes being held in the church. The judges sat either in the old bailiffs' seat or in the Earl of Powis's square seat under the windows.

In the following November (1795), at the Common Hall held before Richard Tudor and Lawton Parry, Esqrs., bailiffs, "The Guildhall of this town having been reported by Mr. Simpson of Shrewsbury, architect, to be in a very dangerous and insecure state", resolved, " that the same be taken down and rebuilt in or as near the same place of its present situation as conveniently may be".

On the 17th of March, 1796, the Great Sessions and Gaol delivery for Montgomeryshire were held in Pool, and the *Cambrian Register*[1] records, "N.B., the Court sat in the *Canal Committee Room*, the Town Hall being deemed unsafe.

In 1796, the funds were raised for rebuilding the Town Hall, by a public subscription, which produced the handsome sum of £1,800, supplemented by the sum of £300 borrowed by the corporation from Messrs. Pugh and Co., bankers, Welshpool. The cost, however, greatly exceeded these amounts, but the deficiency, as well as the loan, were ultimately repaid out of the rents of the corporation property.

In August 1796, the payment of a sum of £3 8s. to Thomas Dax and Humphrey Davies for fitting up the Record Office[2] for the accommodation of the Court of Great Sessions, in consequence of the insecure state of the Town Hall.

In 1798, the Town Hall still remained unfinished, and a balance of £130 4s. 4½d. in the hands of the treasurer was directed to be applied towards its completion; and at length, on the 27th of September 1804, the architects and builders, Messrs. Simpson and Hazeldine of Shrewsbury, were paid £34 13s. as the

[1] Vol. ii, p. 567.
[2] This Record Office stood at the corner of Park Lane, and, in 1791, a contract was entered into between the bailiffs and the county magistrates on the one part, and Joseph Bousfield of Shrewsbury, architect, on the other part, for erecting two cells adjoining, for the sum of sixty pounds (one for males and the other for females), the corporation agreeing to pay one-third of the cost of erection, and one-third of the repairs.

balance due for erecting and finishing the new Town Hall and Market Place.

The accounts and minutes of the corporation have from this time frequent intervals between them.

In 1790, the livery of the servants cost in several items £18 1s.

In 1791, the Earl of Powis offered to erect an elegant pump near the Cross, which was thankfully accepted. A Common Hall was ordered to be held every New Year's Day for auditing the corporation's accounts.

In 1793, John Probert was capital bailiff, and the financial affairs of the corporation seem to have been thoroughly overhauled, and all balances paid in, and arrears ordered to be collected " previous to a Common Hall to be held on the 1st of February next for taking into consideration the distribution to be made under the Act of Parliament to a certain class of burgesses therein mentioned". And a committee was appointed for regulating the distribution.

In 1794, the tenants of the lands which had been valued by Mr. Probert and Mr. R. Tudor were put under agreements for terms of years at increased rents. And in this year the first distribution was made of £44 13s. 10d., amongst a certain class of indigent burgesses, agreeably to the Act of Parliament.

The following is a list of such distribution which appears in the Tensors' Book.

1794	£44	13	10	1818	£40	0	0
1795	14	8	0	1821	31	10	0
1798	1	1	0[1]	1826	15	8	6
1804	50	0	0	1828	20	0	0
1807	30	0	0	1829	25	0	0
1815	60	0	0	1832	35	0	0
1816	30	0	0				

In 1793, items first appear for payment for oil, cotton, etc., used for the public lights at the Town Hall, and possibly elsewhere.

Welshpool, in 1795, had a poetical schoolmaster.

[1] "To Edward Parry, a poor sick burgess."

His name was the Rev. D. Francis, and to his advertisement, dated June 21, 1795, the following lines[1] are appended.

> " Ours will it be, with true paternal care,
> The sprouting scions of your sons to rear;
> To point, where Wisdom to her meed invites,
> And help them fault'ring up her craggy heights.
> To lead the young, the fair idea shoot,
> And ripen all their blossoms into fruit;
> Till forth they shine, conducted by our plan,
> *The contemplating sage, the feeling man;*
> Then now be yours the patronizing smile,
> Befriend exertion, and reward our toil;
> Entrust to our care the pledges of your love,
> And, in success, an arduous task approve.
> And while WELCH POOL to *Honour* now aspires,
> And *Patriotism* glows with purest fires,
> In *Genius* let her also seek renown,
> And add the bay of Science to her crown;
> Thus shall the foster'd Muse exalt her strains,
> And Gratitude reverberate on her plains."

Mr. Francis says, " Ours will it be", and in this he comprehends an assistant, "that from a conscientious regard for the improvement of the young gentlemen committed to his care he had engaged". The " patriotism" he speaks of was doubtless blown into " purest fires" by the Mutiny of the Nore; a fresh event just then, and one exciting considerable attention everywhere.

In 1799, there was an unpleasant dispute between the then Vicar of the parish and the principal parishioners, owing to his being non-resident. He defended himself on the ground that he was chaplain to a peer, which absolved him from the obligation of residence. Upon a letter of remonstrance (couched in terms remarkably impressive) being addressed to him by all his chief parishioners, the Vicar retorted in a poetical effusion, entitled *Pool Blood-hound Hunt*, which, although witty and sarcastic, was of a scurrilous cha-

---

[1] *Bygones*, 1873, p. 155.

racter, and attacked his assailants in a most virulent manner. It gave occasion for an indictment against him for a "scandalous, malicious, and defamatory libel". We are enabled to print a copy of the indictment, which we do, as depicting the state of society in the parish at this epoch, and we fear that it will be admitted by all that the laymen appear to much better advantage than the cleric.

Montgomeryshire to wit.—The Jurors of our Lord the King, upon their oath, present that the Reverend John Pryce, late of Gunley, in the said county of Montgomery, clerk, on the first day of June, in the year of our Lord one thousand seven hundred and ninety-nine, was and from thence continually, until the time of taking this Inquisition, hath been and still is vicar of the vicarage of Pool, in the said county of Montgomery. And the Jurors aforesaid, upon their oath aforesaid, do further present, that the said John Pryce, so being such vicar as aforesaid, on the said first day of June in the year aforesaid, wilfully absented himself from his said vicarage, and continually from thence, until the taking of this Inquisition, resided and abided elsewhere than in at or upon the said vicarage (to wit) at Gunley, in the said county of Montgomery, and out of the said parish of Pool (to wit) at Pool aforesaid, in the county of Montgomery aforesaid. And the Jurors aforesaid, upon their oath aforesaid, do further present that afterwards (to wit) on the eighteenth day of June, in the said year of our Lord one thousand seven hundred and ninety-nine (to wit) at Pool aforesaid, in the said county of Montgomery, one Thomas Jones, one Henry Foulkes, one James Turner, and divers other good and liege subjects of our said Lord the King, then and there being parishioners of the parish of Pool, in the said county of Montgomery, caused and procured a certain letter to be then and there written to the said John Pryce, so being such vicar as aforesaid, of and concerning his the said John Pryce's leaving the said vicarage, and of and concerning his residing at Gunley, out of the said parish of Pool, which said letter they the said Thomas Jones, Henry Foulkes, and James Turner, and the said other good subjects and liege subjects of our said Lord the King, then and there signed with their own proper names, and by and in their several and respective handwriting, and which said letter so signed as aforesaid they the said Thomas Jones, Henry Foulkes, and James Turner, and the said other good and liege

MONTGOMERYSHIRE COLLECTIONS.

COLLECTIONS

HISTORICAL & ARCHÆOLOGICAL

RELATING TO

MONTGOMERYSHIRE

AND ITS BORDERS.

ISSUED BY THE POWYS LAND CLUB FOR THE USE OF ITS MEMBERS.

VOL. XV.

LONDON:
PRINTED FOR THE CLUB BY
WHITING & CO., SARDINIA STREET, LINCOLN'S INN FIELDS.
1882.

"A Ruddy Lion Ramping in Gold."

The Seal of SIR EDWARD DE CHERLETON, LORD OF POWYS, appended to a Charter dated 6th July, 7 Henry V (1418), is adopted as the Seal of the 𝔓𝔬𝔴𝔶𝔰-𝔩𝔞𝔫𝔡 ℭ𝔩𝔲𝔟. This remarkable Seal is not quite perfect, the edge having been splintered away, and the figure in the place of the crest having lost its head, which the engraver has supplied. It appears to have been a round seal, surrounded by an inscription, probably *"Sigillum Edwardi de Cherleton, Domini Powisie"*, of which only the " g" in the word Sigillum, and " wi" in the word Powisie, now remain. The shield in the centre is charged with the *red lion* of Powys—a *lion rampant*—and is probably held up by another lion rampant standing on its hind legs behind the shield, which is clasped by his fore paws. The side supporters, or rather ornamental figures (for it is said that supporters, in the present heraldic sense of the word, were unknown at that period), are wild men sitting astride of lions couchant.—*Mont. Coll.*, vol. vi, p. 293.

MONTGOMERYSHIRE COLLECTIONS.

CONTENTS OF VOL. XV.

Original Proposal for Formation of Club, Rules, and Amended Rules	viii
List of Members	xv
Report of Fifteenth Annual Meeting	xx
Review of the Progress and Prospects of the Powys-land Club	xxv
Classified List of Articles presented to the Powys-land Museum and Library since November 1881	xxx
Alphabetical List of Donors to the Powys-land Museum and Library from its institution to November 1882	xxxvi
Report of Museum Committee	xli
List of Literary Societies with which the Powys-land Club exchanges Publications	xliii
Obituary of Members of the Powys-land Club	xliv

Pedigree of the Family of Kynaston		
Kynaston of	Walford	4
,,	Shotton	4
,,	Hordley	5
,,	Morton	8
,,	Ryton	13
,,	Oteley	15
Genealogical Key Chart of Kynaston family		22
Copy of Inscriptions on Monumental Cup at Hardwick		24
Copy of Inscriptions on Pindar Cup		26

History of the Forden Union Churchyard. By Rev. J. E. Vize, M.A.	27
Montgomeryshire Worthies. By Richard Williams. (*Continued from Vol. XIV, p.* 160)	41
On a Ring Dial found in the Parish of Llansantffraid. By D. W. Evans	71

The Fortresses of Radnorshire on the Borders of Montgomeryshire. By Rev. George Sandford, M.A.	75
Cridia Abbey. By Richard Williams	87
Roads, Bridges, Canals, and Railways in Montgomeryshire. By A. Howell. (*Continued from Vol. XIV, p.* 106)	91
The Bridges 100	
Arms of the Family of Juckes	117
Copy Exemplification of Arms to Edward Jewkes, 1593 117	
Folk-Lore, Superstitions, or What-not, in Montgomeryshire. By Rev. Elias Owen, M.A.	121
The Parish of Forden. By Rev. J. E. Vize, M.A.	155
I. Physical Features and Description . 155	
II. Natural History . . . 163	
i. Ornithology.—British Birds observed in the Vicinity of Forden, by T. C. Vize . . 163	
ii. Botany.—British Flowering Plants found in the Neighbourhood of Forden, by T. C. Vize . 165 List of Cryptogamic Plants found in Forden or its immediate Neighbourhood— (*a*) Fungi . . . 169 (*b*) Lichens . . 177	
iii. Conchology—British Shells 178	
III. Population 180	
List of Magistrates *temp.* Charles II.	183
„ „ „ 33 George III.	185
The Enclosure of Common Lands in Montgomeryshire. II.	191
Pool Quay Weir. By Rev. Aug. Field, Vicar of Pool Quay	197
Montgomeryshire Worthies. By RICHARD WILLIAMS. (*Continued from p.* 70)	203
Pedigree of Pritchard of Ceniarth	225
Parish Registers in Montgomeryshire. By T. W. HANCOCK.	235
Welshpool, Materials for the History of Parish and Borough. By M. C. J. Chapter III (*Continued from Vol. XIII, p.* 428)	249

. Chapter IV.—Ecclesiastical . . .		253
The Churchyard	271	
The Church	275	
Seat-room . .	286	
Gifts to the Church . . .	288	
,, ,, Windows, etc. . .	289	
Monuments in the Church and Inscriptions	292	
Some of the Monumental Inscriptions in the Churchyard . . .	299	
The Communion Plate .	308	
The Registers . .	310	
The Dells	311	
List of the Rectors and Vicars . .	313	
Benefactions and Charities	316	
Abeyant Charities . . .	327	
Appendix—Terriers . . .	334	
Brief for Rebuilding Church, 7 Geo. III. . . .	344	
Miscellaneous Matters . .	346	
Powis Castle—Past and Present. By G. S. and M. C. J. .		361
I. Epoch of the Princes of Powys .	363	
II. ,, Feudal Barons of Powys	369	
III. ,, Barons, Earls, Marquesses, and Dukes of Powis created by patent	388	
IV. The Structure of the Castle . .	398	
Miscellanea, LXXXI to XCI . . .		405

ILLUSTRATIONS.

Seal of Forden House of Industry	39
Woodcut of Ring Dial found in the Parish of Llansantffraid .	73
Lithograph of Stone found near the site of Abbey of Strata Marcella, supposed to be part of a Hexagonal Chimney to face page	199
St. Mary's Church, Welshpool, before the Restoration in 1870 (presented by Mr. D. P. Owen) . . to face	275
Ancient East Window and Font	278
Ground-plan of Church, 1882 . to be mounted between 276 and	277
Altar Tomb and Effigy of Edward Herbert, Earl of Powis, K.G. . . . . . . to face	292
Plan of Vicarial Glebe 1779, showing the portion taken by the Canal Company	349
Powis Castle (presented by Mr. D. P. Owen) . to face	361

Authors alone are responsible for facts and opinions.

PROPOSAL *for a Society or Club, to be called the* "POWYS-LAND CLUB", *for the Collecting and Printing, for the use of its Members, of the Historical, Ecclesiastical, Genealogical, Topographical, and Literary Remains of Montgomeryshire.*

It has occurred to more than one gentleman connected with Montgomeryshire, that it would be desirable to begin an historical and archæological collection for that county.

The county is rich in the remains of former ages, comprising, as it does, nearly the whole of the ancient principality of Upper Powys and other scenes of historic interest, and yet having hitherto formed a portion of Wales which has not received its due proportion of archæological illustration.

A county history is the great desideratum; but, considering the various qualifications required, in one person, to enable him to write a good county history, who is equal to such a herculean task?

It is seldom that in one mind can be found "the profundity of knowledge, the patient and laborious research, the skill in generalisation, the talent for detail, the aptitude for so many and so varied investigations, the taste, energy, and self-sacrificing zeal which can carry such labour to a successful termination". The late Walter Davies was the only man that could be named who would have been equal to the undertaking.

In the absence, however, of a county history, an historical and archæological collection for this county, specifically, would be both valuable and interesting.

It would be, in fact, to carry out, but in more detail with reference to Montgomeryshire, the idea which was broached with respect to all the counties of Wales in the first number of the *Archæologia Cambrensis* in the article—"On the Study and Preservation of National Antiquities."

Following the model of other societies, it is proposed that the collection should include—

1. A *Monasticon*, or a record of all monastic remains, whether buildings, tombs, inscriptions, utensils, seals, etc. [This is already in progress, but, from the few religious houses in the county, will not be extensive.]

2. An *Ecclesiasticon*, or a similar record of all that relates to parochial churches and chapels, whether of the established church, or of any description, etc., and of all objects, such as tombs, crosses, etc., connected with them.

3. A *Castellarium*, a similar record of castellated remains.

4. A *Mansionarium*, a similar collection relating to all ancient manor-houses, mansions, and houses of a certain degree of importance, and to their collected remains.

5. A *Villare* and *Parochiale*, applying to all buildings and remains of towns, villages, parishes, etc., including all public civil buildings, etc.

6. A *Chartularium*, including as complete an account as practicable of all ancient documents referring to the five preceding classes. The manorial history of the county may be illustrated, and the public record office, and the muniment rooms of the magnates of the county would form an almost inexhaustible source of information under this division. It would be proposed to print the original documents *in extenso* where thought of sufficient interest.

7. An *Obituarium*, containing notices of pedigrees of ancient families, notices of celebrated characters, and collections of all that relates to the public and private life of all classes who are or have been inhabitants of the district.

8. An *Ordinary of Arms*, containing authentic copies of all existing remains of mediæval heraldry.—Drawings and copies of inscriptions, etc., on church windows, monuments, etc.

9. The collecting and printing of MS. collections connected with the district, or throwing any light on any of the families of the county.

10. An *Itinerarium*. Notices, plans, and surveys, of all British, Roman, or other ancient roads or ways, etc.

11. Traditions, customs, folk-lore, ballads, etc.

Various topographical and genealogical articles have appeared in publications that are rare and difficult of access, and it would be proposed to reprint such of these articles as may be thought of sufficient interest and value, with such additions as may be procurable; for instance, the topographical accounts of the parishes of Meifod and Llanwnog, which appeared in the *Cambrian Quarterly Review*, and the accounts of Garthbeibio, Llangadfan, and Llanerfyl, and of Llanymynech, that appeared upwards of seventy years ago in the *Cambrian Register*, and such like. They would form models for topographical accounts of other parishes.

And it is wished to reprint several of the articles bearing upon Montgomeryshire which have already appeared in the *Archæologia Cambrensis*.

It is proposed to print the articles in parts, as they are available, and not necessarily in any particular classified order; but when a sufficient number to form a volume is collected, to make the information easily accessible by means of copious *Indices*.

It is also proposed to make such arrangements with the Cambrian Archæological Association as may be found mutually desirable and practicable. It is the wish of the promoters of the scheme to form the closest connection with that well-tried and excellent institution. The scheme may appear extensive, but it will be carried out only so far as materials offer and opportunity occurs.

This preliminary proposal was circulated in the first instance in influential quarters, with the view of testing how far the scheme met with approval, and was likely to be supported.

The collection of two or three facts—in themselves, and, while separate, comparatively unimportant—will often be found to throw light on each other, and will not unfrequently lead to the clearing up of doubtful points, or the discovery of error. In this light all may assist in the work proposed.

"If a collection could be made", said the late Dr. Stanley, Bishop of Norwich, "of all the isolated and floating facts connected with the various branches of topographical knowledge, it is obvious that thus an invaluable body of information and ample store of materials might be amassed, of the utmost importance to the traveller, the antiquarian, the man of science, and the naturalist." The custodian of almost every parochial register may find in it much that is novel and valuable. Any accurate observer who will transcribe all the monumental inscriptions in any church, chapel, or burial place, would render valuable service.

If it meet with support, it is intended to organise and carry it on with the honorary assistance of such as consent to associate themselves for the purpose; the necessary funds for printing and illustrating, transcribing public records, etc., being provided by the subscription of the members. But it is by no means wished to restrict the Association to pecuniary subscribers only. Contributors of archæological information of all the descriptions before indicated would be welcomed as members with as much warmth as pecuniary subscribers.

MORRIS C. JONES,
20, Abercromby Square, Liverpool.
T. O. MORGAN,
Aberystwith.

} *Hon. Secs. pro tem.*

1st *March* 1867.

The Club was constituted on the 1st October 1867; when Part I was issued to the members, and the following Rules adopted:—

ORIGINAL LAWS OF THE POWYS-LAND CLUB.

I. The Club shall consist of not more than one hundred members.

II. The Council shall consist of the following persons, in whom the management of the Club shall be vested, that is to say, the President, Vice-Presidents, the Secretaries, Treasurer, and twelve other Members.

III. That the following gentlemen shall constitute the first Officers and Council of the Club:—

President—The EARL OF POWIS.
Vice-Presidents—The LORD SUDELEY; THE BISHOP OF ST. ASAPH, SIR WATKIN WILLIAMS WYNN, Bart.

Council.

Rev. E. L. BARNWELL, M.A., Melksham, Wilts.	DAVID HOWELL, Esq., Dolguog, Machynlleth
EDMUND BUCKLEY, Esq., M.P., Plas Dinas.	Rev. D. PHILLIPS LEWIS, M.A., Vicarage, Guilsfield.
J. PRYCE DREW, Esq., M.A., Milford, Newtown,	Hon. CHAS. HANBURY TRACY, M.P., Gregynog, Newtown.
Rev. JOHN EDWARDS, M.A., Rectory, Newtown.	PRYCE BUCKLEY WILLIAMES, Esq, Pennant, Welshpool.
Ven. Archdeacon FFOULKES, M.A., Rectory, Llandyssil.	Rev. ROBERT WILLIAMS, M.A., Rectory, Llanfyllin.
ABRAHAM HOWELL, Esq., Rhiewport, Welshpool.	C. W. WILLIAMS WYNN, Esq., M.P., Coed y Maen, Welshpool.

Hon. Treasurer—THOMAS BOWEN, Esq. (Messrs. Beck & Co), Welshpool.

Hon. Secretaries—MORRIS C. JONES, Esq., 20, Abercromby Square, Liverpool (and Gungrog, Welshpool); T. O. MORGAN, Esq., Aberystwith (and Lincoln's Inn).

IV. A General Meeting of the Members shall be held annually, on the first day of the month of October, or on a day soon after, and at such place as the Council shall appoint. And the President, or in his absence one of the Vice-Presidents, shall have power to call Extraordinary General Meetings, on giving, through the Secretaries, a fortnight's notice to the Members.

V. The Council shall be elected at a General Meeting, to continue in office for three years, and be capable of re-election.

VI. The names of the Members proposed to be elected into the Council shall be transmitted by the proposers to the Secretaries one fortnight before the General Meetings; and notice of the persons so proposed shall be forwarded by the Secretaries to all the Members.

VII. At the General Meetings votes for the election of the Council may be given either personally or *by letter* addressed to the Secretaries; but no Member shall be entitled to vote at a General Meeting whose subscription is in arrear.

VIII. Any vacancy which may occur in the Council, or in the offices of Secretaries or Treasurer, shall be provisionally filled up by the Council.

IX. Those gentlemen who have assented or do assent to these rules, and have signified their wish to become Members, shall be deemed original Members of the Society.

X. Subsequent Members may be elected by ballot at any one of the General Meetings, according to priority of application, upon being proposed in writing by two existing Members. One black ball in five shall exclude.

XI. The subscription of each Member shall be paid in advance to the Treasurer, and shall be as follows:—Any Member of the Cambrian Archæological Association who shall become an *original* Member of the Club shall pay the annual sum of half-a-guinea; any other Member of the Club shall pay the annual sum of one guinea. If any Member's subscription shall be in arrear for two years, and he shall neglect to pay his subscription after being reminded by the Treasurer, he shall be regarded as having ceased to be a Member of the Club.

XII. The Council may elect as an Honorary Member any gentleman contributing papers or information such as shall, in their judgment, be in furtherance of the objects of the Club.

XIII. The objects of the Club shall be carried out with the honorary assistance of the Members, and the funds of the Club shall be disbursed in printing and illustrating such information as shall be contributed by the Members, searching for and transcribing public records, etc., and the necessary expenses of the Club.

XIV. The members are earnestly invited to contribute articles and information; and contributors of papers shall be entitled to twelve copies of such articles.

XV. Every member not in arrear of his annual subscription will be entitled to one copy of every publication of the Club, to be delivered as soon as it shall be completed.

XVI. The Council shall determine what numbers of each publication shall be printed, and the copies over and above those required for the Members shall be sold to the public at such time and price as may be fixed by the Council, and the proceeds to be carried to the account of the Club.

XVII. No alteration shall be made in these Laws, except at an Anniversary Meeting; one month's notice of any proposed alteration to be communicated, in writing, to the Secretaries.

At the Second Annual Meeting of the Club, held on the 11th of October 1869, in pursuance of notice given in accordance with Rule XVII, the following alterations in the Laws were made—

"That the Club shall be extended, and shall consist of not more than two hundred members; all additional Members shall pay the annual subscription of one guinea.

"That the Secretary shall be at liberty to admit Members up to that enlarged limit; the applicants for membership who are willing to pay the back subscriptions so as to entitle them to the back parts of the publication of the Club, to have the preference.

"That the Secretaries shall also be at liberty to admit new Members to supply vacancies caused by death, or resignation, or non-payment of subscriptions.

"That the following words be added to Rule XII : 'or may present him with a copy of all or any of the publications of the Club.'"

At the Seventh Annual Meeting of the Powys-land Club, held on the 5th of October 1874, the following were adopted as

"THE RULES OF THE POWYS-LAND MUSEUM AND LIBRARY."

1. The Museum and Library shall be open to the public on Saturdays and Mondays from Ten to Four, on payment by each person of an admission fee of threepence : except on the last Saturday in each month, when from One to Four it shall be open free of charge.

2. An annual family subscription of 5s. shall admit all the members of a family subscribing, and an annual subscription of 2s. 6d. shall admit an individual person, on Saturdays and Mondays, for one year.

3. The Members of the Powys-land Club shall have access to the Museum and Library every day (Sundays excepted) from Ten to Four, and also shall have the privilege of taking therein any personal friends accompanying them, on Tuesdays, Wednesdays, Thursdays, and Fridays.

4. That donors to the Building Fund, to the amount of 10s. or upwards, and their families, shall be admitted free on Saturdays and Mondays, for one year, from the opening of the Museum and Library.

5. Each person visiting the Museum and Library shall be required to enter his or her name in a Visitors' book, to be provided for that purpose.

6. No article or book shall on any account be removed from the Museum and Library, without the special permission of the Committee.

At the Eighth Annual Meeting of the Powys-land Club, held on the 4th of October 1875, in pursuance of notice given in accordance with Rule XVII, an alteration in the laws was made by the adoption of the following additional rule :—

"XVIII. That no dividend, gift, division, or bonus in money shall be made unto or between any of the Members of the Powys-land Club, or of the said Museum or Library, or any other person whatsoever."

And the following alteration and addition to the Rules of the Powys-land Museum and Library were made.

Rule I was altered to read thus:—

"1. That the public shall be admitted to the Museum every week-day, from Ten to Four, on the payment of an admission fee of Threepence, except when the Council shall otherwise determine; and except on the last Saturday in each month, when from One to Four it shall be opened free of charge."

The following additional Rule was adopted:—

"That the Books in the Library shall be open gratuitously to the public, subject to such regulations as shall be made by the Council."

(Signed)   Powis   *President.*

D. P. Lewis.
A. Howell.   } *Three Members of the Council.*
Henry P. Ffoulkes.

R. E. Jones.   } *A Member of the Powys-land Club.*

Morris Chas. Jones.
William V. Lloyd.   } *Honorary Secretaries.*

"I hereby certify that this Society is entitled to the benefit of the Act 6 and 7 Vict., cap. 36, entituled, "An Act to exempt from County, Borough, Parochial, and other Local Rates, Lands and Buildings occupied by Scientific, or Literary Societies."

(Signed)   "J. M. Ludlow,
" Chief Registrar of Friendly Societies,

"The Barrister appointed to certify the Rules of Savings Banks, for the Central Office, London, 19th November 1875."

LIST OF THE MEMBERS

OF THE

POWYS-LAND CLUB.

September 30, 1882.

---

*Those marked * have contributed papers to the " Montgomeryshire Collections".*

Those marked † are Donors of Objects to the Powys-land Museum and Library.

Those marked ‡ have exhibited articles of interest at the Annual Meeting.

†Adnitt, W. H., Esq., Lystonville, Shrewsbury

Babington, Charles C., Esq., F.S.A., 5, Brookside, Cambridge
*†Barrett, Thomas Brettell, Esq., Welshpool
*†Barnwell, Rev. E. L., M.A., Melksham, Wilts
Bates, J. Cadwallader, Esq., Heddon Banks, Wylam-on-Tyne
Beattie, John, Esq., Shortwood, Teddington Park, Middlesex
Beattie, Joseph, Esq., 242, Hagley Road, Edgbaston, Birmingham
‡Beck, Peter Arthur, Esq., Trelydan Hall, Welshpool (*Hon. Treasurer*)
†‡Bennett, Nicholas, Esq., Glanyrafon, Caersws
†Black, Adam William, Esq., 28, York Place, Edinburgh
Bolding, George Frederick, Esq., 204, Hagley Road, Edgbaston, Birmingham
*Bridgeman, Hon. and Rev. Canon, M.A., The Hall, Wigan
Bridgeman, Hon. and Rev. J. R. O., M.A., Rectory, Weston-under-Lyziard, Shifnal
Brisco, Wastel, Esq., Southcott, Reading
‡Buckley, Sir Edmund, Bart., Plas Dinas, Dinas Mawddwy

*Clark, George Thomas, Esq., Dowlais House, Dowlais
Cokayne, George E., Esq., M.A.Oxon., F.S.A., *Norroy King of Arms*, College of Arms, London
†Curling, Mrs., Brookland Hall, Welshpool

‡Davies, Henry, Esq., Town Clerk, Oswestry
*†Davies, Rev. Prebendary, M.A., Moor Court, Kington, Herefordshire
Davies, John D., Esq., Llanidloes
†‡Davies, John Pryce, Esq., Bronfelin, Caersws
Dugdale, John, Esq., Llwyn, Llanfyllin
*†Edwards, Rev. Griffith, M.A., Rectory, Llangadfan, Welshpool

*Edwards, Rev. Canon Wynne, Rectory, Llanrhaiadr-yn-Kinmerch, Denbighshire
†‡Edye, Thomas, Esq., 5, St. Paul's Road, Camden Square, London
*Evans, Rev. D. Silvan, B.D., Rectory, Llanwrin, Machynlleth
†Evans, David Williams, Esq., Clifton, Nottingham, and Glascoed, Llansantffraid
‡Evans, Rev. Edward, M.A., Rectory, Llanfihangel yn Nghwnfa, Llanfyllin, Oswestry
†Evans, Edward, Esq., Bronwylfa, Wrexham
†‡Evans, Edward Bickerton, Esq., Whitbourne Hall, Worcester
†‡Evans, John, Esq., LL.D., F.R.S., Nash Mills, Hemel Hempsted
†Evans, John Hilditch, Esq., Bryn Issa, Pershore, Worcestershire
†Evans, Joseph, Esq., Hurst House, Prescot (*two copies*)
Eyre, Rev. W., St. Beuno's College, St. Asaph

†‡Fardo, George, Esq., Sub-Comptroller, Post Office, Liverpool
Ffoulkes, Ven. Archdeacon, M.A., Rectory, Whittington, Salop
Ffoulkes, W. Wynne, Esq., Old Northgate House, Chester
†‡Field, Rev. Augustus, M.A., Pool Quay, Vicarage, Welshpool
*†‡Fisher, William, Esq., Maesfron, Welshpool
Foljambe, C. S. G., Esq., M.P., Cocklode, Ollerton

†‡Gillart, Richard, Esq., Llynlloed, Machynlleth

Harlech, The Lord, Brogyntyn, Oswestry (*Vice-President*)
†Harrison, George Devereux, Esq., Fronllwyd, Welshpool
Harrison, Colonel John Pryce, 1, Seagrave Place, Cheltenham
Harrison, Robert John, Esq., Caerhowel, Montgomery
Hayman, Rev. Canon Samuel, M.A., Grange-Erin, Douglas, Cork
Herbert, Colonel Geo. Edward, Upper Helmsley Hall, Yorkshire, and Glanhafren, Newtown, Montgomeryshire
Herbert, John Maurice, Esq., Rocklands, Ross
‡Heyward, Colonel John Heyward, Crosswood, Guilsfield
*†‡Hill, Rev. J. E., M.A., Vicarage, Welshpool
†Hilton, Edwin, Esq., Glynhirieth, Llanfair-caereinion
*‡Howell, Abraham, Esq., Rhiewport, Berriew
*Howell, David, Esq., Dolguog, Machynlleth
Howell, Evan, Esq., 4a, St. Paul's Churchyard, London
Hughes, H. R., Esq., Kinmel, St. Asaph
†Hurst, Robert, Esq., Borough Surveyor, Welshpool
Hutchings, Lewis, Esq., Welshpool

Inner Temple Library, London (J. Pickering, Esq., Librarian)

Jehu, Richard, Esq., 21, Cloudesley Street, Islington, London
†Jones, Charles, Esq., Salop Road, Welshpool
†‡Jones, Edward, Esq., Town Clerk, Welshpool
†Jones, Edward Maurice, Esq., Westwood, Welshpool

Jones, John, Esq., Bellan House, Oswestry
*Jones, John, Esq., Staff Commander, R.N., F.R.G.S., Blue Bell, near Welshpool
*†‡Jones, Morris Charles, Esq., F.S.A., F.S.A.Scot., Gungrog, Welshpool (*Honorary Secretary*)
†‡Jones, Morris Patterson, Esq., Heatherlea, 7, Holly Road, Fairfield, Liverpool
‡Jones, Pryce, Esq., Dolerw, Newtown
†Jones, Richard Edward, Esq., Cefn Bryntalch, Abermule, Mont.
Jones, T. Parry, Esq., Park House, Newtown
*†Jones, T. Simpson, Esq., M.A., 77, Chancery Lane, London; and Gungrog, Welshpool
*Jones, William, Esq., Mount Pleasant, Over, Winsford

Kynaston, Rev. W. C. E., M.A., Hardwicke Hall, Ellesmere

‡Londonderry, The Marquis of, K P, Plas, Machynlleth (*Vice-President*)
*‡Leighton, Stanley, Esq., M.P., Sweeney Hall, Oswestry
†‡Lewis, Rev. David Phillips, M.A., Rectory, Llandrinio
Lewis, Lewis, Esq., Newtown Hall, Newtown
†Lewis, Rev. John, M.A., Vicarage, Ford, Salop
Lewis, Samuel, Esq., Holborn Bars, London
Lewis, Rev. T. Wolseley, M.A., Garth Garmon, Cheltenham
Liverpool Free Public Library (Peter Cowell, Esq., Chief Librarian)
*‡Lloyd, J. Y. W., Esq., M.A., Clochfaen, Llanidloes
Lloyd, Henry, Esq., Pentreheilin, Llanymynech, R.S.O., and Dolobran, Meifod
*†Lloyd, Howell William, Esq., 19, Hogarth Road, South Kensington, W.
Lloyd, Mrs. Richard H., Tayles Hill, Ewell, Surrey
†Lloyd, Sampson S., Esq., Moore Hall, Sutton Coldfield, Birmingham, and Dolobran, Meifod
*†‡Lloyd, Rev. William Valentine, R.N., F.R.G.S., Haselbech Rectory, Northampton (*Honorary Secretary*)
†Lovell, Mrs., Llanerchydol, Welshpool

Marsh, Miss Mary, Tybrith, Carno
†Matthews, Rev. Prebendary, M.A., Rectory, Llandisilio, Oswestry
Mickleburgh, John, Esq., Hendomen, Montgomeryshire
Miller, Samuel, Esq., The Court, Abermule, Montgomeryshire
‡Mirehouse, Rev. John, M.A., Colsterworth Rectory, Grantham
‡Morgan, Charles, Esq., Bidlington House, Steyning, Sussex
Morgan, Cornelius, Esq., High Street, Newtown
Morgan, David, Esq., High Street, Welshpool
Morgan, Edward, Esq., Machynlleth
Morgan, George, Esq., The Fron, Newtown
†Morris, Joseph Pugh, Esq., Salop Road, Welshpool
‡Mytton, Devereux Herbert, Esq., Garth, Welshpool
Mytton, Miss, Severn Street, Welshpool

Northumberland, His Grace the Duke of, Alnwick Castle, Northumberland
*†Newill, Thomas, Esq., Powis Castle Park, Welshpool
Nixon, Edward, Esq., Savile House, Methley, Leeds

Oswestry and Welshpool Naturalist Field Club and Archæological Society (Rev. O. W. Fielden, Frankton Rectory, Oswestry, *Sec.*)
†Owen, Arthur Charles Humphreys, Glansevern, Garthmyl, Mont.
†Owen, D. C. Lloyd, Esq., F.R.C.S., 51, Newhall Street, and Penbryn, Rotton Park Road, Edgbaston, Birmingham
†Owen, David Pryce, Esq., Broad Street, Welshpool
*†Owen, Rev. Elias, M.A., Ruthin
†Owen, Rev. R. Trevor, M.A., Vicarage, Llangedwyn
Owen, Rev. Thomas Ketley, Wellington, Salop
*†Owen, T. Morgan, Esq., M.A., Bronwylfa, Rhyl

*†‡Powis, The Earl of, Powis Castle, Welshpool (*President*)
†‡Parker, Rev. F. W., M.A., Rectory, Montgomery
†‡Parker, W. T., Esq., Traethllawn, Welshpool
‡Parry, Love Jones, Esq., F.S.A., Madryn Castle, Pwllheli
‡Perrott, Robert Simcocks, Esq., Bronhyddon, Llansantffraid
Powell, Evan, Esq., Broomcliffe, Llanidloes
†‡Powell, Samuel, Esq., Ivy House, Welshpool
Powys, Bransby William, Esq., 1, Lincoln's Inn Fields, London
‡Pritchard, W. E. Gilbertson, Esq., Ceniarth, Machynlleth
*Price, Lewis R., Esq., 117, St. George's Square, London (*deceased*)
‡Pryce, Mrs. Gunley, Chirbury
†Pryce, Edward S. Mostyn, Esq., Machen House, near Newport, Monmouthshire
†‡Pryce, Elijah, Esq., Trederwen House, Llansantffraid, Oswestry
†Pryce, Thomas, Esq., Whitehall, Batavia
†Pryce, Robert Davies, Esq., Cyffronydd, Welshpool
*Pugh, Wm. Buckley, Esq., Dolfor Hall, Kerry, and Patrington, Hull
Pugh, Thomas, Esq., 408, Sixth Street, Washington, U.S.A.

†Read, Offley Malcolm Crewe, Esq., Llandinam Hall, Llanidloes, and 16, Palace Gardens, London
Rendel, Stuart, Esq., M.P., Plas Dinam, Llanidloes
†Richards, Thomas, Esq., 47, Holland Road, Kensington, London
†Roberts, Rev. Richard, M.A., Vicarage, Amlwch, Anglesea
Roberts, Rev. Robert Jones, M.A., Buttington Vicarage, Welshpool
Robinson, E. F., Esq., M.B., Park Lane, Welshpool
Robinson, George E., Esq., Post Office Chambers, Cardiff
†Rutter, Thomas, Esq., Church Bank, Welshpool

St. Asaph, The Bishop of, The Palace, St. Asaph (*Vice-President*)
Sudeley, The Lord, Toddington, Gloucestershire (*Vice-President*)
Salt, George Moultrie, Esq., Quarry Place, Salop
Salisbury, Rev. E. E. Baylee, B.D., Winceby Rectory, Horncastle, Lincolnshire
Salusbury, Rev. George Augustus, M.A., Westbury Rectory, Salop

*Sandford, Rev. George, M.A., Ecclesall Vicarage, Sheffield
Savin, Thomas, Esq., Oswestry
Sladen, Rev. E. H. Mainwaring, M.A., The Gore, Bournemouth.
Slaughter, Rev. Edward, St. Mary's, Old Bidston Road, Birkenhead
*†Smith, Charles Perin, Esq., Trenton, New Jersey, U.S. America
†Smith, J. Russell, Esq., 36, Soho Square, London
Sotheran, Henry, Esq., 136, Strand, London
Sowerby, Thomas, Esq., M.R.C.S., Welshpool
Squires, Mrs., Fairfield, Clevedon, Somersetshire
Storey, Thomas, Esq., Westfield, Lancaster
†‡Sturkey, Thomas, Esq., Newtown
†Swettenham, William Norman, Esq., M.R.Inst.C.E., County Surveyor, Newtown, Mont.
Swithinbank, George Edwin, Esq., LL.D., Ormleigh, Omerly Park, London, S.E.

Temple, Rev. R., M.A., Melynlog, Oswestry
*†Thomas, Rev. Canon D. R., M.A., Vicarage, Meifod, Welshpool
Tracy, The Hon. Frederick Hanbury, M.P., Penybryn, Montgomery
Trinity College Library, Cambridge (Rev. R. Sinker, M.A., Librarian)
†Tudor, Owen Davies, Esq., 2, Collingham Road, South Kensington, London

†‡Vaughan, Mrs., Brookside, Welshpool
Verney, G. H., Esq., The Cedars, Esher, Surrey

†Wynn, Sir Watkin Williams, Bart., M.P., Wynnstay, Ruabon (*Vice-President*)
*†‡Walker, David, Esq., Architect, 11, Dale Street, Liverpool
Westworth, Robert, Esq., 31, King Street, Liverpool
†‡Wilding, William, Esq., Town Clerk, Montgomery
Williams, Edward, Esq., Broome Hall, Oswestry
Williams, E. W. Colt, Esq., H.M. Inspector of Schools, Hereford
‡Williams, Rev. John, M.A., Rectory, Newtown
*Williams, Rev. Canon Robert, M.A., Rectory, Llanfyllin
*†‡Williams, Richard, Esq., Celynog, Newtown
*Williams, Stephen W., Esq., Penralley, Rhayader
†Williames, Rees Buckley, Esq., Glyncôgen, Berriew, Mont.
†‡Winder, Major Corbett, Vaynor Park, Berriew, Montgomeryshire
Withy, William, Esq., Severn Street, Welshpool
Woods, Sir Albert W., *Garter King of Arms*, College of Arms, London, E.C.
Wright, Philip, Esq., Mellington Hall, Churchstoke, Montgomery
†‡Wynn, Charles Watkin Williams, Esq., Coed-y-Maen, Welshpool
Wynne, W. R. M., Esq., Peniarth, Towyn

After 1st October, 1882.

Price, Mrs. Lewis R., 117, St. George Street, London; and Marrington Hall, Chirbury, Salop

THE FIFTEENTH ANNUAL MEETING.

The Fifteenth Annual Meeting of the Powys-Land Club was held at the Powys-Land Museum and Library, on Monday, the 2nd October 1882. There was a numerous attendance, comprising the Rev. D. P. Lewis, Rector of Llandrinio, Abraham Howell, Esq., P. A. Beck, Esq., (Treasurer), Captain Mytton, Captain John Jones, R.N., W. Fisher, Esq., S. Powell, Esq., C. Howell, Esq., Charles Jones, Esq., W. Withy, Esq., T. Withy, Esq., Charles Howell, Esq., T. Rutter, Esq., James Williams, Esq., A. Field, jun., Esq., Edward Jones, Esq., (Town Clerk), W. T. Parker, Esq., Morris P. Jones, Esq., W. Nevett, Esq., Morris C. Jones, F.S.A., etc. There were numerous ladies present, amongst whom were—Mrs. Harrison (of Caerhowell), Mrs. Lovell, Mrs. Curling, Miss Harrison, Miss Mytton, Miss Davidson, Miss Rownson, Mrs. Morris P. Jones, Miss Morris Jones, Mrs. and Miss Lewis Lewis, Newtown Hall.

It was moved by Mr. HOWELL, and seconded by Mr. MORRIS C. JONES, that the Rev. D. P. Lewis (a Member of the Council), do take the chair.

The SECRETARY read a letter from the Earl of Powis regretting that he was unable to attend, as he was unexpectedly obliged to go up to London on Monday. Also similar communications excusing their attendance were received from the Revs. J. E. Hill, F. W. Parker, Augustus Field, R. J. Roberts, Griffith Edwards, Canon Thomas, and John Lewis; and Messrs. Richard Williams and Morgan Owen.

The CHAIRMAN, after expressing regret at the unavoidable absence of Lord Powis, called upon the Secretary and Treasurer to read the Reports. The Committee's Annual Report was as follows:—

The Annual Report of the Committee to the Annual Meeting of the Powys-land Club, held on the 2nd October 1882.

The Committee, in presenting their Annual Report, have the pleasure of reporting the continued well-doing of the Club.

There have been four deaths during the last year, viz., Mrs. Pugh Johnson of Llanerchydol, the Rev. Joseph McIntosh, Rev. Canon David Williams, and Mr. Lewis R. Price.

Four names have been removed from the roll of Members owing to the non-payment of subscriptions for three years. Eight have resigned. Six new Members have joined the Club.

The finances are in a satisfactory condition. All liabilities have been paid, and there remains a balance of £139 13s. 4d. in hand. It is proposed to transfer £100 of that balance to the building and repair account at Lloyd's Banking Company, to the credit of which there will also shortly be added the promised donation of £100 from Mr. Joseph Evans. There will then be £231 11s. 10d. to the credit of that account, which will enable the Committee to effect some improvements in the Museum and Library, when thought necessary.

The triennial period has arrived for the appointment of the officers of the Society, and the Committee recommend the re-election of the present officers.

Through accidental circumstances—loss of health and other engagements—the literary contributions to the *Montgomeryshire Collections* have not been quite so numerous as in previous years; but the prospect for the future is more encouraging, and it is hoped a successful effort will be made for future work.

The British Museum has been making grants of duplicate objects to provincial museums. The Committee, feeling that museums in small places are apt to be overlooked, and that grants are preferentially made to museums in large towns, have availed themselves of every opportunity of pressing the claims of this hitherto unassisted Museum to participate in this distribution, and their efforts have met with some degree of success. The Library has received, through the instrumentality of Mr. Stuart Rendel, M.P., a donation from the British Museum of twenty-eight volumes of books of a valuable character, which, it is trusted, is only an earnest of further donations of a like kind.

Mr. David Davies, M.P., has also presented a considerable number of Parliamentary Blue Books. These and other additions have increased the Library to about 700 volumes, and have involved the necessity of providing another large book-case, which affords vacant shelf-room for 200 or 300 more volumes, which the Committee hope will soon be filled.

The collection of local portraits has been considerably increased.

The Committee are glad to be able to announce that arrangements have been made for the resuscitation of the Art Classes under the same master (Mr. Cortissos) as before, and that they have granted the Art Classes the use of the Reading-room.

The Hon. Treasurer then read the financial report. (See pp. xxii and xxiii.)

The Chairman, in moving that the Reports then read be adopted and confirmed, and printed and circulated among the Members, said he had been quite unexpectedly called upon to

The Powys-land Club in account with Peter Arthur Beck, Esq., and ending

To Cash paid as follows :—

" Mr. Richards for Printing Report of Meeting and Supplementary Part £20 17 2

" Ditto for Printing Part XXX . . . 56 19 9

" Ditto for Printing Part XXXI . . . 57 15 0

" Paid for Drawing and Lithographing Illustrations, and Copying 12 5 6

" Paid for Postage of Report and Parts XXX and XXXI, to Members; also of back Parts to New Members; Postage of Circulars, collecting Subscriptions, and remitting same, Reporter, etc. . 12 7 11

" Paid for Book-case, etc., for Museum . . 15 19 0

" Balance carried down . . . 139 13 4

£315 17 8

Hon. Treasurer, for the year commencing 1*st October* 1881, 30*th September* 1882.

By Balance in hand	£104	2	8
,, Cash received from Subscriptions as follows :—			
9 Subscriptions from Original Members at 10s. 6d. each	4	14	6
157 Subscriptions from Ordinary Members at £1 1s. each	164	17	0
Special :—			
1 The Earl of Powis .	5	5	0
Arrears received	9	9	0
Subscriptions of next year received in advance from Old Members	10	10	0
8 Members who last year, or previously, paid this year's Subscription in advance.			
11 Continuing and Deceased Members, in arrear, amounting, besides bad debts, to £18 17s. 0d.			
186 Number on List of Members on 30th Sept. 1882.			
Cash received for books sold . . .	11	18	6
,, illustration fund . . .	5	1	0
	£315	17	8
1882, October. By balance in hand brought down .	£139	13	4

occupy that position and was not at all, therefore, prepared with a speech. He afterwards alluded to the valuable gifts of books and of photo-lithographic facsimiles of ancient charters which had been lately made to the Museum and Library by the authorities of the British Museum. The copies of charters, he said, would be found very useful indeed to any person in the neighbourhood who might wish to pursue studies of that kind. A number of Blue Books had also been presented by Mr. David Davies, M.P. Blue Books were not usually considered very amusing reading. He himself had had at various times to read them up for certain purposes, and he could not call them particularly entertaining; they might, however, be useful to persons who wished to acquire information upon special subjects. In connection with archæological research, the reverend gentleman then alluded to the late Egyptian campaign. Had it not been for the numberless researches and discoveries which had been made since the beginning of the century, when Napoleon took French savants with him to Egypt, recent events there would have been watched with the keenest interest by antiquaries. As it was, he thought all who were interested in the remains of an ancient race must be grateful to Sir Garnet Wolseley for moving so rapidly upon Cairo, and thus preserving antiquities of priceless value, which might otherwise have been destroyed through the fanaticism of Arabi Pasha and his followers.

Mr. Howell seconded the motion, which was carried unanimously.

Capt. John Jones proposed, and Mr. Elijah Pryce seconded, that the officers of the Society be re-elected.

The motion was also agreed to.

Mr. Samuel Powell, in a highly eulogistic speech, moved a vote of thanks to the Chairman, and in doing so referred to his services in the cause of archæology, and spoke of him as one of the first antiquaries in Montgomeryshire.

Mr. Edward Jones (Town Clerk) seconded the motion, which was carried with acclamation.

The Chairman, in acknowledging the vote of thanks, said he had lived in the neighbourhood thirty-five years, and had always taken a great interest in its affairs, especially in reference to archæology; but he must strongly disclaim any right to be called one of the first archæologists of Montgomeryshire, or even second or third, in the presence of so distinguished an antiquary, and one who had rendered such signal service to local archæology by the formation of that Museum, and by his labours on behalf of the Powys-land Club, as Mr. Morris Charles Jones.

The CHAIRMAN then proposed a vote of thanks to the Secretary, which was seconded by Mr. A. HOWELL, and cordially adopted.

The SECRETARY briefly replied, and mentioned, with reference to the unavoidable absence of the Earl of Powis, which had naturally caused some disappointment, that the Club had held fourteen Annual Meetings previous to that Meeting, and at eleven of them his lordship had presided. By this public and constant support he had done the Club essential service, for which they were deeply grateful.

A paper, entitled "A Review of the Progress and Prospects of the Powys-land Club", by the Secretary, was taken as read.

A REVIEW OF THE PROGRESS AND PROSPECTS OF THE POWYS-LAND CLUB.

The Club has now run half its sixteenth year, having been commenced on the 1st March 1867.

We propose to review—

I. What has been done.

II. What is still undone; and the prospects of doing the uncompleted work.

I. The Club has been in existence more than half a generation, and the most painful matter connected with it is the ever-recurring dropping off by death of its Members, with all of whom I have been more or less acquainted.

In its whole career it has had 272 Members. Of that number 45 have died, being an average of 3 per annum—not so high an average as might have been expected, considering most of its Members are of mature age, and many in advanced years. One Member is a nonagenarian. Some few have resigned.

Of the original Members, 52 still continue; 32 Members have contributed papers to the *Montgomeryshire Collections*. The present number of the Club, 179.

Financial.—The financial features of the Club have been remarkable. In the fifteen years, the aggregate of its subscriptions, etc., has been £2,894. Of that there has been expended—

In printing . . . . £1,863, or on an average, £124 per ann.
In illustrations, besides gifts . 228 „ 15 „
In fittings for Museum . 246
And investment for repair fund . . . 216
 ——— 462 30 „

In other necessary expenses,
such as postages, circulars,
etc.. . . . . £200, or, on an average, £12 per ann.
Balance in hand . . . 139

The Club has no liabilities, and it has a stock of about twenty complete sets of the *Transactions*, besides incomplete sets, and a large number of wood blocks, all which are worth at least £350.

We may mention parenthetically that this is irrespective of the outlay on the Museum and Library, and the Cottage, which has been raised by special subscriptions, amounting to £1,500, and of the crowded contents of the Museum, and about 700 volumes in the Library, all presented, which have been given by 388 donors. But we consider this the subsidiary—not the main—work of the Club.

We now come to what to us is more important than the financial or mechanical operations of the Club (that is to say) the collecting and printing of the historical and archæological remains of Montgomeryshire. We shall enumerate the subjects in the order in which they appear to us as of the most importance.

I. The Parochial Histories. The histories of fourteen parishes have been completed, and four are in progress; but two of the latter have hung fire for some time.

These may be considered topographical articles mainly, but they comprise more or less the other four branches, which the Club professed to include, viz., the historical, ecclesiastical, genealogical, and literary divisions.

II. The Genealogical Researches have resulted in elaborate disquisitions upon the sheriffs of the county, and many other articles which have thrown much light upon the families sprung from the district, and these we trust will be continued.

One gentleman, to testify his sense of the value of the genealogical collections, and in recognition of the aid he had received therefrom in investigating and establishing his pedigree, has intimated his intention of giving £100 towards the Museum Building Fund, for any future addition or improvement.

III. The Original Documents printed,
The Disquisitions on the Religious Houses,
The Biographical Notices,
The Notices of Antiquities found,
The Heraldic inquiries made,

And other papers on cognate subjects, too numerous to classify and specify, form a mass of information such as has not been collected respecting any other county in Wales.

Without presumption, we may claim for the *Montgomeryshire Collections* to be regarded as a storehouse of material for "the historian, the antiquarian, and the man of science."

With reference to Heraldry, it is intended, if possible, to compile xxvii

a list of those families resident, or being landowners in Montgomeryshire, whose arms are registered in the College of Arms.

In this part of Wales, and perhaps not in Montgomeryshire alone, several bad practices, *heraldically speaking*, prevail.

One is that the possessor of an estate derived from a maternal ancestor, whom he represents, often adopts the maternal coat of arms to the exclusion of his paternal coat; when, in point of fact, he is only entitled to quarter the former with the latter. If he cannot prove his title to arms on the paternal side, he cannot, we conceive, properly use the maternal arms at all.

Another practice is to assume to quarter all the various arms of the families from which he is descended—whether he represents them through heiresses or not. Thus not unfrequently a crowd of unauthorised quarterings is seen on Welsh coats of arms.

The still worse practice is to assume arms to which the assumer has no title.

It is easy to say that heraldry is all nonsense and obsolete. Those who say so, to be consistent, should altogether abstain from the assumption of arms, whether they can prove their descent from armigerous ancestors, or not.

But, on the other hand, if heraldry be recognised or acknowledged as an existing science, no one should assume, unauthorisedly, armorial insignia. If he should use arms which have no authorised existence, the act justly subjects him to ridicule. If he assume arms belonging to another family, it is an infringement of that family's rights, and he is acting under false pretences, holding it out to the world that he is of a family with which he has no proved connection.

There are some few—very few—families who have borne arms from time almost immemorial, which arms are not registered in the College of Arms. The descendants of those families may with just pride bear their unregistered arms. If Foster's *Baronetage* is to be trusted, the arms of one of the most prominent families in Wales are not registered; but who for a moment doubts their authenticity?

But on the other hand, most of the armorial bearings of armigerous families are, as a matter of fact, registered in the College of Arms, and those who can prove their descent, can have their arms confirmed and exemplified by the Heralds' College.

Many have a reasonable tradition—amounting, perhaps, to presumptive evidence—of certain arms having been borne by those from whom they are descended; but have not absolute proof sufficient to satisfy the College of Arms. Such persons, we conceive, should not presume to use the arms without authority; but should apply to the College of Arms—the recognised authority in such matters,—and obtain a grant of the arms, with such difference as the College may impose.

To any Member of the Powys-land Club who should be so minded, not content to assume unauthorised and unauthentic arms, the

Secretary would feel the greatest pleasure in placing his honorary services at their disposal, for the attainment of their wishes, and for placing their heraldic pretensions upon a proper basis.

With reference to the practice of certain well-known arms being worn in common by several families of different names settled in Montgomeryshire, it has been well observed by an experienced genealogist that "such was a confusing and improper usage, as it is clear that only the heir-at-law, or co-heir of some great *homo propositus*, entitled to those arms, could wear them, without substantial difference. Some Cambrian antiquary may be able to say who's who, and all the others should obtain differenced grants."

II. What remains undone, and the prospect of doing it, is the next topic. We think it unnecessary to allude specifically to any other subject than the parochial histories, as they practically comprise all others, although some subjects are often treated separately.

We have seen, of the forty-seven original parishes of which Montgomeryshire consists, parochial histories have been written of fourteen completely and four partially. The aggregate, eighteen, of these only slightly exceeds one-third of the whole number in the County.

Of the remaining twenty-nine original parishes, we have a reasonable expectation of the following eight parishes being speedily undertaken by competent parties, viz. :—

1. Newtown,
2. Llanllwchaiarn, } by Mr. Richard Williams.
3. Llanerfyl, by Rev. Griffith Edwards.
4. Montgomery, by Mr. W. Wilding.
5. Llandrinio,
6. Llandysilio, } by Mr. John Fewtrell.
7. Llanfair Caereinion is in MS.
8. Llanbrynmair, by Mr. Richard Williams.

The Summary would be : Completed . . 14
        Partially done . . 4
        Promised . . . 8
            ——26

Leaving 21 untouched, besides several portions of parishes running into adjoining counties.

The present Secretary and Editor feels that he cannot himself reasonably expect to carry on the work of the Club beyond the twentieth volume, although he is sanguine enough to *aim* at that at least. After that he will be prepared to resign the completion of the work to younger and abler hands. A new series probably would then be commenced; the introduction of new blood may infuse new life into the Club.

He earnestly hopes that during the time his health enables him to pursue the work, he will not appeal in vain to the members and others to complete the parochial histories.

It is hoped that this Review may be the means of stimulating others to commence at least some branch of the work in reference to the remaining parishes.

It is intended to propose to get it done by sections; for instance, to appeal to each Clergyman to write the ecclesiastical chapter of his parish's history—giving an account of his church, communion plate, monumental inscriptions, terriers, lists of rectors and vicars, etc., etc. This alone would be a great step gained in completing the unfinished work. Judging from the past, such an appeal will, it is hoped, meet with a hearty response.

Although we make this special appeal with respect to parochial histories, which we deem of paramount importance, we still hope and beg for the continuance of the series of Biographical, Genealogical and other articles which have been long in progress, and also for reports of any "finds" of antiquities.

We should also greatly appreciate the communication of pedigrees, original documents, and such miscellaneous items of antiquarian interest as we can place in our yearly article, entitled "Miscellanea."

We consider the store of material for the *Montgomeryshire Collections* far from being exhausted, and we look with confidence to the accomplishment (possibly under other auspices) of far greater results than have hitherto been attained.

CLASSIFIED LIST OF ARTICLES,

PRESENTED, BETWEEN NOVEMBER 1881, AND NOVEMBER 1882, TO THE POWYS-LAND MUSEUM AND LIBRARY, WITH THE NAMES OF THE DONORS.*

(Continued from Mont. Coll., Vol. xiv, *p.* xxxv.)

IRON :—
Presented by **(380)** J. E. POUNDLEY (1882).
1. Sword belonging to Rev. James Hamer, Llanfihangel, Captain in the Montgomeryshire Volunteers under Sir Watkin Williams Wynn, Bart., *tempore* George III.

Presented by **(21)** Rev. AUGUSTUS FIELD (1882).
8. An ancient lock.

Presented by **(191)** HERBERT BICKERTON, Liverpool (1882).
2. Five fragments of bomb shells, and a fusé, brought from the sheets of Strasburg by Thomas Bickerton, in October 1870.
3. Three fragments of shells from Porta Pia Gate, Rome, October 12th, 1870.
4. Two ditto from the Bastion and Ramparts of Paris, 1871.

BRASS, ETC. :—
Presented by **(119)** D. W. EVANS (1882).
4. A poke or pocket sundial or viatorium [see *Mont. Coll.*, vol. xv, p. 71].
5. A larger pocket sundial of an elaborate character found at Llansantffraid.

Presented by **(381)** R. HARPER (1882).
1. Engraved copper plate, form of bill of "Edward Bayley, Oak Inn, Pool."

Presented by **(353)** Mrs. SQUIRES.
7. A piece of Indian Armour brought by Col. Burrows from Afghanistan in 1830.

STONE :—
Presented by **(382)** E. T. D. HARRISON (1882).
1. Stone celt, $9\frac{1}{2}$ inches long, 6 inches broad at the widest end.
2. The like, 9 inches long and $4\frac{1}{2}$ broad.

---

* Each donor's name has a large number prefixed, and each of his donations is numbered consecutively with a small number. This is done for the future identification of the donations.

3. The like, 6½ inches long and 3 inches broad. The three were brought from the Fiji Islands.

4. An instrument formed of mahogany 25 inches long and carved, and at one end a branch or fork, in which apparently a flint or metal celt could be fixed with vegetable fibre.

Presented by **(383)** J. Park Harrison (1882).

1. Specimens of flint implements from Cisbury, Sussex.

Presented by **(369)** Roger Kinsey (1882).

1. A circular stone vessel with protuberances or handles or pivots on either side. It is 6 inches in diameter outside and 4½ inches deep. The cavity is round, with a flat bottom 3¾ inches wide and 2½ inches deep. The pivots project 1¼ inches and are 1½ inches thick.

2. Part of a quern, found at Caersws.

Presented by **(384)** Miss Anne Maria Jones, Westwood (1882).

1. A hammer stone found at Westwood, Welshpool, on the excavating of the stables there, measuring 2¾ inches long and 1⅜ inches wide at the broadest place.

Presented by **(344)** James Williams (in exchange for two duplicate fossils (1882).

30. A hammer stone found in the mill race close to the Ford at Pool Quay, measuring 4½ inches long and 2 inches wide at broadest part.

31. Similar hammer found at the same time and place, measuring 3½ inches by 1½ inches.

Presented by **(21)** Rev. Augustus Field (1882).

9. A carved stone forming part of a hexagonal chimney, found on the banks of the Severn, near the site of Strata Marcella Abbey, after the destruction of Pool Quay Weir (see *Mont. Coll.*, vol. xv, p. 197). Also seven stones forming part of the same or a similar chimney, subsequently found at the same place.

Presented by **(86)** C. B. Black (1882).

4. A small stone celt, 2¾ inches long and 1¾ inches broad at the widest part, found in the neighbourhood of Corseul, Brittany ("which place is mentioned by Cæsar as the Capital of the Curiosolites".

Bone :—

Presented by **(383)** J. Park Harrison (1882).

2. Bone Implements (from Peru).

3. Pick of red deer horn and tine of ditto.
   Tools used by miners.

4. Back bone of deer.

Ancient Pottery, Mosaics, Glass, etc. :—

Presented by **(383)** J. Park Harrison (1882).

5. Spindle whorl (from Peru).

Presented by **(114)** T. B. Barrett (1882).

60. A Babylonish brick, 13 inches square and 3 inches thick, with

a cuneiform inscription therein, in a recessed panel, which panel measures 6 inches by 4¾ inches.

In 1859 the late Commodore Jenkins was at Bagdad, and had been engaged in an expedition up the Euphrates, and then received the brick from a friend.

Presented by **(21)** Rev. Augustus Field (1882).

10. Piece of ancient crockery found at Pool Quay.

Presented by **(229)** J. Fewtrell (1882).

An ancient tile, found in Llanymynech Churchyard.

Presented by **(385)** Miss Bickerton (1882).

1. Three specimens of mosaic out of the pavement of the Baths of Caracalla, Rome, (29th November 1876, serpentine green, porphyry red, composition blue).
2. Six bits of modern mosaic from St. Paul's, outside the walls.
3. Six specimens of ancient glass from an old tomb at Ostia.

Presented by **(86)** C. B. Black (1882).

5. *Tabatière* of old Rouen(?) fayence, bought from a person in Corseul, who received it from a peasant, in whose house it had been for a very long time.
6. A more modern *Tabatière*, made of the Grès of Normandie Domfront.

Coins, Medals :—

Presented by **(386)** Miss Edith Kerrison (1882).

Several foreign coins.

Presented by **(101)** D. C. Lloyd Owen (1882).

8. A series of 48 scarce medals, engraved by Thomason, illustrating the Elgin marbles, entitled *Thomason's Metallic Athenian Sculptures*.

Foreign Curiosities :—

Presented by **(382)** E. T. D. Harrison (1882).

A paddle.
A bow.
Two arrows or spears.
5. A ball formed of Calabash.

Presented by **(383)** J. Park Harrison (1882).

6. Miniature bow, Peruvian
7. Weaving stick ,,
8. Alpaca wool for weaving, Peruvian.
9. Charms ,,
10. Woollen string ,,
11. Waist belt apron (?) ,,

Presented by **(386)** Miss Edith Kerrison (1882).

1. Japanese note.

Presented by **(21)** Rev. Augustus Field (1882).

11. A Dutch note.

xxxiii

GEOLOGICAL SPECIMENS :—
Presented by **(385)** MISS BICKERTON (1882).
4. A piece of the Rock of Gibraltar (polished).
PORTRAITS OF MONTGOMERYSHIRE WORTHIES, AND OTHERS :—
Presented by **(114)** T. B. BARRETT (1882).
61. Portrait of the late Dr. Darwin of Shrewsbury, in black outline.
Presented by **(379)** MRS. LOVELL, Llanerchydol (1882).
1. Portrait of David Pugh, Esq., of Llanerchydol, M.P. for the Montgomery Boroughs. Executed by T. Bridge.
BOOKS :—
Presented by **(130)** MORRIS P. JONES (1882).
Ida de Galis, a tragedy of Powis Castle, by Rev. R. W. Morgan, A.M.

Presented by **(374)** SIR JAMES A. PICTON, F.S.A. (1882).
1. Primeval Man, a lecture delivered by him in 1881.

Presented by **(375)** J. PAUL RYLANDS, F.S.A. (1882).
1. Armorial Bearings existing in the churches of Prescot, Wigan, and Liverpool, in the year 1590.
2. Some Account of the Clayton Family, of Thelwall, Co. Chester.

Presented by **(101)** D. C. LLOYD OWEN (1882).
9. The History and Antiquities of the Town of Aberconway and its Neighbourhood, by the Rev. (Canon) R. Williams, 1835.

Presented by **(376)** DAVID DAVIES, M.P. (1882).
1. Numerous Parliamentary Blue Books.

Presented by **(377)** the BRITISH MUSEUM (1882).
1. Fac-similes of Ancient Charters in the British Museum :—
Part i, 1873.
Part ii, 1876.
Part iii, 1877.
Part iv, 1878.
2. Catalogue of Arundel Manuscripts. Coloured plates.
3. Index to the Arundel and the Burney Manuscripts.
4. Catalogue of the Burney Manuscripts.
5. ,, Ancient Manuscripts. Part i. Greek.
. Fragments of the Iliad of Homer, from a Syriac Palimpsest (1851).
7. Additions to the British Museum Manuscripts, 1841-1845.
,, ,, 1846-1847.
,, ,, 1848-1853.
8. Catalogue of Additional Manuscripts, 19,720-24,026. 1854-1860.
9. ,, Additions to the Manuscripts, 1854-1875. Vol. ii.
10. Index to the Catalogue of Additions to the Manuscripts, 1854-1875.

11. Catalogue of the Spanish MSS., P. de Gayangos. 3 Vols.
12. A Guide to the Principal Gold and Silver Coins of the Ancients, from *circ.* B.C. 700 to A.D. 1, with 70 plates. 2nd edition, 1881.
13. A Guide to the Exhibition Galleries.
14. ,, English Medals exhibited in King's Library.
15. ,, Italian Medals.
16. ,, Sculptures of the Parthenon.
17. Græco-Roman Sculptures. Parts i and ii.
18. ,, Sculptures in the Elgin Room.
19. Second Vase Room. Parts i and ii.
20. ,, First and Second Egyptian Rooms.
21. ,, Egyptian Galleries (Vestibule).
22. Printed Books.
23. ,, Autograph Letters, MSS., Original Charters and Seals.

Presented by **(114)** T. B. BARRETT (1881-2).

62. Ancient Chinese Vase of the Ching Dynasty, by P. P. Thomas, 1851.
63. Salmon's State Trials, from Richard II to George II, 1738.
64. The Shropshire Gazetteer, Wem, 1824.
65. An Abridgment of the Records of the Tower of London, from Edward II to Richard III, collected by Sir Robert Cotton, by Wm. Prynne, 1679.
66. Memorials of the English Affairs during the Reigns of Charles I and Charles II, 1682.
67. General Reports of the Commissioners on the Public Records, 1810-1819.
68. The Appendix to Reports, 1819.
69. The General Report, 1837.
70. Original Letters of Eminent Literary Men of the Seventeenth and Eighteenth Centuries (Camden Soc. Publications, 1843).
71. Household Roll of Bishop Swinfield (Camden Soc. Publications, 1854).
72. Political Songs of England from Reign of John to Edward II (Camden Soc. Publication, 1839).

Presented by **(1)** MORRIS C. JONES (1882).

255. Archæological Journal. Vols. i to viii (to complete the set in the Library).
256. An Account of the Rejoicings in Honour of the Coming of Age of Viscount Clive, 1839.

Presented by **(213)** J. Y. W. LLOYD (1882).

3. His Work—History of Powys Fadoc. Vols. i and ii.
Exchanged for a Duplicate Copy of a Book in the Library, 1882.— Ancient Bronze Implements of Great Britain, by John Evans, LL.D., etc.

Presented by **(133)** J. J. HOWARD, LL.D. (1882), in exchange.

Miscellanea Genealogica and Heraldica, 1882.

Presented by **(222)** THE CAMBRIAN ARCHÆOLOGICAL ASSOCIATION (1881-2).
Archæologia Cambrensis. 4th Ser. Vols. xi and xii.

Presented by **(282)** WM. HUGHES (1881).
Salopian Shreds and Patches. Vol. iv, 1880-1.

Presented by **(358)** HISTORICAL SOCIETY OF PENNSYLVANIA (1882).
1. The Pennsylvania Magazine of History and Biography. Vol. iv, Nos. 3 and 4.

ARCHÆOLOGICAL SOCIETIES' TRANSACTIONS received in exchange for the Powys-land Club Publications:—

From **(335)** THE KENT ARCHÆOLOGICAL SOCIETY (1882).
Archæologia Cantiana. Vol. xiv.

From **(223)** THE ROYAL HISTORICAL AND ARCHÆOLOGICAL SOCIETY OF IRELAND (1882).
Journal. Vol. v, 4th Series, No. 50.

From **(225)** THE BERWICKSHIRE NATURALISTS' CLUB (1882).
Transactions, 1880-1.

From **(309)** THE SHROPSHIRE ARCHÆOLOGICAL AND NATURAL HISTORY SOCIETY (1882).
Vol. v, Part 2.

From **(45)** THE BRITISH ARCHÆOLOGICAL ASSOCIATION (1882).
Journal. Vol. xxxvii, Part 4, and Vol. xxxviii, Parts 1, 2, and 3.

From **(293)** THE CAMBRIDGE ANTIQUARIAN SOCIETY (1882).
No. 4 of Vol. iv.
The Church Bells of Cambridgeshire, by J. J. Raven, D.D.

From **(351)** THE BRISTOL AND GLOUCESTERSHIRE ARCHÆOLOGICAL SOCIETY (1881-2).
Transactions, 1876, 1877-8, Parts 1 and 2; 1878-9, Parts 1 and 2; 1880-1, Parts 1 and 2; 1881-2, Part 1; Vol. vi.

From **(72)** THE YORKSHIRE ARCHÆOLOGICAL AND TOPOGRAPHICAL SOCIETY (1882).
Transactions. Parts 26 and 27.

From **(259)** THE HON. SOCIETY OF CYMMRODORION (1882).
Y Cymmrodor. Vol. iv, 2 and 3; Vol. v, 1.

From **(224)** THE ROYAL ARCHÆOLOGICAL INSTITUTE OF GREAT BRITAIN AND IRELAND (1882).
Transactions. Nos. 148a, 151, 152, 153, and 154.

From **(298)** THE LEICESTER LITERARY AND PHILOSOPHICAL SOCIETY (1882).
Transactions. Part 8. From June 1865 to June 1870. (Report of Council, and Transactions for years 1881-82.)

From (**288**) THE ESSEX ARCHÆOLOGICAL SOCIETY (1882).
New series, 1880. Vol. ii, p. 3.

From (**44**) THE LONDON AND MIDDLESEX ARCHÆOLOGICAL SOCIETY (1882).
Transactions. Vol. v, Part 4. History of Marken Hadley, by Rev. F. C. Cass, the Rector. 4to.

From (**297**) THE WILTSHIRE ARCHÆOLOGICAL AND NATURAL HISTORY SOCIETY (1882).
The Magazine. Nos. 57, 58, and 59.

From (**289**) THE ROYAL INSTITUTION OF CORNWALL (1882).
Journal. Vol. vii, Parts 1 and 2.

From (**296**) THE GLASGOW PHILOSOPHICAL SOCIETY (1882).
Proceedings. Vol. xiii, 1. List of Fellows, June 1882.

From (**25**) THE SOCIETY OF ANTIQUARIES OF LONDON (1882).
Proceedings. Vol. viii, No. 5.

From (**295**) THE SUSSEX ARCHÆOLOGICAL SOCIETY (1882).
Sussex Archæological Collections. Vol. xxxii.

From (**46**) THE SURREY ARCHÆOLOGICAL SOCIETY (1882).
Proceedings. Vol. vii, Part 3 ; and Vol. viii, Part 1.

From (**367**) THE SOMERSETSHIRE ARCHÆOLOGICAL AND NATURAL HISTORY SOCIETY.
Proceedings during 1880. Vol. vi, 1881 ; and Vol. vii.

From (**342**) THE SMITHSONIAN INSTITUTION, WASHINGTON.
Smithsonian Report, 1880.
List of Foreign Correspondents to January 1882.

ALPHABETICAL LIST OF DONORS OF ARTICLES AND BOOKS TO THE POWYS-LAND MUSEUM AND LIBRARY,

From its Institution in 1870, to 1st October 1882.

New Donors this Year (1882) marked *.

Abram, W. A., 305
Adnitt, W. H., 123
A Friend, 183
Agnew, Mr., 100
Agnew, Mrs., 319
A Lady, 36
A Military Officer—a native of Montgomeryshire, 338

Andrews, David, 156
Anonymous, 62, 153, 226, 258, 268, 300, 316
Appleton, J. R., 71
Armstrong, Miss H., 188
Astley, Rev. J. R. L., 321
Austin, George, 176

Bamfield, John, 83
Barnes, Thomas, 212
Barnwell, Rev. E. L., 149
Bartlett, W., 256
Barrett, T. B., 114
Beadnall, C. E., 85
Beaver, A. H. D., 323
Beck, Arthur Temple, 175
Bennett, Mrs., 174
Bennett, Nicholas, 54
Beryron, Inglis, 165
Bickerton, Herbert, 191
*Bickerton, Miss, 385
Black, Mrs., 178
Black, A. W., 112
Black, C. B., 86
Bloxam, M. H., 334
Boler, R., 108
Boutel, Rev. Charles, 81
Breese, Edward, F.S.A., 197
*British Museum, 377
Broadstock, T. J., 218
Brown, Graham, 177
Brown, G. A., 221
Burd, Rev. John, 313
Burrill, T. O., 131

Caine, Nathaniel, 263
Caine, Mrs. Nathaniel, 307
Clarke, John, 262
Clarke, Mrs., 68
Clough, C. H., 317
Cockcroft, L. M., 110
Corbett, Major, 58
Cordeaux, Rev. John, 128
Corrie, J. D., 98
Corrie, Miss, 37
Cox, Rev. H. O., 330
Curling, Mrs., 211

*Davies, David, M.P., 376
Davies, Mrs. Elizabeth, 116
Davies, Francis, 308
Davies, Mrs. John, 207
Davies, Rev. John, 38
Davies, J. Pryce, 23
Davies, Mary, 179
Davies, Miss, 193
Davies, Mrs., 88

Davies, Rev. Prebendary, 333
Davies, R. E., 311
Davies, Thomas, 104
Davies, William, 198
Dawkins, Mrs., 303
Dawkins, W. B., 9
Delmar, Captain, 127
Delmar, Charles Athol, 241
Dod, Whitehall, 216
Duke, Rev. W. W., 89

Eaton, James, 158
Eddowes, Mrs., 61
Edmunds, R. J., 364
Edwards, Rev. Griffith, 8
Edye, Thomas, 209
Ellacombe, Rev. H. T., 356
Evans, D. W., 119
Evans, Edward, 239
Evans, Edward (Llanrhaiadr), 340
Evans, E. Bickerton, 210
Evans, Mrs. Hannah, 115
Evans, John, F.R.S., 70
Evans, John Hilditch, 74
Evans, Mrs. J. H., 354
Evans, J. Reginald, 22
Evans, Joseph, 368
Evans, The Misses, 13
Evans, Mrs. Moses, 39
Evans, Rev. T. H., 59
Eyton, Rev. R. W., 332

Fardo, George, 99
Fewtrell, John, 229
Field, Rev. Augustus, 21
Fisher, L., 189
Fisher, William, 6
Forster, Miss, 269
Frith, Rev. E. B. C., 64

Garbet, E., 142
Gillart, Richard, 16
Giovannetti, Miss Zoe, 369
Gough, E. Powell, 55
Graham, John, 247
Grazebrook, George, 306
Gregory, Miss, 285
Grenside, Rev. W. B., 230
Grierson, T. B., 169

Griffiths, Charles, 265
Griffiths, Edward, 78
Griffiths, Sarah, 181
Griffiths, Thomas, 362
Griffithes, Miss, 52
Guilsfield, Vicar & Churchwardens of, 66

Hamer, Edward, 7
Hancock, T. W., 10
Hargreaves, William, 24
*Harper, R., 381
*Harrison, E. D. T., 382
Harrison, G. D., 138
*Harrison, J. Park, 383
Harrison, R. J., 35
Hill, Rev. J. E., 19
Hilton, Edwin, 350
Holder, Frederick, 227
Horn, Mrs., 154
Howard, J. J., LL.D., 133
Howell, C. E., 205
Hudson, Howard, 240
Hudson, Morris J., 367
Hughes, Thomas, 327
Hughes, Miss E., 92
Hughes, Serg. J., 261
Hughes, J. Ceiriog, 194
Hughes, William, 282
Humphreys, Arthur C., 53
Humphreys, Joseph, 67
Hurst, Robert, 365

James, Rev. Thomas, 192
James, William, 155
Jenkins, Mrs. Griffith, 343
Jenkins, John, 281
Jenkins, Richard, 196
Jehu, Edmund, 199
Jehu, John, 228
Johnes, Edward, 249
Johnson, Mrs. Willes, 245
*Jones, Miss A. M., 384
Jones, Charles, 43
Jones, C. W., 129
Jones, D. F., 348
Jones, Edward, 84
Jones, Edward Maurice, 80

Jones, John, 20'
Jones, John, Liverpool, 242, 264
Jones, Mrs. John, 195
Jones, John, Llanrhaiadr, 244
Jones, John, Staff-Commander, R.N., 160
Jones, Rev. Joseph, 42
Jones, Maurice, 102
Jones, Morris C., 1
Jones, Morris P., 130
Jones, Mrs., Church Street, 361
Jones, Mrs., The Farm, 284
Jones, R. E., 144
Jones, Robert, 140
Jones, Robert James, 184, 366
Jones, T. G., 26
Jones, T. Parry, 299
Jones, T. Pugh, 185
Jones, T. S., 109
Jones, Rev. W. B., Meifod, 355
Jones, Mrs. William, 93
Joseph, Joseph, 136

Kendrick, James, M.D., 117
Kennet, Miss, 358
*Kerrison, Miss E., 386
Kerrison, Mrs., 201
*Kinsey, Roger, 388

Latting, J. J., 49
Leighton, Stanley, 134
Lewis, Rev. D. P., 5
Lewis, Rev. John, 252
Lewis, William, 341
Literary Societies :—
  Antiquaries, Society of, London, 25
  Antiquaries, Society of, Scotland, 73
  Berwickshire Naturalists' Club, 255
  Birmingham and Midland Institute, 254
  British Archæological Association, 45
  Bristol and Gloucester Archæological Society, 351

Literary Societies—*continued*
  Cambrian Archæological Association, 222
  Cambridge Antiquarian Society, 293
  Chester Archæological Society, 287
  Cornwall Royal Institute, 289
  Cymmrodorion Society of London, 259
  Essex Archæological Society, 288
  Glasgow Philosophical Society, 296
  Historic Society of Lancashire and Cheshire, 294, 219
  Ireland, Royal Historical and Archæological Association of, 223
  Kent Archæological Society, 335
  Leicester Literary and Philosophical Society, 298
  Liverpool Free Public Library, 337
  Liverpool Literary and Philosophical Society, 286
  London and Middlesex Archæological Society, 44
  Norfolk and Norwich Archæological Society, 291
  *Pennsylvania, Historical Society of, 378
  Royal Archæological Institute of Great Britain, 224
  Smithsonian Institution, Washington, 342
  *Somersetshire Archæological Society, 387
  Suffolk Institute for Architecture, etc., 292
  Surrey Archæological Society, 46
  Sussex Archæological Society, 295
  Wiltshire Archæological Society, 297
  Worcester Diocesan Society, 290
  Yorkshire Archæological and Topographical Society, 72

Lloyd, Howel W., 28
Lloyd, J. Y. W., 213
Lloyd, Mrs. R. H., 237
Lloyd, Sampson S., 76
Lloyd, Rev. W. V., 27
*Lovell, Mrs., 379
Ludger, M., 236
Luton, John, 268
Luxmoore, Miss, 4

McIntosh, Rev. J., 106
Maclardy, Mr., 257
Maginnis, Mrs., 190
Marrat, F. W., 267
Marshall, Rev. H. J., 56
Matthews, Rev. J., 336
Matthews, Miss, 14
Meifod, Vicar and Churchwardens of, 65
Morgan, Charles, 251
Morin, Henry, 96
Morris, Charles, 217
Morris and Co., 187
Morris, Edwin, 121
Morris, E. Rowley, 2
Morris, Henry, 357
Morris, John, 238
Morris, Joseph Pugh, 103
Morris, Miss, 318
Morris, Thomas, 47
Morris, William, 12
Mulholland, R., 204
Mytton, Mrs., 279

Needles, Alfred, 246
Nevett, Frank, 69
Newill, Thomas, 107
Nicholas, Dr. T., 125
Nicholson, W. C., 202

Owen, D. C. Lloyd, 101
Owen, D. P., 215
Owen, Edward, 135
Owen, Rev. Elias, 34
Owen, Mrs., Berriew, 363
Owen, Rev. R. Trevor, 328
Owen, T. Morgan, 352

Powis, the Earl of, 57
Parker, Rev. F. W., 79

xl

Parker, W. T., 80
Parry, Henry, 15
Parry, Love Jones, 214
Parry, R., 200
Passmore, F. R. B., 280
Paterson, William, 111
Paynter, C. E., 320
Phillips, J. Roland, 148
*Picton, Sir J. A., F.S.A., 374
*Poundley, J. E., 380
Powell, Samuel, 118
Powell, W. B., 91
Price, Benjamin, 31
Price, J. E., 371
Price, Miss, 186
Priest, Mr., 182
Pryce, Charles, 124
Pryce, Elijah, 143
Pryce, Miss, 243
Pryce, Mrs., 94
Pryce, Thomas, 302
Pugh, Mrs., 234

Ramage, C. T., 75
Ramage, J. C., 163
Ramage, Mrs., 359
Read, Captain Crewe, 17
Rees, William, 50
Richards, Edward, 232
Richards, Mrs. Jane, 152
Richards, Thomas, 349
Rider, W. E., 157
Rimmer, Richard, 370
Roberts, Askew, 97
Roberts, Mrs., 95
Roberts, Richard, 231
Roberts, Rev. R., 325
Robertson, Mrs., 314
Rogers, Mr., 87
Roper, F.; 113
Rowland, Rev. Thomas, 250
Rush, Mrs., 208
*Rylands, J. Paul, 375

Salter, Edward, 51
Salter, S., junior, 329
Sayce, Miss, 41
Sayce, John, 248
Scott, General, 225

Shepherd, Mr. and Mrs., 105
Sheraton, Henry, 173
Sheraton, Robert, 132
Siddorns, Mr., 206
Sinker, Rev. Robert, 327
Smith, Charles Perrin, 48
Smith, J., 235
Smith, J. Russell, 312
Smith, Worthington G., 314
Squires, Mrs. 353
Stanley, Hon. W. O., 283
Stephens, Mrs., 253
Sturkey, Thomas, 120
Swettenham, F. N., 322

Tallis, J., 345
Thickens, William, 167
Thomas, Charles, 170
Thomas, David, 346
Thomas, Rev. D. R., 146
Thomas, Miss Jane, 139
Thomas, John, 180
Thomas, W. F., 347
Trevor, E. S. R., 60
Tudor, O. D., 304
Turnbull, Dr., 40
Turnbull, Miss G., 266
Turner, Rev. J. J., 11
Turner, Rev. W. H., 330

Underwood, Martin, 77

Vale, Mr. and Mrs., 82
Vaudrey, B. Ll., 172
Vaughan, Mrs. (Dolanog), 166
Vaughan, Thomas, 180
Vaughan, Mrs. T., 122
Vernon, Miss, 162
Vize, Rev. J. E., 326

Walker, David, 30
Ward, John D., 324
Ward, William, 145
Welshpool, Corporation of, 373
Whitlow, Rev. R. W., 137
Wilding, William, 171
Williams, Rev. Canon R., 147
Williams, George, 164
Williams and Gittins, 168

Williams, James, 344	Woollett, Miss, 90
Williams, Rev. John, 32	Wynn, Lady Annora, 126
Williams, J. Graham, 3	Wynn, C. W. W., 63
Williams, Richard, 18	Wynn, Sir W. W., 360
Williams, Richard (Welshpool), 141, 203	Wynne, W. W. E., 29
Williams, Thomas, 339	Yearsley, Mrs., 151
Woodall and Venables, 331	Yearsley, Miss Mary, 150

THE REPORT OF THE POWYS-LAND MUSEUM AND LIBRARY COMMITTEE.

The Museum has been visited by a considerable number of persons, 465 of whom have entered their names in the Visitors' Book, and many more who have not observed that rule. 152 persons have paid the admission fee.

	£	s.	d.
The balance at the beginning of the year was	1	18	0
Admission fees received	2	0	6
	£3	18	6
The expenditure—Income-tax, 15s. 5d.; cleaning, 11s.; firing, 4s.; brooms, etc., 5s. 6d.	£1	15	11
	£2	2	7

	£	s.	d.
The Balance of the BUILDING AND REPAIR FUND on the 1st October, 1881, at Lloyd's Banking Company, Limited, was	£23	4	8
Dividends since received on £200 Debenture Stock:—			
1882, Jan. 17 . . . . £3 18 4			
July 17 . . . . 3 18 4			
	7	16	8
G. Oliver Jones, Esq., donation	0	10	6
	£31	11	10

To which will shortly be added the donation of £100 from Joseph Evans, Esq., and £100 transferred from the general account, making together £231 11s. 10d., which will form a substantial nucleus of a fund for carrying out the full development of the scheme of the Powys-land Museum and Library, by adding to it a School and Gallery of Art, as mentioned in this Committee's Report for the year 1875, and as indicated by the plan thereto attached.

The establishment of a School of Art was contemplated and provided for by the Trust Deed of the Museum Site (see the copy Deed printed as an Appendix to the *Montgomeryshire Collections*, Vol. vii), and the building being available to be used as a Gallery of Art, will enable the Museum Trustees to accept donations of Works of Art, Models from the Antique, and other large ornamental objects which may be offered, and which hitherto they have had no accommodation for, and consequently had to decline—besides providing a Committee-room and other necessary offices.

The Committee congratulate the Members on the prospect of the Institution being completed in its integrity, according to its original design.

The Committee deeply regret that, in consequence of the retirement from business of Mr. Thomas Richards, their long business connection with him, which has been invariably and eminently satisfactory, will terminate. Mr. Richards carries with him into his privacy the best wishes of all who have had business relations with him.

The POWYS-LAND CLUB exchange publications with the following Literary Societies, viz. :—

The Society of Antiquaries of Scotland, Royal Institution, Edinburgh.

The British Archæological Association, 32, Sackville Street, Piccadilly.

The Royal Archæological Institute of Great Britain and Ireland, 16, New Burlington Street.

The Cambrian Archæological Association, 30 and 32, Sardinia Street, Lincoln's Inn Fields, London, W.C.

The Royal Historical and Archæological Association of Ireland. (Rev. J. Graves, Inisnag, Stoneyford, Kilkenny, Hon. Sec.)

The Historic Society of Lancashire and Cheshire, Royal Institution, Liverpool.

The London and Middlesex Archæological Society. (G. H. Birch, Esq., Hon. Sec., 9, Buckingham Street, Strand, London.)

The Surrey Archæological Society, 8, Danes' Inn, Strand, London.

The Yorkshire Archæological and Topographical Society (G. H. Tomlinson, Esq., Huddersfield).

The Birmingham and Midland Institute, Birmingham.

The Berwickshire Naturalist Club (James Hardy, Esq., Old Cambus, Cocksburnspath).

The Honourable Society of Cymmrodorion, London (Secretary, C. W. Jones, Esq , Local Government Board, London).

The Cambridge Antiquarian Society (Rev. S. S. Lewis, F.S.A., Corpus Christi College, Secretary).

The Chester Archæological Society (T. Hughes, Esq., F.S.A., Secretary).

The Literary and Philosophical Society of Liverpool (Royal Institution, Liverpool).

The Essex Archæological Society (H. W. King, Esq., Leigh Hill, Leigh, Essex, Secretary).

The Royal Institution of Cornwall (J. H. Collins, Esq., Truro).

The Sussex Archæological Society (John Edward Price, Esq., 60, Albion Road, Stoke Newington, London, Secretary).

The Suffolk Institute of Archæological and Natural History (Edward Deering, Esq., Bury St. Edmunds).

The Worcester Diocesan Architectural and Archæological Society (J. H. Hooper, Esq., College Green, Worcester, Secretary).

The Wiltshire Archæological Society (Rev. H. A. Olivier, Museum, Devizes).

The Shropshire Archæological and Natural History Society (W. H. Adnitt, Esq., The Museum, Salop, Secretary).

The Leicester Literary and Philosophical Society, Leicester.

The Somersetshire Archæological and Natural History Society (The Castle, Taunton).

The Smithsonian Institution, Washington, U.S.A. (S. Baird, Esq., Assistant-Secretary).

The Bristol and Gloucester Archæological Society (P. Hallet, Esq., Hon. Secretary, Claverton Lodge, Bath).

The Glasgow Philosophical Society, Glasgow.

OBITUARY OF MEMBERS OF THE POWYS-LAND CLUB.

1869.
Jan. 29. CHARLES THOMAS WOOSNAM, Esq., Newtown.
May 23. EDWARD WILLIAMS, Esq., Lloran House, Oswestry.

1870.
May 15. Major-General CHARLES THOMAS EDWARD HINDE.
Oct. 30. Rev. JOHN EDWARDS, M.A., Rector of Newtown.
Nov. 16. Rev. HARRY LONGUEVILLE JONES, M.A.

1871.
Feb. 26. Sir BALDWIN LEIGHTON, Bart., Loton Park, Salop.
Mar. 3. EDWARD EVANS, Esq., Thorneloe House, Worcester.
Mar. 24. PRICE BUCKLEY WILLIAMES, Esq., Pennant.
April 24. GEORGE WOOSNAM, Esq., Newtown.
June 21. WILLIAM PRYCE YEARSLEY, Esq., Welshpool.
July 23. ARTHUR JAMES JOHNES, Esq., Garthmyl.
Dec. 5. JOHN PRYCE DREW, Esq., Milford House, Newtown.
Dec. 12. Rev. JOSEPH JONES, R.C. Church, Welshpool

1872.
April 28. ROBERT MAURICE BONNOR MAURICE, Esq., Bodynfol.

1873.
Sept. 4. Rev. ROBERT JOHN HARRISON, M.A., Caerhowel.
Nov. 13. JOHN GOUGH NICHOLS, Esq., F.S.A.

1874.
April 10. ROBERT DEVEREUX HARRISON, Esq., Fronllwyd, Welshpool.
Nov. 25. R. H. STURKEY, Esq., Meifod.

1875.
Aug. 11. EDWARD WILLIAMS, Esq., of Neuadd faben, Talgarth.
Nov. 4. THOMAS BOWEN, Esq., Welshpool.

1876.
Jan. 5. Mrs. ANN WARBURTON OWEN, Glansevern.
Feb. 10. JOSEPH OWEN JONES, Esq., Fron-y-gog.
May 26. THOMAS TAYLOR GRIFFITH, Esq., Wrexham.
June 15. JOHN RALPH, first LORD HARLECH, Brogynton, Oswestry.
June 18. Rev. JOHN JUDGE, Leighton Vicarage, Welshpool.

1877.
            Rev. CANON JENKINS, Llangyniew Rectory, Welshpool.
April 28. SUDELEY, LORD SUDELEY (*Vice President*).

1878.
June 8. The Ven. ARCHDEACON MORGAN, M.A.
Aug. 5. JOSEPH HUMPHREYS, Esq., The Court, Dogpole, Shrewsbury.
Dec. 5. THOMAS OWEN MORGAN, Esq., of Aberystwith.

1879.
Mar. 28. Rev. ROBERT JONES, B.A., All Saints', Rotherhithe.
April 29. Rev. JENKIN JONES, M.A., Rector of Cerrig y Druidion.
Aug. 3. Rev. THOMAS JAMES, LL.D., F.S.A.
Dec. 12. Rev. J. J. TURNER, M.A.
1880.
Jan. 28. Rev. F. H. THOMAS, Vicar of Chirk, aged 75.
Mar. 5. Rev. D. PRITCHARD PRITCHARD, of Ceniarth.
April 22. Miss HINDE-LLOYD, of Bath.
June 9. WATKIN WILLIAMS EDWARD WYNNE, Esq., of Peniarth, aged 79.
1881.
Feb. 22. Miss JANE DAVIES of Penmaen Dovey.
Mar. 10. EDWARD BREESE, Esq., F.S.A., of Pwllheli.
April 22. JOHN SIDES DAVIES, Esq., M.R.C.S., of Oswestry.
April 26. Rev. Canon ROBERT WILLIAMS, M.A.
Nov. 25. Mrs. PUGH-JOHNSON, Llanerchydol.
1882.
May 6. Rev. JOSEPH McINTOSH, Llanerfyl.
May 24. Rev. Canon DAVID WILLIAMS, Castle Caereinion.
LEWIS R. PRICE, Esq., 117, St. George's Square, London.

CORRIGENDUM.

On page 411, *supra*, the seventh line has, by accident, been misplaced. It should be read before the first line of that page. The passages, when corrected, will read thus:—

MEMORANDUM AS TO THE FAMILY OF HARRISON.

In the *Historical Record of the 52nd Regiment* (*Oxford Light Infantry*), published in 1860, the following notice occurs of the Battle of Bunker's Hill, and of Robert John Harrison (the father of the late Major Robert John Harrison of Caer Howel), having been engaged in it as a volunteer and being wounded:—

" On the 17th June 1775, the Battle of Bunker's Hill was fought, and the 52nd Regiment particularly distinguished itself on the occasion, and suffered severely. Three captains, one sergeant, and twenty rank and file were killed. Amongst the wounded were one major (who afterwards died), one captain, three lieutenants, and two ensigns, '*and volunteer Robert John Harrison*', and seven sergeants and seventy-three rank and file."

MONTGOMERYSHIRE WORTHIES.

By RICHARD WILLIAMS, Newtown.

(Continued from p. 70.)

Owen, Sir Arthur Davies, Knight, of Glansevern, was the eldest son of Owen Owen, Esq., of Cefnhafodau, Llangurig (Sheriff 1766), by Anne his wife, daughter and heiress of Charles Davies, Esq., of Llivior, Berriew. He was brought up to the profession of the law, and became an able and active magistrate, one of the deputy lieutenants for the county, and for many years Chairman of Quarter Sessions. From the formation of the corps of Montgomeryshire Yeomanry Cavalry in 1803 to the time of his death, he was second in command of it. He served the office of High Sheriff in 1814. He was married to Mrs. Pugh, a widow (the mother of David Pugh, Esq., M.P. for many years for the Montgomery Boroughs), whom he survived without having issue. He died October the 18th, 1816, aged 64, and was buried in Berriew Church. His portrait is at Glansevern.—(*Mont. Coll.*, iii, p. 261.)

Owen, Rev. David, M.A., was the second son of Owen Owen, Esq., of Cefnhafodau, Llangurig. He was educated at Trinity College, Cambridge, and in 1777 became Senior Wrangler of that University. He was elected a Fellow of his college, and subsequently ordained priest. Eventually he settled in the island of Campo Bello, in Passamaquoddy Bay, New Brunswick, which belonged to his family, where he died, unmarried, in 1829. His remains were, in accordance with his own request, brought over to England and deposited in the family vault in Berriew Church. His portrait is at Glansevern.—*(Ibid.)*

OWEN, WILLIAM, King's Counsel, of Glansevern, was the third son of Owen Owen, Esq., of Cefnhavodau, Llangurig, and was born in the year 1758. He was educated at the Free Grammar School, Warrington (then conducted by his uncle the Rev. Edward Owen, M.A., see *ante*), from which he proceeded to Trinity College, Cambridge. In 1782 he took his degree of B.A., and was fifth wrangler. Among the members of his own college who graduated at the same time were Professors Porson and Hailstone, Drs. Raine and Wingfield. Mr. Owen and these four gentlemen were afterwards elected Fellows of Trinity College. He subsequently entered upon the study of the law, and was called to the Bar by the honourable society of Lincoln's Inn, of which eventually he became a bencher. For several years he travelled the Oxford and Cheshire Circuits, but afterwards confined his practice chiefly to the Courts of Chancery and Exchequer. He was appointed Commissioner of Bankrupts and (7th Aug. 1818) a King's Counsel. About the year 1821 he relinquished his practice, and retired into the country to reside upon his estate at Glansevern, inherited from his brother, Sir Arthur Davies Owen, where he became a magistrate and deputy lieutenant. During the rest of his life he took an active part in all the public business of the county, and generally presided as Chairman of Quarter Sessions. Mr. Owen was chiefly instrumental in abolishing the Great Sessions and the old system of Welsh judicature, by means of the important evidence he gave on the subject before a Committee of the House of Commons in 1817, and 1820, and otherwise. He was a staunch Whig (or what would now be called a Liberal) in politics, and took a leading part in Montgomeryshire in the great reform agitation which preceded the passing of the Reform Bill in 1832. The County of Montgomery was the first to petition in support of that Bill. He stoutly opposed the original proposal to give the representation of the Montgomery Boroughs to Llanfyllin alone, and it was in a great measure through his exertions that Newtown, Llanidloes, Machynlleth, and Welshpool were admitted to share the representation with Llanfyllin and Montgomery. In 1823 Mr. Owen married Anne Warburton, only child of Capt. Sloughter, and relict of the Rev. Thomas Coupland of the Priory, Chester; but there was no issue of the marriage. Mr. Owen died on the 10th of November 1837, aged 79, and was buried in Berriew Church. A handsome marble monument was there erected to his memory by his widow, which testifies that "he left behind him a name without reproach". His portrait is at Glansevern. The following grant of arms was made 3rd April 1838 to Mrs. Owen "to be placed on any monument or otherwise to the memory of her late husband, the said William Owen, deceased":—*Sable*, a tilting spear erect *or*, the head proper imbued *gules*, between three scaling ladders *argent*, on a chief *ermine*, a fort triple-towered also proper; and for a crest, on a wreath of the colours a wolf salient proper, supporting a scaling ladder as in the arms. Motto, "Toraf cyn plygaf" (I will break before I bend). Mrs. Owen died on the 5th January 1876, aged 93, having survived her second husband over thirty-eight years. Upon her death, by virtue of a deed of settlement executed by her in February 1873, the Glansevern estates devolved upon Arthur Charles Humphreys, Esq., great-grandnephew of Mr. Owen, who, by royal licence, dated 11th November 1876, in pursuance of a clause contained in the settlement, took the surname of Owen after that of Humphreys, and the arms of Owen.—(*Mont. Coll.*, iii, 261; x, 418-21; *Lleyn MSS.*, etc.)

OWEN, WILLIAM, Captain R.N., was the youngest son of David Owen of Cefnhavodau, Llangurig, by Frances, daughter of John Rogers of Cefnyberain, Kerry. He entered the Royal Navy when very young, and in the year 1760, while he was yet but a midshipman, greatly distinguished himself at the taking of Pondicherry from the French, losing his right arm in the action. He was a Lieutenant in 1769, and was shortly afterwards promoted to the command of H.M.S. *Cormorant*, in which he again distinguished himself. Captain Owen was bringing home despatches when he lost his life by an accident at Madras in 1778. He was the father of two distinguished naval officers, Admirals Sir Edward W. C. R. Owen and William F. Owen. His portrait is at Glansevern.—(*Mont. Coll.*, iii, p. 255.)

OWEN, SIR EDWARD WILLIAM CAMPBELL RICHARD, G.C.B., K.H., and Vice-Admiral of the Red, was a son of the above named Captain William Owen, and was born in 1771. He was educated at Hanway School, Chelsea, and entered the navy August 11, 1785, became a Lieutenant November 6, 1793, and Post-Captain November 30, 1798. After the peace of Amiens he was stationed with several sloops and smaller vessels under his orders on the coast of France, and by his activity and zeal kept the enemy in a constant state of alarm, at one time driving their ships on shore, and at another bombarding the towns of Dieppe and St. Valery. Subsequently, in 1806, Commodore Owen (having then hoisted a broad pendant) superintended a very successful attack on Boulogne; and in 1809 accompanied the expedition to Walcheren, where his ability and energy in the discharge of his arduous duties gained for him warm commendation. In 1815 he was made, for his distinguished services, Knight Commander of the Bath; in 1821 he was appointed a Colonel of Marines; and in 1825 advanced to flag rank. From 1828 to 1832 he held the chief command on the East India Station, and from 1841 to 1845 that in the Mediterranean. He was Member of Parliament for Sandwich from 1826 to 1829; became Surveyor-General of Ordnance in 1827; and was a member of the Council of H.R.H. the Duke of Clarence, Lord High Admiral. He was a great favourite with His

Royal Highness, who, after his accession to the throne as William IV, conferred upon him, in 1832, the insignia of the Grand Cross of the Hanoverian Guelphic Order, and it is said proposed to confer a peerage upon him, but, for some reason or other, this proposal was not carried out. In 1834-5 Sir Edward held office again as Clerk of the Ordnance. In January 1846 the Grand Cross of the Order of the Bath was conferred upon him, and a grant of supporters was made to him and recorded at the College of Arms on the 26th of that month. His arms are therein described as—Per saltire *sable* and *gules*, a lion rampant *or*, surrounded by the motto, "Tria juncta in uno." Crest on a wreath of the colours, a stag *argent*, billetty, tripping. Motto, "Flecti non frangi." Sir Edward married, in 1829, Selina, daughter of Captain J. B. Hay, R N. He died October 8th, 1849, at his residence, Windlesham House, Surrey, aged 78. His portrait, by Pickersgill, is at Glansevern.—(*Mont. Coll.*, iii, 256 ; x, 417 ; and xi, 374 ; *Gent. Mag.*, etc.)

OWEN, Vice-Admiral WILLIAM FITZWILLIAM, was the younger and only brother of the above-named Sir Edward Owen, and was born at Manchester in 1773. Having been educated with his brother at Hanway School, Chelsea, where he attained the first rank, he entered the Royal Navy in the summer of 1788 on board the *Culloden*, 74 guns, commanded by his relation, Sir Thomas Rich, and was present at the great battle of the 1st June 1794. Shortly afterwards he sailed in the *Ruby* (64) for the Cape of Good Hope, where he witnessed the capture of a Dutch squadron of three sail of the line and six frigates and sloops in Saldana Bay in August 1796. Returning to England after this exploit, he joined the *London* (98), bearing the flag of Admiral Colpays, with whom he quitted that ship during the mutiny at Spithead in May 1797. For his firmness on that trying occasion he was, in the following month, promoted to the rank of lieutenant, and placed in command of the *Flamer* gun-brig. In this and other vessels he saw much active and harassing service till the close of the first French revolutionary war. At the re-commencement of hostilities he was among the foremost to offer his services, and in July 1803 he was appointed to the command of the *Sea Flower*, a brig of 14 guns. Very shortly afterwards he sailed for the East Indies, where he was employed upon various missions by the Commander-in-Chief. In 1806 he captured *Le Charle*, a French vessel; and, by the exploration of several of the channels between the eastern islands, contributed greatly to the improvement of the charts. Towards the close of the same year he piloted Sir Edward Pellew's squadron through an intricate navigation into Batavia Roads. Here his bravery and skill were conspicuous in the command of a division of armed boats at a successful attack on a Dutch frigate, seven men-of-war brigs, and about twenty armed vessels, for which he was honourably mentioned in the *Gazette*. The following year he assisted in the capture and destruction of the Dutch dockyard, stores, and fleet at Griessik, in Java. In 1808 his ship, the *Sea Flower*, was captured by the French in the Bay of Bengal, and he himself taken prisoner, and carried to the Isle of France, where he was detained until June 1810, when he was exchanged. In May 1809 the rank of commander was conferred upon Mr. Owen, and on his liberation and return to India, he assisted in organising the expedition against the Isle of France, which was taken in December 1810. He subsequently commanded the *Barracouta*, and took part in the operations which led to the surrender, to the British forces, of Batavia in August 1811, having in May of the same year been advanced to post-rank. After acting in command of the *Piedmontaise* for a short time, he was appointed Captain of the *Cornelia* (32 guns), in which he sailed from Batavia Roads in March 1812 with a small squadron to take possession of the commissariat depôt at the eastern end of Sumatra. Having accomplished this, he returned to England in charge of a valuable convoy from China in June 1813. In addition to his other arduous services, Captain Owen materially assisted his friend, Captain Horsburgh, in compiling his well-known *Oriental Navigator;* and employed his leisure in correcting charts and translating from the Portuguese Franzoni's *Sailing Directions.* In March 1815 he was appointed to the surveying service on the lakes of Canada. In August 1821 he was appointed to the corvette *Leven* (24 guns), in which, accompanied by the *Barracouta,* he was for four years employed on the west and east coasts of Africa; and during that period rendered effective aid to General Turner in the Ashantee War. In February 1827 he was commissioned to the *Eden* (26 guns), for the purpose of forming a settlement in the island of Fernando Po, and to complete his surveys of that coast, which occupied him until the close of 1831. He then retired on half-pay, but continued his labours in correcting charts and improving the means of maritime surveying. He and his brother, Sir Edward Owen, having, on the death of their relative the Rev. David Owen (see *ante,* p. 203), become owners of the island of Campo Bello in Passamaquoddy Bay, New Brunswick, and desiring to settle there, Sir Edward surrendered to him his portion. Captain Owen accordingly brought his wife and two daughters there, and for some time energetically occupied himself in the improvement of his estate. He represented the island in the House of Assembly at Fredericton, where he exposed various abuses, and showed himself to be a staunch reformer. Being still anxious to pursue his hydrographical labours, he was appointed to the *Columbia,* a fine steam vessel of 100-horse power, to survey the Bay of Fundy and the coast of Nova Scotia. In December 1847 he was promoted to flag rank, and continued the rest of his life on half-pay. Vice-Admiral Owen had been for many years prior to his death an active Fellow of the Royal Astronomical Society. He was, in conduct and bearing, firm and kind, shrewdly sensible and unostentatious, his manner sometimes bordering on the eccentric; a man of steady resources and unremitting zeal; and a fluent, though blunt speaker. During his latter days his faculties had been for some time declining. He died at St. John's, New Brunswick, on the 3rd of November 1857, at the advanced age of 84 years.—(Hamer's *Hist. of Llangurig; Mont. Coll.*, iii, 257; *Mon. Articles of the R.A. Soc.*, etc.)

OWEN, REV. OWEN, was born at Machynlleth, in 1806, and was educated for the Independent Ministry at the Carmarthen and Highbury Colleges. He was minister for some time at Newport (Monmouth), Liskeard, and Manorbeer; but later in life he joined the Established Church, and emigrated to America, where he practised medicine in Chicago till his death in 1874. He married Mary Anne, daughter of David Beynon, Esq., and granddaughter of John Beynon, Esq., of Trewern, Carmarthenshire, Sheriff of Cardiganshire in 1783. He wrote and published several works under the *nom de plume* "Celatus", each of them containing an acrostic giving his name, and sometimes his address also. The following is a list of them :—1. *The Modern Theme.* A work on education (1848 and 1854). 2. *The Taper for Lighting the Sabbath School Lamps.* A series of lectures to Sunday-school teachers. 3. *A Glass of Wholesome Water.* A plea for total abstinence. 4. *The Shepherd's Voice.* 5. *The Working Saint.* A sermon (1843). 6. *The Sources of Science; or, the Pierian Springs laid open.* Lectures on the benefits arising from scientific institutions (1854). 7. *The Public Pearl; or, Education the People's Right and a Nation's Glory* (1854). The ideas contained in these works are many of them excellent, and in advance of the time in which they were written; but the style is very unattractive, hazy, involved, and sometimes ludicrous. The author was, however, evidently a man of good parts and an enthusiast. He is said to have spent his own and most of his wife's fortune in various well-intentioned, but ill-managed efforts for the public good. His wife also published in 1852 a small illustrated volume of dialogues and poems for the young, entitled *The Early Blossom*, under the *nom de plume* " Celata".

OWEN, RICHARD, of Garth, near Llanidloes, was one of the gentlemen who were deemed to be "fit and qualified to be made Knights of the Royal Oak", an Order intended to be established by King Charles II on his restoration in 1660, as a reward to several of his followers, and the knights of which were to wear a silver medal, with a device of the king in the oak, pendant to a ribbon about their necks. It was thought best, however, to abandon this intention, to avoid jealousies and animosities. Mr. Owen's estate was stated, in the list of gentlemen so intended to be honoured, to be of the value of £800 per annum. His arms were—*Sable,* on a fess, between a lion rampant, in chief *argent*, and a fleur-de-lys in base *or*, three snakes entwined proper. He was the lineal ancestor of the Marchioness of Londonderry, to whom the Garth estate has descended.—(*Gweithiau Gwallter Mechain*, iii, p. 207; *Mont. Coll.*, viii, p. 207.)

OWEN, RICHARD, of Rhiwsaeson, was another of the gentlemen upon whom the Knighthood of the Royal Oak was intended to be conferred. He was the son of Athelstan Owen, Esq., of Rhiwsaeson. His estate was valued at £1,000 per annum. He served the office of Sheriff in 1653. The Rhiwsaeson estate was sold in 1750, and is now the property of Sir Watkin Williams Wynn, Bart.—*(Ibid.)*

OWAIN VYCHAN ab Gruffydd ab Ieuan Llwyd of Llanbrynmair, was a chieftain of Cyfeiliog, to whom his contemporary Lewys Glyn Cothi has addressed a highly eulogistic ode. He is described as a generous friend of the bards, who ever delighted to hear the dulcimer and harp, and was himself a skilful musician as well as accomplished in other respects, and well versed in the laws and customs of his country. From him descended the Owens of Rhiwsaeson and Ynysymaengwyn.—(*L. G. Cothi*, p. 447; *Lewys Dwn*, i, 297, 318.)

PARRY HARRI, a bard of a somewhat eccentric character, born in 1709, the year in which Huw Morris, the celebrated poet, died, as he took a pride in stating. Few of his compositions have been printed. Sion Prys's *Almanack* for 1744 gives an account of an Eisteddfod at Llansantffraid Glyn Ceiriog, the proceedings being opened by Parry with the following *Englyn* :—

"Eisteddwch, ceisiwch ein cân—llu clauar,
 Lle clywir ymddiddan;
 Gosodiad fel gwe' sidan
 Cu rwym glos—y Cymry glân."

He greatly disliked the Methodists and all Dissenters. In W. Howel's (of Llanidloes) *Almanack* for 1774, there are nineteen stanzas by him under the title *Ceryddiad difrifol i'r Methodistiaid*, etc. (a Serious Reproof to the Methodists, etc.). During the last thirty years of his life he was in the habit of going about the country "clera", that is to say, singing and vending songs, carols, and other poetical effusions of his own. In April each year he began to sing his May carol, recounting the events of the past twelvemonth. His muse was simple, homely, and harmless. At the time of his death he was nearly ninety years of age.—(Gwallter Mechain's *Works*, i, p. 466.)

PARRY, ROBERT, a poet of considerable merit, was the son of a clergyman of the same name, and was born near Machynlleth. During his childhood he removed, with his parents, into Denbighshire, his father having been promoted in 1810 to the Vicarage of Eglwysfach in that county. He received a university education, being intended for the Church, but, preferring the life of a farmer, he relinquished the idea of taking Orders. He passed the greater part of his life as a respectable farmer at Plas Efenechtyd and Plas Towerbridge, near Ruthin. He died at the latter place in 1863, and was buried at Eglwysfach. His poem on *Belshazzar's Feast*, the Chair subject at the Denbigh Eisteddfod of 1828, was adjudged to be second best. It is printed in *The Gwyneddion*, being an account of that Eisteddfod; and many of his compositions may be found in the Welsh magazines of those days.—(*Enwogion Cymru.*)

POWELL, VAVASOR, an eminent Nonconformist preacher of the seventeenth century, who, although born out of Montgomeryshire, was so closely connected with the county by descent and marriage, as well as residence within it for some years, and whose name is so intimately associated with the early history of Nonconformity within it, that he may well be regarded as a Montgomeryshire worthy. He was born at Knucklas, in Radnorshire, in the year 1617. His father, Richard Powell, belonged to an ancient Welsh family, who had lived in that neighbourhood a hundred years before him. His mother was of the Vavasors, a family of great antiquity that came from Yorkshire into Wales. His bitter enemies (of whom his sturdy and energetic Nonconformity produced many) have endeavoured to throw discredit upon his origin as well as upon almost every action of his life. Thus Anthony Wood, in his *Athenæ Oxonienses*, with ill-concealed spite, says:—

"Vavasor Powell having often told his friends and the brethren, not without boasting, that he was once a member of Jesus College in Oxon, I shall, therefore, upon his word, number him among these writers. Be it known, therefore, that this person, who was famous in his generation for his ill-name among those that were not of his opinion, was born in the Borough of Knucklas, in Radnorshire, son of Richard Howell, an ale-keeper[1] there, by Penelope, his wife, daughter of Wil-

---

[1] This statement and the other depreciating remarks which follow, are copied from *Strena Vavasoriensis*, or *Hue and Cry*, etc., a scurrilous book written by one Alexander Griffiths, and published about 1652, while Powell was in prison. It is almost entirely a tissue of calumnious falsehoods; to refute which, Charles Lloyd of Dolobran, the Rev. James Quarrel, and others, in 1653 published *Examen et*

liam Vavasor[1] of Newtown, in Montgomeryshire. He was brought up a scholar, saith the publisher of his life, but the writer of *Strena Vavasoriensis* tells us that his employment was to walk guests' horses, by which, finding no great gain at such a petty alehouse, he was elevated in his thoughts for higher preferment, and so became an hostler (I would say groom) to Mr. Isaac Thomas, an innkeeper and mercer in Bishop's Castle in Shropshire."

Walker says that after this he was "a schoolmaster, and at length a preacher at Clun", and charges him with having entered the Church by means of forged Orders, a charge for which there does not seem to have been a particle of foundation. The truth appears to be that, after spending some time at Oxford, he was employed by his uncle, the Rev. Erasmus Powell, to be his curate at Clun, where he also kept a school. He had always been from his childhood, as he himself says in his autobiography, ".very active and forward in the pursuit of the pleasures and vanities of this wicked world..... only drunkenness I much hated", encouraging the sports and pastimes that were then common on the Sabbath. "Being one Lord's Day", he says, "a stander by and beholder of those that broke the Sabbath by divers games, being then myself a reader of Common Prayers, and in the habit of a foolish shepherd, I was ashamed to play with them, yet took as much pleasure therein as if I had, whereupon a godly, grave professor of religion (one of those then called Puritans), seeing me there, came to me, and very soberly and mildly asked me, ' Doth it become you, sir, that are a scholar, and one that teacheth others, to break the Lord's Sabbath thus?'" This re-

Purgamen Vavasoris. The author of the *Strena* describes Powell's father as "a poor Ale-man and Badger of Oatmeal".

[1] William Vavasor was the son of Andrew Vavasor, Sheriff of Montgomeryshire in 1563, and was himself High Constable of the Hundred of Newtown, 39 Eliz. (1596).—See *Mont. Coll.*, iv, p. 274, *note*, where the writer has, however, fallen into the rather serious blunder of stating that Vavasor Powell married his own mother, Penelope Vavasor being his mother, not his wife.

proof caused him to resolve not to transgress again in that manner, and soon afterwards a sermon of the celebrated Puritan preacher, Walter Cradock, deeply impressed him. He forsook his former companions and took to Puritan ways, travelling much in Radnorshire and Breconshire, especially preaching, until the persecution he met with caused him, in August 1842, to leave Wales and go to London. His enemies, however, assert that he was never ordained, and that, being indicted at Radnor for "Nonconformity, forging of Orders, and seditious doctrine, he was with much ado reprieved from the gallows". After passing two years in London, preaching whenever he had an opportunity, he was called to Dartford, in Kent, where he was very successful in his ministry for two years more. In 1646, Wales having been reduced under the power of the Parliament, he wished to return thither, and accordingly applied to the Assembly of Divines, then sitting "for the trial of public preachers", for a certificate. After some demur about ordination, they gave him the following :—

"These are to certify those whom it may concern, that the bearer hereof, Mr. Vavasor Powell, is a man of a religious and blameless conversation, and of able gifts for the work of the Ministry, and hath approved himself faithful therein, which we, whose names are underwritten, do testify— some of our own knowledge, others from credible and sufficient information. And, therefore, he being now called, and desired to exercise his gifts, in his own countrey of Wales, he also having the language thereof,[1] we conceive him fit for that

---

[1] Incidentally, this shows that at that time Welsh was the language generally spoken in Radnorshire. The Rev. Jonathan Williams, in his "History of Radnorshire" (*Arch. Camb.*, 3rd series, iv, p. 547), says that, even in 1747, divine service was performed in all its churches in the Welsh tongue alone. Now there is not, I believe, a single place of worship belonging to the Established Church in Radnorshire where the service is ever conducted in Welsh, and it would probably be hard to find in the whole county a thousand persons who can speak Welsh.

work, and worthy of encouragement therein. In witness whereof we here subscribed our names. Sept. 11, 1646.

" Charles Herle, *Prolocutor.*

" Henry Scudder.
William Greenhill.
Franc. Woodcock.
William Strong.
Joseph Caryl.
William Carter.
Thomas Wilson.
Jer. Burroughs.

Phillip Nye.
Stephen Marshall.
Jer. Whitaker.
Arthur Salwey.
Peter Sterry.
Henry Prince.
Christopher Love.
Tho. Froysell.
Robert Bettes."

On his arrival in Wales he renewed with great energy his former labours, "preaching the Word in season and out of season......insomuch that there was but few, if any, of the churches, chapels, town-halls in Wales, wherein he did not preach Christ, yea, very often upon mountains, and very frequent in fairs and markets ; it was admirable to consider how industrious he was by his often preaching in two or three places a day, and seldom two days in a week throughout the year out of the pulpit ; nay, he would sometimes ride a hundred miles in a week, and preach in every place where he might have admission both day and night." His enemies, of course, called this fanaticism. It is said that he often preached twenty times a week, and that he sometimes spoke and prayed for three, four, nay six and seven hours together ! and that "he had a ready wit, well read in history and geography, a good natural phylosopher, and skilled in physick, which greatly furthered his invention, but above all very powerful in prayer, much indued with the Spirit, and an eloquent man, mighty in the Scriptures, which was so admirably imprinted in his memory, that he was as a concordance wherever he came...... He was exceedingly hospitable : the feasts that he used to make was not for the rich, but the poor and aged, whom he often invited, and supplyed with clothes, shoos, stockings, and all other necessary accommodations. He was very free in

the entertainment of strangers......and great resort
was to him from most parts of Wales and many from
England; and was so free-harted that he would use
to say, he had room for twelve in his beds, a hundred
in his barns, and a thousand in his heart." In 1647
he accompanied, as Chaplain, a portion of the Parliamentary forces into Anglesey, where he narrowly escaped being killed. He was one of those who, on the
20th May 1648, subscribed "the resolutions and engagements of us the gentlemen, ministers, and well-affected of the County of Montgomery", to assist the
Parliament to suppress the insurrection.[1] At this time
he, it appears, lived on his property at Goitre, in Kerry,
Montgomeryshire, where he had built "a fair and
sumptuous house". He was also chiefly instrumental
in obtaining the passing, in February 1649-50, of the
celebrated "Act for the Propagation of the Gospel in
Wales", and was named one of the Commissioners to
carry it out. This Act lasted but for three years,
namely, until 1653. Under it a great number of the
clergy were ejected "for ignorance, scandal", etc.; "yet
not all", he says, "as it was falsely reported; for in
Montgomeryshire, the county where I lived, there were
eleven or twelve never ejected". After deducting
from the list of 330 given by Walker, those who were
pluralists and are named twice, and those who were
unqualified for the ministry, but were employed by the
Commissioners as schoolmasters, the actual number is
reduced in all Wales to about 150. His enemies
charged him with having received enormous sums from
the sequestered benefices, but this he indignantly
denied, saying: "Let me deal freely and truly with all
the world in that particular: I never received by
salary and all other ways put together for my preaching in Wales, from Christians and from the State since
the beginning, which is above twenty years, but between six and seven hundred pounds at most." Fired
with apostolic zeal, he and his fellow-itinerants, be-

[1] Phillip's *Civil War in Wales and the Marches*, vol. ii, p. 373.

sides preaching incessantly, in the short space of fourteen years, presented their countrymen with three editions of the New Testament in Welsh, and one edition of 6,000 copies of the whole Bible. In 1652 Vavasor Powell, " supposing himself able", as Wood says,

" to encounter any minister in Wales, did, after his settlement there, send a bold challenge to any minister or scholar, that opposed him or his brethren, to dispute on these two questions: (1) *Whether your calling or ours (which you so much speak against) be most warrantable, and nearest to the Word of God?* (2) *Whether your mixt ways, or ours of separation, be nearest the Word of God?* This challenge being sent flying abroad 11th of June 1652, it came into the hands of Dr. George Griffith of Llanymynech, in Shropshire, who looking upon it as sent to him, he returned an answer in Latin two days after, with promise, on certain conditions, to dispute with him, either in private or public. On the 19th of the same month, Vav. Powell returned a reply in Latin from Redcastle, but so full of barbarities, that any schoolboy of ten years of age might have done better. After this the Doctor made a Rejoynder in elegant Latin, wherein he corrected Powell for his false grammar, barbarisms, and solecisms, and did set a day whereon they should meet to dispute on the aforesaid questions; but the time, place, and method, with conveniences, being discussed and delayed from time to time, the disputation was not held till the 23rd of July following.[1] At that time, both parties meeting in the company of their friends, Powell's cause fell to the ground, meerly, as 'twas conceived, for want of academical learning, and the true way of arguing. So that he being then much guilty of his own weakness, endeavoured to recover it and his reputation by putting a relation of the dispute in the news book called the *Perfect Diurnal*, as if he had been the conqueror. Which relation, redounding much to the dishonour of the Doctor, he, the said Doctor, did publish a pamphlet, entitled *Animadversion on an Imperfect Relation in the 'Perfect Diurnal'*, etc."

Powell was a staunch Republican, and in 1653 and 1654 he spoke against Oliver Cromwell to his face, preached publicly against him, and wrote letters to him for assuming the Protectorship, for which he was

---

[1] For a fuller account of this disputation, which took place at the New Chapel, Penrhos, see *Mont. Coll.*, iv, p. 161.

more than once imprisoned. For joining with others in a letter of protest against Cromwell's usurpation, he was apprehended by a party of horse "from a day of fasting and prayer at Aberbechan" (Llanllwchaiarn), and taken before Major-Gen. Berry at Worcester, who, however, received him kindly, and did not detain him long. The latter end of 1654 he, at the head of a party of "fanatics", quelled a rising of the Cavaliers at Salisbury, and took an active part in preventing risings in Wales. In 1656 his views upon Baptism were changed, and he was immersed. From that time he must, therefore, be reckoned as a Baptist; but his views were not extreme, and he continued on friendly terms with those who differed from him, saying, "In this of Baptism, as in many other cases, difference in persuasion and practice may well consist with brotherly love and Christian communion." In 1657 he was at Oxford, where, on the 15th July, we find him preaching in the pulpit of All Saints. Being known to be an irreconcileable enemy to the monarchy, he was, upon the approach of the King's restoration, namely, the latter end of February 1659-60, seized and imprisoned at Shrewsbury; and his lands and tenements that had been purchased by him were taken from him. He was very soon removed from Shrewsbury into Montgomeryshire, and there kept in close custody; and upon his refusing to take the oaths of allegiance and supremacy, he was removed to the Fleet Prison in London, where he remained two years. During twelve months he was so closely confined that he was not suffered to go out of his chamber door. This and the offensive smell arising from a dunghill which stood right under his window so impaired his health, that he never afterwards quite recovered it. In 1662 he was again removed to Southsea Castle, near Portsmouth, where he was closely confined five years. In 1667 he was removed by *Habeas Corpus;* and being set at liberty, he retired to Wales, but, before ten months' end, he was again committed to Cardiff Gaol, and in October 1669 again removed to Karoon House (the then Fleet Prison) in Lambeth. It seems that he was allowed to preach occasionally, and had some measure of liberty here. The last sermons he preached were on the 25th of September 1670, many being admitted to hear him. A day or two afterwards, a violent attack of dysentery, from which he never rallied, confined him to his bed; and, after a month's illness, he died peacefully at four o'clock in the afternoon of the 27th of October 1670, in the fifty-third year of his age, and the eleventh of his imprisonment. He was buried at the lower or west end of the burial place in Bunhill Fields, "in the presence of innumerable Dissenters that then followed his corpse". Over his grave was soon afterwards erected an altar monument of freestone, on the "plank" of which was engraved the following epitaph, composed by his friend and biographer, Mr. E. Bagshaw :—

"VAVASOR POWELL, a successful teacher of the past, a sincere witness of the present, and an useful example to the future age, lies here interred, who, in the defection of so many, obtained mercy to be found faithful; for which being called to several prisons, he was there tried, and would not accept deliverance, expecting a better resurrection. In hope of which he finished this life and testimony together, in the eleventh year of his imprisonment, and in the fifty-third year of his age, Octob. 27 an. 1671 (*sic*).[1]

> "In vain oppressors do themselves perplex,
> To find out arts how they the saints may vex.
> Death spoils their plots, and sets the oppressed free,
> Thus Vavasor obtained true liberty.
> Christ him releas'd, and now he's join'd among
> The martyr'd souls, with whom he cries, 'How long!'
> "Rev. vi, 10."

He was the author of several works, all written in English. The following is a list of them :—

1. *Disputation between him and Joh. Goodwin concerning Universal Redemption, held in Coleman Street.* London : 31 December 1649 (London, 1650 quarto).

---

[1] This is evidently an error. The year should be 1670.

2. *Scriptures Concord; or, a Catechism Compiled out of the Words of the Scripture, etc.* London, 1647, octavo, 2nd ed.; 1653, 5th ed.

3. *Several Sermons*, as (1) *Christ Exalted by the Father, God the Father Glorified, and Man's Redemption Finished.* Preached before the Lord Mayor of London. London, 1649, quarto, etc.

4. *Christ and Moses Excellency; or, Sion and Sinai's Glory.* Being a triplex treatise, distinguishing and explaining the two Covenants or the Gospel and Law; and directing to the right understanding, applying and finding of the informing and assuring promises that belong to both Covenants. London, 1650, octavo.

5. *A Dialogue between Christ and a Publican, and Christ and a Doubting Christian.*

6. *Common Prayer Book no Divine Service; or, Twenty-seven Reasons against forming and imposing any human Liturgies or Common Prayer Book, etc.* London, 1661, quarto, 2nd ed.

7. *Arguments to prove that Lord Bishops, Diocesan Bishops, etc., and their Authority, are contrary to the Word of God, and so consequently unlawful, etc.* Also a discovery of the great disparity between Scriptural and Congregational Bishops and Diocesan Bishops. London, 1661, quarto, 2nd ed., corrected and much enlarged.

8. *The Bird in the Cage Chirping, etc.* London, 1661, 2nd ed., octavo. Written in prison.

9. *The Sufferer's Catechism.* Written also in prison.

10. *Brief Narative concerning the Proceedings of the Commissioners in Wales against the ejected Clergy.*

11. *The Young Man's Conflict with the Devil.*

12. *Sinful and Sinless Swearing.*

13. *An Account of his Conversion and Ministry.* ["'Tis a canting and enthusiastical piece."—Wood.]

A Confession of Faith concerning the Holy Scriptures. Some gracious, experimental, and very Choice Sayings and Sentences. Certain Hymns, and his Death-bed Expressions. London, 1671.

14. *A New and Useful Concordance of the Bible:* with the chief acceptations and various significations contained therein. Also marks to distinguish the commands, promises, and threatenings. Lond., 1671, and 1673, 8vo. Mostly done by V. Powell, but finished by N. P. J. F., etc.

15. *Collection of those Scripture Prophecies which relate to the Call of the Jews, and the glory that shall be in the latter Days.* Printed at the end of the Concordance. A second edition in 1673 contained nearly 9,000 additional references; with the addition of Scripture similes, etc.

16. *The Candle of Christ.* (1653.)

Wood adds: "The most ingenious Mrs. Kath. Philipps, of the Priory, of Cardigan, hath among her poetry a *Poem upon the Double Murder of King Charles I*, in answer to a libellous copy of rhimes made by Vav. Powell; but in what book those rhymes are, or whether they were printed by themselves, I cannot tell."

In the year 1671, being that which next followed his death, his biography (written, it is said, by his friend E. Bagshaw) was published under the title: *The Life and Death of Mr. Vavasor Powell, that Faithful Minister and Confessor of Jesus Christ*. Wherein his Eminent Conversion, Laborious, Successful Ministry, Excellent Conversation, Confession of Faith, Worthy Sayings, Choice Experiences, Various Sufferings, and other Remarkable Passages in his Life, and at his Death, are faithfully recorded for Publick Benefit. With some Elogies and Epitaphs by his Friends." This book contains many curious and interesting particulars of his life, persecutions, sufferings, and escapes from peril. Among the latter it is related that—

"At another time one came to a meeting where he preached at *Newtown*, with a full purpose to kill him; but was at that time convinced and converted by the Word, and confessed and begged pardon for his wickedness. . . . . Another time a man of *Welch Pool* entered into an oath to kill him, and designed to attempt it at *Guilsfield* where he preached, where he was also at the same instant converted by the power of the Word. . . . . Another time a woman came with a knife to kill him as he was preaching in a market place at *Machynlleth*, but was prevented. . . . . A soldier shot a brace of bullets at him looking out of his prison window in *Montgomery*, but God preserved him."

His biographer says that gentlemen of the best rank in the counties of Salop, Radnor, Montgomery, etc., saluted him as their kinsman. We also learn that his wife (Katherine) survived him; that he died childless; as to his personal appearance, that he was "in stature mean, yet meek, content," and that he "had a body of steel made, as of purpose, for his never resting, indefatigable spirit." Wood also tells us : "I have been informed by M. Ll., who knew and was acquainted with Vav. Powell .... that, when he preached, a mist or smoak would issue from his head, so great an agitation of spirit he had, etc., and therefore 'twas usually reported by some, especially those that favoured him, that he represented the saints of old time that had rays painted about their heads."

In calmly surveying his character after the lapse of two centuries, while admitting that some of his doctrines and theories were extreme and visionary, and that
" Failings he had, but where is he
From more and greater that is free?"
it is but simple justice to say that his moral character, notwithstanding the foul aspersions of his enemies, was unblemished, his courage undaunted, his zeal and energy fervid and untiring, that he was earnest, sincere, and self-sacrificing to a remarkable degree, and that by his incessant labours, he left an impression upon Wales, so deep and lasting that upwards of two centuries have failed to efface it. (Bagshaw's *Life and Death of Vavasor Powell*, etc. ; Wood's *Athenæ Oxon.* ; Walker's *Sufferings of the Clergy* ; Rees' *Nonconformity in Wales* ; Richards' *Cambro-British Biography* ; *Gwyddoniadur*, etc.)

POWYS, LEWIS, a poet who flourished between 1580 and 1620, of whom little is now known.

PRICE, OWEN, an eminent scholar and tutor, was a native of Montgomeryshire. In 1648, he was made by the Parliament Visitors a scholar of Jesus College, Oxford, where he remained four years, after which he was appointed master of a public school in Wales, where he took pains to imbue his pupils with Presbyterian principles. In 1655, he returned to Oxford, and was made a student of Christ Church. Having taken his degrees in Arts, he became master of the Free School, near Magdalen College, "where, by his industry and good way of teaching, he drew many youths of the city, whose parents were fanatically given", as Wood puts it, "to be his scholars." On the King's restoration, he was ejected for nonconformity, and taught school, in which he much delighted, in Devonshire, Basill's Lee, near Abingdon, and other places, "became useful among the brethren and a noted professor in the art of Pedagogy." He wrote and published: 1. *The Vocal Organ; or, a new art of teaching Orthography, etc.* Oxon, 1665, 8vo. 2. *English Orthography, etc.* Oxon, 1670, 8vo. He died at his house near Magdalen College, Oxford, on November 25th, 1671, and two days afterwards was buried in the church of St. Peter's in the East, "near to the door leading into the belfry". (Wood's *Athen. Oxon.;* Williams's *Em. Welshmen,* etc.)

PRICE, THOMAS, of Llanfyllin, was an eminent antiquary of the seventeenth century. He formed a large collection of Welsh and other MSS. which he sent to the Library of the Vatican in Rome. *(Lleyn MSS.)*

PEDIGREE OF PRITCHARD OF CENIARTH.

THE family of PRITCHARD of Ceniarth, there is strong ground for believing, is a cadet branch of the great house of Mathafarn. It appears to have a common origin with Richard Pugh, Esq., Sheriff, in 1627,[1] claiming to be descended from his brother Edward Pugh.

The following extract from the Mathafarn pedigree in *Lewys Dwnn's Visitations of Wales* (vol. i, 296), shows the descent of Edward Pugh from Hugh ap Evan of Mathafarn.

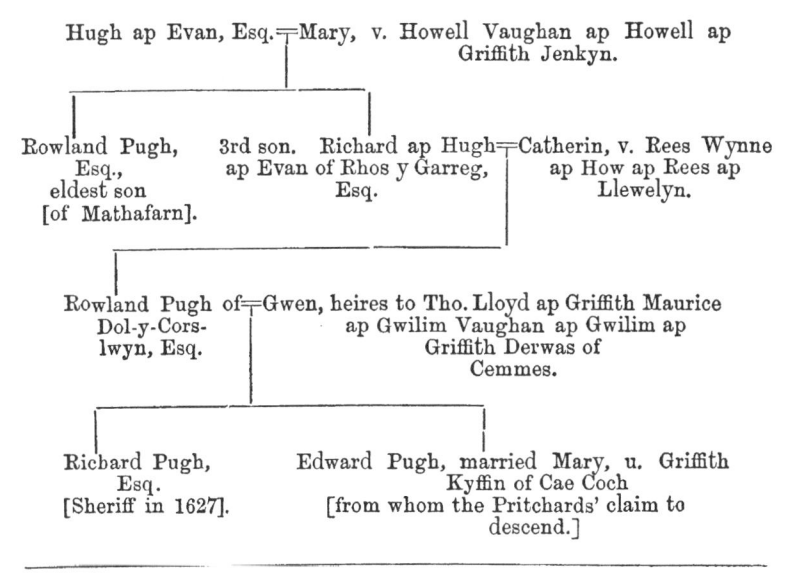

Hugh ap Evan, Esq.=Mary, v. Howell Vaughan ap Howell ap Griffith Jenkyn.

Rowland Pugh, Esq., eldest son [of Mathafarn].

3rd son. Richard ap Hugh=Catherin, v. Rees Wynne ap Evan of Rhos y Garreg, Esq. ap How ap Rees ap Llewelyn.

Rowland Pugh of Dol-y-Corslwyn, Esq.=Gwen, heires to Tho. Lloyd ap Griffith Maurice ap Gwilim Vaughan ap Gwilim ap Griffith Derwas of Cemmes.

Richard Pugh, Esq. [Sheriff in 1627].

Edward Pugh, married Mary, u. Griffith Kyffin of Cae Coch [from whom the Pritchards' claim to descend.]

---

[1] *Mont. Coll.*, vol. ix, p. 73.

The following is a translation[1] of part of an elegy on ROWLAND PRITCHARD, composed by Dafydd Manuel, 1709 :—

> " His was a generous name of an ancient race,
> And he was a branch of a venerable stock ;
> Memorable were their achievements,
> Strong were they to defend.
> Renowned was he in his day,
> Intrepid, of the disposition of Cynfyn :
> The blood of Einion, whom Meirion praises,
> Seisyllt, the magnanimous of old ;
> A beloved chieftain was he.
> Whose gold was scattered over the country ;
> The blood of Madog, whose fame was abroad,
> And whose gold was abundant ;
> The bravest man, and an ancestor (of his)
> Was Howel Goch, the flower of the county,
> Who derived his descent from South Wales ;
> From Gwyddno was his lineage unbroken.
> Of the Lloyds there were a hundred barons.
> He was the arm and strength of the Vaughans,
> The progeny of Llawdden, a renowned race ;
> He was a branch of the stock of Gwaethfoed.
> He bore, as descended from the Lloyds, *or*, lion *sable*,
>   three boar's heads, a sign of distinction ;
> The arms of Cunedda (who will not respect him ?)
> Shall be exalted, as on a chain,
> On thy tomb, gentle Rowland !
> Mournful, dark, and gloomy,
> Is all that here remains after him, like a load of ice !
> Woe ever to the country to have seen his grave !
> Woe to the poor from all parts of Gwynedd !"

[1] By Rev. D. S. Evans, B.D.

THE PEDIGREE
Of the Family of Pritchard of Ceniarth.

1. EDWARD PRITCHARD, son of Rowland Pritchard ap Edward ap Rowland ap Richard ap Hugh ap Evan, married BRIDGET, daughter of Rowland Pugh of Mathafarn (who was granddaughter to Sir Richard Pryse, of Gogerddan). He married, secondly, Lourie. He died 12th September 1698, and was buried in the family vault in Machynlleth church. His wife Lourie died the 24th September 1698, and was buried in the vault in the church. He had one son, Rowland (2) who succeeded him.

2. ROWLAND PRITCHARD (named the seventh) was born 1633; married JANE OWEN of Llynlloedd, who died and was buried in the Pritchards' family vault in Machynlleth church, 26th March 1709. He died the 30th of August 1709, and was buried in the vault in Machynlleth church. His name appears amongst the church officers, thus:—

        Rowland Pritchard, ⎰ 1685.
        Rowland Pugh, ⎱ Church Guardians.
        Edward Jones, Vic.,
            Do.   1687.

He left a son Edward (3).

3. EDWARD PRITCHARD, born . . . . married about 1699 to SARAH LLOYD, daughter of Morgan Lloyd of Caelan, Llanbrynmair, son of Jenkin Lloyd of Clochfaen, descended from Tudor Trevor (see *Mont. Coll.*, vol. ii, p. 276), and by his first wife, who was alive in 1726, as appears by her son's marriage settlement, had twelve children.

    1. Bridgetta, baptised at Machynlleth church, 27th October 1701, and married Evan Evans son of James Evans of Winllan, Cardiganshire. Marriage settlement dated 10th of June 1725.

    2. Jane, baptized at Machynlleth church 26th July 1702, married Hugh Pugh.

    3. ROWLAND (of Ceniarth), baptized at Machynlleth church, 8th July 1704, of whom hereafter as Rowland (4).

    4. Morgan, baptized at Machynlleth church, 9th April 1708.

5. Anne, baptized at the church of Machynlleth, 17th of June, 1709; married Lewis Jukes, and had several children. A widow, and died 3rd January 1777.

6. Sara, baptized at Machynlleth church, 9th December 1711.

7. Margaret, baptized at Machynlleth church 10th November 1714; married .... Lewis of Llanbrynmair 15th January 1742.

8. Susanna, baptized 7th July at Machynlleth church 1716; died 20th August 1716.

9. John, baptized 2nd August 1717; died ....

10. Littleton, baptized 2nd September 1718; died 29th October 1718.

11. Richard, baptized 20th May 1720; died 12th April 1722.

12. Vaughan, baptized 2nd June 1722; married Affrina; had a daughter Gwen, baptized 6th March 1749; he went to Caemardin, Cardiganshire.

Edward Pritchard married, secondly, ELIZABETH OWEN, 10th of August 1734, by whom he had issue; but they died in their infancy.

He married, thirdly, CATHARINE VINCENT, 27th December 1739, by whom he had a daughter Elizabeth, baptized in Machynlleth church, 4th July 1741.

He died the 29th December 1741, and was buried in the Pritchards' family vault in Machynlleth church. His wife survived him, and afterwards married Mr. Hawes of London. They lived at Stratford, and their son was Mr. Hawes, M.P., representing a Liberal constituency in Parliament some years ago. His name is thus recorded in Machynlleth church:—

Edward Pritchard, } 1711.
Thomas Pugh, } Churchwardens.
David Wynn, Rector.

4. ROWLAND PRITCHARD (viz., 8th ap Edward, etc.), baptized in Machynlleth church 8th July 1704; married in 1722 Jane, daughter of Richard Edwards of Gwern Berrai, Darowen, marriage settlement dated 11th October 1726. The trustees were the Rev. Littleton Lloyd, rector of the parish of Llan Llochaiarn, county of Montgomery, gent.; Rowland Edwards of Pant Glas, in the parish of Machynlleth, county of Montgomery, gent.; Edward ab Richard of Bryn Melin, in the

aforesaid county of Montgomery, gent.; Edward Vaughan of the parish of Penegoes, in the county of Montgomery, gent. He died at Morben, 1768, and was buried in the vault in Machynlleth church 3rd September 1768. His name is thus recorded in Machynlleth church :—

> Rowland Pritchard, Ceniarth, } 1745.
> Evan Richard,   } Churchwardens.
> John Owen, rector.

Their children were :—

1. EDWARD, date of baptism not known (of Ceniarth).

2. Bridget, date of baptism not known; married William Hughes, Esquire, of Gogarth, county of Merioneth. (No entry to be found in the Machynlleth church register from 1722 to 1730. The leaves have been cut out. At Darowen there is no entry in the church register from 1720 to 1729.)

3. Richard, baptised 24th June 1731. He married 19th October 1757, Jane, daughter of John Jones, of Eskir Evan and Cwmbychan Bach, and they had four children: Jane, baptized 1st August 1758; she married H. Humphreys. Sarah, baptized 20th October 1760; died unmarried 1837. Rowland, baptised 18th July 1763, died an infant; Mary, baptised 27th April 1765, died unmarried about 1842. Richard Pritchard's will proved 16th May 1810. His name is recorded in Machynlleth church:—" Richard Pritchard, Owen Owen, Churchwardens, Robert Edwards, Rector, 1772."

4. Sarah, baptised 13th December 1735, married Edward Rowlands, Esq., of Rhenfelen, Darowen parish, and had one daughter, who married Humphrey Jones, Esq. of Garthmill, on the 14th November 1775.

5. Mary, baptized 3rd March, 1739, married John Parry, Esq. of Aberystwith, and is now represented by John Parry, Esq., of Glanpaith, Cardiganshire, and the Rev. Thomas Parry, rector of Walthamstow.

6. Jane, the youngest daughter, died unmarried 8th April 1819, aged 83. (She was godmother to Bridget James, who married David Pritchard, of Ceniarth, in November 1819.)

5. EDWARD PRITCHARD (viz., 8th, ap Rowland, etc.), baptized ... married in 1756 to JANE, daughter of David Rees of Maesy-

pandy, Merionethshire (who was born 27th August 1737, and was buried 18th October 1781). He died at Ceniarth in 1810. He had six children.

1. Rowland, born at Morben Isy y Garreg, baptized at Machynlleth church 19th September 1758, died the 1st February 1759.

2. Mary, born at Morben, baptized 29th September 1761, married E. Evans.

3. Elizabeth, born at Morben, baptized 9th February 1764, died the 1st March 1764.

4. EDWARD, born at Morben, baptized at Machynlleth church 25th May 1765 (the eldest surviving son), of whom hereafter.

5. Sarah, born at Morben, baptized 27th September 1766, married Simon Griffiths of Cwmrhaidr, Esquire, 13th October 1803, and had three daughters. Susanna married 1828, Matthew Davis Williams, Esq., of Cwmynfelin, Cardiganshire. They had twelve children. Jane died unmarried at Cwmcynfelin. Catherine, the youngest daughter, died at Lodge Park, Cardiganshire. The Pughes of Cwmrhaidr derive their descent from Elystan Glodrudd, and the family is now represented by George Griffiths Williams, Esq. of Wallog, Cardiganshire.

6. Bridget, born at Morben, baptized 12th November, 1767, married a Mr. Allen[1] of a good Staffordshire family,

---

[1] CARDINAL ALLEN, born 1532, died 1594, was sprung from the same family.—William Allen was born at Rossal in Lancashire. His father, John Allen, was a gentleman of good family and some fortune. William Allen was entered at Oriel College, Oxford, in his fifteenth year, took the degree of B.A. in 1550, being esteemed an honour to the University on account of his great parts, learning and eloquence. In 1558 he was made one of the Canons of York; but on Queen Elizabeth's accession he, as a zealous Catholic, lost all hopes of preferment, and withdrew to Louvain in Spanish Netherlands, where an English College was erected, of which he became the principal support. At this time several persons of great learning, and some of the boldest champions of the Popish cause, resided in this place, with whom he grew into great esteem on account of the strength of his genius and politeness of his manners. The gracefulness of his person, it is said, contributed much to obtain the attention of his associates, for with a majestic presence he had an easy, affable deportment, and with the greatest severity of manners a mildness of speech and behaviour which won the affection of all who conversed with him. He returned to Lanca-

and had four children, two sons and two daughters.
Benjamin, Edward, Marianne and Sarah; Sarah died in
London. The sons are dead. The eldest daughter married
Mr. Baker (who died at Llynlloed, and is buried in the
churchyard in Machynlleth); they had two daughters.
The eldest daughter, Louisa, married Sir David Cunningham, Bart., deceased; the youngest, Catherine, married Major Nangle, Mrs. Nangle died at Toronto, in
Canada. Mrs. Baker married, secondly, William Willats,
Esq., and had one son, William Hale Willats, Esq. of
Denton Court, Canterbury, Kent, educated at Eton, and
took honours at Christ Church College, Oxford.

6. EDWARD PRITCHARD (viz. 9th ap Edward ap Rowland, etc.),
born at Morben, baptized 25th May 1765, married his cousin
BRIDGET, daughter of John Parry, Esq. of Aberystwith, 11th

---

shire for the benefit of his health in 1565, and then laboured to the
utmost of his powers in making converts. He also published several
pamphlets which rendered him obnoxious to the Government, and he
was obliged to conceal himself at the house of the Duke of Norfolk
in Norfolk, and there wrote an apology for his party, viz., *Brief
Reasons concerning the Catholic Faith.* However, he was forced to
make his escape to Flanders in 1568, where he had powerful friends,
and amongst them Sir Christopher Hatton. Wm. Allen then became Canon of Cambray, a considerable preferment, conferred on
him to reward his zeal for the Catholic church. He then became,
through the interest of the Guises, Canon of Rheims, was a friend of
the Jesuits, and considered the chief of the English fugitives abroad,
and with them persuaded King Philip of Spain to undertake the
conquest of England. To facilitate this project, Sixtus V was prevailed on to renew the excommunication against Queen Elizabeth by
his predecessor Pius V. Dr. Allen wrote in defence of this base
proceeding, and to give weight to his writings was created Cardinal
by the title of St. Martin in Montibus, and soon after the King of
Spain gave him an abbey of great value in the kingdom of Naples.
The Pope, having a high opinion of the Cardinal's merit and use in
Consistories, would not allow him to leave Rome. The remainder of
his life was spent there in great honour and reputation, living in
much splendour. He died in the 63rd year of his age, strongly
suspected to have been poisoned by the Jesuits. He was buried
with great pomp in the English College at Rome. His portrait is
in the Vatican, and Mrs. Willats was allowed to have a copy of it,
which is now at her house in Queensgate, London. Lately was discovered the lost deeds of a family estate, that of Ubberley Hall,
near Hanley, the present value being £70,000. The Allen family
had possessed the estate in the male line from the time of the
Conquest, till one hundred years ago, when the deeds were lost, and
from the lack of them, the family were dispossessed in 1828.

January 1803, died the 6th July 1811, aged 46. His widow died the 18th of April 1812, aged 35, *sans* issue : Edward Pritchard was a captain in the Montgomeryshire Militia and a J.P. He left Ceniarth estate to his nephew David (the eldest son of his brother David). A new vault was made for him and his wife in the church at Machynlleth, under the small pew.

7. DAVID PRITCHARD, born at Morben, baptized 3rd February 1769, married SARAH, daughter of Thomas Newell of Shrewsbury, 2nd November 1794, and had nine children.

    1. DAVID (the eldest son, of Ceniarth).

    2. Sarah, died unmarried at 13, Ravensbourn Villas, Stanstead Road, Forest Hill, on 11th October 1879, aged 81 years, buried at Brompton Cemetery.

    3. Edward, married Jane . . . . *sans* issue, and was buried at Brompton Cemetery.

    4. Rowland married, but had no children, and was buried at Brompton Cemetery.

    5. Thomas Newell died at London Wall, aged 59, unmarried, and was buried at Brompton Cemetery, 1862.

    6. Hannah, married Richard Bale, died at Priory Grove, Brompton, without issue, and she and her husband are buried in Brompton Cemetery.

    7. Rice, died unmarried, and was buried by his father in the churchyard of   in the City Road.

    8. Bridget, married William Hawes, and they had a son, Thomas Newell Pritchard, who died unmarried, and was buried in Brompton Cemetery; and a daughter, Hannah Sarah, who married in 1880 Dr. Carmichael of the Isle of Skye.

    9. Richard, died unmarried at 100, London Wall, September 1851, and was buried in a church in the City Road, where his father was buried.

8. DAVID PRITCHARD, born 28th November, 1797, baptized   , married 19th November, 1819, BRIDGET, daughter of Thomas James, merchant and shipowner, Aberystwith (who was born 13th September 1786, and died 11th January 1863), and had issue one daughter, CATHARINE. David Pritchard was the first representative of Ceniarth that was buried in the churchyard. All the eldest sons and their wives were buried in the vault in the church. David Pritchard died 30th December 1859.

PEDIGREE OF PRITCHARD OF CENIARTH. 233

9. CATHARINE, daughter and heiress of David Pritchard, born 20th October 1820, baptised at Ceniarth, married, 10th December 1844, DAVID GILBERTSON (who was born 30th September 1813), third son of W. Cobb Gilbertson, Esq., J.P., Major of the Cardigan Militia, of Cefngwyn, Cardiganshire, by his third wife, Elizabeth, daughter of the Rev. Isaac Williams of Ystrad-teilo, vicar of Llanrhysted, Cardiganshire. William Cobb Gilbertson was nephew and heir of William Jones, Esq. of Dol y Cletwr, High Sheriff for the county of Cardigan, 1766. She has had issue :—

1. DAVID PRITCHARD (10).
2. WILLIAM EDWARD (11).
3. Catharine, born 13th March 1848, at Western House, Old Brompton, baptized at Trinity Church, Brompton.
4. Thomas James, born at 10, Thistle Grove, 18th of June 1854, baptized at St. Mary's Boltons, West Brompton, died at Oak Villa, 16th August 1857, and was buried in the churchyard at Machynlleth.
5. John, born at 10, Thistle Grove, 12th August 1856, educated at Westminster School and Trinity College, Cambridge. He took Holy Orders 1881, and now holds a curacy at Devonport.
6. Elizabeth, born at Oak Villa, 25th June 1858, baptized at St. Mary's Boltons, died at the same place 20th February 1860, buried at Machynlleth.
7. James Williams, born at Oak Villa, Old Brompton, 2nd September 1860, baptized at St. Mary's Boltons, now an undergraduate at Trinity College, Cambridge.
8. Bridget Mary, born at Merrington House, Old Brompton, 2nd January, 1863, baptized at St. Mary's Boltons.
9. Lewis, born at Merrington House 9th October 1865, baptized at St. Mary's Boltons, now at Westminster School.

10. DAVID PRITCHARD, born 13th October 1849, at Western House, Old Brompton, baptized at Trinity Church, married at St. Mary Abbots, Kensington, 5th June 1879, to Cicely Ann, second daughter of Henry Master Feilden, Esq., M.P., of Witton Park, Lancashire. He was educated at King's College School, Westminster School, and Trinity College, Cambridge. He assumed the name of Pritchard, in lieu of that of Gilbertson, on his attaining 21, in accordance with the provisions of his grandfather, David Pritchard's will, by virtue of which he

became possessor of the Ceniarth estate. He was captain of the E Company of the Cambridge Volunteers, when at Trinity College. He took Holy Orders in 1874, and became rector of Watermellock in 1877. He died the 5th of March 1880, and was buried on the 12th of March in the churchyard at Machynlleth.

11. WILLIAM EDWARD GILBERTSON (2nd son), was born at Western House, Old Brompton, 22nd January, 1852, baptized at Trinity Church, Brompton, was also educated at King's College School, Westminster School, and Trinity College, Cambridge. On the death of his elder brother he became the possessor of the Ceniarth estate, and added the surname of PRITCHARD to that of Gilbertson, in pursuance of his grandfather's will.

C. G.

May 1882.

PARISH REGISTERS IN MONTGOMERYSHIRE.

By THOS. W. HANCOCK.

THERE have been various opinions as to the period when parish registers were first kept in England. The *Annals of Shrewsbury* state that they were first kept in 1499. Cole, in his MSS. in the British Museum, mentions having read that they were first commenced in 1501. But the foundation of the system as an established institution is due to Thomas Cromwell, Earl of Essex, Henry VIII's Minister of State, though the precise date of his earlier order is not known. Dr. Thorpe, and Jacob, the author of the *Law Dictionary*, state them to have been instituted by the " Lord Cromwell, Anno 13 Hen. VIII [1521] while he was Vicar-General to the King." Nicholls, in his *History of Leicester*, gives the same date when noticing the register of Cottesbach, which begins in 1558, stating this to be "37 years after the first institution of these parochial records by the Lord Cromwell in the 13th year of Henry VIII." Whittaker, in his *History of Sheffield*, states them to have been kept in pursuance of Cromwell's injunction in 1534. But Dr. Prideaux, Bishop of Worcester, in his directions to churchwardens, says :—" Parish registers were first ordered by the Lord Vicegerent Cromwell in the 30th year of King Henry VIII, 1538, and from thence all parish registers have their beginning."

A brief notice of the history of Cromwell, and his preferments, will assist in forming a conclusion as to the probable correct date of their foundation. Cromwell was the son of a blacksmith at Putney, in Surrey,

and was born about 1490. Early in life he became a
clerk to the English factory at Antwerp, which situation he soon left, and went into several countries as
the secret agent of his sovereign. In 1510 he was
sent on a mission to Rome. On his return he was
taken into the service of Cardinal Wolsey, who obtained for him a seat in the House of Commons, where
he defended his master with great spirit. On the fall
of the Cardinal in 1529, the king took him into his
own service, and gave him several valuable and important places. In 1531 he was knighted, and in
1535 he was appointed Visitor-General of Monasteries.
In July 1536, he was appointed Minister of State in
Ecclesiastical matters, under the title of Vicar-General,
and in September of that year he issued his first set of
injunctions to the clergy, but among which the subject
of parish registers does not appear. In the next year
he issued also certain articles to the clergy; but
nothing is recorded about registration. But in the
injunctions which he sent out in the next following
year, 1538, parish registers form a distinct article in
the same. The date of this order is the 8th September. That the conception of parish registers was
wholly an original creation of his own is doubtful.
For Cardinal Ximenes, Archbishop of Toledo, in
Spain, had instituted a system of parish registering in
that country, with a view to remedy the disorders
which arose by the frequency of divorces there. In a
synod held by him in 1497, he enjoined his clergy to
keep a regular record of marriages and births. It is
highly probable that Cromwell received the idea from
that source. In England, the Papists, however, viewed
the "commaundement geven to the parsons and vycars
off everye parisse that they schulde make a book wher
in to be specyffyyd the names off them that be weddyd
and buryyd and crystynyd", with much fear and distrust, their "mystrust was that somme charges, mor
than hath byn in tymys past, shold growe to them by

this occasyon off regestrynge of thes thynges."[1] The injunction issued by Cromwell, as printed by Burnet, reads as follows:—

"Item, That you and every Parson, Vicar, or Curate within the Diocese, shall for every church keep one Book or Register, wherein he shall write the day and year of every Wedding, Christning and Burying, made within your parish for your time, and so every man succeeding you likewise, and also there insert every person's name that shall be so wedded, christned and buried; and for the safe keeping of the same Book, the parish shall be bound to provide of their common charges one sure coffer, with two locks and keys, whereof the one to remain with you, and the other with the wardens of every such parish, wherein the said Book shall be laid up, which book ye shall every Sunday take forth, and in the presence of the said wardens, or one of them, write and record in the same all the weddings, christnings, and buryings made the week afore; and that done to lay up the book in the said coffer as afore. And for every time the same shall be omitted, the party that shall be in the fault thereof, shall forfeit to the said church 3s. 4d., to be employed on the reparation of the said church."[2]

Following the issue of this injunction in 1538, many registers were immediately commenced, but unfortunately few are now in existence. The restoration of Popery under Philip and Mary did not vitiate this canon touching registration, for Cardinal Pole in 1556, in his Constitutions and Decrees to the Archbishops and Bishops, enjoins that "Visitors" of all parochial churches should "carefully inquire whether the parochial clergy have books in which they set out the names of those who are baptised, with their parents' names, as also the names of those who die, or who contract marriage."[3] The prejudice of the Papists to Cromwell's law had, evidently, to a considerable extent disappeared; but the laxity of enforcing it made it a dead letter. In consequence of the negligence shown to the order, and the irregular and bad keeping of the

[1] Cromwell correspondence in Chapter House, Bundle E.
[2] Burnet's *Hist. of Reformation*, ed. 1715, vol. i, p. 171.
[3] *The Reform of England*. By Cardinal Pole. 12th Decree.

238 PARISH REGISTERS IN MONTGOMERYSHIRE.

books, the Convocation, in Queen Elizabeth's time, found it necessary to renew the admonition. In 1597, the Upper House directed special attention to the matter, that the clergy should show accurate observance to the injunctions, and directed that the books should be of parchment, and the entries should be made in a clear and legible hand. That a chest or coffer should be kept in the church for their preservation, with *three* locks; and that upon every Sabbath day, immediately after morning and evening prayer, the minister and churchwardens should take the parchment book out of the said coffer, and the minister in the presence of the churchwardens should write and record in it the names of all persons christened, with the names of their parents, and all marriages and burials; and that all entries made in it each week should be read publicly in the church on the following Sunday, after morning and evening prayer. That a true copy of this book should be sent from every parish yearly to the Consistory Court of the bishop, where a book was to be kept for recording the same. That the contents of old decayed paper books, containing parish entries, should be fairly rewritten into the new parchment book, and that great care should be taken to secure accuracy in the transcription. That in order to prevent tampering with the contents of the new register books, the resident parson, or in his absence the curate of the parish, together with both churchwardens, should subscribe their names to every separate page.

Montgomery had but recently been outlined into a separate shire when Cromwell's injunction was issued, much of it lay undelimited, remaining only as a part of the large district of Powysland; yet by virtue of the Act of Union, passed in the twenty-seventh year of the King's reign, the county went under English law. Judging by what remains in existence of the Registers of that century, in Wales, it may fairly be assumed that the Montgomeryshire clergy generally became loyally attached to the reformed order of things. The Decree received no readier obedience in any Welsh district than in this. Montgomeryshire has *nine* parishes with Registers dating between 1558 and 1598. Flintshire has *eight*, dating between 1538 and 1598; the parish Register of Gwaenyscor commencing in the memorable year of 1538, and that of Hanmer in the same shire, the next earliest, in 1563. Denbighshire has *six*, the earliest being that of Ruabon, commencing in 1550. Carnarvonshire has *four*, the Conway Register commencing in 1541, and is the second earliest in Wales. Merionethshire has *two*, that of Mallwyd, dating 1586, and Llanderfel, dating 1598. Anglesea has *one*, that of Llansadwrn, dating 1584. In South Wales, two shires only, Carmarthen and Glamorgan, have sixteenth century Registers, but only three now remain between the two counties; the earliest book is that of the parish of St. Ishmael, in Carmarthenshire, dating 1571.

If the existence or absence of Parish Registers be any guide to the progress of the Reformation in Wales in the Sixteenth Century, which I think may be some data to measure its steps, then the spiritual seed fell upon hard ground. Exception may be taken to this doctrine, yet notwithstanding, all things considered, I think it to be one test. The clergy in Wales, as a whole, showed intense apathy to their ecclesiastical and spiritual functions. Matters appear to improve as the government of Elizabeth became more established, and after the Translation of the Scriptures into Welsh in 1588. But praise must be withheld.

The following Table is an arrangement of the parishes in the county, shewing a comparative view of the times of the earliest entries of the Registers.

Churchstoke - - 1558	Llandinam - - - 1594
Guildsfield - - 1573	Berriew - - - 1596
Aberhavesp - - 1578	Manafon - - - 1596
Llansantffraid - - 1582	Forden - - - 1598
Llangyniew - - 1583	Llanfair-Caereinion - 1602

Llanfechain	-	-	1603	Sneyd, or Snead -	-	1665
Hirnant	-	-	1606	Llanwnog -	-	1668
Llanidloes	-	-	1618	Llanymynech	-	1668
Kerry	-	-	1619	Llanmerewig	-	1670
Llanerfyl	-	-	1623	Llanwrin -	-	1676
Trefeglwys	-	-	1623	Tregynon -	-	1678
Llanwddin	-	-	1624	Penegoes -	-	1679
Penstrowed	-	-	1628	Llanrhaiadr-	-	1679
Llangadfan	-	-	1630	Pennant -	-	1680
Darowen	-	-	1633	Mochdref -	-	1682
Welshpool	-	-	1634	Machynlleth	-	1684
Carno	-	-	1638	Llanllugan -	-	1688
Meifod	-	-	1649	Castell Caereinion	-	1689
Bettws	-	-	1655	Montgomery	-	1694
Llanllwchhaiarn	-	-	1658	Llandyssul -	-	1699
Newtown	-	-	1660	Hyssington -	-	1701
Llanwyddelan	-	-	1661	Llangurig -	-	1701
Llandrinio	-	-	1662	Buttington -	-	1708
Llandysilio	-	-	1662	Cemmaes -	-	1711
Llanbrynmair	-	-	1663	Garthbeibio-	-	1718
Llanfihangel	-	-	1663	Llangynog -	-	1720
Llanfyllin	-	-	1664			

In many of the parishes, the Registers show great neatness in the penmanship, and the entries are properly classified. In few instances only are the births, marriages, and deaths entered indiscriminately. Many of the clergy had a predilection for entering them in Latin. In some parishes the entries, apparently, are not in the handwriting of the clergy, but in that of a local professional "writer"; in these instances the entries would be copies only of the notes made by the parson, or, perhaps, by the parish clerk. I happen to know, within my own memory, of cases where the parson left the whole business of registering, and the entire custody of the books to the parish clerk. It will be observed from the preceding Table, as well as from the list of Registers here following, that there exists a great deficiency of years, and great irregularity, which is indicative of gross neglect of the law affecting the keeping of the books. The admonitions of the Bishops in Convocation requiring copies of the Registers to be sent to the Consistory Courts, appear to be wholly unattended to. The vulgar tradition, in some districts, is that their destruction was the work of Oliver Cromwell and the parliamentary party in the revolutionary troubles of the seventeenth century. However guilty this Cromwell may have been, as affects desecration of church fabrics and furniture, so universal a destruction and deficiency as exist in Church Registers can not well be taxed to him ; but their loss is due to another state of things, and to other agents. A glance at the irregular dates, which is also a general fault throughout the Welsh parishes, forces on one the conclusion that the guilty parties were the clergy and churchwardens.

The abstract here next following is intended to give the number of all the Register books in the parishes of the county, up to the commencement of the present century, with notes as to their condition and their defects. It may usefully serve the writers of parish histories, who should verify the same, and enlarge upon it.

1.—ABERHAVESP. R.

 I. Bap., Bur., Marr., 1578-1651.
 II, III. Bap., Bur., 1726-1786 ; Marr., 1726-1753.
 IV. Bap., Bur., 1786-1812.
 V. Marr., 1754-1812.

2.—BERRIEW. V.

 I-IV. Bap., Bur., 1596-1789; Mar., 1596-1764; (deficient, years, 1628-1683).
 V. Bap., Bur., 1790-1812.
 VI, VII. Marr., 1765-1812.

3.—BETTWS-CEDEWAIN.

 I-III. Bap., Bur., 1655-1788 ; Marr., 1655-1753.
 IV. Bap., Bur., 1789-1812.
 V, VI. Marr., 1754-1812.

4.—BUTTINGTON. V.

 I. Bap., Bur., Marr., 1708-1736.
 II. Consists of loose parchment leaves, obliterated, and illegible in many places, contains Baptisms, Burials, and Marriages from the year 1723 to 1735; but it is deficient of the years 1729 to 1732.

III. Bap., 1735-1772; Bur., 1735-1782; Mar., 1735-1754; but is interrupted by IV, which is imperfect.
IV. Bap.,1740-1781; Bur., 1739-1764; Marr.,1740-1754.
V, VI. Bap., 1772-1812.
VII, VIII. Bur., 1782-1812.
IX. Marr., 1754-1800; this is interrupted by X.
X. Marr., 1782-1812.

5.—CARNO. V.

I. Contains Registers, A.D. 1638-1707; but is wanting in entries from 1687 to 1699.
II, III. Entries 1708-1812.
IV. Marriages, 1754-1812.

6.—CASTELL CAEREINION. R.

I. Partly illegible, contains Baptisms, Burials, Marriages, A.D. 1689-1742; but is deficient of years 1733, 1739.
II, III. Bap., Bur., 1743-1803; Marr., 1743-1809.
IV. Bap., 1804-1812.
V. Bur., 1804-1812.
VI. Duplicate of entries in II, III, Marr. 1754-1804.
VII. Marr., 1809-1812.

7.—CEMMAES. R.

I, II. Contain Baptisms, A.D., 1711-1812.
III, IV. Bur., 1711-1812; deficient of 1755.
V. Marr., 1711-1755.
VI, VII. Marr., 1757-1812.

8.—CHURCHSTOKE. V.

I, II. Contain Baptisms, Burials, A.D. 1558-1773; Marriages, 1558-1753.
III, IV. Bap., Bur., 1774-1812.
V. Marr., 1754-1812.

9.—DAROWEN. V.

I. (Parchment), Bap., Bur., Marr., 1633-1689.
II. (Parchment), Bap., Bur., Marr., 1708-1733.
III, IV. (Parchment), Bap., Bur., 1736-1790; Marr., 1736-1753.
V. (Parchment), Bap., Bur., 1791-1812.
VI, VII. Marr., 1754-1812.

10.—FORDEN. V.

I. Bap., Marr., Bur., 1598-1681. The following years are wanting, 1607-1610, 1652, 1680-1681.
II, III. Entries, 1681-1747; year 1745, defective.

PARISH REGISTERS IN MONTGOMERYSHIRE. 243

IV, V. Entries, 1875-1812; the years 1748-1750 appear to have been torn out.
VI. Marr., 1754-1812.
The Chapelry of Trelystan has five volumes of Registers, containing Bap., Bur., Marr., 1660-1812.

11.—GARTHBEIBIO. R.

I, II. Bap., Bur., Marr., 1718-1812.

12.—GUILDSFIELD. V.

I. Bap., Bur., Marr., 1573-1653; deficient 1653-1696.
II, III, IV. Bap., Bur., 1696-1772; Marr., 1696-1753.
V, VI, VII. Bap., Bur., 1773-1812.
VIII, IX. Marr., 1754-1812.

13.—HIRNANT. R.

I, II. Are in a very mutilated state, and scarcely legible; they contain Bap., Bur., Marr., 1606-1783.
III. Bap., Bur., Marr., 1784-1812.

14.—HYSSINGTON. V.

I. Bap., Bur., 1701-1812; Marr., 1701-1753.
II. Marr., 1754-1812.

15.—KERRY. V.

I. Bap., Bur., Marr., 1619-1656.
II. The entries are in a very confused state, 1657-1707.
III, IV. Bap., Bur., Marr., 1708-1812.

16.—LLANBRYNMAIR. R.

I, II. Bap., Bur., Marr., 1663-1738.
III, IV. Bap., Bur., 1749-1812.
V-VII. Marr., 1754-1812.

17.—LLANERVYL. R.

I, II, III. Bap., Bur., 1623-1796; Marr., 1623-1753.
IV. Bap., Bur., 1797-1812.
V. Marr., 1754-1811.

18.—LLANDYSSIL. R.

I, II. Bap., Bur., 1699-1757; Marr., 1699-1754.
III, IV. Bap., Bur., 1758-1812.
V. Marr., 1755-1812.

19.—LLANDYSILIO. V.

I. Bap., Bur., Marr., 1662-1763; interrupted by
II. Bap., Bur., 1753-1812.
III, IV. Marr., 1754-1812.

20.—LLANDRINIO. R.

I. Bap., 1662-1696; Bur., 1662-1667; Marr., 1664-1695.
II. Irregular entries, Bap., 1697-1754; 1763-1774; Bur., 1708-1774; Marr., 1744-1753.
III, IV. Bap., 1775-1812.
V, VI. Bur., 1781-1812.
VII, VIII, IX. Marr., 1754-1812.

21.—LLANDINAM. V.

The Registers are written in Latin from 1594 to 1732.

22.—LLANFAIR CAEREINION. V.

I, II. Very imperfect, Bap., Bur., Marr., 1602-1676.
III, IV. Bap., Bur., Marr., 1680-1701.
V, VI. Bap., Bur., 1723-1772; Marr., 1723-1753.
VII. Bap., 1773-1802; Bur., 1773-1801.
VIII. Bap., Bur., 1803-1812.
IX, X. Marr., 1754-1812.
No Register for 1676-1680, and 1701-1723.

23.—LLANFIHANGEL. YN NGHWNFA.[1] R.

I. Bap., Bur., Marr., 1663-1667.
II. Bap., Bur., Marr., 1693-1698.
III. Bap., Bur., Marr., 1708-1738.
IV. Bap., Bur., 1739-1762; Marr., 1739-1753.
V, VI. Bap., Bur., 1763-1803.
VII. Bap., 1805-1812.
VIII. Bur., 1805-1812.
IX, X, XI. Marr., 1754-1812.

24.—LLANFYLLIN. R.

I. Bap., Bur., Marr., 1664-1727; wanting 1699-1701.
II, III. Bap., Bur., 1728-1787; Marr., 1728-1753.
IV. Bap., Bur., 1789-1812.
V, VI. Marr., 1754-1812.

25.—LLANGADVAN. R.

Registers: Baptisms, Burials, Marriages, 1630-1812; year 1640, deficient; 1641, illegible; 1641-1673, lost; and 1696-1700, 1705-1717, deficient.

---

[1] Llanfihangel *yn Nghwnfa* means St. Michael's Church *in the High Land*, as a distinction from the other St. Michael's *in the Plain* (Llanfihangel *yn Nghentyn*), which is the Welsh name of Alberbury parish. A portion of this latter parish is attached to the county of Montgomery, as also are portions of Llanyblodwel and Worthen.

26.—LLANGURIG. V.
I. Bap., Bur., Marr., 1701-1757 ; but very defective.
II. Bap., Bur., 1758-1812.
III. Marr., 1758-1812.

27.—LLANGYNOG. R.
I. Bap., Bur., Marr., 1720-1749.
II. Bap., 1750-1796 ; Bur., 1850-1802 ; Marr., 1750-1761,
III. Bap., 1797-1812 ; Bur., 1803-1812.
IV. Marr., 1763-1812.

28.—LLANGYNIEW. R.
I. Bap., Bur., Marr., 1583-1683 ; no Register, 1683-1729.
II. Bap., Bur., 1729-1777 ; Marr., 1731-1753 ; no marriages between 1753-1755.
III, IV. Bap., Bur., 1778-1812.
V. Marr., 1755-1812.

29.—LLANIDLOES. V.
I. Bap., Bur., Marr., 1618-1708.
II, III, IV, V, Bap., Bur., Marr., 1711-1812.

30.—LLANLLUGAN. V.
I. Decayed, and several leaves lost; Bap., Bur., Marr., 1688-1702.
II, III. Bap., Bur., Marr., 1731-1804.
IV. Bap., Bur., 1805-1812.

31.—LLANLLWCHHAIARN. V.
I. Partly illegible ; Bap., Bur., Marr., 1658-1729.
II. Bap., Bur., 1730-1792 ; Marr., 1730-1753.
III. Bap., Bur., 1793-1812.
IV. Marr., 1754-1812; (Baptisms, Burials, deficient, 1799-1801.)

32.—LLANMEREWIG. R.
I. Bap., Bur., Marr., 1670-1760; but deficient 1685-1688. They are written in Latin until 1732.
II. Bap., Bur., Marr., 1761-1812.

33.—LLANRHAIADR YN MOCHNANT. V.
I. Bap., Bur., 1679-1692.
II. Bap., Bur., 1695-1713.
III, IV. Bap., 1713-1812.
V, VI. Bur., 1713-1812.
VII, VIII. Marr., 1713-1812.

34.—LLANSANTFFRAID YN MECHAIN. V.

I. Bap., Bur., Marr., 1582-1614.
II. Bap., 1665-1711; Bur., 1688-1711; Marr., 1684-1711.
III. Bap., Bur., 1712-1757; Marr., 1712-1753.
IV. Bap., Bur., 1758-1812.
V. Marr., 1754-1812.

35.—LLANVECHAIN. V.

I, II, III. Bap., Bur., 1603-1812; Marr., 1603-1753.
IV, V. Marr., 1754-1812.

36.—LLANWDDIN. V.

I, II. Registers are in Latin; Bap., Bur., Marr., 1624-1736.
III, IV. Bap., Burr., Marr., 1737-1812.
V. Marr., 1759-1812.

37.—LLANWNOG.

I, II. Bap., Bur., 1668-1809; Marr., 1668-1753. Baptisms deficient, 1774-1783.
III. Bap., Bur., 1810-1812.
IV. Marr., 1754-1812.

38.—LLANWRIN. R.

I. Bap., Bur., Marr., 1676-1781. Deficient 1676-1703.
II. Bap., 1782-1812.
III. Bur., 1782-1812.
IV. Marr., 1782-1812.

39.—LLANWYDDELAN. R.

I, II, III. Imperfect, and partly illegible. Bap., Bur., Marr., 1661-1783.
IV, V. Bap., Bur., 1792-1812.
VI. Marr., 1784-1812.

40.—LLANYMYNECH. R.[1]

I. Bap., Bur., 1668-1722 (imperfect.); Marr., 1668-1753.
II, III. Bap., Bur., 1773-1812.
IV. Marr., 1754-1812.

41.—MACHYNLLETH. R.

I. Bap., Bur., Marr., 1684-1722.
II. Bap., Bur., 1731-1759; Marr., 1734-1753.
III, IV. Bap., Bur., 1760-1812.
V, VI, VII. Marr., 1754-1812.

---

[1] Llanymynech parish occupies a position in three counties,—Montgomery, Salop, and Denbigh.

42.—MANAFON. R.

I. Very imperfect. Bap., 1596-1665; Bur., 1596-1667.
II. Also very imperfect. Bap., Bur., 1678-1718. The entries of Marriages in I and II are very imperfect.
III. Bap., Bur., 1719-1760; Marr., 1719-1753.
IV. Bap., Bur., 1761-1812.
V. Marr., 1754-1812.

43.—MEIFOD. V.

I. Bap., Bur., 1649-1674.
II. Bap., Bur., 1675-1701; Marr., 1677-1702.
III. Bap., Bur., 1702-1812; Marr., 1702-1758.
IV. Marr., 1759-1812.

44.—MOCHDREF, OR MOUGHDREF. V.

I. Bap., Bur., Marr., 1682-1755.
II. Bap., Bur., Marr., 1765-1812.

45.—MONTGOMERY. R.

I, II. Bap., Bur., 1694-1782; Marr., 1694-1753.
III. Bap., Bur., 1782-1812.
IV, V. Marr., 1754-1812.

46.—NEWTOWN. R.[1]

Registers, 1660-1812.

47.—PENEGOES. R.

I. Irregular entries. Bap., Bur., 1679-1770; Marr., 1679-1753; deficient 1722-1745, and interrupted by Vol. II.
II. Bap., Bur., 1763-1812.
III, IV. Marr., 1754-1812.

48.—PENNANT MELANGELL. V.

I. (Latin). Bap., Bur., Marr., 1680-1714.
II. Bap., 1720-1791; Bur., 1720-1790; Marr., 1720-1762.
III. Bap., Bur., 1792-1812.
IV. Marr., 1763-1812.

---

[1] In the case of the Registers of this parish, it is to be feared that the earlier books were plundered by some of the Parliamentary party. It will be observed that the present Registers commence with the year of the downfall of the "Commonwealth", 1660; no other similar case occurs in this county.

248 PARISH REGISTERS IN MONTGOMERYSHIRE.

49.—PENSTROWED. R.
 I. Imperfectly entered and irregular. Bap., Marr., 1628-1707.
 II. Bap., Bur., 1793-1812.
 III. Marr., 1762-1812.

50.—SNEAD, OR SNEYD. R.
 I, II. Bap., Bur., 1665-1812; Marr., 1665-1757.
 III. Marr., 1758-1802.

51.—TREFEGLWYS. V.
 I, II. Bap., Bur., Marr., 1623-1689.
 III. Bap., Bur., Marr., 1695-1722.
 IV. Bap., 1723-1798; Bur., 1723-1812; Marr., 1723-1753.
 V, VI. Bap., 1799-1812.
 VII, VIII. Marr., 1754-1812.

52.—TREGYNON. V.
 I. Bap., Bur., Marr., 1678-1710.
 II. Bap., Bur., Marr., 1712-1753.
 III, IV. Bap., Bur., 1754-1812.
 V. Marr., 1754-1812.

53.—WELSHPOOL. V.
 I. Bap., Bur., Marr., 1634-1703; deficient, years 1703-1708.
 II. Bap., Bur., Marr., 1708-1736.
 III. Bap., 1735-1772; Bur., 1735-1782; Marr., 1735-1754; interrupted by IV.
 IV. Imperfect. Bap., 1740-1781; Bur., 1739-1764; Marr., 1740-1754.
 V, VI. Bap., 1772-1812.
 VII, VIII. Bur., 1782-1812.
 IX. Marr., 1754-1800; interrupted by X.
 X. Marr., 1782-1812.

(To be continued.)

WELSH POOL:

MATERIALS FOR THE HISTORY OF THE PARISH AND BOROUGH.

(Continued from Vol. xiii, page 428.)

It was usual, under the Corporation of the old *régime*, for the Bailiffs, upon their election, to give a "feast", or dinner. One of the last Bailiffs (John Robinson Jones) celebrated his election in a more enduring way, by erecting upon the site of the cross-pump, in the centre of Welshpool, a handsome stone obelisk, surmounted by three gas lamps. It bears the following inscription :—

A.D. 1835.
Erected for the accommodation of the
Inhabitants of Welshpool,
and presented to them
by
JOHN ROBINSON JONES,
of Brithdir, Esquire,
one of the Bailiffs of the Borough.

The cross-pump, thus appropriately decorated, covered a spring, which, in former days, was celebrated for the purity of its water. Amongst many others, the late Dr. Darwin of Shrewsbury, whose large medical practice often brought him to Welshpool, never came to the town without quaffing a bumper of the water, fresh from the cross-pump, which he always pronounced to be of unequalled purity. Unfortunately, in the drainage of the town, through some leakage of the sewers, the well has become contaminated, and the Officer of Health has put his ban upon its once celebrated water for drinking purposes.

In the year 1849, a subscription, promoted chiefly by the late Mr. Edward Morris, was entered into by the inhabitants of the borough, for the purpose of purchasing the tolls payable at fairs held there, from the Lord of the Manor, the Earl of Powis, "with the intention (by discontinuing the collection of the same) of the advancing and promoting the trade and interests of the town". The purchase-money was £400, in consideration of which sum the tolls were conveyed by the Earl to the Corporation by deed dated the 8th May 1849.

The road from Welshpool to Leighton led over the river Severn, which had to be crossed at a ford. Many lamentable accidents having occurred from time to time at this ford, it was at length determined to build a bridge across the Severn. The project came to maturity in the year 1871, when a handsome substantial bridge was opened during the Mayoralty of Mr. Thomas Morris, by whose instrumentality the sum of £1,780, the cost of the erection of the bridge, was raised by public subscription. The bridge bears the following inscription :—

This bridge was erected by public subscription through
the exertions of
THOMAS MORRIS, ESQ.,
During his Mayoralty,
MDCCCLXXI.
Plans executed and works carried out by Fisher
and Dyson, contractors, Huddersfield, under
the inspection of Mr. Robert Carver,
engineer, Leighton.

The Town Hall was enlarged in 1836, and a more convenient Assize Court constructed. But, in consequence of the accommodation afforded by the Court being insufficient, it was resolved to rebuild the Town Hall, and the scheme was carried out in the year of 1873, during the Mayoralty of Mr. David Pryce Owen, who laid the foundation stone, on the 15th September in that year, in the presence of the principal officials of the town and county.

This Town Hall thus rebuilt, at an expense of £6,000

and upwards, exclusive of the cost of the site, affords convenient accommodation for the public purposes for which it is used, and is a great ornament to the town. There has been, also, a considerable further expenditure in providing the market accommodation.

In the year 1874, on the occasion of his retiring from the office of Alderman, and after having served the office of Mayor for the years 1848, 1860, 1861, and 1864, Mr. Abraham Howell presented a gold chain and badge to the Mayor and Corporation of Welshpool, to be worn by the Mayor on public occasions. It is a handsome linked gold chain, comprising twenty-six flat ornamented links and the like number of massive rings, alternately, with an oval badge or pendant, upon the face of which are the Arms of the Borough, "a Castle", surrounded by the words, in blue enamel:—

"The Mayor, Aldermen, and Burgesses of the Borough of Welshpool."

On the back of the badge are the words:—

"Presented by Mr. A. Howell, retiring Alderman 1874."

Each succeeding Mayor has added a link and ring to the chain, upon his retiring from the Mayoralty. The seven links already added bear the following inscriptions:—

1st Link.	E. M. Jones,	1874-5.
2nd Link.	E. M. Jones,	1875-6.
3rd Link.	William Rogers,	1876-7.
4th Link.	Samuel Davies,	1877-8.
5th Link.	W. T. Parker, J.P.	1878-9.
6th Link.	G. D. Harrison,	1879-80.
7th Link.	G. D. Harrison,	1880-1.

List of Mayors of Welshpool since the passing of the Municipal Corporation Act.

Nov. 1835. John Davies Corrie of Dysserth (unanimously elected first Mayor).
„ 1836. Thomas Beck of Llwynderw.
„ 1837. Edward Pugh of Broad Street.

,,	1838.	Joseph Jones of Park Lane.
,,	1839.	Charles Wilding of the Dairy.
,,	1840.	Thomas Bowen of Hendrehen.
Nov.	1841.	Thomas Davies of The Moors.
,,	1842.	Robert Devereux Harrison.
,,	1843.	Morris Jones of Gungrog (died on 10 Dec. 1843, and Thomas Owen, elected in his stead).
,,	1844.	Charles Wilding (2nd time).
,,	1845.	Joseph Jones (2nd time).
,,	1846.	Maurice Lloyd Jones.
,,	1847.	Robert Owen of Broad Street.
,,	1848.	Abraham Howell.
,,	1849.	Thomas Brettell Barrett.
,,	1850.	Thomas Bowen.
,,	1851.	John Williams, High Street.
,,	1852.	William Yearsley.
,,	1853.	Ed. Thompson David Harrison.
,,	1854.	Charles Wilding (3rd time).
,,	1855.	William Yearsley (2nd time)
,,	1856.	Robert Owen (2nd time).
,,	1857.	Robert Devereux Harrison (2nd time).
,,	1858.	Maurice Lloyd Jones (2nd time).
,,	1859.	Thomas Bowen (2nd time).
,,	1860.	Abraham Howell (2ndtime).
,,	1861.	Do. do. (3rd time).
,,	1862.	Ed. Thompson David Harrison (2nd time).
,,	1863.	John Haywood Williams.
,,	1864.	Abraham Howell (4th time).
,,	1865.	Thomas Jones, Clive Place.
,,	1866.	William Withy of The Golfa.
,,	1867.	Ed. Thompson David Harrison (3rd time).
,,	1868.	Do. do. (4th time).
,,	1869.	Griffith Parker of Traethllawn (died Jan. 1, 1870, and Thomas Bowen elected in his stead).
,,	1870.	Thomas Morris of London House.
,,	1871.	Do. do. (2nd time).
,,	1872.	David Pryce Owen.
,,	1873.	Do. do. (2nd time).
,,	1874.	Edward Maurice Jones.
,,	1875.	Do. do. (2nd time).
,,	1876.	William Rogers.
,,	1877.	Samuel Davies.
,,	1878.	William Thomas Parker of Traethllawn.
,,	1879.	George Devereux Harrison.
,,	1880.	Do. do. (2nd time).
,,	1881.	Charles Mytton of Pool Quay.

EDW. JONES, Town Clerk.

Chap. IV.—Ecclesiastical.

The ecclesiastical history of the parish of Welshpool is of considerable interest, and extends back to a very early period.

Among the Welsh saints in the period from the accession of Cystennyn Goronog, A.D. 542, to the death of Maelgwn Gwynedd, A.D. 566, was CYNFELYN,[1] a son of Bleiddyd ab Meirion of the line of Cunedda Wledig, the head of one of the three holy families of the Isle of Britain, and the first who bestowed lands and privileges on the Church in Britain. Cynfelyn was the founder of a Church at Welshpool. His brother Llewelyn is said also to have founded a religious house at Trallwng, now called Welshpool, and to have ended his days in the monastery of Bardsey. It seems probable, according to the analogy of the dedication of Welsh Churches to their founder, that the Church founded by Cynfelyn was dedicated to him,[2] and that it was in connection with the religious society founded by his brother Llewelyn. Llewelyn's establishment may have been of the greater importance, as Welshpool appears to have been known as *Trallwng Llewelyn* for several centuries, possibly to distinguish it from another place called Trallwng.[3]

Gwrnerth the son (or brother, according to some authorities) of Llewelyn is said also to have been a saint at Welshpool, and a religious dialogue in verse between him and his father (or brother) Llewelyn is in the *Myvyrian Archaiology*, the composition of which is attributed to St. Tyssilio.

[From The *Four Ancient Books of Wales*, i, 590.]
Red Book of Hergest III.

Llewelyn and Gwrnerth were two penitent saints at Trallwng in Powys, and it was their custom to meet together during

---
[1] Rees' *Welsh Saints*, p. 260.
[2] A church founded by him in Cardiganshire is called Llangynfelyn. There is "Bryn Gynfelyn" in Llanfechain parish.
[3] *Mont. Coll.*, v, p. 104.

the last three hours of the night and the first three hours of the day to say their matins; and the hours of the day besides. And once upon a time, Llewelyn, seeing the cell of Gwrnerth shut, and not knowing why it was so, composed an Englyn.

 I. Mountain snow—wind about the bush;
  It is the Creator of Heaven that strengthens me,
  Is it asleep that Gwrnerth is?

 II. Mountain snow—God above all things
  It is to him I will pray.
  No; I cannot sleep.

 III. Mountain snow—wind about the house;
  It is so thou speakest.
  What, Gwrnerth, causes that?

 IV. Mountain snow—wind from the south;
  I will utter prime words.
  Most probably it is death.

 V. Mountain snow—white-topped the vale;
  Every one is mild to him by whom he is cherished.
  May the Creator of Heaven deliver thee!

 VI. Mountain snow—white-topped the tree;
  I will speak differently.
  There is no refuge against the decree of Heaven.

 VII. Mountain snow—every rite should be observed
  For fear of distressing anxiety in the day of doom.
  Shall I have the Communion as a favour?

 VIII. Mountain snow—wind about the house;
  It is so thou speakest.
  Alas! my brother, must that be?

 IX. Thou highly-gifted!   I love;
  It is to God I will pray.
  Llewelyn, it is high time I should receive it.

 X. Mountain snow—wind about the hill;
  The Creator of Heaven will have me.
  Is it asleep Llewelyn is?

 XI. Mountain snow—wind from the south;
  I will utter prime words.
  No; I am chanting my hours.

 XII. Mountain snow—it is easily known
  When the wind turns round a wall.
  Knowest thou who says it?

 XIII. Mountain snow—thou bold of speech,
  It is so thou speakest.
  I know not, unless thou wilt say.

XIV. Mountain snow—every assistance
　　 Will receive becoming praise;
　　 Thy brother Gwrnerth is here.

XV. Foremost in the tumult and in energetic action
　　Is every brave one, being impelled by his Awen;
　　What, Gwrnerth, is best for thee?

XVI. The first thing to be aimed at in every usage and action
　　　congenial to the brave,
　　 Is a pure life unto the day of judgment;
　　 The best that I have found is alms-giving.

XVII. Thou highly gifted with good qualities,
　　　The canon is on thy lips;
　　　Tell me what alms the best.

XVIII. Bold the Awen; there is wind over the lake
　　　 When the wave beats around the eminence;
　　　 The best is meat for hunger.

XIX. If meat I cannot obtain,
　　 And with my hands cannot get it,
　　 Say what shall I then do?

XX. Foremost in the tumult and in energetic action
　　Is every brave one, impelled by his Awen;
　　Give clothing to keep from nakedness.

XXI. My clothes I will give,
　　 And myself commend to God;
　　 What recompense shall I then receive?

XXII. What good things thou givest on every opportunity,
　　　Bold in thy privilege keep thy countenance;
　　　And thou shalt have Heaven a hundredfold.

XXIII. Since with the early dawn I love thee,
　　　 It is in the form of verse I am asking,
　　　 With God what one thing is most odious?

XXIV. Advantage, and Awen, and equality
　　　When water will run up the ascent;
　　　The worst of deceit where there is confidence.

XXV. If I practice deceit through confidence,
　　 And to God Supreme confess,
　　 What punishment will befall me?

XXVI. Shouldst thou practice deceit through confidence,
　　　Without faith, without religion, without belief,
　　　Thou shalt have sevenfold penance.

XXVII. I will with the dawn believe thee,
　　　 And for God's sake will ask,
　　　 How shall I obtain Heaven?

XXVIII. Good and evil are not alike,
As wind and smoke when contending;
Do good for the sake of God, who is not wrathful.

XXIX. Bold is the Awen of every one that is patronised;
Horses are apt to run much about in hot weather.
The end of all things is confession.

XXX. What thou doest from all excess,
From deception, and oppression, and arrogance,
For God's sake make a full confession.

Tyssilio, the son of Brochwael Ysgythrog, composed these verses concerning Gwrnerth's coming to perform his devotions with Llewelyn the saint, his companion; and they are called the colloquy of Llewelyn and Gwrnerth.

Gwyddfarch, the founder of the first Church in Meifod, a saint and anchorite of the sixth century, but of unascertained date, is described in the *Iolo MSS.* (104, 501), as "Gwyddfarch ab Llewelyn or Trallwng, Sant ef Bangor Cybi, Môn" (Gwyddfarch, the son of Llewelyn of Trallwng, a saint of the College of Cybi in Anglesea [Holyhead]).

He is elsewhere variously described, and many ingenious surmises have been made to reconcile the discrepancies.[1] In our view the probabilities are that Gwyddfarch was the son of Llewelyn of Welshpool, and if such be the case, the ecclesiastical establishment at Welshpool may, not improbably, have had an earlier origin than that of Meifod. It was at least contemporary. The festival, or wake-day, November 8, of Meifod, is the same as that of Welshpool, which, to us, seems a confirmation of the above view.

The Churches of the Ancient Britons "were built of wood, and covered with reeds or straw".[2] Building Churches of stone was contrary to the usual custom of the Britons[3] before the beginning of the eighth century. Cyntelyn's Church, built doubtless of such perishable materials, has long ago passed away; but there is every probability it stood on the site of the present

[1] See *Mont. Coll.*, x, p. 155; and xi, p. 24.
[2] Rees' *Welsh Saints*, p. 59.
[3] *Ibid.*, 58.

parish Church, which dates back to the thirteenth century.

The genealogy of Cynfelyn and Llewelyn, of which a table has been already printed in the *Montgomeryshire Collections*,[1] shows their descent from two of the three holy families of Wales, and also their probable connection with Marchell, the foundress of the ancient religious house, which was situated in the township of Gungrog fawr, and in the parish of Welshpool. Nothing of its history has come down to us.

The Cistercian Monastery of Strata Marcella (the Latinised form of Ystrad Marchell) was afterwards established, and built upon its foundations, it being apparently the custom of the Romish Church to take possession of the native religious houses, and adopt them. An account of that Abbey has been already printed in the *Montgomeryshire Collections*,[2] to which the reader is referred.

We have already mentioned that Welshpool was long called *Trallwng Llewelyn*, after Llewelyn, the founder of the religious house there; and it is remarkable that different members of the family, from which Llewelyn and his brother Cynfelyn sprang (viz., the sons and grandsons of Cunedda Wledig), gave names to various parts of the district in which they settled, and became the founders of so many clans there located; for instance, Ceredig had Ceredigion, comprising Cardiganshire and part of Carmarthenshire, the word Ceredigion being the plural of Ceredig, and meaning his followers. Arywstli had Arwystley in the western part of Montgomeryshire, and Einion had Caer-Einion in the same county. In the like manner Marchell gave her name to the commote of Ystrad Marchell, which we take to be a strong corroboration of the argument in favour of her being sprung from Cunedda Wledig. This is mentioned as a significant circum-

[1] Vol. iv, p. 11.
[2] See *Mont. Coll.*, iv, 1 and 293; v, 109; vi, 347; viii, 63; x, 397; and xv, 199.

stance, showing the importance of the brothers who founded the religious house and original Church in Welshpool.

It was commonly supposed that the Rectory of Welshpool (together with those of Meifod and Guilsfield) was at one time appropriated to the Abbey of Strata Marcella, and Browne Willis expressly states such to be the case; nevertheless, there does not appear to be any distinct evidence on the subject. It is clear, however, the appropriation could not have been before the year 1265, when Bishop Anian appropriated the Rectory of Berriew to that Abbey, for in that year "an agreement was made between the Rectors of the Mother[1] Church of Myvot (not then the Abbot and Monks of Pole, otherwise they would have been named), and the Rector of the Church of Llanfihangel, about the tithes of certain hamlets in the parish of Alberbury by the oaths of good men before Griffith, the son of Wenoynwen".

If Welshpool was appropriated to the Abbey, it did not long remain so, for we find that in 1272,[2] Anian, Bishop of St. Asaph, requests John, Bishop of Hereford, to enjoin the Prior of Chirbury, to restore the Vill of Kilkewydd to the Rectors of Pole (Welshpool), Bettws (Bettws Cedewen), and Aberriew (Berriew), which Rectors formerly held the said vill. Kilkewydd is a small hamlet, situate in Forden parish, and lying between Pool and Berriew, and on the north side of the Severn. How the Rector of Pole became entitled to hold jointly with Bettws and Berriew this hamlet, is one of the puzzles which the disturbed state of the district during the thirteenth century, with respect to ecclesiastical boundaries, has left for solution.

Anian, Bishop of St. Asaph, at one time claimed the diocesan rule of the Gordowr; but in 1288 the contention was decided in favour of the Bishop of Hereford.

[1] From this we infer Meifod was the mother church of Llanfihangel, otherwise called Alberbury.
[2] Eyton's *Antiquities of Shropshire*, xi, p. 61.

The Rector and Vicar of Welshpool claimed the tithes and parochial jurisdiction of a large portion thereof. The question of parish seems to have survived the question of diocese, for it was not until August 6th,[1] 1289, that Phillip de Orreby (Rector of Worthen), John (Rector of Pole), and Griffith (Vicar of Pole), submitted to the arbitration of Bishop Swinfield (the Bishop of Hereford) their disputes about the tithes of "four vils in the county of Gordowr, viz., Butinton, Hope, Leghton, and Ullstane Mynde (Trelystan)", all which were acknowledged to be in Hereford diocese. With respect to Buttington and Hope, the decision must have been in favour of Welshpool, as the tithes of these vills still belong to it.

There is an award by Richard, Bishop of Hereford, dated July 26, 1289,[2] which well illustrates the topography of the much-changed district of the Gordowr, and shows to what a distant point the incumbents of the parish of Welshpool claimed the parochial jurisdiction. It is a decision concerning the tithes of fourteen vills, in the parts of Gordowr in the diocese of Hereford, which tithes were claimed by Brother Peter de Corcellis, *Corrector* or Prior of the Religious House of the Grandimontane Order at Alberbury on the one part; and by John (son of the Lord Griffin, late Lord of La Pole), Rector of the Church of La Pole, and Griffin Fitz Edenweth, Vicar of the same Church on the other part. The vills enumerated are: Balislee (Bausley), Bragynton (Bragginton), Berlee, Bromrochpol, Bromrochpol *secunda*, Wonynton (Winnington), Wichfield, Perendon, Haregrene (Hargrave), Trifnant (Trevnant), Trif-Bereved (Middletown), Hochelprene, Krigion (Crigion), and Orleton. The seven identified vills will adumbrate the district around the Breidden Hills which contained the eight others.

The Concord before referred to as being made in 1265 (a copy of which is printed in Canon Thomas's *Hist. of the Diocese of St. Asaph*, p. 775, note 4), between the

[1] Eyton's *Antiquities of Shropshire*, vol. ix, p. 103. [2] *Ibid.*, vii, p. 44.

Rector of the Mother Church of Meifod, and the Rector of the Church of Llanfihangel (Alberbury), discloses that there was a dispute, which this "concord" settled, between those parsons, respecting eleven vills, viz., Hagyntâ (Braginton), Bronrocpol, Llanwercheit (Llanfarchell), Billissle (Bausley), Wenaton (Winnington), Wytfild, Trefnant, Pinton (Perendon), Harore (Hargrave), Tref-p'vet (Middletown), and Crew. The text of this document was so obscure and uncertain as to its correctness, that the late Rev. R. C. Eyton (the celebrated Shropshire antiquary) declined to "commit himself very far about it". It will be observed that eight of the vills at least are common to the award of 1289, and the concord of 1265, viz., Bausley, Bromrochpol, Winnington, Perendon, Hargrave, Trefnant, Middletown, Wichfield or Wytfild.

The Concord of 1265 seems to concede to the "Mother Church" of Meifod some rights over the disputed vills. Yet in 1289, twenty-four years afterwards, such conceded rights are entirely ignored, and the contest for the tithes of the disputed vills is arbitrated upon by Bishop Swinfield as between the Rector of Llanfihangel and the Rector and Vicar of Pool (the Rector of Meifod not being mentioned). The effect of the award is not given, but it may be inferred it was adverse to the incumbents of Welshpool, as they have no claim to tithes in these vills at the present time.

These disputes arose, doubtless, owing to the contention between the Bishops of St. Asaph, and the Bishops of Hereford about the limits of their respective dioceses. It is supposed, during the border wars of Henry III's time, the two Llewelyns had been so far successful as to have encroached upon, or at least made debatable a large tract of country, east of the Severn.[1] Anian (II), Bishop of St. Asaph (1268-1293), seems to have taken advantage of this state of things, by arrogating to his diocese portions of the parishes of Alberbury, Worthen,

[1] Eyton, vii, p. 87. *Roll of Household Expenses of Bishop Swinfield* (Camden Society's Publications), p. lxxviii.

and Chirbury. The controversy had begun while Cantilupe was Bishop of Hereford (1275-82). At that prelate's death it was before the Papal Court, and had since been referred back to competent judges on the spot. A jury of Welsh and English had at length been assembled to decide the boundary of the two dioceses of Anian (II), and Richard Swinfield, now Bishop of Hereford. The award was in favour of Hereford, and Bishop Swinfield formally took possession of all the vills within the boundary assigned to him. The settlement, notwithstanding a subsequent effort of Bishop Anian to disturb it, governs generally the question of boundary between these two dioceses at this day; but there are some exceptions, such as Kilkewydd, part of the parish of Forden being on the north side of the river, and part of Berriew on the south. This episcopal contest, doubtless, induced the Rector and Vicar of Welshpool, and the Rectors of Meifod to attempt to profit in the *melée*, and to secure some portion of the spoil. It will be remarked that the Rector of Welshpool was John "son of the Lord Griffin", the then Lord of Powys; and this, perhaps, may account for his claim for the tithes of the Alberbury vills surviving that of the contemporaneous, but perhaps less influential, Rectors of Meifod, and for his claim for Buttington and Hope surviving to this day, although the claim for Leighton and Wlstane Mynd (Trelystan), seems to have failed.

John de la Pole was the third son of Griffith ap Wenwynwyn;[1] and it would appear that the contention about the tithes of the vills in the Gordowr was not a solitary instance of his taste for litigation, for he had in 1290 a dispute with his brother Owen, which was compromised. The fact that the Manor of "Buttington, with its members of Trewern and Hope, under the Barony of Cause", was held by Griffith de la Pole of Peter Corbet,[2] for a knight's fee, and was in 1284 vested in his widow Hawise in the name of dower,

[1] *Mont. Coll.*, i, p. 64. [2] *Ibid.*, p. 49.

explains the reason why John de la Pole, had the parochial jurisdiction of Buttington and Hope confirmed to him by Bishop Swinfield. It was in 1288, and during the incumbency of John de la Pole, Bishop Swinfield visited Shrawardine Church, and returned back to Alberbury. There, in the choir of the conventual Church, "the principal Chaplain of Hawyse,[1] Lady of La Pole", attended, "and for himself and the other Chaplains celebrating at Botington, swore canonical obedience to the Bishop".

In Pope Nicholas' taxation, in 1291, the Rectory of Welsh Pool is classed under *Decanatus de Pola*, and is thus entered:—

	Taxatio.	Decima.
Ecclesia de Pola taxat' Rectoria	8 13 4	17 4
Vicaria	3 6 8	not dec.

It appears as an independent Rectory, and subject to no other Church.[2] The same may be said of "Keygidia" (Guilsfield).

It is convenient here to give the entries of the Rectory and Vicarage of Pool in the *Valor Ecclesiasticus* of Henry VIII for comparison.[3]

Rectoria de Pole.
Valet clare c'o'ibz annis p' scrutin' et exami'ac'
   commission' etc. . . . xxx*l*.
Inde p'x'ma p'te d'no Regi debit' . . lx*s*.
   Vicar' de Pole.
Val' in gross' c'o'ibz annis p' scrutin' and ex-
   ami'ac' commiss, etc. . . xiij*l*. xii*s*. iiij*d*.
Repris' Lactual' ep'o, iij*s*. iiij*d*.; p'cur' annual,
   iij*s*. ix*d*.; p'cur' visit' jux'a rat', xiij*d*. . viij*s*. ij*d*.
Et valet clare co'i'bz annis . . xiij*l*. v*s*. ij*d*.
Inde p'x'ma p'te d'no Regi debit' . . xxvi*s*. vj*d*. 9'

Here, again, it is shown to be an independent Rectory, and in the interval of nearly two centuries and a half between the two documents the income of the Rectory and Vicarage had increased nearly four-fold.

In 1295, during John de la Pole's incumbency, Pool was one of the five towns in which a proclamation was

[1] *Mont. Coll.*, p. 48.   [2] *Ibid.*, ii, p. 87.   [3] *Ibid.*, p. 97.

made, "in the presence of the people assembled together on holy days", of the sentence of excommunication pronounced against Prince Madoc ap· Llewelyn and his adherents who had risen against the new taxes, levied through Sir Roger de Puleston, whom they seized and put to death. Madoc was to be excommunicated by name, and his adherents *en masse*, and the whole of the country that supported him, to be put under interdict, the baptism of infants and the penance of the dying being alone permitted. The execution of the sentence was, however, not so easy, as neither the Bishop nor his officers dared to approach the Prince, or be seen in any of the parts that adhered to him, so that he had to content himself in making proclamation in five principal towns, of which Pool was one.[1]

John de la Pole died in 1303.[2] During his incumbency, parts of the structure of the present Church, which is undoubtedly of the period of the thirteenth century, must have been built, and posssibly, then, the Church may have been re-dedicated to the Virgin Mary. Griffith de la Pole (his father) had in 1275 broken off friendly relations with Llewelyn, and probably from that period was under English influence in ecclesiastical, as well as civil, matters. In ten years afterwards he ended his life, as he had begun it, a subject of an English King. English influence may have induced the Welsh chief to have thrown off the name of the Welsh saint, and, at the instigation of the Monks of the neighbouring Cistercian Abbey of Strata Marcella, to have adopted their practice of re-dedicating the newly-erected Church to St. Mary.

We next come to three transactions which we regard as scandals to the Church and misapplication of funds from the uses for which they were given. Whether such acts are perpetrated, or participated in, by king, bishop, or collegiate corporation, they are equally discreditable.

[1] Willis's *St. Asaph*, ii, App. xxiv, p. 72; Thomas's *History of the Diocese of St. Asaph*, p. 58.
[2] *Mont. Coll.*, i, p. 65.   [3] *Mont. Coll.*, i, p. 34.

The documents, which we shall give in their original texts, so that the exact effect of them can be seen, are three licenses from the king to the three successive bishops of St. Asaph.

No. 1.—1380. License from Richard II to William Spridlington to hold Pool, together with Meifod and Guilsfield, *in commendam*.

Concessit Rex Richardus Secundus, Junii 28 Anno Regni Tertio, et Licentiam dedit pro se et heredibus, quantum in ipso fuit, Willhelmo tunc Episcopo Assavensi, quod ipse de assensu Capituli Ecclesiæ suæ Asaphensis Capellas de la Pole et Kegidva Suæ Diocesis Assavensis Ecclesiæ Parochiali de Meyvot predictæ Diocesis imperpetuum unire et annectere et eandem ecclesiam cum capellis eidem pertinentibus et annexis appropriare, et easdem sic appropriatas, predicto Episcopo et sucessoribus suis Assavensibus, in proprios usus tenere possit imperpetuum.[1]

No. 2.—1401. The like licence from Henry IV to Bishop John Trevor, enabling him to accept a concession made by the Pope.

A.D. 1401.—Pro Episcopo Assaphensi Rex omnibus ad quos, etc., Salutem. Sciatis quod, ut accepimus, sanctissimus in Christo Pater Papa Modernus, ob reverentiam nostram, et consideratione literarum nostrarum sibi nuper directarum. Ac etiam eâ consideratione quod Ecclesia Assaphensis, occasione guerrarum et tribulationum quæ nuper in partibus illis fuerunt multipliciter dampnificata Existit Quod que, eâ occasione, Reverendus Pater Johannis Episcopatus loci prædicti statum suum Episcopalem de fructibus et proficuis Ecclesiæ suæ prædictæ prout retroactis temporibus consuevit honorifice manutenere non potest, de gratia sua speciali concesserit et commiserit potestatem Episcopis Herefordensi, Vulteranensis et Bangorensi quod ipsi seu eorum aliquis Ecclesiam Parochialem de Meyvot cum capellis de Pole et Kegidfa in Diocense Assavensi præfato Johanni Episcopo concedere possint seu possit in commendam Habend. Ecclesiam prædictam cum capellis prædictis et eis gaudendo una cum fructibus et proficuis quibuscumque eisdem spectantibus quamdiu idem Johannes Episcopus (durante vita suâ) Episco-

---

[1] Browne Willis's *Survey of St. Asaph* (by Edwards), Appendix, vol. ii, p. 94.

pus dictæ Ecclesiæ Assaphensis extiterit supportando onera eisdem ecclesiæ et capellis incumbentia prout in bullis præfatis sanctissimi patris inde confectis plenius continetur. Nos de gratia nostra speciali, et ad supplicationem prædicti Johannis Episcopi concessimus et licentiam dedimus præfatis Episcopis Herefordensi Vulteranensis, et Bangorensi quod ipsi seu eorum aliquis dictas Bullas exequi poterunt, seu poterit, et eidem Episcopo quod ipse dictam gratiam Apostolicam secundum formam et effectum earumdem Bullarum acceptari et ea uti poterit absque offensa alicujus statuti Regni nostri incurrenda. In cujus, etc., Teste Rege apud Westmonasterium xxiii die Auguste.

Per Breve de privato sigillo.[1]

No. 3.—1439. The like licence from Henry VI. to Bishop Lowe.

Rex omnibus ad quos, etc. Salutem. Quod cum Lewelinus quondam Episcopus Assavensis Ecclesias de Meyvot, Pola, et Guyldsfeild, de suo patronatu et Advocatione existentes, in quibus Ecclesiis Vicarii sunt et habent [habitant], et separati et dotati nuper unisset Licentia Regia non obtenta ob quam causam Dominus Ricardus nuper Rex Anglie secundus post conquestum, in curia sua presentationem suam ad predictam Ecclesiam de Myvot, cum capellis suis de Pola et Guyldesfeild sic unitis et annexis versus Willhelmum tunc Assavensem Episcopum per defaltam recuperasset. Nos vero premissa considerantes de gratia nostra speciali et ad supplicationem Venerabilis Patris Johannis nunc Episcopi Assavensis Advocationem et Patronatum dictæ Ecclesiæ de Meyvot cum capellis suis de Pola et Guyldesfield predictis sic vocatis eisdem Episcopo cum suis juribus et pertinentiis universis restituimus et eam sibi concessimus, habendum et tenendum sibi et successoribus suis imperpetuum unione et reparatione predictis, seu seisina quacunque in hac parte habita non obstante. Et ulterius considerantes exilitatem dictæ Ecclesiæ Assavensis per Guerras et rebellionem Walliæ, una cum maneriis suis et singulis ornamentis multipliciter destructam, de uberiori nostra gratia concessimus et Licentiam dedimus pro nobis et heredibus nostris, quantum in nobis est, eidem nunc Episcopo, quod ipse dictam Ecclesiam de Meyvot cum capellis suis de Pole et Guyldesfeild appropriare, et eam sic appropriatam una cum eisdem capellis in proprios usus tenere possit sibi et successoribus suis imperpetuum; Statuto de Terris et Tene-

---

[1] Rymer's *Fœdera*, vol. v, p. 222.

mentis ad manum mortuam non ponendis, seu aliquo alio Statuto seu ordinatione in contrarium edito non obstante, proviso semper quod quedam competens summa inter pauperes parochianos earumdem Ecclesiarum singulis annis per loci illius ordinarium distribuatur, juxta formam Statuti inde editi et provisi. In cujus, etc., Teste Rege, apud Manerium suum de Eltham 23 die Februarii.

Per breve de privato sigillo, et pro quadraginta et quinque libris solutis in Hanaperio.[1]

We must refer to the last of these three documents to see the origin of this series of transactions. It was an act of usurpation by William Llewelyn ap Madoc (1357-1376). The licence of 1439 recites that Bishop Llewelyn had "united the churches of Meifod, Pool, and Guilsfield in which churches Vicars were and lived, and were separated and endowed", without obtaining the consent of the King, wherepon Richard II asserted his right to the presentation, and recovered it by default.

From this it can but be inferred that the three churches were independent of each other until they were unlawfully seized and united by Bishop Llewelyn; up to this time they had distinct existences as independent rectories, and nothing we have been able to discover indicates that any one of these churches had any pre-eminence over any. of the others. This unrighteous transaction took place before 1376.

We now revert to the Document No. 1, which is a licence from King Richard II to William, Bishop of St. Asaph, to unite the churches of Pool and Guilsfield to the parish church of Meifod, and to appropriate the three to his own proper use. The same observation applies to this document, that Pool and Guilsfield were not united previously, or why should power be given to unite them? Moreover, this licence only operated during the lifetime of the Bishop to whom it was granted, and the other two licenses had the like limited operation. On the death of each Bishop a new license was necessary.

[1] Browne Willis's *Survey of St. Asaph* (by Edwards), vol. ii, p. 114.

No. 2 is a license from Henry IV to John, Bishop of St. Asaph, by which the King enables the Bishop to hold the parish church of Meifod with its chapels of Pool and Guilsfield *in commendam*, in accordance with the Bull of the Pope which it recites, and which appoints three bishops to inquire into the matter, and give authority to grant such church with its chapels *in commendam*. Without the Royal authority the Bishop could not take advantage of the Papal concession.

Document No. 3 contains the recital we have already set out, and purports, " of our special favour", to restore the advowson and patronage of the three livings to the Bishop, and furthermore, in consideration of the poverty of the See and the manifold injuries it had suffered "by the War and Rebellion of Wales", to give the Bishop licence to appropriate them to his own proper use for ever, the Statute of Mortmain or any other statute or ordinance notwithstanding, provided that a competent sum be distributed amongst the poor parishioners each year by the Ordinary, according to the form of the statute in such case made and provided.

The distribution was to be made according to the statute. What statute we are unable to say. The poor parishioners were to be benefited by a gift of money, in lieu, it is presumed, of spiritual instruction, and no provision was made for the parsons serving the churches.

The little note at the end, however, explains what tapped the source of the Royal "abundant favour". It was not the respect for the Bishop, nor the consideration of the poverty of the See, nor the ruin of the Church, but pelf—"for £85 paid into the Hanaper".

It is said by a high authority:[1] "Ecclesiastically, this parish (Welshpool) has been, from the remotest times, connected with Meifod as one of its daughter churches."

We have most carefully examined all sources within our reach, and we do not find that this tradition is borne out.

It is acknowledged that Gwyddfarch, the founder of the first church in Meifod, is represented as having

[1] Canon Thomas's *History of St. Asaph*, p. 789.

come from Welshpool. We have shown who Cynfelyn was, and that it is highly probable that Gwyddfarch was the son of Llewelyn, who was the brother of Cynfelyn the founder of the original church in Welshpool. If he were not, there must have been two Gwyddfarchs, holy men and saints, in this district—a most improbable supposition.

If Gwyddfarch of Meifod was the nephew of Cynfelyn, is it likely that the nephew would found a church before the uncle? On the contrary is it not more probable, as in the absence of any recorded account we venture to submit, that the uncle would found his church prior, in point of time, to the nephew, and, therefore, that the church at Trallwng, founded by Cynfelyn, was in existence before the church in Meifod, founded by Gwyddfarch? We do not claim for the former church the pre-eminence as the "Mother Church", but only precedence as the "Elder Sister."

The concord of 1265, between Meifod and Alberbury, before referred to, certainly refers to Meifod as the "Mother Church" (of Alberbury, we presume, Pool is not there mentioned), and portions of the tithes of certain townships in Alberbury are apparently awarded to Meifod as such. But did she ever enjoy them? We think not; and that the contention arose from the arrogance of some ambitious rectors of Meifod, for, in twenty-four years afterwards, we find the tithes of the same Townships (or at least eight of them) claimed from Alberbury, by John, Rector de la Pole, the son of the Lord of Powys, Griffith ap Wenwynwyn. In the Award of 1289, not a word is said about the previous claim of the Rectors of Meifod, who are entirely ignored; nevertheless John, the lordly Rector of Pole, is no more successful than Meifod; possibly both were claiming what did not belong to them, but this document and the whole transaction are entirely inconsistent with Meifod then having rights in Alberbury, and in any event do not, in any way, tend to show that Meifod was the Mother Church of Welshpool.

In Pope Nicholas' taxation, 1291, Pole appears as an independent rectory.

In 1295, Pool, not Meifod, is selected as one of the churches in which the proclamation of excommunication against Prince Madoc was read—a significant distinction.

Up to the year 1376 or thereabouts, when Bishop Llewelyn ap Madoc usurped the power to unite the churches *(Ecclesias)* of Meifod, Pool, and Guilsfield, we find Welshpool always mentioned as an independent and distinct rectory, and this unlawful episcopal act is the first occasion where Pool is degraded, in name at least, from an *Ecclesia* to a *Capella*—a conventional degradation only we submit, for, in ancient law proceedings *Capella* may have been changed into *Ecclesia*,[1] but the converse did not hold.

The three licenses calling Pool and Guilsfield chapels to Meifod did not—indeed, could not—convert them into *Capellæ*—the term chapel was used in a conventional sense only—and their independent existence revived immediately after the illegal and repeated annexations were annulled by legal process or ceased by the death of the Bishops.

In the *Valor Ecclesiasticus* of Henry VIII, Pool and Guilsfield again appear as independent rectories, which they continue still to be, notwithstanding the appropriation, or rather misappropriation, of a large proportion of the rectorial tithes by Christ Church College, Oxford, which we as strongly condemn as a breach of morality as well by the King Henry VIII, who perpetrated it, as by the Collegiate authorities, who continuously participate in the (morally) unlawful spoil. We sincerely hope the latter may ere long repent and

---

[1] "In an ancient law book Fitzherbert observes that 'Ecclesia' properly means a parsonage, whence if a presentation were made to a chapel or to a church by the name of *ecclesia*, it changed the name thereof, and it presently commenced a church. When the question was, whether it were *ecclesia, aut capella pertinens ad ecclesiam?* the issue was, whether it had *Baptisterium et sepulturam?* For, if it had the administration of the sacraments and sepulture, it was in law judged a church." (Chambers' *Cyclopædia*, by Rees.)

make restitution of their share of the rectorial tithes to the use of the parish.

In concluding our remarks on this subject, we submit that Bishop Llewelyn's usurpation of the power, and the three Royal licences to three bishops to hold the "Church of Meifod with its chapels of Pool and Guilsfield" *in commendam*, constitute the only evidence that Welshpool was treated or termed as a "chapel" to Meifod, or that Meifod was its Mother Church, except a solitary heading in Browne Willis's *Survey of St. Asaph* (Edwards's ed., vol. i, p. 392) under "Vicars of Meifod", *supposed to be the Mother Church of Guilsfield, Pool, and Buttington*, a supposition for which he gives no authority, and which must be taken for what it is worth.

Until further evidence is adduced we must hold that Welshpool was always an independent rectory, although for a certain specific purpose it was conventionally called a "chapel", and that it is at least coeval, if not anterior, in foundation to Meifod, and that, in fact, Meifod was not its "Mother Church".

This rectory was thus held *in commendam* during the episcopate of Bishop Llewelyn, who occupied the see from 1357-1376; during Bishop Spridlington's episcopate, 1376-1382; Bishop Trevor's, 1395-1411; Bishop Lowe's, 1433-1444. During the intervals in the episcopates of Bishop Child (a Benedictine monk of Battle Abbey), 1382-1390; Bishop Bach (S. T. P. of the Order of Preaching Friars), 1390-1395; and Bishop de Lancaster (Abbot of Valle Crucis), 1411-1433; and in the interval between 1444, the end of Bishop Lowe's episcopate, and 1537, we are not able to find who filled the rectory. It may have been held by each successive Bishop *in commendam*, but Royal licences do not appear to have been obtained.[1]
In 1537, Bishop Warton (the last Romish occupier of

[1] It is said that this parish was impropriated by Cardinal Wolsey to the college he founded in Oxford, but if so (which is doubtful) Henry VIII re-asserted his right to it, and granted it to his new college in Oxford.

the see) appointed Dr. Magnus to the rectory of this parish, and also to those of Meifod and Guilsfield.

In 1546, King Henry VIII resumed his authority over the rectory, and in Dugdale's *Monasticon* (vol. ii, p. 167-70), under the head "St. Winisfrede's Monastery", now Christ Church Oxford, there is the following reference to this parish:

"Lands assigned by his Majesty unto his new College in Oxforde (*Harl. MS.*, Brit. Mus., No. 4316, fo. 56*b*), Anno primo Oct., and in the 00th year of King Henry VIII for lands gevine by his Ma'tie to his new Colledge in Oxeford.

"Vicker xiij*li*. vs. ij*d*. The parsonage of Pole in the same Bishoprick [St. Asaphe] of xxx*li*.."

The Churchyard.—Before we proceed to notice the structure of the present parish Church, we think it will be well to make a few remarks upon the Churchyard in which it stands. The Churchyard is singularly situated on a declivity, on the north side of, and overlooking the town of, Welshpool. The public road, or street, which separates it from the Vicarage grounds, is deeply excavated. About fifty years ago the bank was much reduced,[1] and the Churchyard is propped up from the road by a massive stone wall, with buttresses, which it is inferred was built by the town portion of the parish, for, by the parish books, it appears that that portion of the parish has to repair the wall.

In a charter, or "writing", of *circa* 1324, by which John de Cherleton, Lord of Powys, granted to the burgesses of Pole common of pasture in certain lands, the bounds of such common are described as beginning "from the King's highway, above the Churchyard of the Church of Pole", and ascending to Croys Pluan. This is the earliest mention of the Churchyard we have found.

On 26 June 1825, a communication was opened with the Dean and Chapter of Christ Church, Oxford (the

[1] The road opposite to the entrance to the vicarage was filled up considerably: there are some houses and shops there now considerably below the level of the road. Mr. S. Powell remembers the same houses and shops having flights of steps from the road, their levels then being considerably higher than the road.

impropriate Rectors), who were about effecting an exchange as to "the croft" part of their rectorial glebe adjoining the Churchyard, alleging that in consequence of the increase of population of the parish, the burial ground was much too small and crowded with graves, and it had become absolutely necessary to have additional burial ground, and asking for a grant of half an acre of the croft. After the lapse of seven years, on the 8th February 1832, a reply was received from the Impropriate Rectors, that they would make a grant to the parish of the ground required for the purpose of increasing the parish Churchyard; and, shortly afterwards, a rate of one shilling in the pound was ordered to carry out the arrangement; and, in 1832, upwards of £80 was spent in forming the roads and fences, etc., of the new part of the Churchyard; and, on 21 October 1834, £20 6s. 8d. was paid for consecrating the burial ground.

There is an entrance to the Churchyard at the east corner, where the road is more nearly on a level with the Churchyard; but on the south there is an entrance by a flight of steps, up which the ascent from the road to the level of the Church is no less than about twenty-five feet. This is felt to be an inconvenience for aged and infirm people, for there is no access to the Church without climbing a great ascent. The Church itself is built on a declivity, and the Churchyard ascends behind to a height of many feet, so that a person standing on the "top" of the Churchyard can see over the roof of the Church, and nearly over the tower. There is a lovely and commanding view of the surrounding country from the Churchyard, which is a surprise and a delight to every beholder.

The Churchyard contains two acres and twenty-five perches, including the addition. The repair of the "terrier", or boundary of the Churchyard, is, according to an old terrier of 1730, as follows, viz. : "The stile at the east end is repaired by the Vicar. The wall from thence down to the south side to the Greedle is repaired by the town part of the parish. The Greedle gates by his Grace the Duke of Powis. The wall from the west up to the partition hedge, being twenty yards in length, by the township of Cyffronydd. The rails at the east end to the upper corner of the Churchyard, commonly called the Judge's Hill, by the township of Gyngrog Vawr. The remaining part is to be repaired by the township of Welshtown, Trefnantfechan, Llanerchydol, Dyserth, Stredalfedan, Tyddinprydd, and Trallwmgollen, share and share alike, according to the valuation of the several townships."

The Creedle[1] gates were on the entrance at the west corner, and were repaired by the Duke of Powis and his successors, as lessees of the tithes, under Christ Church College, Oxford.

"Judge's Hill" is mentioned by Richard Davies, the Welshpool quaker, as the place where Edward Evans, a persecuted quaker, who died during his imprisonment, was buried; and Richard Davies incidentally gives the reason why it was so called.

"The jailer of Welshpool was very cruel to Friends, and continued them in that nasty hole, before mentioned, till Edward Evans fell sick (by reason of the dampness and unhealthiness of the room) and died; and the jailer would not suffer us to have his body to be buried, except we would pay the coroner, and so clear him, as if he had no hand in his death; but at last his relations prevailed without a coroner's inquest, and they took and buried him on an hill, on the backside of the steeple-house in Welshpool; and it happened, as they were digging the grave, they found some bones of a man; and, upon inquiry, in some old records, it was said: 'There was an old judge buried there; and the name of that place is called ever since *Judge's Hill*. We had got no burying place of our own then, but were about having one."[2]

The burial is not recorded in the Welshpool parish register. The place is supposed to be the north-west corner of the old Churchyard before it was enlarged, and, possibly, the ground was unconsecrated.

[1] The meaning of the word "Greedle" we have not been able to discover.   [2] Richard Davies's *Autobiography*, 2nd ed., 1765, p. 91.

There formerly stood in the Churchyard an ancient stone cross, all traces of which have disappeared. Formerly, it was the custom, in mortgage deeds, to make the money payable "at or upon the stone crosse, within the Church yeard of the parish Church of Pool, between the hours of seaven and eleaven of the clock in the afternoon". A mortgage deed, dated in 1600,[1] has the appointment for repayment in these terms, and the cross must have been extant at that period; possibly, during the time of the Civil War, this cross was destroyed.

There is a large boulder stone lying in the Churchyard, not far from the porch of the Church, respecting which there are some curious ancient traditions. It is said to have been used by the Druids as an altar, or the centre stone of a circle, upon which offerings were made. Afterwards it found its way to Ystrad Marchell Abbey, and was there used as a throne, upon which the Abbots and other dignitaries of the Church were installed. After the dissolution, this stone with other relics was brought to St. Mary's Church, Welshpool, and upon it men and women, offenders against the laws of Mother Church, had to do penance during morning service. Vavasor Powel, who occasionally preached in the Church during the time of the commonwealth, has been credited with turning this stone, with other objects of superstition, out of the Church. Since then it has been used, within the memory of persons now living, as a place from which the parish Clerk would, on the congregation leaving the Church, proclaim any article that had been found, with the view of discovering the owner.[2]

There was a footpath through the Churchyard, commencing at a stile near the Greedle gates, at the southwest corner, up the west side, and to a stile at the north-west corner, leading across the croft to the Red Lane. This was stopped up, or diverted, when the addition was made to the Churchyard.

A stone pedestal stands in the Churchyard, in front

[1] *Mont. Coll.*, xiv, p. 161.   [2] *Ibid.*, xiv, p. 216.

St Mary's Church, West Port.

Published by R. Owen.   Newman & Co. 48, Watling St, London.

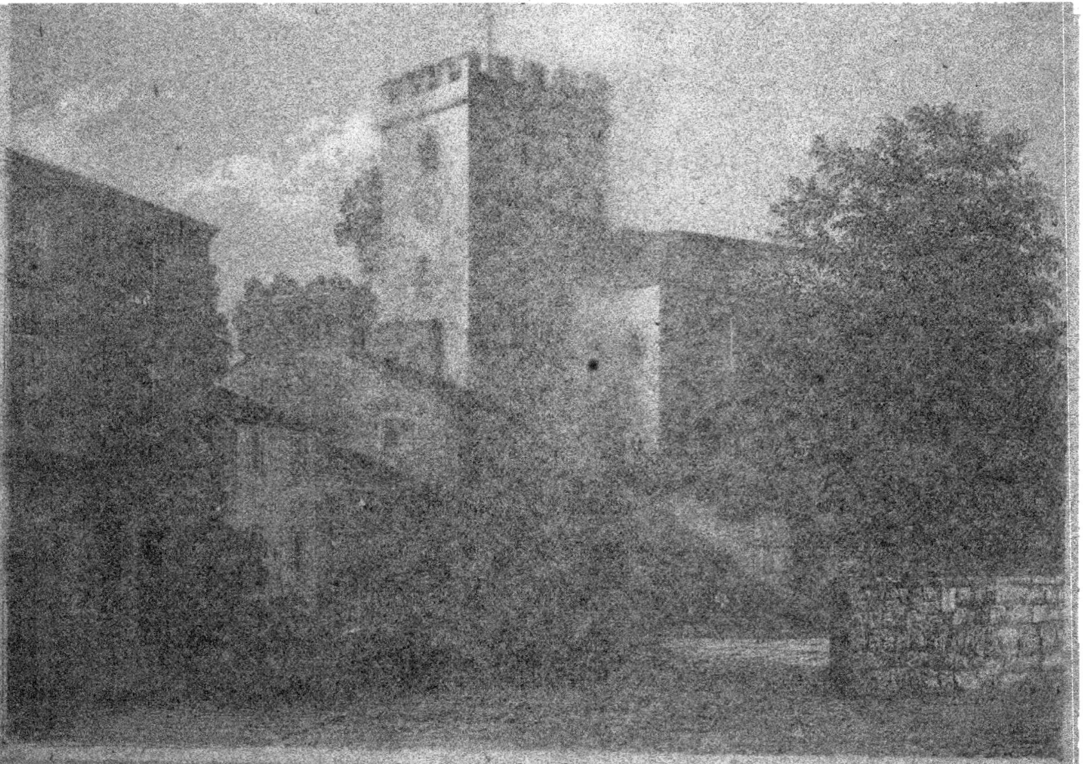

of the porch, upon which there is a brass sun-dial. It is inscribed:—

```
" Samuel Yates         Jno. Owens, jun.
  Thomas Meredith      Jno. Williams.
              Wardens.
                1743.
```

Benj. Radcliffe, Pool.   Lat. 52, 44."

The maker, Benjamin Radcliffe, was a clockmaker in the town. Several clocks of his manufacture are still in existence, and are held in high repute. The sun-dial was presented by Mr. Richard Edmunds in 1810, as appears by an entry amongst the benefactions.

The Church.—The present parish Church of Welshpool is dedicated to "St. Mary the Virgin". The original Church probably would take its name from its founder, Cynfelyn. The re-dedication to St. Mary may, probably, be traced to the influence of the Cistercian Monastery of Strata Marcella, which was situate within the parish. It was a rule of the fraternity that their religious houses should be dedicated to the Virgin,[1] and few Churches in Wales were so dedicated until the thirteenth century. This was, probably, the date of the erection of the present Church, and it is borne out by certain parts, to which we shall advert in detail.

Griffith ap Wenwynwyn, the last of the Princes of Powys, and who merged his Princedom into a feudal Barony under the Crown of England, may probably claim the honour of building the Church. He was a great benefactor to the town of "Pole", and granted the charter by which it was erected into a borough; and, being under English influence, nothing seems more likely than he should confer upon the community, so dependent upon him, the benefit of a suitable Church for the worship of Almighty God. His fourth son, John de la Pole, was Rector of the Church as early as 1289, and is the first Rector of whom we have any record.

[1] Rees' *Welsh Saints*, p. 60.

Prince Griffith, in 1241, a year after Llewelyn ap Iorwerth's death, had Powys-land made over to him as its rightful Prince, and thereupon did feudal service to England. But, in the interval between that date and 1275, many vicissitudes happened, and Griffith had to yield to the force of circumstances, and was not constant to his English allegiance. In 1275, a rupture took place between Llewelyn and Griffith, from which time the territory of the latter came to be placed under English protection. From this time forward the Principality of Powys may be regarded as an English Barony held under the Crown of England like any other Lordship Marcher. From the disturbed state of affairs, prior to this date, it would hardly be safe to think that time could be devoted to ecclesiastical matters.

May we venture to suggest the idea that the Church was rebuilt in or about 1275, in commemoration of the securing of peace, under English protection, after a long and eventful struggle between Griffith and Llewelyn? The most ancient portion of the present structure appears to date from the thirteenth century.

The Structure of the Church.[1]—The Church has been built at various times—the thirteenth, the fourteenth, and the fifteenth, or sixteenth centuries, having each left their remains, while the whole of the nave and south aisle were rebuilt in the eighteenth century—and consisted of a chancel, nave with two aisles of different widths, south porch, and tower. A singular feature about the building is that the nave is of much greater width than the chancel, and so situated that the chancel, instead of being in the centre, lies on the north side, so as almost to suggest that the present nave covers the ground once occupied by a nave and south aisle, and that the present south aisle, which

[1] For the description of the architectural features of the structure of the church we are mainly indebted to Rev. J. E. Hill, M.A., the present vicar; and to an interesting manuscript account left by his predecessor, Archdeacon Clive.

Saint Mary's Church.
Welshpool.
1882

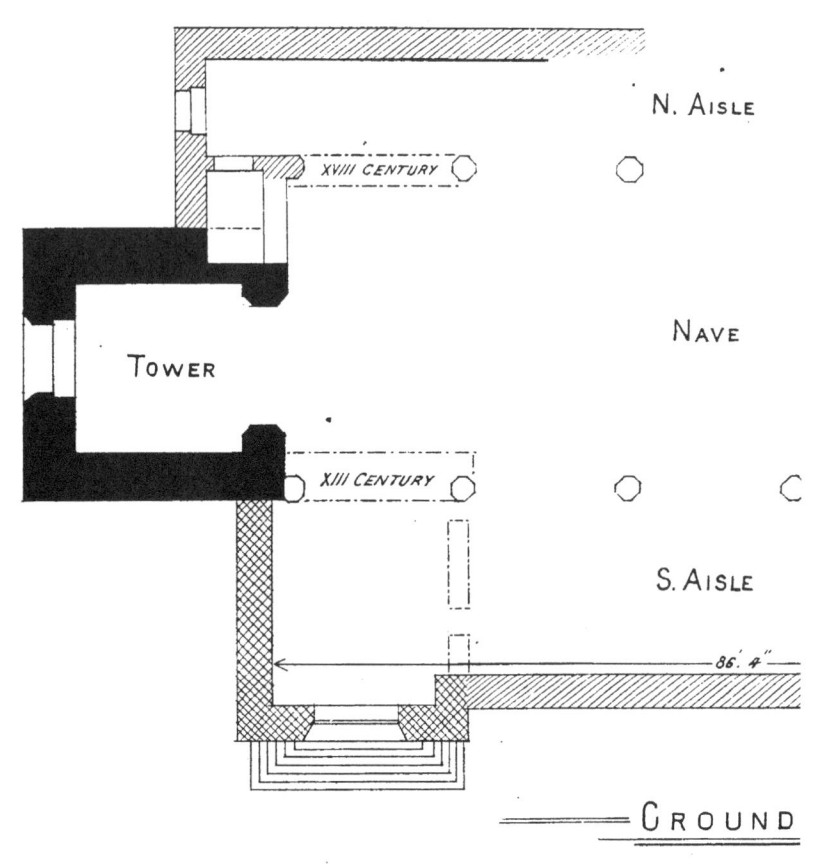

Part black denotes 13th Century with later additions.
,, ▒▒▒ ,, 14th ,,
,, ▨▨▨ ,, 15th or 16th Century, and rebuilt in 18th Century.
,, Plain ,, more recent.
Dotted lines denote old walls removed, with
probable date marked upon same.

ORGAN

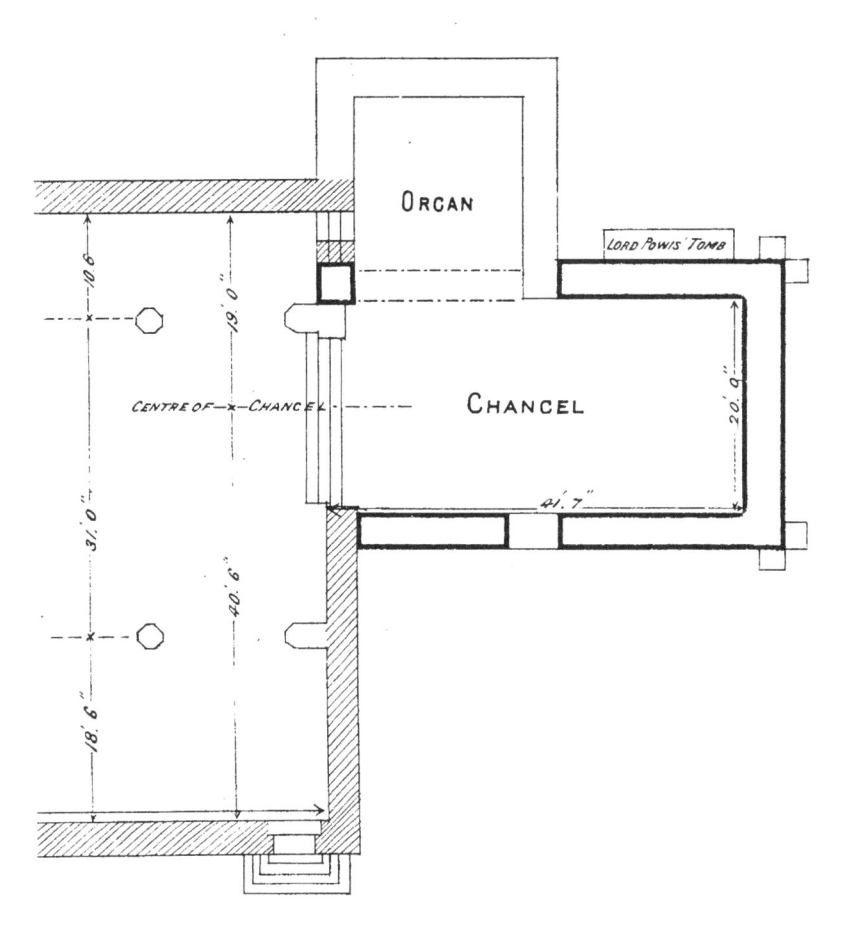

LORD POWIS TOMB

CENTRE OF — x — CHANCEL

CHANCEL

10'.6"
19'.0"
20'.9"
31'.0"
40'.6"
18'.6"
41'.7"

PLAN.

SCALE OF 10   5   0   10   20   30   40 FEET

DRAWN & PRESENTED BY

CHARLES W. JONES, ARCHITEC
LIVERPOOL
Mont. Coll: Vol. XV. — TO BE MOUNTED BETWEEN PP 276 &

projects nearly to the line of the fourteenth century porch, is a more recent addition.

The Thirteenth Century.—Of the Church as it existed in the thirteenth century, there remained one Early English window in the chancel, which had to be removed for the construction of the organ chamber, and has been replaced in the north gable. It is supposed by some that this was the original east window of the Church, and removed later on to the north wall of the chancel.

Of this period was part of the chancel walls, the foundation of which was found to be laid in clay, and not in mortar.

The wall, which, with an old doorway, was also pulled down, in order to lengthen the south aisle by throwing the porch into the Church, was of this period, and apparently at one time extended the whole length of the building, along the line of the present south arcade, part of it still remaining, and forming the foundation of the columns. The respond of a low arch, corresponding very closely with that in the tower, stood in this wall, and also a stoup for holy water, which had been so broken up that it was impossible to preserve it.

A weathering was found in the tower, showing that the eave of the roof had once been lower than the spring of the present arches.

A stone belonging to a circular column of this date (thirteenth century), two feet four inches in diameter, and roughly worked with an axe, and not a chisel, was discovered built in.

The tower, with its foot buttresses, two first storeys, and fine arch, which has been opened out, and jambs repaired, is of the thirteenth century.

The stops at the western sides show that the floor was once at the level to which the nave has been lowered; but, on the east side, there was one nine inches below, showing a Church with a lower level still.

The Fourteenth Century witnessed great changes. The present chancel certainly existed. An east window of that period existed until 1856, and the three other side windows now in the chancel corresponding with it were doubtless then inserted. The east window was found so defective at the repairs in 1856 that it was taken down. A drawing of it, by the late Rev. John Parker of Sweeney, is in the possession of Mr. Stanley Leighton, his nephew, of which we give a sketch. It probably displaced the thirteenth century window which it is hoped has now found a last resting place in the north gable of the organ chamber.

Upon stripping the plaster, the side windows were found to have quoins round them, which were so damaged that new ones with a label added have been inserted. At one time, the quoins of the south-east windows of the south aisle reached some three feet lower. Sedilia of a plain pointed character, with chamfered edges, had once existed and been subsequently removed, and the cill of the windows appears to have been used instead.

The doorway, of this date, in the south porch had to be taken down in order to obviate the necessity of steps inside the church, and an exact copy, so far as possible, was placed in its stead.

The base of a font of this period was found underneath the one which had been of late used, and is now placed in the Powysland Museum.

The other, a large octagonal basin, unpierced, with freely but not inelegantly carved foliage, after, it is said, an Early English pattern, was buried in the churchyard about twenty-four feet in front of the south porch—a Vandal-like act which has caused much surprise. This font is included in the sketch of Rev. J. Parker's drawing of the fourteenth century east window, and was highly spoken of by him.

No foundation of an arcade continuing the south wall of the chancel, such as would account for the curious ground plan of the church, has been observed.

EAST WINDOW IN WELSHPOOL CHURCH TAKEN DOWN IN 1856.
ALSO OLD FONT

A finial belonging to a gable has also been found, and a variety of cut sandstone, showing that much has been destroyed. The screen which existed up to 1728, and which is described in a previous volume[1] as "a peece of antiquity very curiously wainscotted, cut, and neatly carved, in the end of which is six pedestalls, on which, in former days, were the effigies of the Apostles, or some other of the saints, supposed finely cut, to stand with proper distances between each other, which it's a pity it should be thrown down", may have been, and probably was, of this century. It perhaps resembled the Newtown Screen, of which there is an illustration in *Montgomeryshire Collections*, vol. iii, p. 211.

In the *Fifteenth*, or early in the *Sixteenth Century*, the whole of the nave seems to have been rebuilt; the north aisle was added at this time, for its east wall is built against the face of an older one, and its foundations did not extend to the depth of the original nave. The present columns and arches were built, and the nave extended to the present width. The south aisle was thrown out almost to the line of the fourteenth century porch. The tower was probably raised at this time, and the present belfrey storey and windows added. This church was apparently surrounded by a battlemented parapet, which remained on the chancel walls until 1856, and portions of the rest were found to have been re-used for jambs in the windows of 1777. The windows of this church were square-headed, as is found in several other churches of the district.

The panelled roof, supposed to be taken from the Abbey of Strata Marcella, and to have been originally the roof of the refectory, was introduced into the chancel, cutting off the apex of the east window. It may be doubted, however, whether it was not made for the place, as it is constructed so as exactly to fit. It has several shields fixed in the following order, viz.:—

[1] *Mont. Coll.*, xiv, p. 164.

East Window.

```
3           2           1
            4
            5
8           7           6
            9
```

They are numbered according to the order in which they appear as viewed from the East window; the numbers refer to the following :—

The shields in the roof as viewed from the East window :—
No. 1. 1 and 4, *Argent*, a lion rampant *gules*; 2 and 3, *Gules*, a lion rampant *sable*.

2. 1 and 4, *Argent*, three fleurs-de-lis; 2 and 3, *Gules*, three lions pass. *or*.

3. Same as No. 2.

4. *Gules*, a cross *or*, impaling *Azure*, a chevron between three birds *gules*.

5. Party per pale *azure* and *argent*, three eagle's heads *gules*.

6. Party per pale *azure* and *gules*, three lions rampant *sable*.

7. *Gules*, a goat pp. impaling a shield of four quarterings: 1 (?); 2 (?); 3, *Gules*, a lion rampant *or*; 4 (?).

8. Quarterly, 1 *Argent*, a lion rampant *gules*; 2 *Sable*, a lion rampant *or*; 3 *Or*, a lion rampant *sable*; 4 *Gules*, a lion rampant *argent*.

9. (?), On a chevron *gules*, between three birds *or*, impaling *Argent*, a lion rampant *gules*.

Sir Edward Herbert built a gallery in 1588, probably over the rood loft or organ gallery, " extending the width of the chancel".

" For about ten years, from 1728 to 1738, a bitter controversy was carried on in the parish respecting this gallery, which some wished to pull down, others to repair and enlarge. Two of the inhabitants applied to the Court of St. Asaph, and obtained a *quorum interest*, with permission to build a gallery twenty-eight feet by nine, and sell the seats, thus making it a private and not a public gallery, as had been at first suggested. Against this scheme thirty-eight inhabitants protested in an address to Dr. Wynn, Vicar-General, and the project was defeated" (Archdeacon Clive's *MS. Account of the Parish* in the Register).

The result seems to have been that the ancient screen was removed, and a gallery formed and suspended from the roof, intercepting the view of the chancel, and extending over Lord Powis's seat, a frightful object, darkening a great portion of the church. The dimensions were twenty-six feet by nine, and it was divided into twelve pews.[1]

Eighteenth Century.— In the year 1770, the nave of the church being in a ruinous condition, a brief was obtained, which produced £160, and further sums raised by subscription, amounting in the whole to, about £1500; and between 1773 and 1777, the whole was taken down, except, perhaps, the piers and arcades, and rebuilt on the lines of the old foundations. The chief features of this alteration were the introduction of round Hanoverian windows and a low flat ceiling. One of these windows still remains in the North wall of the church.

Six bells, new cast, were placed in the tower in the year 1791.

In 1813, a west gallery was built against the tower in order to put an organ, given by Viscount Clive, the old organ having been destroyed by the Puritans.

About the latter end of the last, and the beginning of the present, century, the population of the parish increased rapidly; many of the wealthier inhabitants had no pews, and the poor were altogether without[2] accommodation. This led to the erection of two galleries.

On the 8th March 1821, a faculty was granted by Dean Shipley, Vicar-General of the Bishop of St. Asaph, on the representation by the Vicar, churchwardens, and other inhabitants of the parish of Pool, that the body of the parish church of Pool was incapable of containing the number of inhabitants of the said parish who for the most part assembled therein to hear divine service read and sermons preached, and all other the worship of Almighty God performed in the said

[1] Archdeacon Clive's *MS. Account.* [2] *Ibid.*

church, and the children of the national schools, and that it would conduce to the accommodation of those persons if a new gallery were erected over the south aisle of the church; and, by such faculty, power was given to the churchwardens, and also to the Viscount Clive (who had undertaken, at his sole cost, the erection of the proposed new gallery), to erect a new gallery with pews and free sittings over the south aisle of the said church, to extend from the east to the west wall, with a staircase leading from the porch, to contain twenty-one open seats at the west end, and eleven pews at the east end; and the twenty-one open pews were confirmed to the churchwardens upon trust, to permit the poor inhabitants of the said parish and the children of the National School to use the same; and the eleven pews were confirmed to the said Viscount Clive as appurtenant to his capital mansion, called Powis Castle, and other dwelling houses of the said Viscount in the parish of Pool, for the use of the said Viscount Clive and his successors, and his and their servants and domestics, tenants, and other owners and occupiers of Powis Castle, and the said dwelling houses, all others being excluded without his or their leave being first obtained.[1]

Another faculty was granted in August 1822, by Dean Shipley. It recites the faculty of the 8th March 1821, and that at a vestry, held on the 8th February 1822, it was resolved that a new gallery should be built on the north aisle of the Church, for removing the National School children and the poor from the south gallery to the north gallery. And also that the old singers' gallery, containing 237 feet, should be taken down, and the owners of the pews there indemnified either by purchase or an equivalent of pews in the south gallery, at their option. And that the pews in the south gallery, after accommodating the owners of pews in the old singers' gallery, should be sold to defray the expense of the intended improvement. And it further recites

[1] The proctor's bill of costs in relation to this faculty amounted to £14 16s. 1d.

that, at a vestry, on the 28 June 1822, it was resolved that the pulpit and reading-desk be removed to the east end of the Church. The faculty, then, grants leave to the Vicar and Churchwardens to erect the north gallery as proposed, and to remove the pulpit and reading-desk to the east end, and to remove the singing gallery, and to indemnify the owner of pews as proposed, and to sell the surplus pews in the south gallery, for the purpose of defraying the expense of erecting the new gallery, provided that the purchasers were owners of dwelling-houses in the parish, to which dwelling-houses the purchased pews were to become appurtenant; and the faculty confirmed all other improvements intended to be made.

These alterations were duly carried out, and effected a great alteration in the Church by removing the "hideous" suspended gallery, and altering the position of the pulpit and reading-desk, from the middle of the Church to the east end of the nave.

The tower of the Church was embattled, and new-roofed. Before this alteration, "the top was like a small slated pyramid, four-sided, with a weather-vane at the top.[1] The bells were recast, and two added, making a peal of eight; and compensation was given to the owners of the pews in the singing gallery.

The arrangement, authorised by the faculty of 1822, for selling the pews in the south gallery, for the purposes of paying the expenses, is a remarkable one, but seems unobjectionable, as the purchasers were confined to owners of dwelling-houses in the parish.

In the chancel is a vault, belonging to the Earl of Powis, made in the year 1772, when the remains of the late Earl of Powis were deposited in it. In 1839, the crown of the vault was lowered, the space between the altar rails enlarged, and new steps laid down by the present Earl.

An old document at Powis Castle records the names of thirteen persons who were buried under the floor of

[1] *Ex. inf.*, Mr. S. Powell.

the chancel, between 1769 and 1779, among whom was Edward Fisher, Priest of Buttington Chapel, buried in the year 1779.[1] The chancel, doubtless, was used as a burial place long before the formation of the vault in 1772, and many illustrious persons buried therein.

In the year 1846, the pews in the chancel, with the consent of the Dean and Chapter of Christ Church, were taken down and replaced by open benches, specially reserved for the use of the poor. The cost of this alteration was defrayed by donations from the Dean and Chapter of Christ Church, and the Vicar of Pool, aided by a grant from the Diocesan Church Building Society.

In 1849 a new parish clock, by Dent, was provided.

In 1852, when the recumbent monument to the Earl of Powis was erected, the sacrarium was enlarged and rearranged, flagged with Yorkshire stone instead of slate, the circular wooden altar rails removed, and brass ones placed across from north to south, and new steps laid down by the present Earl.

In 1852 the church was heated with hot water at a cost of £134.

In the year 1856, the chancel was thoroughly restored by the impropriate Rectors, the Dean and Chapter of Christ Church, Oxford; the battlements were taken down, and a new high-pitched roof constructed; the east wall was taken down, and the fourteenth century window replaced by one of a different design.

At the same time, a new stone arch, with carved corbels, was placed between the chancel and the nave at the expense of the parish.

Before this alteration, there was a branch of ivy in the south-west corner of the chancel, which extended from the roof nearly to the ground inside the Church, but was not allowed to touch the ground, as the tradition ran, that in that event "Llyndu pool would drown Welshpool." The root from which it grew was outside the Church on the wall or battlement, which

[1] Archdeacon Clive's *MS. Account.*

then surrounded the chancel. It was a rare natural curiosity which, unfortunately, at this alteration, was not preserved.

In the year 1866, in consequence of the great difficulties caused by appropriated pews, it was resolved to render the Church free. The Vicar and Churchwardens were authorised to obtain plans for the necessary alterations and restoration of the Church. A faculty was obtained in 1869, and the work was completed in 1871, at a cost of £4,155.

The following alterations were made :—The ceiling of the nave was taken down, and, in its stead, an open roof was constructed of pitch pine,[1] the rafters and principals being cased, and the rest entirely remodelled. The entire flooring of the nave was lowered to the level of the early Church, and, in lieu of enclosed pews, there were provided solid movable benches, constructed of the best wainscoting oak, and with tastefully carved headings. In consequence of lowering the floor, new bases were provided for all the piers of the arcade arches; the north wall was underbuilt, and the body of the Church and chancel laid with new encaustic tiles. A new arcade, with two additional arches, was opened and added to the west end, the only walling forming the internal porch being removed, and a new entrance approached by a massive flight of stone steps was substituted. The organ was removed to an organ-chamber, built for its reception, on the north side of the chancel, to which were added two arches, one large one between the chancel and the organ-chamber, and the other opening from the organ-chamber into the north aisle. The chancel was fitted up with carved oak benches, with decorated heading, for the choir.

Three new stone windows were inserted in the south wall of the Church, with stained glass. By lowering the floor of the Church, the chancel is relatively higher than it was, and is approached by a series of steps.

[1] The flat ceiling over the galleries and the ceiling under the galleries were not removed and still remain.

It is divided from the nave by a low stone screen, ornamented with diaper carving. On the south side stand a triple sedilia, piscina, and credence table.

A reredos was presented by Lucy, Countess of Powis, the principal materials of which are alabaster and marble, the wings being of Caen stone, and inlaid with tiles. In its principal panel is a cross of white marble, the apex of which surmounts the whole structure. Provision was made for heating the interior by a hot-water apparatus, placed under the organ chamber.

The restoration occupied twelve months, and was carried out from the designs of Mr. G. E. Street, A.R.A. By virtue of the faculty obtained, the seats in the body of the Church are free and unappropriated, with the exception of one bench, which is appropriated to the Lord of the Manor, the Earl of Powis, being the second from the front; the front bench is conventionally appropriated for the use of the Mayor and Corporation and Magistrates of the borough, when they attend divine service.

The basement of the tower forms the vestry.

Seat-room of the Church.—The following is a statement as to the sittings in the church which was made in 1838:—

STATEMENT OF SITTINGS IN POOL CHURCH, APRIL 17, 1838.

No. of Pews.		Sittings.	Appropriated.	Free.
42.	Middle Aisle	5 = 210		
17.	Middle to South	5 = 85	385	
18.	South Aisle	5 = 90		
8.	Chancel	5 = 40		40
16.	Middle to North	5 = 80	135	
11.	South Gallery	5 = 55		
6.	Upper end, North Aisle	6 = 36		36
29.	North Aisle	4 = 116		
4.	Under Organ Loft	4 = 16		
10.	Organ Loft	4 = 40	304	
5.	Chancel	4 = 20		
28.*	South Gallery	4 = 112		
2.	Organ Loft	8 = 16	24	
1.	Under Loft	8 = 8		

Carried forward   884   40

No. of Pews.		Sittings.	Appropriated.	Free.
	Brought forward		884	40
18.	South Aisle	3 = 54 ⎫	60	
2.	Under Organ Left	3 = 6 ⎭		
3.	Middle to North	2 = 6	6	
1.	Lord Clive's Pew	14 = 14 ⎫		
1.	Do. South Gallery	9 = 9 ⎪	40	
1.	Jones, Shoemaker	8 = 8 ⎪		
1.	Servants' Pew, South Aisle	9 = 9 ⎭		
North Gallery—free sittings		135 ⎫		375
Do. children		240 ⎭		
	Total appropriated		990	415
	Total free		415	
	Total sittings		1405	

We give this statement as we found it, but we think it over-estimates the capacity of the pews: most of those estimated to contain five, would not comfortably accommodate more than four, adults; this would take off from fifteen to twenty per cent. from the number of the sittings in the body of the church.

By the alteration in the chancel in 1846, as before mentioned, a good many more sittings were provided by open benches for the poor; the precise number we have not been able to ascertain.

The recent alterations of the church in 1871, when the organ gallery was removed, and the chancel refitted for the choir and clergy only, have reduced the number of sittings in the church very considerably, although it must be admitted it has improved the appearance of the church, and conduced to the convenience of the parishioners generally. The nave is now divided into four rows of open benches.

North aisle, containing 26 benches—each 7 feet long— intended for males only, calculated to contain 4 each . . . 104
Two rows of 22 benches—one 14 feet long and the other 14 feet 6 inches long—calculated to contain 8 × 44 = 352; deduct for space occupied by 8 pillars, equivalent to 8 persons' room . . . 344
South aisle, containing 22 benches,—each 10 feet 6 inches long,—calculated to contain 6 each, intended for females only 132

580

Brought forward .	.	580
The chancel . .		30
The galleries are undisturbed.		
South gallery containing 28 pews × 4	112	
Do.　Lord Powis's pew .	9	
North gallery calculated for children	240	
Free sittings . . .	135	
	——	496
		————
		1106

The question of removing the galleries has been contested on one occasion, but the expediency of their remaining seems self-evident from the fact that the body of the church has, according to its present open-bench arrangements, sittings only to seat comfortably 580 adult members of the general parishioners, exclusive of the choir and clergy.

Gifts to the Church.—There are many gifts to the Church in addition to the •reredos above mentioned. A handsome new font, made of Mansfield Woodhouse Magnesian limestone, was presented by the Honourable and Rev. John R. Orlando Bridgeman and Mrs. Bridgeman (daughter of Archdeacon Clive, for 45 years Vicar of this parish), as a memorial to their daughter Georgina Bridgeman, aged six, and is inscribed :—

"Filiæ pientissimæ grati erga Deum quod illa paulisper frui licuit parentes fecerunt MDCCCLXXI."

It is octagonal, on a circular base and pillars, and was reproduced after the fragments of an old one discovered underneath the one last used, which last one, a large octagonal basin unpierced, with rough foliage after an early English pattern, is buried in the churchyard about 24 feet in front of the south porch.

The brass lectern was presented by Miss Corrie of Dysserth, as a memorial of her brother Lieutenant Samuel Corrie, of the 18th Royal Irish, who died in 1867. It is inscribed :—

"The grass withereth, the flower fadeth, but the Word of our God shall stand for ever."

The brass pulpit desk was presented by Mrs. Wolseley Lewis, and the other furniture necessary to the carrying on of divine service, was presented by various ladies of the congregation.

In 1877, a stone pulpit was presented by the Rev. C. J. Bowen, and the Rev. T. Wolseley Lewis and Mrs. Wolseley Lewis, in memory of Thomas Bowen and Mary his wife. It is elaborately carved with gothic designs. It is inscribed :—

"To the Honour and Glory of God,
And in loving memory of
Thomas Bowen and Mary his wife
This pulpit was erected by their children.
1877."

Windows.—The church is rich in stained glass windows. The decorated east window of five lights, in the chancel, was erected in 1856 by public subscription, and contains a series of fifteen medallions representing events in the life of St. Mary the Virgin, viz :—

The Annunciation	St. Joseph's Workshop
The Salutation of Elizabeth	Water made into Wine
The Adoration of the Infant	His Mother and Brethren
Offering of the Magi	standing without
The Presentation in the Temple	With Jesus bearing the Cross
Flight into Egypt	Standing by the Cross
Journey to Jerusalem	Embalming Him
With the Doctors in the Temple	Going Home with St. John.

It also has two shields of arms, viz., the Royal Arms, and *Sable*, on a cross engrailed *argent*, a lion passant *gules*, between four leopard's faces, *az.*, on a chief *or*, a rose of the third, barbed *vert*, seeded of the fifth, between two Cornish choughs ppr.—the arms of Christ Church, Oxford.

There are three other windows in the chancel filled with diaper glass and with armorial bearings. The one in the north wall has three shields :—

1. Party per pale *azure* and *gules*, three lions rampant *argent* (for Herbert Earl of Powis).

2. Same as 1 (Herbert), impaling 1 and 4; *Or,* on a chief *sable,* three escallops of the field; and 2 and 3 *argent,* three roses *gules,* barbed and seeded ppr. (Graham).

3. Same as 1 (Herbert).

The first window in the south side has three shields:—

1. Per pale *azure* and *gules,* three lions rampant *argent* (for Herbert).

2. *Argent,* on a fesse *sable,* three mullets *or* (for Clive).

3. Quarterly, 1 and 4, Clive; 2 and 3 *Sable,* three garbs *or,* on an escutcheon of pretence (Herbert).

The second on south side has also three shields—

1. *Sable,* two keys in saltier endorsed *argent* (See of St. Asaph).

2. *Sable,* on a cross engrailed *argent,* a lion pass. *gu.*, between 4 leopard's heads *azure,* on a chief *or,* a rose of the third, barbed *vert,* seeded of the fifth, between two Cornish choughs ppr. (Christ Church College, Oxford).

3. *Argent,* a castle *azure* (Welshpool Borough Arms).

The most ancient window in the church, and perhaps in that respect the most interesting, is placed in the gable of the organ gallery and is hid by the organ. It contains no armorial bearings or scripture subjects, but is ornamented with some stained glass.

There is also a decorated window at the east end of the nave, the stone-work erected by subscription, and the glass presented by the Earl of Powis. It has a shield of arms at the top Per pale *az.* and *gu.* three lions ramp. *ar.* for Herbert, and contains representations of events from the life of Moses, viz:—

His hands stayed up	An Angel appears to him
Finding of Moses	Keeping his Flock
At the Burning Bush	The Brazen Serpent
The Exodus from Egypt	The Passage of the Red Sea
The Smiting of the Rock	The Rod turned into a Serpent

The Golden Calf

In the year 1876 two of the windows in the north wall were restored from designs by Mr. Street, and filled with stained glass by Wailes of Newcastle. The one window is in memory of Lucy, Countess of Powis, and was erected by public subscription at the cost of £250. It contains representations of events from the life of St. John the Evangelist, viz:—

The Apostle's Call	Baptising a Convert
The Visit to the Sepulchre	Writing the Apocalypse
Leaning on our Lord's Bosom at the Last Supper	Cast into the Cauldron of Boiling Oil.

It is inscribed:—

" To the Glory of God and to the Memory of Lucy, Countess of Powis, who died September 6, A.D. 1875."

The other window was erected to the memory of Mr. Thomas Bowen, Banker, Welshpool, by public subcription, at the like cost of £250. It contains representations of events from the life of St. Peter, viz:—

Walking on the Sea	Healing the Sick
Receiving the Commission, " Feed My Sheep"	Delivered from Prison The Death of Ananias.
Raising Dorcas	

It is inscribed:—

" To the Glory of God and in Memory of Thomas Bowen, Esq., who died November 4th, A.D. 1875."

In 1877, new steps and rails for the approach to the Church from Bull street (now called Church street), were made from designs by Mr. Hurst, at a cost of £160, raised by public subscription.

The royal arms in carved wood, and enblazoned in colours, are now fixed on the west wall of the church. The benefaction table states it was presented by Richard Edmunds in 1802. It contains in the 1st and 4th grand quarterings the following, viz., 1st and 4th, three fleurs-de-lys for France; 2nd and 3rd, three lions passant for England. This is remarkable, as, the arms being presented to the church in 1802, one would not have expected the shield to contain the French fleurs-de-lys, as they were removed, by royal proclamation, from the arms of England upon the first of January 1801.

On each side the royal arms are two flags, formerly

belonging to the Royal Montgomery Militia, which were presented to the church within the last twenty years.

The Monuments in the Church, with copies of the inscriptions thereon.—The principal one is a remarkably handsome monument to Edward Herbert, Earl of Powis, K.G., erected by his widow, Lucy, Countess of Powis, in 1852. The memorial is in the form of an altar-tomb, and is placed under an arched recess in the north wall of the chancel of the church. The style adopted is that of the close of the thirteenth and commencement of the fourteenth centuries. The arch is of the form known as segmental-pointed; it is enriched with carved capitals representing natural foliage, with pateræ, and with an order of foliated ornament. The details are founded upon those of the well-known Chapter-house, of Southwell Minster, Notts. The monument itself is of Derbyshire alabaster. The plinth is richly moulded, and upon it stands a *podium* diapered in a pattern which was suggested by the enrichment of the triforium of the choir of Westminster Abbey. In the centre of this portion are two coats of arms conjoined, the one that of the Earl himself, encircled by the label of the Order of the Garter; the other, the Earl's arms impaled with those of his Countess, the daughter of James, third Duke of Montrose, viz., Quarterly 1st and 4th *or*, on a chief *sa.*, three escallops of the field; 2nd and 3rd *ar.*, three roses *gu.*, barbed and seeded ppr. Upon two shields placed upon either side of the central group are figured the arms of the See of Bangor, *Gu.*, a bend or gutty-de-poix between two mullets pierced *argent*; and those of the See of St. Asaph (old style), *Sa.* a key and a shepherd's crook in saltire, endorsed *ar.* Upon the altar-tomb thus formed lies the effigy of the Earl. He is represented in the robes of a peer, and wearing the collar and other insignia of the Order of the Garter. The head rests upon a cushion, supported by two small seated angels. The hands are joined in prayer, and at the feet, on a cushion, is placed the

Mont: Coll. Vol. XV to face p. 292.

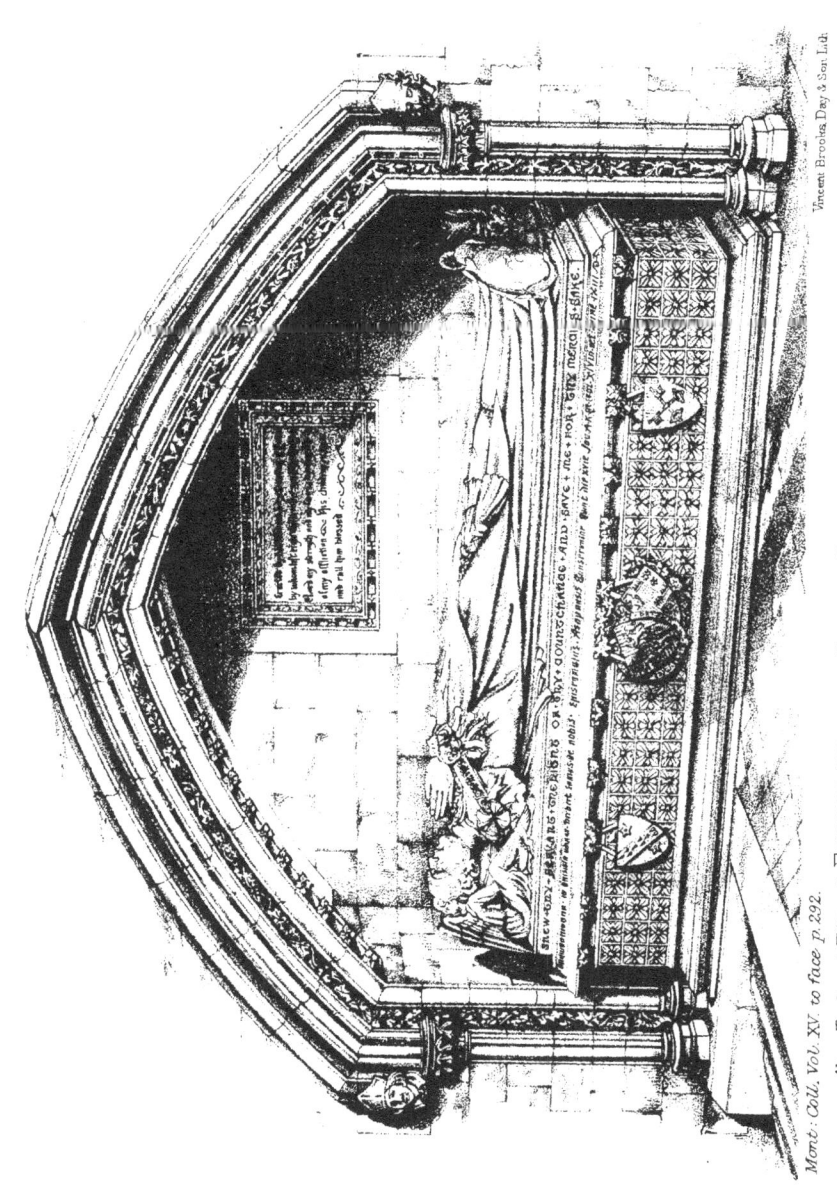

Altar Tomb and Effigy of EDWARD HERBERT, EARL OF POWIS K.G. in the Chancel of S[t] Mary's Church Welshpool.

Vincent Brooks, Day & Son Lith.

Earl's coronet, between an elephant and a griffin, the supporters of the family arms. Upon the margin of the slab, in which the effigy is formed, is inscribed, in sunken Lombardic characters, the text,

"Show Thy servant the light of Thy countenance, and save me for Thy mercies' sake."

Beneath is a raised brass inscription, with ruby ground by Waller, and in old English characters:—

"Hic obdormiscit in Christo EDWARDUS HERBERT, Comes de Powis, Episcopatus Asaphensis Conservator. Obiit die xvii Jan. A.S. MD.CCCXLVIII. Æt. suæ LXIII."

Above the figure itself, upon a brass tablet, enclosed by a moulded border, inserted in the wall-space formed by the comprising arch, the following inscription is engraved;—

"Erected by his widow, Lucy, Countess of Powis, by whom he left eight children, five sons and three daughters.

"'O Lord, my strength and my fortress; my refuge in the day of affliction.'

"'His children shall arise up and call him blessed.'"

The likeness was obtained from a fine portrait at Walcot, by Grant, and a sketch by Sir George Hayter. The sculptor was the late Mr. Edward Richardson, who carried out the work from the design and under the direction of the late Sir George Gilbert Scott, R.A.[1] We give an engraving of this beautiful monument.

On the north wall of the chancel is a mural monument, of a handsome design and formed of different colored marbles, to the memory of Sir Edward Herbert, Knight, the first of the Herbert family who possessed Powis Castle. It has been engraved in the *Montgomeryshire Collections* (vol. v, p. 174). It bears the following emblazoned shields —

[1] We are indebted to Mr. G. Gilbert Scott, F.S.A., architect, for the above description.

Party per pale *azure* and *gules*, three lions rampant *or*, for Herbert, surmounted by a motto, " Christus michi vita." Same arms, on an escutcheon of pretence, *Argent*, on a fesse *azure*, three stag's heads cabossed *or*, for Stanley, surmounted by a motto, " Mors michi lucrum."

Underneath the shields, in two panels, is the following inscription :—

Here lyeth the body of the Right Worshipfull S'R EDWARD HERBERT, Knight, second son to the Right Hon'r'ble S'r Will'm Herbert, Knight, Earl of Pe'broke, Lord Cardiff, and Knight of the most Noble Order of the Garter, and of Anne his wife, sister and sole heir to Sir William Parker, Knight, Lord Pare of Kirkeby Kendall Marmyo' Fitzhughe and St. Quintine, Earle of Essex, Marquess of Northampton, and Knight of the most Noble Order of the Garter, which S'r Edward Herbert married Mary, daughter and sole heire to Thomas Stanley of Standen, in the county of Hertford, Esq., Master of the Mint, anno Domini 1570, yongest sone of Thomas Stanley of Dalgarth, in the county of Cumberland, Esq., which S'r Edward Herbert and Dame Mary his wife had issue four sons and eight daughters (vizt.) William Herbert, Esq., his eldest sonne and heire, who maryed Ladye Mary Elyonor, second daughter to Henry, late Earl of Northumberland, George Herbert seconde sonne, John Herbert third son, and Edward Herbert, fourth son; Elizabeth first daughter, dyed young, Anne second daughter, Joyce the third daughter, Fraunses the forth daughter, Katherine the fyft daughter, Jone the sixt daughter, dyed young, Mary the seventh daughter, and Wenefrede the eighth daughter; which S'r Edward dyed the 23rd day of Marche, anno Domini 1594; and this monument was made at the charge of the said Mary Lady Herbert, the 23rd day of October 1597."

Copy of the inscriptions upon the coffin plates in the vault belonging to the Powis family, underneath the chancel.

1. ELIZABETH CRAVEN, Lady Powis. Died Oct'r 8th, 1762. Aged 63.
2. The Right Honourable HENRY ARTHUR HERBERT, Earl of Powis. Died Sep'r 1772. Aged 70 years.
3. BARBARA ANTONICE HERBERT, Countess of Powis. Died March 12th, 1786. Aged 51 years.

---

[1] *Ex. inf.*, Mr. Tallis, the sexton.

4. The Right Honourable GEORGE EDWARD HENRY ARTHUR HERBERT, Earl of Powis, Viscount Ludlow, and Lord Lieutenant of the Counties of Salop and Montgomery. Died Jan'y 17th, 1801. Aged 46 years.

5. Honourable HARRIET EMILY HERBERT. Died at Meriden, in the county of Warwick, April 28th, 1824. Aged 11 weeks and 1 day.

6. Right Honourable EDWARD HERBERT, Earl of Powis, K.G. Born March 22nd, A.D. 1785. Died Jan. 17th, 1848. Aged 63.

7. The Right Honourable LUCY GRAHAM, Countess of Powis. Born 25th September 1793. Died at Walcot 16th September 1875.

8. Lady HARRIET JANE HERBERT. Born 21st Dec., 1831. Died 21st June, 1880.

Small marble tablet in chancel, not fixed, with arms on shield, *Gules*, a [bird] *argent*, with a crescent *or*. Inscription almost illegible.

Juxta altare jacet sepultum Corpus Gul. Langford A. M., Vicarii ......ecclesiæ.

[rest illegible.]

Chancel, South Wall.—Small brass tablet in frame of carved stone.

MARIANNE, wife of William Clive, Clerk, Vicar of this parish, and daughter of George Tollet of Betley Hall, in the county of Stafford, Esquire, died 16th February 1841, aged 36 years, leaving an infant daughter. "Then I say, brethren, the time is short."—1 Cor. vii, 20.

Two small brass plates in stone frames, with uniform Gothic designs.

The Dame JANE OWEN, formerly of Glan Severn in this county, who died xix February MDCCCXXV, aged 59 years. This Tablet is erected to her beloved memory by her son David Pugh of Llanerchydol, Esq. Her remains repose in a vault in this churchyard.

Sacred to the beloved memory of Lieutenant JOHN CADWALLADER PUGH, late of the Royal Regiment, and youngest son of David and Anne Pugh of Llanerchydol in this county. He died on his passage home from Canada with his regiment 19th July 1851, aged 25 years.

Stone on floor of chancel.

[Infant child] of David......and BRAY. Also Lucy the wife [illegible].

Stone on floor of chancel near door.

Here lyeth ye body of ELIZABETH, ye wife of Thomas Traunter of Pool, gent., who departed this life the 19th day of June, Anno Domini 1692, in......years.

Also the body of THOMAS TRAUNTER of Poole, gent., son of the said Thomas Traunter and Elizabeth his wife, who departed this life this......day of September A.D. 1727, aged 44 years.

Also of MEURIC, son of the said............

North Wall of Church.—White and dove-coloured marble mural monument.

Sacred to the memory of ANN, widow of the late Captain RICHARD PIERCY, R.N., who died March 26, 1848, in the 81st year of her age. This Tablet is erected as a tribute of affection by her sister, Sarah N. Willoughby.

A similar tablet—

Sacred to the memory of ALFRED TEMPLER ERSKINE, the beloved and only son of Alfred H. Cheke, Esq., H.M. Bengal Army. Born at Benares 25th Oct. 1856. Died at Dresden 4th January 1864. "And Jesus called a little child unto Him."—Matt. xviii, 2.

A brass plate surmounted by a floriated Calvary cross, having in the margin a small shield bearing *Or*, on a chief *gules*, three eagles displayed of the field; Crest, Out of a ducal crown a talbot's head, and having the following inscription—

To the glory of God and sacred to the loving memory of ROBERT DEVEREUX HARRISON. Died suddenly April 8th, 1874, aged 60 years. "In the midst of life we are in death."

ALICE GERTRUDE, youngest beloved child of the above, and of Emily his wife, fell asleep January 17th, 1875, aged 1 year and 10 months. They are in peace. This tablet is erected by the widow and mother.

White marble tablet with a border of slate coloured marble—

Sacred to the memory of MARY, widow of the late Reverend WILLIAM WILLIAMS, M.A., Rector of Llanfyllin and Llangadfan, in this county. She died 11th February 1825, aged 79 years.

East Wall of South Aisle.—Small brass plate in an oak frame—
Near to this place rests, in the hope of a joyful resurrection, the body of THOMAS EVANS. Hee died June 3, 1766. Aged 45.
" Affliction sore long time I bore, physicians were in vain
Til death gave ease and God did pleas to ease me of my pain,"
" I know that my Redeemer liveth, and that He shall stand at the latter day upon the earth ; and though after my skin worms destroy this body, yet in my flesh shall I see God."—Job xix, 25, 26.

Small brass plate, with floriated border, let into black marble—
IN LOVING REMEMBRANCE OF A DEAR FATHER, JOHN DAVIES CORRIE OF DYSSERTH, FOR MORE THAN 70 YEARS A CONSTANT WORSHIPPER IN THIS CHURCH. DIED DEC. 20TH, 1878. AGED 81 YEARS. " With the Lord there is mercy, and with Him is plenteous redemption."

South Wall.—Marble tablet—
To the memory of THOMAS PARRY, Esq., of Madras, third son of the late Mr. Parry of Leighton Hall. Died Aug. 14, 1825, aged 59 years. Also of Mrs. JANE BRYAN, sister of the above, late of this town. Died Feb. 16, 1846, aged 95 years. Also of FIELD EVANS, Esq., of Henfaes. Died July 14th, 1853, aged 83 years. This tablet was erected by the niece, daughter, and widow. Also to the memory of ANN, relict of the above FIELD EVANS, Esq. Died March 13th, 1855, aged 77 years.

On the south wall there was formerly a hatchment of the Lloyds of Trevnant—1 and 4 *Sable*, three nag's heads *argent* ; 3 and 4 *Argent*, a chevron *sable*, between three boar's heads of the last—but it was destroyed at the restoration of the church.

White and black marble tablet—
This tablet is erected in memory of EDWARD JONES, surgeon of this town, who, after a long illness, which he bore with resignation, fell asleep in Jesus, March 11th, 1839, aged 49 years. Also of MARTHA, wife of the above, who died on the 18th January 1878, in the 92nd year of her age.

Marble tablet on south wall. Scroll—
Underneath lyeth the body of MORRIS POWELL, gent., who departed this life the 8th of October 1721, aged 68 years. Also the body of JOAN his wife, who departed this life the 29th of March 1729,

aged 92 years. And near this place lyeth the body of ROBERT POWELL, gent., their third son, who departed this life the 25th day of March 1729, aged 42 years.

West end of the Church.—Large mural monument—
Sacred to the memory of ANNE, widow of the late GILBERT ROSS, Esq., of London, who died the 19th of Nov. 1821, aged 93 years. Also of GEORGE ROSS, Esq., of Llanerchydol, youngest son of the above-named Anne and Gilbert Ross. He died July 5th, 1812. aged 42 years. Also of GILBERT ROSS, Esq., of this town, eldest son of Anne and Gilbert Ross. He died Oct. 2, 1815, aged 60 years, Also of GILBERT BUCKLEY ROSS, Esq., only son of the above-named George Ross and Eliza his wife. He died Aug. 1st, 1825, aged 27 years.

Small marble tablet—
Sacred to the memory of CHARLES ROCKE, late of this town, Attorney-at-law, who died 3rd of May, 1779, aged 38. Also of ELIZABETH ROCKE, his daughter, who died 26th February, 1835, aged 68, SARAH ROCKE, second daughter, born June 1st, 1773, died May 1st, 1849.

Small brass plate—
In a vault under this pew, lye the remains of CHARLES ROCKE, attorney, late of this town, who departed this life, May 3rd, 1779, aged 38.

Here lyeth the body of John Owen, of Gungroge Uawre, Gent., who departed this life the vi day of September, aged xliii. An. Dom. MDCLXXXIII.[1]

The next five inscriptions on brass plates are now unfixed, but were formerly either affixed to the walls or to stones on the floor of the church.

Brass plate—
S. M. GULIELME WYNNE, A.M., uicarij huius Ecclesiae vigilantissimi fil. JOANNIS WYNNE de coperieni in Agro Flint Arm. natu guarti viri doctissimi Theologi consummatissmi Equi justique semper tenacissimi qui munus et officium pastorale non tam concionibus [licet facundissimis] quam Vitâ vere Christianâ moribus et nisi Gerrimis perquam digne cohonestavit tantus Vir morte heu nimis maturâ praereptus dulce sui apud omnes desiderium reliquit obiit xii Kal April Anno Dni MDCXCVII, Annos natus xliiii.
Monumentum hocce pietatis et amoris $\mu\nu\eta\mu\acute{o}\sigma\upsilon\nu o\nu$ LMPq moestissima coniux.

---

[1] Extracted by Sir T. E. Winnington, in 1866, from his copy of the *Duke of Beaufort's Progress through Wales.*

Here lyeth the body of SAMUEL DAVIES, Doctor-of-Laws, late vicar of this parish, and of Guilsfield, and treasurer of the Church of Saint Asaph, who in all the worst changes of times continued firme and active in his duty, and a faithfull Shepherd to his Flock, and an indulgent Parent, a Kinde Master, a Peaceable and Hospitable Neighbour, constant in Prayer, reverent in Service, and devout in all Pious actions. He departed this life in the 61st year of his age, March 27th, 1693.

Underneath lyeth the body of JACOB HUMPHREYS, late parish clerk of Pool, who departed this life the 13th day of November, 1738, aged 74 years.

In the memory of Mr. THOMAS LLOYD, Surgeon, who departed this life, 15th July, 1786, in the 30th year of his age.

Sacred to the memory of THOMAS EMPSON, Esq., late Captain in the Montgomeryshire Militia. He died April ye 26th 1789, aged 62 years.

A brass plate, with a shield of arms "Paly of nine," which has been enamelled, but the enamel has been peeled off the face.

Copy[1] of the inscriptions upon the coffin-plates in the vault belonging to the Llanerchydol family, in the churchyard—

1. JANE OWEN, formerly wife of Charles Pugh, Esq., died 11th February, 1782. Aged 61.
2. DAVID PUGH, Junior, Llanerchydol, died September 23rd, 1857, in the 43rd year of his age.
3. DAVID PUGH, Esq., M.P., born 14th August, 1789; died 20th April, 1861.
4. ANNE PUGH, died 8th October, 1863. Aged 70 years.
5. FELECIA HARRIET PUGH, born March 25th, 1825; died August 21st, 1874.
6. CHARLES VAUGHAN PUGH, born 19th May, 1819; died 28th December, 1874.
7. MARGARET ANNE JOHNSON, died 25th November, 1881. Aged 63 years.

Some of the Monumental Inscriptions in St. Mary's Churchyard, Welshpool.—Old head-stones found in Churchyard, now placed at the east end of the Chancel.

Mrs. MARGARET TRAUNTER, of the Turkey liouse, in the parish of Churchstoke, daughter of the undernamed Thomas Traunter, Gent., was buried here the 19th of January, 1779, in the 52nd year of her age.

---

[1] *Ex inf.* Mr. Tallis, the sexton.

I.H.S.—Sacred to the memory of GEORGE, the son of Peter Brown, by Ella his wife, who departed this life the 19th of July, 1809, aged 24 ye[ars].
I left this world in blooming years,
And all my friends in floods of tears,
Therefore, repent while you have t[ime]
For I was taken in my prime.

Also RICHARD, the son of Edward Evans by Elizabeth his wife, who died Oct. 18th, 1814, aged 8 months.

Here lyeth the body of JOHN GRIFFITHS, late of Glanhaueren, gent., who departed this life the thirtieth day of October in the yeare of our Lord God 1710, aged neare 80 yeares.

Here lyeth the body of MARGRET WILLIAMS, yovngest davghter vnto David Williams of Poole, gent., who deceased the xxiii day of April 1684, aged xxv years.

[HERE LY]ETH the body of [Theo]phylvs Lang[fo]rd, the 4th son of Rich— [L]angford of Trevalen, in the covnty of Denbigh, Esqr., an attvrney att law, Deceased the 30th day of Avgvst, An'o Dom' 1667, annoq' ætatis svæ 60.

Here lieth the bodie of —— GRIFFITHES of Glanhaveren, gent., who dyed the tenth day of May, an'o D'm'ni 1685, ab't ye 30th yeare of his age. Here also lyeth the body of ELIZ'TH GRIFFITHES, widd. and relict of John Griffiths, gent., dec'ed, and eldest daughter of Tho' Bray of Marton, in coun' Salop, gent., dec'ed, who departed this life 8th day of January, an'o D'm'i 1719, aged 71 years.

Here lieth the body of EVAN JONES, gent., late of Hem, in Forden, who departed this life the 2nd day of March 1711, in the 78th year of his age.[1]

Near the Chancel.—Monument—
Underneath are deposited the remains of GEORGE DEVEREUX HARRISON, Esq., late Lieut. of H.M. Marines, and second son of the late R. J. Harrison of the Gaer, in this county. Died 20th December 1819, aged 36 years. Also of GEORGE DEVEREUX HARRISON of Welchpool, surgeon, second son of George Devereux Harrison, Esq., who departed this life the 26th day of May 1843, aged 28 years.

Also of MARIANNE GRIFFITHS, eldest daughter of the late Robert Griffiths, Esq., of this town, who departed this life the 20th day of November 1843, aged 62 years.

---

[1] Copied by Rev. W. V. Lloyd in 1858, not existing now (1882).

WELSH POOL. 301

Monument surrounded by pallisading—
Underneath lie the remains of WILLIAM YEARSLEY, late solicitor of this town, who departed this life Aug. 19, 1860, aged 58 years. Underneath lie the remains of JANE, only daughter of William Yearsley, solicitor of this town, and ANNE his wife. She died the 16th day of October 1846, aged 15 years.

Monument surrounded by pallisading—
Underneath are interred the mortal remains of GEORGE GOULD of Golfa, Esq., who departed this life the 18th of May 1835, in the 78th year of his age. Underneath are interred the mortal remains of ELEANOR, widow of the late George Gould of Golfa, Esq., who departed this life the 21st August 1841, aged 88 years.
In memory of THOMAS WITHY of Golfa, Esq., who departed this life the 8th March 1852, aged 79 years. Also of JANE, widow of the above, who departed this life the 5th January 1859, aged 84 years.

Flat stone—
Sacred to the memory of THOMAS YATES, Esq., of this town, who departed this life September 11th, 1841, aged 58. Two infant children—R'D FREDERICK, 3rd son, 24 May 1839, aged 8 years. MAURICE, 25 April 1828, aged 13 months.

Monument—
To the memory of THOMAS JONES, 70 years full surgeon in Her Majesty's Navy. Born in Montgomery 26 Nov. 1733. Died in Pool 18th Feb. 1828. Also of MARY MORRIS JONES, wife of Thomas Jones, surgeon. Born 1743; died 1803.

Monument with railings—
JAMES TURNER of Welchpool, departed this life December 18th, 1806, aged 57 years. MARY, relict of the late James Turner, Esq., of this town, who died 9th January 1833, aged 62 years. WILLIAM TURNER, Esq., of Lincoln's Inn, second son of James and Mary Turner of this town. Died April 18th, 1826, aged 24 years.

Monument surrounded by pallisading—
Sacred to the memory of HENRY, eldest son of Henry Foulkes, Esq., of this town, and Mary his wife, died 3rd May 1792, aged 5 months. Also MARY, wife of Henry Foulkes, Esq., of this town, and daughter of the late Rice Pryce, Esq., and Catherine his wife, of Tycoch Manafon in this county, died 14th February 1814, aged 62 years. Also MARY, eldest daughter of Henry Foulkes, Esq., of this town, and Mary his wife, died 23rd Nov. 1817, aged 30. ANN, second daughter of the late William Foulkes of Penthryn and Trelydan, both in this county, died Sept. 30th, 1843, aged 83. Her end

Y 2

was peace. Also CATHERINE, second daughter, and CHARLOTTE, youngest daughter of Henry and Mary Foulkes, who both died on the same day, Feb. 11, 1818, aged 29 and 25. Also the Rev. HENRY FOULKES, youngest son of the late Henry and Mary Foulkes, died Oct. 2, 1830, aged 33. Also HENRY, seventh son of the late William Foulkes, Esq., and Ann his wife, of Trelydan, in the parish of Guilsfield, and Penthryn in the parish of Berriew, both in this county, died 18th May 1818, aged 61. This tomb was erected by Ann Foulkes as a tribute of affection to the memory of her departed relatives.

Flat stone—

Here, by a beloved daughter, her fond and faithful companion through life, lie the remains of the best of women, of mothers, and of wives, and of one who never lost a friend or made a foe, MARY, relict of the Rev. John Pryce, died 2nd September 1829, aged 88. Sacred to the memory of MARTHA ANN HAMER, relict of the late Henry Hamer, Esq., of Liverpool, and youngest daughter of the late Rev. John Pryce, Gunley, died September 3rd, 1861, aged 80 years. In.........memory of the most affectionate of sisters, the best of daughters, and sincerest of friends, HARRIOTTE PRYCE, died 23rd January 1827, aged 53 years. In memory also of her twin brothers, EDWARD and JOHN PRYCE, who died in infancy 26th of January 1777.

Slate monument (rapidly going to decay)—

Here lie the remains of MARY LLOYD, relict of Thomas Lloyd, Esq., of Trefnant, in the co. of Montgomery. She died the 21st Dec. 1801, aged 77 years.

Head stone—

Sacred to the memory of JOHN PUGH, gent., late of Newtown and since of Severn Street in this town, who died 23rd day of August 1815, aged 71 years.

MOSES EVANS.

" My debts is payd, my grave you see ;
Stay but a while, you will follow mee."

A raised stone—

Underneath this stone are deposited the remains of JOHN SMITH (late of Pool), gentleman, who died the 21st day of January 1793, aged 87 years. Also of MARY SMITH, widow of the above, who died the 12th day of November 1807, aged 75. SUSANNA CORRIE, of Dysserth, in this parish, widow of John Corrie of Vauxhall, in the county of Surrey, gentleman, and daughter of the said Mary Smith by her former husband, John Davies of Dysserth, Esq., died on the 29th day of October 1844, aged 85 years.

In the vault underneath this stone are deposited the remains of MARY ANNE, the beloved wife of John Davies Corrie of Dysserth, in this parish, Esq., obt. 4th December 1838, æt. 35. Also of JOHN DAVIES CORRIE, eldest son of the above, who died on the 24th October 1841, aged 15 years. JOSEPH HARVEY CORRIE, second son of the above, died at Newport, Salop, May 24th, 1843, and was buried there, aged 9 years. Also of EMMA CORRIE, second wife of the above named J. D. Corrie, who died on the 12th November 1856, aged 55 years. Also of JOHN DAVIES CORRIE, who died at Dysserth, December 28th, 1878, aged 81 years.

Raised stone surrounded by dwarf iron railings—

In memory of GRACE, wife of Thomas Evans, Welshpool, who died February 17th, 1796, aged xxxv years.

"Let worms devour my wasting flesh
And crumble all my bones to dust,
My God shall raise my frame anew
At the revival of the just."

Also of THOMAS EVANS, who died February 21st, 1829, aged 66 years.

"Triumphant in his closing eye
The hope of glory shone,
Joy breathed in his expiring sigh
To think the fight was won.
Gently the passing spirit fled,
Sustained by grace divine.
Oh, may such grace on us be shed,
And make our end like thine."

Stone—

In respectful memory of JOHN EVANS late of the Farm, in the parish of Guilsfield, who died May 19th, 1817, aged 83 years.

Another stone—

In respectful memory of MARY, the widow of the late John Evans of the Farm, in the parish of Guilsfield, who died the 21st day of November 1831, in the 90th year of her age.

Monument surrounded by iron pallisading—

In memory of MORRIS JONES of Gungrog, in this county, Esquire. Born 25th March 1776; died 10th December 1843. Also of ELIZABETH, relict of the above. Born 9th January 1785; died 11th March 1868.

Also of ALICE ROSE OGLE. Born 2nd January 1843; died 3rd May 1863. And of FLORENCE MARY KERRISON. Born 2nd July 1856; died 20th October 1856. Grandchildren of the before-named Morris Jones and Elizabeth his wife.

Monument surmounted with cross—

In affectionate remembrance of THOMAS VAUGHAN, late of the Moors in this parish. Born Sept. 30th, 1801 ; died Nov. 5th, 1873.

Flat stone—

In memory of MARY, the wife of Thomas Bowen, the Bank, Welshpool, who died 26 September 1871. Also of THOMAS BOWEN, Banker, of this town, and of Tyddyn, born August 11th, 1805 ; died November 4, 1875.

In memory of EDWARD FARMER, who departed this life March 10th, 1822, aged 67 years. Also, of MARGARET, wife of the above Edward Farmer, who departed this life January 14th, 1833, aged 72 years. In memory of REES FARMER, who departed this life July 27th, 1816, aged 20 years.

" In prime of life I ceased to be,
No doctor could me save ;
Because it was my Maker's will,
To call me to the grave."

Monument surrounded with iron railings.

FRANCIS SHUKER MADDOX, departed this life June the 5th, 1811, in the 23rd year of his age ; sacred to whose memory this tomb is erected as the last tribute of respect by his afflicted parent. Here lieth the body of RICHARD MADDOX, late of this town, Gent., who departed this life January 26th, 1814, aged 88 years. Also, ELIZABETH, wife of John Hopkins, of this town, who departed this life the 7th November 1828, aged 79 years.

Monument—

Sacred to the memory of SARAH, daughter of Edward Jones, Surgeon, and Martha his wife, born February 27th, 1815 ; died February 18th, 1836. In memory of EDWARD JONES, late Surgeon of this town, who departed this life March 11th, 1839, aged 49 years. Also, of MARTHA, wife of Edward Jones, who departed this life January 18th, 1878, aged 92 years.

Head stone—

Sacred to the Memory of EDWARD, son of Edward Jones, and Martha his wife, born 26th November 1819; died 26th August 1823.

Table monument—

In memory of JOSEPH RUTTER, late of this town, School master, died January 4th, 1826, aged 65 years.

Table monument—
Underneath are deposited the remains of WILLIAM JONES, late of Pool, Gentleman, who departed this life November 18th, 1839, aged 79 years.

Flat stone—
Sacred to the memory of WILLIAM PRYCE YEARSLEY, solicitor of this town, born the 18th day of October 1829 ; died the 21st day of June 1871.

Flat stone—
Sacred to the memory of MARGARDT, the wife of Thomas Clarke of Welshpool, died October 20th, 1847, aged 76. Also, Thomas Clarke, who departed this life January 10th, 1849, aged 72.

Flat stone—
Sacred to the memory of SARAH YEARSLEY, born August 2nd, 1801 ; died December 28th, 1869.

Table monument—
Sacred to the memory of DAVID JONES, late maltster of this town, who died the 12th day of March 1818. In memory of DAVID JONES, Dolanog house, coal merchant, died March 25th, 1842, aged 37 years.

Underneath lie the remains of MARY, the wife of Robert Owen, bookseller ; she died December 7th, 1852, aged 53 years. ROBERT OWEN, born February 4th, 1799, died April 6th, 1866. ELIZABETH, daughter of Robert and Mary Owen, born July 11th, 1831, died September 30th, 1875.

Table monument—
In memory of ELIZABETH, wife of Pryce Owen, of this town, late bookseller, who died March 23rd, 1841, aged 66 years. In memory of THOMAS, son of Pryce and Elizabeth Owen ; he died January 3rd, 1854, in the 45th year of his age. In memory of PRYCE OWEN, who departed this life August 2nd, 1857, aged 84 years.

On tomb stones—
Here lie the remains of SAMUEL POWELL, currier, late of this town, who departed this life October 11th, 1809, aged 61 years. Also, underneath this stone lieth the remains of JANE POWELL, the daughter of Samuel and Elizabeth Powell, who departed this life November 1st, 1821, aged 41 years. Sacred to the memory of JAMES POWELL, who departed this life February 5th, 1829, aged 51 years. Sacred to the memory of MATTHEW POWELL, who departed this life July 1st, 1819, aged 31 years. Also, of ELIZABETH POWELL, relict of Samuel Powell, who departed this life November 10th, 1838, aged 86 years.

Sacred to the memory of RICHARD POWELL, Officer of Excise, who departed this life, May 28th, 1827, aged 75 years. Sacred to the memory of THOMAS POWELL, late of Pool, Gentleman, who died the 1st of April 1817, aged 72 years. Also, of JANE, relict of the above named Thomas Powell, who died the 2nd of August 1817, aged 74 years. Sacred to the memory of WILLIAM POWELL, son of Thomas and Jane his wife, who departed this life April 28th, 1812, aged 27 years. Underneath lieth the remains of SAMUEL POWELL, currier, late of this town, who departed this life, July 3rd, 1843, aged 67 years. Also underneath this stone lieth the remains of THOMAS POWELL, who died January 11th, 1864, aged 85 years. In memory of ELIZABETH POWELL, who died August 28th, 1870, aged 80 years. In memory of JOANNA, daughter of Samuel and Joanna Powell, of the Gungrog cottage, who died July 16th, 1861, aged 15 years. Also, of ELIZABETH, eldest daughter of Samuel and Joanna Powell, and wife of William Jones, of Trade Hall in this town, who died July 14th, 1874, aged 30 years. CHARLES POWELL, died July 16th, 1878, aged 24 years.

Handsome stone monument—

In memory of EDWARD MORRIS, Belle vue, Welshpool, late of London house, who died May 29th, 1866, aged 69 years. In memory of MARY ANN, relict of Edward Morris, who died January 4th, 1880, aged 77 years.

Table tomb—

OLIVER JONES, departed this life August 6th, 1812, aged 61.

Small monument—

To the memory of WILLIAM COOK, Junr., who died November 26th, 1812, aged 79. To the memory of SUSANNAH COOK, died . . . . . 1813, aged 15. Also, of SUSANNAH COOK, (illegible).

Two monuments together surrounded with an iron pallisading. The first bears the following inscriptions:—

Underneath lie interred the bodies of JOHN WILLIAMS, who died the 10th day of January 1802, aged 74 years. JOHN MEREDITH WILLIAMS, only son of the above named John Williams, by Susannah, his wife, who died June 17th, 1806, aged 30 years. Also, to the memory of the Rev. JOHN MEREDITH WILLIAMS, of Plas Dolanog, in this County, who died August 31st, 1855, aged 50 years.

The other bears the following—

SUSANNAH, wife of the above named John Williams, who died the 30th day of May 1810, aged 73 years. MARGARETTA MEREDITH, only sister to the above named Susannah Williams, who died the 6th day of June 1811, aged 82 years.

A headstone—
In memory of THOMAS BRADLEY, who died 29th of May 1822, aged 82 years.

A monument surrounded by iron railings—
Sacred to the memory of ELIZABETH, relict of John Moore, late of Crediton, Devon, Gent., who departed this life the 21st of May, 1813, aged 82 years. Also, in memory of ANN, wife of P. L. Serph, who died December 14th, 1837, aged 68 years.

Stone—
In memory of THOMAS BOWEN, who died 9th January, aged 81; SARAH, his wife, who died 5th February 1791; and ELIZABETH, his wife, who died July 1822. PRYCE BOWEN, died December 5th, 1846, aged 85 years.

Monument with pallisading—
In this vault are deposited the remains of ELIZABETH, relict of the late Gilbert Ross, Esq., of this town, who departed this life August 16th, 1825, aged 66. "There's rest in Heaven."
Sacred to the memory of EDWARD PARRY, late of Severn Cottage, who departed this life February 25th, 1825, aged 63. Also, in memory of DAVID PARRY, late of Severn Cottage, who departed this life September 29th, 1856, aged 85 years. Also, of ANN PARRY, daughter of the late John Parry of Leighton Hall, who died 23rd January 1836, aged 49 years. Deservedly loved and universally regretted.

Flat stones—
Here lyeth the body of JOHN COLLEY, Gentleman, who departed this life the 27th day of May 1752, aged 42 years on the 9th September 1751. Here also lyeth the body of JOHN STEPHEN, of Berth ddu, Gent., brother-in-law to the above said John Colley, who departed this life the 31st day of July 1768, in the 51st year of his age.

Head stone—
In memory of RICHARD SAMUEL, who died December 4th, 1811, aged 55 years. MARY SAMUEL, died December 2nd, 1847, aged 102. RICHARD DAVIES, died March 25th, 1824, aged 40. ELIZABETH DAVIES, died March 23rd, 1861, aged 73. All the above were of Welshpool.

Table monument—
In memory of JOHN NEWELL, late of Severn street in this town, who died 24th February 1846, aged 76 years.

308 WELSH POOL.

Head stone—
ADAM BRAY, died November the 19th, 1801, aged 46.

The Communion Plate—1. The Golden Chalice was presented to the Church by Thomas Davies, Esq., in 1662. It bears the following Latin inscription :—

" Thomas Davies, Anglorum in Africæ plagâ occidentali Procurator generalis ob vitam multifariâ Dei misericordiâ ibidem conservatam CALICEM hunc é purissimo auro Guiniano conflatum (*a*), Dei honori et ecclesiæ de Welshpoole ministerio perpetuo sacrum voluit. A quo usu SS. si quis facinorosus eundem Calicem in posterum alienaret (quod avertat Deus) Dei vindicis supremo tribunali pænas luat. Cal. Apr. ix, MDCLXII."

The chalice is stated to be of the value of £168 sterling. In a printed copy of the inscription in several books, between the words "conflatum" and "Dei," at *(a)* the following words have been interpolated :—" clxviii minis valentem." This interpolation probably is the

authority for the value of the chalice. It appears to be of pure gold. It weighs between 30 and 31 ounces, which at £3 17s. 10½d. per ounce (the present standard of value) would give a little more than £120 as the present value of the gold of which it is composed. The cost of the workmanship would add considerably to its value. It is 9½ inches in height, and 4½ inches in its broadest part. It is kept in a curious brass case, which probable formed part of the original gift. A shield of arms is engraved upon it, bearing the following charges: "A lion passant between three fleurs-de-lis", and surmounted with a plume of feathers. "*Ar.*, a lion pass., *sable*, between three fleurs-de-lis, *gu.*," are the armorial bearings, it seems, of the family of Davies of Kynant, as well as of several leading families in Montgomeryshire—Pugh of Mathafarn ; Pryce of Gunley ; and several others.

The identity of the munificent donor, Thomas Davies, has been established in a singular manner. Some years ago a gentleman noticed in the parish church of Lathbury, Newport Pagnell, Buckinghamshire, a brass plate on which there was an inscription to the memory of a Montgomeryshire man, and in which there was a reference to a monument in Welshpool church. Thinking it might be of interest to the Vicar of Welshpool, the gentleman forwarded a rubbing of the inscription to Archdeacon Clive, the then Vicar, who preserved it by pasting it on the cover of one of the Registers. The following is a copy of the rubbing, which speaks for itself.

A shield, a lion passant between three fleurs-de-lis, impaling a lion rampant crowned—

RICHARD DAVIES OF KYNANT, IN THE COUNTY OF MONTGOMERY,
GENT., HEERVNDER BURIED, HEE DECEASED AT THE
HOWSE OF HIS
SON, ISAIAH DAVIES, THEN MINISTER OF THIS PARISH, 20TH DAY
NOVEMBER 1661, AGED 77 YEARES.
HIS SON THOMAS DAVIES, ESQUIRE, AT THAT TIME BEING AGENT GENERALL
FOR THE ENGLISH NATION VPON THE COAST OF AFRICA,
CAVSED A CŒNOTAPH TO BE ERECTED IN THE CHURCH OF
WELSHPOOLE, THE PLACE OF HIS BIRTH, TO THE PIOUS MEMORY
OF HIS FATHER, AND THIS SMALL MEMORIALL FOR SUCH CAMBRIA-
BRITTAINES AS SHALL THIS WAY TRAVAILE.

The cœnotaph is not now in the Church of Welshpool.

2. *A Large Silver Christening Bowl*, now used as an Alms Dish. It bears the following inscription :—

310 WELSH POOL.

The gift of John Edmunds Esq., Chief Bailiff of the Ancient Borough of Welshpoole, in the County of Montgomery, to the Parish of Welshpoole, 1773.

THE CORPORATION SEAL OF

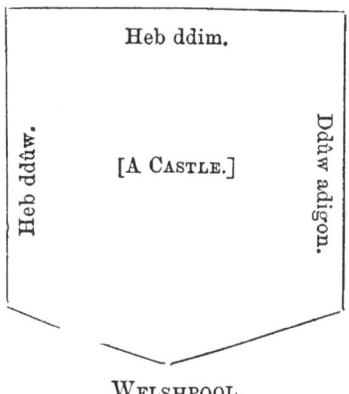

```
┌─────────────────────────┐
│       Heb ddim.         │
│                         │
│ Heb ddŵw.  [A CASTLE.]  Ddŵw adigon. │
│                         │
└──────┐           ┌──────┘
       └───────────┘
```

WELSHPOOL.

John Edmunds was the great-grandfather of Richard John Edmunds, Esq., of Edderton, near Welshpool (where there is a portrait of him); and also of Elizabeth, the wife of Rev. Howel Evans, M.A., Vicar of Oswestry.

3. A Silver paten, inscribed—

A gift for the use of the Communion table to the parish church of Welshpoole, 1715. MARY EDMUNDS.

4. A smaller silver paten, inscribed—

Ecclesiae Paroch'li de Pola D.D., Gulielmus Clive, Vicar. Ann. Dom. MDCCCXLI.

5. A large silver flagon inscribed—

Hoc vas in sacrum hujus ecclesiæ usum dedicavit Johannes Pryce, A. M. Vicarius, Maii die Decimo, 1793.

6. A silver-gilt cup (not inscribed).

Catalogue of the Registers in the Parish Chest, Welshpool, in the year 1819.

	A.D.	A.D.
I. General, containing entries of Baptisms, Burials, and Marriages	from 1634	to 1701
The entries are not to be found	,, 1701	,, 1708

WELSH POOL. 311

II.	General	,,	1708 ,, 1736
III.	Contains Baptisms	,,	1736 ,, 1772
,,	Burials	,,	1736 ,, 1782
,,	Marriages	,,	1736 ,, 1751
IV.	Marriages	,,	1754 ,, 1781
V.	Baptisms	,,	1772 ,, 1812
VI.	Burials	,,	1782 ,, 1811
VII.	Burials	,,	1811 ,, 1812
VIII.	Marriages	,,	1782 ,, 1812
IX.	General Baptisms	,,	1813 ,, 1835
,,	Burials.	,,	1813 ,, 1842
,,	Marriages	,,	1813 ,, 1837

Made by W. Clive, vicar.

Continuation by Rev. J. E. Hill.

X.	Baptisms	,,	1836 ,, 1861
XI.	Baptisms	,,	1861
XII.	Burials	,,	1842 ,, 1858
XIII.	Burials	,,	1858 ,, 1872
XIV.	Burials	,,	1872
XV.	Marriages	,,	1837 ,, 1861
XVI.	Marriages	,,	1861

Bells.—At a vestry meeting held 22nd July 1783, it was ordered that the then present peal of bells be taken down and sent to the foundry to be melted down and recast, at the expense of the whole parish. There were originally but five bells. In 1791, six new bells, new cast, were placed in the tower. These were cast by Mr. Rudhall, who was paid nearly £300. They did not last long, for at a vestry meeting held on the 14th January 1814, the state of the bells was taken into consideration, three of which being cracked and useless, a subscription was set on foot for purchasing eight bells and for the sale of the present six bells to defray part of the expenses, and the Churchwardens were authorised to procure estimates and enter into a contract for a peal of eight bells. The sum of £284 16s. 6d., was collected, and the same is credited in the parish book as the subscription from sundry persons towards purchasing a peal of eight new bells for the parish church. The bells were cast by Meares of London, who received in exchange the old bells and the sum of £242 in cash. The carriage of the old bells to Salop, and of the new bells from Salop, cost £6 17s. 6d., and of the bell wheels from London £2 15s. 6d. By a memorandum on the cover of the Churchwardens' Book, it appears that on August 17th, 1824, the new bells were opened by the Shrewsbury, Chester, and Wrexham ringers, "first peal two hours and fifty minutes." There was a great to-do on the occasion, and considerable expense incurred, possibly to absorb the amount of subscriptions received. On 18th August 1824, £6 5s., was paid for the expenses of the ringers from Chester and Liverpool, and one from Salop; £5 for the travelling expenses of the Wrexham ringers, nine in number; and on the 21st August, John Jones, *Cross Keys*, was paid £9 6s. 6d. for entertaining the Wrexham ringers, and Mr. Whitehall (formerly of the *Oak Inn*), was paid £21 4s. 11d., for entertaining the ringers. One of the bells was recast in 1868. The following interesting inscriptions are moulded upon seven of the bells :—

1st Bell.
In sweetest sound let each its note reveal;
Mine shall be first to lead the dulcet peal.

2nd Bell.
In mazy changes cheer the landscape wide;
Court echo from the Park or Golva's side.

3rd Bell.
And will as sportive fancy counts them o'er,
Shall waft them far on Severn's fertile shore.

4th Bell.
When female virtue weds with manly worth,
We catch the rapture and spread it forth.

5th Bell.
Does battle rage, do sanguine foes contend,
We hail the victor, if he's Britain's friend.

6th Bell.
Hail, patriot George, for whom a nation prays,
That health and peace may crown thy latter days.

WELSH POOL. 313

7th Bell.
This was recast in 1868, and the couplet was not replaced upon it.
8th Bell.
May all whom I shall summon to the grave
The blessing of a well-spent life receive.

List of Rectors—
Circa 1290.—JOHN DE LA POLE, son of Prince Griffith ap Wenwynwyn.
Held *in commendam* by three Bishops of St. Asaph—Spridlington, Trevor, and Lowe.
1537.—Dr. MAGNUS. He was a foundling of Newark-uponTrent in Nottinghamshire, and had the surname of "Amongus" given to him, as being maintained by several people there; or some say, by certain Yorkshire clothiers, who occasionally travelled that way early in the morning, and first found him. Having taken a degree in some university abroad, and at length brought up in literature in one of the universities in England, he became so much noted to King Henry the Eighth, that he was by him not only promoted to several dignities but sent Ambassador to various countries. Among several embassies that he was employed in, was that into Scotland in 1524. Among the dignities he enjoyed were the Archdeaconry of the East Riding of York in 1504; the Sacristy of York Cathedral in the same year; a canonry in the Church of Windsor in 1520; the Mastership of St. Leonard's, York, etc. Among the benefices he had, were the rectories of Bedall in Yorkshire, Guilsfield, and Meifod. Towards the end he founded a free school in the place of his nativity, which he well endowed.

List of Vicars—
1289.—GRIFFITH FITZ EDENWETH.—He is mentioned in the Award of Bishop Swinfield, dated 26 July 1289 (see *supra*, p. 259). He must then have been recently appointed Vicar, for in 1319, "in Septimana Pentecostes", Griffith Vicar " de la Pole", was one of the witnesses examined in the Inquisition *post-mortem* of Griffith, son and heir of William de la Pole, and stated that he was then of the age of sixty years, and that Griffith, son of William de la Pole, was of the age of twenty-nine years, and that he (Griffith Vicar de la Pole) knew this, because he was then parochial chaplain in the

[1] Williams's *Eminent Welshmen*, p. 342.

church of Mallwyd, and baptized the same Griffith, and thus knew his age (*Mont. Coll.*, vol. i, p. 176).

1531.—JOHN LLOYD. Collated by Bishop Standish. ? Vicar also of Guilsfield.

1571.—J. PIERS by T. Davies.

ROBERT CAMMIS.

1575.—WILLIAM MORGAN, A.M., by Hughes. "That imcomparable man for piety and industry, zeal for religion and his country, and a conscientious care of his church and succession, was born at a place called Gwibernant, in the parish of Penmachno, and County of Carnarvon. He was educated at St. John's College, Cambridge, and his first preferment was the Vicarage of Welshpool, to which he was instituted August 8th, 1575. After a residence there of three years he was removed to the Vicarage of Llanrhaiadr yn Mochnant, in Denbighshire, where he finished his great undertaking of translating the Bible into the Welsh language. His original intention was to translate the Pentateuch only, but in consequence of a dispute with his parishioners at Llanrhaiadr,[1] he was obliged to attend Whitgift, Archbishop of Canterbury, at Lambeth. This prelate conceived a high opinion of his abilities, and appointed him his chaplain, and prevailed upon him to undertake the translation of the whole of the Bible into Welsh. About the year 1587, he went to London for the purpose of consigning the work to the press, and for the year during which he was engaged in superintending the printing, he resided with Dr. Gabriel Goodman, Dean of Westminster, of whose hospitality, as well as his general kindness on this occasion, he speaks in terms of the liveliest gratitude in the dedication affixed to this work. This was the first translation of the entire Bible into Welsh, and was published in 1588 in folio. In the same year he was presented to the rectory of Llanfyllin, and also to the sinecure rectory of Pennant Melangell. And in 1504, the sinecure of Denbigh was added to his other preferments. His eminent zeal and learning were at length rewarded by his elevation to the bishopric of Llandaff, to which he was consecrated in 1595, at the express command of Queen Elizabeth. He was translated to St. Asaph in September 1601, and he died there September 10th, 1604, and was interred on the following day in the Cathedral, without any inscription or monument to mark the place of interment."

---

[1] It is said that when they found he was engaged upon the work of translation they complained to the Archbishop of his incompetency for the task.—Thomas's *St. Asaph*, p. 89.

1579.—HUGH DAVIES, Rector of Llanwrin 1562 ; Rector of Llanerfyl 1571 ; Sinecure, Pennant 1577.

1600.—THOMAS KYFFIN, Vicar of Whitford, 1601 ; Vicar of Berriew, and Canon in 1608, and Prebendary of Myfod in 1614. He was a younger son of Richard Kyffin of Glasgoed. He built the vicarage house at Berriew, as appears by the initials of his name (T. K.) and the year (1616), over the hall door. He died in 1622. (*Cambro-Briton*, vol. i, p. 384.)

1622.—RICHARD EVANS, A.M., collated by Bishop Parry, Vicar of Llanrwst, 1618 ; Vicar of Tremeichion, 1619 ; Prebendary, Meifod, 1621 ; Rector, Halkin, 1626 ; Vicar of Llanasa, 1633. Was for fourteen years under sequestration whilst Vicar of Llanasa. (Thomas's *St. Asaph*, p. 104).

1626.—HUMPHREY PENRHYN, collated by Bishop Hanmer.

1632.—WILLIAM LANGFORD, A.M., collated by Bishop Owen, Master of Ruthin School 1626-8 ; Rector of Hen Eglwys 1630 ; Rector of Llanerfyl 1637; Canon 1639 ; Sinecure Rector of Llanfor 1644. For an account of him whilst Vicar of Welshpool see *Montgomeryshire Collections*, vol. xiii, pp. 258-262. A tablet (unfixed) to his memory is in Welshpool Church. See his Monumental Inscription, *supra*, page 295.

1668.—SAMUEL DAVIES, LL.D., collated by Bishop Glenham, Vicar of Guilsfield 1670; Canon 1677 ; Prebendary of Meifod 1685. He was buried in Welshpool Church. See his Monumental Inscription, *supra*, page 299.

1694.—WILLIAM WYNN, collated by Bishop Jones. There is a Latin monumental inscription to his memory in Welshpool Church. See *supra*, page 298.

1697.—JOHN HARDING, M.A., Vicar of Chirbury, where he resided.

1735.—WILLIAM JAMES.

1747.—WILLIAM MORGAN, M.A., collated by Bishop Lisle ; resided for most part in Brecknockshire.

1772.— JOHN PRYCE, M.A., collated by Bishop Shipley,—of Gunley, Fellow of Pembroke College, Oxford (see *Mont. Coll.*, vol. xiv, p. 210). He presented a large silver flagon for the use of the church.

1809.—HENRY JONES WILLIAMS.—At a vestry meeting held 26th June 1825, a committee was appointed "with a request that they should obtain an estimate of the expense of a tablet and a suitable inscription to be put up in the church, and report the same at a future meeting". No report is recorded, nor is there any tablet now in the church.

1819.—WILLIAM CLIVE, M.A., Vicar of Montford, Salop, 1831 ; Archdeacon of Montgomery 1844 ; Hon. Canon 1849 ;

Residentiary Canon 1854; resigned 1861; Rector of Blymhill, diocese of Lichfield, 1865; Rural Dean of Brewood. He was a nephew of Robert Lord Clive, who died in 1775. During his incumbency many improvements were made in the church. In 1819 national schools were built at a cost of £250, exclusive of grants. In 1825 and 1826 £1,500 was laid out on the church, increasing the accommodation by 300 free sittings. In 1838 the Belan school was built at a cost of £307. In 1856 the chancel was rebuilt by the impropriate rectors at a large cost (probably £1,000 or more), and a new east window of stained glass inserted by public subscription, and a chancel arch was built by the parish at an expense of £80. Christ Church was built at a cost of £6,000. The Vicarage house was also rebuilt at his own expense. He also presented to the church a small silver paten. The total expenditure on these matters relating to the church establishment and educational purposes very considerably exceeded the sum of ten thousand pounds during Archdeacon Clive's long incumbency of forty-five years.

1865.—JOHN EDWARD HILL, M.A., collated by Bishop Short, Curate of Ashburton 1848-50; Welshpool 1850-1865. In 1871, during his incumbency, the parish church was restored at a cost of not less than £5000, including the various costly gifts of reredos, pulpit, and church furniture; and two stained glass windows were put in, as memorial windows, at a cost of £500.

Table of Benefactions in the Porch of the Church [on panels].

1. Arthur Blainey, Esq., gave the sum of Twenty pounds....
Mr. Kynaston gave the sum of Twenty pounds.....
The Rev. J. Pryce, Vicar, gave the sum of five pounds five shillings, a subscription towards the rebuilding of this church.
The Corporation of Pool gave the sum of one hundred pounds.
Mr. David Pugh gave the sum of Twenty pounds.

2. John Edmunds, Esq., Chief Bailiff of this borough, presented the parish with a handsome Christening Bowl, Anno Domini 1773.

3. The Rev. J. Pryce, Vicar of this parish, presented an elegant Silver Flagon as an addition to the Communion service, Anno Dom. 1793.

4. The Right Honourable Lord Viscount Clive presented an elegant* Organ to the parishioners of this parish, opened on the Nativity of our Saviour, 1813.

6. Elijah Phillips, gent., bequeathed the sum of £100 to be laid

out at interest or invested in lands, and the interest and rents thereof to be distributed amongst the poor of this parish on the first day of January yearly for ever in money by the vicar and churchwardens for the time being. Rd. Tudor, Jno. Briscoe, trustees.

7. Richard Tudor, gent., bequeathed to the parish of Pool the interest of one hundred pounds to be paid yearly to the Master of this Church School for teaching ten poor boys, natives of and poor inhabitants in the town of Pool.

N.B.—The vicar for the time being is trustee for these legacies.

8. Richard Tudor, gent., also bequeathed the interest of 40 pounds yearly to a petty schoolmaster or mistress for teaching 10 poor boys and girls, natives and inhabitants of the said town of Pool.

Also the interest on 80 pounds yearly for apprenticing out one poor boy, a native and inhabitant of the aforesaid town of Pool.

9. Richard Tudor also bequeathed the interest on 50 pounds to be given on St. Thomas's Day yearly for ever to such poor as are of and chargeable to the middle division of Pool, excepting the sum of ten shillings, which is to be distributed by the churchwardens amongst the poor of the upper and lower divisions of the parish of Pool.

10. Thomas Davies, gent., gave a Chalice of pure gold for the use of the Communion, A.D. 1662.

Mrs. Mary Edmunds also gave for the use of the Communion one Silver Salver and a Damask Cloth, A.D. 1715.

11. Lord Viscount Hereford gave to this church an elegant pair of Chandeliers.

Clopton Phrys, Esq., gave a handsome Pulpit.

Price Jones, Esq., gave a new Bible and Common Prayer, A.D. 1776.

12. Richard Edmunds, Esq., of the Exchequer of Pleas London, gave to his native parish the Royal Arms which adorn this church A.D. 1802.

13. Richard Edmunds, Esq., also gave a handsome Dial Plate placed on a pedestal south of this church, A.D. 1810.

14. The Rt. Hon. the Earl of Powis gave the sum of £100. Wm. Mostyn Owen, Esq., the sum of £30, A.D. 1775.

15. Small panel with old royal arms thereon, 1778.

16. Sir Watkin Williams Wynn, Baronet, gave the sum of £100. John Chichester, Esq., the sum of £31 10s., A.D. 1775.

17. David Pugh, Esq., of Llanerchydol, by a liberal donation defrayed the entire expense of extending the gallery for the accommodation of the Welshpool choir, A.D. 1818.

18. Thomas Langford, gent., bequeathed to this parish the sum of four pounds for clothing of eight poor old industrious persons with shoes, stockings, and whitecloth coats, to be given on the first Sunday in November yearly, under the direction of Henry Wynne, Esq., and Henry Parry, clerk, their heirs and assignees for ever trustees for the same.

19. Edward Parry, gent., bequeathed to the Vicar and Churchwardens of the middle division of Pool the sum of 170 pounds in trust, to be laid out in good security, or vested in lands, and that the interest of £100 thereof to be paid to the Chief Master of this Church School for teaching eight poor boys, natives of this town, to read and write.

20. Mr. Edward Parry also left seventy pounds, part of the aforesaid £170, the interest thereof to be laid out yearly in purchasing 6 upper garments for six poor persons having a legal settlement in the middle division of the parish of Pool yearly for ever. A.D. 1770.

21. Jos. Pursell, gent., bequeathed to the Vicar and Churchwardens of the middle division of the parish of Pool the sum of fifty pounds, to be placed out at interest, the produce thereof to be paid yearly on New Year's Day for ever to such poor persons as have legal settlements in the said division.

22. Miss Elizabeth Lloyd, Spinster of the parish of Guilsfield, bequeathed to the Vicar and Churchwardens of the parish of Pool and their successors for the time being the interest on £90 to be distributed in bread in the following manner, viz.: That is amongst such of the said poor as shall be most religious and shall most frequently attend divine service, and who shall be found attending the same on the first Sunday in Advent, Christmas Day, New Year's Day, the first Sunday in Lent, Good Friday, Ascension Day, and the first Sunday in August for ever.

In the years 1855 and 1857, Thomas Lloyd Dickin, Esq., of Welshpool, and his sister, Sarah Dickin, bequeathed £150 each, which, under their wills and an order of the County Court, is vested in the Vicar and Churchwardens for the time being, and John Buckley Williams, Esq., or his successor, owner of certain estates, and the interest laid out annually at their discretion for the benefit of the poor belonging to or resident in the parish.

CHARITIES OF WELSHPOOL.

The Burgesses' Land.—John de Cherleton, Lord of Powys, by his charter bearing date 17 Edward II,[1] confirmed to his beloved burgesses of the community of the town of Pool, common of pasture daily for their cattle of all kinds in certain lands "which Lord Owen, son of Lord Gruffith ap Gwenwynwyn of famous memory, his predecessor, had perambulated for the use and profit of the said burgesses." The bounds are defined by the charter, and were nearly adjoining the town, and bounded on one side by the churchyard.

[1] *Mont. Coll.*, vii, p. 335.

The land continued an open field or common from that time until the year 1761, when an Act for enclosing the same was obtained.[1] One tenth was allotted to the then Lord of Powis, and the remainder to the Bailiffs, Aldermen, and Burgesses, who had power given them to lease for twenty-one years.

The Act enacts—

That the clear rents of the lands, allotted to the Corporation of Pool should in the first place be applied towards building, repairing, beautifying, enlarging, and maintaining in good condition and repair the public edifices belonging to the said Borough and Corporation of Pool (which were greatly gone to decay), and the surplus of such rents and profits, after answering the purposes aforesaid, should be paid and applied from time to time for the benefit and relief of the poor and distressed burgesses of the said Borough of Poole, in such manner as the Bailiffs, Aldermen, and Burgesses, and their successors for the time being should order or appoint.

At the time of the Charity Commissioners' Report (1838), the land is stated thereby to consist of eleven fields and a small wood, total quantity being seventy-five acres, and the total income £136 15s. per annum. But in 1863, when the Smithfield was formed, certain exchanges were made with the Earl of Powis.

In 1864, the following was the rental of the property—

No.	Tenant.	Holding.	Quantity. A. R. P.	Year's Rent.
1	Rich. Goolden	Ceunant Croft	... ...	Conveyed in exchange to the Earl of Powis
2	Wm. Rowlands	Little Ceunant Croft	3 0 27	£12
3	Do.	Further Ceunant Croft	4 1 24	£16 10s.
4	Do.	Gwernygo	... ...	Conveyed in exchange to Earl of Powis
5	Richard Owen	Coedywlad Piece	10 1 24	£18
6	Thos. Morris	Hill Field	6 3 6	£21
7	Do.	North Corner Piece	8 3 27	£13 10s.
8	Do.	East Corner Piece	12 1 28	£31
9	Do.	Quarry Piece	7 3 22	£25
10	Thos. Dudley	South Corner Piece	10 0 38	£26 4s.
11	William Withy	Hither Croft	2 0 10	£5
12	Smithfield and Approaches	... ...	5 1 9	£28 10s. conveyed to Corporation in exchange by Earl of [Powis
			71 2 15	£196 14s.

[1] See *Mont. Coll.*, vol. xii, p. 268.

According to the last (1881) printed account of the corporation accounts the rental appears to be £243 6s.

Between 1846 and 1877 various sums, amounting to £19,000, have been borrowed by the corporation on security of the " Corporation Town Hall and tolls", " Smithfield and the corporation land", " portion of the Town Hall lands, rents, and rates, etc.;" and the same have been applied "in erecting the Assize Courts", " erection of the Smithfield", and " the erection of the Town Hall and market", and are redeemable by a sinking fund, for providing which £2,171 4s. 10d. has been laid out in consols. It will take a long time to redeem this large sum of money. Whether the corporation were justified in attempting, or had power to postpone, the rights of the " poor burgesses", by mortgaging the fee simple of the charity lands, is a matter into which we shall not enter.

The last sum that was disbursed amongst the poor burgesses out of the surplus of the rents was £20, in January 1824. But the Charity Commissioners add, " there will be no distribution for the future until the debts are paid"; an event which is in the distant future.

Tudor and Parry's Charities and the Church School.
—The first story over the church porch was at one time used as a school room. The first mention of it that we have found is an entry in the Churchwardens' book under the date of 18 February 1774, when it was ordered (*inter alia*) " that the walls of the porch be sufficiently raised, and that there be made a door leading out of the porch into the middle of the south aisle, and *that proper windows be fixed in the school room."*

It is not easy to determine whether the school room was then formed by raising the roof of the porch, or whether only new windows were to be fixed in a school room already existing; perhaps the latter may be the more probable, as the church school was in existence in 1770.

About 1770, Edward Parry bequeathèd to the Vicar

and Churchwardens of the middle division of Welshpool £170; the interest on £100 to be paid to the chief master of the Church School for teaching eight poor boys, natives of the town, to read and write; and the interest on £70, the remaining part thereof, to be laid out yearly in purchasing six upper garments for six poor persons having a legal settlement in the middle division of the parish of Pool, yearly for ever. It appears, also, that Richard Tudor, by his will (the date unknown), gave the sum of £100 to be laid out at interest, the same to be given to the schoolmaster who should, for the time being, teach a grammar or Latin school, in the church school of the parish of Pool, for teaching ten boys, natives of Pool; and, if there were no such schoolmaster, the legacy was to go to the testator's nephew, Richard Tudor.

Richard Tudor is a name that occurs in the list of bailiffs of Welshpool not less than four times in the eighteenth century, viz., in 1718, 1730, 1749, and in 1796.[1] It may be conjectured that the testator was the bailiff of the first three periods, and the nephew the bailiff of the last period. If this conjecture be correct, the date of the will may be in the last half of the century, and the school probably in existence for some time previously.

In 1797, there was some dispute about the appointment of the schoolmaster, and the vicar's rights in the matter were ignored, and the vicar appealed to the bishop. In that year there is a letter extant from Dean Shipley to the vicar, in which the dean says, that he had read over his papers with the bishop, and as it did not appear that he (the vicar) was invested with any positive authority to appoint a schoolmaster, and as the will seemed to imply that he was not one of the trustees (whoever they might be), for in the latter part it mentioned "the trustees or overseers", and "the vicar or curate", clearly distinguishing the two latter from the former, and as the parish had hitherto

[1] *Mont. Coll.*, xii, p. 318.

submitted to his (the vicar's) appointment of a master, they were of opinion that it would be most prudent in him to coincide in their choice in the present instance. Should they be so blind to their own interest as to appoint an immoral or otherwise unjustly exceptionable man, he would have his remedy against them.

There was a poetical schoolmaster in Welshpool in 1795 (see *Mont. Coll.*, xiv, p. 207) who may have been the person whose appointment had been contested with the vicar, between whom and the parishioners at that time there was a bad feeling, which came to a violent crisis in 1799.

About 1815-20 William Owen, an able poet and an excellent schoolmaster, kept the school for some time in the school-room over the porch of the church. The father of Mr. Richard Williams was in school with him there. William Owen afterwards removed to Newtown. He was an accomplished musician and was a native of Carnarvonshire, and a Calvinistic Methodist.[1]

Francis Bray kept the school for some time, and on his death the scholars were transferred to the school of his brother, Job Bray, which was held in Stanley Street; the charity scholars were placed in a part of the school room apart from Job Bray's private pupils. Job Bray during the life of his brother Francis, kept a school in Church Street, adjoining a blacksmith's shop which formerly stood at the corner near the church steps. The house in which Job Bray lived is now occupied by Mr. William Jones.[2]

On the 19th March 1824, it appears by the parish books that the school room was then ordered to be removed from the parish church, and it was determined either to build or hire a school room.

The Charity Commissioners' Report in 1838 states that there had been no school held in the church, so as to constitute a church school, for many years, in consequence of the church having been enlarged. It had been customary to hire a room wherein the school was

[1] *Ex inf.* Mr. R. Williams.   [2] *Ex inf.* Mr. S. Powell.

held, and the rent, amounting to £6 per annum, was paid out of the church rates. The school, at the time of the investigation, was closed in consequence of the schoolmaster having absconded, and it was submitted by the minister and churchwardens whether the interest of the legacies left for the purposes of education could not be paid to the master of the national school on condition of his teaching gratis the required number of children. Under the circumstances, it seemed to the Commissioners no better course could be pursued. Neither grammar nor Latin had been taught in the church school for nearly fifty years, the education had consisted of reading, writing, and arithmetic. The interest of £40 was paid to a schoolmistress (who kept a petty school), for which she taught ten young children of the Middle Division in reading.

The interest of £80 was annually employed towards apprenticing one boy of the town of Welshpool; the selection was made by the Vicar from the elder boys in the school. The interest of the £50 was distributed, with other charities, on New Year's Day. The funds were disbursed by the parish authorities in the best way they could for the purposes of the charity; but, in 1837, the matter was submitted to the Charity Commissioners. By a letter dated 6 June 1837, the Charity Commissioners, by their clerk, stated that

"The state of the Church School at Welshpool, and the gift of Richard Tudor and Edward Parry to the schoolmaster, had been laid before the Commissioners, and that under the circumstances they saw no objection to the course proposed to be pursued of paying the interest of the benefactions (so long, at least as the Church School is suspended), to the master of the National School, on the condition of his teaching gratis the number of children required by the Will of Tudor."

This has since been done.

Pursell's Charity.—Joseph Pursell, gentleman, bequeathed to the Vicar and Churchwardens of the Middle Division of the parish of Pool, the sum of £50, to be placed out at interest, and the produce to be paid yearly on New Year's Day, to such persons as had a legal settlement in the Division.

Philip's Charity.—Elijah Philip, gentleman, by will, date unknown, bequeathed the sum of £100, the interest to be distributed amongst the poor of the parish on the 1st of January yearly in money, by the Vicar and Churchwardens for the time being. The £100 was laid out in the purchase of a farm situate in the parish of Llanfihangel, called Gwnfa, and conveyed to the churchwardens in 1755. It consists of a small farmhouse and about thirty-one acres of land. In 1797 the farm was leased by the Vicar and Churchwardens to Edward and John Parry for seven years, at the yearly rent of £8 8s. It is described in the lease as a barn, stable, cowhouse, and lands, then occupied by John Davies. It was then let at £10, but has subsequently been let at £13, per annum, so that it produces a good return for the capital invested; but, on several occasions, costly repairs have had to be done. Previous to the 12th of January 1816 a considerable outlay had been made on the Gwnfa farm, which it was determined should be reimbursed to the parish out of the annual rent; £5 annually only being given to the poor every New Year's Day until the whole debt was paid. In April 1846 a sum of £83 10s. 1d. was authorised to be paid, £75 out of the rates, and £8 10s. 1d. out of the church alms; the £75 was repaid by instalments out of the rents.

In 1842, Thomas Evans was tenant of the farm, and the Rev. R. Pughe, Rector of Llanfihangel, sent an estimate for the repairs of the building at £20, or, if rebuilt, £50.

In 1876, with the consent of the Charity Commissioners, the Vicar and Churchwardens gave notice to their tenant, John Evans, that the tenancy should remain unaffected by the Agricultural Holdings (England) Act 1875, which was acknowledged by the tenant..

Lloyd's Charity.—Elizabeth Lloyd, spinster, of the parish of Guilsfield, bequeathed to the Vicar and Churchwardens of the parish of Pool, and their successors for the time being, the interest on £90 to be distributed in bread among such of the poor as should be most religious, and should most frequently attend Divine Service, and should be found attending the same on the first Sunday in Advent, Christmas Day, New Year's Day, the first Sunday in Lent, Good Friday, Ascension Day, and the first Sunday in August, for ever.

At the time of the Charity Commissioners' Report (1838), the following is a summary of the charities given away in sums of money to the poor.

	£	s.	d.
Rent of Gwnfa Estate (Elijah Phillips's Charity)	10	0	0
Tudor's	2	5	0
Pursell's	2	10	0
Miss Lloyd's	4	10	0

The distribution of the above amounts was made on the 1st of January in the parish church by the Vicar, who was assisted by the Churchwardens and Overseers. It was given away in sums varying from 6d. to 2s. 6d., chiefly to the female parishioners. This mode of distribution was considered by the parish to be injurious, and they were advised to adopt some more beneficial arrangement.

On the 10th of November 1836 the Commissioners made a written recommendation:—

"That the distribution of the Charities belonging to Welshpool, which are given away by the Minister, Churchwardens, and Overseers in money, should in future be made in larger sums to worthy and deserving objects not receiving parochial relief, in order that the charity may be made a reward for good character, and not an inducement to dissipation."

The following is a summary of the charities, and of the mode in which they are now distributed:—

				£	s.	d.
Parry	£70	6 gowns, Mid. Division		2	16	0
Parry	100	National School		4	0	0
Tudor	100	Ditto		4	0	0
Carried forward	£270	Carried forward	£10	16	0

	£		£	s.	d.
Brought forward	270	Brought forward	10	16	0
Tudor	40	Dame's School (Infant)	1	12	0
Do.	80	Apprentice	3	4	0
Do.	50	Poor, New Year's Day ⎫			
Jos. Pursell	50	Ditto ⎬	16	16	0
Lloyd and Sarah Dickin	300	Ditto ⎭			
Balance from Church Alms	20	For Religious Poor who attend Church	3	12	0
Eliz. Lloyd	90				
	£900		£36	0	0

This £900 was placed on mortgage on freehold land, Sept. 1881.

Philip's £100 purchased a farm in Llanfihangel; rent (£12) distributed on New Year's Day.

Langford's Charity.—Thomas Langford, gent., bequeathed to the parish the sum of £4 for clothing eight poor industrious persons with shoes, stockings, and white cloth coats, to be given on the first Sunday in November, yearly. This charity has long been paid as a rent-charge on the Golfa estate in the parish of Welshpool, and has been usually distributed by the owner thereof.

By a document dated 28th June 1837, under the hands of five of the Charity Commissioners, which recited that:—

"It appeared that the property belonging to the Charity funded by Thomas Langford, for clothing eight poor persons with shoes, stockings, and white cloth coats, of the parish of Welshpool, consists only of one annuity not exceeding £50; that is to say, of one annuity, a rent-charge of £4, issuing out of the Golfa estate in Welshpool parish, then belonging to the Rev. Richard Pugh, and that there were no existing Trustees qualified to received the same."

The said Commissioners, in pursuance of the powers contained in the Act, empowered the resident Minister and the Churchwardens for the time being of the parish of Welshpool, to receive the said annuity and apply the same according to the purposes of the said charitable donation.

Lady Harriet Herbert's Memorial Charity. — In

1881 the sum of £312 10s. was raised by public subscription for "perpetuating the memory of the estimable qualities of the late Lady Harriet Herbert", the youngest daughter of Edward Herbert, Earl of Powis, K.G., and great granddaughter of Robert, Lord Clive, who died 21st June 1881, and the fund was vested in trustees upon the following trusts, viz., to invest the same, and to apply the income under the direction of the Earl of Powis, or his successor or successors for the time being, as the owner or owners of Powis Castle, and the Vicar and Mayor of Welshpool respectively for the time being, in money, fuel, clothing, medical and nursing aid, and food, or otherwise, for the relief of such cases of distress or need as they or any two of them in their discretion shall from time to time think fit.

Miss Charlotte Clive's Charity.—By her will, dated the 2nd July 1855, and a subsequent codicil, Miss Charlotte Clive (the sister of Archdeacon Clive) bequeathed to the Vicar and Churchwardens of Welshpool the sum of £200 (less legacy duty £20) upon trust to invest the same, and to apply the income, on the 1st day of January in each year, "either in clothing or in such other manner as her trustees should think most for the benefit of the poor residents in the said parish of Welshpool".

The said sums of £312 10s., and £180, and a further sum of £7 10s. (money in the hands of the Vicar and Churchwardens for charitable purposes), making together £500, were invested by them on mortgage of freehold property, by deed dated the 28th December 1881.

ABEYANT CHARITIES.

Jervis's Charity.—It is stated in an old benefaction table that Mrs. Ann Jervis (in 1741) left 20s. a year for the benefit of the poor housekeepers of Pool, payable out of an estate called David Mason's, which in 1838 belonged to Dr. Mytton, but the payment had been discontinued, probably, the Charity Commissioners say (but they give no authority for the statement), on the ground of its being void by the statute of mortmain.

On the 9th of January 1829 the matter was brought before the vestry, and it appeared, by a report laid before the meeting, that Dr. Mytton offered to permit any gentleman to inspect the writings in his possession relative to Mason's tenement, and to pay what should be justly due to the poor housekeepers of Pool from that property, with the legacy of Mrs. Ann Jervis. A professional man was appointed to see Mr. Mytton and to inspect the award in Guilsfield parish church, and any other documents which he may have tending to elucidate and establish the claim of the parish. There is no record of the result of the inquiry.

The Almshouse.—The Terrier of 1791 states that "there is an almshouse founded by the late Mr. Parry for eight poor persons, with the annual sum of 10s. each." The almshouse is situate near the west entrance to the churchyard, and consists of eight rooms, each of which is inhabited by an aged woman, who has been a decayed housekeeper; the selection being made by the Vicar. The repairs, up to the time of the Charity Commissioners' Report in 1838, had been paid by the parish out of the poors' rate. It is now (1882) not in a good state of repair, but very antiquated, and rather dilapidated.

By his will, dated 20th of April 1741, "Thomas Parry of Welshpoole, in the county of Montgomeryshire, gentleman, gave all his messuages and lands whatever in Gungrouge Fawre, Gungrouge Vechan, Dyserth, Llanverchidol, Tyddin Predd, Trallwn and Cletterwood, unto his son, Humphrey Parry, upon this special trust, that he pay within twelve months of his (testator's) decease, to the poore of the parish of Poole £50, to be laid out at interest by the said Humphrey Parry, the yearly interest to be paid to the most old and indigent poor of the said parish, always preferring those poor in the almshouse, and the charge of repairing the same yearly, which is first yearly to be deducted by the said Humphrey Parry." He mentions Humphrey, Mary and Jane, daughters of his son, Humphrey Parry; Elizabeth Parry and Catherine Parry, daughters of his son Thomas Parry; Edward Parry and Hector Parry, children of his son Edward Parry; Thomas Traunter his grandson; and his daughter Mary Traunter, widow.

The almshouse seems to have been in existence before the date of this will, and it does not appear who founded it. The statement in the Commissioners' Report that it was "founded by Mr. Parry", would lead to the inference that the testator founded it in his lifetime; but of this there is no evidence.

By his will dated 23rd May 1769, and proved at London 28th of July 1769, Humphrey Parry of the town of Llanfyllin, gent., gave his wife Mary a life interest in all his property in Montgomeryshire, and, after her decease, gave his property unto his two daughters, Mary Lloyd and Jane Griffiths, in tail; and, in default of issue, unto his grandson, Francis Dorsett, in fee. To him, also, he gave his property in Oswestry. The testator mentions Mary Lloyd; Jane Griffiths; his grandaughter Sydney Dorsett; his granddaughters, Mary Dorsett and Ursula Dorsett; and his granddaughter Blanche Dorsett. He ratified to the poor of Pool the £50 legacy bequeathed by his father, deducting only 10s. annually towards the repair of the almshouse; he gave residue to wife, who proved the will.

It seems probable that the endowment of £4 was the produce of the legacy left by Thomas Parry, but how it became so much as £4 is not known. The property belonging to the Parrys devolved upon their descendant, Mr. Humphrey Parry Dorsett.

At a vestry meeting of the Pool Lower Division on 9th February 1827, it was ordered that the almshouse near the church be whitewashed, and the front thereof be put in proper repair at the present time at the expense of this Division.

On 9th January 1829 Mr. Groom, one of the churchwardens, laid before the vestry the following letter from Mr. Matthew Griffiths, who appears to have been the tenant of the *Bull Inn*, Welshpool, under Mr. Humphrey Parry Dorsett, in answer to one addressed by Mr. Groom to him.

"Bishop's Castle, 7th Jan. 1829.

"DEAR SIR,—I received your letter this morning, and hereunder is the account in my book:—

			£	s.	d.
"1796. Jan. 1.	Paid 7 poor women in Almshouse 5s. each		1	15	0
„ Dec. 26.	Paid 8 poor women 5s. each		2	0	0
1797. April 15.	Paid 8 poor women 5s. each		2	0	0
„ Dec. 30.	Paid 8 poor women 5s. each		2	0	0
1798. April.	Paid 7 poor women 5s. each		1	15	0
„ Dec. 25.	Paid 7 poor women 5s. each		1	15	0
Easter, 1799.	Paid 7 poor women 5s. each		1	15	0

"The reason that 8 were paid and 7 were paid as far that I can recollect that dwelling must be void by the death of a poor woman. You will see by the dates that it was paid twice in each year. I was allowed what I paid out of my rent by Mr. Dorsett's agents. Any further information that I can give I beg you will command me, as I am always very sorry when I hear of a charity being abused or neglected. I am, dear sir, yours truly,

"MATTHEW GRIFFITHES.

"It must be due at Easter and Christmas."

On 4 June 1843, at a vestry meeting, it was ordered that, in the event of any future repairs being required for the almshouse, that a meeting of the three divisions of the parish be called for the purpose of ascertaining the amount of such required repairs, and to agree to the means of payment.

In the Charity Commissioners' Report of 1838, it is stated "that the payment of 10s. to each person inhabiting the almshouses had been discontinued since the year 1799, and it was stated to have been chargeable upon the *Bull* public-house in Welshpool. The last owner, Humphrey Parry Dorsett, allowed that amount to be deducted from the rent, but no reference is made to this rent-charge in the conveyance (dated 1804) to the present owner, Mr. William Jones of Welshpool, who, in consequence, had refused to continue the payment." The Commissioners, also, mention statements made with the view of showing that the sum of £4 was a voluntary payment of the Dorsett family, but the legacy shows that this was not really the case. It also states that the property, including the "*Bull Inn,* was advertised in the *Shrewsbury Chronicle* on the 7th December 1792 (the sale to take place on 3rd January 1793), but no mention was made there of any rent-charge on the estate."

The following is a copy of the advertisement which appeared in the *Shrewsbury Chronicle* of that date :—

MONTGOMERYSHIRE ESTATES.

To be Sold by Auction at the Royal Oak, in Pool, in the County of Montgomery, on Thursday the 3rd day of January 1793, in the following Lots. The Sale to begin at three o'clock.

Lot I.—The Bull Inn, in the Town of Pool, in the possession of Mr. Thomas Rogers, together with two small Dwellings adjoining, with Stabling for about thirty horses, a good Yard, and every convenience for carrying on the business of an Inn ; with five pieces of Land within a quarter of a mile of the said Inn, known by the names of Maes-yn-Gerrig, Cae-Nant-Gwyn, the Borfa-Greens, and Little-meadow, containing 16A. 1R. 2P.

Lot II.—Two Pieces of Land in the holding of the said Thomas Rogers, called the Clover Piece, and Evan Arthur's Piece, within half a mile of the Town of Poole, adjoining the Turnpike Road from Pool to Shrewsbury on the North, and the River Severn on the South, containing 6A. 1R. 14P.

Lot III.—A Piece of Land in the holding of the said Thomas Rogers, called the Lower-close-person, within a quarter of a mile of Poole, containing 4A. 1R. 15P.

Lot IV.—A Modern-Built House, with a good Garden, in the Centre of the Town of Pool, in possession of Mr. John Bromley.

Lot V.—A Dwelling-House and Two Stables, adjoining Lot the 4th, with a Garden and Orchard held therewith, in the possession of Mr. Thomas Morris.

Lot VI.—A Dwelling House adjoining Lot the 5th, in the possession of Mr. John Pugh, Ironmonger, with the Garden held therewith of nearly a quarter of an acre.

Lot VII.—Two Pieces of Pasture Land called Fron Llwyd, near the Turnpike Gate upon the Upper Road from Pool to Guilsfield, in the holding of Mr. John Pugh, containing 10A. 2R. 9P.

Lot VIII.—A Piece of Land, called Little Henfas-Gerrig, within a quarter of a mile of Pool, adjoining the Turnpike Road from Pool to Shrewsbury, containing 1A. 20P.

Lot IX.—A Tenement called the Blue Bell Farm, in the holding of Mr. Richard Edwards, consisting of a Farm House, Barn, with two Bays and Thrashing floor, a Cow-house, with six Pieces of Land adjoining, containing 13A. 2R. 38P.

Lot X.—A Croft in the holding of the said Richard Edwards, within a quarter of a mile of Pool, lying between Lot the 9th and the Turnpike Road to Guilsfield, containing 2R. 3P.

Lot XI.— A Piece of Meadow Land called Little Maes-y-Dentir, in the holding of Mrs. Lloyd, lying nearly adjoining the New Road from Pool to the Severn, within half a mile of Pool, containing 2A. 2R. 30P.

Lot XII.—Three Pieces of Pasture and Meadow Land in the holding of Mr. Joseph Morris, called the Meadows and the Dry-piece, situated upon the bank of the Severn, near Lot the 11th, containing 11A. 1R. 31P.

Lot XIII.—A Malt Kiln in the holding of the said Joseph Morris, situate near the Bridge in Lower Church Street.

Lot XIV.—A House and Garden in the holding of Mr. Samuel Turner, situate near the Bridge in Lower Church Street, adjoining Lot the 13th.

Lot XV.—A House and Garden adjoining Lot the 14th, in the holding of Mr. Jacob Humphreys.

Lot XVI.—A House and Garden in Upper Church Street, in the holding of Mr. Richard Samuel.

Lot XVII.—A House in the holding of Richard Morris, adjoining Lot the 14th.

Lot XVIII.—A House and Garden adjoining the Bridge in Upper Church Street, in the holding of Mr. Edward Lloyd.

Lot XIX.—A Garden adjoining the Church Yard, in the holding of Mr. John Williames, Attorney, containing 1R. 17P.

Lot XX.—An Orchard and Garden in the holding of Mr. Jacob Humphreys, containing 1A. 3R. 12P.

Lot XXI.—A Pew in the Middle Aisle, close to the Reading Desk, in the holding of Miss Vaughan.

Lot XXII.—A Pew in the same Aisle, near the Pulpit, in the holding of Mrs. Jones, Widow.

Lot XXIII.—A House, Barn, and Lands in Desert, in the holding of Thomas Hughes, late Austin's, containing 6A. 1R. 19P

Lot XXIV.—A House in two Dwellings and a Stable, in Buttington village, and three small Closes of Land, in the holding of Mr. Thomas Phipps, containing 2A. 11P., with Right of Common on the Long Mountain.

Lot XXV.—A House, Barn, Garden, and three small Pieces of Land, in the Township of Gungrog, in the holding of Tudor Edwards, containing 3A. 30P.

Lot XXVI.—A Farm House, Barn, and several Pieces of Land in the Parish of Buttington, adjoining the Turnpike Road from Pool to Shrewsbury, with a Right of Common upon the Long Mountain, in the occupation of Mr. Vaughan, of Gungrog, containing 17A. 1R. 36P.

Lot XXVII.—A Farm in Desert, in the holding of Mr. Arthur Pierce, containing 26A. 2R. 11P.

Lot XXVIII.—A Farm and Lands in Hope, in the holding of Mr. Thomas Jones, with a Sheep-walk upon the Long Mountain, containing 8A. 35P.

N.B.—Lots 1st, 4th, 5th, 6th, 9th, 14th, 15th, 16th, and 17th, have Pews in Pool Church belonging to them.

☞ For further Particulars apply to Mr. Arthur Davies, Surveyor; or to Mr. John Lloyd, Attorney, at Oswestry.

By a document dated 28th June 1837, under the hands and seals of the Charity Commissioners, after reciting that it appeared that the property belonging to the charity founded by —— Parry for eight poor persons in the Almshouse in Welshpool, consisted only of one annuity not exceeding £50, viz., an annuity of £4 issuing out of a public-house called the *Bull*, now belonging to Mr. Jones, and that there were no existing heirs qualified to receive the same, the Commissioners empowered the ministers and churchwardens to receive and apply the same according to the purposes of the said charitable donation. The Terrier of 1849 (*infra*, p. 343) states that part of the property was purchased by David Pugh, Esq., of Llanerchydol, upon which the annuity is supposed to have been charged, or upon the *Bull Inn*.

Humphrey Parry had three daughters, Mary Lloyd and Jane Griffiths (mentioned in his will), and Margaret, who married Francis Dorsett of Oswestry (a cousin of Francis Dorsett of Glascoed), who was in the profession of the law. He had probably two sons and three daughters. The sons were Francis Dorsett (mentioned in his grandfather, Humphrey Parry's will), and Humphrey Parry Dorsett, in whom, eventually, the Welshpool property ultimately vested, and who paid the annuity of £4 per annum up to the year 1799. Humphrey Parry Dorsett died without issue. His sister Mary was married to John Owen of Oswestry. John Owen had three sons, viz., John Owen of Broadway, who died without issue; George Dorsett Owen, who died 3rd November 1852 at Oswestry; and Charles Brown Owen. George Dorsett Owen has an eldest son, the Rev. John Maurice Dorsett Owen, M.A., Vicar of Holy Trinity, Bromley.

APPENDIX.

The following are three Terriers of the Parish in 1730 [*or* 1750 *or* 1760], 1791, *and* 1849.

A TERRIER of the buildings, glebe lands, tythes, etc., belonging to the Vicarage of Poole, in the Diocese of St. Asaph, Anno Dom. 1730.

A vicarage-house, containing one cellar, five ground-rooms, four rooms above stairs, one closet, one garret, one seat in the church; one barn containing three bays and a threshing floor; one stable with a little room adjoining; one garden; one orchard; one piece of glebe land adjoining to the north side of the churchyard, called the Croft, containing three acres or thereabouts; one piece of ground near the upper end of Poole Town, called the Vicar's Close, containing two acres or thereabouts; one small plot of ground, called the Vicar's garden, bounded on one side by Maes Gwestyd, on the other side by Maurice Jones's house, and butting on the street, containing about a quarter of an acre; One piece near Mr. Griffith Griffith's tan-house, called the Vicar's Close, containing about three-quarters of an acre; one small parcel in a piece of Mr. Thomas Parry's, called the Lower Close y Person, about the value of 5s. per year; such another parcel of the same value in the lands of Sir Charles Lloyd, shooting from the aforementioned parcel across the river Lledan, and extending itself in length from the said river to the high road that leads from Poole to Severn; one small parcel intermixt with Sir Charles Lloyd's lands in an inclosure called Erw Cant, about the value of one shilling and sixpence per year.

As to the tythes, one-fourth part of all within the parishes of Pool and Buttington is paid to the Vicar of Poole, excepting the demesne of Powis Castle, which claims a modus of two pounds per year, and Buttington Farm, which claims a modus at 17s. 6d. per year. The Abbey lands also refuse to pay tythes.

The repair of the Terrier of the Churchyard is as follows, viz., the stile-gate at the east end is repaired by the Vicar; the wall from thence down the south side to the greedle is repaired by the town part of the parish; the greedle-gates by His Grace the Duke of Powis; the wall from thence up the west to the partition hedge, being twenty yards in length, by the Township of Cyfronydd; the rails at the east end, from the Vicar's stile to the upper corner of the churchyard, commonly called the Judge's Hill, by the Township of Gyngrog Vawr. The remaining part of the fence is to be repaired by the Townships of Welshtown, Trefnant fechan, Llan y chidol, Dysarth, Stredal fedan, Tyddin prydd, and Trallwmgollen, share and share alike, according to the valuations of the several townships.

Witnesses.—John Harding, Vicar; William Evans, Curate; T. Pryce,[1] Vicar of Welshpool; F. Bromley,[1] Curate of Welshpool; Samuel Hodson;[2] Joseph Morris;[3] Richard Parry; the mark of × Emmanuel Jones,[4] Churchwardens.

This is a true copy of the original Terrier, faithfully compared and examined by

JOHN JONES, Deputy Registrar.

A TRUE TERRIER of all the glebe lands, messuages, tenements, tythes, portions of tythes, and other rights, belonging to the Vicarage and Parish Church of Welch Pool, in the county of Montgomery and Diocese of St. Asaph, now in the use and possession of the Rev. John Pryce there or his tenants, taken, made, and renewed, according to the Old Evidences and the knowledge of the antient inhabitants, at a Vestry holden this 15th day of July, pursuant to a due legal notice given in church on Sunday last for that purpose, and exhibited in the primary visitation of the Right Rev. Father in God, Lewis, Lord Bishop of St. Asaph, holden at Welchpool, 1791.

Imprimis, a Vicarage, built partly of brick and part of timber, lathe, plaister, and covered with tile, containing one cellar and five rooms below, viz., two parlours, a kitchen, pantry, and brewhouse, with four lodging-rooms, one storeroom, and one garret above, with a seat in the church next the desk, containing four sittings belonging to the said Vicarage House. *Item*, one timber barn containing one threshing floor and two bays, with a wood house, stable, and coach-house, and a small loft above all adjoining to the said barn, and under the same roof and covered with thatch, with a yard fenced in before the whole range of said building on the south side by pailing and quickset hedge. *Item*, one garden in the south side of the Vicarage House containing one rood and one perch,

---

[1] *Quere*, if the date was not 1750 or 1760, these two gentlemen were children in 1730, if even then born.

[2] Samuel Hodson ditto. He, in 1816, was a farmer in Montgomery.

[3] Joseph Morris lived at the *Sun Inn*.

[4] Emmanuel Jones lived at Coed y dinas.

with an orchard adjoining on the west side thereof, containing 34 perches, bounded by the river Lleyden on the west, and the Close Person on the south, the fence around them belonging to the Vicar to repair. *Item,* one small terras or courtyard on the north front of the said Vicarage is compass'd with a stone and brick wall abutting on the turnpike road, about thirteen yards long and eleven feet wide. *Item,* one small yard adjoining to the west end of the said Vicarage, with a pump therein.

The glebe lands are as follows :—*Imprimis,* one small parcel of land in a field of Mr. Dorsett's, late Mr. Parry's, of Welch Pool, called Maes y Dendas, adjoining to Close y Person, extending sixty yards or thereabouts in length down to the river Lleyden, and in breadth about seventeen yards, from the south ffence of the said Close y Person into the aforesaid field, as appears by the mere stones now fixed in the boundaries thereof; as also another parcel of land opposite the aforementioned, westerly extending itself from the said river Lleyden to the old high road, that formerly led from Pool to Severn, across a meadow called Maes y fellin, now belonging to the Earl of Powis, but lately the property of Mr. Joddrell and Sir Charles Lloyd, containing about half an acre, part of which is now cut through by the canal. *Item,* a parcel of land in the Henvais, in length about six hundred yards, and ten yards in breath, in an inclosure adjoining southward to Dommin Gastell meadow. *Item,* one parcel of land called the Vicar's Meadow, containing one acre and twenty-eight perches, bounded on the east by the tan-house yard, and orchard; on the south, by Thomas Griffiths' yard, and Mr. Stephen's lands by the Llundy meadows; on the west, by a meadow of the late Mr. Bromley's, now the property of the Earl of Powis; on the north, no part of the ditch, or fence around the said meadows, belongs to the Vicar to repair, or clear, except half of the ditch or watercourse on the north or east sides only within the said meadow; which meadow is now exchanged, with the consent of the Bishop, for land adjoining to Close y Person, and bounded on the east by a road to Dommin's Mill, and on the south by the canal. *Item,* one small plot of garden ground called the Vicar's Garden, bounded by Maes gwastett on the one side, on the other by Maurice Jones's house and the High street of Welshpool, containing twenty-six perches, with a sheep-fold and stands for cattle between it and the said street, on part of which ground is now erected by the Commissioners of the Turnpike a small house which they claim as their property. *Item,* one parcel of land at the upper end of the Town of Pool, containing two acres, two roods, and thirty-four perches, with a small plot of garden ground at the east end below, with a road or suffrance between the said close and garden to a piece of land belonging to Miss Davies, of Dyserth, the said road and garden containing together about one rood and three perches, the east and west end of the said close's fence are repaired by the Vicar, with the north upper end of the same, but the north lower side is repaired by the tenants of Dyserth, and all the south side by the late Mr. Palmer's tenants. *Item*, one parcel of land called the Vicar's Croft, adjoining to the north side of the churchyard, containing about three acres and nineteen perches, the ffence on the north and east side thereof are repaired by the Vicar, the west side by the several proprietors whose gardens and land are thereunto adjoining, except about ten yards next the churchyard stile, which is repaired by the Vicar, as a fence to a small plot of garden ground below, bounded on the south by Mr. Williams's garden, and on the east by the churchyard, containing about six perches, belonging to the Vicar.

As to the tithes, one fourth part of the tithe of hay and corn, with wool and lamb and all other small tithes whatsoever, throughout the parishes of Pool and Buttington, are paid in kind to the Vicar of Welshpool, except within the demesne only of Powis Castle, where they pay no wool and lamb or any small tithes, and throughout only the thirtieth part of hay and corn, whereof the Vicar hath the fourth, and receives forty shillings in money, but which forty shillings only they now pay and claim as a modus for the whole. Except also the demesne of Buttington Hall farm, where no wool or lamb is paid or any other small tithe, and they throughout the fortieth part of hay and corn (as appears in an ancient Terrier), whereof the Vicar hath a fourth part and receives seventeen and sixpence in money, which seventeen shilling and sixpence only they now pay and claim as a modus for the whole farm. As to the Easter dues, they are paid throughout the parishes of Pool and Buttington in the following manner, viz: tenpence from every married couple, and fivepence from every widow, and widower, and from every unmarried person above the age of sixteen, twopence, and of every tradesman twopence for his trade beside the sum above.

As to the Church, its repairs, fence, utensils, etc., they are as follows: the church is repaired by the parish in general, and the chancel by the Earl of Powis, as lessee of the great tithes belonging to Christ Church in Oxford. The fence of the churchyard is as follows, viz: the style and gate at the east end are repaired by the Vicar, and the wall from thence along the south side with the steps and so on to the greedle gate, are repaired by the town part of the parish, and the greedle gate by the Earl of Powis; and the wall from thence up the west side, being about twenty yards, by the township of Cyffronyth, and from thence up to the stile by the township of Trehelig, and from the stile along the north side called the Judges' Hill, by the several townships of Welshtown, Trefnant fechan, Llanerchidol, Dyserth, and Stredal vechan, Tyddin Prydd, Trallwm gollen, share and share alike: and from thence down the east side to the Vicar's stile by the township of Gungrog fawr. The books and utensils of the church are as follows, viz., one English Bible and Common Prayer, one Welch Bible and Common Prayer, one folio volume of the whole Duty of Man, two surplices, two velvet cushions for the pulpit, one green fringed cloth, one damask table cloth, with two napkins for the communion table, one solid gold cup containing one wine quart, weight thirty-four ounces, the gift of Thomas Davies, late of Pool; one silver cup guilt within and cover, weighing nineteen ounces and half; one silver salver for bread of brass [sic] metal, ditto two handsome brass chandeliers in the middle aisle the gift of the late Lord Viscount Hereford, two pair of small brass branches on the pulpit and desk the gift of John Owen, of Penrhos, Esquire. There are also in the steeple six new bells, lately cast at the expence of the parish.

As to the legacies, there are many bequeathed by several persons to the poor of the parish, all regularly inscribed on cards in the church and faithfully applied. There are also two charity schools, founded by the late Messrs. Parry and Tudor, for instructing a few poor children of the Middle Division to read and write, and the interest of £150 for clothing poor persons in the Middle Division, and for apprenticing one poor boy in Middle Division and for apprenticing one boy in ditto, annually. Mr. Thomas Langford has also left the sum of four pounds for cloathing eight poor persons annually of the parish, and there is likewise an Alms House, founded by the late Mr. Parry for eight poor persons, with the annual sum of ten shillings each.

The clerk is appointed and chosen by the Vicar. His annual stipend from the parish is four pounds, his burial fees is three shillings and sixpence, and his marriage fees one shilling.

The Vicar's fees for a licensed wedding are six shillings, for an unlicensed three shillings and sixpence, for the burial of an extra parochial corps one shilling; out of the tenpence Easter dues the clerk has fourpence, and out of the fivepence for ditto he has twopence.

WELSH POOL. 339

This is a true copy of the Terrier belonging to the Vicarage and Parish of Welshpool, in the County of Montgomery, and Diocese of St. Asaph, as witness our hands this fourteenth day of July 1791. E. Lloyd, Abraham Jones, the mark × of Arthur Pearce, William Griffiths, Churchwardens; George Baker, William Pain, Richard Brown, Jeremiah Nicholas, Henry Owens, George Bibby, Inhabitants.

This present copy was taken and revised July 2nd, 1799, by Francis Bromley, Curate; William Clarke, Edward Pryce, the mark × of John Edwards, Churchwardens.

JOHN PRYCE, Vicar.

Endorsed on the back of the said Terrier. In regard to the payment of fforty shillings only as a modus for the demesne of Powis Castle, and that of seventeen shillings and sixpence for Buttington Hall farm, I am not prepared fully to admit the legality thereof, though in other respects I conceive the statement in the Terrier to be accurate. As witness my hand,

JOHN PRYCE, Vicar of Welchpool.

This copy was taken and revised July 2nd, 1799, by me,

FRANCIS BROMLEY, Curate.

A copy of a true note and TERRIER of all the glebes, lands, meadows, gardens, orchards, houses, stocks, implements, tenements, portions of tithes, and other rights belonging to the Vicarage and Parish Church of Welshpool, in the County of Montgomery, and Diocese of St. Asaph, now in the use and occupation of Rev. William Clive, Clerk, or his tenants, taken, made, and renewed, according to the old evidences of knowledge of the ancient inhabitants, by the appointment of the Right Rev. Father in God, Thomas Vowler, Lord Bishop of St. Asaph, under the communication hereunto attached, and of which communication the following is a copy:—

"We, Thomas Fowler, Bishop of St. Asaph, do hereby, in pursuance of the 87th Canon, appoint the Rev. William Clive, Clerk, Vicar of the Parish and Parish Church of Welshpool, in the County of Montgomery, and Diocese of St. Asaph: and John Davies Corrie, of Dyserth, in the Parish of Welshpool, aforesaid, gentleman; Charles Wilding, of Powis Castle in the same parish, gentleman; Robert Devereux Harrison, of the same parish, gentleman; Edward Pugh of the same parish, gentleman; Field Evans, of the same parish, gentleman; William Yearsley, of the same parish, gentleman; Moses Evans, of the same parish, grocer; Robert Owen, of the same parish, bookseller; John Williams, of the same parish, chymist; William Clarke, of the same parish, writer; John Williams, of the same parish, confectioner; and Edward Morris, of the same parish, mercer; together with the Churchwardens of the said parish of Welshpool, to take, make, and renew a true note and terrier of all the glebe lands, meadows, gardens, orchards, houses, stocks, implements, tenements, and portion of tithes out of the said parish, and other rights belonging to the Vicarage of Welshpool. Witness my hand, this 13th day of March 1849.

"THOMAS VOWLER, St. Asaph."

Imprimis, One slated dwelling-house, in length seventy-six feet, and in breadth thirty-six feet, without the wall; one brewhouse, milkroom and larder, being altogether thirty-one feet in length, and seventeen feet in breadth; one skullery, nine feet by nine feet; one servants' hall, fifteen feet by thirteen feet; all of stone and slated. One coach-house, twenty-three feet by thirteen feet.

Item, one stone building, thirty-nine feet by eighteen feet, containing a coachhouse, a stable with two stalls, and cowhouse, with four tyings.

Item, one garden, one field, and plantation.

Item, pleasure ground and shrubbery adjoining the Vicarage house, all of which are contiguous, and the outside boundary (including all and no other premises), commencing from the canal bridge eastward, over which the road passes to Dommen's Mill is as follows: the canal south-east as far as the sluice from the Llydan brook, thence the said brook south-west to the Bull bridge, thence the turnpike road from Pool to Shrewsbury north-west, and north as far as a small building now used as a cooper's shop. From this point a wall faced with brick to the north-east, one hundred and ninety-six feet in length, and then in the same direction, a stone wall in length one hundred and seventy-five feet, which same wall is then turned at a right angle and continued one hundred and forty-nine feet in a straight line (with the exception of an opening eleven feet wide, now used as an approach by the Venerable Archdeacon Clive to a tenement of his), up to the road leading to Dommin's Mill, and from this junction the north-east boundary is a stone wall three hundred and fifteen feet in length, extending by the the side of the said road into the canal bridge first mentioned, all which premises are particularly delineated and set forth in the map inserted in the margin of this Terrier. The fence from the cooper's shop to the Dommens's Mill is repaired by the owners of the contiguous properties, namely: the said Archdeacon Clive, a Mr. Edward Bryan, Mr. John Wall, and Mr. James Roberts; that which runs alongside of the Dommen's Mill road is repaired by the Vicar, and also the fence from the

Cooper's shop southward to the end of the wall, which is also set forth in the map, forty-five feet below the lower end of the Red Lion Street. The whole acreage of this portion of the glebe, within the boundary above described, is six acres and four perches. A Portion of the before mentioned glebe land, called Close y person, together with a garden adjoining, was about twenty-five years ago had in exchange from the Dean and Chapter of Christ Church for a piece of land adjoining the churchyard and garden. And also a field and garden, bounded by Maes gwastad on the west side, on the south by a garden the property of the Earl of Powis, on the east by a garden the property of Mr. Edmunds, on the north by the High street of Pool, containing twenty-six perches, the sheep folds and stands for cattle between it and the street.

The churchyard contains two acres and twenty-five perches. The church is repaired by the parish in general; the chancel by the Dean and Chapter of Christ Church; the east gate is repaired by the Vicar, and the west by the Dean and Chapter of Christ Church; and the whole fence by the parish in general.

Item, a rent paid by the Earl of Powis for some intermixed and unascertained land in Welshtown, the sum of ten shillings per annum.

Item, the Chapel house and garden at the Belan, containing one rood and twelve perches. Scite of the National Schools, with frontage, yard, and premises adjoining.

The Vicarial portion of the tithes of Pool parish, including two pounds modus for tithes of the ancient demesne of Powis Castle, including also the sums formerly paid for Easter dues, which the Vicar of Pool pays to the Curate of Buttington, the sum of one hundred and sixty-five pounds, ten shillings. *Item*, the sum of fifty pounds by grant from the Dean and Chapter of Christ Church.

The books and utensils of the church are as follows, namely: one folio Bible, one folio Common Prayer Book, one Common Prayer quarto for the parish clerk, two altar services for the Communion Table, two books of offices, one velvet cushion for the pulpit, one woollen cloth fringed for the Communion Table, one damask large cloth, four damask cloth napkins, five surplices, one solid gold cup containing one wine quart, weight thirty ounces, the gift of Thomas Davies, late of Pool, one silver cup gilt, weighing nineteen ounces, one silver salver for bread, the gift of Mrs. Mary Edmunds, one silver paten, one silver basin for collecting alms, the gift of John Edmunds, Esquire, one small plate very old, a carved stone font, two brass chandeliers in the middle aisle the gift of the late Viscount Hereford.

There are also in the steeple eight bells, and twelve small hand bells, the King's Arms, the Ten Commandments, one church clock, two biers, two hearse cloths, one parish chest with three locks, one iron chest for registers, one iron chest containing the communion service, one old chest made of wood. The seats in the church have been repaired time immemorial, by the respective owners. The north gallery, containing nineteen benches, is entirely free; and the chancel, containing eight benches, is also altogether free. The register books are in number, twelve.

No. 1. Including births, deaths, and marriages from the year 1634 to 1701.

No. 2. Including births, deaths, and marriages from 1708 to 1735 (from 1701 to 1708 being missing).

No. 3. Contains baptisms from 1735 to 1772; burials 1735 to 1782; marriages from 1735 to 1754.

No. 4. Contains marriages, 1754 to 1782.

No. 5. Contains baptisms from 1772 to 1812.

No. 6. Contains burials from 1782 to 1811.

No. 7. Contains marriages from 1784 to 1812.

No. 8. Contains burials from 1811 to 1812.

No. 9. Contains baptisms from 1813 to 1835; burials from 1813 to 1842; marriages from 1813 to 1837.

No. 10. Contains baptisms from 1836 to 1849.

No. 11. Burials from 1842 to 1849.

No. 12. Marriages from 1837 to 1849.

The Vicar's fees are, for a wedding by license ten shillings and sixpence, for a wedding by banns seven shillings and sixpence, publication of banns one shilling; for every burial one shilling; for churching one shilling. The fee of one shilling formerly paid at the christening is not demanded by the present Vicar.

The clerk is chosen and appointed by the Vicar. His annual stipend from the parish is four pounds. For bell sheaf and Easter dues, by commutation, seven pounds thirteen shillings. His fees for a wedding by license, five shillings; for a wedding by banns, two shillings and sixpence; churching, sixpence; burial, sixpence. The sexton's fee for making a grave, four shillings and sixpence; ditto for infants, three shillings and sixpence.

As to the legacies bequeathed for the benefit of this parish they are as follows, namely: an almshouse for eight poor persons, founded by the late Mr. Parry, with the annual sum of ten shillings each. This sum was paid by the late Mr. William Jones, shoemaker, the owner of the Bull Inn, and lands be-

WELSH POOL.

longing thereto, and supposed to have been charged on those lands, or on lands purchased by David Pugh, Esquire, of Llanerchydol, but it has not been paid for several years past, and the parish officers have no documents or other evidence which would justify them in suing for its recovery. A small privy has been erected on a portion of a yard belonging to the Almshouse by Mr. John Williams, for which he pays to the Vicar and Churchwardens an annual rent of one shilling.

By the late Mr. Richard Tudor the sum of one hundred pounds; also the sum of forty pounds for instructing a few poor children of the Middle Division to read and write; and also the sum of fifty pounds, the interest to be distributed in money, the whole secured by mortgage at $4\frac{1}{2}$ per cent. Also by the said Mr. Tudor, the interest of eighty pounds, for apprenticing one poor boy of the Middle Division of Pool, now on mortgage at $4\frac{1}{2}$ per cent.

And .... bequeathed the sum of fifty pounds, which is secured on the second district of the Montgomeryshire Roads, the interest of which is to be distributed annually.

Mrs. Elizabeth Phillip bequeathed the sum of one hundred pounds, the interest of which is to be distributed annually. A farm called Cwmfryn, in the parish of Llanfihangel, in this County, was purchased with this legacy, and which said farm is now let at the annual rent of fourteen pounds.

Thomas Langford, gentleman, bequeathed to this parish the sum of four pounds yearly, for clothing eight poor persons. This is paid from the Golfa estate, belonging to the late George Gould, Esquire.

Mr. Edward Parry the sum of one hundred pounds, the interest to be paid for teaching eight poor boys of the Middle Division to read and write. The said Edward Parry also bequeathed seventy pounds, the interest of which to be laid out in purchasing six upper garments for the poor persons belonging to the Middle Division. The said one hundred and seventy pounds is secured by mortgage at $4\frac{1}{2}$ per cent.

Miss Elizabeth Lloyd bequeathed the interest of ninety pounds to be distributed annually in bread, which is also secured on the said second district of Roads. The Vicar for the time is trustee for the Tudor legacies, and the Vicar and Churchwardens for the time being for all the other legacies.

In testimony of the truth of the before mentioned particulars and of every of them, we, the minister, churchwardens, and inhabitants, have set our hands this first day of June, in the year of our Lord one thousand eight hundred and forty-nine.

W. CLIVE, Vicar.

Churchwardens.	Inhabitants.	
John Griffiths,	Jno. D. Corrie,	Morris Evans,
George Brown,	Chas. Wilding,	R. Owen,
James Eddowes,	R. D. Harrison,	John Williams,
James Farr.	W. Yearsley.	W. Y. Clarke,
	Edward Pugh,	John Williams,
	Field Evans,	Edward Morris.

Brief for re-building Welshpool Church. 7 George III.

"George the third, by the Grace of God, of Great Britain, France, and Ireland, King, Defender of the Faith, and so forth : To all and singular, Archbishops, Bishops, Archdeacons, Deans, and their Officials, Parsons, Vicars, Curates, and all other spiritual persons; and to all Teachers and Preachers of every separate congregation, and also to all Justices of the Peace, Mayors, Sheriffs, Bailiffs, Constables, Churchwardens, Chapelwardens, Head Boroughs, Collectors for the Poor and their Overseers, and also to all Officers of Cities, Boroughs and Towns Corporate ; and to all other our Officers, Ministers, and subjects whomsoever they may be, as well within liberties as without, to whom these presents shall come, greeting. Whereas, it hath been represented unto us, as well upon the humble petition of the Minister, Churchwardens, and Inhabitants of the Parish of Pool, in the County of Montgomery, as also by certificate under the hands and seals of our trusty and well beloved Sir John Powell Pryce, Bart., Pryce Jones and Thomas Lloyd, Esquires, Justices of the Peace for our said County of Montgomery, assembled at their General Quarter Sessions, holden at Pool aforesaid, in and for our said County, on the fourth day of November in the sixth year of our Reign. That the Parish Church of Pool aforesaid is a very ancient structure, and notwithstanding the parishioners have laid out considerable sums of money in repairing the said Church, yet the same is become so ruinous that they cannot assemble therein, for the public worship of Almighty God, without imminent dangers of their lives, and that the said Church cannot any longer be supported, but must be wholly taken down and rebuilt. That the truth of the premises hath been made appear to our said Justices in their General Quarter Sessions aforesaid, not only by the oaths of the said petitioners, but also by the oaths of able and experienced workmen, who have carefully viewed the said Church, and made an estimate of the charge of taking down and rebuilding the same, which (moderately computed) amounts to the sum of £2,500 and upwards, which sum the said parishioners are unable to raise among themselves, being chiefly tenants at rack rents and burdened with numerous poor. They have therefore most humbly besought us to grant unto them our most gracious Letters Patent, licence and protection, under our great Seal of Great Britain to empower them to ask, collect, and receive the alms, benevolence, and charitable contributions of all our loving subjects throughout

England, our town of Berwick-on-Tweed, our Counties of Flint, Denbigh, and Radnor in Wales; and from house to house through our Counties of Montgomery, Salop, Stafford, Worcester, and Hereford, to enable them to rebuild the Parish Church of Pool, aforesaid: Unto which their humble request we have graciously condescended, not doubting but that when our instructions, for promoting so pious a work, shall be made known to our loving subjects, they will readily and chearfully contribute their endeavours for accomplishing the same. Know ye therefore that of our special grace and favour, we have given and granted and by these our Letters Patent under our great Seal of Great Britain We do give and grant unto the Minister, Churchwardens, and Inhabitants of the parish of Pool aforesaid, and to their Deputy and Deputies, the Bearer and Bearers, hereof (authorized as is hereinafter directed), full power, licence, and authority to ask, collect, and receive, the alms, benevolence, and charitable contributions of all our loving subjects, within all and every our Counties, Cities, Towns, Boroughs, Hamletts, Cinque Ports, Districts, Parishes, Chapelries, and all other places whatsoever throughout England, our Town of Berwick-on-Tweed, our Counties of Flint, Denbigh, and Radnor in Wales; and from house to house throughout the Counties of Montgomery, Salop, Stafford, Worcester, and Hereford, to enable them to take down and rebuild the Parish Church of Pool aforesaid. And therefore, in pursuance of the tenor of an Act of Parliament, made in the fourth year of the reign of Queen Anne, intituled, 'An Act for the better collecting Charities, in Briefs, by Letters Patent, preventing abuses in relation to such Charities,' our will and pleasure is, and we do hereby (for the advancement of these our pious intentions) require and command all Ministers, Teachers, and Preachers, Churchwardens, Chapelwardens, and the Collectors of this Brief, and all others concerned, that they and every of them observe the directions in the said Act contained, and do in all things conform themselves thereunto. And that when the printed copies of these presents shall be tendered unto you the respective Ministers, and Curates, Churchwardens, and Chapelwardens, and to the respective Teachers and Preachers of every separate congregation, and to any person who teaches or preaches in any meeting of the people called Quakers, that you and every of you, under the penalties to be inflicted by the said Act do receive the same. And you the respective Ministers and Curates, Teachers and Preachers, and persons called Quakers, are by all persuasive motives and arguments, earnestly to exhort your respective congregations and assemblies, to a liberal contribution of their Charities for the purpose aforesaid. And for the Churchwardens and Chapelwardens, together with the Minister, or some of the substantial inhabitants of the several parishes and chapelries, and all other places whatsoever within our Counties of Montgomery, Salop, Stafford, Worcester, and Hereford, are hereby required to go from house to house upon the week days, the publication of these presents, to ask and receive from the parishioners, as well masters and mistresses, or servants, and others in their families, their christian and charitable contributions, and to take the names in writing of such as shall contribute thereunto, and the sum and sums by them respectively given, and indorse the whole sums upon the printed Briefs in words of length, and subscribe the same with your own proper hands, together with the name of the parish or place where, and the time when collected, and to enter the same in the public books of account kept for such parish and chapelry respectively, and the sum and sums collected, together with the printed briefs so indorsed, you are to deliver to the Deputies and Agents authorised to receive the same. And we do by these presents nominate, constitute, and appoint the Right Rev. the Lord Bishop of St. Asaph, Sir John Powell Pryce, Bart.; Pryce Jones, Thomas Lloyd, Henry Wynne, Henry Parry, Esquires; William Coupland, James Henings, John Meredith, David Parry, Gentlemen; the Rev. Salusbury Pryce, Juckes Egerton, Randolph Parry, Henry Newcomb, David Davies, Edward Price, Clerks; Thomas Stevenson and John Stevenson, Gentlemen, Trustees and Receivers of the Charity to be collected, by virtue of these presents, with power to them, or any three or more of them, to give Deputations to such Collectors as shall be chosen by the said Petitioners, or the major part of them. And the said Trustees, or any three or more of them, to give Deputations to such Collectors as shall be chosen by the said Petitioners, or the major part of them. And the said Trustees, or any three or more of them, are to make and sign all necessary orders, and do all other reasonable acts for the due and regular collection of this Brief, and the advancement of the said Charity, and to see that the moneys, when collected, be applied, as far as may be, in answering the true intent and meaning of these presents. And, lastly, our will and pleasure is that no person or persons shall collect and receive any the printed Briefs, or moneys collected thereon, but such only as shall be so deputed, and made the Bearer and Bearers of these presents or duplicates thereof. In witness whereof we have caused these our letters to be made patent, and to continue in force for one whole year from Michaelmas Day next, and no longer. Witness ourself at Westminster, the 7th day of July in the seventh year of our reign.

"BILLINGSLEY."

[No seal attached].
Add. MSS. B, vii, 12. 7 George III.

MISCELLANEOUS MATTERS.

AN ACCOUNT of the tithe, hay, and grass arising in the township of ·Trallwmgollen in the years 1765 and 1766, which tithe the tenants and landowners have refused to set forth in kind, or pay the following customary rates for the same.

WELSH POOL.

Tithes for the year 1765.

					£	s.	d.
Anne Parry, widow, for Tithe of	65	acres of	hay		3	5	0
Idem,	,,	15	,,	barley	1	2	6
Mr. Robert Palmer,	,,	25	,,	hay	1	5	0
Solomon Jones,	,,	17	,,	hay	0	17	0
Idem,	,,	30	,,	lent grain	2	15	0
Joseph Lee,	,,	15	,,	hay	0	15	0
Edward Jones,	,,	26	,,	hay	1	6	0
Mr. William Thomas,	,,	28	,,	hay	1	8	0
Mr. Richard Evans,	,,	8	,,	hay	0	8	0
Idem,	,,	5	,,	wheat	0	10	0
Idem,	,,	4	,,	barley	0	6	0
Mr. Turner,	,,	3	,,	hay	0	3	0

Tithes for the year 1766.

					£	s.	d.
Anne Parry, widow, for Tithe of	88	acres of	hay		4	8	0
Idem,	,,	18	,,	wheat	1	16	0
Mr. Birkitt,	,,	30	,,	hay	1	10	0
Solomon Jones, and tenant	,,	17	,,	hay	0	17	0
Idem,	,,	12	,,	wheat	1	4	0
Idem, lent grain		18			1	7	0
Joseph Lee,	,,	15	,,	hay	0	15	0
John Lewis,	,,	10	,,	hay	0	10	0
Thomas Jones,	,,	4	,,	hay	0	4	0
Mr. William Thomas,	,,	28	,,	hay	1	8	0
Idem, for wheat,	,,	8	,,		0	16	0
Mr. Robert Palmer,	,,	25	,,	hay	1	5	0
Mr. Richard Evans,	,,	8	,,	hay	0	8	0
Idem,	,,	3	,,	barley	0	7	6
Mr. Turner,	,,	3	,,	hay	0	3	0

Valuation by Watson in 1776, addressed to Rev. Mr. Price, Gunley, of Wheat, etc., within the parish of Welshpool.

	Value.
	£ s. d.
Cyfronydd.—Wheat, 20 acres; barley, 19; oates, 21; hay, 21	13 16 6
Trallwm gollen.—Wheat, 8 acres; barley, 6; oates, — hay, 71; wheat, 14; barley, 29; oates, 11; hay, 11 In ditto, and modus of 1-40th.	13 3 10
Dyserth.—Wheat, 18 acres; barley, 24; oates, 38; hay, 35	21 12 7
Stredal Vechan.—Wheat, 14 acres; barley, 21; oates, 21, Hay, 18	13 8 6
Tythyn Prydd.— Wheat 38 acres; barley, 42; oates, 30; hay, 42	28 18 3
Trevnant Vechan.—Wheat 12 acres; barley, 16; oates, 20; hay, 9.	10 13 0

VOL. XV.   B B

348 WELSH POOL.

	£	s.	d.
Welch Town.—Wheat, 13; barley, 17; oates, 25; Hay, 56	20	13	0
Llanerchidol.—Wheat 61 acres; barley, 43; oates, 64; hay, 69	38	2	3
Gongrog Vawr.—Wheat, 40; barley, 47; oates, 43; hay, 61	34	0	6
	£207	5	8

    Vicar's share . £51 16s. 5d.
    Due to Chapter 155 9s. 3d.

BUTTINGTON—
Hop[*e*].—Wheat 48; barley, 24; oates, 56; hay, 56.
Clutterwood.—Wheat, 8; barley, 7; oates, 29; hay, 7.
Clutterwood.—Wheat, 70; barley, 52; oates, 54; straw, 72.
Trewern.—Wheat, 50; barley, 26; oates, 76; straw, 76.

	£	s.	d.
Value of Buttington tithe	120	11	0

    Vicar's share £30 2s. 9d.
    Due to Chapter £90 8s. 3d.

THE VICARIAL GLEBE in the parishes of Pool and Buttington extracted from the Tithe Commutation particular.

No. on Map.   a. r. p.
450. Church and churchyard . . . 2 0 25
467. Vicarage House, offices, garden,
   shrubberies, stable, etc. . 2 2 3
468. Close (alias Close y person had in exchange from the Dean and Chapter of Christ Church College,
   Oxford) . . . 3 1 11
   Plantation   . 0 0 30
                 ———
                    6 0 4
   Garden in Pool Town held by Edward Williams 0 0 32
   A rent paid by the Earl of Powis for some intermixed and unassessed land in Welsh town,
   10s. per annum.
443. Chapel, house, and garden below . . 1 12 0
828a. Scite of the new church (Christ Church) and
   churchyard . . . 1 1 16

Vicarial portion of tithes, Pool parish, including £2
 modus for tithes of ancient demesne of Powis
 Castle, including also the sum formerly paid for
 Easter dues 165 10 0

WELSH POOL. 349

	£ s. d.
Ditto of Buttington parish, including 17s. 6d. for Buttington Hall Ancient Demesne, including the sum paid for Easter dues, which the Vicar of Pool payd to the Curate of Buttington £11 10s. .	. 106 10 0
	£272 0 0

		A. R. P.
Buttington.—Schoolroom, church, and churchyard		. 0 1 26
Vicarage house and garden	1 31	
Piece of land	2 23	
		—— 1 0 14
Selte of Trewern Chapel of Ease		. 0 0 8

ANNUAL VALUE of land destroyed and injured by making the Montgomeryshire Canal in the parish of Pool as valued by Mr. Bowman, Earl of Powis, and Vicar of Pool, per annum, £6 12s., payable from Lady Day 1796.   [Signed]   T. Withy, 20 June 1780.

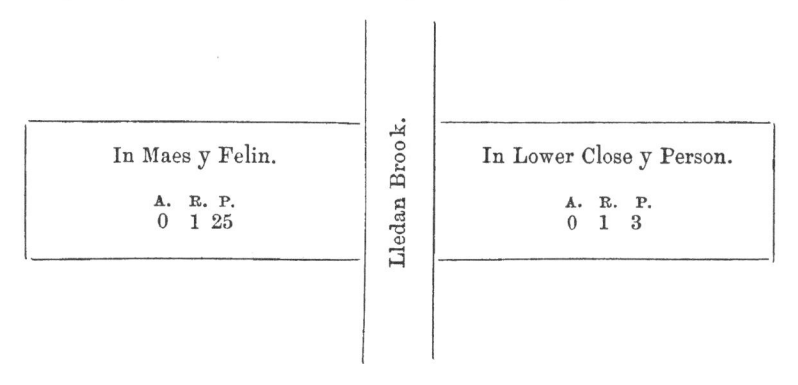

In Maes y Felin.	Lledan Brook.	In Lower Close y Person.
A. R. P. 0 1 25		A. R. P. 0 1 3

PLAN of the Rev. Mr. Pryce's Glebe in Maes y Felin and Lower Glebe y Person as surveyed April 6, 1779, by O. Bibby.

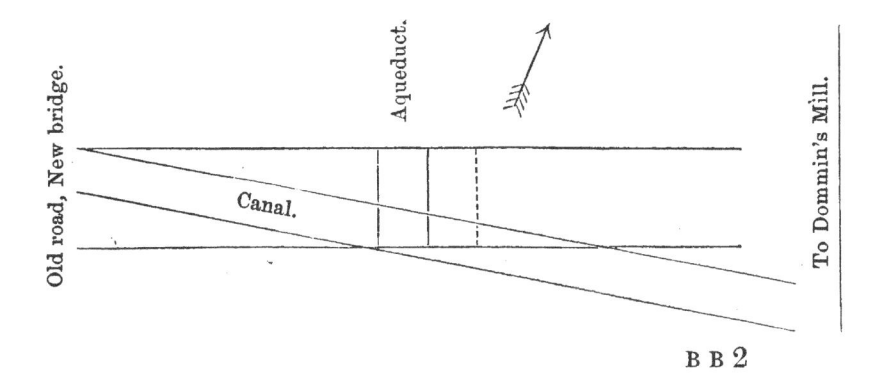

Old road, New bridge. — Canal. — Aqueduct. — To Dommin's Mill.

B B 2

Declaration of Patronage.

By a document, which is called "Declaration of Patronage by Subscribers", dated 26th June 1844, addressed to the Bishop of St. Asaph and the Vicar of Welshpool, pursuant to the Act of 1 and 2 William IV, the undersigned Hugh, Duke of Northumberland and Charlotte Florentia Duchess of Northumberland, Lady Harriet Clive, The Hon. Robert Henry Clive, David Pugh, John Arthur Lloyd, Panton Corbett, Henry Clive, Richard Griffithes Parry, The Right Hon. C. W. W. Wynn (as executors of the late Sir W. W. Wynn, Bart.), Charles Wilding, Thomas Beck, Edward Pugh, Joseph Jones, Henry Jones, Joseph Newill, Thomas Penson, William Clive, Edward Herbert Earl of Powis, and Edward James Herbert, commonly called Viscount Clive, members of the Church of England, give notice:—

That according to the last return of the population of the said parish of Pool, the population of the parish of Pool amounted to 2,000 persons and upwards, i.e.d., 4,626 persons, and that the only church for the performance of divine worship according to the rites of the United Church of England and Ireland then existing therein, viz., the parish church of St. Mary's, in Pool aforesaid, does not afford accommodation for more than one-third of the inhabitants for attendance on divine service according to the rites aforesaid, i.e.d., the said church does not afford accommodation for more than 1,300 persons.

That a new church or chapel has been built in the said parish, and is nearly completed, and the expense incurred and to be incurred in and about the erection and fitting up of the said new church would amount to the sum of £6,000, or rather less, which had been or would be defrayed by the subscriptions of divers well-disposed persons.

That it is intended to appropriate and devote such new church to the performance of divine service according to the rites of the United Church of England and Ireland.

That such new church or chapel will afford accommodation for 800 persons.

And they, the undersigned, Edward Herbert Earl of Powis, and Edward James Herbert, commonly called Viscount Clive, did thereby declare an intention of providing a perpetual yearly rent-charge of upwards of £40 to be secured on lands of adequate value by way of endowment for such new church, in addition to the pew-rents arising from the said church, and of providing a fund for the repairs of the said church in manner following, viz., a perpetual rent-charge of £15, being of the value of £300 and upwards, and equal in value to £5 upon every £100 of the original cost of erecting and fitting up of such new church, to be secured upon lands of adequate value. And also a further sum to be reserved annually out of the pew-rents of the said church, after the rate of £5 for every £100 of the gross value of the repair fund so to be provided as last aforesaid.

And they, the whole of the undersigned persons, did thereby further declare their intention of setting apart or appropriating one-third at least of the sittings in such new church to be for ever as free sittings, subject to such determination as the Lord Bishop of the said Diocese might come to in pursuance of the Act of the 1 and 2 Victoria, entitled, "An Act to amend and render more effectual the Church Building Acts", as to whether the same should be free, or whether the same or any part thereof should be let at such low rents as the Lord Bishop might from time to time direct. And that the said new church was adapted to the convenience of that part of the inhabitants of the said parish of Pool, for which such additional accommodation was necessary.

Correspondence showing what had been done in the Parish.

In 1839, Archdeacon Clive wrote to the Dean and Chapter of Christ Church, Oxford, asking for a contribution to the new church about to be built at Welshpool. He stated that in 1819, upwards of £300 was raised by subscription, exclusive of a grant from the National Society, and two school rooms built for the education of two hundred and fifty children on the national system. In the year 1825 and 1826, £1,500 or more was laid out by the inhabitants without a rate, increasing the accommodation of the church, three hundred being free sittings. That another school room, commenced in 1838, had just been completed, the contract being £307. It was situate in a township three miles from the parish church, and had been licensed for Divine Service. A grant of £25 was obtained from the National Society.

The reply was that it was an invariable principle with the Dean and Chapter, where their property consisted of tithes, to make their contribution in aid of endowments *alone*. Therefore they declined to contribute towards the structure of the new church, although they would not be unwilling to make some contribution towards the support of the minister.

In 1844 the Dean and Chapter's lease of the great tithes of this parish to the Earl of Powis expired, and they enquired as to their position, with which they seemed unacquainted, and shewed a desire to grant a further endowment.

In 1846 Archdeacon Clive again wrote a letter to the Dean and Chapter of Christ Church, Oxford, in which he makes several interesting statements. That since his incumbency two National Schools had been erected, one in the town and another in a distant township, which was licensed for divine service. That by means of two galleries in the parish church, five hundred sittings had been provided for, three hundred being free. That for these works £2,100 had been raised in the neighbourhood. In 1839 a first stone of a new church was laid, which had since been completed at a cost of £6,000, consisting entirely of voluntary contributions. That Lord Powis having charged his estates with £100 per annum for the endowment, at that time it was thought the minister would be sufficiently endowed. The subscriptions falling short it was found necessary to take the amount of the repair fund, and the salary for the vestry clerk, and other expenses out of this endowment, so that in fact the nett income of the endowment does not amount to more than £75. That the living of Pool is £273, and when the Curate's salary is deducted is £173. The population stated at 4,626, but really 5,000, and the extent of the parish is six miles in length and three in breadth. This second appeal was not successful.

In 1847 the Dean and Chapter offered to lease their glebe to the Vicar.

Reservation of Road to Frochas.

In 1847, Mr. David Pugh wished to stop up the lane running by Llanerchydol lodge, making it enter higher up the Ceunant road Mr. J. Lyon Winder and Mr. Robinson Jones were the justices appointed to "view" the proposed alteration. They assented to the alteration on condition of Mr. Pugh reserving "to the Vicar and Churchwardens of Welshpool, to have egress and regress up his private drive and the same to their successors." And Mr. Pugh gave an undertaking accordingly, and stated, "he felt every anxiety to make as good a road for the accommodation of the clergymen agreeable to his undertaking." The road was required for the purpose of their cottage lecture at the Frochas.

Correspondence as to the state of the Chancel and the repair thereof.

On the 11th June 1853, the Vicar brought before the Dean and Chapter the state of the chancel of Welshpool Church. He states in his letter,

"The original church appears to have been built about the fourteenth century. The nave fell down and was rebuilt in 1774, the tower and chancel remaining. The chancel must at that time have been in a very dilapidated state, for the battlements are all gone, and the upper part of the wall has been rebuilt in a most slovenly way, with bricks and rubble stone; at the same time square brick columns were reared inside to support the roof, the end of the beams having decayed. The late Earl of Powis, at that time the lessee of the tithes, removed these wretched props and restored the ceiling. The buttresses have been examined by experienced builders, and it is their decided opinion that they were erected long after the original structure, and have proved in consequence rather injurious than otherwise. The north and south windows are in a tolerable state of repair, and two of them have been filled with quarries by the present Earl of Powis. The light from the east window is so strong as to be painful to the congregation, and as consequently, a wish has been shewn on the part of the parish to put in stained glass. With a view to this improvement, I have had the stone work examined, and obtained an estimate which I forward. The whole structure, walls and roof, are I fear in a very crazy condition."

He appealed for the Dean and Chapter to send an architect, and to repair the structure, and mentioned that Mr. Scott on a cursory inspection, had thought the mullions of the east window could be preserved. This led to a correspondence which lasted for four years. In the first letter, 7th April 1853, the question of their being only part owners of the tithes was raised, and that therefore they should only bear part of the repairs. The repairs were estimated at £145, and the Dean and Chapter thought perhaps rebuilding would be better and cheaper than patching at that cost. They offered £100, upon those interested undertaking the repairs of the whole structure, but the Vicar at once vetoed that. He stated

"The walls are very rotten and shakey, and the roof in a bad state; amongst other dilapidations the stone framework of the east window is much decayed."

And he asked only for the restoration of the stone work, he undertaking to put in a stained glass window by subscription.

In 1854 an application for a monument being put up in the chancel was discouraged by the Dean and Chapter, but any fee received they offered to give to some charitable object.

In 1855, Mr. Bland, architect, was employed, but was very dilatory. His report was submitted to Mr. Pountney Smith of Shrewsbury, on 12th May, 1855. On 30th November following, the Dean and Chapter were excessively surprised by the estimates of Mr. Pountney Smith, who had trebled Mr. Bland's figures, and they resolved to employ their college surveyor, Mr. Bruton.

On 5th April 1856, the question was raised as to the parishioners building the chancel arch, which Mr. Billinge thought necessary, and not a part of the chancel. On the 22nd May 1856, allusion is made to the joint ownership of the tithes, and the consequent joint liability of the Vicar with the Rectors. On 8th June 1856, a communication was made that Mr. John Billinge was appointed architect, the difference of opinion between Mr. Pountney Smith and the college surveyor being so wide. When the church was rebuilt the chancel arch was neglected to be rebuilt, which was part and parcel of the church, which the parishioners were bound to rebuild, and until that was done the chancel could not be repaired. On 30th June 1856, Mr. Bland was again employed. On 2nd June, 1856, the Vicar replied on the subject of the share the Vicar might be called upon to take in the reparation of the chancel, and exonerated himself from the liability on the following grounds:—First, that the Terrier of 1791 said, the repairs were done by the Impropriate Rectors' lessee; second, that in point of fact, the Impropriate Rectors had always done the repairs; thirdly, the Vicar had never before been called upon. This letter did not settle the question, which was persisted in. This drew from the Vicar the following trenchant letter which was effectual. He says,—

"I am very sorry to learn from your letter received this morning that in all probability the repairs of the chancel of Welshpool Church will not be done before the winter, and that the Chapter, though the matter has been before them since the year 1853, have not yet ascertained whether there is a legal obligation on the Vicar of Pool to bear a part of the expense, or if there is such an obligation, in what proportion he is bound to contribute. When you refer to the custom where great tithes are divided, you omit to notice what is I believe not customary, that in this case the Chapter receive three-fourths of the small or Vicarial Tithes. With respect to the point in question, it has been the custom from time immemorial for the lessee to bear all the cost of repairs, and I am informed by the Agent at Powis Castle, that these repairs have been done, not in compliance with ancient usage, but under express covenant in the lease. In the first, to which he refers, it is stated, 'And also at their own cost and charges, repair and uphold the chauncel of the Parish Churches of Myvode, Poole,' etc. And again in the last lease, A.D. 1828, there is a similar covenant limited in that case to Pool and Buttington, Lord Powis having renewed for those parishes only. And in advertizing their tithes that year, the College admits its liability and publishes it, for with reference to Lot 1, part of Pool parish, there is the following notice, 'The purchasers of this Lot must covenant to keep the chancel of the Parish Church of Welshpool in repair.'

"I presume that the Chapter has amongst its records all this information, and it would, before renewing their call upon the Vicar to take a share in the expense of repairing the chancel, have referred to it, and if they did, I must be allowed to express my surprise that it was not deemed sufficient on behalf of the Vicar, against the only conflicting evidence hitherto produced.

"I may add that there is amongst the old papers, in the office at Powis Castle, a copy of a Faculty to build a gallery at the east end of the church, in which the following sentence occurs, 'and consent of my Lord Duke of Powis being had to make a stair-case out of *his* chancel.' The document is dated 1728; and in another paper bearing date also 1728 about the same matter, there is the following sentence, 'If a stair-case is permitted to be made in the Chauncel, which belongs to Christ Church Colledge in Oxford, and of which Colledge my Lord Powis holds it with the tithes of the parish by leave only,' etc. There are also other letters which confirm the opinion that the chancel belongs wholly to the Chapter, and has ever been repaired by their representative.

"I am glad to find that Mr. Billinge intends to retain the waggon roof in the chancel, so that there will be no alteration in the interior, and in this case, though I should desire a stone arch, I cannot call upon the parishioners to put it up. I intend to apply for voluntary subscriptions to place painted glass in the east window, and I hope to receive from the Chapter, as a contribution, the cost of a plain window, which will be saved."

The correspondence hitherto had been conducted by Dr. Bull, the treasurer, but the reply was from Dean Liddell, giving up the point and agreeing to do the whole repair of the chancel, on condition of receiving a guarantee that the chancel arch should be done by the parish. The building of this arch was estimated at £75, and the architect's charge £5 = £80; which the Vicar undertook to provide.

The following memorandum is in the handwriting of Mr. C. Wilding, formerly Agent to the Earl of Powis, and probably was the source of information from which the Vicar's letter was written. It gives some further details which we think it well to preserve.

"Whatever may be stated in ancient Terriers with respect to Pool Chancel, the custom has been (so long that the memory of man does not go against it) for the College Lessee to bear all cost of repair. Not only in more recent periods, as for instance towards the close of the lease of 1805, when in seven years, to 1822, there was expended by the Lessee nearly £300, four years of which period were during the incumbency of the Rev. H. J. Williams, who was appointed to the

Living in opposition to the then Lessees, as was his predecessor, and at earlier periods, the Powis Castle family, being Roman Catholics (then also Lessees), could not have any influence, and whose interest could not but be adverse to that of the Vicar upon this point. But moreover, this was under an express covenant in the College Lease as follows, 'And also at his own cost and charges repair, and uphold the chancels of the Parish Churches of Myvode, Poole,' etc. The like was also required in the last Lease of 1828, limited in that case to Poole and Buttington, Lord Powis having renewed for these two parishes only. The College further supported their *sole* claim to the chancel by requiring or accepting a sum of money as consideration for the erection of a monument to the late Earl of Powis.

"If the College is *now* right, much wrong has been done to their former lessees, by their being compelled by covenant to bear the whole charge of repair of the Chancel. It might also be said the College proclaimed *its own liability* to the *world*, as in the advertizement of 1828, it is said in reference to Lot 1 (part of Pool Parish), ' The purchaser of this Lot *must* covenant to keep the chancel of the Parish Church of Welshpool in repair.'

"Since writing the foregoing I have referred to other old papers, relating to a dispute between parties in the town, as to converting the organ gallery into pews ; this you will recollect as the old 'singers' gallery. I don't know who was the Vicar, but he could hardly escape being party, or if not a partizan, one who must have been interested in anything affecting the chancel, if the College present view is a right one; but the chancel is dealt with only as Lord Powis's, or as Lord Powis, as lessee of Christ Church College. The suit as to the organ gallery was a very protracted one, and conducted with much 'spleen' in some of the papers, of which there is a large bundle. I presume there was a 'family seat', as in one paper endorsed 1728, it says, 'supposing [my Lord Duke] he used his own seat in person, the gallery would be offensive from noise,' &c. Of course as a Roman Catholic he did not use it in person.

"It appears by some of the papers that the organ was demolished by the Puritans in the civil war.

"C.W., 12th June 1856."

"It may be added that all applications for permission to bury in the chancel have been made solely to the College Lessee, and given, as possessing sole right. No notice whatever is taken of the Vicar ; these are of early date."

Augmentation of Living.

On the 9th November 1848, the Dean and Chapter of Christ Church, Oxford, put their seal to the Deed of Augmentation, securing the Vicar of Welshpool £50 per annum (the sum which brought up his income to the limit which the Act of

Parliament imposes on ecclesiastical bodies). The Dean and Chapter of that time expressed objections to mural tablets being placed in the chancel, and suggested a high scale of fees for such a privilege, with the view of deterring them. The deed of augmentation was not, by some mishap, registered. At the same time they allotted £30 to Buttington.

In 1866, the Dean and Chapter were intending to withdraw one-half of it, but they were induced to continue it, on the condition they should be at liberty hereafter to reconsider the question.

Belan.

Previous to 1866, the Dean and Chapter of Christ Church, made a grant of £50 a year for the maintenance of certain services in an outlying district, viz. the Belan. They proposed to withdraw in 1866, but upon representations to them that the same necessity existed they consented to continue it.

The Bishop of St. Asaph (Dr. Short), being asked in 1868, if baptisms could be administered at the Belan, replied, "If the Lord's Supper is administered, it seems *a fortiori* that the sacrament of baptism should be administered also, and of course, churchings. The only objection to baptism is, that the register is apt to get out of order, for the school room cannot have a separate register. But, if the officiating clergyman can regularly transmit the register of the baptism performed in the Belan, and it be duly entered in the Welshpool register, and your wish that it should be so, I have no objection to the children being brought to the Belan." Upon being asked to grant a licence, the bishop replied, "No licence is necessary, the performance takes place on your discretion with my sanction."

Annexation of Gungrog Fechan to Welshpool.

By an order in Council made at the Court at Osborne House, Isle of Wight, on the 29th day of Feb. 1868, present the Queen's most excellent Majesty in Council, the township of GUNGROG FECHAN was separated from the parish of Guilsfield, and united to the parish of Welshpool for ecclesiastical purposes. After reciting the Act of 1 and 2 Victoria, intituled, "An Act to abridge the holding of Benefices in plurality, and to make better provision for the residence of the Clergy." And that the Lord Bishop of St. Asaph, had drawn up, together with a scheme, a representation in writing, bearing date the 21st day of January 1868, and had transmitted the same to the Archbishop of Canterbury, in the words and figures following [which being of local interest we give in full]:—

"To the most Reverend Charles Lord Archbishop of the Province of Canterbury.

"I, Thomas Vowler, Lord Bishop of St. Asaph, do hereby represent to your Grace, that there is [in] the County of Montgomery, and my Diocese of St. Asaph, the Vicarage of Guilsfield, the parish whereof comprizes amongst other places the township of GUNGROG FECHAN, the limits and boundaries whereof are well known and defined.

" That the said township is situate at the extreme end of the said parish of Guilsfield, and is in a great measure surrounded by the parish of Welshpool, in the said County of Montgomery, and in my Diocese of St. Asaph, to which last mentioned parish it might be more conveniently annexed for ecclesiastical purposes.

"That according to the last census, the population of the said parish of Guilsfield including the said township, is 1956 (that of the said township being estimated at 300), and of the said parish of Welshpool is 4,752.

" That the majority of the persons residing within the limits of the said township, are distant about three miles from their parish church of Guilsfield, whilst they are about half a mile from the parish church of Welshpool, to which said last mentioned church they are and have been in the habit of resorting.

" That the said Parish Church of Welshpool, and the Chapel-of-Ease of Christ Church within the said parish, afford accommodation for the inhabitants of the said parish of Welshpool, and for the persons residing within the said township.

" That the persons residing within the limits of the said township, are liable to contribute to rates for the repair of the said Parish Church of Guilsfield.

" That the patronage of a right of presentation or collation to the Vicarages of Guilsfield and Welshpool belongs to me in right of my See of St. Asaph, and the Rev. David Phillips Lewis is the present Incumbent of the said Vicarage of Guilsfield, and the Rev. John Edward Hill is the present Incumbent of the said Vicarage of Welshpool.

" That it appears to me that, under the provisions of the Act of Parliament passed in the session holden in the first and second years of the reign of Her present Majesty, chapter 106, the said township of Gungrog Fechan may be separated from the said parish of Guilsfield, and united and annexed to the said parish of Welshpool for ecclesiastical purposes.

" That pursuant to the direction contained in the 26th section of the said Act, I have prepared the following scheme, which together with the consent thereto of the Incumbents of the said Vicarages of Guilsfield and Welshpool, and of myself in particular, I do submit to your Grace, to the intent that your Grace may, if on full consideration and enquiry you shall be satisfied with such scheme, certify the same, and such consent by your report to Her Majesty in Council.

"*The Scheme above referred to.*—That the said township of Gungrog Fechan shall be separated from the parish of Guilsfield, and united and annexed to and be deemed part and parcel of the said parish of Welshpool aforesaid for ecclesiastical purposes.

"That the said township shall be subject to the same ecclesiastical jurisdiction as the said parish of Welshpool, and the Incumbent of Welshpool shall have exclusive care of souls within the limits of the same township.

"That all fees and other ecclesiastical dues and payments for churchings, marriages, burials, and other ecclesiastical offices, solemnized and performed within the said parish of Welshpool, in respect of the said township of Gungrog Fechan, shall henceforth belong to the Incumbent, Clerk, and Sexton of the said parish of Welshpool.

"That the tithe rent-charge, and other payments in lieu of tithes, of the said township, shall not be affected by the proposed separation, but shall continue payable as before.

"That the parishioners within the said township shall be liable, in common with the other inhabitants of the said parish of Welshpool, to all rates, charges, and assessments, which may henceforth be made for the repair and maintenance of the Parish Church of Welshpool, and the expenses incidental to the due performance of Divine Service therein, and shall be exempt from all rates, charges, and assessments to be made for and in respect of the said parish church of Guilsfield, or any church or chapel in the said parish of Guilsfield.

"That the parishioners within the said township shall be entitled to accommodation in the Parish Church of Welshpool, and in the said Chapel-of-Ease of Christ Church, Welshpool, but shall henceforth [not] be entitled to any accommodation in the Parish Church of Guilsfield aforesaid, except nevertheless any person or persons (if any), possessing a legal right by Faculty or otherwise to the exclusive use of any pews or sittings in the said Parish Church of Guilsfield, and who may not be willing to relinquish and give up the same.

"Given under my hand, this 21st June 1868.

"THOMAS VOWLER, St. Asaph.'

Also reciting the consent of the Bishop and two Vicars, and the certificate, by the Archbishop, of the said scheme, and consent to and his satisfaction with such scheme, to the intent that an Order in Council, may issue for carrying the aforesaid scheme into effect :

Then, therefore, Her Majesty in Council by and with the advice of her said Council, was pleased to approve of the said scheme of the Bishop of St. Asaph, and to order, and it was therefore ordered, that the same be carried into effect.

Income of Vicar.

The average gross income for the seven years ending 1866 was £321 5s., and the out-goings £73 4s., leaving the net income of £248 1s.

In 1873 the Church Extension Society made a grant to the Vicar of £50 per annum for an additional curate, on condition of additional services being held.

LEIGHTON BRIDGE.—Note to page 250, *supra*. The melancholy circumstance that led to the building of this bridge seems worthy of record. On the 5th March 1870, the river Severn was very high, and the current dangerously rapid; the old ferryman named Holloway ferried Mrs. Morris and her daughter across the river, and after landing them, returned with a passenger on the way to Welshpool. After leaving the bank of the river, the old ferryman accidentally fell into the water. Mrs. Morris rushed to the boat-house for assistance; his wife alone was at hand, and came to the river's side in time only to see her husband floating down the turbulent stream, and then sinking in deep water. The river was dragged from the 5th to the 30th March, when the body was found, Mr. Thomas Morris happening to be on the spot. An inquest was held, and a verdict of "accidentally drowned" was returned, with a presentment by the jury (of which Mr. T. Morris was foreman) strongly representing to the authorities the necessity of a bridge being built on this part of the river, on the ground that scarcely a year elapsed without some person being drowned in crossing the ferry.

On the following 9th November, Mr. Thomas Morris was elected Mayor of Welshpool, and the above melancholy circumstance made so strong an impression on his mind that he never rested until the recommendation of the jury was carried out, and a bridge was erected, which is a lasting memorial of his public spirit.

Published by R. Owen, Welshpool.

POWIS CASTLE.
MONTGOMERYSHIRE.

Newman & Co. 48 Watling St. London.

POWIS CASTLE.

POWIS CASTLE.
PAST AND PRESENT.

A HALO of glory lingers around the venerable pile of Powis Castle,[1] which partakes of the joint properties of castle and mansion, and is situated about one mile from Welshpool. It has been identified with the aspirations and affections of Central Wales for nearly 800 years, and been known, as a bulwark of independence, a senate-house for council, a scene of bardic song, and a temporary prison-house for political offenders. No Welshman can pass by it, as if it were an ordinary spot on the earth's surface. While he gazes on its towers, he feels the latent sentiment of nationality springing anew, as if the spirit, which animated the momentous events that have rendered the fortress illustrious, still hovered round, with power to attract all who may in future approach it. Its annals have been conspicuous and graphic, when Powysland formed an independent kingdom, and frequently exacted satisfaction from its neighbours

"For foul despiteous scathe and scorn," (*Scott*)

and subsequently in feudal times, and finally during the proprietorship of the noble family of Herbert.

We may be permitted to draw aside the pall of oblivion, and survey with the eye of the imagination the diademed Prince of Powys in his spacious hall, distinguished by the *Eudorchawg*, or chain of twisted gold links, the badge of Celtic royalty, and armlets, and anklets, of the same metal, peculiar to the Princes of Powys as independent sovereigns, and the national

[1] It has been called "Poole Castle", "Castle de la Pole", "The Pool Castle", "Castell Côch yn Mhowys", "Red Castle" during the Civil War in the reign of Charles I, and subsequently Powis Castle.

banner, emblazoned with the Black Lion of Powys, while we listen to the bard, arrayed in a sky-blue mantle, appealing to the glorious recollections of bygone ages, and his roll of exploits reverberating through successive centuries, and behold the martial retainers, partaking of the foaming beverage of the Hirlas Horn, and ready to shed the last drop of their blood for the honour, or security, of their fatherland. From the ramparts of Castell Coch Wenwynwyn, 'the wolf of Plinlimmon,' and 'torch of Pengwern,' at the head of 'his tall men,' or champions of Wales, led on his gallant followers to many fields of enterprize and renown, and engaged in perilous conflicts with Norman chivalry—

"Wolves of war,
They kept their border well; they did their part;
Their fame is full; their lot is praise and song."—*Southey.*

Wenwynwyn indignantly rejected the obsolete claims of Llewelyn ap Iorwerth, Prince of Gwynedd, to a supremacy over all the Welsh princes, and held him at defiance.

Our lot, however, is cast in more peaceful times—

"For see! the martial vision fails;
The glimmering spears are seen no more;
The shouts of war die on the gales,
Or sink in Severn's lonely roar.
For chiefs, intent on bloody deed,
And Vengeance, shouting o'er the slain,
Lo! highborn Beauty rules the steed,
Or graceful guides the silken rein."—*Scott.*

We can also give the reins to our fancy, as we pass in review the Barons of Powys with their sparkling coronets, ranked among the 'majores Barones' of South Britain, but divided in their sympathies between attachment to their Norman patrons, and to their tenants and dependents, who were still loyal to the descendants of their native princes in a home endeared by the prestige of a thousand national associations.

We have also many mementoes of the devoted loyalty, sufferings, and heavy losses of William, first Lord

Powis, in the protracted struggle between Charles I and his Parliament, and discern with delight and admiration the unequivocal marks of architectural taste, which has imparted to Powis Castle a prominent place among 'the stately homes' of the British aristocracy in modern times.

We propose to divide the history of the Castle into three epochs :—

I. When it was in the possession of the Princes of Powys, and their ordinary residence.

II. When it was in the possession of the feudal Barons of Powys, and writs of summons were issued in right of their tenure thereof. And

III. When it became the property and seat of the noble house of Herbert, who, as owners thereof, received creation by patent, and became Peers of the realm by patents of creation, renewed on several occasions.

I. The first mention which history makes of Powis Castle, is about A.D. 1109, when Cadwgan ap Bleddyn ap Cynfyn sought an asylum at Tre'r Llyn, or Trallyn, now Welshpool, and, having reduced the country to some kind of order, and restored the courts of judicature, in which he sat in person to administer justice, he began to erect a castle, but, having been treacherously murdered by his nephew Madoc ap Ririd, he left the building unfinished. It was continued by his kinsman, Wenwynwyn ap Owen Cyfeiliog, who succeeded his father Owen in the government of this part of Powysland, and, on its completion, it appeared a low-roofed edifice of red stone, while a ditch and palisade were, in addition to the commanding situation, its most important defences.

Wenwynwyn[1] in very early life took his part in the desultory warfare, that sprang up among the Norman

[1] Sir Walter Scott in his novel of the *Betrothed*, chap. i, alludes incorrectly to Castell Coch, or "the Red Castle", since better known by the name of Powis Castle, as in latter times the princely seat of the Duke of Beaufort, and misrepresents Wenwynwyn as childless.

chieftains on the border, or embroiled him with his countrymen in North and South Wales.

In the lifetime of his father he conquered the cantred of Arwystli, probably from the Princes of South Wales, to whom it had been given, by Henry II, in 1171.

In the year 1191, in consequence of the depredations committed by the Welsh on the inhabitants of the Marches, Hubert, Archbishop of Canterbury, in the absence of King Richard I, came with a powerful army and besieged the Castle. He met with a vigorous resistance, and the garrison disdained to capitulate to a beleaguering host, thrice exceeding their own in numbers, till the walls had been sapped by a company of miners. Forthwith the English forces repaired and strengthened its defences, and having quartered a strong garrison within its walls returned to England.

But Wenwynwyn, chagrined by the loss of his principal stronghold, determined to put forth all his energies in the hope of its recovery. He proceeded to lay siege to it, and it was shortly delivered up to him on the same terms, which his own men had previously received at the hands of the English commander, as we learn from Yorke's *Royal Tribes in the Pentarchia*—

" Wenwynwyn, sanguinis hæres,
Ante obitum patris totam subjecit Arustli,
Inde Polæ castrum, quod vi subjecerat Anglus,
Conditione pari, qua perdidit ante, recepit."

T. Evans, in his *Topography and History of North Wales*, p. 881, citing Hoveden and Stowe, says that the event happened in 1197.

The Prince of Powys Uchaf, being dissatisfied with the arbitrary pretensions of the Prince of Gwynedd, was subsequently induced to go over to the English side, and consented to become a vassal to King John, and to hold his territory *in capite* of the King of England. But when Llewelyn ap Iorwerth, Prince of Gwynedd, on his return from South Wales, which he had been visiting as paramount sovereign, was apprised of the fact, that Wenwynwyn had broken the national league, and renewed his oaths of allegiance to King John, he despatched some friendly ecclesiastics to remonstrate with the Prince of Powys Uchaf. On their intervention, however, proving unsuccessful, the indignant monarch of Cymrû Oll led an army into Wenwynwyn's territory, in 1233, and ravaged it with fire and sword, and dismantled his castle at Pool, which, from the colour of the stone, was then called Castell Côch, or the Red Castle in Powysland. Wenwynwyn, bending under the weight of years and overwhelming reverses of fortune, fled for refuge to Ranulph, Earl of Chester, and shortly afterwards closed his troublous career.

Llewelyn ap Iorwerth, Prince of Gwynedd, conferred the realm of Powys Uchaf on Griffith ap Madoc, Prince of Powys Isaf, and Lord of Dinas Bran.

In the year 1241, Griffith ap Wenwynwyn regained his hereditary territories, becoming, however, a feudal tenant in chief of the English monarch, Henry the Third. He remained true to his allegiance for many years, and his loyalty survived the first outburst of Welsh glory and success in the early triumphs of Llewelyn ap Griffith, Prince of Gwynedd. It was not until his country had been conquered by Llewelyn, and lost to the English beyond all reasonable hope of recovery, that he joined the standard of his native country, and, on entering into an alliance, offensive and defensive, with the victorious Llewelyn, received back from him his territory, to be held of the Prince of Gwynedd. This state of things was temporarily recognized by the King of England, who acknowledged in perilous times the claims of Llewelyn, and consented to his receiving the fealty and homage of all the Barons of Wales. Thus Powysland and its Castle were once more annexed to the principality of Wales, and continued in that union for about twelve years.

But a rupture occurred, about the year 1275, between Llewelyn ap Griffith, Prince of Gwynedd, and Griffith ap Wenwynwyn, Prince of Powys Uchaf, whereby the territory and the castle of the latter lapsed once more under English protection.

In 1274, Llewelyn had visited Dolforwyn, and complained of the deceit and disloyalty of the Prince of Powys Uchaf, and dispossessed him of Arwystli, and thirteen townships of Cyfeiliog, and taken away with him, as a hostage, his eldest son, Owen, to Gwynedd.

Early[1] in the year 1275, Llewelyn ap Griffith, being in his palace at Aber, entertained his brother David as a guest, together with David's retainers, and expected, with friendly hospitality, the arrival of Owen ap Griffith ap Wenwynwyn, to share their social board, and the pleasures of the chase. Prince Owen arrived, but the knights, who were to have accompanied him, were prevented from coming by the bad weather, which rendered many parts of the country impassable. David, being much troubled by this circumstance, left his brother's court abruptly, and Owen, disconcerted, and fearing that one or other of his accomplices might betray him, made full confession to Llewelyn of a plot formed by Prince David, who, desiring to obtain the sovereignty of Wales, had intended on a certain night during his sojourn to conduct Owen with his knights to Llewelyn's sleeping place, that they might murder him. Owen had been won to promise his aid in this conspiracy by David's offer of his daughter in marriage, endowed either with Cydewin and Ceri, or with the private patrimony of Llewelyn in Perfeddwlad. The Prince of Wales, being informed of these particulars, cited David to appear at Rhuddlan, and answer to the charge of treason. David refused to do so, unless furnished with a safe conduct; an accusation was, therefore, formally drawn up, and a day fixed for him to appear and answer it; but, before that day arrived, he had mustered a strong band of armed men, left his abode, found refuge with Llewelyn's enemies, and with them commenced a series of predatory incursions upon Llewelyn's territories.

Meanwhile the Prince of Wales, having learned that

[1] Williams's *History of Wales*, p. 391.

sealed documents, embodying the terms of this treasonable compact, were kept at Castell Tre'r Llyn, near Welshpool, as Powis Castle was then called, in the safe custody of Owen's mother, sent messengers thither to demand them. Griffith ap Wenwynwyn, Prince of Powys Uchaf, Owen's father, received the messengers, offered them hospitable accommodation for the night, and promised to accompany them on the morrow into Llewelyn's presence; but, having thus plausibly beguiled them, he cast them into a deep dungeon.

He then fortified his castle with more than a hundred men and arms, laying in provisions and all other things necessary for the siege and defence of a castle, and, having raised the standard of war on the greater tower, and burned the houses outside, as was the custom in time of war, he himself, with his family, went over to the prince's enemies, and committed gross outrages and depredations in his lands, in 1281.

This throws some light upon the state of the castle at that time, and that it had more towers than one—the greater tower being used for hoisting the standard; whether the houses burnt would be in the town of Pole, or dwellings immediately adjoining the castle, it is not now possible to determine.

The remonstrances addressed to Griffith by the deputation of Welsh ecclesiastics were in vain, and he forthwith hastened to Shrewsbury, where he concerted with Prince David fresh schemes of treason.

In his will[1] dated in 1277-8, Griffith in almost royal language disposes of his lands amongst his sons, giving to his eldest son, Owen, 'all his land of Sorlanherth hudol (Llannerchudol), which would include the Castle.

The will proceeds, " We will also and concede to our said son, Owen, and his heirs, that, if they should happen to build or restore any castle, and the community of the same Owen, or his heirs, should be called together for this purpose, the whole community belonging to the lands of our said sons should take their part in

[1] *Mont. Coll.*, i, p. 38.

this common aid, according to that, which the said Owen's tenants should do, or should be bound to do, free from all contradiction or impediment from his said brothers, or their heirs."

From this paragraph it seems probable, that the Castle of Pole was not in a good state of repair, but required rebuilding, or restoration.[1]

On June 9th, 1281, King Edward addressed a letter to the Prince of Gwynedd, informing him, that he had instructed his justiciaries to decide the long-pending cause between the Prince of Gwynedd and Griffith ap Wenwynwyn, in accordance with the laws and customs of Wales, but the promise of speedy adjudication was not fulfilled, and the Prince of Gwynedd, provoked by repeated delays, and irritated by fruitless summonses, was rendered at length fiercely indignant by King Edward's absolute refusal to bring the case into court, unless the Prince would consent to have it tried by English laws. He once more risked the fortunes of war, and perished by an untimely fate in the following year on the banks of the Yrfon, near Builth, Brecknockshire.

Owen ap Griffith, the last Prince of Powys Wenwynwyn, known as Lord de la Pole from his residence, Powis Castle, near Welshpool, was summoned to a Parliament held at Shrewsbury, and acknowledging his domains to be possessed under the Crown of England *in capite*, under the title of Free Baronage, he resigned to the King, his heirs, and the Crown of England, the

[1] At Welshpool, close east of the Railway station, is a mound, somewhat mutilated by the formation of a bowling green, which, in a map of 1629, is called Domine (Domen) Castell, and near which is, or was, a mill called the Domen Mill. It appears from an inquest in 1299, that William de Bollers had certain tenements in Mariton under John Fitz Reginald by the service of providing one soldier in time of war at the mote of Pole (*ad motam de Pola*) armed with a bow, two arrows, and a bolt. He was to serve for a night and a day. See Eyton's *Antiquities of Shropshire*, xi, 91. This has been supposed to relate to Powis, or Powis Castle; but surely the Mote of Pole is more likely to be the above-mentioned mound.—*Mont. Coll.*, vol. x, p. 348.

name and crown of a prince (*"nomen et circulum principatus"*). Thus he surrendered his princely prerogatives, and descended to the position of a feudal Baron of England.

This important circumstance, affecting the nationality of Powys Uchaf, determines our first epoch, and we hasten by transition to our second period, the epoch of the Feudal Barons of Powys.

II.—The epoch of the Feudal Barons of Powys. Owen ap Griffith married Hawyse, daughter of Philip Corbet, Baron of Caus, and by her had an only daughter, Hawyse Gadarn, or the Hardy, so called for her resolute defence of her hereditary rights. Tradition reports, that she was called upon to resist the claims of her four uncles, Llewelyn, John, Griffith Vychan, and David, who questioned the eligibility of a female to succeed to the family dignities, but this report does not seem to be well founded except in its reference to Griffith Vychan, her bitter and frequent opponent.

At the death of Owen, in 1293, *Inquisitiones post mortem* were held, which give at great length the details of his princely possessions. They were held at La Pole, and the Castle of La Pole. That relating to Machynlleth[1] is said to belong to "the honour of the Castle of La Pole *(pertinentem ad honorem castri de la Pole)*. The Inquisition relating to Llanerchydol manor comprises the Castle, and says he was seized at the time of his death of

" Soetlanverwodel, with the adjacent hamlets, by service of the Barony of Pole.

" Also the easements of the houses within the curtilage, the herbage of the garden, and the pasture round the castle, of the annual value of ixs.

" Also that there were cc acres of arable land in the demesne, every one of which is of the value of iid., xxxiiis. and iiijd."

---

[1] *Mont. Coll.*, vii, p. 321.

The value of the Castle, gardens, and park being only £2 4s. 4d., in 1293, is a striking instance of the rise of the value of landed property in the last six centuries.

Hawyse Gadarn, by the influence of Edward II, August 26th, 1309, became the wife of John de Cherleton, born in 1268, elder son of Sir Allan de Cherleton, of Apley, co. Salop, who in her right acquired the feudal Barony of Powys, held *in capite*, and the Castle, from the English Crown, and was summoned to Parliament 26th July, 1313,[1] as Dominus Powys, and from that period to 25th July, 1353.

Sir John de Cherleton took a leading part in the military and parliamentary transactions of his time. In conjunction with his wife's uncle, Griffith de la Pole, in 1310, he was requested to allow 400 soldiers to be raised in the Lordship of Powys, and summoned to give aid against the Scots on several occasions, and summoned to Parliament at Westminster in 1313, again in 1314, and required to raise 500 soldiers from his lordship of Powys, again 200 from his lordship of Builth, and 300 from Powys in 1317, and to raise 500 foot soldiers from Powys in 1319. He is addressed as one of the "majores barones" in 1318. In 1322, he was in arms against the king at the battle of Boroughbridge, after which he surrendered himself. Summoned again to raise 500 men in 1325, and again in the following year, he regained the confidence of his sovereign. He is variously called Sire Johan de Cherleton, Dominus de Powys, and Seigneur de Powis in the military writs. He was engaged for awhile as Lord Chief Justice of Ireland. Among other manors, on which inquisition was taken at his death, 49 Edw. III, are found Mathraval, Keveilioc, Arustle, Castrum de Pole, etc.

---

[1] Nov. 6, 1313, an order in Council had been issued to the effect that Monsieur Griffith de la Pole, Monsire Fouk Lestrange, and their allies, were not to be apprehended or molested for the part which they had taken in the siege of Pole Castle, nor for the depredations which they had committed in the lands of Powys and la Pole, and elsewhere in that neighbourhood.—*Mont. Coll.*, vol. i, p. 71.

In accordance with the religious practice of the age, Sir John de Cherleton enriched the foundation of the Franciscan Friars at Shrewsbury, where his wife's grandfather, Griffith ap Wenwynwyn, her father Owen, herself and husband were buried. Time has not yet destroyed the last memorials of these two noble persons. An inscription under the figure of Sir John de Cherleton, in a window of St. Mary's Church at Shrewsbury, asks the passenger to pray for Monsieur Sir John de Cherleton, who caused this glazing to be made, and for Dame Hawyse his *companion,* this unusual term signifying a union with royalty.

Griffith de la Pole,[1] the son of Prince Owen and Joanna, did not live to attain his majority. In the first year, however, of Edward II, though still a minor, he appears to have had the custody of the Castle of Pole, together with all the lands and tenements, which were of Owen de la Pole deceased, assigned to him by the King's gift, and in the following year, by charter dated at Windsor on July 14th, 1308, under the king's privy seal, the king concedes to his beloved valet, Griffith, son of Owen de la Pole, the custody of the lands and tenements, which were of John and David, sons of Griffith de la Pole, which they held of him *in capite* on the days of their death, and which were in the king's hands by reason of the minority of (the same) Griffith de la Pole, the nephew and heir of the said John and David, to hold together with all the rights belonging to the said custody until the full age of the same Griffith, paying thereof to the king in each year into his treasury, at the customary terms, the value of the aforesaid lands and tenements during the aforesaid custody. He died under age, in June 1309 ; and in the same year, Walter de Gloucester, the king's escheator, had orders to take in hand the lands and tenements, which were of Griffith, son and heir of Owen de la Pole, deceased. The inquest was held at La Pole on the Wednesday before the feast of St. Lawrence in

[1] *Mont. Coll.*, vol. i, 55.

the 3rd year of Edward II, August 10th, 1309. The jury found, that he had held of the king by barony, and for his homage and fealty, the castle of La Pole in the country of Powys, with two parts of the vill of la Pole, and the other tenements below mentioned, namely, the vill of Disserth, as a member of la Pole, Llanerthudel, the vills of Trevenant and Castell, certain tenements at Selveyn, the vills of Tidinprid, Trallungolleyn, and Gaer, with rents from Bruchtyr, Estrodelvedan, etc. He had held also other extensive estates in Powysland. The whole was held of the king by the service before mentioned, and the profits arising from the whole amounted in all to £190 6s. 11d. Hawyse was his sister and nearest heir, and she was eighteen years of age on the feast of St. James, the Apostle, last past, July 25th, 1309.

It is not evident, that all the uncles of Hawyse Gadarn were strongly opposed to the succession of their niece, Hawyse Gadarn, to the estate of her ancestors. Three uncles were already dead, two of whom, being ecclesiastics, could have left no legitimate issue. Griffith Vychan, however, the fifth in age, was undoubtedly opposed to the claims of his niece, and levied considerable forces, with which he besieged Pool Castle unsuccessfully, and continued in his enmity apparently to the end of his career. Hawyse Gadarn seems to have enjoyed a semi-regal authority in Powysland, in subjection to the English crown.

There is an old tradition, which seems to have originated with Dr. Powel, that this lady's uncles, Llewelyn, John, Griffith Vychan, and David, upon the death of their nephew Griffith, laid claim to their brother's lands, alleging, for a cloak to their usurpation, that by the gafel she could not, as a female, inherit her father's lands. But her cause was taken up by the king, who gave her in marriage to Sir John de Cherleton, a gentleman of his bedchamber, and ordered Roger de Mortimer to go to her rescue. By Mortimer's assistance, their machinations were defeated, and resulted in a decision from the Crown to the effect, that their estates should be limited to their heirs male, and on failure of such should revert to Hawyse and her heirs. It is, nevertheless, true, that the lands of all her uncles, with the exception of those of William de la Pole, the Lord of Mawddy, did eventually revert to the heirs of Hawyse. "Joh'es de Charlton, et Hawisia uxor ejus dixerunt, quod ipsi tenent terram de Powys, ut jus et hereditatem ipsius Hawysiæ, et quod ipsi habent in terris illis omnem regalem libertatem."

But the paramount authority, or supremacy, of the King of England is clearly asserted, for Sir John Cherleton has to appear before the council of the King, "coram concilio Domini Regis," and King Edward II proposes terms of pacification after the unsuccessful siege of Pool Castle.

Griffith Vychan[1] was certainly a person of some importance in Powysland, for a writ of Edward II, dated June 18th, 1310, not only makes him a commissioner to levy forces in Wales for the then proposed invasion of Scotland, but definitely names him, and John de Cherleton, as the persons, who, it was expected, would allow a contingent of four hundred men to be enlisted in their land of Powys.

In the year 1312, Griffith de la Pole asserted a claim to Pool Castle, and, raising a great power of the Welsh, laid siege to that fortress. In that year he disposed of his estate at Longnor, co. Salop, to provide himself with funds necessary to carry on his perilous enterprise. He was foiled, however, in his design, chiefly through the intervention of Roger de Mortimer, of Wigmore, whom Edward II instructed to support Hawyse and her husband. But the English King was not altogether unfavourable to him, for in the year 1313, November 6th, an order in council was issued to the effect, that Monsieur Griffith de la Pole, Monsire Fouk Lestrange, and their allies, were not to be apprehended or molested for the part, which they had taken in the

[1] *Mont. Coll.*, vol. i, p. 65.

siege of Pool Castle, nor for the depredations which they had committed in the lands of Powys, and La Pole, and elsewhere in that neighbourhood. In the same year, Griffith de la Pole complained to the king in council, that he had been disseized of his land in Powys, and prayed for redress. Judgment was deferred until the next session of Parliament. The stake was great, and the hostilities in fact amounted to a civil war between the contending parties. Not long after this, in the spring of the year 1316, we find him again at war with John de Cherleton and Hawyse his wife, and the king's mandate was issued to the contending parties, ordering them, under penalty of forfeiture, to cease from hostilities, and citing them to appear before him on the quindene of the next Easter, to prosecute their suit, and receive justice thereupon. On March 8th, 1316, the king's writ was directed to all his bailiffs, etc., informing them, that he had sent John de Crumwell to those parts (Powysland) to enforce his mandate. It is next recorded, that John and Hawyse had ceased from hostilities on their side, and in all things obeyed the king's orders; but Griffith continued his depredations in open defiance of the king's commands, and, on April 3rd, the sheriff of Shropshire was ordered to go himself to Griffith and make known to him the contents of the former mandate. On the quindene of Easter aforesaid, John de Cherleton in person, and Hawyse by her attorney, duly appeared before the king's council at Westminster, and placed themselves in the king's hands. But the sheriff of Shropshire stated that he had been to the town of Pole, and being unable to find Griffith either there or in the parts about la Pole, or elsewhere in his bailiwick, he had fully notified the contents of the king's writ to Philip de Smethcote, Griffith's *locum tenens*, and many others of the land of la Pole, and he further stated that he had also notified the same to Griffith himself, at his lands and tenements at Dendor in Powys, by Edmund de Langedon and Walter de Burghton, in the presence of Peter Corbet, and Thomas de Wynnesbury. However, Griffith appeared not either in person or by his attorney, and apparently judgment went by default.

Nevertheless, a writ of November 1st, 1318, names Griffith de la Pole as one of the adherents of Thomas, Earl of Lancaster, who were pardoned for all felonies and trespasses up to the 7th of August preceding.

In 1328, Griffith de la Pole complains to the king and his council that Sir John de Cherleton, in the time of King Edward II, had forcibly ejected him from his land of Dendour and Mecheyn Iscoit in Powys, which he had held of the king *in capite*, and of which land he had been seized for upwards of thirty years, as of his rightful inheritance.

A memorandum occurs in the Parliament Rolls of 1330, to the intent, that the king, having heard that Mons. Johan de Cherleton and Mons. Griffith de la Pole, by reason of the dispute, which had so long continued between them, had assembled men-at-arms, and collected opposing forces, which were great evils and vexations in breach of the peace, and in the facilities they afforded them for invading the parts of Wales and the Marches, his Majesty forbade the said Mons. Johan and Mons. Griffith de la Pole, then present in the same Parliament, under pain of forfeiture, to assemble men-at-arms, or levy them, or cause them to be levied, on the one side or the other, for the purpose of engaging in war, or perpetrating any other evil, or to make forcible entrance upon any castles, manors, lands, or tenements, or to do anything in breach of the peace, or to the terror of the people. And the said Mons. Johan and Mons. Griffith were informed by the king, that if either of them wished to make any complaint of the other, they must do so in the form of a petition, and the king would adjudicate thereon.

This is the last we hear of Griffith de la Pole. There is no doubt of the fact that his pretensions were formidable, and that his hostilities rendered the tenure of the Castle of Pool by Sir John de Cherleton and his wife, Hawyse, insecure, for it required the Royal forces of England to aid Sir John de Cherleton in the defeat of his rival. His death put an end to the uncertainty of the issue of the contest, and Sir John de Cherleton and Hawyse, his wife, were left in undisturbed possession of the Castle, and its territorial appanage.

Pending this long contention, John de Cherleton exercised all the rights of dominion, and, among other matters, granted a charter to the burgesses of Pole, in which he styled himself Lord of Pole, and issued it from his Castle of Pole.

In it he gives the burgesses of Pole the liberty of apprehending all fugitives and felons, evidently for the purpose of putting down the adherents of Griffith de la Pole, then asserting his right to the Castle of Pole.

Whatever the Castle may have consisted of before Sir John de Cherleton's marriage with Hawyse, the heiress of the Princes of Powys, the present structure owes its foundation to the English Baron, who, to maintain the influence of the English Crown, under whom he held the Castle and Barony, maintained an English garrison in Welshpool, and naturally set himself to make Castle Trellyn a fabric worthy of the castle-building age, in which he lived.

We shall reserve the proofs, that Sir John de Cherleton was the builder of the present Castle, and proceed to record what few historical facts are extant respecting it during his time, and that of his successors.

The Castle and estates devolved for three generations in the direct line. Upon the deaths of his son, John de Cherleton (II), "Dominus de Powys", in 1360, and of his grandson, John de Cherleton (III), "de Powys", in 1374, the *Inquisitiones post mortem*, then severally held, found, that each of them died possessed of the Castle and Manor of La Pole.[1]

His great grandson, John de Cherleton (IV) de Powys, had an engagement with Owen Glendower, in

[1] *Mont. Coll.*, i, p. 278, *et seq.*

1401, and defeated him. It is probable, that this was the occasion, when the suburbs of Welshpool were ravaged and burnt; possibly the contest may have been in defence of the Castle, then an important fortress. He died in 1401, leaving no issue, when his Castle and estates devolved upon his brother and heir, Edward de Cherleton. It is remarkable that, in that year, amongst the subjects brought before the Privy Council, the matters of the land of Powys and Castle de la Pole, which had lately come into the king's hand, were brought forward, and the custody thereof was committed to Lord Burnell. Nevertheless, shortly afterwards, Edward de Cherleton took possession of the Castle and land inherited by him from his brother, but the times were troublous, and the rebellion was then raging. In 1403, we find him writing a letter to the Privy Council—a very early specimen of letter writing—urging the despatch of reinforcements. That letter is expressed to be written at the Castle de la Pole.

In 1404, Edward de Cherleton was authorised by the Council to make a truce as to his Castle of Pole.

The charters, granted by Edward de Cherleton to the burgesses of Pole in 1406, show how much that borough was treated as an English garrison. It is given "*apud castrum nostrum de Pola*", whilst two other charters, granted it, are given "*apud manerium de Mathraval*".

In this charter, amongst the witnesses, are "John Fitz Piers, Captain of our Castle of Pole, John Kendall, our constable there", showing it had a garrison properly officered. His predecessors do not mention such officers, except his brother John de Cherleton, and they both probably had to appoint such officers in consequence of the attacks, to which they were subjected during the rebellion of Owen Glendower. We will give a list of officers mentioned in one of the charters, indicating the almost royal state, which the Lords of Powis displayed during the *régime* of the Cherletons :—

21st January, 1411.
David Holbach, our Seneschal of Powys.
Matthew ap Ieuan, his locum tenens.
Wilhelmus Piers, our receiver.
Hugo Say, our Constable and Captain of our Castle of Pole.
Peter Barbour, our Chaplain.

There existed a chapel on the top of the Castle, in which religious services were performed until recent times.

In 1409, when Glendower again began to make a great head, and Edward de Cherleton's estate suffered greatly, the King directed a writ to him to raise forces, and suppress vigorously this new disturbance, and to keep his Castle garrisoned, and not to permit any of his estates to be deserted.

In 1417, Sir John Oldcastle, Lord Cobham, the celebrated Lollard, being pursued by Henry V with great perseverance, took refuge in Powysland, in Broniarth, in the parish of Guilsfield, and just outside the boundary of the Borough of Welshpool, and was there captured by Edward de Cherleton, Lord of Powys, with the aid of Sir Griffith Vaughan, his brothers, and humble dependents. Upon his capture, Sir John Grey was sent down by Parliament to take charge of him, and took him to Pool Castle, and afterwards to London, where he was hanged as a traitor, and burnt as a heretic. This visit of Sir John Grey to Pool Castle led to his marriage with Joane, the eldest daughter of Sir Edward de Cherleton, who survived him. Sir John Grey was present on 3rd April, 1421, at the battle at Beaugè in France, where, with many others, he was slain.

Edward de Cherleton died on 14th March, 1421, being then seized of the Castle and Manor of Pole, and its attendant manors, leaving his second wife surviving, who afterwards married John de Sutton, fourth Baron Dudley. She, and her second husband, in her right, occupied the Castle for many years. She was deceased in 1479, when she was found by inquest to be seized of the Ville of Pole.

Upon the death of Edward de Cherleton, his great possessions passed to his two daughters and co-heiresses, Joane, then aged twenty-one, and already the widow of Sir John Grey, and Joyce, then aged eighteen, and soon afterwards married to Sir John Tiptoft.

From 1421, when Edward de Cherleton died, until about 1541, the castle was held in coparcenery by his daughters and co-heiresses, and their respective descendants, and, strange to say, each daughter, and her descendants, assumed the title of " Powys", and this circumstance shows how the possession of this castle and the appendant estates, or even of a moiety or undivided share thereof, in these early times, when the peerage law was unsettled, was deemed competent to confer upon the possessor a Barony by tenure. We are not able to trace the fact except by inquisitions *post mortem*, and some other fragmentary information, but that such was the case will undoubtedly appear.

We propose, in the first instance, to trace the devolution of the moiety, or undivided share of the castle and lands belonging to the elder daughter, Joane, and then the moiety of the younger daughter, Joyce, until the entirety became re-united in one possessor.

Joane, the eldest daughter, on the death of her father, had livery of her paternal inheritance, of which the Lordship of Powys was part. She died in 1425, seized, according to the inquisition after her death, of the Castle of Pole, and divers lands thereunto abutting, with the keep there (" *cum le dungeon ibidem* ") and other large possessions. The keep was the principal tower or stronghold of the castle, and situate in the innermost court. Its lower part was commonly used as a prison, and probably was in this instance.

Although the Castle of Pole is mentioned in the Inquisition, a part only of the castle was inherited by her, probably the portion surrounding the keep or stronghold of the castle, for her sister's heirs were, as it will appear, seized of a moiety of the castle, called the " Utterward."

"Near Trallhwn, on the south side", writes Camden, in his *Britannia* in 1580, "is a castle called, from the reddish stones of which it is built, Castle Kôch, where within the same walls are two castles, belonging to the Lord of Powys, the other to Baron Dudley."

In 1425, upon the death of Joane, her eldest son, Henry Grey, succeeded to her Powys possessions, and, when knighted, was called Dominus Powys.

In 1438, by a minute of Privy Council, dated 5th May, it was accorded that, by a warrant under the privy seal, "the Jaylor of (ye Castel of) Poole be directed to remove certain prisoners to the Castel of Shrowesbury." From this fragmentary minute, it seems as if the Castle of Poole was used as a gaol for the confinement of State prisoners. "Le Dungeon," or the keep, has been already mentioned in the inquisition *post mortem* of Joane, mother of Sir Henry Grey.

For a century afterwards the castle must have been used as a gaol, for Leland, writing about 1544, says:

"In all, Hy Powis is not one castle, that evidently aperithe by manifest ruins of waulis; and *they were* wont to bring, in tymes past, in the old Lord Duddley's days, theyr prisoners to Welshpool . . . . And in Low Pois is but onely the Castle of the Walche Poole."

In 1441-2, the Greys and Tiptofts effected a partial partition of the estates, but they continued to hold the Castle of Pole in moieties for another century.

In 1447, a tragic occurrence took place at the Castle of Pool. Sir Griffith Vaughan, who was one of the active agents in arresting Sir John Oldcastle, the Lollard chief, was himself eventually taken off in a violent manner. It seems certain that, having refused to obey a summons of Henry Grey, Lord of Powis, to perform some feudal service, he was beheaded in the courtyard of Pool Castle, and, as appears by the elegies, by the violation of a safe conduct granted to him. Lewis Glyn Cothi describes the land of Powys, as being in a state of consternation on hearing of the foul deed.

One motive, that has been suggested, is that Sir Griffith arrogantly asserted his right, through his grandmother, an heiress fourth in descent from Wenwynwyn, Prince of Powys Uchaf, to a portion of the Lordship of Powys, which incited Henry Grey to commit this treacherous and cruel act.

Soon afterwards, in 1450, Henry Grey himself died, being seized, according to his inquisition *post mortem*, of the Castle and Manor of Pool (but we presume a moiety of the castle is meant), and leaving his son and heir, Richard Grey, who succeeded him in his honours and estates, and a daughter Elizabeth, who married Sir Humphrey Kynaston, and whose descendants, John Kynaston, Esq., and Sir John Kynaston Powell, severally, in 1732 and 1800, preferred claims for the abeyant barony of Powys.

Richard Grey, Lord Powys, was a Yorkist, but at Ludford, in 1459, with many others, laid down his arms, and was glad to compound for his life by the forfeiture of his estates, which, however, was not enforced.

He died in 1465, possessed of a moiety of the Castle of Pole, and his son John succeeded him, and obtained livery of his lands on his coming of age in 1480. He sat in the House of Lords, as Lord "Grey de Powys", and died in 1497, leaving a son and heir, John, who was never summoned to Parliament. They must in succession have possessed the castle, but no record appears thereof. John, Lord Grey, died in 1504, at the age of 19, having been married, under curious circumstances,[1] to Margaret, daughter of Edward, Lord Dudley, K.G., leaving a son and successor, Edward, then only a year old.

The Greys were a short-lived family, five of them in succession succeeded to their family inheritance when infants, and in the short space of 83 years four generations of them passed away.

It is convenient now to advert to the devolution of

[1] *Mont. Coll.*, vol. i, p. 345.

the other moiety of the castle, belonging to the younger daughter and co-heiress of Sir Edward de Cherleton.

Joyce, the second daughter, married Sir John Tiptoft, who, in consequence of this marriage, was summoned to Parliament, and, although designated in the summons as "John Tiptoft, Cavalier" only, he bore the title of Powys.

In 1446, Joyce de Tiptoft, described as "Domina Powys", died, and was buried at Enfield. A splendid monumental brass was erected to her memory, and a rubbing of it is in the Powysland Museum. Her son, John de Tiptoft, succeeded to a moiety of the castle, and to her lands, and was created Earl of Worcester, and in his patent of creation is called Lord Tiptoft and Powys.

In 1470, John, Earl of Worcester, died, and by inquisition is found to have died seized of the moiety of the Castle of Pole, called the "Utterward", with the Lordship of Powys, and his son Edward de Tiptoft succeeded him, when only two years old, and died in 1485. He left no issue, and upon his death his heirs were his aunts Philippa, wife of Thomas de Roos, Joane, wife of Sir Edmund Ingoldsthorpe, Knight, and Joyce, the wife of Edmund de Sutton, son and heir of John de Sutton, Baron Dudley. Only the children of Joyce, the wife of Edmund de Sutton, appear to have become connected with the Powys estate, and, therefore, we conclude, upon the division of Edward de Tiptoft's estates amongst his three aunts, the Powys estate fell to the lot of Joyce.

Sir Edmund de Sutton died in the lifetime of his father, John de Sutton, fourth Baron Dudley; and upon the latter's death in 1482, the moiety of the Castle of Poole devolved upon John Sutton, fifth Baron Dudley.

There were no less than four marriages of the Suttons with the Cherleton Grey and Tiptoft families, and they resulted in a curious concatenation of events.

The first-mentioned marriage of John, first Baron

Sutton of Dudley, with Isabel, daughter of John de Cherleton, Lord of Powys, probably led to the subsequent connections; but we do not find that he, by his marriage, became entitled to, or connected with, any part of the Powys estates.

The second marriage of John, fourth Baron Sutton of Dudley, with the widow of Edward de Cherleton, led to his being seated at the castle, now called Powis Castle, in right of his wife. She was deceased in 1479, and was by inquest found to be seized at her death of the Ville of Pole. After the battle of Bloreheath, where he was wounded, he received from Henry VI the stewardship of Montgomery and Chirbury for life, to be executed personally, or by deputy.

There was also, as mentioned previously, a matrimonial connection between the Grey branch of the family and the Dudley family, for Lord Grey of Powys married Margaret, daughter of Edward, Lord Dudley.

The fourth marriage naturally followed the second marriage; Sir Edmund de Sutton, the son of John, fourth Baron of Dudley, married Joyce, daughter of John, Lord Tiptoft, by Joyce, his wife, the granddaughter and heiress of Edward de Cherleton, Lord of Powys, whose widow the father had married. By this alliance, Edmund de Sutton became possessed of a moiety of the Castle and Barony of Powys, and also the two important manors of Cyfeiliog and Arwystli, which remained in his descendants for three generations. Their younger son, Robert Sutton, who assumed the name of Dudley, was steward of Powys, or at least of the Dudley portion of Powys, and probably of these manors. Two, at least, of the direct descendants and heirs of Sir Edmund de Sutton and Joyce, his wife, took the title of "Powes", apparently in right of the tenure by them successively of a moiety of the castle and estates. We shall proceed to adduce evidence of this being the case.

Their eldest son was John Sutton, fifth Baron of Dudley, summoned to Parliament from 1483 to 1487.

We have found no evidence of his having assumed the title of Powes, but there can be little doubt of his having done so, as his son unquestionably did, for the partial proprietorship of Powys Castle frequently conferred the title of Powys by tenure, and his maternal grandfather and uncle had previously assumed this title of Powys.

His son was Edward Sutton, sixth Baron of Dudley, summoned to Parliament from 1492 to 1529. He, undoubtedly, assumed the title of Dudley "*and Powes*". In the epitaph of his two sons (who died 1501 and 1504), formerly in Hinley Church, he is designated as "Domini Edward Sutton, Militis, Domini Dudley et Powes." In a document dated 1534, Edward Sutton is described as "Lord Dudley and Powys", and he there seems to represent the Lordship or Barony of Powys, and assumes to make a covenant or engagement with the Steward, Constable, and Lieutenant of Oswestry for the extradition of criminals found in their respective jurisdictions, and for other like purposes.

His son was John Sutton, seventh Baron, but was never summoned to Parliament. That he was designated "Lord Powes", is shown in convincing evidence by the accomplished genealogist, Rev. W. V. Lloyd, in an episode in his biographical sketch of one of the Montgomeryshire Sheriffs, Thomas Ireland.[1] Mr. Lloyd mentions Robert Dudley, younger brother of John, Lord Dudley, and great uncle to John, seventh Baron, and says :—

"In the volume of the Stafford MSS. are some depositions by this Robert Dudley, taken 30 Henry VIII, 1538, in which he states that he dwelleth in Shrewsbury, and has dwelled there twenty years and more, and also was brother to the late Lord Dudley, grandfather to the *Lord Powes* that now is."

Mr. Lloyd points out that the Lord Powes here referred to was John Dudley, seventh Baron, and not, as Mr. Blakeway erroneously supposes, Edward Grey, the last of the line, and proceeds to remark :—

[1] *Mont. Coll.*, vol. ix, p. 95.

"As the Greys and Tiptofts, representing Joan and Joyce, the co-heiresses of Sir Edward de Cherleton, Lord of Powys, used the title of Powys at the same time (see the Herald's opinion in 'Feudal Barons of Powys', *Mont. Coll.*, vol. i, pp. 388-9), so did in 1538 their representatives, the Greys and Sutton Dudleys. This would shew that the attainder in 1470 of Robert Dudley's uncle, John, Lord Tiptoft, and Earl of Worcester, had not deprived his representative, John, seventh Baron Dudley, ' Lord Powes', of a right to his portion of the Barony of Powys. This is further confirmed by the remarks of Leland in his antiquarian tour, about the year 1544, [which is subsequently quoted], and gives the status of the Barony at the time in the actual division of the Castle of Powys between the Lords Powys of the houses of Grey and Dudley."

We therefore conclude upon this evidence, adduced by Mr. Lloyd, that John, seventh Baron Dudley, in 1538 was designated Lord Powes. About 1540, Lord Quondam, as the seventh Lord Dudley and "Powes" was called, must have disposed of his moiety of the Castle of Poole and his portion of Powys to his coparcenery owner, Edward Grey.

This unfortunate peer was an improvident man, and was cozened out of his Dudley Castle and estates by John Dudley, Duke of Northumberland, and became dependent on his friends, and thus acquired the name of "Lord Quondam".[1]

Leland refers to Pole Castle thus:—[2]

"Walshe Pole had 2 Lord Marchers Castles within one wall, the Lord Powis naimed Grey, and the Lord Dudly callyd Sutton, but now the Lord Powys hathe bothe in his hond. The Lord Duddeley parte is almost fallen downe. The Lord Powys part is meally good. Castel Cough, in English, Red castle, standith on a rokke of dark redd colorid stone. It hath ii separated wardes, whereof the one was the Lord Duddeleys.

[1] In 1534, Lord Dudley, described as Edward, who seems to have died in 1530, and probably means his successor John, seventh Baron Dudley, made an agreement with the steward and other officers of the Lordship of Oswestry for the exchange of prisoners and other purposes. He here assumed to act, as the principal owner of Powys, and is called Lord Dudley and Powys, and we may infer, that his portion of Powys abutted on the Lordship of Oswestry.

[2] *Mont. Coll.*, vol. xiii, p. 206.

Now both long to the Lord Powys. The Walsche Pole is in compas almost as much as a little toune."

The hopeless state of the affairs of the seventh Lord Dudley was probably the cause of his parting with the Dudley portion of the Barony of Powys to the Greys, a family, however, which itself soon afterwards came to an ignoble end.

Upon the alienation of Lord Quondam of his moiety of the Barony of Powys, the Lord Dudleys, his descendants, abandoned the use of the title of "Powes", the assumption, and the abandonment, alike showing that it was regarded solely as a territorial dignity.

Thus, shortly after 1540, and probably before 1544, when Leland wrote, the proprietorship of the moiety of the castle assigned to Joyce, the younger daughter of Sir Edward de Cherleton, had become vested in the Greys, the proprietors of the other moiety.

In 1552, Edward Grey, Lord of Powys, died without lawful issue, and thus the barony fell into abeyance. But he made a will, by which he devised his Barony and Manor of Powys, and his Castle and Manor of Pool, and all his lordships in the County of Montgomery, to Edward Grey, his illegitimate son by Jane Orwell, daughter of Sir Lewis Orwell, Knight, in tail general. To this ignoble disposal of his fine estate came this unfortunate peer; having no lawful progeny he made his bastard son his representative, and heir.

On his father's death, the son, Edward Grey, was only four years old; nevertheless, he is recorded as having received the complimentary offer of cake and wine on his passage through Shrewsbury to his father's funeral. His subsequent life was a continued worry, owing to this great estate coming to him. In less than three years the Vernons, who afterwards claimed the abeyant barony, began to put forward their claims.

Edward Grey came of age in 1568, and he lost no time in fortifying his title to the bulk of his father's estates by conveying to Edward Kynaston the Manors of Plas yn Dinas and Trewern, then worth £500 per annum, as a consideration for Edward Kynaston assigning to Edward Grey all his title as heir-at-law of Edward Grey, Lord of Powys, to the other side. But this did not suffice, it was too great a prize to be held by his feeble and ignoble hands. The judgments of a retributive providence were supposed to have descended on Sir Griffith Vaughan, and the Cherletons and the Greys, who were concerned in the base apprehension of Sir John Oldcastle, Lord Cobham.

In 1587 (29 Elizabeth) an important event took place, no less than the transfer, by sale, from Edward Grey, the illegitimate son and universal legatee of Edward Grey, the last Lord of Powys, to Sir Edward Herbert, the second son of William, the chivalrous Earl of Pembroke, of Pool Castle, and the seventeen dependent manors; in which family of Herbert during the succeeding three centuries this great estate has remained.

It is worthy of remark that Jane Orwell, the mother of the last Edward Grey, subsequent to the death of Edward Grey, Lord of Powys, married John Herbert, the brother of Sir Edward Herbert. In 1596 she addressed a letter to Edward Kynaston, and subscribed herself as his kinswoman, Jane Powys; and John Herbert, her husband, subscribed himself as his kinsman, and in a postscript to the same letter John Herbert addressed Edward Kynaston as "Cosyn". It seems great assurance on her part, that she should assume the title and designation of Powys, for she would not be entitled to the tenure even for life of Powys Castle and Lordship. If she had had possession, such tenure might possibly have been considered to confer the title, but she could not have been in possession of the castle, for in 1590 Sir Edward Herbert dates a letter from Poole Castle. Thus ignobly terminates the period of the possession of the castle by the Feudal Barons of the line of the Cherletons and their descendants.

For nearly three hundred years the Feudal Barons occupied Poole Castle, embracing the period, when the last spark of Cambrian nationality was extinguished, to be rekindled for a few years during the adventurous career of Owen Glendower ; the persecution of the Lollards, the wars of the Roses, the elevation of a Welshman, in the person of Henry VII, to the English throne, and the eventful Reformation of the Church of England.

None of these barons was more distinguished than Sir John de Cherleton, the husband of Hawyse Gadarn. Brave, learned, hospitable, wealthy, and successful in the vindication of his rights, "like a well-graced actor" he left the stage of life.

The Dudleys were generally devoid of ambition and enterprise, but aspiring and fortunate in their matrimonial alliances, and the seventh Lord was unfitted to cope with the rapacity of his kinsman, and the difficulties of his position, and incapable of preserving the moiety of the castle and domain of his forefathers.

The Greys were remarkable as a short-lived family, gallant and hasty, and ever ready to encounter danger for its own sake. The decapitation of Sir Griffith Vychan, by the command of Henry, second Lord Grey, within the walls of his castle, in 1477, without the authority of judge and jury, and in spite of a safe conduct, was an act of violence indicative of the impetuosity of the family, but utterly unjustifiable and universally condemned. It was a twofold misfortune, that the castle and its magnificent appanage of lands should have been left, in an inauspicious hour, to an illegitimate scion of the house, who parted at successive times with the princely possessions of his ancestors without an adequate effort to retain the splendid inheritance.

III.—The third epoch in the annals of Powis Castle embraces the period, when the Herberts, proprietors of the mansion and its adjacent domain, became peers of the realm by creation.

Powis Castle was transferred from the descendants

of Wenwynwyn in the male line to his descendants in the female line, as represented by the Cherletons, Tiptofts, Dudleys, and Greys, and, through ages of twofold proprietorship, to the possession of the Herberts, who have duly prized the venerable fabric, endeared by a thousand historical associations. They have uniformly acknowledged, by their devotedness to public interests, and the welfare of their numerous tenantry, the obligations, as well as the privileges, arising from a large estate, and evinced those qualities which best promote the welfare of society.

After a short possession of Powis Castle for seven years, Sir Edward Herbert died in 1594, and was succeeded by his eldest son, William, who was made a Knight of the Bath at the coronation of James I, and created Baron "Powys of Powys" by Charles I in 1629.

We have seen how the possession of the Castle and domain belonging to it have been treated as a barony by tenure, even by those who had only an undivided share therein. The same principle soon came to be applied, when the possession shifted from the indigenous owners to the family of Herberts; but the practice became different. In the first case, the barony was called into existence by writ of summons, or the possessor assumed the title of Powys in right of the tenure, whether of the entirety, or an undivided interest; whereas, in the latter case, the possession of the Castle and the appendant manors was treated by the Crown, as a title for the exercise of the Royal Prerogative by creating the possessor a baron or peer of the realm by patent, according to the recent practice or custom of peerage law, since writs of summons had, as a rule, ceased to be issued.[1] There have been three

[1] Mr. J. Gough Nichols took a similar view in his Review, entitled the "Barony of Powys", printed as an appendix to *Mont. Coll.*, vol. ii. On p. 21, Mr. Nichols thus expresses himself:—"We view the case thus. As a territorial dignity or Barony by tenure, the title is actually and virtually enjoyed by the present Lord of Powis Castle; to whom and his descendants in the male line the title has

instances of this creation by patent, in right of the possession or tenure of the Castle and appendant manors, viz. :—

1. William Herbert, as first Baron Powys (to which we have just adverted).

2. Henry Arthur Herbert, as Baron and Earl of Powis, in 1748, the identical year, in which he succeeded to Powis Castle.

3. Edward, second Lord Clive (in the Irish peerage), as Earl of Powis, consequent on his marriage with Henrietta Antonia Herbert, the heiress of the Powis possessions.

On the breaking out of the Civil War between Charles I and his Parliament, William, first Lord Powis, declared himself to be a supporter of the Royal cause, fortified his castle, and placed in it a strong garrison, of which he took the command in person.

One end of the gallery at Powis Castle communicates with the state bed-room, which is preserved in the same order, as when prepared for the reception of Charles I, who was expected to sleep in this stronghold, when on his route to Chester in 1644.

On Wednesday, October 2nd, 1644, Sir Thomas Myddleton and his forces drew near by moonlight to the Castle, and waited until about two o'clock A.M. for the going down of the moon before the commencement of the attack, and then approached the precincts of the formidable fortress. The gates were all closed, but the rich booty within the Castle made the assailants anxious, and impatient for an attack. The mastergunner, John Arundel, was ordered to place a petarre against one of the gates. It was fired, and burst open the gate, and, in spite of many showers of stone flung from the Castle by the defenders, the infantry of Sir Thomas Myddleton, commanded by Major Henry Ket and Captain Hugh Massey, rushed into the works, and so stormed the Castle-gate, and possessed themselves

been confirmed after modern usage *by patent*, as in earlier times it was confirmed to the Cherletons and Greys by writs, which according to the practice of that day summoned them to Parliament."

of the old and new Castle, and of all the plate, provisions, and goods there deposited. They captured Lord Powis, and his brother and two sons, three captains and one lieutenant, eighty officers and common soldiers. Red Castle had been deemed of sufficient strength to hold out a year's siege against ten thousand assailants. Sir Thomas Myddleton sent Lord Powis prisoner to the garrison of Wem, and from thence to London on his parole, where he stayed at his lodging in the Strand.

Red Castle was occupied by the Parliamentarians to the time of the Restoration in 1660.

It appears by a manuscript in the library at Powis Castle, that this fortress, together with that of Montgomery, inclusive of their outworks, was ordered by the Parliament to be demolished, but, by a decree of the Council of State, dated April 28th, 1660, it is stated that the Red Castle in Wales did not belong to the State, and that the owners and proprietors thereof, having given security that it should not be employed or made use of to the disturbance of the peace of the nation, or prejudicial to the Parliament and Commonwealth, it is commanded that the former decree, made for demolishing the above-named Castle, be rescinded, with the exception only of the outworks, and the making of some breaches in the walls in order to make it indefensible in case of any future insurrection against the government and authority of the Parliament. After these injunctions had been carried into effect, it was delivered into the possession of its legitimate proprietors.

In 1684, the Duke of Beaufort, the President of the Council of the Marches of Wales, made a tour through Wales in almost regal state, and in the course of his progress he visited Welshpool and Powis Castle. An account of this progress has been printed in a costly (privately printed) volume. From a copy of this splendid work, we may give the following extracts:—

"*Saturday, July* 19*th,* 1684.—His Grace the Duke of Beaufort left Ludlow in order to his general visitation of his commands in Wales, and arrived this day at Powis Castle, commonly called Red Castle, having been mett in his way by the chiefest of the gentry of that part of Shropshire, who conducted him through Bishop's Castle. And the said gentlemen of that county, having brought him to their confines, His Grace was mett soon after by those of the county of Montgomery, the first shire of this progress of North Wales, and at a convenient place in the road was their troop drawn up, the officers being in very noble equippage. Advancing further towards Welshpool, His Grace found the foot likewise drawn up, with all their officers at ye head of them, where he saw them exercise, and make several good volleyes. The horse in like manner performed their duty.

"*Saturday, July* 19*th.*—His Grace the Duke of Beaufort lay that night at Powis Castle, from whence, the following day being Sunday, July 20th, he went, accompanied by the Earl of Worcester, Sir John Talbot, and a great number of knights, militia officers, and gentlemen, besides the officers of his family, Ludlow, and attendants, to the Church of Welshpool, where divine service was read, and a loyal sermon preached by the Rev. ——, the militia foot, with their respective officers, makeing a guard for his passing and returne through ye town, where the magistracy also attended him in their formalities; after which His Grace, the Earle of Worcester, Lord Herbert of Cherbury, Sir John Talbot, and most of the gentlemen of Montgomeryshire, were very nobly entertained at Powis Castle, though neither the Earle of Powis nor his Countess was there.

"From Powis Castle the Duke proceeded to Lloydiarth (Llwydiarth), where he was sumptuously entertained by the Member for the Borough of Montgomery, Edward Vaughan, and on

"*Thursday, July* 31*st,* 1684, His Grace left Lloydiarth, arrived again at Powis Castle, vulgarly called Red Castle, being formed, founded, and hewn out of a high red rock in Montgomeryshire, where he was mett by Her Grace the Lady Duchess of Beaufort, the Marchioness of Worcester, and other noble ladys, His Grace's daughters, with four coaches and six horses, and attendants suitable. Here were noble entertainments repeated, and their Graces rested the day following, being August 1st, 1684.

"*Saturday, August* 2nd, 1684.—The Duke of Beaufort, Lord President of Wales, departed from the Castle of Powys onwards on his journey to that of Ludlow."

After awhile another danger equally formidable—a second tempest of civil dissension—threatened the stability of the House of Herbert of Powis Castle, and arose from the same cause—devoted loyalty to the Stuart dynasty. William, Marquis of Montgomery and Duke of Powis, resolutely shared the fortunes of his Royal Master, James II, and was outlawed for not returning from the Continent within a certain period, and submitting to the new Government. William III granted the Montgomeryshire and Northamptonshire estates of Lord Powis to the Earl of Rochfort, April 1st, 1696.

In 1715, the Duke of Powis was committed to the Tower on the suspicion of abetting the cause of the Pretender. In 1722, when milder measures were adopted by the Government, William, second Marquis and Duke of Powis, obtained restitution of his estates, and of all his titles, except the dukedom. He found his old Castle much altered, and in some respects beautified. The terrace had been formed, and the ceiling and the walls of the great staircase and the ceiling of the dining-room had been painted by Lanscroon, who had tastefully pourtrayed the coronation of Queen Anne. But the Dutchman, Lord Rochfort, is said to have carried away all that he deemed worth taking of the pictures and furniture, as well as the family records. An account of the expenses incurred in obtaining a reversal of the attainder is extant. They amounted to £294 7s. 8d. .

In November 1727, part of Powis Castle was burnt down. There is an old plan extant of the part of the Castle, which was then burnt, shewing the storeroom, still-house, brew-house, bakehouse, laundry, slaughterhouse, candle-house, and common room, where the ashes lay, extending a length of 169 feet. This circumstance is mentioned by Lord Lyttelton in a letter written 1756, describing his tour through Wales, and his visit to Powis Castle. The ballroom, of the same dimensions as the gallery, was formerly connected with the main building by a portion of the Castle, which was destroyed by fire, so that it is now detached from it. There is a plate of Powis Castle, published by Buck in 1742, which is dedicated to the Duke and Marquis of Powis. It shews the gardens and terrace, ornamented in the French style of decoration, which was probably effected by this nobleman.

Upon the death of William, third titular Duke of Powis, unmarried, in 1748, the various titles became extinct, and Powis Castle and his large estates devolved, under the provisions of his will, upon his kinsman, Henry Arthur, Lord Herbert of Chirbury of the third creation, who was in the same year created Earl of Powis, Viscount Ludlow, and Baron Powis of Powis Castle, 27th May, 21 George II ; and three years afterwards he married Barbara, the niece of the third Marquis, and titular Duke of Powis. He raised in 1745 a regiment of foot, in order to suppress the rebellion under the Pretender to the Throne. He died at Bath, September 11th, 1772, but was buried at Welshpool. He was succeeded in his titles by his only son, George Edward Henry Arthur, who became Lord Lieutenant and *Custos Rotulorum* of Montgomeryshire, and died unmarried in 1801, when his estates passed temporarily to his only surviving sister, Lady Henrietta Antonia, who had married in 1784 Edward, second Lord Clive.

His Lordship's remains lay in state in Powis Castle, and the public were admitted to view them at midnight before the funeral. The interment took place by torchlight, under the chancel of Welshpool Church. The second Lord Clive, who, as Governor of Madras, had acquired additional *éclat* for the distinguished name he bore, received the thanks of both Houses of Parliament for his eminent services during the Mahratta war, May 3rd, 1804, and on the 12th day of the same month was advanced to the vacant earldom of Powis, and among other titles, to the Barony of Powis, of Powis Castle, Co. Montgomery.

His son, Edward, Lord Clive, adopted, March 9th, 1807, the surname and arms of Herbert, as much venerated in Montgomeryshire, for the public services of his kinsmen, as beloved for their private worth and benevolence, and succeeded to the chief estates of his maternal ancestors at Powis Castle, Lymore, and Llyssin.

Powis Castle was described by Bingley, in his *Tour in North Wales*, in 1814, as being in a most neglected and dilapidated state; but Lord Clive resolved to repair and enlarge it. He married, February 9th, 1818, Lucy, third daughter of the third Duke of Montrose, and shortly afterwards, in the decade between 1820 and 1830, and at the large cost of £16,000, availed himself of the architectural skill of Sir Robert Smirke,[1] who strove to harmonize the different portions of the Castle of various dates, to obliterate the traces of defective taste, and to

"Consult the genius of the place in all."—*Pope*.

Among the numerous guests who partook of the hospitality of the second Earl of Powis, in his enlarged and beautiful seat, were two members of the Royal Family, the Duchess of Cambridge, and her younger daughter, the Princess Mary, now Duchess of Teck.

In the Memoirs of the celebrated statesman, Lord

[1] See Timbs' *Ancient Castles*.

Palmerston, by Lord Dalling, vol. iii, p. 88, we meet with a remark of his Lordship concerning the recent improvements in the Castle, and its further capabilities, in a letter to his brother, Sir William Temple.

"Nov. 26, 1841.—We passed a day at Powis Castle, where we found Powis in high force. Powis has improved his Castle sensibly, and slowly; but he has yet a great deal to do to make it as comfortable as it is capable of being made."

His Lordship preserved the See of St. Asaph from extinction, and was a candidate for the Chancellorship of the University of Cambridge in 1847. He was Lord Lieutenant of Montgomeryshire, and a Knight of the Garter. He was succeeded, January 17th, 1848, by his eldest son, Edward James, third Earl of Powis, who is Lord Lieutenant of the County of Montgomery, and High Steward of the University of Cambridge.

The Corporation of Welshpool have the Castle engraved on their Seal, as their armorial insignia, and in their old Parish Church there is a stained window, where there is an heraldic shield, bearing *Az.*, a castle *or*, which is the only reliable authority for the tinctures of the blazon which has yet been discovered. The shield has been in another instance emblazoned *gules.*

The pool, Llyn dû, which gave its name to Welshpool, and was so long associated with the mansion in the neighbourhood, is now enclosed within the spacious park of Powis Castle.

Castle Côch has borne the battle and the breeze for many centuries. The "sharp scythe of conflict" has committed its ravages around its walls. The devouring flames have preyed upon its ancient chambers; but amid the changes of time, and fall of dynasties, the descendant of Wenwynwyn still resides in the venerable home of his ancestors, and retains among his countrymen the ascendant of a bygone age.

DESCENT OF THE EARL OF POWIS FROM THE PRINCES OF UPPER POWYS.

WENWYNWYN, Prince of Powys Uchaf.⊤=Margaret, d. of Robert, Lord Corbet of Caus.

Griffith ap Wenwynwyn.⊤=

William de la Pole, fourth son of Griffith, Lord of Mawddy, co.⊤=Gladousa. Merioneth.

Griffith de la Pole ⊤=

William ap Griffith de la Pole.⊤=Margaret, d. and co-heir of Thomas ap Llewelyn ap Owen, Lord of Ioaood.

John de la Pole.⊤=Elizabeth, d. and heir of Sir Fulk Corbet of Wattlesburgh.

Fulk, Lord of Mawddy, died 1414, s. p.   Elizabeth, sole heiress to her⊤=Hugh Burgh. brother Fulk.

Sir John Burgh.⊤=Jane, d. and co-heir of Sir Wm. Clopton of Clopton and Radbroke.

Elizabeth Burgh.⊤=William Newport of High Ercall, co. Salop.

John Newport.⊤=Alice, d. of ——, Swinnerton, co. Stafford.

Thomas Newport.⊤=Anne, d. of Sir Richard Corbet of Moreton Corbet, Knt., co. Salop.

Sir Richard Newport.⊤=Margaret, d. and sole heir of Sir Thomas Bromley, Knight.

Magdalene Newport.⊤=Richard Herbert of Montgomery Castle.

Edward, 1st Lord Herbert of Chirbury.⊤=Mary Herbert of St. Julian's, co. Monmouth.

Richard, 2nd Lord Herbert of Chirbury.⊤=Lady Mary Egerton, d. of 1st Earl of Bridgwater.

Florence Herbert.⊤=Richard Herbert of Dolguog, and Oakley Park.

Francis Herbert of Dolguog⊤=Mary, d. of Rowland Baugh of Stonehouse, co. and Oakley Park. Salop.

Henry Arthur Herbert, created Earl⊤=Barbara, niece of Wm. Herbert, 3rd of Powis 1748.   Duke of Powis.

Lady Henrietta Antonia Herbert.⊤=Edward, 2nd Lord Clive, created Earl of Powis 1804.

Edward Herbert, 2nd Earl of Powis, K.G.⊤=Lady Lucy Graham, 3rd d. of Duke of Montrose.

EDWARD JAMES HERBERT, 3rd Earl of Powis, appointed Lord Lieutenant of Montgomeryshire, in 1877.

IV. The structure demands our careful observation. We are indebted for the following account of the site and structure of Powis Castle, and the date of its building, to a valuable paper of the Rev. C. H. Hartshorne, in the *British Archæological Journal*, vol. xvii, pp. 22-28.

"The situation, in which Sir John Cherleton built his Castle of Powis, was highly favourable for the chief objects, that urged its erection, personal security, and defence. Placed on a rock, and surrounded by a ravine, which on the south side has been formed into a terraced garden of unusual extent, and loveliness, where Flora and Ceres alternately contend on five successive plateaux for the pre-eminence; and strengthened on the north by two darkly yawning fosses, which even at the present day have lost none of their pristine horror, it commands a view of unrivalled magnificence. The deep blue heights of the Breidden partially close the distance to the east, forming so grand a feature in the landscape, that even the busy town of Pool beneath, and the fertile valley, through which the majestic Severn rolls its pellucid waters, almost escape observation. On the north it is shut in by an extensive park, remarkable for its varied undulations, and for its venerable oaks, silvered over by the lichens of a thousand years, a domain perpetually enchanting us by the picturesqueness of its sylvan beauty, by its contrasts of rock and verdure, its craggy dells, its sunny slopes, its silence only broken by the browsing deer, and soothing us by its natural wildness and its solitude. In wandering amid this peaceful scenery, we soon forget the

"Embattled house, whose massy keep,
Flung from yon cliff a shadow large, and cold,
There dwelt the gay, the beautiful, the bold."

We forget too, amid the pensive shade, the long line of events, that has rendered so many points of view from the Castle deserving attention. For it is a memorable district, a land, that has witnessed numerous conflicts between the Britons under Caractacus and the Roman conquerors, between the English and the Welsh, and the Welsh and the Danes, in distinct view of Powis Castle; perhaps in the blue heights of Breidden, or Moel Golfa, probably on the summit of Caer Digol, the Roman invaders engaged in the final struggle, a struggle the most memorable of all events in our history. Still later was this part of Powysland the battlefield of Danes and Saxons, the latter assisted by the Welsh, when the Northmen were defeated at Buttington.

" The erection of Powis Castle by Sir John de Cherleton is an indisputable fact. The character of the building precisely agrees with the architectural style of the time. In truth its age may be very closely made out, as it is almost certain that he built it between the years 1310 and 1315. Even from the details of the masonic marks under the two great gateways, there is sufficient reason for assigning it to this particular period, since these entrances exhibit the marks observable at Alnwick and Dunstanboro', and the date of these castles can be fixed to a year.

" Little need be said about the building, as it is neither spacious, nor yet remarkable for its singularity, or decoration. It may be briefly described, as an Edwardian keep, consisting of four massive round towers, the two on the north and south sides being connected with a short curtain wall, which has internally encroached on the area for the purposes of modern accommodation. Therefore, viewed from the small enclosure, very little evidence appears to shew its antiquity, but under the archways, and looked at from without, very little of the recent additions are discernible. The chimneys are remarkable for their loftiness, and plain circular forms.

" Orginally, the Castle was entered over the fosse at the western extremity, in the usual manner across a drawbridge, and under a gate house. These portions however are removed, and the present entrance is through a porter's lodge erected in 1668. Within the keep there are insertions of this period.

"A large embattled building of a very uncommon kind lies to the left, as the keep is approached from without. This was formerly the chief hall. The crenelles on the summit are crowded, and smaller than usual.

"Immediately on reaching the keep, the visitor's attention is struck by a handsome Jacobean portal, affixed so as to conceal the old Edwardian entrance, and a great deal of this work exists within and without the keep.

"If we may judge from the two dates, that are found in the gallery, as well as on the curious ceiling of the bedchambers, in the western towers, these additions were made in 1593 and 1594, and would consequently be the work of Sir Edward Herbert, second son of Sir William Herbert, Earl of Pembroke, while the gateway, just mentioned, was added by his great grandson, William, the first Earl of Powis, so created in 1674, Marquis of Powis 1687, outlawed in 1689. He was even created Marquis of Montgomery and Duke of Powis by James II, after his abdication; but these titles were never recognised in England."

Upon the occasion of the meeting of the Cambrian Archæological Association in Welshpool, in 1856, not much information repecting the building was elicited; but we proceed to give the little that can be gleaned. We quote from a newspaper report of the meeting. It is remarked, that "the magnitude of this fine pile of building is observed with the greatest effect, on the road leading from Montgomery, whence its embattled turrets are seen rising above the magnificent trees, by which they are nearly surrounded. The principal entrance is a gateway, between two massive round towers. In front, it is approached by two immense and tastefully laid-out terraces, rising one above the other, adorned with statues, etc. On the grand staircase is some fine tapestry with the date 1705, and the work on the ceiling represents the coronation of Queen Anne. Mr. J. H. Parker stated, that he was disappointed in not finding, as he had expected from the exterior, a grand hall, an interesting old kitchen, with a pantry and a buttery, and other characteristics of an old castle. But he found everything altered, beginning at the time of Elizabeth, when the interior appears to have been entirely rebuilt, and of this period, with a small part of the time of the reign of Henry VIII, the interior consists. And even this had been, to some extent, obliterated with the alterations, which have gone on from that period to our own time. The Castle was interesting as a fine specimen of the times of Elizabeth and James I. The gallery, which is of this period, is a good one, and as far as the remains of the original work extend, is quite equal to any of its kind. Of the original arrangements of Powis Castle it is almost impossible to say anything, although the fortifications may in some degree be traced. There was a drawbridge, with an entrance gate of the thirteenth century, but by reason of its plain characters it was difficult to say whether this gate was of the thirteenth or fourteenth century. The postern gate is ornamented with a moulding, and marked with the arms of the family. This he believed to be of the time of Henry VIII. The most ancient part of the Castle was the roof, and there were some mouldings and chimneys of Henry VIII or earlier than that period.

Mr. W. W. E. Wynne stated he found, on one side of the Castle, quoins which shewed that the wall had been extended.

The Earl of Powis stated, that it would not be necessary to say, that great alterations must have taken place to convert the Castle from a fortress into a place of residence. Because, if they took the period fixed upon by Mr. Parker, which was that of James I, those were very different times to those when two lords had two castles, with the same precincts. Considerable changes seem to have been made about the time of James II, of which the gallery and some of the ceilings were. Then came the second period after the restoration, when alterations were made after the Royalists had been living in Holland, and France. The French taste is seen in the terraces and balustrades, and in the leaden figures of shepherds and shepherdesses. It is evident from the stair balconies, that the entrance was made at this time ; this is evident by the arms, which are at the top of the staircase. These alterations were made by the third Earl of Powis. After this came the Revolution of 1688, when the Castle was in the hands of the Crown for some fourteen years. From that time nothing was done until thirty years ago, when the windows of the Castle were altered from the old white French sash, such as are still in the greenhouses below, and which are the same as those in châteaux in France. These were replaced by the present windows, very much to the improvement of the Castle, as the Earl could from recollection testify. The only alteration, that had been made within the last thirty years was the raising of the eastern turret one storey, which was a great improvement to the appearance. In the olden time the principal entrance to the Castle was through the iron gates, which are not now made much use of. In those days carriages were not much used, and people rode along the northern side of the Castle along the edge of the moat,[1] but when carriages came more into fashion, it was found inconvenient for people to ascend so large a number of steps, after leaving their carriages. The other entrance thus came to be most used. Thus the anomaly existed here, which was to be seen at a neighbouring house, Vaynor Park, where the entrance was also through the stable yard. They had always considered the ballroom as the most ancient part, this was rebuilt by the Earl's great uncle a century ago. A fire occurred at the Castle about that time, and as[2] no plan remained, it was im-

[1] In the plate of Powis Castle in Boswell's *Antiquities of England and Wales* (1786) this road is shown.
[2] There is a plan showing the portion burnt (See *supra*, p. 394), of which the Earl did not appear to be aware.

possible to say, whether the banqueting hall existed at that place.

With respect to that ancient work, the sundial terrace, which the Rev. James Parker had remarked was a very remarkable feature in the place, a good many years ago, a gentleman considered of great taste in his day, Mr. "Capability" Brown, proposed to his (the Earl's) great uncle to destroy that work by blasting, so as to have a smooth surface all round. This advice, very fortunately for archæologists, and for the subsequent possessors of Powis Castle, was not taken, but the reply was, that, if ever it were blown up, he hoped Mr. Brown would be on the top of it.

From the summit of a hill in the spacious park, two miles distant from the Castle, may be seen in clear weather the mountains of Plinlimmon, Cader Idris, Snowdon, the Arans, the Arenigs, and other towering heights. Nature is less changeable than man, and presents the same magnificent features, which justified the selection of this locality as the seat of government eight centuries ago, and still arrests the admiring eye of the spectator.

"Aberfraw's royal halls" have perished. Even "the great palace of Dinevawr", the residence of Rhodri Mawr, is in ruins; the princely fortress of Mathraval has "not left a rack behind", and Powys has resigned its place among the nations.

"Farewell the neighing steed, and the shrill trump,
The spirit-stirring drum, the ear-piercing fife,
The Royal Banner."—*Shakespeare.*

The sky-blue mantle of the Bard has disappeared, and "the lyric torrent, strong and free", has declined in its volume and force. The Hîrlas Horn is rarely seen at the festive board.

"A thousand years their cloudy wings expand
Around me, and a dying Glory smiles
O'er the far times."—*Byron.*

The royal court of the Principality of Powys is only visible in a dim and distant perspective. The social principle has altogether triumphed over the spirit of the feudal age. Yet Powis Castle, from its stately aspect, imposing site, its "harvest of renown", and memorials of Welsh Nationality, as from the stroke of the enchanter's wand, recalls bygone ages to the recollection.

"Stat magni nominis umbra."

The prestige of historical exploits is still felt. A moral claim of influence is acknowledged to exist, not less than the majesty, which surrounds a king, or the stern authority of a feudal age, and it consists in duties faithfully performed, and benefits cordially conferred by its proprietors, and in kindred sympathies. The flight of ages, and the innovations of modern society have not impaired, or weakened, the associations, that are yet paramount in Powysland, and cluster around the time-honoured walls of Powis Castle.

"It will be a bond
Of love, and brotherhood, when all beside
Hath been dissolved."—*Southey's Madoc.*

G. S.
M. C. J.

MISCELLANEA.

(*Continued from Vol.* xiv, *page* 407.)

LXXXI.

EXTRACTS FROM ANCIENT MONTGOMERYSHIRE WILLS.

WILL, 1548. (5, Populwell.) " S'R DAVYD ELIS,[1] preeste, to be bur. in the parryshe churche of Poole... to the reparacons of a certeyne bridge called Bottingtons,[2] twentie shillinges...to the reparacons of the bridge called Telkevy the other twentie shillinges...to Davyd lloyde ap Roberte[3] of the towne of pole my grave horsse...Residue...to Roberte lloyde ap Davyd... Elsabethe Meyvoyde, and to Elys Myvoyde." In "Sentence" (1549-50) he is described as of the diocese of St. Asaph, and the attempt of Robert ap Edward, testator's next of kin, to impugn the will, is unsuccessful.

" Ego JOH'ES WAGHAN cli'cus primo die...Maij 1527°. My bodie to be buried in saint Mary Church[4] yarde...unto the High aulter of saint Martins xij*d*...unto Sir Richard Burnell, curate of saint petirs, one of these iij thinges, that is to say, my decretall orelles, my coverlett, or my matteres, unto sir Robert Bayly my booke of Tully pistelle...unto sir Thomas Yardeley my book of a dieta...unto sir William Savege ij*s*. besides the dutie between hym and me before...unto sir Richard Addeney, xx*d*.... my brother Lewes to have and to holde the close and the tithe

[1] Vicar of Welshpool; but not previously known as such. A " David ap Elis" is given as Rector of Llanfechan. No date.

[2] Buttington and Kilkewydd Bridges are both within two miles of the Town of Welsh Pool, and cross the Severn. The one is in the parish of Welsh Pool and the other in the parish of Forden.

[3] David Lloyd (second son of) ap Robert Lloyd of Welsh Pool and Nantcribba, ap David Lloyd Vaughan of Marrington and Hafodwen.— *Mont. Coll.*, Vol. iii, 145.

[4] St. Mary Church, probably Llanfair in Caedewain, *i.e.*, Newtown, and in the same Deanery are Berriew and Manavon. The earliest Rector given in Browne Willis is Richard ap Griffith, 1537.

ale as he was wonte to have...I bequeth and charge Edwarde ap Evan loyd vjs. viijd., to pay to the church of the Berrowe...unto the church of Mannevon xxs...unto my brother sir Hugh Waghan, which is parson of saint Martins, xiijli....John Morys, clarke of saint Martens...Hijs testibus, sir Owen Powle, vicar of abarow, Roger Adeney, John Griffith, and John Mores, clerke there." Proved 10 May 1527. (Folio 19, "Porch.")

WILL, 1550. (15, Coode.) WILLIAM COWPER (of Thurgarton, Notts?) " To Richard Cowp' my sonne my manor llawligan,[1]... Mongumerie...Also all my maris, felies, folys & coltes remayning in the mountayns in Walis and in the said manor...Item my ferme or lease of the parsonage of llangaure in the said countie...to my said sonne Richard Cowp'...Item one annuitie of lijs. viijd. w'ch I have yerely receyvid oute of the Treasorers office of the Cowrte of Agmentacions, & grantid and going " owte of the landes of llanligan aforesaid, sometyme being a priorie, and now in the Kings Ma'tie handes.

1553-4. (26, Tashe.) "JAMES LECHE of Newtowne in Wales, in the countie of Mungomery, Esquier." All lands, etc., not otherwise disposed of in this will to Elizabeth his wife and Anne his daughter for their lives. Remainder to Charles Price, his said daughter Anne's son. Lands in Haberhaves to wife and daughter Sage for their lives; remainder to James, son of said daughter Sage. To son, Anthony Leche, interest and term of years in the farm of Manlogho Landylowe Singlemans. Testator died in London. D. R. T.

LXXXII.

A CURIOUS CHAPTER IN MONTGOMERYSHIRE HISTORY.

Chancery Division, before Mr. Justice Kay, March 8th, 1882.

WILLIAMS *v.* WILLIAMS.—This was an action to recover from the executors of a deceased gentleman the sum of £321, which had been expended in having the body of the deceased cre-

---

[1] The site of Llanllugan Nunnery was granted 37 Hen. VIII to Sir Henry D'Arcy. The rectory or parsonage of Llanfair (Caereinion) was an impropriation. Browne Willis states (*Mitred Abbeys*, ii, 316) that "in 1553 here remained in charge £2 10s. 8d. in annuities." The last Prioress was Rose Lewis. For an account of Llanllugan Nunnery, see *Mont. Coll.*, vol. ii, p. 301.

mated. The claim was made by a Miss Eliza Williams [of Henllys, Manafon] against the executors of the late Dr. Crookenden, who was a Roman Catholic, and whose remains were buried in the Brompton Cemetery in unconsecrated ground. An application was made to the Home Secretary to exhume the body of Dr. Crookenden, which was granted to the plaintiff, who was sister of the wife of the deceased. Dr. Crookenden wrote Miss Williams a letter, in which he directed that she was to have his body cremated as soon after his death as possible. In a codicil to his will, he directed that the plaintiff was to receive his body from his executors, who were to pay all the expenses to which Miss Williams might be put in carrying his wishes into effect. He further directed that the calcined remains should be put into a Wedgwood vase which he had bequeathed to the plaintiff for that purpose. The deceased was buried on December 23, 1875, and it was with the consent of the relatives that the plaintiff applied to the Home Office for the license to exhume the body for the purpose of cremation. If objection were taken to her suggestion, she asked that the remains be interred in consecrated ground. The Home Office granted the license for the removal of the body to a churchyard [Manafon] in Montgomeryshire, but refused to allow it to be exhumed for the purpose of cremation. The plaintiff, however, had taken means to have the wishes of the deceased carried into effect, and she now sought to recover the expense to which she had been put. Mr. Higgins, Q.C., for the plaintiff; and Mr. Rigby, Q C., for the defendants. His lordship said that in law there was no property in a dead body; at the same time, it was part of the duty of the executors to provide for the proper burial of the deceased. By the law of this country no man had a right to dispose of his body by will, or in any other way; and the direction that his body was to be given to Miss Williams, who was not one of his executors, was void and could not be enforced. A question might arise as to whether the burning of the body was permissible under the law of this country. He was decidedly of opinion that cremation was illegal in this country. The plaintiff had obtained the license from the Home Office under false pretences, as it was only granted for the purpose of being buried in consecrated ground. He was bound to say, however, that the plaintiff had acted from the best of motives. In the circumstances, the action had failed, and must be dismissed with costs.[1]

[1] From *Reynolds' Newspaper*, 12th March 1882. The *Law Reports* (Chancery Division) for September, 1882, contain a full report of the case.

[The ashes have been placed in a jar and are buried, or rather, as I am informed, placed under a grating in Manafon churchyard.—R. W.]

LXXXIII.
STRATA MARCELLA ABBEY.

Extract from Eyton's *Antiquities of Shropshire*, vol. vi, p. 225.

" Roger Fitz Madoc was enfeoffed, early in the thirteenth century, in half Picklescott by the coparcenery of Smethcott. Robert Fitz Madoc granted this moiety of Picklescott to the ' White Monks of Pole', as the *Haughmond Chartulary* expresses it, meaning the Cistercian Convent of Ystrat Marchel. The second Richard de Linley (with his daughter, Alice), quitclaimed ' to God and St. Mary, and to all the Saints, and to the Abbot and Monks of Pole, all their right in that part of the whole vill of Picklescott which Robert Madoc had given and which was of the fee of Alice's ancestors.'

"The Abbot and Convent of Strattmarkel gave this land to Thomas Corbet of Caus, in exchange for certain land in the Haye, of Thomas Corbet, about Caus."

See *Mont. Coll.*, vol. iv, p. 313 (and note), where the grant of Thomas Corbet of part of " Hayes " is mentioned as a " donation", whereas this extract shews it to be an " exchange." The transaction took place, Eyton says, between 1227 and 1235.

LXXXIV.
THE HARGRAVE AND BEACON RING.

Extract of a letter from the Rev. R. W. Huntley, vicar of Alberbury, to Sir Richard Jenkins, G.C.B.

" Dec. 11th, 1840.

"I take the liberty, as Vicar of the Parish in which the Hargrave lies, to give you what I consider the origin of that name.

" In the reign of Alfred, the Danes made, among their many invasions, the following campaign in England: They sailed up the Thames, sacked London, Reading, Oxford, and Cricklade, and that line of country generally. At Cricklade, fortifying their gallies, they compelled the Saxons to transport their light boats over the Cotswold ridge, till they launched them in the Severn, a land carriage of some 25 miles perhaps. They then sailed up the Severn, sacking Gloucester, Worcester, Bridgenorth, Shrewsbury, and Welshport. This campaign gives a good idea of what the nation then suffered, and of the wild and predatory mode of warfare which those northmen or sea-kings then followed.

"Alfred, at this time, was engaged with another Danish party in Devonshire and the west of England generally. He detached, however, one of his Thanes, named Ord-helm, a name which, if interpreted, means Wielder of the Hammer. This personage led his forces after them, and at Welshpool slow-footed justice overtook the marauders. The Danes found themselves, after some hammering, compelled to entrench themselves in that very beautiful specimen of Danish fortifications, BEACON RING, on the Long Mountain. Here Ord-helm blocked them up. When they had been compelled to eat their horses by famine, the Danes made a general sortie, and a battle took place in which they were totally defeated, fled towards Pontesbury, where they were again attacked and routed, and in their final retreat, meeting with some forces that were sent to sustain Ord-helm, were finally overthrown at Quatt, near Bridgenorth. All this success, however, was not witnessed by Ordhelm. He fell in the hour of victory, in the battle in the Long Mountain—no doubt having wielded his Hammer with crushing effect. What became of his body is not stated, but the words "The Hargrave" seem to say he was buried there; "Her" or "Har" being Saxon for a leader of an army, and "grave", as now, meaning the place of interment.

"This morceau of history is to be found in the *Saxon Chronicles*; and, as probably indicating the name of your ancient family holding in my parish, I thought it might interest you." T. B. B.

LXXXV.
PUGH OF MATHAFARN.

Copies of monumental inscriptions in Conway church :—

"ELIZABETH COYTMOR, fifth child of George Coytmor, gent., by Mary, his wife, died 4th March 1709."

"Margaret Coytmor, third and youngest daughter of Rupert Coytmor, of Coytmor, Esqre., who exchanged this life for a better the 29th day of September 1634. 'She is not dead but liveth.' Mar. ye 5th, ver. ye 39th."

"George Coytmore, died 17th Sept. 1738, aged 66, also Margaret, his wife, 21st August 1757, aged 78."

"HERE LYETH THE BODY
OF ROWLAND PVGH
OF MATHAVERNE IN THE
COVNTY OF MOVNTGOME
RY ESQVIER WHO
DIED ON ST. STEVEN'S
DAY ANNO DOMINI
1644."

Rowland Pugh married Elizabeth, second daughter to Sir Richard Pryse of Gogerddan, Co. Cardigan, and had two daughters. He was Sheriff, 1609 and 1626. His second wife was Mary, daughter of James Lewis Coedmore, and he was M.P. for Montgomery, 1588-9.[1]

St. Stephen's Day being the day after Christmas Day, makes it probable that Rowland Pugh was on a visit to his father-in-law (Coytmor) at Conway, and so died away from home. The Coytmors are said to have lived at what is known as the Bishop's Palace, above and adjoining Plas Mawr in Conway Town. Part of the old house is still standing, and there is a curiously carved chimney-piece left. The house is presently occupied in several tenements, mostly as a tramp's lodging house. H. L. Squires.

LXXXVI.

Memorandum as to the Family of Harrison.

In the *Historical Record of the 52nd Regiment* (*Oxford Light Infantry*), published in 1860, the following notice occurs of the Battle of Bunker's Hill and

[1] *Mont. Coll.*, vol. v, p. 494, where his second wife is stated to be Mary, daughter of James Lewis, of Coedmore. See *Mont. Coll.*, vol. II, p. 312, note 2, where he is stated to be "supposed to be dead, but yet known to be in plain life."

Robert John Harrison (of Caer Howel), having been engaged in it as a volunteer and being wounded :—

"On the 17th June 1775, the Battle of Bunker's Hill was fought, and the 52nd Regiment particularly distinguished itself on the occasion, and suffered severely." Three captains, one sergeant, and twenty rank and file of Robert John Harrison (the father of the late Major) were killed. Amongst the wounded were one major (who afterwards died), one captain, three lieutenants, and two ensigns, *"and volunteer Robert John Harrison"*, and seven sergeants and seventy-three rank and file.

RICHARD HARRISON, Lieutenant in the 2nd Battalion 30th (or Cambridgeshire) Regiment of Foot, who was son of the said Robert John Harrison, and younger brother of Major R. J. Harrison of Caerhowel, was present at the Battle of Waterloo, and the following is a copy of letter written by him four days after that battle to his sister, Mrs. Laugher :—

"Camp near Bavey in France,
"*June 22nd*, 1815.

"MY DEAR CON,—I wrote to you some time before leaving Antwerp in answer to your last letter, and have never got an answer; however, I avail myself of the present moment just to give you a line to say that I am still in the land of the living. The French made a sudden movement, and we marched from our cantonments at Soignies on the 16th, and were severely engaged that evening. Finding in the morning that the enemy were in great force, we fell back to a stronger position on the 17th; and on the 18th a general action took place, in which Napoleon and Lord Wellington were fairly opposed to each other, the French certainly in much greater numbers. You will perceive that our division have been particularly engaged; our brigade have only about six hundred men left out of two thousand. The French particularly attacked our division; in short, the brunt of the action fell upon us, and our fellows behaved most gallantly. Our brigade was attacked in square by cavalry, artillery, and the best French infantry; but we kept our ground, when the reserve came up, and we gained a most complete victory, taking fifteen thousand prisoners and upwards of one hundred and fifty pieces of cannon. We have been advancing ever since. This is our second day's march in France, and I have not seen a French soldier; they retreat in the greatest disorder. You will perhaps see my name amongst the wounded. I was returned contrary to my own wishes, not thinking it severe enough to be returned for; though I have been touched once in the leg and twice in the left arm, neither are of any consequence. But I have to regret many a fine fellow; we have twenty-one officers of the regiment, and three parts of the men, killed and wounded.

"We are just going to advance, therefore must conclude.
"I remain, my dear Con,
"Your affectionate brother,
"RD. HARRISON."

LXXXVII.
ANCIENT CLUBS IN MONTGOMERYSHIRE.[1]

KERRY CONVIVIAL CLUB.—About the year 1765 there appears to have been a sporting or convivial club in Kerry village, each member having an armchair of his own with a brass plate let in at the back of it, with his initials and a motto engraved upon it. There were at least twelve of them, all made of mahogany, and uniform in shape and size, and they at one time belonged to the late Mr. R. P. Long of Dolforgan, but at his sale they were purchased by the late Mr. Robert Pryce, of the *Herbert Arms Inn*, Kerry; and his widow still owns them. Five or six of the chairs are in good order and condition, and I found the *disjecta membra* of the remaining half dozen in a lumber room upstairs; but three of the brass plates are missing. The following are the inscriptions on the nine plates which I was able to find:—

"R. F.—Natale solum."
"C. P.—Quis ulla aliena sibi credat mala?"
"J. O.—Better to hunt in fields for health unbought,
    Than fee the doctor for a nauseous draught."

[1] See vol. xiii, p. 177.

" J. H.—Curo et rogo, 1765."
" W. H.—Ex fumo dare Lucem."
" T. M. E.—Equis Canibusque."
" B. L.—Afiach pob trwmgalon."
"W. M.—Insanire juvat."
" S. H.—May we see Heav'n at last
When we see no more hounds."

R. W.

LXXXVIII.
Robert Owen, the Philanthropist.
Supplemental Note to supra, p. 70.

The following notice of Robert Owen occurs in an article by Mr. W. J. Thoms, entitled "Gossip of an old Bookworm", and published in *The Nineteenth Century*, vol. x, p. 873, December 1881.

"In the year 1858, Lord Brougham insisted upon my paying him a visit at Brougham Hall, and a most pleasant and interesting ten days I spent there. . . . . My noble host, one morning, gave me a pamphlet, which he had just received by post and just read, saying 'read that, and tell me what you think of it.' It was Mrs. Ryves' *Appeal for Royalty*, written for the *Morning Post* by Mr. Macdonald, an *attaché* of that paper and a friend of Mr. Ryves. When I returned it to him the next morning, and told him it was a repetition of her mother's book on 'Junius,' full of absurd misstatements based upon the reputed evidence of dead witnesses, he told me to keep the book, and startled me by saying, 'The Duke of Kent used to allow her £400 a year!' On my expressing my doubts as to the Duke's ability to do so, he replied, sharply, 'Robert Owen told me so.' The fact being, as it turned out afterwards, that Owen of Lanark had advanced her £400 per annum for three years, at the intervention of the Duke of Kent, and which £1,200 Her Majesty very liberally repaid."

In 1868, a proposal was made for the erection of a monument to the memory of ROBERT OWEN in Newtown, the place of his birth and death, and the Local Board of that town was applied to by some of his admirers for permission for the erection of a monument in some prominent position in the town. The Local Board gave a decided negative to the proposal, and, from correspondence which appeared in the public prints at the time, such refusal was grounded on the irreligious and pernicious character of Robert Owen's writings and principles. The alleged modification of his views before his death was not given the weight to which many thought it was entitled. His friends in Manchester and elsewhere being thus prevented by local obstacles from erecting in Newtown a fitting memorial of the philanthropist, put one up in Kensal Green Cemetery, London, and contented themselves with the memorial which had been placed in the churchyard belonging to the old Parish Church of Newtown, which consisted of a simple table tomb-stone surrounded by a low iron railing, with the following inscriptions on its four sides, viz. :—

On the North Side.—" Erected by public subscription, 1861."

South Side.—" In memory of Robert Owen, the philanthropist, born at Newtown, May 14th, 1771, died at Newtown, November 17th, 1858."

East Side.—" Robert Owen, father of the philanthropist, died March 14th, 1804."

West Side.—" Ann Owen, mother of the philanthropist, died July 13th, 1803, aged 68 years."

LXXXIX.
LLANGOLLEN.
Thursday 19 *July* 1877.

From beyond the wide ocean, where sunsets tinge with gold
The domes and lofty mountains, on heaven's blue vault unroll'd ;
Again I come, *Llangollen*, through thy lovely vale to roam,
A pilgrim to the ancient shrine of an ancestral home.
The joyous foam-toss'd waters, glancing in rapid flight,
The stone bridge, Norman-arched, picturesquely in sight ;
The cascade lightly springing from beneath its leafy lair,
With gentle murmurs filling the ardent summer air ;
The distant azure mountains, with white cloud diadems ;
The brooklets ever rippling within the verdant glens.
The scene is very charming, but holds me not in thrall,
As the grand historic interest, which far surpasses all.
The *Eglwyseg* mountains rise fantastic towards the sky,
The *Vreiddins* to the eastward, form ramparts broad and high ;
And the fortress of *Prince Eliseg*, on *Dina's* lofty brow,
Casts the shadow of its ruins in the valley far below.
The maiden-driven donkeys trail up the steep hill side,
Where *Brochwel*, Prince, with sword and spear, the Saxon foe defied,
And clash'd the bossed buckler, and shouted the battle song,
Which through successive centuries has ever since roll'd on ;
And famous *Crucis Abbey*, with ivy-festoon'd wall, ·

MISCELLANEA. 415

And *Eliseg's* hoary records, which a thousand years recall—
Telling of Princely heroes, who rul'd this land of yore,—
All these have lur'd me hither, and, if I may add more,
The "*Royal*" cheer awaiting me, upon the Dee's fair shore.
But there is still another land, beneath the setting sun,
Whose portals wide are open thrown, whene'er my wand'ring's done;
A land of forests, mountains, of lakes and flowing stream,
A land of beauty that we love with loyalty supreme.
Philadelphia. C. P. S.

XC.
DOCUMENTS RELATING TO QUAKER BURIAL-GROUNDS IN MERIONETHSHIRE.

To all Christian people to whom these presents shall come or may concern, more especially to our beloved friends, ABRAHAM DARBY of Colebrookdale, in the county of Salop, ironmaster, JOHN YOUNG, of the town of Salop, in the said county of Salop, mercer, JOHN LEWIS, of Haverfordwest, in the county of Pembroke, ironmaster, WILLIAM REYNOLDS, of the town of Carmarthen, in the county of Carmarthen, maltster, JOHN GOODWIN, of Eskirgoch, in the county of Montgomery, gentleman, EDWARD JONES of Talcoed, in the county of Radnor, gentleman, and RANDLE OWEN of Talcoed aforesaid, gentleman, ELLIS LEWIS OWEN of Tyddyn y Garreg, in the county of Merioneth, and HUGH ROWLAND OWEN of Dewisbren, in the said county of Merioneth, gentleman, send greeting in our Lord God everlasting.

Whereas Owen Lewis Owen of Tyddyn y Garreg, esquire (now long since deceased), was in his lifetime (that is to say) in the year of our Lord 1646, seized in his demesne of a good and indefeasible estate of inheritance of and in that ancient capital messuage and demesne lands thereto belonging, called TYDDYN Y GARREG aforesaid, and other lands and tenements in the township of Garthgynfawr, and of certain other lands and tenements in the township of Nanney, in the said county of Merioneth, and soon after was convinced of the principles of truth as held by the people called Quakers, whereupon he the said Owen Lewis Owen separated, set apart, and enclosed a certain piece of ground at Tyddyn y Garreg aforesaid, for a burying place for the people called Quakers, to bury their dead. And whereas the said Owen Lewis Owen left several issue, of whom Lewis Owen, his eldest son and heir, was one, and Rowland Owen was another, and which said Lewis

Owen, the eldest son, is long, since dead, having left issue (by Ellenor his wife, daughter of Ellis Morris of Dolegyn, in the said county of Merioneth, esquire, also long since deceased), Owen Lewis Owen, also deceased, and the said Ellis Lewis Owen, and several other issue, grandchildren of the said Owen Lewis Owen first above named, and which Rowland Owen, the other son of the said Owen Lewis Owen first above named is also long since dead, having left several issue, of which the said Hugh Rowland Owen is his only son and heir, and one of the grandchildren of the said Owen Lewis Owen first above named.

And whereas Owen Humphreys of Llwyn du, in Llwyngwril, in the said county of Merioneth, esquire, now long since deceased, was in his lifetime (that is to say) in the year of our Lord 1646, seized in his demesne of a good and indefeasible estate of inheritance of and in that ancient capital messuage, tenement, and lands called Llwyn du aforesaid, and other messuages, lands, and tenements in Llwyngwril aforesaid, in the said county of Merioneth, and soon after was convinced of the principles of truth as held by the people called Quakers, whereupon he the said Owen Humpheys separated, set apart, and enclosed a certain piece of ground called Bryn y Tallwyn, a part of Llwyn du demesne, for a burying place for the said people called Quakers, to bury their dead.

And whereas the said Owen Lewis Owen, grandson of the said Owen Lewis Owen first above named, intermarried with Anne Humphreys, granddaughter of the said Owen Humphreys, and daughter and sole heir of Humphrey Owen Humphrey, sometime of Llwyn du, also deceased, who was the eldest son and heir of the said Owen Humphreys, and had male issue, the present Lewis Owen of Tyddyn y Garreg aforesaid, esquire, their eldest son and Humphrey Owen of Llwyn du aforesaid gentleman, their youngest son.

And whereas the said Owen Lewis Owen (grandson of the said Owen Lewis Owen first above named), and the said Anne his wife (granddaughter of the said Owen Humphrey), for settling and conveying the ancient inheritance of him the said Owen Lewis Owen (the grandson) upon the present Lewis Owen, Esq., and his heirs for ever, and for the settling and conveying the ancient inheritance of the said Anne upon the present Humphrey Owen, the younger and his heirs for ever, by certain indentures of lease and release, bearing date respectively the 23rd and 24th day of February, in the twelfth year of the reign of his present Majesty King George II, over Great Britain and so forth, and in the year of our Lord

MISCELLANEA. 417

1738 (the release being made or mentioned to be made between
him the said Owen Lewis Owen (the grandson) and the said
Anne his wife of the one part, and the said Ellis Lewis Owen
and Hugh Rowland Owen of the other part, did convey and
assure all their several inheritances unto the said Ellis Lewis
Owen and Hugh Rowland Owen and their heirs, to the several
uses therein mentioned (that is to say) as for touching and concerning the reversion, remainder, and inheritance of all and
singular the several and respective messuages, mills, lands, tenements, and hereditaments lying in Garthgynfawr and Nanney,
being the inheritance of the said Owen Lewis Owen (the grandson) immediately from and after the end, expiration, forfeiture,
or other determination of the several and respective estates for
life therein limited, as the same should severally and respectively end and determine, and charged and chargeable with
the several and respective annuities or rent-charges therein
mentioned (save and except the garden and burying-place of
Tyddyn y Garreg, part of the inheritance of the said Owen
Lewis Owen (the grandson) where persons of the persuasion,
community, or society of Quakers did use to bury their dead,
with free ingress, egress, and regress thereto and therefrom,
as often as occasion for burying should require), to the use
and behoof of the present Lewis Owen of Tyddyn y Garreg,
being the eldest son of the said Owen Lewis Owen (the grandson) by the said Anne his wife, and of the heirs of the body
of him the said Lewis Owen lawfully issuing, and in default of
such issue to the use and behoof of the present Humphrey
Owen of Llwyn du, second son of him the said Owen Lewis
Owen (grandson), begotten on the body of the said Anne, and
of the heirs of the body of the said Humphrey Owen, lawfully
issuing with other remainders over. And as for touching and
concerning the several and respective messuages, lands, tenements, hereditaments, and other the premises lying in the
township of Llwyngwril aforesaid, with their and every of
their appurtenances, being the inheritance of the said Anne
surrendered from and after the surrender, forfeiture, or other
determination of the several and respective estates for lives of
them the said Owen Lewis Owen (the grandson) and Anne his
wife, in the said indenture of release limited, and as the same
should severally and respectively end and determine (save and
except the garden or burying place at Llwyn du, part of the
last mentioned premises, where persons of the persuasion
community, or society of Quakers did use to bury their dead,
with free ingress, egress, and regress thereto and therefrom,
as often as occasion for burying should require). Then to the

use and behoof of the present Humphrey Owen of Llwyn du, second son of the said Owen Lewis Owen (the grandson) by the said Anne his wife, and of the heirs of the body of him the said Humphrey Owen, lawfully issuing with remainders over. And as to touching and concerning the garden or piece of ground on and part of the lands of Owen Lewis Owen (the grandson), called Tyddyn y Garreg, and also the garden or piece of ground on a part of the lands of Llwyn du, being part of the inheritance of the said Anne, the wife of him the said Owen Lewis Owen (the grandson) in both which gardens or parcels of ground the families of the said Owen Lewis Owen (the grandson) and Anne his wife, and others of the persuasion, community, or society of Quakers, had theretofore used to bury their dead, whereof no use was in the said indenture of release before limited, the sam should be and remain to the use and behoof of all severally the persons called Quakers to bury their dead in, when and as often as they should think fit and occasion should require. And the said Ellis Lewis Owen, and Hugh Rowland Owen and their heirs, should stand and be seized of both the said pieces or parcels of ground last mentioned, to the use and behoof of the community or society of the persons aforesaid, called Quakers, and of every person or persons of that persuasion, to bury their dead there, with liberty of ingress, egress, and regress thereto and therefrom as often as they should require, and to none other intent or purpose whatsoever, as in and by the said in part recited indenture of release (relation being thereunto had) may more fully and at large appear.

Now know Ye, that we the said Ellis Lewis Owen and Hugh Rowland Owen (being mortal), and very much relying upon the integrity of the said Abraham Darby, John Jewry, John Lewis, William Reynolds, John Goodwin, Edward Jones, and Randle Owen, have by these presents granted, assyned, and set over, and do for us and our respective heirs, grant, assign, and set over the said two said pieces or parcels of ground called Tyddyn y Garreg Burying Ground and Llwyn du Burying Ground, unto them the said Abraham Darby, John Young, John Lewis, William Reynolds, John Goodwin, Edward Jones, and Randle Owen, their heirs and assigns, to have and to hold the said two pieces or parcels of ground called the Tyddyn y Garreg Burying Ground and Llwyn du Burying Ground, unto them the said Abraham Darby, John Young, John Lewis, William Reynolds, John Goodwin, Edward Jones, and Randle Owen, their heirs and assigns for ever, in trust to and for the only proper use and behoof of the community or society of the persons called Quakers, and of every person and persons of that persuasion, to bury his her or their dead there, with free liberty of ingress, egress, and regress thereto or therefrom, as often as occasion shall require, and to none other use, intent, or purpose whatsoever. In witness whereof we, the said Ellis Lewis Owen and Hugh Rowland Owen, have hereunto put our hands and seals the 2nd day of December, in the thirty-eighth year of the reign of our Sovereign Lord George II, by the grace of God of Great Britain, France, and Ireland, King, Defender of the Faith, and so forth, and in the year of our Lord 1756.

      ELLIS LEWIS OWEN (L.S.)
      HUGH ROWLAND OWEN. (L.S.)

Sealed and delivered (the parchment being first legally stampt) in the presence of
    HUMPHREY OWEN of Lwyndû,
    LEWIS OWEN of Tyddyn y Garreg,
    ROBERT OWEN of Pont Philip.

Summary of Subsequent Deeds Relating to Tyddyn y Garreg and Llwyn du Graveyards.

26th and 27th January, 1777.—Indentures of Lease and Release for conveyance of Tyddyn y Garreg and Llwyn du Graveyards, from John Young and John Lewis to Richard Reynolds, Abraham Darby, John Rose, Caleb Birchall, William Holtham, George Parker, Rowland Owen, and George Young.

24th and 25th July, 1816.—Indentures of Lease and release for conveyance of same graveyards from *Richard Reynolds and *George Young, surviving Trustees, to *Bernard Dickenson, of Coalbrookdale, ironmaster; *Francis Darby, of same place, ironmaster; *John Reynolds, of Ketley, ironmaster; *William Morgan, of Coalbrookdale, miller; William Norris, of same place, accountant; Joseph Gibbons, of Swansea, broker; °John Bevington, of same place, china manufacturer; Jonathan Rees, of Neath, ironmonger; *Evan Rees the younger, of Skinner Street, London, window glass merchant; °John Lewis, of Ebbw Vale, agent; °Summers Harford, and °John Lloyd Harford, of the same place, ironmasters; and *Henry Habbeley Price, of Neath Abbey, engineer.

Those marked * were deceased in 1854. Those marked ° had ceased then to be members of the Society of Friends.

William Norris, of Coalbrookdale, solicitor, acted for the vendors. He says: "We wish the clause respecting recent graves to be retained, omitting the penalty part, trusting herein to the purchasers as they in regard to title must to us.

We doubt not that you in your parts do respect your dead, and so we trust we do here. And it is in part, at least, because we have this trust in you that we entrust the dead to you." He objected to the term "reverend" being used, on scripture grounds. "We find not in the Old or New Testament the word applied to men; no 'Rev. Moses, or Daniel, Matthew, or Paul.'" I. H. E.

Family of Lewis of Tyddyn y Garreg.

NOTE.—Owen Lewis, or Owen Lewis Owen (the party mentioned in the first recital of the deed of 1756) was a Justice of the Peace of Merionethshire in Cromwell's time, and suffered imprisonment in Bala, and some of his property was seized about 1662 (see Besse's *Sufferings* and Richard Davies's *Autobiography*). "In 1690, the widow of this Owen Lewis, and his son Ellis Lewis, removed from Wales to Mount Mellick, Ireland. Here they remained until 1708, when they emigrated to Pennsylvania, Owen Lewis's widow having previously married Owen Roberts, formerly of Wales. In 1713, Ellis Lewis, son of Owen Lewis, married Elizabeth Newlin, of a family rich and connected with the Provincial Government. From this marriage has descended a well-known family of those parts. of high respectability, and eminent for having given a Chief Justice to the State." The Lewises of Tyddyn y Garreg were the progenitors of the Lewises of Dolgan, or at least the two families were akin. John Henry Lewis of Dolgan was High Sheriff of Merioneth in 1835. His father, James Lewis, was the Architect of Bethlehem Hospital in London. The American family are very desirous of obtaining a copy of the pedigree of the family of Lewis of Tyddyn y Garreg, showing the early descent of the family.

XCI.

EXTENT MAWR, MERIONETH.

Agreement as to depasturing on Alt Dolgelly, the 28th of August, 1654, and copied by John Edwards in August 1799.

A note of an Agreement made between Griffith Nanney, Esq., John Lloyd, Esq., Robert Vaughan, Esq., Tuder Vaughan, David Ellis, Owen Lewis, Ellis Morris, Griffith Lloyd ap Ellisey, Owen Tuder, Richard Humphreys, and Howel Vaughan, of the one part, and Lewis ap John Griffith, Griffith Simon, John William, Griffith ap Robert, Lewis ap Rees, Ellis Lewis ap Tuder, Sir Richard Lloyd, and Lewis Anwyl, of the other part.

First.—It is agreed by and between the said parties that the parcell of land called EXTENT MAWR shall yearly, at or upon the 15th of April (O.S.) be kept from depasturing with any cattel thereupon until the 19th day of June (O.S.) then next following, upon ye proportionable costs and charges of the persons in the said lands interested.

Likewise, It is agreed that upon ye 19th day June (O.S.) yearly, the persons hereunto named shall drive in and depasture such proportion of cattell as is sett down at their several names in the Schedule annexed, and the said cattell there to continue untill the tenth day of July next following.

Likewise, It is agreed that, upon the 18th day of July (O.S.) yearly the said lands shall again be kept from depasture until the 10th day of August (O.S.) then next following, and then that the said persons before mentioned shall turne and drive in the like proportion there to continue. If, therefore, any of them respectively shall find cause, till the 30th September thence next following. And then and from thence forward yearly till the 15th April (O.S.) thence next following.

The said land shall be inter-commoned by the said partyes interested therein with all sorts of cattell at their respective places.

Likewise, That there shall be yearly chosen three or more of the said persons in the lands interested, to be overseers of the said lands, and also to take care for the ordering, fencing, keeping, and providing of one or more to keep and oversee the lands upon the costs and charges of the persons interested proportionable at their respective charges, and also for the taxing the chief rent proportionable as aforesaid.

Likewise, That there shall be common of turbary for all the persons interested and their undertenants, provided that the turffes cutt by them, or any of them, shall not be thence removed until the ground be once depastured upon and made bare.

Likewise, It is agreed that such of the partys interested as bord upon Extent Mawr shall well and sufficiently hedge, fence and enclose their lands, so adjoining to Extent Mawr, at their own costs and charges.

Likewise, It is agreed that whosoever shall turne voluntarily or willingly drive in any more cattell than what is annexed and layd down to their several names, from the 15th day of April yearly untill ye 30th day of September yearly, or turne any at all upon such times as are hereby appointed for the keeping of the said lands, shall lose the benefitt of any trust, benefit, profitt, interest, or advantage in or unto the said lands foresaid. In witness whereof the partys have hereunto putt their hands.

GRIFFITH NANNEY.	OWEN TUDER.
JOHN LLOYD.	RICHARD HUMPHREYS.
ROBERT VAUGHAN.	ELLIS MORRIS.
TUDER VAUGHAN.	The marke of ELLIS LEWIS
DAVID ELLIS.	TUDER.
OWEN LEWIS.[1]	The marke of JOHN WILLIAM.
GRIFFITH LLOYD.	The marke of GRIFFITH SIMON.

Cows.
Sir Richard Lloyd's allowance ...... for Bryn y Castell and Tir Extent bach 9
Griffith Nanney, Esq., Plâs y Brithdu . . . 7
Jo'n Lloyd for Trefeilia, Hafod, Cae Tyddyn, Ednyfed, and Pen yr allt 18
Robert Vaughan, Esq., for the 2 ten'ts called Gwengraig Uchaf . 7
Tuder Vaughan for Cefn Coch ucha and issa . . 7
Howell Vaughan for Gwengraig eitha and Kefn y clawdd . 8
David Ellis for Gwanas 6
Owen Lewis for Tythyn Mawr and Tyddyn y Garreg . 16
Ellis Morris for Dolgyn Uchaf . . . 5
Richard Humphrey for Tythyn Pwll, *alias* Coed . 8
Lewis Jo'n Griffith for Dewisbren and Dreberfeder . 9
Owen Tuder for Pandu 'r Gorder and Maes Coch . 8
Griffith Simon for Cwmcorysyl . . 8
Jo'n Williams for the half of Gwengraig issa . 5
Griffith ap Robert for the halfe of Gwengraig issa . 8
Griffith Lloyd ap Elliseg for Frith yr enrych and Dregerrig . 6
Lewis ap Rees for [illegible] and Maes yr helme . 5
Lewis Anwyl for Tyddyn y frath . 5
Ellis Lewis ap Tuder for Cwm Curynch . . . 6

The number of all the cattell that are to be pastured in the said grounds at the time appointed are . . . 151

[This is a copy taken 30th August 1799, by John Edwards, Dolgelly, taken from a copy dated 23rd day of September 1703, by Ow. Lewis.] J. H. E.

[1] The person mentioned in the first recital of the deed on p. 415.

DA   Collections historical &
740   archaeological relating to
M7C6   Montgomeryshire and its
v.14   borders

PLEASE DO NOT REMOVE
CARDS OR SLIPS FROM THIS POCKET

UNIVERSITY OF TORONTO LIBRARY

WS - #0002 - 230922 - C0 - 229/152/27 [29] - CB - 9780656104666 - Gloss Lamination